CLASSICS OF WESTERN THOUGHT

Volume
I

The Ancient World

FOURTH EDITION

CLASSICS OF WESTERN THOUGHT

Under the General Editorship of
Thomas H. Greer
Michigan State University

Volume **I**
The Ancient World
FOURTH EDITION
Edited by Donald S. Gochberg
Michigan State University

Volume **II**
Middle Ages, Renaissance, and Reformation
FOURTH EDITION
Edited by Karl F. Thompson
Michigan State University

Volume **III**
The Modern World
FOURTH EDITION
Edited by Edgar E. Knoebel
Michigan State University

Volume **IV**
The Twentieth Century
Edited by Donald S. Gochberg
Michigan State University

CLASSICS OF WESTERN THOUGHT

Volume
I

The Ancient World

FOURTH EDITION

Edited by
Donald S. Gochberg
Michigan State University

HARCOURT BRACE JOVANOVICH, PUBLISHERS
San Diego   New York   Chicago   Austin   Washington, D.C.
London   Sydney   Tokyo   Toronto

Copyright © 1988, 1980, 1968, 1964 by Harcourt Brace Jovanovich, Inc.

ISBN: 0-15-507682-5

Library of Congress Catalog Card Number: 87-81142

Printed in the United States of America

Introduction to
the *Classics* Series

Writings by the great minds of the Western tradition offer modern Westerners the best possible introduction to their humanistic heritage. To provide such an introduction, the editors of this series have brought together works that we consider classics of the Western tradition—of Western *thought*, in the broad sense. For the most part, these volumes of primary documents are intended for use in college-level courses in humanities or the history of civilization, normally in the company of a brief narrative text. One such text, designed especially for use with this series, is my *Brief History of the Western World*, Fifth Edition (Harcourt Brace Jovanovich, 1987).

The number and range of documents in Western civilization are, of course, enormous, and good reasons can always be advanced for choosing one work over another. We have sought works that are truly *classic*, that is to say, valuable both for their intrinsic merit and for having exerted a paramount influence on their own and later times—works that display judgment applied to observation as well as creative thought and literary skill. In deciding upon the length and quantity of selections, we have aimed to keep in balance two considerations: having each selection long enough to give a clear view of the author's ideas and, at the same time, offering selections from a substantial number of the foremost writers.

The documents appear for the most part in chronological order, in four manageable volumes: *The Ancient World* (Volume I); *Middle Ages, Renaissance, and Reformation* (Volume II); *The Modern World* (Volume III); and *The Twentieth Century* (Volume IV). Each document is introduced by a brief account of the author's life, his or her role in the shaping of the Western tradition, and the significance of the particular work. As in the selection of the writings themselves, we have kept student and instructor constantly in mind.

In this Fourth Edition of the first three volumes of the *Classics*, we have added a number of documents especially suited to the interests of today's readers. (These are noted specifically in the editor's preface to each of the revised volumes.) Most of the selections in the preceding edition have been kept; in several instances they now appear in attractive new translations. Clear and concise footnotes have been extended throughout these volumes in order to explain parts of documents that might otherwise be obscure. As a result of all these improvements, we believe that readers will find these *Classics*, more than ever, an enjoyable aid to understanding the Western intellectual heritage.

Thomas H. Greer
General Editor

Preface to
the Fourth Edition

This first volume of the *Classics of Western Thought* series contains some of the enduring thought and expression of the ancient world, spanning a period of more than two thousand years (from Gilgamesh to Augustine) Given the necessary limitations of any single volume, we can present only a representative sample of the literary treasures of those early civilizations. We are the heirs to a rich and varied legacy, whose sources are spread over the whole of antiquity.

The Fourth Edition of *The Ancient World* is organized so that first we follow the Greeks. We see their heroic qualities as defined by Homer, the relationship of character to fate as explored by Sophocles. Our readings of the Greeks end with their philosophical search for rational answers to the questions of goodness and excellence, of truth and justice, and of proper aesthetic form. Greek culture, of course, was not without its irrational elements. (The gods, after all, had their favorites.) But it was the moderation, harmony, and balance of the Greek classical ideal that spread throughout the Mediterranean world, finding expression in literature and the arts (what we now call the humanities) and serving as a model for *a way of life*.

Next we observe the wider Roman political vision. Breaking down the borders of the old Greek city-states, the Romans established a broad community of humankind resting on government and law. Justly, they could boast with Pliny that the mission of Rome was "to give to humanity human culture, and in a word become for all peoples in the whole world their one and only country." The Romans—adapting, interpreting, and extending Greek culture—succeeded where Athens had failed. They gave humanity their own ideal of a *universal* human order.

As Roman imperial unity began to weaken by the late third century A.D., however, a feeling of profound malaise spread throughout the ancient world. A sense of political and moral frustration, as well as a realization of the imperfect nature of earthly life, led to an urgent search for supernatural meaning and guidance and ultimately to the rise—from Jewish roots—of Christianity. Gone was the unique Greek view of human beings that included an unprecedented confidence in their potential excellence and a bold reliance on their power of reason. Our last group of readings thus serves as witness to the Judeo-Christian perception of human frailty, of God's omnipotent goodness, and of the quest for a moral order in which the divine will is revealed in the affairs of humanity. The ideal of the Christian saint eventually replaced Aristotle's classical ideal of the "high-minded man" who did his utmost to fulfill his uniquely human powers. The Middle Ages had arrived.

Despite the fluctuations of passing centuries, the ideals we identify with ancient Greece, Rome, and Judea were to live on in radically altered times. Today, in the thermonuclear age, those concepts and practices still offer fascinating and useful approaches to the perennial problems of our lives' value and meaning.

This Fourth Edition of *The Ancient World* rests securely on the solid foundation constructed by the distinguished editor of the previous editions, Professor Emeritus of Humanities Stebelton H. Nulle. It also owes a special debt to the General Editor of the *Classics* series, Thomas H. Greer, for his constant guidance and encouragement; his *Brief History of the Western World* is designed to accompany the entire series. The choice of selections and the editorial apparatus were also influenced by the critical judgments of thousands of undergraduates who have been reading *The Ancient World* and commenting liberally on its selections for a quarter of a century. One of those students, Richard F. Lebed, assisted in the preparation of this edition.

Every selection has been evaluated once again for its enduring quality and for its readability to the present generation of students. Moreover, there are seven totally new selections: Aesop's *Fables*, Plato's *Apology*, Aristotle's *Poetics*, Tacitus' *Germania*, Petronius' *Satyricon*, Apuleius' *The Golden Ass*, and *The Epic of Gilgamesh*. These new selections were chosen for their varied literary forms as well as for their historical or cultural interest.

Just as fluency in the ancient languages has generally diminished in our time, the availability of excellent translations has increased.

Accordingly, new translations have been used for eight of the previous edition's selections: Sophocles' *Oedipus the King*; Aristophanes' *Lysistrata*; the historical narratives of Herodotus, Thucydides, and Livy; Plutarch's *Life of Marcus Cato*; three of Horace's *Odes*; and Saint Augustine's *The City of God*. The older translations that remain have been modernized in phrasing and punctuation.

Some selections from the previous edition have been expanded. For example, Book XXIII of *The Iliad* ("The Funeral and the Games") has been added to Book I. In Herodotus' *History* we can now see the fatal pride of the Persian emperor as he raises his vast army and marches to conquer Greece. We can now read Thucydides' account of the debate that preceded the Peloponnesian War and of the devastating plague that followed "Pericles' Funeral Oration" about the Athenian ideal. Two additional *Odes* of Horace are included, and there are two more biblical selections: Job and the Letter of Paul to the Romans.

The headnotes of this edition are generally more complete, with added biographical and historical information. Footnotes now explain all foreign words, allusions, and obscure terms. The footnotes also call attention to the *relationships* among the varied selections. The new editorial apparatus is *informative*—usually not interpretive—giving readers sufficient background to develop their own critical judgments.

Donald S. Gochberg

Contents

CLASSICS OF WESTERN THOUGHT

Volume
I

The Ancient World

FOURTH EDITION

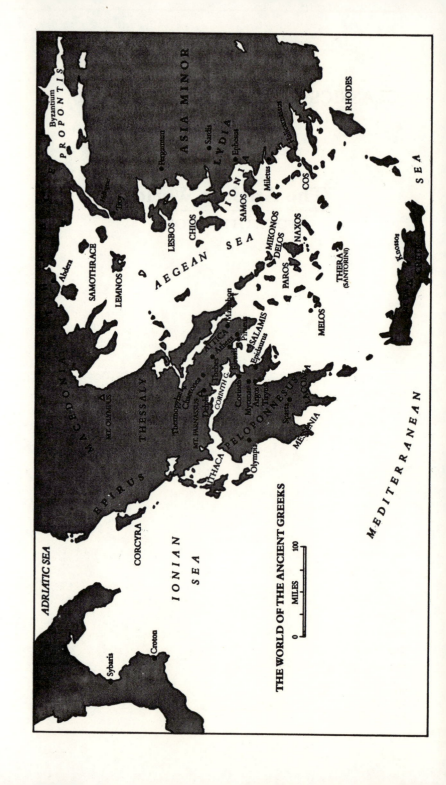

THE WORLD OF THE ANCIENT GREEKS

1

Homer

The Iliad

*L*ITERATURE *probably began with oral poetry. The* epic *is among the earliest forms of such poetry—sung by bards who memorized and doubtless modified thousands of lines. It is, typically, a long narrative poem about some great struggle (for example, a war between great powers that ultimately destroys a civilization). The style is lofty and serious, and the central figure is a hero whose actions affect the fate of the whole group—his city, tribe, nation, or race. The "traditional" epic (also called "primary" or "folk" epic) was shaped by a poet or poets out of historical and legendary materials about their glorious past triumphs. Homer was such a shaper. According to ancient traditions he lived as a professional entertainer in the early Greek settlements on the eastern edge of the Aegean Sea around the eighth century* B.C. *In any case the oldest surviving epics of Western civilization,* The Iliad *and* The Odyssey, *have been attributed to him. His poems certainly tell of a time long before his own, for the accepted date of the fall of Troy (Ilium), the event that occurs right after* The Iliad's *story and before* The Odyssey's, *is 1184* B.C. *And whatever the facts of their creation, there is no doubt that across the centuries of Western literature these poems have been widely read and admired.*

The Iliad *is not only the tale of a war but more centrally the story of Achilles, its tragic hero, and the customs of his era and class; indeeed, the work might more properly have been called* The Achilleid. *As the poem begins, nine years of war between the Achaeans (Greeks) and the Trojans have passed, and Troy still stands. Helen, the Achaean woman whose desertion of her husband, King Menelaus, for the Trojan prince Paris is the cause of the war,*

THE ILIAD Homer, *The Iliad,* trans. E. V. Rieu (London: Penguin Books, 1950), I, 23–29; XXIII, 412–436. Copyright © E. V. Rieu, 1950. Reproduced by permission of Penguin Books Ltd.

still resides among the Trojans. So far, all the Achaeans have to show for their efforts to recapture her are the spoils of raids carried out in the region around the walled city. Nevertheless, as our selection of Book One shows, the events of these raids have brought matters to a crisis by inspiring the anger of Achilles toward his military chief, King Agamemnon. Achilles' withdrawal from the siege threatens the Achaean cause; for, by all opinion (including his own), he has excelled all others in battle and is indispensable to Achaean victory.

As we read of the quarrel between the hero and Agamemnon, brother of Menelaus and commander of the combined Achaean armies, we see Achilles' tragic flaw—imperious, uncontrolled, unrelenting anger—which has led him to retire sullenly from battle. What follows, in the absence of his prowess, is a sharp reversal for his comrades—and for him, worse still, the death of Patroclus, his dearest friend. Our second excerpt, Book Twenty-Three of The Iliad, shows the rituals of the funeral for Patroclus and the athletic contests in his heroic memory. (Such funeral games were among the origins of athletic competition in the Western world.)

The narrative of The Iliad is filled largely with descriptions of ups and downs in the long combat and of the part played in it by the gods. More significantly, it also reveals the aristocratic interests and lifestyle of those Greeks who first heard the poem recited and of those who, later, were the first to read it. The climax of this epic work comes not with the predestined fall of Troy but with the struggle of Achilles to recover from his anger. It is this personal victory, this restoration of the "divine order," that satisfies the gods and the moral sense of the ancient Greeks.

The Odyssey continues Homer's narrative with the story of the aftermath of the war. It focuses upon the homecoming of another war hero, resourceful King Odysseus. Having offended Poseidon, god of the sea, he must spend ten years on the difficult journey. When he arrives at his own rocky island of Ithaca, alone and disguised, Odysseus takes bloody revenge on those who had abused his kingdom's hospitality during his absence. The Odyssey ends with restoration of the "proper" social order in Ithaca.

Homer's original audience regarded the poems as part of their ancestral history. Thus, they already knew the main lines of the story. (Troy must fall, Achilles must eventually die before Troy's defeat, Odysseus must—after many adventures—make his way home, etc.) The audience's fascination with the epics, therefore, lay in the poet's skill—his development of character and beauty of language.

The epic poems of Homer have been translated many times from the original Greek and have been presented in several forms. One of the most charming and readable prose *versions is that by the English scholar E. V. Rieu. The following excerpts from* The Iliad *are taken from his translation.*

BOOK I: THE QUARREL

The Wrath of Achilles is my theme, that fatal wrath which, in fulfilment of the will of Zeus,[1] brought the Achaeans[2] so much suffering and sent the gallant souls of many noblemen to Hades, leaving their bodies as carrion for the dogs and passing birds. Let us begin, goddess of song,[3] with the angry parting that took place between Agamemnon King of Men[4] and the great Achilles son of Peleus. Which of the gods was it that made them quarrel?

It was Apollo, Son of Zeus and Leto, who started the feud, when he punished the King for his discourtesy to Chryses, his priest, by inflicting a deadly plague on his army and destroying his men. Chryses had come to the Achaean ships to recover his captured daughter. He brought with him a generous ransom and carried the chaplet [wreath] of the Archer-god Apollo on a golden staff in his hand. He appealed to the whole Achaean army, and most of all to its two commanders, the sons of Atreus.[5]

'My lords, and you Achaean men-at-arms; you hope to sack King Priam's city and get home in safety. May the gods that live on Olympus grant your wish—on this condition, that you show your reverence for the Archer-god Apollo Son of Zeus by accepting this ransom and releasing my daughter.'

[1]The chief of those twelve major gods who reside on Mount Olympus in northern Greece; he controls the heavens and exerts his considerable authority over the other gods.

[2]The ancient Greeks. Occasionally, Homer also refers to these warriors as Danaans (descendants of the legendary King Danaus), or as Argives.

[3]An invocation: for his great task Homer is requesting the aid of Calliope, Muse (patron goddess) of epic poetry.

[4]Agamemnon, king of Mycenae and the commander-in-chief of the expedition against Troy, was a kind of lord paramount or first among equals, for many other kings took part in the expedition.

[5]Agamemnon and his brother, Menelaus, king of Sparta. Homer's frequent reference to ancestry reflects a consciousness and pride of family among such warriors.

The troops applauded. They wished to see the priest respected and the tempting ransom taken. But this was not all to King Agamemnon's liking. He cautioned the man severely and rudely dismissed him.

'Old man,' he said, 'do not let me catch you loitering by the hollow ships to-day, nor coming back again, or you may find the god's staff and chaplet a very poor defence. Far from agreeing to set your daughter free, I intend her to grow old in Argos, in my house, a long way from her own country, working at the loom and sharing my bed. Off with you now, and do not provoke me if you want to save your skin.'

The old man trembled and obeyed him. He went off without a word along the shore of the sounding sea. But when he found himself alone he prayed fervently to King Apollo, Son of Leto of the Lovely Locks. 'Hear me, god of the Silver Bow, Protector of Chryse and holy Cilla, and Lord Supreme of Tenedos.[6] Smintheus,[7] if ever I built you a shrine that delighted you, if ever I burnt you the fat thighs of a bull or a goat, grant me this wish. Let the Danaans pay with your arrows for my tears.'

Phoebus Apollo heard his prayer and came down in fury from the heights of Olympus with his bow and covered quiver on his back. As he set out, the arrows clanged on the shoulder of the angry god; and his descent was like nightfall. He sat down opposite the ships and shot an arrow, with a dreadful twang from his silver bow. He attacked the mules first and the nimble dogs; then he aimed his sharp arrows at the men, and struck again and again. Day and night innumerable fires consumed the dead.

For nine days the god's arrows rained on the camp. On the tenth the troops were called to Assembly by order of Achilles—a measure that the white-armed goddess Here[8] prompted him to take, in her concern for the Danaans whose destruction she was witnessing. When all had assembled and the gathering was complete, the great runner Achilles rose to address them:

'Agamemnon my lord, what with the fighting and the plague, I fear that our strength will soon be so reduced that any of us who are not

[6]Chryse (home of Chryses) and Cilla are towns near Troy; Tenedos is an island off the coast.

[7]Another name for Apollo, Olympian god of light, youth, medicine, music, archery, and prophecy. Smintheus literally means "mouse god." Since mice and rats are carriers of plague, Chryses' using the name of Smintheus as one of the titles by which he addresses Apollo is appropriate for the plague that will follow his prayer.

[8]Here (more often spelled Hera) is Zeus's sister and queen. She favors the Greeks; many of the gods take sides in this earthly battle.

dead by then will be forced to give up the struggle and sail for home. But could we not consult a prophet or priest, or even some interpreter of dreams—for dreams too are sent by Zeus—and find out from him why Phoebus Apollo is so angry with us? He may be offended at some broken vow or some failure in our rites. If so, he might accept a savoury offering of sheep or of full-grown goats and save us from the plague.'

Achilles sat down, and Calchas son of Thestor rose to his feet. As an augur,[9] Calchas had no rival in the camp. Past, present and future held no secrets from him; and it was his second sight, a gift he owed to Apollo, that had guided the Achaean fleet to Ilium. He was a loyal Argive, and it was in this spirit that he took the floor.

'Achilles,' he said, 'my royal lord, you have asked me to account for the Archer-King Apollo's wrath; and I will do so. But listen to me first. Will you swear to come forward and use all your eloquence and strength to protect me? I ask this of you, being well aware that I shall make an enemy of one whose authority is absolute among us and whose word is law to all Achaeans. A commoner is no match for a king whom he offends. Even if the king swallows his anger for the moment, he will nurse his grievance till the day when he can settle the account. Consider, then, whether you can guarantee my safety.'

'Dismiss your fears,' said the swift Achilles, 'and tell us anything you may have learnt from Heaven. For by Apollo Son of Zeus, the very god, Calchas, in whose name you reveal your oracles, I swear that as long as I am alive and in possession of my senses not a Danaan of them all, here by the hollow ships, shall hurt you, not even if the man you mean is Agamemnon, who bears the title of our overlord.'

At last the worthy seer plucked up his courage and spoke out. 'There is no question,' he said, 'of a broken vow or any shortcoming in our rites. The god is angry because Agamemnon insulted his priest, refusing to take the ransom and free his daughter. That is the reason for our present sufferings and for those to come. The Archer-King will not release us from this loathsome scourge till we give the bright-eyed lady back to her father, without recompense or ransom, and send holy offerings to Chryse. When that is done we might induce him to relent.'

Calchas sat down, and the noble son of Atreus, imperial Agamemnon, leapt up in anger. His heart was seething with black passion and his eyes were like points of flame. He rounded first on Calchas, full of menace.

[9]An interpreter of omens, considered invaluable by ancient armies.

'Prophet of evil,' he cried, 'never yet have you said a word to my advantage. It is always trouble that you revel in foretelling. Not once have you fulfilled a prophecy of something good—you have never even made one! And now you hold forth as the army's seer, telling the men that the Archer-god is persecuting them because I refused the ransom for the girl Chryseis, princely though it was. And why did I refuse? Because I chose to keep the girl and take her home. Indeed, I like her better than my consort, Clytaemnestra. She is quite as beautiful, and no less clever or skilful with her hands. Still, I am willing to give her up, if that appears the wiser course. It is my desire to see my people safe and sound, not perishing like this. But you must let me have another prize at once, or I shall be the only one of us with empty hands, a most improper thing. You can see for yourselves that the prize I was given is on its way elsewhere.'

The swift and excellent Achilles leapt to his feet. 'And where,' he asked, 'does your majesty propose that our gallant troops should find a fresh prize to satisfy your unexampled greed? I have yet to hear of any public fund we have laid by. The plunder we took from captured towns has been distributed, and it is more than we can ask of the men to reassemble that. No; give the girl back now, as the god demands, and we will make you triple, fourfold, compensation, if Zeus ever allows us to bring down the battlements of Troy.'

King Agamemnon took him up at once. 'You are a great man, Prince Achilles, but do not imagine you can trick me into that. I am not going to be outwitted or cajoled by you. "Give up the girl," you say, hoping, I presume, to keep your own prize safe. Do you expect me tamely to sit by while I am robbed? No; if the army is prepared to give me a fresh prize, chosen to suit my taste and to make up for my loss, I have no more to say. If not, I shall come and help myself to your prize, or that of Aias; or I shall walk off with Odysseus'. And what an angry man I shall leave behind me! However, we can deal with all that later on. For the moment, let us run a black ship down into the friendly sea, give her a special crew, embark the animals for sacrifice, and put the girl herself, Chryseis of the lovely cheeks, on board. And let some Councillor of ours go as captain—Aias, Idomeneus, the excellent Odysseus, or yourself, my lord, the most redoubtable man we could choose—to offer the sacrifice and win us back Apollo's favour.'

Achilles the great runner gave him a black look. 'You shameless schemer,' he cried, 'always aiming at a profitable deal! How can you expect any of the men to give you loyal service when you send them on a raid or into battle? It was no quarrel with the Trojan spearmen that brought *me* here to fight. They have never done *me* any harm. They have never lifted cow or horse of mine, nor ravaged any crop that the deep soil of Phthia grows to feed her men; for the roaring seas and many a dark range of mountains lie between us. The truth is that we joined the expedition to please you; yes, you unconscionable cur, to get satisfaction from the Trojans for Menelaus and yourself—a fact which you utterly ignore.[10] And now comes this threat from you of all people to rob me of my prize, my hard-earned prize, which was a tribute from the ranks. It is not as though I am ever given as much as you when the Achaeans sack some thriving city of the Trojans. The heat and burden of the fighting fall on me, but when it comes to dealing out the loot, it is you that take the lion's share, leaving me to return exhausted from the field with something of my own, however small. So now I shall go back to Phthia. That is the best thing I can do—to sail home in my beaked ships. I see no point in staying here to be insulted while I pile up wealth and luxuries for you.'

'Take to your heels, by all means,' Agamemnon King of Men retorted, 'if you feel the urge to go. I am not begging you to stay on my account. There are others with me who will treat me with respect, and the Counsellor Zeus is first among them. Moreover, of all the princes here, you are the most disloyal to myself. To you, sedition, violence and fighting are the breath of life. What if you *are* a great soldier—who made you so but God? Go home now with your ships and your men-at-arms and rule the Myrmidons. I have no use for you; your anger leaves me cold. But mark my words. In the same way as Phoebus Apollo is robbing me of Chryseis, whom I propose to send off in my ship with my own crew, I am going to pay a visit to your hut and take away the beautiful Briseis, your prize, Achilles, to let you know that I am more powerful than you, and to teach others not to bandy words with me and openly defy their King.'

This cut Achilles to the quick. In his shaggy breast his heart was torn between two courses, whether to draw his sharp sword from his side, thrust his way through the crowd, and kill King Agamemnon, or to control himself and check the angry impulse. He was deep in this inward conflict, with his long sword half unsheathed, when Athene[11] came down to him from heaven at the instance of the white-armed goddess Here, who loved the two lords equally and was fretting for

[10]It was Agamemnon who personally persuaded the Greek princes to undertake a war to recover Helen, the wife of Menelaus.

[11]Daughter of Zeus, goddess of wisdom, who favors the Greek side. At this moment Athene brings some self-control to Achilles.

them both. Athene stood behind him and seized him by his golden locks. No one but Achilles was aware of her; the rest saw nothing. He swung round in amazement, recognized Pallas Athene at once—so terrible was the brilliance of her eyes—and spoke out to her boldly: 'And why have you come here, Daughter of aegis-bearing[12] Zeus? Is it to witness the arrogance of my lord Agamemnon? I tell you bluntly— and I make no idle threats—that he stands to pay for this outrage with his life.'

'I came from heaven,' replied Athene of the Flashing Eyes, 'in the hope of bringing you to your senses. It was Here, goddess of the White Arms, that sent me down, loving the two of you as she does and fretting for you both. Come now, give up this strife and take your hand from your sword. Sting him with words instead, and tell him what you mean to do. Here is a prophecy for you—the day shall come when gifts three times as valuable as what you now have lost will be laid at your feet in payment for this outrage. Hold your hand, then, and be advised by us.'

'Lady,' replied Achilles the great runner, 'when you two goddesses command, a man must obey, however angry he may be. Better for him if he does. The man who listens to the gods is listened to by them.'

With that he checked his great hand on the silver hilt and drove the long sword back into its scabbard, in obedience to Athene, who then set out for Olympus and the palace of aegis-bearing Zeus, where she rejoined the other gods.

Not that Achilles was appeased. He rounded on Atreides[13] once again with bitter taunts. 'You drunken sot,' he cried, 'with the eyes of a dog and the courage of a doe! You never have the pluck to arm yourself and go into battle with the men or to join the other captains in an ambush—you would sooner die. It pays you better to stay in camp, filching the prizes of anyone that contradicts you, and flourishing at your people's cost because they are too feeble to resist—feeble indeed; or else, my lord, this act of brigandage would prove your last.

'But mark my words, for I am going to take a solemn oath. Look at this staff.[14] Once cut from its stem in the hills, it can never put out leaves or twigs again. The billhook stripped it of its bark and foliage;

---

[12]In Homer the aegis is a thundercloud; in the works of later writers it is a garment of Athene.

[13]Son of Atreus: Agamemnon. The Atreidae were of a family famous in Greek legend.

[14]A speaker in the Assembly claimed the group's attention so long as he held the staff which had been handed to him by a herald.

it will sprout no more. Yet the men who in the name of Zeus safeguard our laws, the Judges of our nation, hold it in their hands. By this I swear (and I could not choose a better token) that the day is coming when the Achaeans one and all will miss me sorely, and you in your despair will be powerless to help them as they fall in their hundreds to Hector killer of men. Then, you will tear your heart out in remorse for having treated the best man in the expedition with contempt.'

The son of Peleus finished, flung down the staff with its golden studs, and resumed his seat, leaving Atreides to thunder at him from the other side. But Nestor now leapt up, Nestor, that master of the courteous word, the clear-voiced orator from Pylos, whose speech ran sweeter than honey off his tongue. He had already seen two generations come to life, grow up, and die in sacred Pylos, and now he ruled the third. Filled with benevolent concern, he took the floor. 'This is indeed enough to make Achaea weep!' he said. 'How happy Priam[15] and Priam's sons would be, how all the Trojans would rejoice, if they could hear of this rift between you two who are the leaders of the Danaans in policy and war. Listen to me. You are both my juniors. And what is more, I have mixed in the past with even better men than you and never failed to carry weight with them, the finest men I have ever seen or shall see, men like Peirithous and Dryas, Shepherd of the People, Caeneus, Exadius, the godlike Polyphemus and Aegeus' son, Theseus of heroic fame. They were the strongest men that Earth has bred, the strongest men pitted against the strongest enemies, a savage, mountain-dwelling tribe whom they utterly destroyed. Those were the men whom I left my home in Pylos to join. I travelled far to meet them, at their own request. I played my independent part in their campaign. And they were men whom not a soul on earth to-day could face in battle. Still, they listened to what I said and followed my advice. You two must do the same; you will not lose by it. Agamemnon, forget the privilege of your rank, and do not rob him of the girl. The army gave her to him: let him keep his prize. And you, my lord Achilles, drop your contentious bearing to the King. Through the authority he derives from Zeus, a sceptred king has more than ordinary claims on our respect. You, with a goddess for Mother, may be the stronger of the two; yet Agamemnon is the better man, since he rules more people. My lord Atreides, be appeased. I, Nestor, beg you to relent towards Achilles, our mighty bulwark in the stress of battle.'

[15]King of Troy and father of Hector.

'My venerable lord, no one could cavil at what you say,' replied King Agamemnon. 'But this man wants to get the whip-hand here; he wants to lord it over all of us, to play the king, and to give us each our orders, though I know one who is not going to stand for that. What if the everlasting gods did make a spearman of him? Does that entitle him to use insulting language?

Here the noble Achilles broke in on the King: 'A pretty nincompoop and craven I shall be called if I yield to you at every point, no matter what you say. Command the rest, not me. I have done with obedience to you. And here is another thing for you to ponder. I am not going to fight you or anybody else with my hands for this girl's sake. You gave her to me, and now you take her back. But of all else I have beside my good black ship, you shall not rob me of a single thing. Come now and try, so that the rest may see what happens. Your blood will soon be flowing in a dark stream down my spear.'

The two stood up, when the war of words was over, and dismissed the Assembly by the Achaean fleet. Achilles, with Patroclus and his men, made off to his trim ships and huts; while Atreides launched a fast vessel on the sea, chose twenty oarsmen to man her, and after embarking the cattle to be offered to the god, fetched Chryseis of the lovely cheeks and put her on board. The resourceful Odysseus went as captain, and when everyone was in, they set out along the highways of the sea.

Meanwhile Agamemnon made his people purify themselves by bathing. When they had washed the filth from their bodies in the salt water, they offered a rich sacrifice of bulls and goats to Apollo on the shore of the unharvested sea; and savoury odours, mixed with the curling smoke, went up into the sky.

While his men were engaged on these duties in the camp, Agamemnon did not forget his quarrel with Achilles and the threat he had made to him at the meeting. He called Talthybius and Eurybates, his two heralds and obedient squires, and said to them: 'Go to the hut of Achilles son of Peleus, take the lady Briseis into your custody, and bring her here. If he refuses to let her go, I shall come in force to fetch her, which will be all the worse for him.'

He sent them off, and with his stern injunction in their ears, the two men made their unwilling way along the shore of the barren sea, till they reached the encampment and ships of the Myrmidons, where they found the prince himself sitting by his own black ship and hut. It gave Achilles no pleasure to see them. They came to a halt, too timid and abashed before the prince to address him and tell him what they wanted. But he knew without being told, and broke the silence. 'Heralds,' he said, 'ambassadors of Zeus and men, I welcome you. Come forward. My quarrel is not with you but with Agamemnon, who sent you here to fetch the girl Briseis. My lord Patroclus, will you bring the lady out and hand her over to these men? I shall count on them to be my witnesses before the happy gods, before mankind, before the brutal king himself, if the Achaeans ever need me again to save them from disaster. The man is raving mad. If he had ever learnt to look ahead, he would be wondering now how he is going to save his army when they are fighting by the ships.' Patroclus did as his friend had told him, brought out Briseis of the lovely cheeks from the hut, and gave her up to the two men, who made their way back along the line of ships with the unhappy girl.

Withdrawing from his men, Achilles wept. He sat down by himself on the shore of the grey sea, and looked across the watery wilderness. Then, stretching out his arms, he poured out prayers to his Mother.[16] 'Mother, since you, a goddess, gave me life, if only for a little while, surely Olympian Zeus the Thunderer owes me some measure of regard. But he pays me none. He has let me be flouted by imperial Agamemnon son of Atreus, who has robbed me of my prize and has her with him now.'

Achilles prayed and wept, and his Lady Mother heard him where she sat in the depths of the sea with her old Father. She rose swiftly from the grey water like a mist, came and sat by her weeping son, stroked him with her hand and spoke to him. 'My child,' she asked him, 'why these tears? What is it that has grieved you? Do not keep your sorrow to yourself, but tell me so that we may share it.'

Achilles of the swift feet sighed heavily. 'You know,' he said; 'and since you know, why should I tell you the whole story? We went to Thebe, Eëtion's sacred city; we sacked the place and brought back all our plunder, which the army shared out in the proper way, choosing Chryseis of the lovely cheeks as a special gift for Atreides. Presently Chryses, priest of the Archer-god Apollo, came to the ships of the bronze-clad Achaeans to set free his daughter, bringing a generous ransom and carrying the chaplet of the Archer Apollo on a golden staff in his hand. He importuned the whole Achaean army, but chiefly its

[16]Achilles' mother, Thetis, was a divine sea-nymph, a daughter of Nereus, the Old Man of the Sea. This appeal to her includes the first reference to the hero's tragically short lease on life.

two leaders, the Atreidae. The troops showed by their applause that they wished to see the priest respected and the tempting ransom taken. But this was not at all to Agamemnon's liking. He sent him packing, with a stern warning in his ears. So the old man went home in anger; but Apollo listened to his prayers, because he loved him dearly, and let his wicked arrows fly against the Argive army. The men fell thick and fast, for the god's shafts rained down on every part of our scattered camp. At last a seer who understood the Archer's will explained the matter to us. I rose at once and advised them to propitiate the god. This made Agamemnon furious. He leapt to his feet and threatened me. And now he has carried out his threats: the bright-eyed Achaeans are taking the girl to Chryse in a ship with offerings for the god, while the King's messengers have just gone from my hut with the other girl Briseis, whom the army gave to me.

'So now, if you have any power, protect your son. Go to Olympus, and if anything you have ever done or said has warmed the heart of Zeus, remind him of it as you pray to him. For instance, in my father's house I have often heard you proudly tell us how you alone among the gods saved Zeus the Darkener of the Skies from an inglorious fate, when some of the other Olympians—Here, Poseidon and Pallas Athene—had plotted to throw him into chains. You, goddess, went and saved him from that indignity. You quickly summoned to high Olympus the monster of the hundred arms whom the gods call Briareus, but mankind Aegaeon, a giant more powerful even than his father. He squatted by the Son of Cronos with such a show of force that the blessed gods slunk off in terror, leaving Zeus free.

'Sit by him now, clasp his knees,[17] and remind him of that. Persuade him, if you can, to help the Trojans, to fling the Achaeans back on their ships, to pen them in against the sea and slaughter them. That would teach them to appreciate their King. That would make imperial Agamemnon son of Atreus realize what a fool he was to insult the noblest of them all.'

'My son, my son!" said Thetis, bursting into tears. 'Was it for this I nursed my ill-starred child? At least they might have left you carefree and at ease beside the ships, since Fate has given you so short a life, so little time. But it seems that you are not only doomed to an early death but to a miserable life. It was indeed an unlucky day when I brought

---

[17]The sacred posture of the kneeling suppliant was to clasp the knees of the person appealed to with one hand and to reach for his chin with the other.

you into the world. However, I will go to snowcapped Olympus to tell Zeus the Thunderer all this myself, and see whether I can move him. Meanwhile, stay by your gallant ships, keep up your feud with the Achaeans, and take no part in the fighting. Yesterday, I must tell you, Zeus left for Ocean Stream to join the worthy Ethiopians at a banquet, and all the gods went with him. But in twelve days' time he will be back on Olympus, and then you may rest assured that I shall go to his Bronze Palace, where I will throw myself at his feet. I am convinced that he will hear me.'

· Thetis withdrew, leaving Achilles to his grief for the gentle lady whom they had forced him to give up. Meanwhile Odysseus and his men reached Chryse with the sacred offerings. When they had brought their craft into the deep waters of the port, they furled the sail and stowed it in the black ship's hold, dropped the mast neatly into its crutch by letting down the forestays, rowed her into her berth, cast anchor, made the hawsers [ropes] fast, and jumped out on the beach. The cattle for the Archer-god were disembarked, and Chryseis stepped ashore from the seagoing ship. Odysseus of the nimble wits led the girl to the altar and gave her back to her father. 'Chryses,' he said, 'Agamemnon King of Men has ordered me to bring you your daughter and to make ceremonial offerings to Phoebus on the Danaans' behalf, in the hope of pacifying the Archer-King, who has struck their army a grievous blow.' Then he handed the lady over to her father, who welcomed his daughter with joy.

The offerings destined to do honour to the god were quickly set in place round the well-built altar. The men rinsed their hands and took up the sacrificial grains.[18] Then Chryses lifted up his arms and prayed aloud for them: 'Hear me, God of the Silver Bow, Protector of Chryse and of holy Cilla, and Lord Supreme of Tenedos! My last petition found you kind indeed: you showed your regard for me and struck a mighty blow at the Achaean army. Now grant me a second wish and save the Danaans from their dreadful scourge.' Thus the old man prayed; and Phoebus Apollo heard him.

When they had made their petitions and scattered the grain, they first drew back the animals' heads, slit their throats and flayed them. Then they cut out slices from the thighs, wrapped them in folds of fat and laid raw meat above them. These pieces the old priest burnt on the faggots, while he sprinkled red wine over the flames and the young

---

[18]Grains of barley were sprinkled between the horns of the sacrificial animal.

men gathered round him with five-pronged forks in their hands. When the thighs were burnt up and they had tasted the inner parts, they carved the rest into small pieces, pierced them with skewers, roasted them thoroughly, and drew them all off.

Their work done and the meal prepared, they fell to with a good will on the feast, in which all had equal shares. When their thirst and hunger were satisfied, the stewards filled the mixing-bowls to the brim with wine,[19] and after first pouring out a few drops in each man's cup,[20] served the whole company. And for the rest of the day these young Achaean warriors made music to appease the god, praising the Great Archer in a lovely song, to which Apollo listened with delight.

When the sun set and darkness fell, they lay down for sleep by the hawsers of their ship. But as soon as Dawn had lit the East with rosy hands, they set sail for the great Achaean camp, taking advantage of a breeze the Archer-god had sent them. They put up their mast and spread the white sail. The sail swelled out, struck full by the wind, and a dark wave hissed loudly round her stem as the vessel gathered way and sped through the choppy seas, forging ahead on her course. Thus they returned to the great Achaean camp, where they dragged their black ship high up on the mainland sands and underpinned her with long props. This done, they scattered to their several huts and ships.

Now all this time Achilles the great runner, the royal son of Peleus, had been sitting by his fast ships, nursing his anger. He not only kept away from the fighting but attended no meetings of the Assembly, where a man can win renown. He stayed where he was, eating his heart out and longing for the sound and fury of battle.

Eleven days went by, and at dawn on the twelfth the everlasting gods returned in full strength to Olympus, with Zeus at their head. Thetis, remembering her son's instructions, emerged in the morning from the depths of the sea, rose into the broad sky and reached Olympus. She found all-seeing Zeus sitting away from the rest on the topmost of Olympus' many peaks. She sank to the ground beside him, put her left arm round his knees, raised her right hand to touch his chin, and so made her petition to the Royal Son of Cronos. 'Father Zeus, if ever I have served you well among the gods, by word or deed, grant me a wish and show your favour to my son. He is already singled

---

[19]In the ancient world wine was usually diluted with water; hence, the mixing-bowls.

[20]Before the whole company drank its wine, the steward put a few drops in each man's cup to be poured out on the ground as a liquid offering (libation) to the god.

out for early death, and now Agamemnon King of Men has affronted him. He has stolen his prize and kept her for himself. Avenge my son, Olympian Judge, and let the Trojans have the upper hand till the Achaeans pay him due respect and make him full amends.'

The Marshaller of the Clouds made no reply to this. He sat in silence for a long time, with Thetis clinging to his knees as she had done throughout. At last she appealed to him once more: 'Promise me faithfully and bow your head, or else, since you have nothing to lose by doing so, refuse; and I shall know that there is no god who counts for less than I.'

Zeus the Cloud-gatherer was much perturbed. 'This is a sorry business!' he exclaimed. 'You will make me fall foul of Here, when she rails at me about it, as she will. Even as things are, she scolds me constantly before the other gods and accuses me of helping the Trojans in this war. However, leave me now, or she may notice us; and I will see the matter through. But first, to reassure you, I will bow my head—and the immortals recognize no surer pledge from me than that. When I promise with a nod, there can be no deceit, no turning back, no missing of the mark.'

Zeus, as he finished, bowed his sable brows. The ambrosial locks rolled forward from the immortal head of the King, and high Olympus shook.

The affair was settled, and the two now parted. Thetis swung down from glittering Olympus into the salt sea depths, while Zeus went to his own palace. There the whole company of gods rose from their chairs in deference to their Father. There was not one that dared to keep his seat as he approached; they all stood up to greet him. Zeus sat down on his throne; and Here, looking at him, knew at once that he and Thetis of the Silver Feet, the Daughter of the Old Man of the Sea, had hatched a plot between them. She rounded instantly on Zeus. 'What goddess,' she asked, 'has been scheming with you now, you arch-deceiver? How like you it is, when my back is turned, to settle things in your own furtive way. You never of your own accord confide in me.'

'Here,' the Father of men and gods replied, 'do not expect to learn all my decisions. You would find the knowledge hard to bear, although you are my Consort. What it is right for you to hear, no god or man shall know before you. But when I choose to take a step without referring to the gods, you are not to cross-examine me about it.'

'Dread Son of Cronos,' said the ox-eyed Queen, 'what are you suggesting now? Surely it never was my way to pester you with questions. I have always let you make your own decisions in perfect peace. But now I have a shrewd idea that you have been talked round by Thetis of the Silver Feet, the Daughter of the Old Man of the Sea. She sat with you this morning and clasped your knees. This makes me think that you have pledged your word to her to support Achilles and let the Achaeans be slaughtered at the ships.'

'Madam,' replied the Cloud-compeller, 'you think too much, and I can keep no secrets from you. But there is nothing you can *do*, except to turn my heart even more against you, which will be all the worse for yourself. If things are as you say, you may take it that my will is being done. Sit there in silence and be ruled by me, or all the gods in Olympus will not be strong enough to keep me off and save you from my unconquerable hands.'

This made the ox-eyed [large-eyed] Queen of Heaven tremble, and curbing herself with an effort she sat still. Zeus had daunted all the other Heavenly Ones as well, and there was silence in his palace, till at last Hephaestus the great Artificer[21] spoke up, in his anxiety to be of service to his Mother, white-armed Here. 'This is unbearable!' he exclaimed. 'A pretty pass we are coming to, with you two spoiling for a fight about mankind and setting the gods at loggerheads. How can a good dinner be enjoyed with so much trouble in the air? I do advise my Mother, who knows well enough what is best, to make her peace with my dear Father, Zeus, or she may draw another reprimand from him and our dinner be entirely spoilt. What if the Olympian, the Lord of the Lightning Flash, the strongest god in Heaven, should feel disposed to blast us from our seats? No, Mother, you must humbly ask his pardon, and the Olympian will be gracious to us again.'

As he said this, Hephaestus hurried forward with a two-handled cup and put it in his Mother's hand. 'Mother,' he said, 'be patient and swallow your resentment, or I that love you may see you beaten, here in front of me. A sorry sight for me—but what could I do to help you? The Olympian is a hard god to pit oneself against. Why, once before when I was trying hard to save you, he seized me by the foot and hurled me from the threshold of Heaven. I flew all day, and as the sun sank I fell half-dead in Lemnos, where I was picked up and looked after by the Sintians.'

[21]Hephaestus, son of Zeus and Here, is the god of fire and the metallic crafts. Being lame he is the only Olympian god not formed perfectly.

The white-armed goddess Here smiled at this, and took the beaker from her Son, still smiling. Hephaestus then went on to serve the rest in turn, beginning from the left, with sweet nectar which he drew from the mixing-bowl; and a fit of helpless laughter seized the happy gods as they watched him bustling up and down the hall.[22]

So the feast went on, all day till sundown. Each of them had his equal share and they all ate with zest. There was music too, from a beautiful Harp played by Apollo, and from the Muses,[23] who sang in turn delightfully. But when the bright lamp of the Sun had set, they all went home to bed in the separate houses that the great lame god Hephaestus had built for them with skillful hands. Olympian Zeus, Lord of the Lightning, also retired to the upper room where he usually slept, and settled down for the night, with Here of the Golden Throne beside him.

BOOK XXIII: THE FUNERAL AND THE GAMES

While the city of Troy gave itself up to lamentation,[24] the Achaeans withdrew to the Hellespont,[25] and when they reached the ships, dispersed to their several vessels. Only the battle-loving Myrmidons were not dismissed. Achilles kept his followers with him and addressed them. 'Myrmidons,' he said, 'lovers of the fast horse, my trusty band; we will not unyoke our horses from their chariots yet, but mounted as we are, will drive them past Patroclus and mourn for him as a dead man should be mourned. Then, when we have wept and found some solace in our tears, we will unharness them and all have supper here.'

The Myrmidons with one accord broke into lamentation. Achilles led the way, and the mourning company drove their long-maned horses three times round the dead, while Thetis stirred them all to

[22]The sight of the lame god (instead of the usual attractive servers) hobbling around them with the nectar turned the carefree gods to laughter. Thus, the tension of the Zeus-Here argument was relieved, as Hephaestus had intended.

[23]Nine goddesses, daughters of Zeus and Mnemosyne (goddess of memory); each one of the Muses encouraged and protected a different art or science.

[24]The Trojans are mourning Hector, their greatest warrior, whom Achilles had killed (in Book XXII). Achilles had returned to the battle (which he had left in Book I) in order to seek revenge for his dearest friend, Patroclus, killed by Hector. The funeral for Patroclus had been delayed until after Achilles' revenge had been achieved.

[25]The ancient name for the Dardanelles; overlooked by the high walls of Troy, they are the straits separating Europe from Asia.

weep without restraint. The sands were moistened and their warlike panoply was bedewed with tears, fit tribute to so great a panic-maker. And now the son of Peleus, laying his man-killing hands on his comrade's breast, led them in the melancholy dirge: 'Rejoice, Patroclus, even in the Halls of Hades. I am keeping all the promises I made you. I have dragged Hector's body here, for the dogs to eat it raw; and at your pyre I am going to cut the throats of a dozen of the highborn youths of Troy, to vent my anger at your death.'

Achilles, when he had finished, thought of one more indignity to which he could subject Prince Hector. He flung him down on his face in the dust by the bier of Menoetius' son.[26] His soldiers then took off their burnished bronze equipment, unyoked their neighing horses, and sat down in their hundreds by the ship of the swift son of Peleus, who had provided for them a delicious funeral feast. Many a white ox fell with his last gasp to the iron knife, many a sheep and bleating goat was slaughtered, and many a fine fat hog was stretched across the flames to have his bristles singed. Cupfuls of blood were poured all round the corpse.

Meanwhile Prince Achilles, the swift son of Peleus, was taken by the Achaean kings to dine with the lord Agamemnon, though they had hard work to make him come, still grieving for his comrade as he was. When they reached Agamemnon's hut they told the clear-voiced heralds to put a big three-legged cauldron on the fire in the hope of inducing Achilles to wash the clotted gore from his body. But he would not hear of such a thing. He even took a vow and said: 'By Zeus, who is the best and greatest of the gods, it shall be sacrilege for any water to come near my head till I have burnt Patroclus, made him a mound and shorn my hair, for I shall never suffer again as I am suffering now, however long I live. But for the moment, though I hate the thought of food, we must yield to necessity and dine. And at dawn, perhaps your majesty King Agamemnon will order wood to be collected and everything to be provided that a dead man ought to have with him when he travels into the western gloom, so that Patroclus may be consumed by fire as soon as possible and the men return to their duties when he is gone.'

They readily agreed and set to with a will on the preparation of their supper, in which they all had equal shares. They ate with zest, and when they had satisfied their thirst and hunger they retired for the

---

[26]Menoetius was the father of Patroclus.

night to their several huts. But the son of Peleus groaning wearily lay down on the shore of the sounding sea, among his many Myrmidons, but in an open space, where the waves were splashing on the beach. His splendid limbs were exhausted by his chase of Hector to the very walls of windy Ilium; but he had no sooner fallen into a sleep that soothed and enfolded him, resolving all his cares, than he was visited by the ghost of poor Patroclus, looking and talking exactly like the man himself, with the same stature, the same lovely eyes, and the same clothes as those he used to wear.

It halted by his head and said to him: 'You are asleep: you have forgotten me, Achilles. You neglect me now that I am dead; you never did so when I was alive. Bury me instantly and let me pass the Gates of Hades. I am kept out by the disembodied spirits of the dead, who have not let me cross the River and join them, but have left me to pace up and down forlorn on this side of the Gaping Gates.[27] And give me that hand, I beseech you; for once you have passed me through the flames I shall never come back again from Hades. Never again on earth will you and I sit down together, out of earshot of our men, to lay our plans. For I have been engulfed by the dreadful fate that must have been my lot at birth; and it is your destiny too, most worshipful Achilles, to perish under the walls of the rich town of Troy. And now, one more request. Do not let them bury my bones apart from yours, Achilles. Let them lie together, just as you and I grew up together in your house, after Menoetius brought me there from Opus as a child because I had had the misfortune to commit homicide and kill Amphidamas' boy by accident in a childish quarrel over a game of knucklebones. The knightly Peleus welcomed me to his palace and brought me up with loving care. And he appointed me your squire. So let one urn, the golden vase your lady Mother gave you, hold our bones.'

'Dear heart,' said the swift Achilles, 'what need was there for you to come and ask me to attend to all these things? Of course I will see to everything and do exactly as you wish. But now come nearer to me, so that we may hold each other in our arms, if only for a moment, and draw cold comfort from our tears.'

With that, Achilles held out his arms to clasp the spirit, but in vain. It vanished like a wisp of smoke and went gibbering underground. Achilles leapt up in amazement. He beat his hands together and in his desolation cried: 'Ah then, it is true that something of us does survive even in the

---

[27]Ghosts could not enter Hades, the underworld of the dead, until their bodies were properly buried or cremated.

Halls of Hades, but with no intellect at all, only the ghost and semblance of a man; for all night long the ghost of poor Patroclus (and it looked exactly like him) has been standing at my side, weeping and wailing, and telling me of all the things I ought to do.' Achilles' outcry woke the Myrmidons to further lamentation, and Dawn, when she stole up to them on crimson toes, found them wailing round the pitiable dead.

Meanwhile King Agamemnon sent mules and men from every part of the encampment to fetch wood. The officer in charge of the party was Meriones, the squire of the lovable Idomeneus. The men carried woodman's axes in their hands together with stout ropes, and the mules walked ahead of them. They went up dale and down by many a zigzag path, and came at last to the spurs of Ida of the many springs. There they set to work with a will felling the tall oaks with their long-bladed axes, and trees came crashing down. The Achaeans split the logs and then roped them to the mules, who cut up the ground with their feet in their efforts to haul them down to the plain through the tangled undergrowth. The woodcutters too all carried logs, by order of Meriones, squire to the amiable Idomeneus. When they reached the shore, they laid them neatly down at the spot where Achilles planned to build a great mound for Patroclus and himself.

Having stacked this huge supply of wood all round the site, they sat down and waited there in a body. Achilles then gave orders for his war-loving Myrmidons to put on their bronze and for every charioteer to yoke his horses. They hurried off and got into their armour, and the fighting men and drivers mounted their cars. The horse led off, and after them came a mass of infantry one could not count. In the middle of the procession Patroclus was carried off by his own men, who had covered his body with the locks of hair they had cut off and cast upon it. Behind them Prince Achilles supported the head, as the chief mourner, who was despatching his highborn comrade to the Halls of Hades.

When they came to the place appointed for them by Achilles, they put Patroclus down and quickly built him a noble pile of wood. But now a fresh idea occurred to the swift and excellent Achilles. Stepping back from the pyre, he cut off from his head an auburn lock he had allowed to grow ever since its dedication to the River Spercheus.[28] Then he looked out angrily across the wine-dark sea and said: 'Spercheus, is this your answer to my father Peleus' prayers? He promised you that at my home-coming from Troy I should cut off this lock for

[28]The Spercheus was the river of Achilles' homeland. It was common in ancient Greece for boys to dedicate a lock of hair to the local river's god.

you and make you the rich offering of fifty rams, sacrificed beside your very waters, where you have a precinct and a fragrant altar. That was the old king's vow; but you have denied him what he prayed for. And now, since I shall never see my own country again, I propose to part with this lock and give it to my lord Patroclus.'

As he spoke, he put the lock in the hands of his beloved comrade. His gesture moved the whole gathering to further tears, and sunset would have found them still lamenting, if Achilles had not had a sudden thought. He went up to Agamemnon and said: 'My lord Atreides, you are the man to whom the troops will listen. Of course they can mourn as much as they wish; but for the moment I ask you to dismiss them from the pyre and tell them to prepare their midday meal. We that are the chief mourners will see to everything here, though I should like the Achaean commanders to remain.'

On hearing what Achilles wished, Agamemnon King of Men dismissed the troops to their trim ships; but the chief mourners stayed where they were and piled up wood. They made a pyre a hundred feet in length and breadth, and with sorrowful hearts laid the corpse on top. At the foot of the pyre they flayed and prepared many well-fed sheep and shambling cattle with crooked horns. The great-hearted Achilles, taking fat from all of them, covered the corpse with it from head to foot, and then piled the flayed carcasses round Patroclus. To these he added some two-handled jars of honey and oil, leaning them against the bier; and in his zeal he cast on the pyre four high-necked horses, groaning aloud as he did so. The dead lord had kept nine dogs as pets. Achilles slit the throats of two and threw them on the pyre. Then he went on to do an evil thing—he put a dozen brave men, the sons of noble Trojans, to the sword, and set the pyre alight so that the pitiless flames might feed on them.[29] This done, he gave a groan and spoke once more to his beloved friend: 'All hail from me, Patroclus, in the very Halls of Hades! I am keeping all the promises I made you. Twelve gallant Trojans, sons of noblemen, will be consumed by the same fire as you. For Hector son of Priam I have other plans—I will not give him to the flames, I will throw him to the dogs to eat.'

But in spite of this threat from Achilles the dogs were not given access to the corpse of Hector. Day and night, Zeus' Daughter

---

[29]The fat would help the corpse to burn. The other items are intended to accompany the dead nobleman on his journey. Honey and oil are provisions; horses and dogs are companions; the Trojan captives will be Patroclus' servants. Since Homer states that Achilles did "an evil thing," we must assume that such a human sacrifice was most un-Greek and reveals a vestige of Achilles' tragic flaw.

Aphrodite kept them off, and she anointed him with ambrosial oil of roses, so that Achilles should not lacerate him when he dragged him to and fro. Moreover, Phoebus Apollo caused a dark cloud to sink from the sky to the ground and settle on the corpse, covering the whole area in which it lay, so that the heat of the sun getting at this side and that should not wither the skin on his sinews and his limbs too soon.[30]

There was some delay with the body of Patroclus also: the pyre refused to kindle. But a remedy suggested itself to the swift and excellent Achilles. Standing clear of the pyre, he prayed and offered splendid offerings to the two winds, Boreas of the North and Zephyr of the Western Gale. He made them rich libations from a golden cup and implored them to come so that the wood might kindle readily and the bodies quickly be cremated. Iris[31] heard his prayers and sped off to convey his message to the Winds, who had all sat down together to a banquet in the draughty house of the Western Gale. Iris came running up, and when they saw her standing on the stone threshold, they all leapt up to their feet and each invited her to come and sit beside him. But she excused herself, and went on to deliver her message. 'I have no time to sit down,' she said. 'I must get back to Ocean Stream and the Ethiopians' land, where they are entertaining the immortals at a sacrificial banquet I am anxious not to miss. But I have a message from Achilles for you, Boreas and the Western Gale. He is praying to you and promising you splendid offerings if you will come and kindle the pyre under the body of Patroclus, for whom the whole Achaean army is mourning.'

Her message delivered, Iris went off, and the two Winds rose uproariously, driving the clouds before them. In a moment they were out at sea, blowing hard and raising billows with their noisy breath. When they came to the deep-soiled land of Troy, they fell upon the funeral pile and the fire blazed up with a terrific roar. Howling round the pyre they helped each other all night long to fan the flames; and all night long the swift Achilles, using a two-handled cup which he replenished from a golden mixing-bowl, poured out libations, drenched the earth with wine, and called on the spirit of the unhappy Patroclus. As a father weeps when he is burning the bones of a son who has died on his wedding-day and left his stricken parents in despair, Achilles wept

---

[30]Aphrodite, goddess of love and female beauty, and Apollo both favored the Trojan side.

[31]Goddess of the rainbow and a messenger of the gods.

as he burned his comrade's bones, moving round the pyre on leaden feet with many a deep groan.

At the time when the Morning Star comes up to herald a new day on earth, and in his wake Dawn spreads her saffron mantle over the sea, the fire sank low, the flames expired, and the Winds set out for home across the Thracian Sea, where the roaring waves ran high. Achilles was exhausted. Turning from the pyre he sank to the ground and instantly fell fast asleep. But the other chieftains, who had joined King Agamemnon, would not let him be, and the whole party now approached him. Roused by their voices and footsteps, he sat up and told them what he wanted done. 'My lord Atreides,' he said, 'and you other leaders of the united Achaeans; make it your first task to put out with sparkling wine whatever portions of the pyre the flames have reached. Then we must collect my lord Patroclus' bones, being careful to distinguish them, though that will not be difficult, as he lay in the center of the pyre, separated from the rest, who were burnt on the verge of it, horses and men together. We will put the bones in a golden vase and seal it with a double layer of fat, against the time when I myself shall have vanished in the world below. As for his barrow,[32] I do not ask you to construct a very large one, something that is seemly but no more. Later you can build a big and high one, you Achaeans that are left in the well-found ships when I am gone.'

They went about the business as the swift son of Peleus had directed. First they put out with sparkling wine all parts of the funeral pyre in which the flames had done their work and the ash had fallen deep. Then, with tears on their cheeks, they collected the white bones of their gentle comrade in a golden vase, closed it with a double seal of fat, laid it in his hut and covered it with a soft linen shroud. Next they designed his barrow by laying down a ring of stone revetments round the pyre. Then they fetched earth and piled it up inside.

When the troops had built the monument, they made as if to go. But Achilles stopped them and told them all to sit down in a wide ring where the sports were to be held. For these he brought out prizes from the ships—cauldrons and tripods; horses, mules, and sturdy cattle; grey iron and women in their girdled gowns.

The first event was a chariot race, for which he offered the following splendid prizes: for the winner, a woman skilled in the fine crafts, and a tripod with ear-shaped handles, holding two-and-twenty pints; for

[32]Burial mound.

the runner-up, a mare six years old and broken in, with a little mule in her womb; for the third man, a fine kettle holding four pints, untarnished by the flames and still as bright as ever; for the fourth, two talents [weights] of gold; and for the fifth, a two-handled pan, as yet untouched by fire.

Achilles stood up to announce the contest to the Argives. 'My lord Atreides and Achaean men-at-arms, these are the prizes that await the winning charioteers. Of course, if we were holding sports in honour of some other man, it is I who would walk off to my hut with the first prize, for you don't need me to tell you that my horses are the best of all, being immortal and a present from Poseidon[33] to my father Peleus, who passed them on to me. But I and my splendid pair will not compete; they are in mourning for their glorious driver. How kind Patroclus was to them, always washing them down with clean water and then pouring olive-oil on their manes! No wonder they stand there and grieve for him. Their manes are trailing on the ground and in their sorrow they refuse to move. However, the event is open to anyone else in the whole army who believes in his horses and the build of his chariot. So take your places now.'

This announcement from Achilles brought out the ablest charioteers. The first to spring to his feet was Admetus' son Eumelus King of Men, who was an excellent horseman. Next, the mighty Diomedes son of Tydeus, who harnessed the horses of the breed of Tros that he had taken earlier from Aeneas on the occasion when Apollo saved their master's life. Then red-haired Menelaus son of Atreus, scion of Zeus, who yoked a fast pair, Aethe, a mare of Agamemnon's, and his own horse Podargus. Aethe had been presented to Agamemnon by Echepolus son of Anchises, on condition that he need not go with him to windy Ilium but could stay at home in comfort—he happened to be a very rich man, who lived in Sicyon of the broad lawns. This was the mare that Menelaus yoked—she was champing to be off. The fourth man to harness his long-maned horses was Antilochus. He was the noble son of the magnanimous King Nestor son of Neleus, and his chariot-horses were of Pylian breed.[34] His father now went up to him and gave him some useful hints, though he knew his business well enough himself.

[33]Brother of Zeus; god of the sea, of earthquakes, and of horses.

[34]Since Homer's epics focus on aristocrats almost exclusively, this passage giving the family backgrounds of the contestants and even of their horses is quite typical.

'Antilochus,' said Nestor, 'young as you are, you stand well with Zeus and Poseidon and they have taught you the whole art of driving horses. So there is no great need for me to put you right. But expert though you are at wheeling round the turning-post, your horses are very slow, and I am afraid you will find this a great handicap. Yet even if the other pairs are faster, their drivers do not know a single trick that is not known to you. So you must fall back, my friend, on all the skill that you can summon, if you do not wish to say good-bye to the prizes. It is skill, rather than brawn, that makes the best lumberman. Skill, again, enables a steersman to keep a straight course over the wine-dark sea when his good ship is yawing in the wind. And it is by his skill that one driver beats another. The average man, leaving too much to his chariot and pair, is careless at the turn and loses ground to one side or the other; his horses wander off the course and he does not correct them. But the cunning driver, though behind a slower pair, always has his eye on the post, and wheels close in; he is not caught napping when the time comes to use the oxhide reins and stretch his horses; he keeps them firmly in hand and watches the man who is leading.

'Now let me tell you something to look out for. It is obvious enough; you cannot miss it. There is a dead tree-stump, an oak or pine, standing about six feet high. It has not rotted in the rain, and it is flanked by two white stones. The road narrows at this point, but the going is good on both sides of the monument, which either marks an ancient burial or must have been put up as a turning-post by people of an earlier age. In any case it is the turning-post that my lord Achilles has chosen for this race. As you drive round it you must hug it close, and you in your light chariot must lean just a little to the left yourself. Call on your off-side horse, touch him with the whip and give him rein; but make the near horse hug the post so close that anyone might think you were scraping it with the nave of your wheel. And yet you must be careful not to touch the stone, or you may wreck your horses and smash up your car, which would delight the rest but not look well for you. So use your wits, my friend, and be on the lookout; for if you could overtake them at the turning-post, no one could catch you up or pass you with a spurt, not even if he came behind you with Adrestus' thoroughbred, the great Arion, who was sired in heaven, or the famous horses of Laomedon, the best that Troy has bred.'

Having thus expounded the whole art of horsemanship to his son, King Nestor went back to his seat. Meriones was the fifth man to get his horses ready. And now they all mounted their chariots and cast their lots into a helmet, which Achilles shook. The first lot to jump out was that of Antilochus son of Nestor; then came that of King Eumelus, followed by that of Atreus' son, the spearman Menelaus. Meriones drew the fourth starting-place, and the last fell to Diomedes, the best man of them all. They drew up side by side and Achilles showed them the turning-point, far away on level ground. He had posted the venerable Phoenix, his father's squire, as an umpire there, to keep an eye on the running and report what happened.

At one and the same moment they all gave their horses the whip, shook the reins on their backs and set them going with a sharp word of command. The horses started off across the plain without a hitch and quickly left the ships behind. The dust that rose from underneath their chests hung in the air like a storm-cloud or a fog, and their manes flew back in the wind. At one moment the chariots were in contact with the fruitful earth and at the next were bounding high in the air. The heart of each driver as he stood in his car and struggled to be first was beating hard. They yelled at their horses, who flew along in a cloud of dust.

But it was not till their galloping teams had rounded the mark and were heading back to the grey sea that each man showed his form and the horses stretched themselves. The fast mares of Eumelus now shot out of the ruck, and next came Diomedes' stallions of the breed of Tros, close behind, with very little in it. It looked as though at any moment they might leap into Eumelus' car. They were flying along with their heads just over him, warming his back and his broad shoulders with their breath. In fact Diomedes would have overhauled Eumelus then and there or made it a dead heat, if Phoebus Apollo, who was still angry with Tydeus' son, had not knocked the shining whip out of his hand. Diomedes, when he saw Eumelus' mares going better than ever and his own horses slowing down for lack of anything to spur them on, was so angry that the tears poured down his cheeks. But Athene had had her eye on Apollo when he fouled Diomedes. She sped after the great man, gave him back his whip and put fresh spirit in his horses. Moreover she was so enraged that she chased Eumelus too and used her powers as a goddess to break the yoke of his chariot, with the result that his mares ran off on their own and the shaft crumpled up on the ground, while Eumelus himself was flung out of the car and came down by the wheel. The skin was taken off his elbows, mouth and nose; his forehead was bruised; his eyes were filled with tears, and he was robbed of speech. Meanwhile Diomedes swept round the wreck-age with his powerful horses, having left the others well behind. Athene filled his pair with strength and let their master triumph.[35]

Next after Diomedes came red-haired Menelaus, Atreus' son; and next again Antilochus, who was shouting at his father's horses and urging them to spurt like Diomedes' pair. 'Show me your best paces now,' he cried. 'I am not asking you to race that pair ahead, the gallant Diomedes' horses, whom Athene has just speeded up so as to make her favourite win. But do catch up Atreides' pair and don't get left behind by them. Be quick about it too; or Aethe will be turning up her nose at you—and she a mare. Why are you hanging back, my friends? I tell you frankly what you can expect. No more attentions from King Nestor's hands for you! He will slit your throats without a moment's hesitation if you take it easy now and leave us with the smaller prize. So after them full tilt! Trust me to find a way of slipping past them where the track is narrow. I shall not miss my chance.'

His horses, taking their master's threat to heart, went faster for a little while, and very soon Antilochus, that veteran campaigner, saw a place where the sunken road grew narrow. It ran through a gulley: water piled up by the winter rains had carried part of it away and deepened the whole defile. Menelaus was in occupation of the track, making it difficult for anyone to come abreast of him. But Antilochus did not keep to it. He drove a little off it to one side, and pressed Menelaus hard. Menelaus was alarmed and shouted at him: 'You are driving madly, Antilochus; hold in your horses. The track is narrow here. It soon gets wider—you could pass me there. Be careful you don't hit my chariot and wreck us both.'

But Antilochus, pretending that he had not heard him, plied his lash and drove more recklessly than ever. They both ran on for about the distance that a quoit [discus] will carry when a young man casts it with a swing of the arm to test his strength. Then Menelaus' pair gave way and fell behind. He eased the pace himself, on purpose, fearing that the powerful horses might collide in the road and upset the light chariots, in which case their masters, through their eagerness to win, would find themselves rolling in the dust. But red-haired Menelaus managed to give the other a piece of his mind. 'Antilochus,' he cried, 'you are the

---

[35]The frequently "unfair" interference by the gods to benefit their human favorites is demonstrated here. Usually, however, this divine action merely helps to fulfill the appropriately inevitable: "Diomedes, the best man of them all," will win the chariot race.

most appalling driver in the world. We were mistaken when we thought you had some sense. Well, have it your own way; but all the same, you shall not carry off the prize till you have answered on your oath for this affair.'

Then Menelaus turned to his horses. 'Don't stop,' he shouted at them. 'Don't stand and mope. That pair ahead of you will weaken in the leg far sooner than you. They are neither of them as young as they were.' His horses, frightened by their master's reprimand, sped on with a better will and soon were close behind the other pair.

Meanwhile from their seats in the ring the spectators were looking out for the horses, who were rapidly approaching in a cloud of dust. Idomeneus the Cretan King was the first to see them. He was sitting well above the rest on high ground outside the ring, and when he heard a driver shouting in the distance he knew the voice. He also recognized one of the leading horses, who showed up well, being chestnut all over but for a round white patch like the full moon which he had on his forehead. Idomeneus stood up and called to the other spectators: "My friends, Captains and Counsellors of the Argives; am I the only one who can see the horses or do you see them too? It seems to me that a new pair are leading, and the driver also looks different. Eumelus' mares, who were ahead on the outward lap, must have come to grief out there, for I certainly saw them leading at the turning-post and now I cannot see them anywhere, though I have searched the whole Trojan plain. Perhaps Eumelus dropped his reins: he couldn't steer his horses round the mark and had an accident as he was wheeling. Yes, that is where he must have been tossed out and smashed his chariot, while his mares went wild and bolted. But do get up and have a look yourselves. I cannot be quite sure, but the leading man looks like an Aetolian to me, yes, one of our Argive kings, the son of horse-taming Tydeus, Diomedes himself.'

But Aias the Runner and son of Oïleus contradicted him rudely. 'Idomeneus,' he said, 'why must you be for ever showing off? Those high-stepping mares out there have a long way yet to go; and you are not by any means the youngest man among us, nor do you own the sharpest pair of eyes. Yet you are always laying down the law. Here among your betters you really must control your tongue. That pair in front is the same that led before, Eumelus' mares. And there's Eumelus, in the chariot, with the reins in his hands.'

The commander of the Cretans took offence at this. 'Aias,' he retorted, 'you are a most cantankerous, ill-natured fellow, and quite unlike an Argive in your lack of courtesy. But come now, let us have a bet about the leading pair. We'll stake a tripod or cauldron, and have King Agamemnon as our referee. You'll learn the truth when you pay up.'

Aias the Runner rose in fury to give Idomeneus an insolent repartee; and the quarrel would have gone still further if Achilles himself had not leapt to his feet and intervened. 'Aias and Idomeneus,' he said, 'stop quarrelling. This interchange of insults is a breach of good manners which you would be the first to condemn in others. Why not sit down in the ring and keep your eyes on the horses? They will soon be coming along, all out for victory. Then each of you can recognize them for himself and pick out the winners and the second pair.'

By now Diomedes was very close. He was driving with the whip, swinging his arm right and back for every lash, and making his horses leap high in the air as they sped on to finish. Showers of dust fell on their driver all the time, and as the fast pair flew over the ground the chariot overlaid with gold and tin came spinning after them and scarcely left a tyre-mark on the fine dust behind.

Diomedes drew up in the middle of the arena, with the sweat pouring to the ground from his horses' necks and chests. He leapt down from his glittering car and leant his whip against the yoke. Sthenelus, his gallant equerry, made short work of the prizes. He took possession promptly, giving the tripod with the ear-shaped handles to his exultant men and telling them to lead the woman off. Then he unyoked the horses.

Antilochus son of Nestor was the next man to drive up. He had beaten Menelaus not by any turn of speed but by a trick. Yet even so Menelaus and his fast horses came in close behind. There was no more in it than the space that separates a horse from the wheel of his master's car when he strains in the harness and pulls him along, trotting so close in front that the tip of his tail keeps brushing the tyre and there is hardly any gap, however far he runs. There was no more than that between Menelaus and the peerless Antilochus. It is true that at the time of the incident Menelaus had been left as much as a disk-throw in the rear. But he soon came up with him. Aethe's mettle had begun to tell—she was Agamemnon's lovely mare—and on a longer course Menelaus would have passed him. It would not even have ended in a dead heat.

Meriones, Idomeneus' worthy squire, came in a spear-throw behind the famous Menelaus. His long-maned horses were the slowest pair in the race, and he himself was the poorest racing-driver.

The last of them all to arrive was Admetus' son Eumelus. He was dragging his handsome chariot himself and driving his horses in front of him. When he saw this, the swift and excellent Achilles was sorry for the man. He stood up in the ring and made a suggestion: 'The best driver of the lot has come in last. Let us give him a prize, as is only fair. Make it the second, for of course Diomedes takes the first.'

Everyone welcomed this idea, and Achilles, encouraged by the men's applause, was about to give the mare to Eumelus, when Antilochus, King Nestor's son, jumped up and lodged a formal protest with the royal son of Peleus. 'My lord Achilles,' he cried, 'I shall resent it keenly if you do as you suggest. You are proposing to rob me of my prize because Eumelus' chariot and horses came to grief—as did Eumelus, though he drives so well. The fact is that he ought to have prayed to the immortal gods; then he would never have come in last in the race. However, if you are sorry for the man and fond of him, there is plenty of gold in your hut, and copper and sheep, and you have women-servants too and splendid horses. Choose something later on from these and let him have an even better prize than mine. Or hand it to him now and hear the troops applaud you. But I will not give up this mare. Anyone who cares to try can come and fight me for her with his fists.'

This speech drew a smile from the swift and excellent Achilles. He had always liked Antilochus, his comrade-in-arms, and was delighted with him now. He gave him a gracious answer: 'Antilochus, if you really wish me to send for something extra from my hut and give it to Eumelus as a consolation prize, I will do even that for you. I will give him the cuirass [breastplate] I took from Asteropaeus. It is made of bronze and plated with bright tin all over. It is a gift that he will value.'

But this was not all. Menelaus had by no means forgiven Antilochus and he now got up in a very ugly mood. A herald handed him the speaker's staff and called for silence. Then Menelaus spoke, looking the king he was. 'Antilochus,' he said, 'you used to be a very sensible fellow. Now see what you have done! By cutting in across me with your own far slower pair, you have made my driving look contemptible and robbed my horses of a win. My lords, Captains and Counsellors of the Argives, I appeal to you to judge between the two of us impartially, so that none of our men-at-arms will be able to say: "It was only by lying that Menelaus beat Antilochus and walked off with the mare. His horses really were much slower. It is his rank and power that bring him out on top." No, on second thoughts, I will hear the case myself. And I am not afraid that any Danaan will accuse me of injustice: it will be fairly tried. Antilochus, my lord, come forward here in the proper way; stand in front of your chariot and pair, holding the pliant whip you always drive with; touch your horses; and swear in the name of the Earth-shaker and Girdler of the World[36] that you did not hold up my chariot by a deliberate foul.'

'Enough,' said the wise Antilochus. 'I am a much younger man than you, King Menelaus, and you, my senior and my better, know well enough how a young man comes to break the rules. His mind is quicker, but his judgment not so sound. Forgive me then, and of my own accord I will let you have the mare I won. Moreover, should you ask for something more or better of my own, I would rather give it to you at once than fall for ever out of your majesty's favour and perjure myself before the gods.'

With that, great Nestor's son led the mare over and handed her to Menelaus, whose heart was warmed like the dew that hangs on ears of corn when the fields bristle with a ripening crop. Thus, Menelaus, was the heart within you warmed, and this was the answer that you gave:

'Antilochus, it is my turn to yield: I cannot be angry with you now. You have never been impulsive or unbalanced, though this was certainly a case where the high spirits of youth got the better of discretion. But another time be careful not to overreach your betters. No other Achaean would have found me so easy to placate. But you have suffered much and laboured hard in my behalf, and so have your noble father and your brother. I therefore accept your apology. And not only that, I will give you the mare though she is mine, to show our countrymen here that there is no pride or malice in me.'

With that, he handed over the mare to Noemon, one of Antilochus' men, and himself took the shining kettle. Meriones, who had come in fourth, took the fourth prize, two talents of gold. The fifth, the two-handled pan, remained unclaimed. Achilles gave this to Nestor. He carried it across the ring to him and said: 'Here, my venerable lord, is a keepsake for you also. Let it remind you of Patroclus' funeral, for you will not see the man himself among us any more. The prize I am

[36]Poseidon; in his capacity as god of horses he would be the appropriate guarantor of the oath.

giving you has no relation to the sports; for I know that you will not be boxing or wrestling, nor entering for the foot-race or the javelin-throwing. Your years sit too heavily on you for that.'

As he spoke, Achilles put the prize in Nestor's hands. Nestor was delighted and made him a speech. 'Yes, my dear boy, you are quite right in all you say: I am infirm of limb. My feet are not so steady now, my friend, and my arms no longer swing out lightly from the shoulder as they did. Ah, if only I were still as young and vigorous as I was when the Epeans buried my lord Amarynceus at Buprasion and his sons held funeral sports in honour of their royal father. There was not a man to match me there, either among the Epeans or the Pylians themselves or the mettlesome Aetolians. In the boxing I beat Clytomedes son of Enops. Ancaeus of Pleuron took me on at wrestling and I won. In the foot-race I defeated Iphiclus, who was a good man; and with the javelin I cast farther than Phyleus, and Polydorus too. It was only in the chariot-race that I was beaten, by the two Moliones, who grudged me this event and cut across me in the crowd, because a win for them meant that after all the chief prize stayed at home. Those two were twins. One of them used to drive from start to finish, while the other plied the whip.

'That is the kind of man I was. Now, I must leave this sort of thing to younger men and take the painful lessons of old age to heart. But at that time I stood in a class by myself. Well, you must get on with your own friend's funeral sports. Meanwhile I accept your gift with pleasure. I am delighted to think that you always realize how well disposed I am to you, and never let a chance go by of paying me the respect that our countrymen owe me. May the gods reward you graciously for what you have done.'

When he had heard all that Nestor had to say by way of thanks, Achilles made his way through the crowd of spectators and brought out the prizes for the boxing-match. For the victor in this painful sport, he fetched and tethered in the ring a sturdy mule, six years old and broken in—which is a hard job in the case of mules. For the loser there was a two-handled mug. Standing up, Achilles announced the contest to the Argives: 'My lord Atreides and Achaean men-at-arms, these are the prizes for which I want to see our two best men put up their fists and box to a finish. Apollo's favourite, the man who comes off best in everyone's opinion here, can take this sturdy mule to his own hut. The loser will receive this two-handled mug.'

There rose at once a huge fine-looking fellow called Epeius son of

Panopeus, who was a champion boxer. He put his hand on the sturdy mule and said: 'Come on, the man who wants to carry off the mug. The mule is mine, and nobody is going to knock me out and take her, for I maintain that I am the best boxer here. True, I am not so good at fighting—no one can be a champion all round—but isn't that enough? At any rate, I'll tell you what I mean to do. I am going to tear the fellow's flesh to ribbons and smash his bones. I recommend him to have all his mourners standing by to take him off when I have done with him.'

This challenge was received in complete silence. The only man who dared to take it up was the heroic Euryalus, the son of King Mecisteus, Talaus' son, who, after Oedipus had fallen, went to Thebes for the funeral sports and there beat all the Cadmeians.[37] Euryalus was got ready for the fight and was warmly encouraged by his famous cousin Diomedes, who wanted very much to see him win. He helped him on with his shorts, and bound on his hands the well-cut oxhide thongs. When the two men were dressed they stepped into the middle of the ring; they both put up their mighty hands, and they fell to. Fist met fist; there was a terrible grinding of jaws; and the sweat began to pour from all their limbs. Presently Euryalus took his eye off his man, and the excellent Epeius, leaping at the chance, gave him a punch on the jaw which knocked him out. His legs were cut from under him and he was lifted by the blow like a fish leaping up from the weed-covered sands and falling back into the dark water, when the North Wind sends ripples up the beach. His chivalrous opponent gave him a hand and set him on his legs. His followers gathered round and supported him across the ring on trailing feet, spitting clots of blood, with his head lolling on one side. He was still senseless when they put him down in his own corner. They had to go and fetch the mug themselves.

Losing no time, the son of Peleus brought out and displayed fresh prizes, for the third event, the all-in wrestling. For the winner there was a big three-legged cauldron to go on the fire—it was worth a dozen oxen by Achaean reckoning—and for the loser he brought forward a woman thoroughly trained in domestic work, who was valued at four oxen in the camp. Achilles stood up to announce the contest to the Argives, and called for a couple of entries for the new event. The

---

[37]The reference is to the funeral games for Oedipus, descendant of Cadmus and King of Thebes, who had unknowingly killed his father and married his mother. The Oedipal tradition was to be further developed by the fifth-century B.C. tragedian Sophocles. (See selection 3.)

great Telamonian Aias rose at once, and so did the resourceful Odysseus, who knew all the tricks. The two put on their shorts, stepped into the middle of the ring, and gripped each other in their powerful arms. They looked like a couple of those sloping rafters that a good builder locks together in the roof of a high house to resist the wind. Their backs creaked under the pressure of their mighty hands; the sweat streamed down; and many blood-red weals sprang up along their sides and shoulders. And still they tussled on, each thinking of the fine cauldron that was not yet won. But Odysseus was no more able to bring down his man, and pin him to the ground, than Aias, who was baffled by Odysseus' brawn. After some time, when they saw that they were boring the troops, the great Telamonian Aias said: 'Royal son of Laertes, Odysseus of the nimble wits; either you or I must let the other try a throw. What happens afterwards is Zeus' business.'

With that, he lifted Odysseus off the ground. But Odysseus' craft did not desert him. He caught Aias with a kick from behind in the hollow of the knee, upset his stance, and flung him on his back, himself falling on Aias' chest. The spectators were duly impressed. But now the stalwart admirable Odysseus had to try a throw. He shifted Aias just a little off the ground, but he could not throw him. So he crooked a leg round Aias' knee, and they both fell down, cheek by jowl, and were smothered in dust. They jumped up and would have tried a third round, if Achilles himself had not risen to his feet and interposed. He told them they had struggled quite enough and must not wear each other out. 'You have both won,' he said. 'Take equal prizes and withdraw. There are other events to follow.' The two men readily accepted his decision, and after wiping off the dust put on their tunics.

The son of Peleus went on at once to offer prizes for the foot-race. The first was a mixing-bowl of chased silver, holding six pints. It was the loveliest thing in the world, a masterpiece of Sidonian craftsmanship, which had been shipped across the misty seas by Phoenician traders and presented to King Thoas when they put in at his port. Then Euneus son of Jason had given it to the lord Patroclus in payment for Lycaon, Priam's son; and now Achilles offered it as a prize in honour of his dead friend to the runner who should come in first in the foot-race. The runner-up was to have a large, well-fattened ox; and the third and last man half a talent of gold. Achilles stood up, announced the contest and invited competitors to come forward. Aias the Runner and son of Oïleus jumped up at once; so did Odysseus of the nimble wits; and they were followed by Nestor's son Antilochus, who was the fastest of the younger men. The three of them toed the line, and Achilles pointed out the turning-post.

They went all out from scratch. Aias soon shot ahead; but very close behind him came the good Odysseus, close as a girdled woman brings the shuttle to her breast as she carefully draws it along to get the bobbin past the warp. So little was there in it. Odysseus' feet were falling in the tracks of Aias before the dust had settled down again; and he kept up so well that his breath fanned Aias' head. He was straining every nerve to win, and all the Achaeans cheered him, shouting encouragement to a man who was doing all he could already. As they drew near the finish, Odysseus offered up a silent prayer to Athene of the Flashing Eyes: 'Hear me, goddess. I need your valuable aid. Come down and speed my feet.' Pallas Athene heard his prayer, and she lightened all his limbs.

They were just about to dash up to the prizes, when Aias slipped in full career. This was Athene's doing, and it happened where the ground was littered with dung from the lowing cattle that were slaughtered by the swift Achilles for Patroclus' funeral. So Aias had his mouth and nostrils filled with cattle-dung, while the much-enduring excellent Odysseus, having caught him up and finished, carried off the silver bowl. The illustrious Aias took possession of the farmyard ox. Then he stood there with his hands on one of the animal's horns, and as he spat out dung, remarked to the spectators: 'Damnation take it! I swear it was the goddess tripped me up—the one who always dances attendance, like a mother, on Odysseus.'

But they only laughed at him, delightedly. And now Antilochus came in. He took the last prize with a smile and made them a speech. 'Friends,' he said, 'I'll tell you something that you know already. The gods still favour the old crowd; for though Aias is only a little older than myself, Odysseus over there is the product of an earlier generation, a relic of the past. But his old age, as they say, is green; and it's a hard job to beat him in a race—for any of us but Achilles.'

This compliment to Achilles the great runner drew a reply from the prince himself. 'Antilochus,' he said, 'I cannot allow your tribute to go unrewarded. You have won a half-talent of gold: I will give you another.' And he handed the gold to Antilochus, who received it with delight.

The son of Peleus now brought out and put down in the ring a long-shadowed spear, a shield and a helmet, the arms that Patroclus had taken from Sarpedon. Then he stood up and told the Argives what was coming next. He said: 'I want our two best men to fight each other for these prizes before the assembled troops. They must put on their armour and use naked weapons. To the one who first gets through the other's guard, pinks his man and draws blood, I will give this Thracian sword, with its fine silver mounting, which I took from Asteropaeus. The armour here will be shared between the combatants and I will also give them a good dinner in my hut.'

His challenge was taken up by the great Telamonian Aias and by Tydeus' son, the powerful Diomedes. Each armed himself on his own side of the ring, and the pair advanced on each other in the centre, in fighting mood and looking so fierce that all the spectators held their breath. They came within range. They charged three times, and when they had tried three lunges at each other, Aias succeeded in piercing Diomedes' rounded shield. But the bronze failed to reach his flesh: he was saved by the breast-plate underneath. It was now Diomedes' turn. Thrusting repeatedly above the rim of Aias' large shield he touched him on the neck with his glittering spear-point. The spectators were so terrified for Aias that they called upon the combatants to stop and share the prizes. However, the prince awarded Diomedes the big sword, which he handed to him with its scabbard and its well-cut baldric.[38]

The next prize offered by the son of Peleus was a lump of pig iron which had already done service as a quoit in the powerful hands of Eëtion, and had been carried off on board ship with his other possessions by the swift and excellent Achilles after he had killed him. Achilles stood up, announced the contest and invited competitors to come forward. 'This lump is big enough,' he pointed out, 'to keep the winner in iron for five years or more, even if his farm is out in the wilds. It will not be lack of iron that sends his shepherd or his ploughman in to town. He will have plenty on the spot.'

In response to this, the dauntless Polypoetes rose to throw the disk. So did the highborn and powerful Leonteus, and Telamonian Aias and the noble Epeius. They stood in a row and the good Epeius picked up the weight and hurled it with a swing. But the spectators only laughed

---

[38]The ornamented belt, worn diagonally from shoulder to hip, that supports the sword.

at his effort. Leonteus, offshoot of Ares,[39] was the next to throw. Then the great Telamonian Aias cast with his mighty hand and passed the marks of all the others. But when it came to the dauntless Polypoetes' turn, he overshot the whole field by the distance to which a herdsman can send a boomerang flying on its crooked course among a herd of cows. There was a loud applause, and the mighty Polypoetes' men got up and carried off their king's prize to the hollow ships.

Archery came next, and for this Achilles offered prizes of violet-coloured iron in the form of ten double-headed and ten single-headed axes. He set up the mast of a blue-prowed ship a long way off on the sands; and for a target he had a fluttering pigeon tied to it by the foot with a light cord. 'The man who hits the pigeon,' said Achilles, 'can take the whole set of double-headed axes home with him. If anyone hits the string and not the bird, he won't have done so well, but he can have the single axes.'

The great Prince Teucer and Meriones, Idomeneus' worthy squire, rose to compete and shook lots in a bronze helmet. It fell to Teucer to shoot first, and he quickly let fly an arrow with tremendous force. But he had forgotten to promise the Archer-King a pleasing sacrifice of firstling lambs, and he failed to hit the bird—Apollo grudged him that success. Yet he did strike the cord by which the bird was tethered, near its foot. The sharp arrow severed the string and the pigeon shot up into the sky, leaving the string to dangle down. The Achaeans roared. But Meriones, who had been holding an arrow ready while Teucer aimed, snatched the bow hastily from Teucer's hands and promptly vowed a pleasing sacrifice of firstborn lambs to the Archer-King Apollo. He saw the pigeon fluttering high overhead beneath the clouds, and as she circled there he hit her from below, plumb in the wing. His arrow went clean through, came down at his feet and stuck in the earth, while the bird settled on the mast of the blue-prowed ship with drooping head and plumage all awry. In a moment she was dead and fell to the ground a long way from the man who had shot her. The spectators were lost in admiration. Meriones carried off the set of ten double axes, and Teucer took the single axes to the hollow ships.

Finally the son of Peleus brought into the ring a long-shadowed spear and an unused cauldron with a floral pattern, worth an ox. He put these down, and the javelin-throwers rose to compete. The two

[39]God of war.

men that stood up were imperial Agamemnon, Atreus' son, and Meriones, Idomeneus' worthy squire. But the swift and admirable Achilles interposed, saying: 'My lord Atreides, we know by how much you excel the rest of us and that in throwing the spear no one can compete with your prowess. Accept this prize and take it with you to the hollow ships. But if you are agreeable, let us give the spear to my lord Meriones. That is what I at all events suggest.'[40]

To this decision, Agamemnon King of Men made no demur. So Achilles gave the bronze spear to Meriones, and the King handed his own beautiful prize to his herald Talthybius.

---

[40]Achilles concludes the games with a compliment and a gift for his commander, Agamemnon. He thus completes his public reconciliation.

2

Aesop

Fables

NOT all early Greek literature is as *aristocratic and "high-minded" as Homer's epics. There is also a tradition of folk wisdom, carried at first by the spoken word from generation to generation—through parable and fable. The "classic" originator of such popular tales in the Western world is Aesop.*

Little reliable information exists about this author, although many fascinating stories have come down to us. Herodotus, the fifth century B.C. Greek historian (selection 4), tells us that Aesop had been a slave on the Aegean island of Samos in the sixth century B.C. and that he was murdered by natives of the holy city of Delphi. (They were later directed by their oracle to pay compensation to the grandson of Aesop's owner.) The fact that such influential ancient authors as Herodotus, the historians Xenophon and Plutarch, the playwright Aristophanes, the philosophers Plato and Aristotle all mention Aesop's fables demonstrates that they were frequently repeated and commonly known. We cannot be sure, however, how closely our current versions follow Aesop's original tales. So potent, in fact, was Aesop's name that any fable might have been labelled as his. Some editions, therefore, total over seven hundred fables. The text that we call Aesop's today is based mainly on two collections: one in Latin verse by Phaedrus, a freed slave of the first century A.D., and—about two centuries later—one in Greek verse by Babrius.

The form of the Aesopic fable is that of a brief anecdote focused on a single event and designed to teach some principle of successful living. The characters of the fable are often animals endowed with human speech and personal qualities. Each quality fits the stereotype for that creature; for example, the fox is

THE FABLES OF AESOP   Aesop, *The Fables of Aesop*, ed. and trans. Joseph Jacobs (London, Macmillan & Co., 1894). Adapted by the editor.

untrustworthy, the lamb naive and helpless, the wolf cruel, the lion noble, the ant industrious. These animals, as well as the people in the fables, become easily recognized images of human types. The concluding moral of each story, sometimes added to the text centuries later, is drawn from common human experience and, therefore, makes an easily understood lesson.

Although the language of the fables is spare and simple, the ancients did not consider them only as children's literature. Their point of view is really adult and often satirical. Aesop, for example, is said by Phaedrus to have told the Athenians the story of "The Frogs Desiring a King" when they expressed discontent with their ruler.

The English translation from which the following selected fables are taken was intended for popular reading and remains true to the spirit of gentle satire and common wisdom associated with the name of Aesop.

THE FROGS DESIRING A KING

The frogs were living as happy as could be in a marshy swamp that just suited them; they went splashing about caring for nobody and nobody troubling with them. But some of them thought that this was not right, that they should have a king and a proper constitution, so they determined to send up a petition to Jove [Jupiter] to give them what they wanted. "Mighty Jove," they cried, "send unto us a king that will rule over us and keep us in order." Jove laughed at their croaking, and threw down into the swamp a huge Log, which came down—*kerplash*—into the swamp. The Frogs were frightened out of their lives by the commotion made in their midst, and all rushed to the bank to look at the horrible monster; but after a time, seeing that it did not move, one or two of the boldest of them ventured out towards the Log, and even dared to touch it; still it did not move. Then the greatest hero of the Frogs jumped upon the Log and commenced dancing up and down upon it, thereupon all the Frogs came and did the same; and for some time the Frogs went about their business every day without taking the slightest notice of their new King Log lying in their midst. But this did not suit them, so they sent another petition to Jove, and said to him: "We want a real king; one that will really rule over us." Now this made Jove angry, so he sent among them a big Stork that soon set to work gobbling them all up. Then the Frogs repented when too late.

Better no rule than cruel rule.

THE DOG AND THE REFLECTION

It happened that a Dog had got a piece of meat and was carrying it home in his mouth to eat it in peace. Now on his way home he had to cross a plank lying across a running brook. As he crossed, he looked down and saw his own reflection in the water beneath. Thinking it was another dog with another piece of meat, he made up his mind to have that also. So he made a snap at the image in the water, but as he opened his mouth the piece of meat fell out, dropped into the water and was never seen more.

Beware lest you lose the substance by grasping at the reflection.

THE TOWN MOUSE AND THE COUNTRY MOUSE.

Now you must know that a Town Mouse once upon a time went on a visit to his cousin in the country. He was rough and ready, this cousin, but he loved his town friend and made him heartily welcome. Beans and bacon, cheese and bread, were all he had to offer, but he offered them freely. The Town Mouse rather turned up his long nose at this country fare, and said: "I cannot understand, Cousin, how you can put up with such poor food as this, but of course you cannot expect anything better in the country; come you with me and I will show you how to live. When you have been in town a week you will wonder how you could ever have stood a country life." No sooner said than done: the two mice set off for the town and arrived at the Town Mouse's residence late at night. "You will want some refreshment after our long journey," said the polite Town Mouse, and took his friend into the grand dining-room. There they found the remains of a fine feast, and soon the two mice were eating up jellies and cakes and all that was nice. Suddenly they heard growling and barking. "What is that?" said the Country Mouse. "It is only the dogs of the house," answered the other. "Only!" said the Country Mouse. "I do not like that music at my dinner." Just at that moment the door flew open, in came two huge mastiffs, and the two mice had to scamper down and run off. "Good-by, Cousin," said the Country Mouse. "What! going so soon?" said the other. "Yes," he replied;

"Better beans and bacon in peace than cakes and ale in fear."

ANDROCLES AND THE LION

A slave named Androcles once escaped from his master and fled to the forest. As he was wandering about there he came upon a Lion lying down moaning and groaning. At first he turned to flee, but finding that the Lion did not pursue him, he turned back and went up to him. As he came near, the Lion put out his paw, which was all swollen and bleeding, and Androcles found that a huge thorn had got into it, and was causing all the pain. He pulled out the thorn and bound up the paw of the Lion, who was soon able to rise and lick the hand of Androcles like a dog. Then the Lion took Androcles to his cave, and every day used to bring him meat from which to live. But shortly afterwards both Androcles and the Lion were captured, and the slave was sentenced to be thrown to the Lion, after the latter had been kept without food for several days. The Emperor and all his Court came to see the spectacle, and Androcles was led out into the middle of the arena. Soon the Lion was let loose from his den, and rushed bounding and roaring towards his victim. But as soon as he came near to Andro-cles he recognised his friend, and fawned upon him, and licked his hands like a friendly dog. The Emperor, surprised at this, summoned Androcles to him, who told him the whole story. Whereupon the slave was pardoned and freed, and the Lion let loose to his native forest.

Gratitude is the sign of noble souls.

THE BELLY AND THE MEMBERS

One fine day it occurred to the Members of the Body that they were doing all the work and the Belly was having all the food. So they held a meeting, and after a long discussion, decided to strike work till the Belly consented to take its proper share of the work. So for a day or two the Hands refused to take the food, the Mouth refused to receive it, and the Teeth had no work to do. But after a day or two the Members began to find that they themselves were not in a very active condition: the Hands could hardly move, and the Mouth was all parched and dry, while the Legs were unable to support the rest. So thus they found that even the Belly in its dull quiet way was doing necessary work for the Body, and that all must work together or the Body will go to pieces.

THE WOLF IN SHEEP'S CLOTHING[1]

A wolf found great difficulty in getting at the sheep owing to the vigilance of the shepherd and his dogs. But one day it found the skin of a sheep that had been flayed and thrown aside, so it put it on over its own pelt and strolled down among the sheep. The Lamb of that sheep, whose skin the Wolf was wearing, began to follow the Wolf in the Sheep's clothing; so, leading the Lamb a little apart, he soon made a meal of her, and for some time he succeeded in deceiving the sheep, and enjoying hearty meals.

Appearances are deceptive.

THE FOX AND THE GRAPES

One hot summer's day a Fox was strolling through an orchard till he came to a bunch of Grapes just ripening on a vine which had been trained over a lofty branch. "Just the thing to quench my thirst," said he. Drawing back a few paces, he took a run and a jump, and just missed the bunch. Turning round again with a One, Two, Three, he jumped up, but with no greater success. Again and again he tried after the tempting morsel, but at last had to give it up, and walked away with his nose in the air, saying: "I am sure they are sour."

It is easy to despise what you cannot get.

THE ANT AND THE GRASSHOPPER

In a field one summer's day a Grasshopper was hopping about, chirping and singing to its heart's content. An Ant passed by, bearing along with great toil an ear of corn he was taking to the nest.

[1]Note the similarity to "The Sermon on the Mount" (Matthew, 7:15), where Jesus says, "Beware of false prophets, who come to you in sheep's clothing but inwardly are ravenous wolves."

"Why not come and chat with me," said the Grasshopper, "instead of toiling and moiling in that way?"

"I am helping to lay up food for the winter," said the Ant, "and recommend you do the same."

"Why bother about winter?" said the Grasshopper; "we have got plenty of food at present." But the Ant went on its way and continued its toil. When the winter came the Grasshopper had no food, and found itself dying of hunger, while it saw the ants distributing every day corn and grain from the stores they had collected in the summer. Then the Grasshopper knew

It is best to prepare for the days of necessity.

THE YOUNG THIEF AND HIS MOTHER

A young man had been caught in a daring act of theft and had been condemned to be executed for it. He expressed his desire to see his Mother, and to speak with her before he was led to execution, and of course this was granted. When his Mother came to him he said: "I want to whisper to you," and when she brought her ear near him, he nearly bit it off. All the bystanders were horrified, and asked him what he could mean by such brutal and inhuman conduct. "It is to punish her," he said. "When I was young I began with stealing little things, and brought them home to Mother. Instead of rebuking and punishing me, she laughed and said: 'It will not be noticed.' It is because of her that I am here to-day."

"He is right, woman," said the Priest; "the Lord hath said:

"Train up a child in the way he should go; and when he is old he will not depart therefrom."

AVARICIOUS AND ENVIOUS

Two neighbours came before Jupiter and prayed him to grant their hearts' desire. Now the one was full of avarice, and the other eaten up with envy. So to punish them both, Jupiter granted that each might have whatever he wished for himself, but only on condition that his neighbor had twice as much. The Avaricious man prayed to have a room full of gold. No sooner said than done; but all his joy was turned to grief when he found that his neighbour had two rooms full of the precious metal. Then came the turn of the Envious man, who could not bear to think that his neighbour had any joy at all. So he prayed that he might have one of his own eyes put out, by which means his companion would become totally blind.

Vices are their own punishment.

THE GOOSE WITH THE GOLDEN EGGS

One day a countryman going to the nest of his Goose found there an egg all yellow and glittering. When he took it up it was as heavy as lead and he was going to throw it away, because he thought a trick had been played upon him. But he took it home on second thoughts, and soon found to his delight that it was an egg of pure gold. Every morning the same thing occurred, and he soon became rich by selling his eggs. As he grew rich he grew greedy; and thinking to get at once all the gold the Goose could give, he killed it and opened it only to find,— nothing.

Greed often overreaches itself.

HERCULES AND THE WAGGONER

A Waggoner was once driving a heavy load along a very muddy way. At last he came to a part of the road where the wheels sank halfway into the mire, and the more the horses pulled, the deeper sank the wheels. So the Waggoner threw down his whip, and knelt down and prayed to Hercules the Strong. "O Hercules, help me in this my hour of distress," said he. But Hercules appeared to him, and said:

"Tut, man, don't sprawl there. Get up and put your shoulder to the wheel."

The gods help them that help themselves.

THE OLD MAN AND DEATH

An old labourer, bent double with age and toil, was gathering sticks in a forest. At last he grew so tired and hopeless that he threw down the bundle of sticks, and cried out: "I cannot bear this life any longer. Ah, I wish Death would only come and take me!"

As he spoke, Death, a grisly skeleton, appeared and said to him: "What wouldst thou, Mortal? I heard thee call me."

"Please, sir," replied the woodcutter, "would you kindly help me to lift this bundle of sticks on to my shoulder?"

We would often be sorry if our wishes were gratified.

3

Sophocles

Oedipus the King

*D*RAMATIC *tragedy represents the chief literary achievement of Athens in the Golden Age and one of the noblest products of the human imagination. Its development was encouraged by the extraordinary awareness and maturity of outlook that characterized the Athenian populace in the sixth and fifth centuries B.C. Poets of genius found an audience of comparable taste and feeling, and those who wrote tragedies had a favorable climate in which to present both their interpretations of Hellenic traditions and ideals and their own insights into the nature of human life and destiny. Of these dramatists the three considered supreme were Aeschylus, Sophocles, and Euripides. They were the only Greek tragedians to have some of their works preserved complete—to the benefit of later generations.*

Throughout his long life Sophocles (ca. 496–406 B.C.) had every advantage: aristocratic education, wealth, good looks, success, and, above all, the inspiration of living in Athens during the Golden Age. He is said to have been victorious twenty-four times in the great annual dramatic competitions. Unfortunately, of the more than one hundred twenty plays he wrote, only seven survive. The most famous of these, Oedipus the King, *dates from about 429 B.C. (the year of the statesman Pericles' death); it is regarded not only as his masterpiece but as one of the most influential tragedies of all time. In the following century the philosopher Aristotle would use this play as a model of what a "perfect" tragedy should be. (See his* Poetics, *selection 13.) In our own century Sigmund Freud, the founder of psychoanalysis, would label the "Oedipus complex"—a son's love for his mother and rivalry with his father—one of the most powerful expressions of instinctive drives.*

OEDIPUS THE KING   "Oedipus the King," from *The Three Theban Plays,* by Sophocles, translated by Robert Fagles. Copyright © 1977, 1979, 1982 by Robert Fagles. Reprinted by permission of Viking Penguin, Inc.

Since the Oedipus legend was already well known to Sophocles' audience, their interest lay in watching the main character's responses to the working out of his fate. As interpreted by Sophocles the legend deals with the relationship of humans to the divine order. Since, to the Athenians of Sophocles' time, divine order and justice were considered identical, King Oedipus—who had unintentionally broken the moral code guaranteed by the Olympian gods—is made to suffer horribly. (He had unknowingly killed his father and married his mother.) Whether or not his punishment is just by human standards is irrelevant to the judgment of the gods. It is their will that humans should know themselves and thus realize their limitations. At the end of the play, the self-blinded Oedipus, having come to know the moral code through suffering, emerges a wiser man, more aware of life's meaning than he ever had been as a confident, proud ruler.

This acceptance of divine law and of human limitations was not the private viewpoint of Sophocles alone. The sentiments of the Chorus, whose dramatic role was to comment upon and to express general opinion, showed that the belief that human beings should know themselves and the gods' demands was part of the consciousness of Athenian citizens. The miracle of Periclean Athens was based in part upon the result of this belief: faith that each individual has the potential to face harsh realities, even the prospect of ultimate doom, with courage and dignity. Both the suffering of Oedipus—stirring the emotions of pity and fear—and his grandeur in adversity are evidence of such potential and the essence of tragedy. The Greek attitude, then, was one of awe and wonder at the uniqueness of human beings and their inherent moral capacity for achieving harmony with the divine will. This attitude is the core of that philosophy that came to be known as humanism.

Characters

OEDIPUS, *King of Thebes*

A PRIEST *of Zeus*

CREON, *brother of Jocasta*

A CHORUS *of Theban citizens and their* LEADER

TIRESIAS, *a blind prophet*

JOCASTA, *the queen, wife of Oedipus*

A MESSENGER *from Corinth*

A SHEPHERD

A MESSENGER *from inside the palace*

ANTIGONE, ISMENE, *daughters of Oedipus and Jocasta*

Guards and attendants

Priests of Thebes

[Editor's note on events leading up to the action of the play: A son had been born to King Laius and Queen Jocasta of the ancient Greek city-state of Thebes. The birth was not a happy event, however, for the god Apollo's oracle had issued a frightful prophecy: the child was destined to kill his father and breed children by his mother. Attempting to evade their fate, Laius and Jocasta gave the infant to one of their slaves, a shepherd, ordering him to abandon it on the mountainside where he customarily grazed his flock. So that the child might not crawl to safety, they also ordered its ankles pierced with an iron pin. The shepherd, however, took pity on the mutilated child and passed him on to another shepherd from the rich city-state of Corinth.

Polybus and Merope, king and queen of Corinth, were childless and gratefully rewarded their slave who had brought them such a beloved gift. They raised the child as their own, giving him the name of Oedipus ("Swollen-foot"). The boy grew to sturdy intelligent manhood, a prince of Corinth, assuming himself to be the true son of Polybus and Merope. Accused of lowly birth by a party drunkard, Oedipus—not totally comforted by the assurances of his loving "parents"—journeyed to the sacred oracle of Apollo at Delphi to determine the truth.

Told at Delphi of his terrible fate (but not of his natural parents), Oedipus vowed to outwit the prophecy by never returning to Corinth. During his flight he killed, at a crossroads, a man on a chariot who was trying to force him off the road. He also killed all but one of the man's five attendants. Travelling farther, Oedipus encountered a monstrous Sphinx that had been strangling travellers on the road to Thebes who could not answer its riddle. Oedipus succeeded in answering the riddle, causing the Sphinx to destroy itself. Received joyfully as a hero by the Thebans whose king had been recently murdered—according to reports—by a band of thieves, Oedipus married Queen Jocasta, raised a family of two sons and two daughters, and ruled in peace and prosperity for fifteen years until a terrible plague infected the city.]

TIME AND SCENE. *The royal house of Thebes. Double doors dominate the façade; a stone altar stands at the center of the stage.*

Many years have passed since Oedipus solved the riddle of the Sphinx and ascended the throne of Thebes, and now a plague has struck the city. A procession of priests enters; suppliants,[1] broken and despondent, they carry branches wound in wool and lay them on the altar.

The doors open. Guards assemble. Oedipus comes forward majestic but for a telltale limp, and slowly views the condition of his people.

OEDIPUS

Oh my children, the new blood of ancient Thebes,
why are you here? Huddling at my altar,
praying before me, your branches wound in wool.
Our city reeks with the smoke of burning incense,
rings with cries for the Healer[2] and wailing for the dead.
I thought it wrong, my children, to hear the truth
from others, messengers. Here I am myself—
you all know me, the world knows my fame:
I am Oedipus.

Helping a Priest to his feet.

Speak up, old man. Your years,
your dignity—you should speak for the others.
Why here and kneeling, what preys upon you so?
Some sudden fear? some strong desire?
You can trust me; I am ready to help,
I'll do anything. I would be blind to misery
not to pity my people kneeling at my feet.

PRIEST

Oh Oedipus, king of the land, our greatest power!
You see us before you, men of all ages

[1]A suppliant (or supplicant) is a person who begs a favor of another person. In this opening scene the suppliants are priests who, because of the plague, have given up hope—except through divine intervention. They carry olive or laurel branches wound with tufts of wool. The branches are laid on the altar of the god Apollo to whom supplication is made and left there until the request is granted. (At the end of this scene with the priests, Oedipus will tell them to take the branches away, as if his actions will fulfill the suppliants' request.)

[2]A title of Apollo, patron god of medicine, music, archery and prophecy. As he did at the beginning of *The Iliad* (selection 1), Apollo sometimes expresses his anger by sending down his arrows in the form of plague.

clinging to your altars. Here are boys,
still too weak to fly from the nest,
and here the old, bowed down with the years,
the holy ones—a priest of Zeus myself—and here
the picked, unmarried men, the young hope of Thebes.
And all the rest, your great family gathers now,
branches wreathed, massing in the squares,
kneeling before the two temples of queen Athena[3]
or the river-shrine where the embers glow and die
and Apollo sees the future in the ashes.[4]

                             Our city—
look around you, see with your own eyes—
our ship pitches wildly, cannot lift her head
from the depths, the red waves of death . . .
Thebes is dying. A blight on the fresh crops
and the rich pastures, cattle sicken and die,
and the women die in labor, children stillborn,
and the plague, the fiery god of fever hurls down
on the city, his lightning slashing through us—
raging plague in all its vengeance, devastating
the house of Cadmus.[5] And Black Death luxuriates
in the raw, wailing miseries of Thebes.

Now we pray to you. You cannot equal the gods,
your children know that, bending at your altar.
But we do rate you first of men,
both in the common crises of our lives
and face-to-face encounters with the gods.
You freed us from the Sphinx;[6] you came to Thebes
and cut us loose from the bloody tribute we had paid

---

[3]Goddess of wisdom and daughter of Zeus (chief of the gods).

[4]The priests of Apollo's temple read the future from the patterns they see in the ashes of the burned sacrificial animals.

[5]Founder of Thebes, ancestor of Laius and Oedipus.

[6]A monster with the body of a winged lion, the breasts and head of a woman. From a high rock near Thebes, she gave every passerby the following riddle: "What walks on four legs in the morning, on two at noon, and on three in the evening?" The Sphinx strangled and devoured all those who failed the answer. Oedipus answered correctly that it was Man who (in early life) first crawls on hands and knees, then (in adulthood) walks upright, and finally (in old age) needs a cane as a third "leg." Furious at having been correctly answered, the Sphinx leaped from her rock and was destroyed.

that harsh, brutal singer. We taught you nothing,
no skill, no extra knowledge, still you triumphed.
A god was with you, so they say, and we believe it—
you lifted up our lives.
                                So now again,
Oedipus, king, we bend to you, your power—
we implore you, all of us on our knees:
find us strength, rescue! Perhaps you've heard
the voice of a god or something from other men,
Oedipus . . . what do you know?
The man of experience—you see it every day—
his plans will work in a crisis, his first of all.

Act now—we beg you, best of men, raise up our city!
Act, defend yourself, your former glory!
Your country calls you savior now
for your zeal, your action years ago.
Never let us remember of your reign:
you helped us stand, only to fall once more.
Oh raise up our city, set us on our feet.
The omens were good that day you brought us joy—
be the same man today!
Rule our land, you know you have the power,
but rule a land of the living, not a wasteland.
Ship and towered city are nothing, stripped of men
alive within it, living all as one.

OEDIPUS

                                My children,
I pity you. I see—how could I fail to see
what longings bring you here? Well I know
you are sick to death, all of you,
but sick as you are, not one is sick as I.
Your pain strikes each of you alone, each
in the confines of himself, no other. But my spirit
grieves for the city, for myself and all of you.
I wasn't asleep, dreaming. You haven't wakened me—
I've wept through the nights, you must know that,

groping, laboring over many paths of thought.
After a painful search I found one cure:
I acted at once. I sent Creon,
my wife's own brother, to Delphi—
Apollo the Prophet's oracle—to learn
what I might do or say to save our city.

Today's the day. When I count the days gone by
it torments me . . . what is he doing?
Strange, he's late, he's gone too long.
But once he returns, then, then I'll be a traitor
if I do not do all the god makes clear.

PRIEST

Timely words. The men over there are signaling—
Creon's just arriving.

OEDIPUS

*Sighting Creon, then
turning to the altar.*

                    Lord Apollo,
let him come with a lucky word of rescue,
shining like his eyes!

PRIEST

Welcome news, I think—he's crowned, look,
and the laurel wreath is bright with berries.[7]

OEDIPUS

We'll soon see. He's close enough to hear—

*Enter Creon from the side; his face
is shaded with a wreath.*

[7]Traditionally, a laurel crown was a sign that the wearer brought good news.

Creon, prince, my kinsman, what do you bring us?
What message from the god?

CREON

                              Good news.
I tell you even the hardest things to bear,
if they should turn out well, all would be well.

OEDIPUS

Of course, but what were the god's *words?* There's no hope
and nothing to fear in what you've said so far.

CREON

If you want my report in the presence of these . . .

>   *Pointing to the priests while*
>   *drawing Oedipus toward the palace.*

I'm ready now, or we might go inside.

OEDIPUS

                              Speak out,
speak to us all. I grieve for these, my people,
far more than I fear for my own life.

CREON

                              Very well,
I will tell you what I heard from the god.
Apollo commands us—he was quite clear—
"Drive the corruption[8] from the land,
don't harbor it any longer, past all cure,
don't nurse it in your soil—root it out!"

---

[8]The blood of a murdered man, prior to the act of his being revenged, was thought of as
  a spreading stain that polluted not only the killer but also those who innocently came
  into contact with him.

OEDIPUS

How can we cleanse ourselves—what rites?
What's the source of the trouble?

CREON

Banish the man, or pay back blood with blood.
Murder sets the plague-storm on the city.

OEDIPUS

                                        Whose murder?
Whose fate does Apollo bring to light?

CREON

                                Our leader,
my lord, was once a man named Laius,
before you came and put us straight on course.

OEDIPUS

                                        I know—
or so I've heard. I never saw the man myself.

CREON

Well, he was killed, and Apollo commands us now—
he could not be more clear,
"Pay the killers back—whoever is responsible."

OEDIPUS

Where on earth are they? Where to find it now,
the trail of the ancient guilt so hard to trace?

CREON

"Here in Thebes," he said.
Whatever is sought for can be caught, you know,
whatever is neglected slips away.

OEDIPUS

But where,
in the palace, the fields or foreign soil,
where did Laius meet his bloody death?

CREON

He went to consult an oracle, he said,
and he set out and never came home again.

OEDIPUS

No messenger, no fellow-traveler saw what happened?
Someone to cross-examine?

CREON

No,
they were all killed but one. He escaped,
terrified, he could tell us nothing clearly,
nothing of what he saw—just one thing.

OEDIPUS

What's that?
One thing could hold the key to it all,
a small beginning give us grounds for hope.

CREON

He said thieves attacked them—a whole band,
not single-handed, cut King Laius down.

OEDIPUS

A thief,
so daring, wild, he'd kill a king? Impossible,
unless conspirators paid him off in Thebes.

CREON

We suspected as much. But with Laius dead
no leader appeared to help us in our troubles.

OEDIPUS

Trouble? Your *king* was murdered—royal blood!
What stopped you from tracking down the killer
then and there?

CREON

           The singing, riddling Sphinx.
She . . . persuaded us to let the mystery go
and concentrate on what lay at our feet.

OEDIPUS

                            No,

I'll start again—I'll bring it all to light myself!
Apollo is right, and so are you, Creon,
to turn our attention back to the murdered man.
Now you have *me* to fight for you, you'll see:
I am the land's avenger by all rights
and Apollo's champion too.
But not to assist some distant kinsman, no,
for my own sake I'll rid us of this corruption.
Whoever killed the king may decide to kill me too,
with the same violent hand—by avenging Laius
I defend myself.

To the priests.

           Quickly, my children.
Up from the steps, take up your branches now.

To the guards.

One of you summon the city here before us,
tell them I'll do everything. God help us,
we will see our triumph—or our fall.

*Oedipus and Creon enter
the palace,
followed by the guards.*

PRIEST

Rise, my sons. The kindness we came for
Oedipus volunteers himself.
Apollo has sent his word, his oracle—
Come down, Apollo, save us, stop the plague.

The priests rise, remove their
branches and exit to the side.

Enter a Chorus, the citizens of
Thebes, who have not heard the news
that Creon brings. They march
around the altar, chanting.[9]

CHORUS

                              Zeus!
Great welcome voice of Zeus, what do you bring?
What word from the gold vaults of Delphi
comes to brilliant Thebes? I'm racked with terror—
                    terror shakes my heart
and I cry your wild cries, Apollo, Healer of Delos[10]
I worship you in dread . . . what now, what is your price?
some new sacrifice? some ancient rite from the past
come round again each spring—
              what will you bring to birth?
Tell me, child of golden Hope
      warm voice that never dies!

---

[9]This "ode" (song) of the chorus is really a supplication of a number of gods, begging relief from the plague.

[10]A small island in the Aegean Sea, according to myth the birthplace of Apollo and his twin sister Artemis; it was a place sacred to Apollo's worshippers.

You are the first I call, daughter of Zeus
deathless Athena—I call your sister Artemis,
heart of the market place enthroned in glory,
                              guardian of our earth—
I call Apollo, Archer astride the thunderheads of heaven—
O triple shield against death, shine before me now!
If ever, once in the past, you stopped some ruin
launched against our walls
                    you hurled the flame of pain
far, far from Thebes—you gods
        come now, come down once more!
                                                        No, no
the miseries numberless, grief on grief, no end—
too much to bear, we are all dying
O my people . . .
    Thebes like a great army dying
and there is no sword of thought to save us, no
and the fruits of our famous earth, they will not ripen
no and the women cannot scream their pangs to birth—
screams for the Healer, children dead in the womb
        and life on life goes down
                you can watch them go
    like seabirds winging west, outracing the day's fire
down the horizon, irresistibly
        streaking on to the shores of Evening
                                                        Death
so many deaths, numberless deaths on deaths, no end—
Thebes is dying, look, her children
stripped of pity . . .
    generations strewn on the ground
unburied, unwept, the dead spreading death
and the young wives and gray-haired mothers with them
cling to the altars, trailing in from all over the city—
Thebes, city of death, one long cortege
        and the suffering rises
                wails for mercy rise
    and the wild hymn for the Healer blazes out
clashing with our sobs our cries of mourning—
    O golden daughter of god, send rescue
    radiant as the kindness in your eyes!

Drive him back!—the fever, the god of death
                              that raging god of war
not armored in bronze, not shielded now, he burns me,
battle cries in the onslaught burning on—
O rout him from our borders!
Sail him, blast him out to the Sea-queen's chamber
                              the black Atlantic gulfs
      or the northern harbor, death to all
where the Thracian surf comes crashing.
Now what the night spares he comes by day and kills—
the god of death.

                        O lord of the stormcloud,
you who twirl the lightning, Zeus,[11] Father,
thunder Death to nothing!

Apollo, lord of the light, I beg you—
      whip your longbow's golden cord
showering arrows on our enemies—shafts of power
champions strong before us rushing on!

Artemis, Huntress,
torches flaring over the eastern ridges—
                              ride Death down in pain!

God of the headdress gleaming gold, I cry to you—
your name and ours are one, Dionysus—[12]
   come with your face aflame with wine
      your raving women's cries
   your army on the march! Come with the lightning
come with torches blazing, eyes ablaze with glory!
Burn that god of death that all gods hate!

[11]The lightning bolt was the special symbol and instrument of Zeus.

[12]God of wine, drunken revelry, fertility and rebirth. His mother, Semele, was a daughter of Cadmus, royal founder of Thebes ("your name and ours are one, Dionysus"); his father was Zeus. His followers were often intoxicated, releasing wild emotions. The origins of drama, itself, are associated with the ritual re-enactment of events in the life of Dionysus.

*Oedipus enters from the palace to
address the Chorus, as if addressing
the entire city of Thebes.*

OEDIPUS

You pray to the gods? Let me grant your prayers.
Come, listen to me—do what the plague demands:
you'll find relief and lift your head from the depths.

I will speak out now as a stranger to the story,
a stranger to the crime. If I'd been present then,
there would have been no mystery, no long hunt
without a clue in hand. So now, counted
a native Theban years after the murder,
to all of Thebes I make this proclamation:
if any one of you knows who murdered Laius,
the son of Labdacus, I order him to reveal
the whole truth to me. Nothing to fear,
even if he must denounce himself,
let him speak up
and so escape the brunt of the charge—
he will suffer no unbearable punishment,
nothing worse than exile, totally unharmed.

Oedipus pauses, waiting for a reply.

                            Next,

if anyone knows the murderer is a stranger,
a man from alien soil, come, speak up.
I will give him a handsome reward, and lay up
gratitude in my heart for him besides.

Silence again, no reply.

But if you keep silent, if anyone panicking,
trying to shield himself or friend or kin,
rejects my offer, then hear what I will do.
I order you, every citizen of the state
where I hold throne and power: banish this man—
whoever he may be—never shelter him, never

speak a word to him, never make him partner
to your prayers, your victims burned to the gods.
Never let the holy water touch his hands.
Drive him out, each of you, from every home.
He is the plague, the heart of our corruption,
as Apollo's oracle has revealed to me
just now. So I honor my obligations:
I fight for the god and for the murdered man.

Now my curse on the murderer. Whoever he is,
a lone man unknown in his crime
or one among many, let that man drag out
his life in agony, step by painful step—
I curse myself as well . . . if by any chance
he proves to be an intimate of our house,
here at my hearth, with my full knowledge,
may the curse I just called down on him strike me!

These are your orders: perform them to the last.
I command you, for my sake, for Apollo's, for this country
blasted root and branch by the angry heavens.
Even if god had never urged you on to act,
how could you leave the crime uncleansed so long?
A man so noble—your king, brought down in blood—
you should have searched. But I am the king now,
I hold the throne that he held then, possess his bed
and a wife who shares our seed . . . why, our seed
might be the same, children born of the same mother
might have created blood-bonds between us
if his hope of offspring hadn't met disaster—[13]
but fate swooped at his head and cut him short.
So I will fight for him as if he were my father,
stop at nothing, search the world
to lay my hands on the man who shed his blood,
the son of Labdacus descended of Polydorus,
Cadmus of old and Agenor, founder of the line:
their power and mine are one.
                              Oh dear gods,
my curse on those who disobey these orders!

[13]That is, if Laius had fathered children by his queen, Jocasta, now married to Oedipus.

Let no crops grow out of the earth for them—
shrivel their women, kill their sons,
burn them to nothing in this plague
that hits us now, or something even worse.
But you, loyal men of Thebes who approve my actions,
may our champion, Justice, may all the gods
be with us, fight beside us to the end!

LEADER

In the grip of your curse, my king, I swear
I'm not the murderer, cannot point him out.
As for the search, Apollo pressed it on us—
he should name the killer.

OEDIPUS

                Quite right,
but to force the gods to act against their will—
no man has the power.

LEADER

                Then if I might mention
the next best thing . . .

OEDIPUS

                The third best too—
don't hold back, say it.

LEADER

                I still believe . . .
Lord Tiresias sees with the eyes of Lord Apollo.
Anyone searching for the truth, my king,
might learn it from the prophet, clear as day.

OEDIPUS

I've not been slow with that. On Creon's cue
I sent the escorts, twice, within the hour.
I'm surprised he isn't here.

LEADER

                        We need him—
without him we have nothing but old, useless rumors.

OEDIPUS

Which rumors? I'll search out every word.

LEADER

Laius was killed, they say, by certain travelers.

OEDIPUS

I know—but no one can find the murderer.

LEADER

If a man has a trace of fear in him
he won't stay silent long,
not with your curses ringing in his ears.

OEDIPUS

He didn't flinch at murder,
he'll never flinch at words.

> *Enter Tiresias, the blind prophet, led
> by a boy with escorts in attendance.
> He remains at a distance.*

LEADER

Here is the one who will convict him, look,
they bring him on at last, the seer, the man of god.
The truth lives inside him, him alone.

OEDIPUS

                        O Tiresias,
master of all the mysteries of our life,
all you teach and all you dare not tell,

signs in the heavens, signs that walk the earth!
Blind as you are, you can feel all the more
what sickness haunts our city. You, my lord,
are the one shield, the one savior we can find.

We asked Apollo—perhaps the messengers
haven't told you—he sent his answer back:
"Relief from the plague can only come one way.
Uncover the murderers of Laius,
put them to death or drive them into exile."
So I beg you, grudge us nothing now, no voice,
no message plucked from the birds, the embers
or the other mantic ways within your grasp.
Rescue yourself, your city, rescue me—
rescue everything infected by the dead.
We are in your hands. For a man to help others
with all his gifts and native strength:
that is the noblest work.

TIRESIAS

How terrible—to see the truth
when the truth is only pain to him who sees!
I knew it well, but I put it from my mind,
else I never would have come.

OEDIPUS

What's this? Why so grim, so dire?

TIRESIAS

Just send me home. You bear your burdens,
I'll bear mine. It's better that way,
please believe me.

OEDIPUS

Strange response—unlawful,
unfriendly too to the state that bred and raised you;
you're withholding the word of god.

TIRESIAS

                                        I fail to see
that your own words are so well-timed.
I'd rather not have the same thing said of me . . .

OEDIPUS

For the love of god, don't turn away,
not if you know something. We beg you,
all of us on our knees.

TIRESIAS

                        None of you knows—
and I will never reveal my dreadful secrets,
not to say your own.

OEDIPUS

What? You know and you won't tell?
You're bent on betraying us, destroying Thebes?

TIRESIAS

I'd rather not cause pain for you or me.
So why this . . . useless interrogation?
You'll get nothing from me.

OEDIPUS

                        Nothing! You,
you scum of the earth, you'd enrage a heart of stone!
You won't talk? Nothing moves you?
Out with it, once and for all!

TIRESIAS

You criticize my temper . . . unaware
of the one *you* live with, you revile me.

OEDIPUS

Who could restrain his anger hearing you?
What outrage—you spurn the city!

TIRESIAS

What will come will come.
Even if I shroud it all in silence.

OEDIPUS

What will come? You're bound to *tell* me that.

TIRESIAS

I'll say no more. Do as you like, build your anger
to whatever pitch you please, rage your worst—

OEDIPUS

Oh I'll let loose, I have such fury in me—
now I see it all. You helped hatch the plot,
you did the work, yes, short of killing him
with your own hands—and given eyes I'd say
you did the killing single-handed!

TIRESIAS

                                        Is that so!
I charge you, then, submit to that decree
you just laid down: from this day onward
speak to no one, not these citizens, not myself.
You are the curse, the corruption of the land!

OEDIPUS

You, shameless—
aren't you appalled to start up such a story?
You think you can get away with this?

TIRESIAS

                                        I have already.
The truth with all its power lives inside me.

OEDIPUS

Who primed you for this? Not your prophet's trade.

TIRESIAS

You did, you forced me, twisted it out of me.

OEDIPUS

What? Say it again—I'll understand it better.

TIRESIAS

Didn't you understand, just now?
Or are you tempting me to talk?

OEDIPUS

No, I can't say I grasped your meaning.
Out with it, again!

TIRESIAS

I say you are the murderer you hunt.

OEDIPUS

That obscenity, twice—by god, you'll pay.

TIRESIAS

Shall I say more, so you can really rage?

OEDIPUS

Much as you want. Your words are nothing—
futile.

TIRESIAS

          You cannot imagine . . . I tell you,
you and your loved ones live together in infamy,
you cannot see how far you've gone in guilt.

OEDIPUS

You think you can keep this up and never suffer?

TIRESIAS

Indeed, if the truth has any power.

OEDIPUS

                              It does
but not for you, old man. You've lost your power,
stone-blind, stone-deaf—senses, eyes blind as stone!

TIRESIAS

I pity you, flinging at me the very insults
each man here will fling at you so soon.

OEDIPUS

                              Blind,
lost in the night, endless night that nursed you!
You can't hurt me or anyone else who sees the light—
you can never touch me

TIRESIAS

                    True, it is not your fate
to fall at my hands. Apollo is quite enough,
and he will take some pains to work this out.

OEDIPUS

Creon! Is this conspiracy his or yours?

TIRESIAS

Creon is not your downfall, no, you are your own.

OEDIPUS

                                        O power—

wealth and empire, skill outstripping skill
in the heady rivalries of life,
what envy lurks inside you! Just for this,

the crown the city gave me—I never sought it,
they laid it in my hands—for this alone, Creon,
the soul of trust, my loyal friend from the start
steals against me . . . so hungry to overthrow me
he sets this wizard on me, this scheming quack,
this fortune-teller peddling lies, eyes peeled
for his own profit—seer blind in his craft!

Come here, you pious fraud. Tell me,
when did you ever prove yourself a prophet?
When the Sphinx, that chanting Fury kept her deathwatch here,
why silent then, not a word to set our people free?
There was a riddle, not for some passer-by to solve—
it cried out for a prophet. Where were you?
Did you rise to the crisis? Not a word,
you and your birds, your gods—nothing.
No, but I came by, Oedipus the ignorant,
I stopped the Sphinx! With no help from the birds,
the flight of my own intelligence hit the mark.

And this is the man you'd try to overthrow?
You think you'll stand by Creon when he's king?
You and the great mastermind—
you'll pay in tears, I promise you, for this,
this witch-hunt. If you didn't look so senile
the lash would teach you what your scheming means!

LEADER

I'd suggest his words were spoken in anger,
Oedipus . . . yours too, and it isn't what we need.
The best solution to the oracle, the riddle
posed by god—we should look for that.

TIRESIAS

You are the king no doubt, but in one respect,
at least, I am your equal: the right to reply.
I claim that privilege too.
I am not your slave. I serve Apollo.
I don't need Creon to speak for me in public.

So,
you mock my blindness? Let me tell you this.
You with your precious eyes,
you're blind to the corruption of your life,
to the house you live in, those you live with—
who *are* your parents? Do you know? All unknowing
you are the scourge of your own flesh and blood,
the dead below the earth and the living here above,
and the double lash of your mother and your father's curse
will whip you from this land one day, their footfall
treading you down in terror, darkness shrouding
your eyes that now can see the light!
                                        Soon, soon
you'll scream aloud—what haven won't reverberate?
What rock of Cithaeron[14] won't scream back in echo?
That day you learn the truth about your marriage,
the wedding-march that sang you into your halls,
the lusty voyage home to the fatal harbor!
And a load of other horrors you'd never dream
will level you with yourself and all your children.

There. Now smear us with insults—Creon, myself
and every word I've said. No man will ever
be rooted from the earth as brutally as you.

OEDIPUS

Enough! Such filth from him? Insufferable—
what, still alive? Get out—
faster, back where you came from—vanish!

TIRESIAS

I'd never have come if you hadn't called me here.

OEDIPUS

If I thought you'd blurt out such absurdities,
you'd have died waiting before I'd had you summoned.

---

[14]The mountain on which the infant Oedipus had, supposedly, been left to die.

TIRESIAS

Absurd, am I? To you, not to your parents:
the ones who bore you found me sane enough.

OEDIPUS

Parents—who? Wait . . . who is my father?

TIRESIAS

This day will bring your birth and your destruction.

OEDIPUS

Riddles—all you can say are riddles, murk and darkness.

TIRESIAS

Ah, but aren't you the best man alive at solving riddles?

OEDIPUS

Mock me for that, go on, and you'll reveal my greatness.

TIRESIAS

Your great good fortune, true, it was your ruin.

OEDIPUS

Not if I saved the city—what do I care?

TIRESIAS

Well then, I'll be going.

To his attendant.

Take me home, boy.

OEDIPUS

Yes, take him away. You're a nuisance here.
Out of the way, the irritation's gone.

*Turning his back on Tiresias,
moving toward the palace.*

TIRESIAS

                              I will go,
once I have said what I came here to say.
I'll never shrink from the anger in your eyes—
you can't destroy me. Listen to me closely:
the man you've sought so long, proclaiming,
cursing up and down, the murderer of Laius—
he is here. A stranger,
you may think, who lives among you,
he soon will be revealed a native Theban
but he will take no joy in the revelation.
Blind who now has eyes, beggar who now is rich,
he will grope his way toward a foreign soil,
a stick tapping before him step by step.

Oedipus enters the palace.

Revealed at last, brother and father both
to the children he embraces, to his mother
son and husband both—he sowed the loins
his father sowed, he spilled his father's blood!

Go in and reflect on that, solve that.
And if you find I've lied
from this day onward call the prophet blind.

Tiresias and the boy exit to the side.

CHORUS

                              Who—
who is the man the voice of god denounces
resounding out of the rocky gorge of Delphi?
     The horror too dark to tell,
whose ruthless bloody hands have done the work?
His time has come to fly
     to outrace the stallions of the storm
                    his feet a streak of speed—

Cased in armor, Apollo son of the Father
lunges on him, lightning-bolts afire!
And the grim unerring Furies[15]
                    closing for the kill.
                                        Look,
the word of god has just come blazing
flashing off Parnassus' snowy heights![16]
        That man who left no trace—
after him, hunt him down with all our strength!
Now under bristling timber
        up through rocks and caves he stalks
                        like the wild mountain bull—
cut off from men, each step an agony, frenzied, racing blind
but he cannot outrace the dread voices of Delphi
ringing out of the heart of Earth,
        the dark wings beating around him shrieking doom
                        the doom that never dies, the terror—
The skilled prophet scans the birds and shatters me with terror!
I can't accept him, can't deny him, don't know what to say,
I'm lost, and the wings of dark foreboding beating—
I cannot see what's come, what's still to come . . .
and what could breed a blood feud between
        Laius' house and the son of Polybus?
I know of nothing, not in the past and not now,
no charge to bring against our king, no cause
to attack his fame that rings throughout Thebes—
        not without proof—not for the ghost of Laius,
        not to avenge a murder gone without a trace.

Zeus and Apollo know, they know, the great masters
        of all the dark and depth of human life.
But whether a mere man can know the truth,
whether a seer can fathom more than I—
there is no test, no certain proof
        though matching skill for skill
a man can outstrip a rival. No, not till I see
these charges proved will I side with his accusers.

[15]Avengers of crime, especially directed against killers of their own kin when no earthly
    avenger was available.

[16]A mountain range overlooking the shrine of Apollo at Delphi.

We saw him then, when the she-hawk[17] swept against him,
saw with our own eyes his skill, his brilliant triumph—
> there was the test—he was the joy of Thebes!
> Never will I convict my king, never in my heart.

Enter Creon from the side.

CREON

My fellow-citizens, I hear King Oedipus
levels terrible charges at me. I had to come.
I resent it deeply. If, in the present crisis,
he thinks he suffers any abuse from me,
anything I've done or said that offers him
the slightest injury, why, I've no desire
to linger out this life, my reputation a shambles.
The damage I'd face from such an accusation
is nothing simple. No, there's nothing worse:
branded a traitor in the city, a traitor
to all of you and my good friends.

LEADER

> True,
but a slur might have been forced out of him,
by anger perhaps, not any firm conviction.

CREON

The charge was made in public, wasn't it?
I put the prophet up to spreading lies?

LEADER

Such things were said . . .
I don't know with what intent, if any.

CREON

Was his glance steady, his mind right
when the charge was brought against me?

[17]The Sphinx.

LEADER

I really couldn't say. I never look
to judge the ones in power.

The doors open. Oedipus enters.

Wait,
here's Oedipus now.

OEDIPUS

You—here? You have the gall
to show your face before the palace gates?
You, plotting to kill me, kill the king—
I see it all, the marauding thief himself
scheming to steal my crown and power!

Tell me,
in god's name, what did you take me for,
coward or fool, when you spun out your plot?
Your treachery—you think I'd never detect it
creeping against me in the dark? Or sensing it,
not defend myself? Aren't you the fool,
you and your high adventure. Lacking numbers,
powerful friends, out for the big game of empire—
you need riches, armies to bring that quarry down!

CREON

Are you quite finished? It's your turn to listen
for just as long as you've . . . instructed me.
Hear me out, then judge me on the facts.

OEDIPUS

You've a wicked way with words, Creon,
but I'll be slow to learn—from you.
I find you a menace, a great burden to me.

CREON

Just one thing, hear me out in this.

OEDIPUS

Just one thing,
don't tell me you're not the enemy, the traitor.

CREON

Look, if you think crude, mindless stubbornness
such a gift, you've lost your sense of balance.

OEDIPUS

If you think you can abuse a kinsman,
then escape the penalty, you're insane.

CREON

Fair enough, I grant you. But this injury
you say I've done you, what is it?

OEDIPUS

Did you induce me, yes or no,
to send for that sanctimonious prophet?

CREON

I did. And I'd do the same again.

OEDIPUS

All right then, tell me how long is it now
since Laius . . .

CREON

Laius—what did *he* do?

OEDIPUS

Vanished,
swept from sight, murdered in his tracks.

CREON

The count of the years would run you far back . . .

OEDIPUS

And that far back, was the prophet at his trade?

CREON

Skilled as he is today, and just as honored.

OEDIPUS

Did he ever refer to me then, at that time?

CREON

                                          No,
never, at least, when I was in his presence.

OEDIPUS

But you did investigate the murder, didn't you?

CREON

We did our best, of course, discovered nothing.

OEDIPUS

But the great seer never accused me then—why not?

CREON

I don't know. And when I don't, *I* keep quiet.

OEDIPUS

You do know this, you'd tell it too—
if you had a shred of decency.

CREON

                              What?
If I know, I won't hold back.

OEDIPUS

                   Simply this:
if the two of you had never put heads together,
we'd never have heard about *my* killing Laius.

CREON

If that's what he says . . . well, you know best.
But now I have a right to learn from you
as you just learned from me.

OEDIPUS

                          Learn your fill,
you never will convict me of the murder.

CREON

Tell me, you're married to my sister, aren't you?

OEDIPUS

A genuine discovery—there's no denying that.

CREON

And you rule the land with her, with equal power?

OEDIPUS

She receives from me whatever she desires.

CREON

And I am the third, all of us are equals?

OEDIPUS

Yes, and it's there you show your stripes—
you betray a kinsman.

CREON

                    Not at all.
Not if you see things calmly, rationally,
as I do. Look at it this way first:
who in his right mind would rather rule
and live in anxiety than sleep in peace?
Particularly if he enjoys the same authority.
Not I, I'm not the man to yearn for kingship,
not with a king's power in my hands. Who would?

No one with any sense of self-control.
Now, as it is, you offer me all I need,
not a fear in the world. But if I wore the crown . . .
there'd be many painful duties to perform,
hardly to my taste.
                            How could kingship
please me more than influence, power
without a qualm? I'm not that deluded yet,
to reach for anything but privilege outright,
profit free and clear.
Now all men sing my praises, all salute me,
now all who request your favors curry mine.
I'm their best hope: success rests in me.
Why give up that, I ask you, and borrow trouble?
A man of sense, someone who sees things clearly
would never resort to treason.
No, I've no lust for conspiracy in me,
nor could I ever suffer one who does.

Do you want proof? Go to Delphi yourself,
examine the oracle and see if I've reported
the message word-for-word. This too:
if you detect that I and the clairvoyant
have plotted anything in common, arrest me,
execute me. Not on the strength of one vote,
two in this case, mine as well as yours.
But don't convict me on sheer unverified surmise.

How wrong it is to take the good for bad,
purely at random, or take the bad for good.
But reject a friend, a kinsman? I would as soon
tear out the life within us, priceless life itself.
You'll learn this well, without fail, in time.
Time alone can bring the just man to light;
the criminal you can spot in one short day.

LEADER

                                    Good advice,
my lord, for anyone who wants to avoid disaster.
Those who jump to conclusions may be wrong.

OEDIPUS

When my enemy moves against me quickly,
plots in secret, I move quickly too, I must,
I plot and pay him back. Relax my guard a moment,
waiting his next move—he wins his objective,
I lose mine.

CREON

          What do you want?
You want me banished?

OEDIPUS

          No, I want you dead.

CREON

Just to show how ugly a grudge can . . .

OEDIPUS

               So,
still stubborn? you don't think I'm serious?

CREON

I think you're insane.

OEDIPUS

          Quite sane—in my behalf.

CREON

Not just as much in mine?

OEDIPUS

          You—my mortal enemy?

CREON

What if you're wholly wrong?

OEDIPUS

No matter—I must rule.

CREON

Not if you rule unjustly.

OEDIPUS

Hear him, Thebes, my city!

CREON

My city too, not yours alone!

LEADER

Please, my lords.

Enter Jocasta from the palace.

Look, Jocasta's coming,
and just in time too. With her help
you must put this fighting of yours to rest.

JOCASTA

Have you no sense? Poor misguided men,
such shouting—why this public outburst?
Aren't you ashamed, with the land so sick,
to stir up private quarrels?

To Oedipus.

Into the palace now. And Creon, you go home.
Why make such a furor over nothing?

CREON

My sister, it's dreadful . . . Oedipus, your husband,
he's bent on a choice of punishments for me,
banishment from the fatherland or death.

OEDIPUS

Precisely. I caught him in the act, Jocasta,
plotting, about to stab me in the back.

CREON

Never—curse me, let me die and be damned
if I've done you any wrong you charge me with.

JOCASTA

Oh god, believe it, Oedipus,
honor the solemn oath he swears to heaven.
Do it for me, for the sake of all your people.

The Chorus begins to chant.

CHORUS

    Believe it, be sensible
      give way, my king, I beg you!

OEDIPUS

    What do you want from me, concessions?

CHORUS

    Respect him—he's been no fool in the past
    and now he's strong with the oath he swears to god.

OEDIPUS

    You know what you're asking?

CHORUS

                      I do.

OEDIPUS

                      Then out with it!

CHORUS

    The man's your friend, your kin, he's under oath—
    don't cast him out, disgraced
    branded with guilt on the strength of hearsay only.

OEDIPUS

Know full well, if that's what you want
you want me dead or banished from the land.

CHORUS

                                        Never—
no, by the blazing Sun, first god of the heavens!
     Stripped of the gods, stripped of loved ones,
let me die by inches if that ever crossed my mind.
But the heart inside me sickens, dies as the land dies
and now on top of the old griefs you pile this,
your fury—both of you!

OEDIPUS

                              Then let him go,
even if it does lead to my ruin, my death
or my disgrace, driven from Thebes for life.
It's you, not him I pity—your words move me.
He, wherever he goes, my hate goes with him.

CREON

Look at you, sullen in yielding, brutal in your rage—
you'll go too far. It's perfect justice:
natures like yours are hardest on themselves.

OEDIPUS

Then leave me alone—get out!

CREON

                              I'm going.
You're wrong, so wrong. These men know I'm right.

*Exit to the side. The Chorus turns to
Jocasta.*

CHORUS

     Why do you hesitate, my lady
          why not help him in?

JOCASTA

Tell me what's happened first.

CHORUS

Loose, ignorant talk started dark suspicions
and a sense of injustice cut deeply too.

JOCASTA

On both sides?

CHORUS

Oh yes.

JOCASTA

What did they say?

CHORUS

Enough, please, enough! The land's so racked already
or so it seems to me . . .
End the trouble here, just where they left it.

OEDIPUS

You see what comes of your good intentions now?
And all because you tried to blunt my anger.

CHORUS

My king,
I've said it once, I'll say it time and again—
   I'd be insane, you know it,
senseless, ever to turn my back on you.
You who set our beloved land—storm-tossed, shattered—
straight on course. Now again, good helmsman,
steer us through the storm!

*The Chorus draws away, leaving
Oedipus and Jocasta side by side.*

JOCASTA

                              For the love of god,
Oedipus, tell me too, what is it?
Why this rage? You're so unbending.

OEDIPUS

I will tell you. I respect you, Jocasta,
much more than these . . .

                                        Glancing at the Chorus.

Creon's to blame, Creon schemes against me.

JOCASTA

Tell me clearly, how did the quarrel start?

OEDIPUS

He says *I* murdered Laius—I am guilty.

JOCASTA

How does he know? Some secret knowledge
or simple hearsay?

OEDIPUS

                              Oh, he sent his prophet in
to do his dirty work. You know Creon,
Creon keeps his own lips clean.

JOCASTA

                                        A prophet?
Well then, free yourself of every charge!
Listen to me and learn some peace of mind:
no skill in the world,
nothing human can penetrate the future.
Here is proof, quick and to the point.

An oracle came to Laius one fine day
(I won't say from Apollo himself

but his underlings, his priests) and it said
that doom would strike him down at the hands of a son,
our son, to be born of our own flesh and blood. But Laius,
so the report goes at least, was killed by strangers,
thieves, at a place where three roads meet . . . my son—
he wasn't three days old and the boy's father
fastened his ankles, had a henchman fling him away
on a barren, trackless mountain.

                              There, you see?
Apollo brought neither thing to pass. My baby
no more murdered his father than Laius suffered—
his wildest fear—death at his own son's hands.
That's how the seers and their revelations
mapped out the future. Brush them from your mind.
Whatever the god needs and seeks
he'll bring to light himself, with ease.

OEDIPUS

                                 Strange,
hearing you just now . . . my mind wandered,
my thoughts racing back and forth.

JOCASTA

What do you mean? Why so anxious, startled?

OEDIPUS

I thought I heard you say that Laius
was cut down at a place where three roads meet.

JOCASTA

That was the story. It hasn't died out yet.

OEDIPUS

Where did this thing happen? Be precise.

JOCASTA

A place called Phocis, where two branching roads,
one from Daulia, one from Delphi,
come together—a crossroads.

OEDIPUS

When? How long ago?

JOCASTA

The heralds no sooner reported Laius dead
than you appeared and they hailed you king of Thebes.

OEDIPUS

My god, my god—what have you planned to do to me?

JOCASTA

What, Oedipus? What haunts you so?

OEDIPUS

                                        Not yet.
Laius—how did he look? Describe him.
Had he reached his prime?

JOCASTA

                              He was swarthy,
and the gray had just begun to streak his temples,
and his build . . . wasn't far from yours.

OEDIPUS

                                        Oh no no,
I think I've just called down a dreadful curse
upon myself—I simply didn't know!

JOCASTA

What are you saying? I shudder to look at you.

OEDIPUS

I have a terrible fear the blind seer can see.
I'll know in a moment. One thing more—

JOCASTA

                                      Anything,
afraid as I am—ask, I'll answer, all I can.

OEDIPUS

Did he go with a light or heavy escort,
several men-at-arms, like a lord, a king?

JOCASTA

There were five in the party, a herald among them,
and a single wagon carrying Laius.

OEDIPUS

                              Ai—
now I can see it all, clear as day.
Who told you this at the time, Jocasta?

JOCASTA

A servant who reached home, the lone survivor.

OEDIPUS

So, could he still be in the palace—even now?

JOCASTA

No indeed. Soon as he returned from the scene
and saw you on the throne with Laius dead and gone,
he knelt and clutched my hand, pleading with me
to send him into the hinterlands, to pasture,
far as possible, out of sight of Thebes.
I sent him away. Slave though he was,
he'd earned that favor—and much more.

OEDIPUS

Can we bring him back, quickly?

JOCASTA

Easily. Why do you want him so?

OEDIPUS

                         I'm afraid,
Jocasta, I have said too much already.
That man—I've got to see him.

JOCASTA

                       Then he'll come.
But even I have a right, I'd like to think,
to know what's torturing you, my lord.

OEDIPUS

And so you shall—I can hold nothing back from you,
now I've reached this pitch of dark foreboding.
Who means more to me than you? Tell me,
whom would I turn toward but you
as I go through all this?

My father was Polybus, king of Corinth,
My mother, a Dorian, Merope. And I was held
the prince of the realm among the people there,
till something struck me out of nowhere,
something strange . . . worth remarking perhaps,
hardly worth the anxiety I gave it.
Some man at a banquet who had drunk too much
shouted out—he was far gone, mind you—
that I am not my father's son. Fighting words!
I barely restrained myself that day
but early the next I went to mother and father,
questioned them closely, and they were enraged
at the accusation and the fool who let it fly.
So as for my parents I was satisfied,
but still this thing kept gnawing at me,
the slander spread—I had to make my move.
                         And so,
unknown to mother and father I set out for Delphi,

and the god Apollo spurned me, sent me away
denied the facts I came for,
but first he flashed before my eyes a future
great with pain, terror, disaster—I can hear him cry,
"You are fated to couple with your mother, you will bring
a breed of children into the light no man can bear to see—
you will kill your father, the one who gave you life!"
I heard all that and ran. I abandoned Corinth,
from that day on I gauged its landfall only
by the stars, running, always running
toward some place where I would never see
the shame of all those oracles come true.
And as I fled I reached that very spot
where the great king, you say, met his death.

Now, Jocasta, I will tell you all.
Making my way toward this triple crossroad
I began to see a herald, then a brace of colts
drawing a wagon, and mounted on the bench . . . a man,
just as you've described him, coming face-to-face,
and the one in the lead and the old man himself
were about to thrust me off the road—brute force—
and the one shouldering me aside, the driver,
I strike him in anger!—and the old man, watching me
coming up along his wheels—he brings down
his prod, two prongs straight at my head!
I paid him back with interest!
Short work, by god—with one blow of the staff
in this right hand I knock him out of his high seat,
roll him out of the wagon, sprawling headlong—
I killed them all—every mother's son!

Oh, but if there is any blood-tie
between Laius and this stranger . . .
what man alive more miserable than I?
More hated by the gods? *I* am the man
no alien, no citizen welcomes to his house,
law forbids it—not a word to me in public,
driven out of every hearth and home.

And all these curses I—no one but I
brought down these piling curses on myself!
And you, his wife, I've touched your body with these,
the hands that killed your husband cover you with blood.

Wasn't I born for torment? Look me in the eyes!
I am abomination—heart and soul!
I must be exiled, and even in exile
never see my parents, never set foot
on native earth again. Else I'm doomed
to couple with my mother and cut my father down . . .
Polybus who reared me, gave me life.
                                    But why, why?
Wouldn't a man of judgment say—and wouldn't he be right—
some savage power has brought this down upon my head?

Oh no, not that, you pure and awesome gods,
never let me see that day! Let me slip
from the world of men, vanish without a trace
before I see myself stained with such corruption,
stained to the heart.

LEADER

My lord, you fill our hearts with fear.
But at least until you question the witness,
do take hope.

OEDIPUS

                    Exactly. He is my last hope—
I'm waiting for the shepherd. He is crucial.

JOCASTA

And once he appears, what then? Why so urgent?

OEDIPUS

I'll tell you. If it turns out that his story
matches yours, I've escaped the worst.

JOCASTA

What did I say? What struck you so?

OEDIPUS

       You said *thieves*—
he told you a whole band of them murdered Laius.
So, if he still holds to the same number,
I cannot be the killer. One can't equal many.
But if he refers to one man, one alone,
clearly the scales come down on me:
I am guilty.

JOCASTA

     Impossible. Trust me,
I told you precisely what he said,
and he can't retract it now;
the whole city heard it, not just I.
And even if he should vary his first report
by one man more or less, still, my lord,
he could never make the murder of Laius
truly fit the prophecy. Apollo was explicit:
my son was doomed to kill my husband . . . my son,
poor defenseless thing, he never had a chance
to kill his father. They destroyed him first.

So much for prophecy. It's neither here nor there.
From this day on, I wouldn't look right or left.

OEDIPUS

True, true. Still, that shepherd,
someone fetch him—now!

JOCASTA

I'll send at once. But do let's go inside.
I'd never displease you, least of all in this.

         Oedipus and Jocasta enter the
         palace.

CHORUS

Destiny guide me always
Destiny find me filled with reverence
         pure in word and deed.
Great laws tower above us, reared on high
born for the brilliant vault of heaven—
     Olympian Sky their only father,
nothing mortal, no man gave them birth,
their memory deathless, never lost in sleep:
within them lives a mighty god, the god does not grow old.

Pride breeds the tyrant
violent pride, gorging, crammed to bursting
     with all that is overripe and rich with ruin—
clawing up to the heights, headlong pride
crashes down the abyss—sheer doom!
     No footing helps, all foothold lost and gone.
But the healthy strife that makes the city strong—
I pray that god will never end that wrestling:
god, my champion, I will never let you go.

But if any man comes striding, high and mighty
     in all he says and does,
no fear of justice, no reverence
for the temples of the gods—
     let a rough doom tear him down,
repay his pride, breakneck, ruinous pride!
If he cannot reap his profits fairly
     cannot restrain himself from outrage—
mad, laying hands on the holy things untouchable!

         Can such a man, so desperate, still boast
         he can save his life from the flashing bolts of god?
             If all such violence goes with honor now
                 why join the sacred dance?

Never again will I go reverent to Delphi,
     the inviolate heart of Earth
or Apollo's ancient oracle at Abae

or Olympia[18] of the fires—
    unless these prophecies all come true
for all mankind to point toward in wonder.
King of kings, if you deserve your titles
    Zeus, remember, never forget!
You and your deathless, everlasting reign.

      They are dying, the old oracles sent to Laius,
      now our masters strike them off the rolls.
          Nowhere Apollo's golden glory now—
              the gods, the gods go down.

                    Enter Jocasta from the palace,
                    carrying a suppliant's branch
                    wound in wool.

JOCASTA

Lords of the realm,[19] it occurred to me,
just now, to visit the temples of the gods,
so I have my branch in hand and incense too.

Oedipus is beside himself. Racked with anguish,
no longer a man of sense, he won't admit
the latest prophecies are hollow as the old—
he's at the mercy of every passing voice
if the voice tells of terror.
I urge him gently, nothing seems to help,
so I turn to you, Apollo, you are nearest.

                    Placing her branch on the altar,
                    while an old herdsman enters from
                    the side, not the one just summoned
                    by the King but an unexpected
                    Messenger from Corinth.

[18]Site of the ancient Olympic festival where, among the sacred places, there was a famous temple of Zeus.

[19]Jocasta is addressing the chorus.

I come with prayers and offerings . . . I beg you,
cleanse us, set us free of defilement!
Look at us, passengers in the grip of fear,
watching the pilot of the vessel go to pieces.

MESSENGER

*Approaching Jocasta and the
Chorus.*

Strangers, please, I wonder if you could lead us
to the palace of the king . . . I think it's Oedipus.
Better, the man himself—you know where he is?

LEADER

This is his palace, stranger. He's inside.
But here is his queen, his wife and mother
of his children.

MESSENGER

                    Blessings on you, noble queen,
queen of Oedipus crowned with all your family—
blessings on you always!

JOCASTA

And the same to you, stranger, you deserve it . . .
such a greeting. But what have you come for?
Have you brought us news?

MESSENGER

                    Wonderful news—
for the house, my lady, for your husband too.

JOCASTA

Really, what? Who sent you?

MESSENGER

                             Corinth.
I'll give you the message in a moment.
You'll be glad of it—how could you help it?—
though it costs a little sorrow in the bargain.

JOCASTA

What can it be, with such a double edge?

MESENGER

The people there, they want to make your Oedipus
king of Corinth, so they're saying now.

JOCASTA

Why? Isn't old Polybus still in power?

MESSENGER

No more. Death has got him in the tomb.

JOCASTA

What are you saying? Polybus, dead?—dead?

MESSENGER

                                   If not,
if I'm not telling the truth, strike me dead too.

JOCASTA

                                 To a servant.

Quickly, go to your master, tell him this!

You prophecies of the gods, where are you now?
This is the man that Oedipus feared for years,
he fled him, not to kill him—and now he's dead,

quite by chance, a normal, natural death,
not murdered by his son.

OEDIPUS

Emerging from the palace.

Dearest,

what now? Why call me from the palace?

JOCASTA

Bringing the Messenger closer.

Listen to *him*, see for yourself what all
those awful prophecies of god have come to.

OEDIPUS

And who is he? What can he have for me?

JOCASTA

He's from Corinth, he's come to tell you
your father is no more—Polybus—he's dead!

OEDIPUS

Wheeling on the Messenger.

What? Let me have it from your lips.

MESSENGER

Well,

if that's what you want first, then here it is:
make no mistake, Polybus is dead and gone.

OEDIPUS

How—murder? sickness?—what? what killed him?

MESSENGER

A light tip of the scales can put old bones to rest.

OEDIPUS

Sickness then—poor man, it wore him down.

MESSENGER

That,
and the long count of years he'd measured out.

OEDIPUS

So!
Jocasta, why, why look to the Prophet's hearth,
the fires of the future? Why scan the birds
that scream above our heads? They winged me on
to the murder of my father, did they? That was my doom?
Well look, he's dead and buried, hidden under the earth,
and here I am in Thebes, I never put hand to sword—
unless some longing for me wasted him away,
then in a sense you'd say I caused his death.
But now, all those prophecies I feared—Polybus
packs them off to sleep with him in hell![20]
They're nothing, worthless.

JOCASTA

There.
Didn't I tell you from the start?

OEDIPUS

So you did. I was lost in fear.

JOCASTA

No more, sweep it from your mind forever.

[20]Actually, a reference to Hades, the underworld realm of all the dead souls whose bodies
had been properly buried.

OEDIPUS

But my mother's bed, surely I must fear—

JOCASTA

                         Fear?
What should a man fear? It's all chance,
chance rules our lives. Not a man on earth
can see a day ahead, groping through the dark.
Better to live at random, best we can.
And as for this marriage with your mother—
have no fear. Many a man before you,
in his dreams, has shared his mother's bed.
Take such things for shadows, nothing at all—
Live, Oedipus,
as if there's no tomorrow!

OEDIPUS

                    Brave words,
and you'd persuade me if mother weren't alive.
But mother lives, so for all your reassurances
I live in fear, I must.

JOCASTA

                But your father's death,
that, at least, is a great blessing, joy to the eyes!

OEDIPUS

Great, I know . . . but I fear *her*—she's still alive.

MESSENGER

Wait, who is this woman, makes you so afraid?

OEDIPUS

Merope, old man. The wife of Polybus.

MESSENGER

The queen? What's there to fear in her?

OEDIPUS

A dreadful prophecy, stranger, sent by the gods.

MESSENGER

Tell me, could you? Unless it's forbidden
other ears to hear.

OEDIPUS

                    Not at all.
Apollo told me once—it is my fate—
I must make love with my own mother,
shed my father's blood with my own hands.
So for years I've given Corinth a wide berth,
and it's been my good fortune too. But still,
to see one's parents and look into their eyes
is the greatest joy I know.

MESSENGER

                        You're afraid of that?
That kept you out of Corinth?

OEDIPUS

                        My *father*, old man—
so I wouldn't kill my father.

MESSENGER

                    So that's it.
Well then, seeing I came with such good will, my king,
why don't I rid you of that old worry now?

OEDIPUS

What a rich reward you'd have for that.

MESSENGER

What do you think I came for, majesty?
So you'd come home and I'd be better off.

OEDIPUS

Never, I will never go near my parents.

MESSENGER

My boy, it's clear, you don't know what you're doing.

OEDIPUS

What do you mean, old man? For god's sake, explain.

MESSENGER

If you ran from *them*, always dodging home . . .

OEDIPUS

Always, terrified Apollo's oracle might come true—

MESSENGER

And you'd be covered with guilt, from both your parents.

OEDIPUS

That's right, old man, that fear is always with me.

MESSENGER

Don't you know? You've really nothing to fear.

OEDIPUS

But why? If I'm their son—Merope, Polybus?

MESSENGER

Polybus was nothing to you, that's why, not in blood.

OEDIPUS

What are you saying—Polybus was not my father?

MESSENGER

No more than I am. He and I are equals.

OEDIPUS

My father—
how can my father equal nothing? You're nothing to me!

MESSENGER

Neither was he, no more your father than I am.

OEDIPUS

Then why did he call me his son?

MESSENGER

You were a gift,
years ago—know for a fact he took you
from my hands.

OEDIPUS

No, from another's hands?
Then how could he love me so? He loved me, deeply . . .

MESSENGER

True, and his early years without a child
made him love you all the more.

OEDIPUS

And you, did you . . .
buy me? find me by accident?

MESSENGER

I stumbled on you,
down the woody flanks of Mount Cithaeron.

OEDIPUS

So close,
what were you doing here, just passing through?

MESSENGER

Watching over my flocks, grazing them on the slopes.

OEDIPUS

A herdsman, were you? A vagabond, scraping for wages?

MESSENGER

Your savior too, my son, in your worst hour.

OEDIPUS

                                        Oh—
when you picked me up, was I in pain? What exactly?

MESSENGER

Your ankles . . . . they tell the story. Look at them.

OEDIPUS

Why remind me of that, that old affliction?

MESSENGER

Your ankles were pinned together; I set you free.

OEDIPUS

That dreadful mark—I've had it from the cradle.

MESSENGER

And you got your name from that misfortune too,
the name's still with you.[21]

OEDIPUS

                        Dear god, who did it?—
mother? father? Tell me.

MESSENGER

                    I don't know.
The one who gave you to me, he'd know more.

[21]Oedipus' name means, literally in Greek, "swollen foot."

OEDIPUS

What? You took me from someone else?
You didn't find me yourself?

MESSENGER

                              No sir,
another shepherd passed you on to me.

OEDIPUS

Who? Do you know? Describe him.

MESSENGER

He called himself a servant of . . .
if I remember rightly—Laius.

                              Jocasta turns sharply.

OEDIPUS

The king of the land who ruled here long ago?

MESSENGER

That's the one. That herdsman was *his* man.

OEDIPUS

Is he still alive? Can I see him?

MESSENGER

They'd know best, the people of these parts.

                              *Oedipus and the Messenger turn to
                              the Chorus.*

OEDIPUS

Does anyone know that herdsman,
the one he mentioned? Anyone seen him

in the fields, in town? Out with it!
The time has come to reveal this once for all.

LEADER

I think he's the very shepherd you wanted to see,
a moment ago. But the queen, Jocasta,
she's the one to say.

OEDIPUS

                Jocasta,
you remember the man we just sent for?
Is *that* the one he means?

JOCASTA

                  That man . . .
why ask? Old shepherd, talk, empty nonsense,
don't give it another thought, don't even think—

OEDIPUS

What—give up now, with a clue like this?
Fail to solve the mystery of my birth?
Not for all the world!

JOCASTA

             Stop—in the name of god,
if you love your own life, call off this search!
My suffering is enough.

OEDIPUS

            Courage!
Even if my mother turns out to be a slave,
and I a slave, three generations back,
you would not seem common.

JOCASTA

                Oh no,
listen to me, I beg you, don't do this.

OEDIPUS

Listen to you? No more. I must know it all,
see the truth at last.

JOCASTA

                        No, please—
for your sake—I want the best for you!

OEDIPUS

Your best is more than I can bear.

JOCASTA

                                You're doomed—
may you never fathom who you are!

OEDIPUS

                                        To a servant.

Hurry, fetch me the herdsman, now!
Leave her to glory in her royal birth.

JOCASTA

Aieeeeee—
            man of agony—
that is the only name I have for you,
that, no other—ever, ever, ever!

                                Flinging through the palace doors.
                                A long, tense silence follows.

LEADER

Where's she gone, Oedipus?
Rushing off, such wild grief . . .
I'm afraid that from this silence
something monstrous may come bursting forth.

OEDIPUS

Let it burst! Whatever will, whatever must!
I must know my birth, no matter how common
it may be—must see my origins face-to-face.
She perhaps, she with her woman's pride
may well be mortified by my birth,
but I, I count myself the son of Chance,
the great goddess, giver of all good things—
I'll never see myself disgraced. She is my mother!
And the moons have marked me out, my blood-brothers,
one moon on the wane, the next moon great with power.
That is my blood, my nature—I will never betray it,
never fail to search and learn my birth!

CHORUS

Yes—if I am a true prophet
          if I can grasp the truth,
     by the boundless skies of Olympus,
at the full moon of tomorrow, Mount Cithaeron
you will know how Oedipus glories in you—
you, his birthplace, nurse, his mountain-mother!
And we will sing you, dancing out your praise—
you lift our monarch's heart![22]
     Apollo, Apollo, god of the wild cry
               may our dancing please you!

                                        Oedipus—
               son, dear child, who bore you?
Who of the nymphs who seem to live forever
mated with Pan,[23] the mountain-striding Father?
Who was your mother? who, some bride of Apollo
the god who loves the pastures spreading toward the sun?
     Or was it Hermes,[24] king of the lightning ridges?
Or Dionysus, lord of frenzy, lord of the barren peaks—
did he seize you in his hands, dearest of all his lucky finds?—

[22]In its own state of ignorance, the chorus optimistically expects only good to come
from Oedipus' discovering the truth of his parentage.

[23]A woodland god, patron of shepherds and their flocks.

[24]The divine messenger of the gods, a son of Zeus. Pan, Hermes, and Dionysus all
preferred to live in the wild woods and mountains—like Mount Cithaeron.

found by the nymphs, their warm eyes dancing, gift
to the lord who loves them dancing out his joy!

*Oedipus strains to see a figure
coming from the distance. Attended
by palace guards, an old Shepherd
enters slowly, reluctant to approach
the king.*

OEDIPUS

I never met the man, my friends . . . still,
if I had to guess, I'd say that's the shepherd,
the very one we've looked for all along.
Brothers in old age, two of a kind,
he and our guest here. At any rate
the ones who bring him in are my own men,
I recognize them.

Turning to the Leader.

But you know more than I,
you should, you've seen the man before.

LEADER

I know him, definitely. One of Laius' men,
a trusty shepherd, if there ever was one.

OEDIPUS

You, I ask you first, stranger,
you from Corinth—is this the one you mean?

MESSENGER

You're looking at him. He's your man.

OEDIPUS

To the Shepherd.

You, old man, come over here—
look at me. Answer all my questions.
Did you ever serve King Laius?

SHEPHERD

                              So I did . . .
a slave, not bought on the block though,
born and reared in the palace.

OEDIPUS

Your duties, your kind of work?

SHEPHERD

Herding the flocks, the better part of my life.

OEDIPUS

Where, mostly? Where did you do your grazing?

SHEPHERD

                                        Well,
Cithaeron sometimes, or the foothills round about.

OEDIPUS

This man—you know him? ever see him there?

SHEPHERD

*Confused, glancing from the
Messenger to the King.*

Doing what?—what man do you mean?

OEDIPUS

Pointing to the Messenger.

This one here—ever have dealings with him?

SHEPHERD

Not so I could say, but give me a chance,
my memory's bad . . .

MESSENGER

No wonder he doesn't know me, master.
But let me refresh his memory for him.
I'm sure he recalls old times we had
on the slopes of Mount Cithaeron;
he and I, grazing our flocks, he with two
and I with one—we both struck up together,
three whole seasons, six months at a stretch
from spring to the rising of [the star] Arcturus in the fall,
then with winter coming on I'd drive my herds
to my own pens, and back he'd go with his
to Laius' folds.

To the Shepherd.

Now that's how it was,
wasn't it—yes or no?

SHEPHERD

Yes, I suppose . . .
it's all so long ago.

MESSENGER

Come, tell me,
you gave me a child back then, a boy, remember?
A little fellow to rear, my very own.

SHEPHERD

What? Why rake up that again?

MESSENGER

Look, here he is, my fine old friend—
the same man who was just a baby then.

SHEPHERD

Damn you, shut your mouth—quiet!

OEDIPUS

Don't lash out at him, old man—
you need lashing more than he does.

SHEPHERD

Why,
master, majesty—what have I done wrong?

OEDIPUS

You won't answer his question about the boy.

SHEPHERD

He's talking nonsense, wasting his breath.

OEDIPUS

So, you won't talk willingly—
then you'll talk with pain.

The guards seize the Shepherd.

SHEPHERD

No, dear god, don't torture an old man!

OEDIPUS

Twist his arms back, quickly!

SHEPHERD

God help us, why?—
what more do you need to know?

OEDIPUS

Did you give him that child? He's asking.

SHEPHERD

I did . . . I wish to god I'd died that day.

OEDIPUS

You've got your wish if you don't tell the truth.

SHEPHERD

The more I tell, the worse the death I'll die.

OEDIPUS

Our friend here wants to stretch things out, does he?

Motioning to his men to apply torture.

SHEPHERD

No, no, I gave it to him—I just said so.

OEDIPUS

Where did you get it? Your house? Someone else's?

SHEPHERD

It wasn't mine, no, I got it from . . . someone.

OEDIPUS

Which one of them?

Looking at the citizens.

Whose house?

SHEPHERD

No—
god's sake, master, no more questions!

OEDIPUS

You're a dead man if I have to ask again.

SHEPHERD

Then—the child came from the house . . .
of Laius.

OEDIPUS

      A slave? or born of his own blood?

SHEPHERD

                               Oh no,
I'm right at the edge, the horrible truth—I've got to say it!

OEDIPUS

And I'm at the edge of hearing horrors, yes, but I must hear!

SHEPHERD

All right! His son, they said it was—his son!
But the one inside, your wife,
she'd tell it best.

OEDIPUS

My wife—
she gave it to you?

SHEPHERD

Yes, yes, my king.

OEDIPUS

Why, what for?

SHEPHERD

To kill it.

OEDIPUS

Her own child,
how could she?

SHEPHERD

She was afraid—
frightening prophecies.

OEDIPUS

What?

SHEPHERD

        They said—
he'd kill his parents.

OEDIPUS

But you gave him to this old man—why?

SHEPHERD

I pitied the little baby, master,
hoped he'd take him off to his own country,
far away, but he saved him for this, this fate.
If you are the man he says you are, believe me,
you were born for pain.

OEDIPUS

                O god—
all come true, all burst to light!
O light—now let me look my last on you!
I stand revealed at last—
cursed in my birth, cursed in marriage,
cursed in the lives I cut down with these hands!

*Rushing through the doors with a
great cry. The Corinthian
Messenger, the Shepherd and
attendants exit slowly to the side.*

CHORUS

    O the generations of men
the dying generations—adding the total

of all your lives I find they come to nothing . . .
         does there exist, is there a man on earth
who seizes more joy than just a dream, a vision?
And the vision no sooner dawns than dies
blazing into oblivion.

You are my great example, you, your life,
your destiny, Oedipus, man of misery—
I count no man blest.

              You outranged all men!
       Bending your bow to the breaking point
you captured priceless glory, O dear god,
and the Sphinx came crashing down,
          the virgin, claws hooked
like a bird of omen singing, shrieking death—
like a fortress reared in the face of death
you rose and saved our land.

From that day on we called you king
we crowned you with honors, Oedipus, towering over all—
mighty king of the seven gates of Thebes.

But now to hear your story—is there a man more agonized?
More wed to pain and frenzy? Not a man on earth,
the joy of your life ground down to nothing
O Oedipus, name for the ages—
  one and the same wide harbor served you
               son and father both
son and father came to rest in the same bridal chamber.
How, how could the furrows your father plowed
bear you, your agony, harrowing on
in silence O so long?

           But now for all your power
Time, all-seeing Time has dragged you to the light,
judged your marriage monstrous from the start—
the son and the father tangling, both one—
O child of Laius, would to god
  I'd never seen you, never never!

Now I weep like a man who wails the dead
and the dirge comes pouring forth with all my heart!
I tell you the truth, you gave me life
my breath leapt up in you
and now you bring down night upon my eyes.

Enter a Messenger from the palace.

MESSENGER

Men of Thebes, always the first in honor,
what horrors you will hear, what you will see,
what a heavy weight of sorrow you will shoulder . . .
if you are true to your birth, if you still have
some feeling for the royal house of Thebes.
I tell you neither the waters of the Danube
nor the Nile can wash this palace clean.
Such things it hides, it soon will bring to light—
terrible things, and none done blindly now,
all done with a will. The pains
we inflict upon ourselves hurt most of all.

LEADER

God knows we have pains enough already.
What can you add to them?

MESSENGER

The queen is dead.

LEADER

Poor lady—how?

MESSENGER

By her own hand. But you are spared the worst,
you never had to watch . . . I saw it all,
and with all the memory that's in me
you will learn what that poor woman suffered.

Once she'd broken in through the gates,
dashing past us, frantic, whipped to fury,
ripping her hair out with both hands—
straight to her rooms she rushed, flinging herself
across the bridal-bed, doors slamming behind her—
once inside, she wailed for Laius, dead so long,
remembering how she bore his child long ago,
the life that rose up to destroy him, leaving
its mother to mother living creatures
with the very son she'd borne.
Oh how she wept, mourning the marriage-bed
where she let loose that double brood—monsters—
husband by her husband, children by her child.

And then—

but how she died is more than I can say. Suddenly
Oedipus burst in, screaming, he stunned us so
we couldn't watch her agony to the end,
our eyes were fixed on him. Circling
like a maddened beast, stalking, here, there,
crying out to us—

Give him a sword! His wife,

no wife, his mother, where can he find the mother earth
that cropped two crops at once, himself and all his children?
He was raging—one of the dark powers pointing the way,
none of us mortals crowding around him, no,
with a great shattering cry—someone, something leading him on—
he hurled at the twin doors and bending the bolts back
out of their sockets, crashed through the chamber.
And there we saw the woman hanging by the neck,
cradled high in a woven noose, spinning,
swinging back and forth. And when he saw her,
giving a low, wrenching sob that broke our hearts,
slipping the halter from her throat, he eased her down,
in a slow embrace he laid her down, poor thing . . .
then, what came next, what horror we beheld!

He rips off her brooches, the long gold pins
holding her robes—and lifting them high,
looking straight up into the points,
he digs them down the sockets of his eyes, crying, "You,

you'll see no more the pain I suffered, all the pain I caused!
Too long you looked on the ones you never should have seen,
blind to the ones you longed to see, to know! Blind
from this hour on! Blind in the darkness—blind!"
His voice like a dirge, rising, over and over
raising the pins, raking them down his eyes.
And at each stroke blood spurts from the roots,
splashing his beard, a swirl of it, nerves and clots—
black hail of blood pulsing, gushing down.

These are the griefs that burst upon them both,
coupling man and woman. The joy they had so lately,
the fortune of their old ancestral house
was deep joy indeed. Now, in this one day,
wailing, madness and doom, death, disgrace,
all the griefs in the world that you can name,
all are theirs forever.

LEADER

                Oh poor man, the misery—
has he any rest from pain now?

                            A voice within, in torment.

MESSENGER

                    He's shouting,
"Loose the bolts, someone, show me to all of Thebes!
My father's murderer, my mother's—"
No I can't repeat it, it's unholy.
Now he'll tear himself from his native earth,
not linger, curse the house with his own curse.
But he needs strength, and a guide to lead him on.
This is sickness more than he can bear.

                            The palace doors open.

                  Look,
he'll show you himself. The great doors are opening—
you are about to see a sight, a horror
even his mortal enemy would pity.

Enter Oedipus, blinded, led by a boy. He stands at the palace steps, as if surveying his people once again.

CHORUS

                    O the terror—
the suffering, for all the world to see,
the worst terror that ever met my eyes.
What madness swept over you? What god,
what dark power leapt beyond all bounds,
beyond belief, to crush your wretched life?—
godforsaken, cursed by the gods!
I pity you but I can't bear to look.
I've much to ask, so much to learn,
so much fascinates my eyes,
but you . . . I shudder at the sight.

OEDIPUS

                    Oh, Ohhh—
the agony! I am agony—
where am I going? where on earth?
    where does all this agony hurl me?
where's my voice—
    winging, swept away on a dark tide—
  My destiny, my dark power, what a leap you made!

CHORUS

To the depths of terror, too dark to hear, to see.

OEDIPUS

        Dark, horror of darkness
  my darkness, drowning, swirling around me
  crashing wave on wave—unspeakable, irresistible
              headwind, fatal harbor! Oh again,
    the misery, all at once, over and over
    the stabbing daggers, stab of memory
raking me insane.

CHORUS

No wonder you suffer
twice over, the pain of your wounds,
the lasting grief of pain.

OEDIPUS

Dear friend, still here?
Standing by me, still with a care for me,
the blind man? Such compassion,
loyal to the last. Oh it's you,
I know you're here, dark as it is
I'd know you anywhere, your voice—
it's yours, clearly yours.

CHORUS

Dreadful, what you've done . . .
how could you bear it, gouging out your eyes?
What superhuman power drove you on?

OEDIPUS

Apollo, friends, Apollo—
he ordained my agonies—these, my pains on pains!
But the hand that struck my eyes was mine,
mine alone—no one else—
I did it all myself!
What good were eyes to me?
Nothing I could see could bring me joy.

CHORUS

No, no, exactly as you say.

OEDIPUS

What can I ever see?
What love, what call of the heart
can touch my ears with joy? Nothing, friends.
Take me away, far, far from Thebes,
quickly, cast me away, my friends—

this great murderous ruin, this man cursed to heaven,
  the man the deathless gods hate most of all!

CHORUS

Pitiful, you suffer so, you understand so much . . .
I wish you'd never known.

OEDIPUS

                    Die, die—
  whoever he was that day in the wilds
who cut my ankles free of the ruthless pins,
  he pulled me clear of death, he saved my life
  for this, this kindness—
                    Curse him, kill him!
  If I'd died then, I'd never have dragged myself,
  my loved ones through such hell.

CHORUS

Oh if only . . . would to god.

OEDIPUS

                          I'd never have come to this,
    my father's murderer—never been branded
  mother's husband, all men see me now! Now,
    loathed by the gods, son of the mother I defiled
    coupling in my father's bed, spawning lives in the loins
that spawned my wretched life. What grief can crown this grief?
          It's mine alone, my destiny—I am Oedipus!

CHORUS

How can I say you've chosen for the best?
Better to die than be alive and blind.

OEDIPUS

What I did was best—don't lecture me,
no more advice. I, with *my* eyes
how could I look my father in the eyes

when I go down to death? Or mother, so abused . . .
I've done such things to the two of them,
crimes too huge for hanging.
                                            Worse yet,
the sight of my children, born as they were born,
how could I long to look into their eyes?
No, not with these eyes of mine, never.
Not this city either, her high towers,
the sacred glittering images of her gods—
I am misery! I, her best son, reared
as no other son of Thebes was ever reared,
I've stripped myself, I gave the command myself.
All men must cast away the great blasphemer,
the curse now brought to light by the gods,
the son of Laius—I, my father's son!

Now I've exposed my guilt, horrendous guilt,
could I train a level glance on you, my countrymen?
Impossible! No, if I could just block off my ears,
the springs of hearing, I would stop at nothing—
I'd wall up my loathsome body like a prison,
blind to the sound of life, not just the sight.
Oblivion—what a blessing . . .
for the mind to dwell a world away from pain.

O Cithaeron, why did you give me shelter
Why didn't you take me, crush my life out on the spot?
I'd never have revealed my birth to all mankind.

O Polybus, Corinth, the old house of my fathers,
so I believed—what a handsome prince you raised—
under the skin, what sickness to the core.
Look at me! Born of outrage, outrage to the core.

O triple roads—it all comes back, the secret,
dark ravine, and the oaks closing in
where the three roads join . . .
You drank my father's blood, my own blood
spilled by my own hands—you still remember me?
What things you saw me do? Then I came here
and did them all once more!

Marriages! O marriage,
you gave me birth, and once you brought me into the world
you brought my sperm rising back, springing to light
fathers, brothers, sons—one deadly breed—
brides, wives, mothers. The blackest things
a man can do, I have done them all!

No more—
it's wrong to name what's wrong to do. Quickly,
for the love of god, hide me somewhere,
kill me, hurl me into the sea
where you can never look on me again.

*Beckoning to the Chorus as they
shrink away.*

Closer,

it's all right. Touch the man of sorrow.
Do. Don't be afraid. My troubles are mine
and I am the only man alive who can sustain them.

*Enter Creon from the palace,
attended by palace guards.*

LEADER

Put your requests to Creon. Here he is,
just when we need him. He'll have a plan, he'll act.
Now that he's the sole defense of the country
in your place.

OEDIPUS

Oh no, what can I say to him?
How can I ever hope to win his trust?
I wronged him so, just now, in every way.
You must see that—I was so wrong, so wrong.

CREON

I haven't come to mock you, Oedipus,
or to criticize your former failings.

Turning to the guards.

You there,
have you lost all respect for human feeling?
At least revere the Sun, the holy fire
that keeps us all alive. Never expose a thing
of guilt and holy dread so great it appalls
the earth, the rain from heaven, the light of day!
Get him into the halls—quickly as you can.
Piety demands no less. Kindred alone
should see a kinsman's shame. This is obscene.

OEDIPUS

Please, in god's name . . . you wipe my fears away,
coming so generously to me, the worst of men.
Do one thing more, for your sake, not mine.

CREON

What do you want? Why so insistent?

OEDIPUS

Drive me out of the land at once, far from sight,
where I can never hear a human voice.

CREON

I'd have done that already, I promise you.
First I wanted the god to clarify my duties.

OEDIPUS

The god? His command was clear, every word:
death for the father-killer, the curse—
he said destroy me!

CREON

So he did. Still, in such a crisis
it's better to ask precisely what to do.

OEDIPUS

You'd ask the oracle about a man like me?

CREON

By all means. And this time, I assume,
even you will obey the god's decrees.

OEDIPUS

                                    I will,
I will. And you, I command you—I beg you . . .
the woman inside, bury her as you see fit.
It's the only decent thing,
to give your own the last rites. As for me,
never condemn the city of my fathers
to house my body, not while I'm alive, no,
let me live on the mountains, on Cithaeron,
my favorite haunt, I have made it famous.
Mother and father marked out that rock
to be my everlasting tomb—buried alive.
Let me die there, where they tried to kill me.

Oh but this I know: no sickness can destroy me,
nothing can. I would never have been saved
from death—I have been saved
for something great and terrible, something strange.
Well let my destiny come and take me on its way!

About my children, Creon, the boys at least,
don't burden yourself. They're men;
wherever they go, they'll find the means to live.
But my two daughters, my poor helpless girls,
clustering at our table, never without me
hovering near them . . . whatever I touched,
they always had their share. Take care of them,
I beg you. Wait, better—permit me, would you?
Just to touch them with my hands and take
our fill of tears. Please . . . my king.
Grant it, with all your noble heart.

If I could hold them, just once, I'd think
I had them with me, like the early days
when I could see their eyes.

> *Antigone and Ismene, two small
> children, are led in from the palace
> by a nurse.*

What's that?
O god! Do I really hear you sobbing?—
my two children. Creon, you've pitied me?
Sent me my darling girls, my own flesh and blood!
Am I right?

CREON

Yes, it's my doing.
I know the joy they gave you all these years,
the joy you must feel now.

OEDIPUS

Bless you, Creon!
May god watch over you for this kindness,
better than he ever guarded me.
Children, where are you?
Here, come quickly—

> *Groping for Antigone and Ismene,
> who approach their father
> cautiously, then embrace him.*

Come to these hands of mine,
your brother's hands, your own father's hands
that served his once bright eyes so well—
that made them blind. Seeing nothing, children,
knowing nothing, I became your father,
I fathered you in the soil that gave me life.

How I weep for you—I cannot see you now . . .
just thinking of all your days to come, the bitterness,
the life that rough mankind will thrust upon you.

Where are the public gatherings you can join,
the banquets of the clans? Home you'll come,
in tears, cut off from the sight of it all,
the brilliant rites unfinished.
And when you reach perfection, ripe for marriage,
who will he be, my dear ones? Risking all
to shoulder the curse that weighs down my parents,
yes and you too—that wounds us all together.
What more misery could you want?
Your father killed his father, sowed his mother,
one, one and the selfsame womb sprang you—
he cropped the very roots of his existence.

Such disgrace, and you must bear it all!
Who will marry you then? Not a man on earth.
Your doom is clear: you'll wither away to nothing,
single, without a child.

Turning to Creon.

            Oh Creon,
you are the only father they have now . . .
we who brought them into the world
are gone, both gone at a stroke—
Don't let them go begging, abandoned,
women without men. Your own flesh and blood!
Never bring them down to the level of my pains.
Pity them. Look at them, so young, so vulnerable,
shorn of everything—you're their only hope.
Promise me, noble Creon, touch my hand.

*Reaching toward Creon, who draws
back.*

You, little ones, if you were old enough
to understand, there is much I'd tell you.
Now, as it is, I'd have you say a prayer.
Pray for life, my children,
live where you are free to grow and season.
Pray god you find a better life than mine,
the father who begot you.

CREON

                              Enough.
You've wept enough. Into the palace now.

OEDIPUS

I must, but I find it very hard.

CREON

Time is the great healer, you will see.

OEDIPUS

I am going—you know on what condition?

CREON

Tell me. I'm listening.

OEDIPUS

Drive me out of Thebes, in exile.

CREON

Not I. Only the gods can give you that.

OEDIPUS

Surely the gods hate me so much—

CREON

You'll get your wish at once.

OEDIPUS

                              You consent?

CREON

I try to say what I mean; it's my habit.

OEDIPUS

Then take me away. It's time.

CREON

Come along, let go of the children.

OEDIPUS

No—
don't take them away from me, not now! No no no!

*Clutching his daughters as the
guards wrench them loose and take
them through the palace doors.*

CREON

Still the king, the master of all things?
No more: here your power ends.
None of your power follows you through life.

*Exit Oedipus and Creon to the
palace. The Chorus comes forward
to address the audience directly.*

CHORUS

People of Thebes, my countrymen, look on Oedipus.
He solved the famous riddle with his brilliance,
he rose to power, a man beyond all power.
Who could behold his greatness without envy?
Now what a black sea of terror has overwhelmed him.
Now as we keep our watch and wait the final day,
count no man happy till he dies, free of pain at last.

Exit in procession.

4

Herodotus

History

*D*RAMATIC *tragedy (exemplified
by selection 3) was a leading humanistic endeavor that flourished during the
Golden Age. The same century also saw the emergence of history (that is, the
written record of contemporary events—in prose) as a new way of preserving
the deeds of mankind from oblivion. (Epic poetry had been the old way.) The
appearance of history might be described as a result of the Greek spirit of
rational inquiry into tradition and as an attempt to do for mankind what the
nature-philosophers had done by rational inquiry into the physical world. But
the immediate inspiration for the earliest surviving prose work of Western
literature was patriotic: the great national effort of the Persian Wars (490–445
B.C.)*

*Herodotus (ca. 484–ca. 425 B.C.) has been called the "Father of History"
because of his literary skill and the clarity with which he explores the causes of
human actions. He was born in Asia Minor at Halicarnassus—a Greek city
chafing under Persian control. After an unsuccessful revolt by the inhabitants,
Herodotus, as a young man, went into exile; thereafter, although he loved
Athens, was much acclaimed there, and made it his home, he spent much of his
life wandering through the lands of the eastern Mediterranean and even into
Egypt, Babylonia, and the Black Sea.*

*It was during these long travels that Herodotus set out to record the leading
events of the Persian Wars. His main object was to describe the rival worlds of
Greece and Persia as seen through a single mind; for this purpose he put*

HISTORY   Herodotus, *The Histories*, trans. Aubrey de Selincourt, rev. A. R. Burn
(London: Penguin Books, 1954, rev. 1972), pp. 443–47, 452, 453, 456–57, 458–59, 464,
465–66, 475–77, 511–15, 517–20; 50, 51–59, 59–61, 72, 73, 75–77. Copyright © the Estate
of Aubrey de Selincourt, 1954, copyright © A. R. Burn, 1972. Reproduced by permission of Penguin Books Ltd.

together the vast and varied materials he had gathered on his travels. He was the first to make past events the object of research and verification. This bold and original undertaking he called by the Greek word historia *("researches"). They "are here set down to preserve the memory of the past by putting on record the astonishing achievements both of our own and of other peoples; and more particularly, to show how they [Greeks and Persians] came into conflict." Judged by modern standards, his* History *is unsatisfactory in many ways; he depended, in many cases, on unreliable sources. It is, however, a work of striking impartiality and tolerance, as the following two episodes suggest. Even in the patriotic saga of the Greek stand at Thermopylae, Herodotus treats the Persian enemies and their culture with respect.*

Herodotus wrote his History *for recitation before a public audience, not to be read privately; for it was as a public teller of tales that he made his living. Like Homer before him, therefore, he reflected commonly held ethical and heroic values. However skeptical Herodotus might have been about some of the particulars, he kept in mind the need to hold the interest and approval of the listening audience. As a consequence the work is full of fascinating stories, some of them drawn from the folklore of the Middle East—as is the Croesus-Solon story in this selection. It is an example of the moral sequence demonstrated throughout the* History *and much of Greek literature:* prosperity-pride-ruin. *"For most of those [cities] which were great once are small today; and those which used to be small were great in my own time. Knowing, therefore, that human prosperity never abides long in the same place, I shall pay attention to both alike."*

ACCOUNT OF THE PERSIAN INVASION

After the conquest of Egypt, when he was on the point of taking in hand the expedition against Athens, Xerxes[1] called a conference of the leading men in the country, to find out their attitude towards the war and explain to them his own wishes. When they met, he addressed them as follows: 'Do not suppose, gentlemen, that I am departing from precedent in the course of action I intend to undertake. We Persians have a way of living, which I have inherited from my predecessors and propose to follow. I have learned from my elders that ever since Cyrus[2]

[1]King of Persia from 485 to 465 B.C., invaded Greece in 480 B.C.
[2]Founder of the Persian Empire (559–529 B.C.), father of Cambyses.

deposed Astyages and we took over from the Medes the sovereign power we now possess, we have never yet remained inactive. This is God's guidance, and it is by following it that we have gained our great prosperity. Of our past history you need no reminder; for you know well enough the famous deeds of Cyrus, Cambyses, and my father Darius, and their additions to our empire. Now I myself, ever since my accession, have been thinking how not to fall short of the kings who have sat upon this throne before me, and how to add as much power as they did to the Persian empire. And now at last I have found a way to win for Persia not glory only but a country as large and as rich as our own—indeed richer than our own[3]—and at the same time to get satisfaction and revenge. That, then, is the object of this meeting—that I may disclose to you what it is that I intend to do. I will bridge the Hellespont[4] and march an army through Europe into Greece, and punish the Athenians for the outrage they committed upon my father and upon us.[5] As you saw, Darius himself was making his preparations for war against these men; but death prevented him from carrying out his purpose. I therefore on his behalf, and for the benefit of all my subjects, will not rest until I have taken Athens and burnt it to the ground, in revenge for the injury which the Athenians without provocation once did to me and my father. These men, you remember, came to Sardis with Aristagoras the Milesian, a subject of ours, and burnt the temples and sacred groves; and you know all too well how they served our troops under Datis and Artaphernes,[6] when they landed upon Greek soil. For these reasons I have now prepared to make war upon them, and, when I consider the matter, I find several advantages in the venture; if we crush the Athenians and their neighbours in the Peloponnese,[7] we shall so extend the empire of Persia that its boundaries will be God's own sky, so that the sun will not look down upon any land beyond the boundaries of what is ours. With your help I shall pass through Europe from end to end and make it all one country. For if what I am told is true, there is not a city or nation in the

---

[3]Xerxes greatly overstates the size and wealth of the Greek city-states.

[4]The strait separating Europe from Asia, near the site of ancient Troy.

[5]In 499 B.C. some ethnic Greeks on the coast of Asia Minor had revolted against Darius, their Persian king. With the aid of Athenian infantry, the rebels had burned the city of Sardis. Focussing his revenge on Athens, Darius invaded Greece in 490 B.C. but was defeated at Marathon near Athens. He died while preparing a new invasion which his son, Xerxes, would now push forward.

[6]Persian commanders in the failed campaign of 490 B.C.

[7]The southern portion of Greece.

world which will be able to withstand us, once these are out of the way. Thus the guilty and the innocent alike shall bear the yoke of servitude.

'If, then, you wish to gain my favour, each one of you must present himself willingly and in good heart on the day which I shall name; whoever brings with him the best equipped body of troops I will reward with those marks of distinction held in greatest value by our countrymen. That is what you must do; but so that I shall not appear to consult only my own whim, I will throw the whole matter into open debate, and ask any of you who may wish to do so, to express his views.'

The first to speak after the king was Mardonius. 'Of all Persians who have ever lived,' he began, 'and of all who are yet to be born, you, my lord, are the greatest. Every word you have spoken is true and excellent, and you will not allow the wretched Ionians[8] in Europe to make fools of us. It would indeed be an odd thing if we who have defeated and enslaved the Sacae, Indians, Ethiopians, Assyrians, and many other great nations for no fault of their own, but merely to extend the boundaries of our empire, should fail now to punish the Greeks who have been guilty of injuring us without provocation. Have we anything to fear from them? The size of their army? Their wealth? The question is absurd; we know how they fight; we know how slender their resources are. People of their race we have already reduced to subjection—I mean the Greeks of Asia, Ionians, Aeolians, and Dorians.[9] I myself before now have had some experience of these men, when under orders from your father I invaded their country; and I got as far as Macedonia—indeed almost to Athens itself—without a single soldier daring to oppose me. Yet, from what I hear, the Greeks are pugnacious enough, and start fights on the spur of the moment without sense or judgement to justify them. When they declare war on each other, they go off together to the smoothest and levellest bit of ground they can find, and have their battle on it—with the result that even the victors never get off without heavy losses, and as for the losers—well, they're wiped out. Now surely, as they all talk the same language, they ought to be able to find a better way of settling their differences: by negotiation, for instance, or an interchange of views—indeed by anything rather than fighting. Or if it is really impossible to avoid coming

[8]Greek "tribal" group that included both those in Asia Minor who had revolted against their Persian lords in 499 B.C. and their kinsmen in Athens, the source of Ionian power.

[9]All three Greek tribal groups—Ionian, Aeolian, and Dorian—had some of their population migrate to Asia Minor where they had become subjects of the Persian Empire.

to blows, they might at least employ the elements of strategy and look for a strong position to fight from. In any case, the Greeks, with their absurd notions of warfare, never even thought of opposing me when I led my army to Macedonia.

'Well then, my lord, who is likely to resist you when you march against them with the millions of Asia at your back, and the whole Persian fleet? Believe me, it is not in the Greek character to take so desperate a risk. But should I be wrong and they be so foolish as to do battle with us, then they will learn that we are the best soldiers in the world. Nevertheless, let us take this business seriously and spare no pains; success is never automatic in this world—nothing is achieved without trying.'

Xerxes' proposals were made to sound plausible enough by these words of Mardonius, and when he stopped speaking there was a silence. For a while nobody dared to put forward the opposite view, until Artabanus, taking courage from the fact of his relationship to the king—he was a son of Hystaspes and therefore Xerxes' uncle—rose to speak. 'My lord,' he said, 'without a debate in which both sides of a question are expressed, it is not possible to choose the better course. All one can do is to accept whatever it is that has been proposed. But grant a debate, and there is a fair choice to be made. We cannot assess the purity of gold merely by looking at it: we test it by rubbing it on other gold—then we can tell which is the purer. I warned your father—Darius my own brother—not to attack the Scythians, those wanderers who live in a cityless land. But he would not listen to me. Confident in his power to subdue them he invaded their country, and before he came home again many fine soldiers who marched with him were dead. But you, my lord, mean to attack a nation greatly superior to the Scythians: a nation with the highest reputation for valour both on land and at sea. It is my duty to tell you what you have to fear from them: you have said you mean to bridge the Hellespont and march through Europe to Greece. Now suppose—and it is not impossible—that you were to suffer a reverse by sea or land, or even both. These Greeks are said to be great fighters—and indeed one might well guess as much from the fact that the Athenians alone destroyed the great army we sent to attack them under Datis and Artaphernes. Or, if you will, suppose they were to succeed upon one element only—suppose they fell upon our fleet and defeated it, and then sailed to the Hellespont and destroyed the bridge: then, my lord, you would indeed be in peril. It is no special wisdom of my own that makes me argue as I do; but just such a disaster as I have suggested did, in fact, very nearly overtake us when your father bridged the Thracian Bosphorus and the Danube to take his army into Scythia. You will remember how on that occasion the Scythians went to all lengths in their efforts to induce the Ionian guard to break the Danube bridge, and how Histiaeus, the lord of Miletus, merely by following the advice of the other Ionian despots instead of rejecting it, as he did, had it in his power to ruin Persia. Surely it is a dreadful thing even to hear said, that the fortunes of the king once wholly depended upon a single man.

'I urge you, therefore, to abandon this plan; take my advice and do not run any such terrible risk when there is no necessity to do so. Break up this conference; turn the matter over quietly by yourself, and then, when you think fit, announce your decision. Nothing is more valuable to a man than to lay his plans carefully and well; even if things go against him, and forces he cannot control bring his enterprise to nothing, he still has the satisfaction of knowing that is was not his fault—the plans were all laid; if, on the other hand, he leaps headlong into danger and succeeds by luck—well, that's a bit of luck indeed, but he still has the shame of knowing that he was ill prepared.

'You know, my lord, that amongst living creatures it is the great ones that God [Zeus] smites with his thunder, out of envy of their pride. The little ones do not vex him. It is always the great buildings and the tall trees which are struck by lightning. It is God's way to bring the lofty low. Often a great army is destroyed by a little one, when God in his envy puts fear into the men's hearts, or sends a thunderstorm, and they are cut to pieces in a way they do not deserve. For God tolerates pride in none but Himself. Haste is the mother of failure—and for failure we always pay a heavy price; it is in delay our profit lies—perhaps it may not immediately be apparent, but we shall find it, sure enough, as times goes on. . . .

'This, my lord, is the advice I offer you. . . .'

All the Persian nobles who had attended the conference hurried home to their respective provinces; and as every one of them hoped to win the reward which Xerxes had offered, no pains were spared in the subsequent preparations, and Xerxes, in the process of assembling his armies, had every corner of the continent ransacked. For the four years following the conquest of Egypt the mustering of troops and the provision of stores and equipment continued, and towards the close of the fifth Xerxes, at the head of his enormous force, began his march.

The army was indeed far greater than any other in recorded history. . . .

There was not a nation in Asia that he did not take with him against Greece; save for the great rivers there was not a stream his army drank from that was not drunk dry. Some nations provided ships, others formed infantry units; from some cavalry was requisitioned, from others horse-transports and crews; from others, again, warships for floating bridges, or provisions and naval craft of various kinds. . . .

In Sardis Xerxes' first act was to send representatives to every place in Greece except Athens and Sparta with a demand for earth and water and a further order to prepare entertainment for him against his coming. This renewed demand for submission was due to his confident belief that the Greeks who had previously refused to comply with the demand of Darius would now be frightened into complying with his own. It was to prove whether or not he was right that he took this step.

He then prepared to move forward to Abydos, where a bridge had already been constructed across the Hellespont from Asia to Europe. Between Sestos and Madytus in the Chersonese there is a rocky headland running out into the water opposite Abydos. It was here not long afterwards that the Greeks under Xanthippus the son of Ariphron took Artaÿctes the Persian governor of Sestos, and nailed him alive to a plank—he was the man who collected women in the temple of Protesilaus at Elaeus and committed various acts of sacrilege. This headland was the point to which Xerxes' engineers carried their two bridges from Abydos—a distance of seven furlongs.[10] One was constructed by the Phoenicians using flax cables, the other by the Egyptians with papyrus cables. The work was successfully completed, but a subsequent storm of great violence smashed it up and carried everything away. Xerxes was very angry when he learned of the disaster, and gave orders that the Hellespont should receive three hundred lashes and have a pair of fetters [leg shackles] thrown into it. I have heard before now that he also sent people to brand it with hot irons. He certainly instructed the men with the whips to utter, as they wielded them, the barbarous and presumptuous words: 'You salt and bitter stream, your master lays this punishment upon you for injuring him, who never injured you. But Xerxes the King will cross you, with or without your permission. No man sacrifices to you, and you deserve the neglect by your acid and muddy waters.' In addition to punishing the Hellespont Xerxes gave orders that the men responsible for building the bridges

---

[10]A furlong is a unit of distance equal to 220 yards, an eighth of a mile. (The translator has here converted Greek into English measurements.)

should have their heads cut off. The men who received these invidious orders duly carried them out, and other engineers completed the work. . . .

No sooner had the troops begun to move than the sun vanished from his place in the sky and it grew dark as night, though the weather was perfectly clear and cloudless. Xerxes, deeply troubled, asked the Magi[11] to interpret the significance of this strange phenomenon, and was given to understand that God meant to foretell to the Greeks the eclipse of their cities—for it was the sun which gave warning of the future to Greece, just as the moon did to Persia. Having heard this Xerxes continued the march in high spirits.

The army, however, had not gone far when Pythius the Lydian, in alarm at the sign from heaven, was emboldened by the presents he had received to come to Xerxes with a request. 'Master,' he said, 'there is a favour I should like you to grant me—a small thing, indeed, for you to perform, but to me of great importance, should you consent to do so.' Xerxes, who thought the request would be almost anything but what it actually turned out to be, agreed to grant it and told Pythius to say what it was he wanted. This generous answer raised Pythius' hopes, and he said, 'My lord, I have five sons, and it happens that every one of them is serving in your army in the campaign against Greece. I am an old man, Sire, and I beg you in pity to release from service one of my sons—the eldest—to take care of me and my property. Take the other four—and may you return with your purpose accomplished.'

Xerxes was furiously angry. 'You miserable fellow,' he cried, 'have you the face to mention your son, when I, in person, am marching to the war against Greece with my sons and brothers and kinsmen and friends—*you*, my slave, whose duty it was to come with me with every member of your house, including your wife? Mark my words: it is through the ears you can touch a man to pleasure or rage—let the spirit which dwells there hear good things, and it will fill the body with delight; let it hear bad, and it will swell with fury. When you did me good service, and offered more, you cannot boast that you were more generous than I; and now your punishment will be less than your impudence deserves. Yourself and four of your sons are saved by the entertainment you gave me; but you shall pay with the life of the fifth, whom you cling to most.'

Having answered Pythius in these words Xerxes at once gave orders that the men to whom such duties fell should find Pythius' eldest son

---

[11]Persian priest-oracles.

and cut him in half and put the two halves one on each side of the road, for the army to march out between them. The order was performed.

From the European shore Xerxes watched his troops coming over under the whips. The crossing occupied seven days and nights without a break. There is a story that some time after Xerxes had passed the bridge, a native of the country thereabouts exclaimed: 'Why, O God, have you assumed the shape of a man of Persia, and changed your name to Xerxes, in order to lead everyone in the world to the conquest and devastation of Greece? You could have destroyed Greece without going to that trouble.' . . .

As nobody has left a record, I cannot state the precise number of men provided by each separate nation, but the grand total, excluding the naval contingent, turned out to be 1,700,000.[12] The counting was done by first packing ten thousand men as close together as they could stand and drawing a circle round them on the ground; they were then dismissed, and a fence, about navel-high, was constructed round the circle; finally other troops were marched into the area thus enclosed and dismissed in their turn, until the whole army had been counted. After the counting, the army was reorganized in divisions according to nationality. . . .

Having sailed from one end to the other of the line of anchored ships, Xerxes went ashore again and sent for Demaratus,[13] the son of Ariston, who was accompanying him in the march to Greece. 'Demaratus,' he said, 'it would give me pleasure at this point to put to you a few questions. You are a Greek, and a native, moreover, of by no means the meanest or weakest city in that country—as I learn not only from yourself but from the other Greeks I have spoken with. Tell me, then—will the Greeks dare to lift a hand against me? My own belief is that all the Greeks and all the other western peoples gathered together would be insufficient to withstand the attack of my army—and still more so if they are not united. But it is your opinion upon this subject that I should like to hear.'

'My lord,' Demaratus replied, 'is it a true answer you would like, or merely an agreeable one?'

'Tell me the truth,' said the king: 'and I promise that you will not suffer by it.' Encouraged by this Demaratus continued: 'My lord, you

[12]Herodotus' figure is impossibly huge. The estimates of modern scholars are, nevertheless, still impressive. They range from 100,000 to 400,000 combatants in the Persian army, and from 700 to 1000 ships in the navy.

[13]A former king of Sparta who had been dethroned by his own countrymen on a false charge of illegitimacy.

bid me speak nothing but the truth, to say nothing which might later be proved a lie. Very well then; this is my answer: poverty is my country's inheritance from of old, but valour she won for herself by wisdom and the strength of law. By her valour Greece now keeps both poverty and bondage at bay.

'I think highly of all Greeks of the Dorian lands, but what I am about to say will apply not to all Dorians, but to the Spartans only. First then, they will not under any circumstances accept terms from you which would mean slavery for Greece; secondly, they will fight you even if the rest of Greece submits. Moreover, there is no use in asking if their numbers are adequate to enable them to do this; suppose a thousand of them take the field—then that thousand will fight you; and so will any number, greater than this or less.'

Xerxes laughed. 'My dear Demaratus,' he exclaimed, 'what an extraordinary thing to say! Do you really suppose a thousand men would fight an army like mine? Now tell me, would *you*, who were once, as you say, king of these people, be willing at this moment to fight ten men single-handed? I hardly think so; yet, if things in Sparta are really as you have described them, then, according to your laws, you as king ought to take on a double share—so that if every Spartan is a match for ten men of mine, I should expect you to be a match for twenty. Only in that way can you prove the truth of your claim. But if you Greeks, who think so much of yourselves, are all of the size and quality of those I have spoken with when they have visited my court—and of yourself, Demaratus—there is some danger of your words being nothing but an empty boast. But let me put my point as reasonably as I can—how is it possible that a thousand men, or ten thousand, or fifty thousand, should stand up to an army as big as mine, especially if they were not under a single master, but all perfectly free to do as they pleased? Suppose them to have five thousand men: in that case we should be more than a thousand to one! If, like ours, their troops were subject to the control of a single man, then possibly for fear of him, in spite of the disparity in numbers, they might show some sort of factitious courage, or let themselves be whipped into battle; but, as every man is free to follow his fancy, it is not conceivable that they should do either. Indeed, my own opinion is that even on equal terms the Greeks could hardly face the Persians alone. We, too, have this thing that you were speaking of—I do not say it is common, but it does exist; for instance, amongst the Persians in my bodyguard there are men who would willingly fight with three Greeks together. But you know nothing of such things, or you could not talk such nonsense.'

'My lord,' Demaratus answered, 'I knew before I began that if I spoke the truth you would not like it. But, as you demanded the plain truth and nothing less, I told you how things are with the Spartans. Yet you are well aware that I now feel but little affection for my countrymen, who robbed me of my hereditary power and privileges and made me a fugitive without a home—whereas your father welcomed me at his court and gave me the means of livelihood and somewhere to live. Surely it is unreasonable to reject kindness; any sensible man will cherish it. Personally I do not claim to be able to fight ten men—or two; indeed I should prefer not even to fight with one. But should it be necessary—should there be some great cause to urge me on—then nothing would give me more pleasure than to stand up to one of those men of yours who claim to be a match for three Greeks. So it is with the Spartans; fighting singly, they are as good as any, but fighting together they are the best soldiers in the world. They are free—yes—but not entirely free; for they have a master, and that master is Law, which they fear much more than your subjects fear you. Whatever this master commands, they do; and his command never varies: it is never to retreat in battle, however great the odds, but always to stand firm, and to conquer or die. If, my lord, you think that what I have said is nonsense—very well; I am willing henceforward to hold my tongue. This time I spoke because you forced me to speak. In any case, I pray that all may turn out as you desire.'

Xerxes burst out laughing at Demaratus' answer, and good-humouredly let him go.

After the conversation I have recorded above, Xerxes . . . continued his march through Thrace towards Greece.

●   ●   ●

The position, then, was that Xerxes was lying with his force at Trachis in Malian territory, while the Greeks occupied the pass[14] known locally as Pylae—though Thermopylae is the common Greek name. Such were the respective positions of the two armies, one being in control of all the country from Trachis northward, the other of the whole mainland to the south. The Greek force which here awaited the coming of Xerxes was made up of the following contingents: 300 heavy-armed infantry from Sparta, 500 from Tegea, 500 from Mantinea, 120 from Orchomenus in Arcadia, 1000 from the rest of Arcadia; from Corinth there were 400, from Phlius 200, and from Mycenae 80.

[14]The width of the pass, the distance between a high cliff and the sea, was only about fourteen yards.

In addition to these troops from the Peloponnese, there were the Boeotian contingents of 700 from Thespiae and 400 from Thebes. The Locrians of Opus and the Phocians had also obeyed the call to arms, the former sending all the men they had, the latter one thousand. The other Greeks had induced these two towns to send troops by a message to the effect that they themselves were merely an advance force, and that the main body of the confederate [allied] army was daily expected; the sea, moreover, was strongly held by the fleet of Athens and Aegina and the other naval forces. Thus there was no cause for alarm—for, after all, it was not a god who threatened Greece, but a man, and there neither was nor ever would be a man who was not born with a good chance of misfortune—and the greater the man, the greater the misfortune. The present enemy was no exception; he too was human, and was sure to be disappointed of his great expectations.

The appeal succeeded, and Opus and Phocis sent their troops to Trachis. The contingents of the various states were under their own officers, but the most respected was Leonidas the Spartan, who was in command of the whole army. Leonidas traced his descent directly back to Heracles,[15] through Anaxandrides and Leon (his father and grandfather), Anaxander, Eurycrates, Polydorus, Alcamenes, Teleches, Archelaus, Agesilaus, Doryssus, Labotas, Echestratus, Agis, Eurysthenes, Aristodemus, Aristomachus, Cleodaeus—and so to Hyllus, who was Heracles' son. He had come to be king of Sparta quite unexpectedly, for as he had two elder brothers, Cleomenes and Dorieus, he had no thought of himself succeeding to the throne. Dorieus, however, was killed in Sicily, and when Cleomenes also died without an heir, Leonidas found himself next in the succession. He was older than Cleombrotus, Anaxandrides' youngest son, and was, moreover, married to Cleomenes' daughter. The three hundred men whom he brought on this occasion to Thermopylae were chosen by himself, all fathers of living sons. He also took with him the Thebans I mentioned, under the command of Leontiades, the son of Eurymachus. The reason why he made a special point of taking troops from Thebes, and from Thebes only, was that the Thebans were strongly suspected of Persian sympathies, so he called upon them to play their part in the war in order to see if they would answer the call, or openly refuse to join the confederacy. They did send troops, but their secret sympathy was

[15]It was common for aristocrats to trace their lineage back to some famous hero. For a Spartan warrior, Heracles (Roman Hercules) would have been an especially appropriate ancestor as he was noted for his strength, courage, and endurance.

nevertheless with the enemy. Leonidas and his three hundred were sent by Sparta in advance of the main army, in order that the sight of them might encourage the other confederates to fight and prevent them from going over to the enemy, as they were quite capable of doing if they knew that Sparta was hanging back; the intention was, when the Carneia was over (for it was that festival which prevented the Spartans from taking the field in the ordinary way), to leave a garrison in the city and march with all the troops at their disposal. The other allied states proposed to act similarly; for the Olympic festival happened to fall just at this same period. None of them ever expected the battle at Thermopylae to be decided so soon—which was the reason why they sent only advance parties there.

The Persian army was now close to the pass, and the Greeks, suddenly doubting their power to resist, held a conference to consider the advisability of retreat. It was proposed by the Peloponnesians generally that the army should fall back upon the Peloponnese and hold the Isthmus; but when the Phocians and Locrians expressed their indignation at this suggestion, Leonidas gave his voice for staying where they were and sending, at the same time, an appeal for reinforcements to the various states of the confederacy, as their numbers were inadequate to cope with the Persians.

During the conference Xerxes sent a man on horseback to ascertain the strength of the Greek force and to observe what the troops were doing. He had heard before he left Thessaly that a small force was concentrated here, led by the Lacedaemonians [Spartans] under Leonidas of the house of Heracles. The Persian rider approached the camp and took a thorough survey of all he could see—which was not, however, the whole Greek army; for the men on the further side of the wall which, after its reconstruction, was now guarded, were out of sight. He did, none the less, carefully observe the troops who were stationed on the outside of the wall. At that moment these happened to be Spartans, and some of them were stripped for exercise, while others were combing their hair. The Persian spy watched them in astonishment; nevertheless he made sure of their numbers, and of everything else he needed to know, as accurately as he could, and then rode quietly off. No one attempted to catch him, or took the least notice of him.

Back in his own camp he told Xerxes what he had seen. Xerxes was bewildered; the truth, namely that the Spartans were preparing themselves to die and deal death with all their strength, was beyond his comprehension, and what they were doing seemed to him merely absurd. Accordingly he sent for Demaratus, the son of Ariston, who had come with the army, and questioned him about the spy's report, in the hope of finding out what the behaviour of the Spartans might mean. 'Once before,' Demaratus said, 'when we began our march against Greece, you heard me speak of these men. I told you then how I saw this enterprise would turn out, and you laughed at me. I strive for nothing, my lord, more earnestly than to observe the truth in your presence; so hear me once more. These men have come to fight us for possession of the pass, and for that struggle they are preparing. It is the common practice of the Spartans to pay careful attention to their hair when they are about to risk their lives. But I assure you that if you can defeat these men and the rest of the Spartans who are still at home, there is no other people in the world who will dare to stand firm or lift a hand against you. You have now to deal with the finest kingdom in Greece, and with the bravest men.'

Xerxes, unable to believe what Demaratus said, asked further how it was possible that so small a force could fight with his army. 'My lord,' Demaratus replied, 'treat me as a liar, if what I have foretold does not take place.' But still Xerxes was unconvinced.

For four days Xerxes waited, in constant expectation that the Greeks would make good their escape; then, on the fifth, when still they had made no move and their continued presence seemed mere impudent and reckless folly, he was seized with rage and sent forward the Medes and Cissians[16] with orders to take them alive and bring them into his presence. The Medes charged, and in the struggle which ensued many fell; but others took their places, and in spite of terrible losses refused to be beaten off. They made it plain enough to anyone, and not least to the king himself, that he had in his army many men, indeed, but few soldiers. All day the battle continued; the Medes, after their rough handling, were at length withdrawn and their place was taken by Hydarnes and his picked Persian troops—the King's Immortals—who advanced to the attack in full confidence of bringing the business to a quick and easy end. But, once engaged, they were no more successful than the Medes had been; all went as before, the two armies fighting in a confined space, the Persians using shorter spears than the Greeks and having no advantage from their numbers.

On the Spartan side it was a memorable fight; they were men who

[16]Allies of the Persians.

understood war pitted against an inexperienced enemy, and amongst the feints they employed was to turn their backs on a body and pretend to be retreating in confusion, whereupon the enemy would pursue them with a great clatter and roar; but the Spartans, just as the Persians were on them, would wheel and face them and inflict in the new struggle innumerable casualties. The Spartans had their losses too, but not many. At last the Persians, finding that their assaults upon the pass, whether by divisions or by any other way they could think of, were all useless, broke off the engagement and withdrew. Xerxes was watching the battle from where he sat; and it is said that in the course of the attacks three times, in terror for his army, he leapt to his feet.

Next day the fighting began again, but with no better success for the Persians, who renewed their onslaught in the hope that the Greeks, being so few in number, might be badly enough disabled by wounds to prevent further resistance. But the Greeks never slackened; their troops were ordered in divisions corresponding to the states from which they came, and each division took its turn in the line except the Phocian, which had been posted to guard the track over the mountains. So when the Persians found that things were no better for them than on the previous day, they once more withdrew.

How to deal with the situation Xerxes had no idea; but just then, a man from Malis, Ephialtes, the son of Eurydemus, came, in hope of a rich reward, to tell the king about the track which led over the hills to Thermopylae—and thus he was to prove the death of the Greeks who held the pass.[17] . . .

The Greeks at Thermopylae had their first warning of the death that was coming with the dawn from the seer Megistias, who read their doom in the victims of sacrifice;[18] deserters, too, came in during the night with news of the Persian flank movement, and lastly, just as day was breaking, the look-out men came running from the hills. In council of war their opinions were divided, some urging that they must not abandon their post, others the opposite. The result was that the army split: some dispersed, contingents returning to their various cities,

[17]The track led *around* the pass, to the rear of the Greek forces. (Ephialtes came from the local region. Some ten years later, when he had returned from his place of refuge, Ephialtes was assassinated.)

[18]Cattle and sheep were the most usual victims of the ritual sacrifice to the gods of the Greeks. (Note Odysseus' offering in Book One of *The Iliad*—selection 1, pp. 13–14.) Seers told the future by examining the animals' entrails.

while others made ready to stand by Leonidas. It is said that Leonidas himself dismissed them, to spare their lives, but thought it unbecoming for the Spartans under his command to desert the post which they had originally come to guard. I myself am inclined to think that he dismissed them when he realized that they had no heart for the fight and were unwilling to take their share of the danger; at the same time honour forbade that he himself should go. And indeed by remaining at his post he left a great name behind him, and Sparta did not lose her prosperity, as might otherwise have happened; for right at the outset of the war the Spartans had been told by the Delphic oracle[19] that either their city must be laid waste by the foreigner or a Spartan king be killed. . . .

I believe it was the thought of this oracle, combined with his wish to lay up for the Spartans a treasure of fame in which no other city should share, that made Leonidas dismiss those troops; I do not think that they deserted, or went off without orders, because of a difference of opinion. Moreover, I am strongly supported in this view by the case of the seer Megistias, who was with the army—an Acarnanian, said to be of the clan of Melampus—who foretold the coming doom from his inspection of the sacrificial victims. He quite plainly received orders from Leonidas to quit Thermopylae, to save him from sharing the army's fate. He refused to go, but he sent his only son, who was serving with the forces.

Thus it was that the confederate troops, by Leonidas' orders, abandoned their posts and left the pass, all except the Thespians and the Thebans who remained with the Spartans.[20] The Thebans were detained by Leonidas as hostages very much against their will; but the Thespians of their own accord refused to desert Leonidas and his men, and stayed, and died with them. They were under the command of Demophilus the son of Diadromes.

In the morning Xerxes poured a libation to the rising sun, and then waited till it was well up before he began to move forward. This was according to Ephialtes' instructions, for the way down from the ridge

---

[19]Delphi, on the Greek mainland, was the site of the ancient world's most famous oracle. Questioners would come there seeking advice on matters concerning religious ritual, morality, and the course of the future. (Note Oedipus' journey to Delphi.)

[20]Some modern estimates number the total Greek forces under Leonidas, including his 300 Spartans, at about 7,000 men. Before the final stand, when most of the units were allowed to march away, 1,100 stayed with the Spartans.

is much shorter and more direct than the long and circuitous ascent.[21] As the Persian army advanced to the assault, the Greeks under Leonidas, knowing that they were going to their deaths, went out into the wider part of the pass much further than they had done before; in the previous days' fighting they had been holding the wall and making sorties from behind it into the narrow neck, but now they fought outside the narrows. Many of the invaders fell; behind them the company commanders plied their whips indiscriminately, driving the men on. Many fell into the sea and were drowned, and still more were trampled to death by their friends. No one could count the number of the dead. The Greeks, who knew that the enemy were on their way round by the mountain track and that death was inevitable, put forth all their strength and fought with fury and desperation. By this time most of their spears were broken, and they were killing Persians with their swords.

In the course of that fight Leonidas fell, having fought most gallantly, and many distinguished Spartans with him—their names I have learned, as those of men who deserve to be remembered; indeed, I have learned the names of all the three hundred. Amongst the Persian dead, too, were many men of high distinction, including two brothers of Xerxes. . . .

There was a bitter struggle over the body of Leonidas; four times the Greeks drove the enemy off, and at last by their valour rescued it. So it went on, until the troops with Ephialtes were close at hand; and then, when the Greeks knew that they had come, the character of the fighting changed. They withdrew again into the narrow neck of the pass, behind the wall, and took up a position in a single compact body—all except the Thebans—on the little hill at the entrance to the pass, where the stone lion in memory of Leonidas stands to-day. Here they resisted to the last, with their swords, if they had them, and, if not, with their hands and teeth, until the Persians, coming on from the front over the ruins of the wall and closing in from behind, finally overwhelmed them with missile weapons.

Of all the Spartans and Thespians who fought so valiantly the most signal proof of courage was given by the Spartan Dieneces. It is said that before the battle he was told by a native of Trachis that, when the

---

[21]The instructions allowed time for the troops led by Ephialtes to reach the rear of the Greek force at about the same time as the main Persian frontal attack.

Persians shot their arrows, there were so many of them that they hid the sun. Dieneces, however, quite unmoved by the thought of the strength of the Persian army, merely remarked: 'This is pleasant news that the stranger from Trachis brings us: if the Persians hide the sun, we shall have our battle in the shade.'. . .

The dead were buried where they fell, and with them the men who had been killed before those dismissed by Leonidas left the pass. Over them is this inscription, in honour of the whole force:

> *Four thousand here from Pelops' land*
> *Against three million once did stand.*

The Spartans have a special epitaph; it runs:

> *Go tell the Spartans, you who read:*
> *We took their orders, and are dead.*

[Editor's note: After the battle at Thermopylae the Persians continued their advance. The Athenians evacuated their city which was captured by the Persians who burned down the temples on the Acropolis (the high citadel which dominated the city). In the following months, however, there was a great naval battle in the narrow waters between the island of Salamis and the mainland; there was also a major land battle near Plataea. On both occasions the Persians were totally routed. After those battles never again did a Persian military force threaten the European mainland.]

• • •

CROESUS-SOLON STORY

Having started with the Ephesians, Croesus subsequently attacked all the Ionian and Aeolian cities in turn on various pretexts, substantial or trivial, according to what ground of complaint he could find against them. He forced all the Asiatic Greeks[22] to pay him tribute, and then turned his attention to ship-building in order to attack the islanders. . . .

In the course of time Croesus subdued all the peoples west of the river Halys,[23] except the Cilicians and Lycians. The rest he kept in subjection. . . .

[22]The Asiatic Greeks are those, of whichever tribal origin, living in Asia Minor (modern Turkey).

[23]A river in the central region of Asia Minor.

When all these nations had been added to the Lydian empire, and Sardis[24] was at the height of her wealth and prosperity, all the great Greek teachers of that epoch, one after another, paid visits to the capital. Much the most distinguished of them was Solon the Athenian, the man who at the request of his countrymen had made a code of laws for Athens.[25] He was on his travels at the time, intending to be away ten years, in order to avoid the necessity of repealing any of the laws he had made. That, at any rate, was the real reason of his absence, though he gave it out that what he wanted was just to see the world. The Athenians could not alter any of Solon's laws without him, because they had solemnly sworn to give them a ten years' trial.

For this reason, then—and also no doubt for the pleasure of foreign travel—Solon left home and, after a visit to the court of Amasis in Egypt, went to Sardis to see Croesus.

Croesus entertained him hospitably in the palace, and three or four days after his arrival instructed some servants to take him on a tour of the royal treasuries and point out the richness and magnificence of everything. When Solon had made as thorough an inspection as opportunity allowed, Croesus said: 'Well, my Athenian friend, I have heard a great deal about your wisdom, and how widely you have travelled in the pursuit of knowledge. I cannot resist my desire to ask you a question: who is the happiest man you have ever seen?'

The point of the question was that Croesus supposed himself to be the happiest of men. Solon, however, refused to flatter, and answered in strict accordance with his view of the truth. 'An Athenian,' he said, 'called Tellus.'

Croesus was taken aback. 'And what,' he asked sharply, 'is your reason for this choice?'

'There are two good reasons,' said Solon, 'first, his city was prosperous, and he had fine sons, and lived to see children born to each of them, and all these children surviving: secondly, he had wealth enough by our standards; and he had a glorious death. In a battle with the neighbouring town of Eleusis, he fought for his countrymen, routed the enemy, and died like a soldier; and the Athenians paid him the high honour of a public funeral on the spot where he fell.'

[24]The capital of the Lydian empire; Croesus was its last king (560–546 B.C.).

[25]Solon, (*ca.* 640–*ca.* 560 B.C.), an Athenian statesman and legislator who was elected to end civil conflict in 594. He achieved this by enacting his famous legal reforms. His meeting with Croesus, described by Herodotus, is chronologically doubtful.

All these details about the happiness of Tellus, Solon doubtless in-tended as a moral lesson for the king; Croesus, however, thinking he would at least be awarded second prize, asked who was the next hap-piest person whom Solon had seen.

'Two young men of Argos,' was the reply; 'Cleobis and Biton. They had enough to live on comfortably; and their physical strength is proved not merely by their success in athletics, but much more by the following incident. The Argives were celebrating the festival of Hera,[26] and it was most important that the mother of the two young men should drive to the temple in her ox-cart; but it so happened that the oxen were late in coming back from the fields. Her two sons therefore, as there was no time to lose, harnessed themselves to the cart and dragged it along, with their mother inside, for a distance of nearly six miles, until they reached the temple. After this exploit, which was witnessed by the assembled crowd, they had a most enviable death—a heaven-sent proof of how much better it is to be dead than alive. Men kept crowding round them and congratulating them on their strength, and women kept telling the mother how lucky she was to have such sons, when, in sheer pleasure at this public recognition of her sons' act, she prayed the goddess Hera, before whose shrine she stood, to grant Cleobis and Biton, who had brought her such honour, the greatest blessing that can fall to mortal man.

'After her prayer came the ceremonies of sacrifice and feasting; and the two lads, when all was over, fell asleep in the temple—and that was the end of them, for they never woke again.

'The Argives had statues made of them, which they sent to Delphi, as a mark of their particular respect.'

Croesus was vexed with Solon for giving the second prize for hap-piness to the two young Argives, and snapped out: 'That's all very well, my Athenian friend; but what of my own happiness? Is it so utterly contemptible that you won't even compare me with mere com-mon folk like those you have mentioned?'

'My lord,' replied Solon, 'I know God [Zeus] is envious of human prosperity and likes to trouble us; and you question me about the lot of man. Listen then: as the years lengthen out, there is much both to see and to suffer which one would wish otherwise. Take seventy years as the span of a man's life: those seventy years contain 25,200 days, without counting intercalary months. Add a month every other year, to make the seasons come round with proper regularity, and you will

[26]Sister and wife of Zeus, queen of the Olympian gods.

have thirty-five additional months, which will make 1,050 additional days. Thus the total of days for your seventy years is 26,250, and not a single one of them is like the next in what it brings. You can see from that, Croesus, what a chancy thing life is. You are very rich, and you rule a numerous people; but the question you asked me I will not answer, until I know that you have died happily. Great wealth can make a man no happier than moderate means, unless he has the luck to continue in prosperity to the end. Many very rich men have been unfortunate, and many with a modest competence have had good luck. The former are better off than the latter in two respects only, whereas the poor but lucky man has the advantage in many ways; for though the rich have the means to satisfy their appetites and to bear calamities, and the poor have not, the poor, if they are lucky, are more likely to keep clear of trouble, and will have besides the blessings of a sound body, health, freedom from trouble, fine children, and good looks.

'Now if a man thus favoured dies as he has lived, he will be just the one you are looking for: the only sort of person who deserves to be called happy. But mark this: until he is dead, keep the word "happy" in reserve. Till then, he is not happy, but only lucky.

'Nobody of course can have all these advantages, any more than a country can produce everything it needs: whatever it has, it is bound to lack something. The best country is the one which has most. It is the same with people: no man is ever self-sufficient—there is sure to be something missing. But whoever has the greatest number of the good things I have mentioned, and keeps them to the end, and dies a peaceful death, that man, my lord Croesus, deserves in my opinion to be called happy.

'Look to the end, no matter what it is you are considering. Often enough God gives a man a glimpse of happiness, and then utterly ruins him.'

These sentiments were not of the sort to give Croesus any pleasure; he let Solon go with cold indifference, firmly convinced that he was a fool. For what could be more stupid than to keep telling him to look at the 'end' of everything, without any regard to present prosperity?

After Solon's departure, nemesis[27] fell upon Croesus, presumably because God was angry with him for supposing himself the happiest of men. It began with a dream he had about a disaster to one of his sons: a dream which came true. He had two sons: one with a physical

[27]Divinely inflicted punishment. (Nemesis was the Greek goddess who punished especially those humans guilty of *hubris*, excessive pride or insolence toward the gods.)

disability, being deaf and dumb; the other, named Atys, as fine a young man as one can fancy. Croesus dreamt that Atys would be killed by a blow from an iron weapon. He woke from the dream in horror, and lost no time in getting his son a wife, and seeing to it that he no longer took the field with the Lydian soldiers, whom he used to command. He also removed all the weapons—javelins, spears and so on—from the men's rooms, and had them piled up in the women's quarters, because he was afraid that some blade hanging on the wall might fall on Atys' head.

The arrangements for the wedding were well in hand, when there came to Sardis an unfortunate stranger who had been guilty of man-slaughter. He was a Phrygian,[28] and related to the Phrygian royal house. This man presented himself at the palace and begged Croesus to cleanse him from blood-guilt according to the laws of the country (the ceremony is much the same in Lydia as in Greece): and Croesus did as he asked. When the formalities were over, Croesus, wishing to know who he was and where he came from, said: 'What is your name, stranger, and what part of Phrygia have you come from, to take refuge with me? What man or woman did you kill?'

'Sire,' the stranger replied, 'I am the son of Gordias, and Midas was my grandfather. My name is Adrastus. I killed my brother by accident, and here I am driven from home by my father and stripped of all I possessed.'

'Your family and mine,' said Croesus, 'are friends. You have come to a friendly house. If you stay in my dominions, you shall have all you need. The best thing for you will be not to take your misfortune too much to heart.' Adrastus, therefore, took up his residence in the palace.

Now it happened just at this time that Mount Olympus[29] in Mysia was infested by a monstrous boar. This tremendous creature used to issue from his mountain lair and play havoc with the crops, and many times the Mysians had taken the field against him, but to no purpose. The unfortunate hunters received more damage than they were able to inflict. As a last resource the Mysians sent to Croesus.

'Sire,' the messengers said, 'a huge beast of a boar has appeared amongst us, and is doing fearful damage. We want to catch him, but we can't. Please, my lord, send us your son with a party of young men, and some dogs, so that we can get rid of the brute.'

[28]A native of Phrygia, a country in the central region of Asia Minor.
[29]Not the European peak, but another Olympus in northwestern Asia Minor.

Croesus had not forgotten his dream, and in answer to this request forbade any further mention of his son.

'I could not send him,' he said; 'he is just married, and that keeps him busy. But I will certainly send picked men, with a complete hunting outfit, and I will urge them to do all they can to help rid you of the animal.'

This answer satisfied the Mysians; but at that moment Atys, who had heard of their request, entered the room. The young man, finding that Croesus persisted in his refusal to let him join the hunting party, said to his father: 'Once honour demanded that I should win fame as a huntsman and fighter; but now, father, though you cannot accuse me of cowardice or lack of spirit, you won't let me take part in either of these admirable pursuits. Think what a figure I must cut when I walk between here and the place of assembly! What will people take me for? What must my young wife think of me? That she hasn't married much of a husband, I fear! Now, father, either let me join this hunt, or give me an intelligible reason why what you're doing is good for me.'

'My son,' said Croesus, 'of course you are not a coward or anything unpleasant of that kind. That is not the reason for what I'm doing. The fact is, I dreamt that you had not long to live—that you would be killed by an iron weapon. It was that dream that made me hasten your wedding; and the same thing makes me refuse to let you join in this enterprise. As long as I live, I am determined to protect you, and to rob death of his prize. You are my only son, for I do not count that wretched cripple, your brother.'

'No one can blame you, father,' Atys replied, 'for taking care of me after a dream like that. Nevertheless there is something which you have failed to observe, and it is only right that I should point it out to you. You dreamt that I should be killed by an iron weapon. Very well: has a boar got hands? Can a boar hold this weapon you fear so much? Had you dreamt that I should be killed by a boar's tusk or anything of that sort, your precautions would be justified. But you didn't: it was a weapon which was to kill me. Let me go, then. It is only to hunt an animal, not to fight against me.'

'My boy,' said Croesus, 'I own myself beaten. You interpret the dream better than I did. I cannot but change my mind, and allow you to join the expedition.'

The king then sent for Adrastus the Phrygian, and said to him: 'Through no fault of your own, Adrastus, you came to me in great distress and with an ugly stain on your character. I gave you ritual purification, welcomed you to my house, and have spared no expense to entertain you. Now I expect a fair return for my generosity: take charge of my son on this boar-hunt; protect him from footpads and cut-throats on the road. In any case it is your duty to go where you can distinguish yourself: your family honour demands it, and you are a stalwart fellow besides.'

'Sire,' Adrastus answered, 'under ordinary circumstances I should have taken no part in this adventure. A man under a cloud has no business to associate with those who are luckier than himself. Indeed I have no heart for it, and there are many reasons to prevent my going. But your wishes make all the difference. It is my duty to gratify you in return for your kindness: so I am ready to do as you ask. So far as it lies in my power to protect your son, you may count on his returning safe and sound.'

When Adrastus had given his answer, the party set out, men, dogs, and all. They made their way to Olympus and kept their eyes open for the boar. As soon as they spotted him, they surrounded him and let fly with spears—and then it was that the stranger—Adrastus, the very man whom Croesus had cleansed from the stain of blood—aimed at the boar, missed him, and struck the king's son. Croesus' dream had come true.

A messenger hurried off to Sardis, and Croesus was told of the encounter with the boar and the death of his son. The shock of the news was dreadful; and the horror of it was increased by the fact that the weapon had been thrown by the very man whom the king had cleansed from the guilt of blood. In the violence of his grief Croesus prayed to Zeus, calling on him as God of Purification to witness what he had suffered at the hands of his guest; he invoked him again under his title of Protector of the Hearth, because he had unwittingly entertained his son's murderer in his own house; and yet again as God of Friendship, because the man he had sent to guard his son had turned out to be his bitterest enemy.

Before long the Lydians arrived with the body, followed by the unlucky killer. He took his stand in front of the corpse, and stretching out his hands in an attitude of submission begged the king to cut his throat there and then upon the dead body of his son.

'My former trouble,' he said, 'was bad enough. But now that I have ruined the man who absolved me of my guilt, I cannot bear to live.'

In spite of his grief Croesus was moved to pity by these words.

'Friend,' he said, 'as you condemn yourself to death, there is nothing more I can require of you. Justice is satisfied. This calamity is not your fault; you never meant to strike the blow, though strike it you did. Some God is to blame—some God who long ago warned me of what was to happen.'

Croesus buried his son with all proper ceremony; and as soon as everything was quiet after the funeral, Adrastus—the son of Gordias, the grandson of Midas: the man who had killed his brother and ruined the host who gave him purification—convinced that he was the unluckiest of all the men he had ever known, stabbed himself and fell dead upon the tomb.

For two years Croesus grieved for the death of his son, until the news from Persia put an end to his mourning: Cyrus . . . had destroyed the empire of Astyages, and the power of Persia was steadily increasing. This gave Croesus food for thought, and he wondered if he might be able to check Persian expansion before it had gone too far. With this purpose in view he at once prepared to try his luck with the oracles, and sent to Delphi, to Abae in Phocis, to Dodona, to the oracles of Amphiaraus and Trophonius, and to Branchidae in Milesia. These were the Greek ones which he consulted, but, not content with them, he sent also to the oracle of Ammon in Libya. His object was to test the knowledge of the oracles, so that if they should prove to be in possession of the truth he might send a second time and ask if he should undertake a campaign against Persia.

The Lydians whom Croesus sent to make the test were given the following orders: on the hundredth day, reckoning from the day on which they left Sardis, they were to consult the oracles, and inquire what Croesus, son of Alyattes and king of Lydia, was doing at that moment. The answer of each oracle was to be taken down in writing and brought back to Sardis. No one has recorded the answer of any of the oracles except that of Delphi; here, however, immediately the Lydians entered the shrine for their consultation, and almost before the question they had been told to ask was out of their mouths, the Priestess gave them, in . . . verse, the following reply:

> *I count the grains of sand on the beach and measure the sea;*
> *I understand the speech of the dumb and hear the voiceless.*
> *The smell has come to my sense of a hard-shelled tortoise*
> *Boiling and bubbling with lamb's flesh in a bronze pot:*
> *The cauldron underneath is of bronze, and of bronze the lid.*

The Lydians took down the Priestess' answer and returned with it to Sardis.

When the other messengers came back with the answers they had received, Croesus opened all the rolls and read what they contained. None had the least effect upon him except the one which contained the answer from Delphi. But no sooner had this one been read to him than he accepted it with profound reverence, declaring that the oracle at Delphi was the only genuine one in the world, because it had succeeded in finding out what he had been doing. And indeed it had; for after sending off the messengers, Croesus had thought of something which no one would be likely to guess, and with his own hands, keeping carefully to the prearranged date, had cut up a tortoise and a lamb and boiled them together in a bronze cauldron with a bronze lid.

So much for the answer from Delphi. As to the oracle of Amphiaraus, there is no record of what answer the Lydians received when they had performed the customary rites in the temple; all I can say is, that Croesus believed this oracle too to be in possession of the truth.

Croesus now attempted to win the favour of the Delphian Apollo[30] by a magnificent sacrifice. Of every kind of appropriate animal he slaughtered three thousand; he burnt in a huge pile a number of precious objects—couches overlaid with gold or silver, golden cups, tunics, and other richly coloured garments—in the hope of binding the god more closely to his interest; and he issued a command that every Lydian was also to offer a sacrifice according to his means. After this ceremony he melted down an enormous quantity of gold into one hundred and seventeen ingots about eighteen inches long, nine inches wide, and three inches thick; four of the ingots were of refined gold weighing approximately a hundred and forty-two pounds each: the rest were alloyed and weighed about a hundred and fourteen pounds. He also caused the image of a lion to be made of refined gold, in weight some five hundred and seventy pounds. This statue, when the temple at Delphi was burnt down, fell from the gold bricks which formed its base and lies to-day in the Corinthian treasury. It lost about two hundred pounds weight in the fire, and now weighs only three hundred and seventy pounds.

This was by no means all that Croesus sent to Delphi; there were also two huge mixing-bowls, one of gold which was placed on the right-hand side of the entrance to the temple, the other of silver, on the left. . . . These, then, were the offerings which Croesus sent to Delphi; to the shrine of Amphiaraus, the story of whose valour and misfortune

[30]Apollo—son of Zeus and god of medicine, music, archery, and prophecy—was the patron god of the oracle at Delphi.

he knew, he sent a shield of solid gold and a spear, also of solid gold throughout, both shaft and head; the shield and spear were still at Thebes in my own day, in the temple of Apollo.

The Lydians who were to bring the presents to the temples were instructed by Croesus to ask the oracles if he should undertake the campaign against Persia, and if he should strengthen his army by some alliance. On their arrival, therefore, they offered the gifts with proper ceremony and put their question in the following words: 'Croesus, King of Lydia and other nations, in the belief that these are the only true oracles in the world, has given you gifts such as your power of divination deserves, and now asks you if he should march against Persia and if it would be wise to seek an alliance.' To this question both oracles returned a similar answer; they foretold that if Croesus attacked the Persians, he would destroy a great empire, and they advised him to find out which of the Greek states was the most powerful, and to come to an understanding with it.

Croesus was overjoyed when he learnt the answer which the oracles had given, and was fully confident of destroying the power of Cyrus. To express his satisfaction he sent a further present to Delphi of two gold staters [coins] for every man, having first inquired how many men there were. The Delphians in return granted in perpetuity to Croesus and the people of Lydia the right of citizenship for any who wished, together with exemption from dues, front seats at state functions and priority in consulting the oracle.

When Croesus had given the Delphians their presents, he consulted the oracle a third time, for one true answer had made him greedy for more. On this occasion he asked if his reign would be a long one. The Priestess answered:

> *When comes the day that a mule shall sit on the Median throne,*
> *Then, tender-footed Lydian, by pebbly Hermus*[31]
> *Run and abide not, nor think it shame to be a coward.*

This reply gave Croesus more pleasure than anything he had yet heard; for he did not suppose that a mule was likely to become king of the Medes,[32] and that meant that he and his line would remain in power

---

[31]A river that flows past the Lydian capital city of Sardis.

[32]Herodotus appears to use the names of the Medes and Persians interchangeably. Actually, Cyrus, the founder of the Persian empire, had conquered the Medes in 550 B.C. Thereafter, they occupied a prominent place in his empire.

forever. He then turned his attention to finding out which of the Greek states was the most powerful, with a view to forming an alliance. . . .

When Croesus started for home after the battle in Pteria, Cyrus was sure that he would disband his army as soon as he arrived; so after consideration he found that his best course was to press on to Sardis with all speed before the Lydian forces had time to muster again. This was no sooner determined than done. Indeed he was his own messenger—for so swift was his advance into Lydia that Croesus had no news that he was on the way. This unexpected turn of events put Croesus into a very difficult position; however, he made an attempt to resist the invader. (In those days, by the way, there were no stouter or more courageous fighters in Asia than the Lydians. They were cavalrymen, excellent horsemen, and their weapon was the long spear.)

The armies met on level ground in front of Sardis . . . Both sides suffered heavy losses, but finally the Lydians, forced to retire, were driven within the city walls, where they were besieged by the Persians. . . .

In this way Sardis was captured by the Persians and Croesus taken prisoner, after a reign of fourteen years and a siege of fourteen days. The oracle was fulfilled; Croesus had destroyed a mighty empire—his own.

The Persians brought their prisoner into the presence of the king, and Cyrus chained Croesus and placed him with fourteen Lydian boys on a great pyre that he had built; perhaps he intended them as a choice offering to some god of his, or perhaps he had made a vow and wished to fulfil it; or it may be that he had heard that Croesus was a godfearing man, and set him on the pyre to see if any divine power would save him from being burnt alive. But whatever the reason, that was what he did; and Croesus, for all his misery, as he stood on the pyre, remembered with what divine truth Solon had declared that no man could be called happy until he was dead. Till then Croesus had not uttered a sound; but when he remembered, he sighed bitterly and three times, in anguish of spirit, pronounced Solon's name.

Cyrus heard the name and told his interpreters to ask who Solon was; but for a while Croesus refused to answer the question and kept silent; at last, however, he was forced to speak. 'He was a man,' he said, 'who ought to have talked with every king in the world. I would give a fortune to have had it so.' Not understanding what he meant, they renewed their questions and pressed him so urgently to explain, that he could not longer refuse. He then related how Solon the Athenian once came to Sardis, and made light of the splendour which he saw there, and how everything he said had proved true, and not only for him but for all men and especially for those who imagine themselves fortunate—had in his own case proved all too true.

While Croesus was speaking, the fire had been lit and was already burning round the edges. The interpreters told Cyrus what Croesus had said, and the story touched him. He himself was a mortal man, and was burning alive another who had once been as prosperous as he. The thought of that, and the fear of retribution, and the realization of the instability of human things, made him change his mind and give orders that the flames should at once be put out, and Croesus and the boys brought down from the pyre. But the fire had got a hold, and the attempt to extinguish it failed. The Lydians say that when Croesus understood that Cyrus had changed his mind, and saw everyone vainly trying to master the fire, he called loudly upon Apollo with tears to come and save him from his misery, if any of his gifts had been pleasant to him. It was a clear and windless day; but suddenly in answer to Croesus' prayer clouds gathered and a storm broke with such violent rain that the flames were put out.

This was proof enough for Cyrus that Croesus was a good man whom the gods loved; so he brought him down from the pyre and said, 'Tell me, Croesus, who was it who persuaded you to march against my country and be my enemy rather than my friend?'

'My lord,' Croesus replied, 'the luck was yours when I did it, and the loss was mine. The god of the Greeks encouraged me to fight you: the blame is his. No one is fool enough to choose war instead of peace—in peace sons bury fathers, but in war fathers bury sons. It must have been heaven's will that this should happen.'

Cyrus had his chains taken off and invited him to sit by his side. He made much of him and looked at him with wonder, as did everyone who was near enough to see.

5

Xenophon

The Laws and Customs of the Spartans

*T*HE *heroic stand at Thermopylae of the three hundred Spartans (described by Herodotus in the preceding selection) was a clear fulfillment of the code under which they had been reared. Sparta (also called Lacedaemon) had admirers beyond its own borders, particularly among aristocrats and the wealthy. In the late fifth century* B.C. *pro-Spartan, anti-democratic sentiment was strong among followers of the Athenian philosopher Socrates and among supporters of the reactionary government set up in Athens by the victorious Spartans after the disastrous Peloponnesian War (431–404* B.C.*). That war had set the Greek city-states against each other, with Athens and Sparta as the primary antagonists.*

One of the followers of Socrates was Xenophon (ca. 430-ca. 355 B.C.*), a middle-class property-holding Athenian. After the downfall of the reactionary party he was among those Greeks who, in 401* B.C.*, joined the mercenary army of a prince who claimed the throne of Persia. The collapse of this expedition led to a perilous retreat of hundreds of miles through Persian territory to the Black Sea and safety. Later, Xenophon campaigned under the king of Sparta against the Persians. During his long absence from Athens, he was declared an exile and his property was confiscated. For the next twenty years Xenophon lived in retirement on an estate given him by the Spartans, whom he greatly admired. With ample opportunity to observe directly, he fully embraced the values the Spartans placed on their social organization and customs. He enjoyed his years as a country gentleman on Spartan-held territory, hunting and writing vigorously.*

THE LAWS AND CUSTOMS OF THE SPARTANS   Xenophon, *The Government of Lacedaemon*, in *Xenophon's Minor Works*, trans. J. S. Watson (London: Bell [Bohn Classical Library], 1878), 204–209, 212–221. Adapted by the editor.

Xenophon's best-known work is the Anabasis *("March Up Country"), a spirited account of the long retreat, of which he had been the leader. He also wrote three books about Socrates, and a history continuing from where Thucydides left off in his* History of the Peloponnesian War *(see selection 6). His* Laws and Customs of the Spartans, *reprinted here in part, is perhaps the most detailed account of the Spartan way of life available to us. We can see clearly the rigid, proud conservatism in a society where "senators" had to be at least sixty years of age and members of the citizens' assembly (a merely consultative body) had to be at least thirty.*

The influence of Sparta, in proportion to its population, is quite astonishing. In 480 B.C., when King Leonidas fought the Persians at Thermopylae, there were only about eight thousand Spartan citizens; by the time Xenophon settled in their territory, less than a century later, there were only about two thousand.

Not long after Xenophon's death, this regimented society—whose creation is attributed to Lycurgus, an ancient (and probably legendary) lawgiver— broke down forever. Perhaps this occurred precisely because of that same soldierly, stubborn inflexibility that Xenophon regards as a unique asset. In any case the enacting of that code, which he sees as the basic cause of Spartan greatness, can be dated at about 600 B.C. (The original cause of the code may very well have been the Spartans' need to control their helots [serfs], *who vastly outnumbered their citizen-masters.)*

Of all the distinction won by Sparta at Thermopylae and, later, in the Peloponnesian War, nothing remained but an aristocratic warrior tradition. It was a tradition, however, destined for a long life. Through Xenophon and Plato, and later Plutarch, the Spartan ideal of breeding and discipline passed on to the ruling classes of Europe, whose education, from the fifteenth century to the mid-twentieth, was based on the Greek and Roman classics.

THE REGULATIONS OF LYCURGUS RESPECTING MARRIAGE AND THE TREATMENT OF CHILDREN

But reflecting once how Sparta, one of the least populous of states, had proved the most powerful and celebrated city in Greece, I wondered by what means this result had been produced. When I proceeded, however, to contemplate the institutions of the Spartans, I wondered no longer.

Lycurgus, who made the laws[1] for them, by obedience to which they have flourished, I not only admire, but consider to have been in the fullest sense a wise man; for he rendered his country preëminent in prosperity, not by imitating other states, but by making ordinances contrary to those of most governments.

With regard, for example, to the procreation of children, that I may begin from the beginning, other people feed their young women, who are about to produce offspring, and who are of the class regarded as well brought up, on the most moderate quantity of vegetable food possible, and on the least possible quantity of meat, while they either keep them from wine altogether, or allow them to use it only when mixed with water; and as the greater number of the men engaged in trades are sedentary, so the rest of the Greeks think it proper that their young women should sit quiet and spin wool. But how can we expect that women thus treated should produce a vigorous progeny? Lycurgus, on the contrary, thought that female slaves were competent to furnish clothes; and, considering that the production of children was the noblest duty of the free, he enacted, in the first place, that the female should practice bodily exercises no less than the male sex; and he then appointed for the women contests with one another, just as for the men, expecting that when both parents were rendered strong, a stronger offspring would be born from them.

Observing, too, that the men of other nations, when women were united to husbands, associated with their wives during the early part of their intercourse without restraint, he made enactments quite at variance with this practice; for he ordained that a man should think it shame to be seen going in to his wife, or coming out from her. When married people meet in this way, they must feel stronger desire for the company of one another, and whatever offspring is produced must thus be rendered far more robust than if the parents were satiated with each other's society.

In addition to these regulations, he also took from the men the liberty of marrying when each of them pleased, and appointed that they should contract marriages only when they were in full bodily vigour, deeming this injunction also conducive to the production of an excellent offspring. Seeing also that if old men chanced to have young wives, they watched their wives with the utmost strictness, he made a law quite opposed to this feeling; for he appointed that an old man should introduce to his wife whatever man in the prime of life he

[1]These laws of Sparta had not been written down, but were learned and practiced from generation to generation.

admired for his corporeal and mental qualities, in order that she might have children by him. If, again, a man was unwilling to associate with his wife, and yet was desirous of having proper children, he made a provision also with respect to him, that whatever women he saw likely to have offspring, and of good disposition, he might, on obtaining the consent of her husband, have children by her. Many similar permissions he gave; for the women are willing to have two families, and the men to receive brothers to their children, who are equal to them in birth and standing, but have no claim to share in their property.

Let him who wishes, then, consider whether Lycurgus, in thus making enactments different from those of other legislators, in regard to the procreation of children, secured for Sparta a race of men eminent for size and strength.

ON THE TRAINING AND EDUCATION OF CHILDREN

Having given this account of the procreation of children, I wish also to detail the education of those of both sexes. Of the other Greeks, those who say that they bring up their sons best set slaves over them to take charge of them, as soon as the children can understand what is said to them, and send them, at the same time, to schoolmasters, to learn letters, and music, and the exercises of the palaestra.[2] They also render their children's feet delicate by the use of sandals, and weaken their bodies by changes of clothes; and as to food, they regard their appetite as the measure of what they are to take. But Lycurgus, instead of allowing each citizen to set slaves as guardians over his children, appointed a man to have the care of them all, one of those from whom the chief magistrates are chosen; and he is called the paedonomus. He invested this man with full authority to assemble the boys, and, if he found that any one was negligent of his duties, to punish him severely. He assigned him also some of the grown-up boys as whip-carriers, that they might inflict whatever chastisement was necessary; so that great dread of disgrace, and great willingness to obey, prevailed among them.

Instead, also, of making their feet soft with sandals, he enacted that they should harden them by going without sandals; thinking that, if they exercised themselves in this state, they would go up steep places with far greater ease, and descend declivities with greater safety; and that they would also leap, and skip, and run faster unshod, if they had their feet inured to doing so, than shod. Instead of being rendered

---

[2]A public area used for athletic training.

effeminate, too, by a variety of dresses, he made it a practice that they should accustom themselves to one dress throughout the year; thinking that they would thus be better prepared to endure cold and heat.

As to food, he ordained that they should exhort the boys to take only such a quantity as never to be oppressed with overeating, and not to be strangers to living somewhat frugally; supposing that, being thus brought up, they would be the better able, if they should be required, to support toil under a scarcity of supplies, would be the more likely to persevere in exertion, should it be imposed on them, on the same quantity of provisions, and would be less desirous of sauces, more easily satisfied with any kind of food, and pass their lives in greater health. He also considered that the fare which rendered the body slender would be more conducive to increasing its stature than that which expanded it with nutriment. Yet that the boys might not suffer too much from hunger, Lycurgus, though he did not allow them to take what they wanted without trouble, gave them liberty to steal certain things to relieve the cravings of nature; and he made it honourable to steal as many cheeses as possible. That he did not give them leave to form schemes for getting food because he was at a loss what to allot them, I suppose no one is ignorant; as it is evident that he who designs to steal must be wakeful during the night, and use deceit, and lay plots; and, if he would gain anything of consequence, must employ spies. All these things, therefore, it is plain that he taught the children from a desire to render them more dexterous in securing provisions, and better qualified for warfare.

Some one may say, "Why, then, if he thought it honourable to steal, did he inflict a great number of whiplashes on him who was caught in the act?" I answer, that in other things which men teach, they punish him who does not follow his instructions properly; and that the Spartans accordingly punished those who were detected as having attempted to steal in an improper manner. These boys he gave in charge to others to whip them at the altar of Diana Orthia; designing to show by this enactment that it is possible for a person, after enduring pain for a short time, to enjoy pleasure with credit for a long time. It is also shown by this punishment that, where there is need of activity, the inert person benefits himself the least, and occasions himself most trouble.

In order, too, that the boys, in case of the paedonomus being absent, may never be in want of a president, he appointed that whoever of the citizens may happen at any time to be present is to assume the direction of them, and to enjoin whatever he may think advantageous for them, and punish them if they do anything wrong. By doing this, Lycurgus has also succeeded in rendering the boys much more modest; for neither boys nor men respect any one so much as their rulers. And that if, on any occasion, no full-grown man happen to be present, the boys may not even in that case be without a leader, he ordained that the most active of the grown-up youths take the command of each band; so that the boys there are never without a superintendent.

It appears to me that I must say something also of the boys as objects of affection; for this has likewise some reference to education. Among the other Greeks, a man and boy either form a union, as among the Boeotians, and associate together, or, as among the Eleians, the men gain the favour of the youths by means of attentions bestowed upon them; but there are some of the Greeks who prohibit the suitors for the boys' favours from having the least conversation with them. But Lycurgus, acting contrary to all these people also, thought proper, if any man, being himself such as he ought to be, admired the disposition of a youth, and made it his object to render him a faultless friend, and to enjoy his society, to bestow praise upon him, and regarded this as the most excellent kind of education; but if any man showed that his affections were fixed only on the bodily attractions of a youth, Lycurgus, considering this as most unbecoming, appointed that at Lacedaemon suitors for the favours of boys should abstain from intimate connexion with them, not less strictly than parents abstain from such intercourse with their children, or children of the same family from that with one another. That such a state of things is disbelieved by some, I am not surprised; for in most states the laws are not at all adverse to the love of youths; but Lycurgus, for his part, took such precautions with reference to it.

•   •   •

MEALS TAKEN IN PUBLIC. ON TEMPERANCE

The employments which Lycurgus appointed for each period of life have now been almost all specified. What mode of living he instituted for all the citizens, I will next endeavour to explain.

Lycurgus, then, having found the Spartans, like the other Greeks, taking their meals at home, and knowing that most were guilty of excess at them, caused their meals to be taken in public, thinking that his regulations would thus be less likely to be transgressed. He appointed them such a quantity of food, that they should neither be overfed nor feel stinted. Many extraordinary supplies are also furnished from what is caught in hunting, and for these the rich sometimes contribute bread; so that the table is never without provisions, as long as they design the meal to last, and yet is never expensive.

Having put a stop likewise to all unnecessary drinking, which weakens alike the body and the mind, he gave permission that every one should drink when he was thirsty, thinking that the drink would thus be most innoxious and most pleasant. When they take their meals together in this manner, how can any one ruin either himself or his family by gluttony or drunkenness? In other states, equals in age generally associate together, and with them modesty has but very little influence; but Lycurgus, at Sparta, mixed citizens of different ages, so that the younger are for the most part instructed by the experience of the older. It is a custom at these public meals, that whatever any one has done to his honour in the community is related; so that insolence, or disorder from intoxication, or any indecency in conduct or language, has there no opportunity of showing itself. The practice of taking meals away from home is also attended with these advantages, that the people are obliged to walk in taking their departure homewards, and to be careful that they may not stagger from the effects of wine, knowing that they will not remain where they dined, and that they must conduct themselves in the night just as in the day; for it is not allowable for any one who is still liable to military duty to walk with a torch.

As Lycurgus observed, too, that those who, after taking food, exercise themselves, become well-complexioned, plump, and robust, while those who are inactive are puffy, unhealthy-looking, and feeble, he did not neglect to give attention to that point; and as he perceived that when any one engages in labour from his own inclination, he proves himself to have his body in efficient condition, he ordered that the oldest in each place of exercise should take care that those belonging to it should never be overcome by taking too much food. With regard to this matter, he appears to me to have been by no means mistaken; for no one would easily find men more healthy, or more able-bodied, than the Spartans; for they exercise themselves alike in their legs, in their hands, and in their shoulders.

RULES REGARDING CHILDREN, SLAVES, AND PROPERTY

In the following particulars, also, he made enactments contrary to the usage of most states; for in other communities each individual has the control over his own children, and servants, and property; but Lycurgus, wishing to order things so that the citizens might enjoy some advantage from one another, unattended with any reciprocal injury, ordained that each should have authority not only over his own children, but over those of others. But when a person is conscious that his fellow-citizens are fathers of the children over whom he exercises authority, he must exercise it in such a way as he would wish it to be exercised over his own. If a boy, on any occasion, receive blows from another boy, and complain of that boy to his father, it is considered dishonourable in the father not to inflict additional blows on his son. Thus they trust to one another to impose nothing disgraceful on the children.

He enacted also that a person might use his neighbour's servants, if he had need of them. He introduced, too, a community of property in hunting-dogs; so that those who require them call on their owner to hunt, who, if he is not at leisure to hunt himself, cheerfully sends them out. They use horses also in like manner; for whoever is sick, or wants a vehicle, or desires to go to some place speedily, takes possession of a horse, if he sees one anywhere, and, after making proper use of it, restores it.

Nor, in regard to the following point, did he allow that which is customary among other people should be practised among his countrymen. For when men, from being overtaken by night in hunting, are in want of provisions, unless they have previously furnished themselves with them, he directed that, in such a case, those who have partaken of what they need, leave the rest ready for use, and that those who require a supply, having opened the seals, and taken as much as they want, seal the remainder up again and leave it. As they share thus, then, with one another, those who possess but little participate, whenever they are in need, in all the produce of the country.

RESTRICTIONS ON THE EMPLOYMENTS OF THE SPARTANS

The following practices, too, Lycurgus established in Sparta, at variance with those of the rest of Greece. In other communities all gain as much by traffic[3] as they can; one cultivates land, another trades by sea, another engages in general commerce, another maintains himself by

[3]That is, by commerce.

art. But at Sparta, Lycurgus prohibited free men from having any connexion with traffic, and enjoined them to consider as their only occupation whatever secures freedom to states. How, indeed, could wealth be eagerly sought in a community where he had appointed that the citizens should contribute equally to their necessary maintenance, and should take their meals in common, and had thus provided that they should not desire wealth with a view to sensual gratifications? Nor had they, moreover, to get money for the sake of clothing; for they think themselves adorned, not by expensive raiment, but by a healthy personal appearance. Nor have they to gather money for the purpose of spending it on those who eat with them, since he has made it more honourable for a person to serve his neighbours by bodily exertion, than by putting himself to pecuniary expense; making it apparent that the one proceeds from the mind, and the other from fortune.

From acquiring money by unjust means, he prohibited them by such methods as the following. He instituted, in the first place, such a kind of money, that, even if but ten minae[4] came into a house, it could never escape the notice either of masters or of servants; for it would require much room, and a carriage to convey it. In the next place, gold and silver are searched after, and, if they are discovered anywhere, the possessor of them is punished. How, then, could gain by traffic be an object of pursuit, in a state where the possession of money occasions more pain than the use of it affords pleasure?

OBEDIENCE TO THE MAGISTRATES AND LAWS

That at Sparta the citizens pay the strictest obedience to the magistrates [officials] and laws, we all know. I suppose, however, that Lycurgus did not attempt to establish such an excellent order of things, until he had brought the most powerful men in the state to be of the same mind with regard to it. I form my opinion on this consideration, that, in other states, the more influential men are not willing even to appear to fear the magistrates, but think that such fear is unbecoming free men; but in Sparta, the most powerful men not only put themselves under the magistrates, but even count it an honour to humble themselves before them, and to obey, when they are called upon, not walking, but running; supposing that if they themselves are the first to pay exact

[4]Large iron coins (really weights) of the Spartans.

obedience, others will follow their example; and such has been the case. It is probable, also, that the chief men established the offices of the Ephors[5] in conjunction with Lycurgus, as they must have been certain that obedience is of the greatest benefit, alike in a state, and in an army, and in a family; and they doubtless considered that the greater power magistrates have, the greater effect will they produce on the citizens in enforcing obedience. The Ephors, accordingly, have full power to impose a fine on whomsoever they please, and to exact the fine without delay; they have power also to degrade magistrates even while they are in office, and to put them in prison, and to bring them to trial for their life. Being possessed of such authority, they do not, like the magistrates in other states, always permit those who are elected to offices to rule during the whole year as they choose, but, like despots and presidents in gymnastic contests, punish on the instant whomsoever they find acting at all contrary to the laws.

Though there were many other excellent contrivances adopted by Lycurgus, to induce the citizens to obey the laws, the most excellent of all appears to me to be, that he did not deliver his laws to the people until he had gone, in company with the most eminent of his fellow-citizens, to Delphi, and consulted the god whether it would be more beneficial and advantageous for Sparta to obey the laws which he had made. As the god replied that it would be more beneficial in every way, he at once delivered them, deciding that it would be not only illegal, but impious, to disobey laws sanctioned by the oracle.

INFAMY AND PENALTIES OF COWARDICE

It is deserving of admiration, too, in Lycurgus, that he made it a settled principle in the community, that an honourable death is preferable to a dishonourable life; for whoever pays attention to the subject will find that fewer of those who hold this opinion die than of those who attempt to escape danger by flight. Hence we may say with truth, that safety attends for a much longer period on valour than on cowardice; for valour is not only attended with less anxiety and greater pleasure, but is also more capable of assisting and supporting us. It is evident, too, that good report [reputation] accompanies valour; for almost everybody is willing to be in alliance with the brave.

[5]A five-man board, elected annually, that had nearly unlimited executive powers, except command in war.

How he contrived that such sentiments should be entertained, it is proper not to omit to mention. He evidently, then, intended a happy life for the brave, and a miserable one for the cowardly. In other communities, when a man acts as a coward, he merely brings on himself the name of coward, but the coward goes to the same market, and sits or takes exercise, if he pleases, in the same place with the brave men; at Sparta, however, every one would be ashamed to admit a coward into the same tent with him, or to allow him to be his opponent in a match at wrestling. Frequently, too, a person of such character, when they choose opposite parties to play at ball, is left without any place; and in forming a chorus he is thrust into the least honourable position. On the road he must yield the way to others, and at public meetings he must rise up, even before his juniors. His female relatives he must maintain at home, and they too must pay the penalty of his cowardice, since no man will marry them. He is also not allowed to take a wife, and must at the same time pay the customary fine for being a bachelor. He must not walk about with a cheerful expression, or imitate the manners of persons of blameless character; else he will have to receive whipping from his betters. Since, then, such disgrace is inflicted on cowards, I do not at all wonder that death is preferred at Sparta to a life so dishonourable and infamous.

HONORS PAID TO OLD AGE. ENCOURAGEMENT OF VIRTUE

Lycurgus seems to me to have provided also, with great judgment, how virtue might be practised even to old age; for by adding to his other enactments the choice of senators at an advanced stage of life,[6] he caused honour and virtue not to be disregarded even in old age.

It is worthy of admiration in him, too, that he attached consideration to the old age of the well-deserving; for by making the old men arbiters in the contest for superiority in mental qualifications, he rendered their old age more honourable than the vigour of those in the meridian of life. This contest is deservedly held in the greatest esteem among the people, for gymnastic contests are attended with honour, but they concern only bodily accomplishments; the contest for distinction in old age involves a decision respecting merits of the mind. In propor-

---

[6]The twenty-eight senators, along with the two hereditary kings, formed the principal law-making body of Sparta (the Council of Elders); the senators were elected for life and had to be over sixty years of age.

tion, therefore, as the mind is superior to the body, so much are contests for mental eminence more worthy of regard than those concerning bodily superiority.

Is it not highly worthy of admiration, also, in Lycurgus, that when he saw that those who are disinclined to practice virtue are not qualified to increase the power of their country, he obliged all the citizens of Sparta to cultivate every kind of virtue publicly. As private individuals, accordingly, who practise virtue, are superior in it to those who neglect it, so Sparta is naturally superior in virtue to all other states, as it is the only one that engages in a public cultivation of honour and virtue. Is it not also deserving of commendation, that, when other states punish any person that injures another, Lycurgus inflicted no less punishment on any one that openly showed himself unconcerned with becoming as good a man as possible? He thought, as it appears, that by those who make others slaves, or rob them, or steal anything, the individual sufferers only are injured, but that by the unprincipled and cowardly whole communities are betrayed; so that he appears to me to have justly imposed the heaviest penalties on such characters.

He also imposed on his countrymen an obligation, from which there is no exception, of practising every kind of political virtue; for he made the privileges of citizenship equally available to all those who observed what was enjoined by the laws, without taking any account either of weakness of body or scantiness of means; but if any one was too indolent to perform what the laws prescribed, Lycurgus appointed that he should be no longer counted in the number of equally privileged citizens.

That these laws are extremely ancient is certain; for Lycurgus is said to have lived in the time of the Heracleidae;[7] but, ancient as they are, they are still very new to other communities; for, what is the most wonderful of all things, all men extol such institutions, but no state thinks proper to imitate them.

OF THE SPARTAN ARMY

The regulations which I have mentioned are beneficial alike in peace and in war; but if any one wishes to learn what he contrived better than other legislators with reference to military proceedings, he may attend to the following particulars.

[7]Children of the legendary Greek hero Heracles.

In the first place, then, the Ephors proclaim the age limits for the citizen draft to the army; artisans (non-citizens) are also called by the same order to serve supplying the troops. For the Spartans provide themselves in the field with an abundance of all those things which people use in a city; and of whatever instruments an army may require in common, orders are given to bring some on waggons, and others on beasts of burden, as by this arrangement anything left behind is least likely to escape notice.

For engagements in the field he made the following arrangements. He ordered that each soldier should have a purple robe and a brazen shield; for he thought that such a dress had least resemblance to that of women, and was excellently adapted for the field of battle, as it is soonest made splendid, and is longest in growing soiled. He permitted also those above the age of puberty to let their hair grow, as he thought that they thus appeared taller, more manly, and more terrifying in the eyes of the enemy. . . .

6
Thucydides

History of the Peloponnesian War

*T*HE *Persian Wars, described in Herodotus' account of the heroic Greek stand at Thermopylae (selection 4), were the prelude to Greek glory; the Peloponnesian War (431–404 B.C.), fought mainly between Athens and Sparta, brought suffering and disaster to Greece. In the years following the victory over the Persians, the democratic city-state of Athens expanded into imperial power by using the financial contributions from other city-states, intended for the common defense of Greece, to build up the powerful Athenian navy and its own economic prosperity. Thus, the conflict with Sparta, which had the stronger army, was "inevitable" (the historian Thucydides tells us) because of "the growth of Athenian power and the fear which this caused in Sparta."*

The task of recording and analyzing that bitter struggle of Greek against Greek fell to Thucydides (ca. 460–ca. 400 B.C.). Born in Athens to an aristocratic and wealthy family, Thucydides was chosen in 424 B.C. to command a fleet against the Spartans in the northern Aegean Sea. For allowing himself to be outmaneuvered and defeated by the enemy, he was exiled and did not return to Athens until 404. Thucydides thus had ample opportunity to observe the Peloponnesian War from both sides; he spent his twenty years of exile in various parts of Greece, recording the tragedy of his own times. Behind his narrative lay the deeper purpose of searching for an answer to the following question: "Why had Athens, with the fairest prospects of victory, been beaten?" Thucydides' History is, in essence, an analysis of the causes of the Athenian defeat; hence, it has been well described as a study in the pathology of imperialism and war.

HISTORY OF THE PELOPONNESIAN WAR   Thucydides, *History of the Peloponnesian War,* trans. Rex Warner (London: Penguin Books, 1954), pp. 75–76, 143–156, 400–408. Copyright © Rex Warner, 1954. Reproduced by permission of Penguin Books Ltd.

173

Thucydides' own reflections on issues and motives are found in the forty or more "set speeches" for which the History *is famous. These speeches—which appear as direct quotations from the individual participants, but were actually written by Thucydides—represent a common device in ancient Greek literature. Like the oration and the dialogue they must be accounted for by the importance of the spoken word in Greek culture. Thucydides, describing his method, stated that "while keeping as closely as possible to the general sense of the words that were actually used, [I] . . . make the speakers say what, in my opinion, was called for by each situation."*

The first speech in the following group of selections gives a foreigner's view of the Athenian character. It shows clearly a sharp contrast to the Spartan traits described by Xenophon (selection 5). This contrast is further developed in the second selection, the most famous speech of the History—*the "Funeral Oration" by Pericles, the leading Athenian statesman, in honor of those who had died in the war's first campaign. Like Abraham Lincoln's "Gettysburg Address," which bears many similarities to Pericles' speech, it is both an appeal to patriotism and a reasoned explanation of a free and open democracy's superiority to rival forms of government.*

In the summer following the public funeral a dreadful plague broke out among the people crowded inside the walls of Athens. The city lost more than a quarter of its inhabitants, a blow from which it never fully recovered. (Pericles died in the following year from the lingering effects of the plague.) Thucydides, too, was a victim, but he recovered. His medical and sociological description of the plague's symptoms and results, included here, is remarkable for its scientific objectivity.

The last excerpt is "The Melian Dialogue," in which the monstrous realities of the conflict are stripped bare. To the question, "Why was Athens beaten?" Thucydides implies the answer that Athens, deprived of Pericles' strong but humanely moderate leadership, pursued a policy of barbarous extremism. At Melos, after some fifteen years of brutalizing war, the Athenians justified their empire solely on the grounds of self-serving power.

Thucydides says he composed his History *(which breaks off, unfinished, among the events of 411 B.C.) so that its readers could "understand clearly the events which happened in the past and which (human nature being what it is) will, at some time or other and in much the same ways, be repeated in the future." It was written "to last forever." The* History *is impartial and reflective, conveying both the Periclean ideals favored by Thucydides and the later moral degeneration and disillusionment that result when the life of reason is sacrificed for wealth and power. There is in his writing none of the sentiment or supernaturalism that make the recitations of Herodotus so entertaining, but lovers of Thucydides' objectivity and human insight have hailed him as the supreme historian of all time.*

THE DEBATE AT SPARTA AND DECLARATION OF WAR [432 B.C.][1]

. . . You have never yet tried to imagine what sort of people these Athenians are against whom you will have to fight—how much, indeed how completely different from you. An Athenian is always an innovator, quick to form a resolution and quick at carrying it out. You, on the other hand, are good at keeping things as they are; you never originate an idea, and your action tends to stop short of its aim. Then again, Athenian daring will outrun its own resources; they will take risks against their better judgement, and still, in the midst of danger, remain confident. But your nature is always to do less than you could have done, to mistrust your own judgement, however sound it may be, and to assume that dangers will last forever. Think of this, too: while you are hanging back, they never hesitate; while you stay at home, they are always abroad; for they think that the farther they go the more they will get, while you think that any movement may endanger what you have already. If they win a victory, they follow it up at once, and if they suffer a defeat, they scarcely fall back at all. As for their bodies, they regard them as expendable for their city's sake, as though they were not their own; but each man cultivates his own intelligence, again with a view to doing something notable for his city. If they aim at something and do not get it, they think that they have been deprived of what belonged to them already; whereas, if their

---

[1]Representatives from Corinth, a city-state bitterly hostile to Athens, have called together at Sparta an assembly of delegates from other Greek cities. After giving the others a chance to air their grievances against Athenian aggression, the Corinthians speak, pointing out Athenian encroachments upon the territories of others and urging immediate invasion of Attica, the home region of Athens. (Sparta had the only army that could effectively oppose Athens.) In this excerpt the Corinthians address the Spartans and urge them to action, contrasting Spartan caution to Athenian quickness and versatility. At the conclusion of the speeches, Sparta and her allies would declare war against Athens.

enterprise is successful, they regard that success as nothing compared to what they will do next. Suppose they fail in some undertaking; they make good the loss immediately by setting their hopes in some other direction. Of them alone it may be said that they possess a thing almost as soon as they have begun to desire it, so quickly with them does action follow upon decision. And so they go on working away in hardship and danger all the days of their lives, seldom enjoying their possessions because they are always adding to them. Their view of a holiday is to do what needs doing; they prefer hardship and activity to peace and quiet. In a word, they are by nature incapable of either living a quiet life themselves or of allowing anyone else to do so.

•   •   •

PERICLES' FUNERAL ORATION [430 B.C.]

In the same winter[2] the Athenians, following their annual custom, gave a public funeral for those who had been the first to die in the war. These funerals are held in the following way: two days before the ceremony the bones of the fallen are brought and put in a tent which has been erected, and people make whatever offerings they wish to their own dead. Then there is a funeral procession in which coffins of cypress wood are carried on wagons. There is one coffin for each tribe, which contains the bones of members of that tribe. One empty bier is decorated and carried in the procession: this is for the missing, whose bodies could not be recovered. Everyone who wishes to, both citizens and foreigners, can join in the procession and the women who are related to the dead are there to make their laments at the tomb. The bones are laid in the public burial-place, which is in the most beautiful quarter outside the city walls. Here the Athenians always bury those who have fallen in war. The only exception is those who died at Marathon,[3] who, because their achievement was considered absolutely outstanding, were buried on the battlefield itself.

When the bones have been laid in the earth, a man chosen by the city for his intellectual gifts and for his general reputation makes an

[2]431–430 B.C.

[3]The site, twenty-six miles from Athens, where the Athenians defeated the first Persian invasion (490 B.C.).

appropriate speech in praise of the dead, and after the speech all depart. This is the procedure at these burials, and all through the war, when the time came to do so, the Athenians followed this ancient custom. Now, at the burial of those who were the first to fall in the war Pericles, the son of Xanthippus, was chosen to make the speech. When the moment arrived, he came forward from the tomb and, standing on a high platform, so that he might be heard by as many people as possible in the crowd, he spoke as follows:

'Many of those who have spoken here in the past have praised the institution of this speech at the close of our ceremony. It seemed to them a mark of honour to our soldiers who have fallen in war that a speech should be made over them. I do not agree. These men have shown themselves valiant in action, and it would be enough, I think, for their glories to be proclaimed in action, as you have just seen it done at this funeral organized by the state. Our belief in the courage and manliness of so many should not be hazarded on the goodness or badness of one man's speech. Then it is not easy to speak with a proper sense of balance, when a man's listeners find it difficult to believe in the truth of what one is saying. The man who knows the facts and loves the dead may well think that an oration tells less than what he knows and what he would like to hear: others who do not know so much may feel envy for the dead, and think the orator over-praises them, when he speaks of exploits that are beyond their own capacities. Praise of other people is tolerable only up to a certain point, the point where one still believes that one could do oneself some of the things one is hearing about. Once you get beyond this point, you will find people becoming jealous and incredulous. However, the fact is that this institution was set up and approved by our forefathers, and it is my duty to follow the tradition and do my best to meet the wishes and the expectations of every one of you.

'I shall begin by speaking about our ancestors, since it is only right and proper on such an occasion to pay them the honour of recalling what they did. In this land of ours there have always been the same people living from generation to generation up till now, and they, by their courage and their virtues, have handed it on to us, a free country. They certainly deserve our praise. Even more so do our fathers deserve it. For to the inheritance they had received they added all the empire we have now, and it was not without blood and toil that they handed it down to us of the present generation. And then we ourselves, assembled here today, who are mostly in the prime of life, have, in most directions, added to the power of our empire and have organized our State in such a way that it is perfectly well able to look after itself both in peace and in war.

'I have no wish to make a long speech on subjects familiar to you all: so I shall say nothing about the warlike deeds by which we acquired our power or the battles in which we or our fathers gallantly resisted our enemies, Greek or foreign. What I want to do is, in the first place, to discuss the spirit in which we faced our trials and also our constitution and the way of life which has made us great. After that I shall speak in praise of the dead, believing that this kind of speech is not inappropriate to the present occasion, and that this whole assembly, of citizens and foreigners, may listen to it with advantage.

'Let me say that our system of government does not copy the institutions of our neighbours. It is more the case of our being a model to others, than of our imitating anyone else. Our constitution is called a democracy because power is in the hands not of a minority but of the whole people. When it is a question of settling private disputes, everyone is equal before the law; when it is a question of putting one person before another in positions of public responsibility, what counts is not membership of a particular class, but the actual ability which the man possesses. No one, so long as he has it in him to be of service to the state, is kept in political obscurity because of poverty. And, just as our political life is free and open, so is our day-to-day life in our relations with each other. We do not get into a state with our next-door neighbour if he enjoys himself in his own way, nor do we give him the kind of black looks which, though they do no real harm, still do hurt people's feelings. We are free and tolerant in our private lives; but in public affairs we keep to the law. This is because it commands our deep respect.

'We give our obedience to those whom we put in positions of authority, and we obey the laws themselves, especially those which are for the protection of the oppressed, and those unwritten laws which it is an acknowledged shame to break.

'And here is another point. When our work is over, we are in a position to enjoy all kinds of recreation for our spirits. There are various kinds of contests and sacrifices regularly throughout the year; in our own homes we find a beauty and a good taste which delight us every day and which drive away our cares. Then the greatness of our city brings it about that all the good things from all over the world flow in to us, so that to us it seems just as natural to enjoy foreign goods as our own local products.

'Then there is a great difference between us and our opponents, in our attitude towards military security. Here are some examples: Our city is open to the world, and we have no periodical deportations in order to prevent people observing or finding out secrets which might be of military advantage to the enemy. This is because we rely, not on secret weapons, but on our own real courage and loyalty. There is a difference, too, in our educational systems. The Spartans, from their earliest boyhood, are submitted to the most laborious training in courage; we pass our lives without all these restrictions, and yet are just as ready to face the same dangers as they are. Here is a proof of this: When the Spartans invade our land, they do not come by themselves, but bring all their allies with them; whereas we, when we launch an attack abroad, do the job by ourselves, and, though fighting on foreign soil, do not often fail to defeat opponents who are fighting for their own hearths and homes. As a matter of fact none of our enemies has ever yet been confronted with our total strength, because we have to divide our attention between our navy and the many missions on which our troops are sent on land. Yet, if our enemies engage a detachment of our forces and defeat it, they give themselves credit for having thrown back our entire army; or, if they lose, they claim that they were beaten by us in full strength. There are certain advantages, I think, in our way of meeting danger voluntarily, with an easy mind, instead of with a laborious training, with natural rather than with state-induced courage. We do not have to spend our time practising to meet sufferings which are still in the future; and when they are actually upon us we show ourselves just as brave as these others who are always in strict training. This is one point in which, I think, our city deserves to be admired. There are also others:

'Our love of what is beautiful does not lead to extravagance; our love of the things of the mind does not make us soft. We regard wealth as something to be properly used, rather than as something to boast about. As for poverty, no one need be ashamed to admit it: the real shame is in not taking practical measures to escape from it. Here each individual is interested not only in his own affairs but in the affairs of the state as well: even those who are mostly occupied with their own business are extremely well-informed on general politics—this is a peculiarity of ours: we do not say that a man who takes no interest in politics is a man who minds his own business; we say that he has no business here at all. We Athenians, in our own persons, take our decisions on policy or submit them to proper discussions: for we do not think that there is an incompatibility between words and deeds; the worst thing is to rush into action before the consequences have been properly debated. And this is another point where we differ from other people. We are capable at the same time of taking risks and of estimating them beforehand. Others are brave out of ignorance; and, when they stop to think, they begin to fear. But the man who can most truly be accounted brave is he who best knows the meaning of what is sweet in life and of what is terrible, and then goes out undeterred to meet what is to come.

'Again, in questions of general good feeling there is a great contrast between us and most other people. We make friends by doing good to others, not by receiving good from them. This makes our friendship all the more reliable, since we want to keep alive the gratitude of those who are in our debt by showing continued goodwill to them: whereas the feelings of one who owes us something lack the same enthusiasm, since he knows that, when he repays our kindness, it will be more like paying back a debt than giving something spontaneously. We are unique in this. When we do kindnesses to others, we do not do them out of any calculations of profit or loss: we do them without afterthought, relying on our free liberality. Taking everything together then, I declare that our city is an education to Greece, and I declare that in my opinion each single one of our citizens, in all the manifold aspects of life, is able to show himself the rightful lord and owner of his own person, and do this, moreover, with exceptional grace and exceptional versatility. And to show that this is no empty boasting for the present occasion, but real tangible fact, you have only to consider the power which our city possesses and which has been won by those very qualities which I have mentioned. Athens, alone of the states we know, comes to her testing time in a greatness that surpasses what was imagined of her. In her case, and in her case alone, no invading enemy is ashamed at being defeated, and no subject can complain of being governed by people unfit for their responsibilities. Mighty indeed are the marks and monuments of our empire which we have left. Future ages will wonder at us, as the present age wonders at us now. We do not need the praises of a Homer, or of anyone else whose words may delight us for the moment, but whose estimation of facts will fall short of what is really true. For our adventurous spirit has forced an entry into every sea and into every land; and everywhere we have left behind us everlasting memorials of good done to our friends or suffering inflicted on our enemies.

'This, then, is the kind of city for which these men, who could not bear the thought of losing her, nobly fought and nobly died. It is only natural that every one of us who survive them should be willing to undergo hardships in her service. And it was for this reason that I have spoken at such length about our city, because I wanted to make it clear that for us there is more at stake than there is for others who lack our advantages; also I wanted my words of praise for the dead to be set in the bright light of evidence. And now the most important of these words has been spoken. I have sung the praises of our city; but it was the courage and gallantry of these men, and of people like them, which made her splendid. Nor would you find it true in the case of many of the Greeks, as it is true of them, that no words can do more than justice to their deeds.

'To me it seems that the consummation which has overtaken these men shows us the meanings of manliness in its first revelation and in its final proof. Some of them, no doubt, had their faults; but what we ought to remember first is their gallant conduct against the enemy in defence of their native land. They have blotted out evil with good, and done more service to the commonwealth than they ever did harm in their private lives. No one of these men weakened because he wanted to go on enjoying his wealth: no one put off the awful day in the hope that he might live to escape his poverty and grow rich. More to be desired than such things, they chose to check the enemy's pride. This, to them, was a risk most glorious, and they accepted it, willing to strike down the enemy and relinquish everything else. As for success or failure, they left that in the doubtful hands of Hope, and when the reality of battle was before their faces, they put their trust in their own selves. In the fighting, they thought it more honourable to stand their ground and suffer death than to give in and save their lives. So they fled from the reproaches of men, abiding with life and limb the brunt of battle; and, in a small moment of time, the climax of their lives, a culmination of glory, not of fear, were swept away from us.

'So and such they were, these men—worthy of their city. We who remain behind may hope to be spared their fate, but must resolve to keep the same daring spirit against the foe. It is not simply a question of estimating the advantages in theory. I could tell you a long story (and you know it as well as I do) about what is to be gained by beating the enemy back. What I would prefer is that you should fix your eyes every day on the greatness of Athens as she really is, and should fall in love with her. When you realize her greatness, then reflect that what made her great was men with a spirit of adventure, men who knew their duty, men who were ashamed to fall below a certain standard. If they ever failed in an enterprise, they made up their minds that at any rate the city should not find their courage lacking to her, and they gave to her the best contribution that they could. They gave her their lives, to her and to all of us, and for their own selves they won praises that never grow old, the most splendid of sepulchres—not the sepulchre in which their bodies are laid, but where their glory remains eternal in men's minds, always there on the right occasion to stir others to speech or to action. For famous men have the whole earth as their memorial: it is not only the inscriptions on their graves in their own country that mark them out; no, in foreign lands also, not in any visible form but in people's hearts, their memory abides and grows. It is for you to try to be like them. Make up your minds that happiness depends on being free, and freedom depends on being courageous. Let there be no relaxation in face of the perils of the war. The people who have most excuse for despising death are not the wretched and unfortunate, who have no hope of doing well for themselves, but those who run the risk of a complete reversal in their lives, and who would feel the difference most intensely, if things went wrong for them. Any intelligent man would find a humiliation caused by his own slackness more painful to bear than death, when death comes to him unperceived, in battle, and in the confidence of his patriotism.

'For these reasons I shall not commiserate with those parents of the dead, who are present here. Instead I shall try to comfort them. They are well aware that they have grown up in a world where there are many changes and chances. But this is good fortune—for men to end their lives with honour, as these have done, and for you honourably to lament them: their life was set to a measure where death and happiness went hand in hand. I know that it is difficult to convince you of this. When you see other people happy you will often be reminded of what used to make you happy too. One does not feel sad at not having some good thing which is outside one's experience: real grief is felt at the loss of something which one is used to. All the same, those of you who are of the right age must bear up and take comfort in the thought of having more children. In your own homes these new children will prevent you from brooding over those who are no more, and they will be a help to the city, too, both in filling the empty places, and in assuring her security. For it is impossible for a man to put forward fair and honest views about our affairs if he has not, like everyone else, children whose lives may be at stake. As for those of you who are now too old to have children, I would ask you to count as gain the greater part of your life, in which you have been happy, and remember that what remains is not long, and let your hearts be lifted up at the thought of the fair fame of the dead. One's sense of honour is the only thing that does not grow old, and the last pleasure, when one is worn out with age, is not, as the poet said, making money,[4] but having the respect of one's fellow men.

'As for those of you here who are sons or brothers of the dead, I can see a hard struggle in front of you. Everyone always speaks well of the dead, and, even if you rise to the greatest heights of heroism, it will be a hard thing for you to get the reputation of having come near, let alone equalled, their standard. When one is alive, one is always liable to the jealousy of one's competitors, but when one is out of the way, the honour one receives is sincere and unchallenged.

'Perhaps I should say a word or two on the duties of women to those among you who are now widowed. I can say all I have to say in a short word of advice. Your great glory is not to be inferior to what God has made you, and the greatest glory of a woman is to be least talked about by men, whether they are praising you or criticizing you. I have now, as the law demanded, said what I had to say. For the time being our offerings to the dead have been made, and for the future their children will be supported at the public expense by the city, until they come of age. This is the crown and prize which she offers, both to the dead and to their children, for the ordeals which they have faced. Where the rewards of valour are the greatest, there you will find also the best and bravest spirits among the people. And now, when you have mourned for your dear ones, you must depart.'

[4]A reference to that worldly view exemplified by a well-known remark of Simonides (*ca.* 556–*ca.* 468 B.C.), a famous poet and businessman. When criticized for his love of money, he replied that since he had been deprived by old age of all other pleasures, he could still be comforted by profit.

THE PLAGUE [430 B.C.]

In this way the public funeral was conducted in the winter that came at the end of the first year of the war. At the beginning of the following summer the Peloponnesians[5] and their allies, with two-thirds of their total forces as before, invaded Attica, again under the command of the Spartan King Archidamus, the son of Zeuxidamus. Taking up their positions, they set about the devastation of the country.

They had not been many days in Attica before the plague first broke out among the Athenians. Previously attacks of the plague had been reported from many other places in the neighbourhood of Lemnos[6] and elsewhere, but there was no record of the disease being so virulent anywhere else or causing so many deaths as it did in Athens. At the beginning the doctors were quite incapable of treating the disease because of their ignorance of the right methods. In fact mortality among the doctors was the highest of all, since they came more frequently in contact with the sick. Nor was any other human art or science of any help at all. Equally useless were prayers made in the temples, consultation of oracles, and so forth; indeed, in the end people were so overcome by their sufferings that they paid no further attention to such things.

The plague originated, so they say, in Ethiopia in upper Egypt, and spread from there into Egypt itself and Libya and much of the territory of the King of Persia. In the city of Athens it appeared suddenly, and the first cases were among the population of Piraeus,[7] where there were no wells at that time, so that it was supposed by them that the Peloponnesians had poisoned the reservoirs. Later, however, it appeared also in the upper [central] city, and by this time the deaths were greatly increasing in number. As to the question of how it could first have come about or what causes can be found adequate to explain its powerful effect on nature, I must leave that to be considered by other writers, with or without medical experience. I myself shall merely describe what it was like, and set down the symptoms, knowledge of which will enable it to be recognized, if it should ever break out again. I had the disease myself and saw others suffering from it.

[5]The Peloponnesian peninsula forms the south of Greece; its dominant city-state was Sparta.

[6]An island in the Aegean Sea colonized by kinsmen of the Athenians.

[7]The chief port of Athens, five miles from the central city.

That year, as is generally admitted, was particularly free from all other kinds of illness, though those who did have any illness previously all caught the plague in the end. In other cases, however, there seemed to be no reason for the attacks. People in perfect health suddenly began to have burning feelings in the head; their eyes became red and inflamed; inside their mouths there was bleeding from the throat and tongue, and the breath became unnatural and unpleasant. The next symptoms were sneezing and hoarseness of voice, and before long the pain settled on the chest and was accompanied by coughing. Next the stomach was affected with stomach-aches and with vomitings of every kind of bile that has been given a name by the medical profession, all this being accompanied by great pain and difficulty. In most cases there were attacks of ineffectual retching, producing violent spasms; this sometimes ended with this stage of the disease, but sometimes continued long afterwards. Externally the body was not very hot to the touch, nor was there any pallor: the skin was rather reddish and livid, breaking out into small pustules and ulcers. But inside there was a feeling of burning, so that people could not bear the touch even of the lightest linen clothing, but wanted to be completely naked, and indeed most of all would have liked to plunge into cold water. Many of the sick who were uncared for actually did so, plunging into the water-tanks in an effort to relieve a thirst which was unquenchable; for it was just the same with them whether they drank much or little. Then all the time they were afflicted with insomnia and the desperate feeling of not being able to keep still.

In the period when the disease was at its height, the body, so far from wasting away, showed surprising powers of resistance to all the agony, so that there was still some strength left on the seventh or eighth day, which was the time when, in most cases, death came from the internal fever. But if people survived this critical period, then the disease descended to the bowels, producing violent ulceration and uncontrollable diarrhea, so that most of them died later as a result of the weakness caused by this. For the disease, first settling in the head, went on to affect every part of the body in turn, and even when people escaped its worst effects, it still left its traces on them by fastening upon the extremities of the body. It affected the genitals, the fingers, and the toes, and many of those who recovered lost the use of these members; some, too, went blind. There were some also who, when they first began to get better, suffered from a total loss of memory, not knowing who they were themselves and being unable to recognize their friends.

Words indeed fail one when one tries to give a general picture of this disease; and as for the sufferings of individuals, they seemed almost beyond the capacity of human nature to endure. Here in particular is a point where this plague showed itself to be something quite different from ordinary diseases: though there were many dead bodies lying about unburied, the birds and animals that eat human flesh either did not come near them or, if they did taste the flesh, died of it afterwards. Evidence for this may be found in the fact that there was a complete disappearance of all birds of prey: they were not to be seen either round the bodies or anywhere else. But dogs, being domestic animals, provided the best opportunity of observing this effect of the plague.

These, then, were the general features of the disease, though I have omitted all kinds of peculiarities which occurred in various individual cases. Meanwhile, during all this time there was no serious outbreak of any of the usual kinds of illness; if any such cases did occur, they ended in the plague. Some died in neglect, some in spite of every possible care being taken of them. As for a recognized method of treatment, it would be true to say that no such thing existed: what did good in some cases did harm in others. Those with naturally strong constitutions were no better able than the weak to resist the disease, which carried away all alike, even those who were treated and dieted with the greatest care. The most terrible thing of all was the despair into which people fell when they realized that they had caught the plague; for they would immediately adopt an attitude of utter hopelessness, and, by giving in in this way, would lose their powers of resistance. Terrible, too, was the sight of people dying like sheep through having caught the disease as a result of nursing others. This indeed caused more deaths than anything else. For when people were afraid to visit the sick, then they died with no one to look after them; indeed, there were many houses in which all the inhabitants perished through lack of any attention. When, on the other hand, they did visit the sick, they lost their own lives, and this was particularly true of those who made it a point of honour to act properly. Such people felt ashamed to think of their own safety and went into their friends' houses at times when even the members of the household were so overwhelmed by the weight of their calamities that they had actually given up the usual practice of making laments for the dead. Yet still the ones who felt most pity for the sick and the dying were those who had had the plague themselves and had recovered from it. They knew what it was like and at the same time felt themselves to be safe, for no one caught the disease twice, or, if he did, the second attack was never fatal. Such people were congratulated on all sides, and they themselves were so elated at the time of their recovery that they fondly imagined that they could never die of any other disease in the future.

A factor which made matters much worse than they were already was the removal of people from the country into the city,[8] and this particularly affected the incomers. There were no houses for them, and, living as they did during the hot season in badly ventilated huts, they died like flies. The bodies of the dying were heaped one on top of the other, and half-dead creatures could be seen staggering about in the streets or flocking around the fountains in their desire for water. The temples in which they took up their quarters were full of the dead bodies of people who had died inside them. For the catastrophe was so overwhelming that men, not knowing what would happen next to them, became indifferent to every rule of religion or of law. All the funeral ceremonies which used to be observed were now disorganized, and they buried the dead as best they could. Many people, lacking the necessary means of burial because so many deaths had already occurred in their households, adopted the most shameless methods. They would arrive first at a funeral pyre that had been made by others, put their own dead upon it and set it alight; or, finding another pyre burning, they would throw the corpse that they were carrying on top of the other one and go away.

In other respects also Athens owed to the plague the beginnings of a state of unprecedented lawlessness. Seeing how quick and abrupt were the changes of fortune which came to the rich who suddenly died and to those who had previously been penniless but now inherited their wealth, people now began openly to venture on acts of self-indulgence which before then they used to keep dark. Thus they resolved to spend their money quickly and to spend it on pleasure, since money and life alike seemed equally ephemeral. As for what is called honour, no one showed himself willing to abide by its laws, so doubtful was it whether one would survive to enjoy the name for it. It was generally agreed that what was both honourable and valuable was the pleasure of the moment and everything that might conceivably contribute to that pleasure. No fear of god or law of man had a restraining

---

[8]This was done because of the war raging outside the city's walls.

influence. As for the gods, it seemed to be the same thing whether one worshipped them or not, when one saw the good and the bad dying indiscriminately. As for offences against human law, no one expected to live long enough to be brought to trial and punished: instead everyone felt that already a far heavier sentence had been passed on him and was hanging over him, and that before the time for its execution arrived it was only natural to get some pleasure out of life.

This, then, was the calamity which fell upon Athens, and the times were hard indeed, with men dying inside the city and the land outside being laid waste.

•   •   •

THE MELIAN DIALOGUE [416 B.C.]

The Athenians also made an expedition against the island of Melos. . . .

The Melians are a colony from Sparta. They had refused to join the Athenian empire like the other islanders, and at first had remained neutral without helping either side; but afterwards, when the Athenians had brought force to bear on them by laying waste their land, they had become open enemies of Athens.

Now the generals Cleomedes, the son of Lycomedes, and Tisias, the son of Tisimachus, encamped with the above force in Melian territory and, before doing any harm to the land, first of all sent representatives to negotiate. The Melians did not invite these representatives to speak before the people, but asked them to make the statement for which they had come in front of the governing body and the few. The Athenian representatives then spoke as follows:

'So we are not to speak before the people, no doubt in case the mass of the people should hear once and for all and without interruption an argument from us which is both persuasive and incontrovertible, and should so be led astray. This, we realize, is your motive in bringing us here to speak before the few. Now suppose that you who sit here should make assurance doubly sure. Suppose that you, too, should refrain from dealing with every point in detail in a set speech, and should instead interrupt us whenever we say something controversial and deal with that before going on to the next point? Tell us first whether you approve of this suggestion of ours.'

The Council of the Melians replied as follows:

'No one can object to each of us putting forward our own views in a calm atmosphere. That is perfectly reasonable. What is scarcely consistent with such a proposal is the present threat, indeed the certainty, of your making war on us. We see that you have come prepared to judge the argument yourselves, and that the likely end of it all will be either war, if we prove that we are in the right, and so refuse to surrender, or else slavery.'

ATHENIANS. If you are going to spend the time in enumerating your suspicions about the future, or if you have met here for any other reason except to look the facts in the face and on the basis of these facts to consider how you can save your city from destruction, there is no point in our going on with this discussion. If, however, you will do as we suggest, then we will speak on.

MELIANS. It is natural and understandable that people who are placed as we are should have recourse to all kinds of arguments and different points of view. However, you are right in saying that we are met together here to discuss the safety of our country and, if you will have it so, the discussion shall proceed on the lines that you have laid down.

ATHENIANS. Then we on our side will use no fine phrases saying, for example, that we have a right to our empire because we defeated the Persians, or that we have come against you now because of the injuries you have done us—a great mass of words that nobody would believe. And we ask you on your side not to imagine that you will influence us by saying that you, though a colony of Sparta, have not joined Sparta in the war, or that you have never done us any harm. Instead we recommend that you should try to get what it is possible for you to get, taking into consideration what we both really do think; since you know as well as we do that, when these matters are discussed by practical people, the standard of justice depends on the equality of power to compel and that in fact the strong do what they have the power to do and the weak accept what they have to accept.

MELIANS. Then in our view (since you force us to leave justice out of account and to confine ourselves to self-interest)—in our view it is at any rate useful that you should not destroy a principle that is to the general good of all men—namely, that in the case of all who fall into danger there should be such a thing as fair play and just dealing, and that such people should be allowed to use and to profit by arguments that fall short of a mathematical accuracy. And this is a principle which affects you as much as anybody, since your own fall would be visited by the most terrible vengeance and would be an example to the world.

ATHENIANS. As for us, even assuming that our empire does come to an end, we are not despondent about what would happen next. One is not so much frightened of being conquered by a power which rules over others, as Sparta does (not that we are concerned with Sparta now), as of what would happen if a ruling power is attacked and defeated by its own subjects. So far as this point is concerned, you can leave it to us to face the risks involved. What we shall do now is to show you that it is for the good of our own empire that we are here and that it is for the preservation of your city that we shall say what we are going to say. We do not want any trouble in bringing you into our empire, and we want you to be spared for the good both of yourselves and of ourselves.

MELIANS. And how could it be just as good for us to be the slaves as for you to be the masters?

ATHENIANS. You, by giving in, would save yourselves from disaster; we, by not destroying you, would be able to profit from you.

MELIANS. So you would not agree to our being neutral, friends instead of enemies, but allies of neither side?

ATHENIANS. No, because it is not so much your hostility that injures us; it is rather the case that, if we were on friendly terms with you, our subjects would regard that as a sign of weakness in us, whereas your hatred is evidence of our power.

MELIANS. Is that your subjects' idea of fair play—that no distinction should be made between people who are quite unconnected with you and people who are mostly your own colonists or else rebels whom you have conquered?

ATHENIANS. So far as right and wrong are concerned they think that there is no difference between the two, that those who still preserve their independence do so because they are strong, and that if we fail to attack them it is because we are afraid. So that by conquering you we shall increase not only the size but the security of our empire. We rule the sea and you are islanders, and weaker islanders too than the others; it is therefore particularly important that you should not escape.

MELIANS. But do you think there is no security for you in what we suggest? For here again, since you will not let us mention justice, but tell us to give in to your interests, we, too, must tell you what our interests are and, if yours and ours happen to coincide, we must try to persuade you of the fact. Is it not certain that you will make enemies of all states who are at present neutral, when they see what is happening here and naturally conclude that in course of time you will attack them too? Does not this mean that you are strengthening the enemies you have already and are forcing others to become your enemies even against their intentions and their inclinations?

ATHENIANS. As a matter of fact we are not so much frightened of states on the continent. They have their liberty, and this means that it will be a long time before they begin to take precautions against us. We are more concerned about islanders like yourselves, who are still unsubdued, or subjects who have already become embittered by the constraint which our empire imposes on them. These are the people who are most likely to act in a reckless manner and to bring themselves and us, too, into the most obvious danger.

MELIANS. Then surely, if such hazards are taken by you to keep your empire and by your subjects to escape from it, we who are still free would show ourselves great cowards and weaklings if we failed to face everything that comes rather than submit to slavery.

ATHENIANS. No, not if you are sensible. This is no fair fight, with honour on one side and shame on the other. It is rather a question of saving your lives and not resisting those who are far too strong for you.

MELIANS. Yet we know that in war fortune sometimes makes the odds more level than could be expected from the difference in numbers of the two sides. And if we surrender, then all our hope is lost at once, whereas, so long as we remain in action, there is still a hope that we may yet stand upright.

ATHENIANS. Hope, that comforter in danger! If one already has solid advantages to fall back upon, one can indulge in hope. It may do harm, but will not destroy one. But hope is by nature an expensive commodity, and those who are risking their all on one cast[9] find out what it means only when they are already ruined; it never fails them in the period when such a knowledge would enable them to take precautions. Do not let this happen to you, you who are weak and whose fate depends on a single movement of the scale. And do not be like those people who, as so commonly happens, miss the chance of saving themselves in a human and practical way, and, when every clear and distinct hope has left them in their adversity, turn to what is blind and vague, to prophecies and oracles and such things which by encouraging hope lead men to ruin.

---

[9] That is, one throw of the dice.

MELIANS. It is difficult, and you may be sure that we know it, for us to oppose your power and fortune, unless the terms be equal. Nevertheless we trust that the gods will give us fortune as good as yours, because we are standing for what is right against what is wrong; and as for what we lack in power, we trust that it will be made up for by our alliance with the Spartans, who are bound, if for no other reason, than for honour's sake, and because we are their kinsmen, to come to our help. Our confidence, therefore, is not so entirely irrational as you think.

ATHENIANS. So far as the favour of the gods is concerned, we think we have as much right to that as you have. Our aims and our actions are perfectly consistent with the beliefs men hold about the gods and with the principles which govern their own conduct. Our opinion of the gods and our knowledge of men lead us to conclude that it is a general and necessary law of nature to rule whatever one can. This is not a law that we made ourselves, nor were we the first to act upon it when it was made. We found it already in existence, and we shall leave it to exist for ever among those who come after us. We are merely acting in accordance with it, and we know that you or anybody else with the same power as ours would be acting in precisely the same way. And therefore, so far as the gods are concerned, we see no good reason why we should fear to be at a disadvantage. But with regard to your views about Sparta and your confidence that she, out of a sense of honour, will come to your aid, we must say that we congratulate you on your simplicity but do not envy you your folly. In matters that concern themselves or their own constitution the Spartans are quite remarkably good; as for their relations with others, that is a long story, but it can be expressed shortly and clearly by saying that of all people we know the Spartans are most conspicuous for believing that what they like doing is honourable and what suits their interests is just. And this kind of attitude is not going to be of much help to you in your absurd quest for safety at the moment.

MELIANS. But this is the very point where we can feel most sure. Their own self-interest will make them refuse to betray their own colonists, the Melians, for that would mean losing the confidence of their friends among the Hellenes [Greeks] and doing good to their enemies.

ATHENIANS. You seem to forget that if one follows one's self-interest one wants to be safe, whereas the path of justice and honour involves one in danger. And, where danger is concerned, the Spartans are not, as a rule, very venturesome.

MELIANS. But we think that they would even endanger themselves for our sake and count the risk more worth taking than in the case of others, becuase we are so close to the Peloponnese that they could operate more easily, and because they can depend on us more than on others, since we are of the same race and share the same feelings.

ATHENIANS. Goodwill shown by the party that is asking for help does not mean security for the prospective ally. What is looked for is a positive preponderance of power in action. And the Spartans pay attention to this point even more than others do. Certainly they distrust their own native resources so much that when they attack a neighbour they bring a great army of allies with them. It is hardly likely therefore that, while we are in control of the sea, they will cross over to an island.

MELIANS. But they still might send others. The Cretan sea is a wide one, and it is harder for those who control it to intercept others than for those who want to slip through to do so safely. And even if they were to fail in this, they would turn against your own land and against those of your allies left unvisited by Brasidas.[10] So, instead of troubling about a country which has nothing to do with you, you will find trouble nearer home, among your allies, and in your own country.

ATHENIANS. It is a possibility, something that has in fact happened before. It may happen in your case, but you are well aware that the Athenians have never yet relinquished a single siege operation through fear of others. But we are somewhat shocked to find that, though you announced your intention of discussing how you could preserve yourselves, in all this talk you have said absolutely nothing which could justify a man in thinking that he could be preserved. Your chief points are concerned with what you hope may happen in the future, while your actual resources are too scanty to give you a chance of survival against the forces that are opposed to you at this moment. You will therefore be showing an extraordinary lack of common sense if, after you have asked us to retire from this meeting, you still fail to reach a conclusion wiser than anything you have mentioned so far. Do not be led astray by a false sense of honour—a thing which often brings men to ruin when they are faced with an obvious danger that somehow affects their pride. For in many cases men have still been able to see the dangers ahead of them, but this thing called dishonour, this word, by its own force of seduction, has drawn them into a state where they have surrendered to an idea, while in fact they have fallen voluntarily

[10]A successful Spartan general.

into irrevocable disaster, in dishonour that is all the more dishonourable because it has come to them from their own folly rather than their misfortune. You, if you take the right view, will be careful to avoid this. You will see that there is nothing disgraceful in giving way to the greatest city in Hellas [Greece] when she is offering you such reasonable terms—alliance on a tribute-paying basis and liberty to enjoy your own property. And, when you are allowed to choose between war and safety, you will not be so insensitively arrogant as to make the wrong choice. This is the safe rule—to stand up to one's equals, to behave with deference toward one's superiors, and to treat one's inferiors with moderation. Think it over again, then, when we have withdrawn from the meeting, and let this be a point that constantly recurs to your minds—that you are discussing the fate of your country, that you have only one country, and that its future for good or ill depends on this one single decision which you are going to make.

The Athenians then withdrew from the discussion. The Melians, left to themselves, reached a conclusion which was much the same as they had indicated in their previous replies. Their answer was as follows:

'Our decision, Athenians, is just the same as it was at first. We are not prepared to give up in a short moment the liberty which our city has enjoyed from its foundation for 700 years. We put our trust in the fortune that the gods will send and which has saved us up to now, and in the help of men—that is, of the Spartans; and so we shall try to save ourselves. But we invite you to allow us to be friends of yours and enemies to neither side, to make a treaty which shall be agreeable to both you and us, and so to leave our country.'

The Melians made this reply, and the Athenians, just as they were breaking off the discussion, said:

'Well, at any rate, judging from this decision of yours, you seem to us quite unique in your ability to consider the future as something more certain than what is before your eyes, and to see uncertainties as realities, simply because you would like them to be so. As you have staked most on and trusted most in Spartans, luck, and hopes, so in all these you will find yourselves most completely deluded.'

The Athenian representatives then went back to the army, and the Athenian generals, finding that the Melians would not submit, immediately commenced hostilities and built a wall completely round the city of Melos, dividing the work out among the various states. Later they left behind a garrison of some of their own and some allied troops to blockade the place by land and sea, and with the greater part of their army returned home. The force left behind stayed on and continued with the siege. . . .

Meanwhile the Melians made a night attack and captured the part of the Athenian lines opposite the market-place. They killed some of the troops, and then, after bringing in corn [grain] and everything else useful that they could lay their hands on, retired again and made no further move, while the Athenians took measures to make their blockade more efficient in future. So the summer came to an end.

In the following winter . . . the Melians again captured another part of the Athenian lines where there were only a few of the garrison on guard. As a result of this, another force came out afterwards from Athens under the command of Philocrates, the son of Demeas. Siege operations were now carried on vigorously and, as there was also some treachery from inside, the Melians surrendered unconditionally to the Athenians, who put to death all the men of military age whom they took, and sold the women and children as slaves. Melos itself they took over for themselves, sending out later a colony of 500 men.

7

Aristophanes

Lysistrata

WE know little of Aristophanes, the *foremost comic playwright of the ancient world, beyond what is revealed in his eleven surviving comedies. He was born around 450 B.C., lived most of his life in or near Athens, and died around 388 B.C. Most of the more than forty plays he is known to have written were composed during the events of the dreadful Peloponnesian War against Sparta and its allies (see selection 6).*

The interests, attitudes, and spirit displayed in his works suggest that Aristophanes was an intellectual of a conservative turn of mind and lively wit. Since (as is frequently true of satirical comedy) some of his words of ridicule refer to local affairs, modern readers may miss his point. The translator, therefore, must sometimes change the playwright's references to things more familiar to modern readers—without losing Aristophanes' biting energy, wild plot-action, or "instructional" intent.

Although comedy was his medium, he often wrote plays that were shocking in language, plot, and subject. Clearly, Aristophanes sought to do more than entertain. In addition to being funny, his plays were serious and critical appeals to the reasoning minds of his Athenian audience. Lysistrata, *the play presented here, is one of three surviving comedies in which he ridicules the stupidity of Greeks fighting Greeks. First staged in 411 B.C., less than two years after the worst Athenian disaster of the War (the expedition to Sicily), the play has since been used as a sharp protest against modern wars. And, while poking fun at the sexual game, the play also makes a provocative statement in favor of women's rights. (It should be noted that, although women are the leading*

LYSISTRATA   From *Lysistrata* by Aristophanes, translated by Douglass Parker. Copyright ©1964 by William Arrowsmith. Reprinted by arrangement with New American Library, New York, New York.

figures in the plot, all parts were played by male *actors—in keeping with the rules of Greek theater.)*

Nothing testifies more convincingly to the values cherished in fifth-century Athens (the "Golden Age") than the fact that Lysistrata was produced there with public support, even while the state was enduring the later years of a devastating war. It is also significant that, after the defeat of Athens, such productions ceased and what is known as the Old Comedy (of which Aristophanes' plays are the prime examples) became, like the Golden Age, a thing of the past.

The Old Comedy clearly shows its origins in the ancient Dionysiac fertility revels. An Old Comedy's plot, typically, focuses on the working out of some fantastic idea; for example, building a "Socratic" Utopia (as in The Clouds) or conducting a "sex strike" against war (as in Lysistrata). There is, usually, an agon (contest) between those for and those against the idea. Towards the end, the idea is put into action; and the play, typically, closes in a komos (a party or celebration) of happy reconciliation. (In fact, the two Greek root words of "comedy," komos and oide, mean "party song.") Although the social criticisms voiced in Aristophanes' plays seem to have had little effect on the course of Athenian history, the plays would become the foundation of Western comic drama.

Characters of the Play

LYSISTRATA
KLEONIKE } *Athenian women*[1]
MYRRHINE

LAMPITO, *a Spartan woman*
ISMENIA, *a Boiotian girl*
KORINTHIAN GIRL

[1]As often happens in ancient Greek comedy, some of the characters' names match their roles; for example, *Lysistrata* means, in Greek, "dismisser of armies"; *Kleonike* means "dried weed"; *Myrrhine* suggests a slang word for the female sexual organ; *Kinesias*, the name of Myrrhine's husband, is derived from the Greek verb *kinein* ("to move") and is used here as a punning reference to the movements of intercourse. (The letter "K," as shown here in the English equivalent of the Greek letter, is often shown in other translations as "C.")

POLICEWOMAN
KORYPHAIOS [Chorus Leader] OF THE MEN
CHORUS OF OLD MEN *of Athens*
KORYPHAIOS [Chorus Leader] OF THE WOMEN
CHORUS OF OLD WOMEN *of Athens*
COMMISSIONER *of Public Safety*
FOUR POLICEMEN
KINESIAS, *Myrrhine's husband*
CHILD *of Kinesias and Myrrhine*
SLAVE
SPARTAN HERALD
SPARTAN AMBASSADOR
FLUTE-PLAYER
ATHENIAN WOMEN
PELOPONNESIAN WOMEN
PELOPONNESIAN MEN
ATHENIAN MEN

SCENE: *A street in Athens. In the background, the Akropolis;*[2] *center, its gateway, the Propylaia. The time is early morning. Lysistrata is discovered alone, pacing back and forth in furious impatience.*

LYSISTRATA
Women!
Announce a debauch in honor of Bacchos,[3] a spree for Pan,[4] some footling fertility fieldday, and traffic stops—the streets are absolutely clogged with frantic females banging on tambourines. No urging for an orgy!
　　　　But *today*—there's not one woman here.

Enter Kleonike.

　　　　Correction: one. Here comes my next door neighbor.—Hello, Kleonike.

[2]The steep plateau dominating the city; upon its crest were built the major temples. The greatest of these, the Parthenon, contained a gold and ivory statue of Athene—and the city's treasury.

[3]Bacchos (Dionysos) was the god of wine, revelry, and fertility; he was also the patron god of the drama.

[4]A woodland god of flocks and shepherds.

KLEONIKE

Hello to *you,*
Lysistrata.—But what's the fuss? Don't look so
barbarous, baby; knitted brows just aren't your
style.

LYSISTRATA

It doesn't matter, Kleonike—I'm on fire
right down to the bone. I'm positively ashamed to
be a woman—a member of a sex which can't even
live up to male slanders! To hear our husbands talk,
we're *sly:* deceitful, always plotting, monsters of
intrigue. . . .

KLEONIKE

Proudly.

That's us!

LYSISTRATA

And so we agreed to meet
today and plot an intrigue that really deserves the
name of monstrous . . . and WHERE are the
women?
Slyly asleep at home—they won't get up for
anything!

KLEONIKE

Relax, honey. They'll be here. You know a
woman's way is hard—mainly the way out of the
house: fuss over hubby, wake the maid up, put the
baby down, bathe him, feed him . . .

LYSISTRATA

Trivia. They
have more fundamental business to engage in.

KLEONIKE

Incidentally, Lysistrata, just why are you calling this
meeting? Nothing teeny, I trust?

LYSISTRATA

Immense.

KLEONIKE

Hmmm.

And pressing?

LYSISTRATA

    Unthinkably tense.

KLEONIKE

          Then where IS
everybody?

LYSISTRATA

    Nothing like that. If it were, we'd
already be in session. Seconding motions. —No, *this*
came to hand some time ago. I've spent my nights
kneading it, mulling it, filing it down. . . .

KLEONIKE

Too bad. There can't be very much left.

LYSISTRATA

          Only this:
the hope and salvation of Hellas lies with the
WOMEN!

KLEONIKE

    Lies with the women? Now *there's*
a last resort.

LYSISTRATA

    It lies with us to decide affairs of
state and foreign policy.
          The Spartan Question:
Peace or Extirpation?

KLEONIKE

    How *fun!*
          I cast an Aye for
Extirpation!

LYSISTRATA

    The Utter Annihilation of every last
Boiotian?[5]

KLEONIKE

    AYE!—I mean Nay. Clemency, please, for
those scrumptious eels.[6]

LYSISTRATA

    And as for Athens . . . I'd
rather not put the thought into words. Just fill in the

---

[5]Boiotia is a region near Athens; its cities were allied with Sparta.

[6]Eels from Boiotia, in short supply because of the war, were considered a great delicacy in Athens.

blanks, if you will. —To the point: If we can meet
and reach agreement here and now with the girls
from Thebes and the Peloponnese,[7] we'll form an
alliance and save the States of Greece!

KLEONIKE

Us? Be
practical. Wisdom from women? There's nothing
cosmic about cosmetics—and Glamor is our only
talent. All we can do is *sit*, primped and painted,
made up and dressed up,

Getting carried away in spite of her argument.

ravishing in saffron
wrappers, peekaboo peignoirs, exquisite negligees,
those chic, expensive little slippers that come from
the East . . .

LYSISTRATA

Exactly. You've hit it. I see our way
to salvation in just such ornamentation—in slippers
and slips, rouge and perfumes, negligees and
decolletage. . . .

KLEONIKE

How so?

LYSISTRATA

So effectively that not one
husband will take up his spear against another. . . .

KLEONIKE

Peachy!

I'll have that kimono dyed . . .

LYSISTRATA

. . . or
shoulder his shield . . .

KLEONIKE

. . . squeeze into
that daring negligee . . .

LYSISTRATA

. . . or unsheathe
his sword!

[7]Thebes is in Boiotia; the Peloponnese is a peninsula, forming the southern part of
Greece, and includes Sparta.

KLEONIKE

        . . . and buy those slippers!

LYSISTRATA

Well, now. Don't you think the girls should be here?

KLEONIKE

Be here? Ages ago—they should have flown!

She stops.

But no. You'll find out. These are authentic
Athenians: no matter what they do, they do it late.

LYSISTRATA

But what about the out-of-town delegations? There
isn't a woman here from the Shore; none from
Salamis . . .[8]

KLEONIKE

        That's quite a trip. They usually get on
board at sunup. Probably riding at anchor now.

LYSISTRATA

I thought the girls from Acharnai would be here
first. I'm especially counting on them. And they're
not here.

KLEONIKE

        I think Theogenes' wife[9] is under way.
When I went by, she was hoisting her sandals . . .

Looking off right.

But look! Some of the girls are coming!

*Women enter from the right. Lysistrata looks off to the left where more—a ragged
lot—are straggling in.*

LYSISTRATA

And more over here!

KLEONIKE

        Where did you find *that* group?

---

[8]An island just across the bay from the port of Athens and under its control. (Lysistrata's
plan is to gather women from cities both allied with and opposed to Athens.)

[9]Theogenes was a member of the political group in Athens that was urging agressive
continuation of the war.

LYSISTRATA
They're from the outskirts.

KLEONIKE

Well, that's something. If
you haven't done anything else, you've really ruffled
up the outskirts.

Myrrhine enters guiltily from the right.

MYRRHINE

Oh, Lysistrata, we aren't late,
are we?

Well, *are* we?

Speak to me!

LYSISTRATA

What is it,
Myrrhine? Do you want a medal for tardiness?
Honestly, such behavior, with so much at stake . . .

MYRRHINE
I'm sorry. I couldn't find my girdle in the dark. And
anyway, we're here now. So tell us all about it,
whatever it is.

KLEONIKE

No, wait a minute. Don't begin just
yet. Let's wait for those girls from Thebes and the
Peloponnese.

LYSISTRATA

Now *there* speaks the proper attitude.

*Lampito, a strapping Spartan woman, enters left, leading a pretty Boiotian girl
(Ismenia) and a huge, steatopygous [fat-buttocked]Korinthian.*

And here's our lovely Spartan.

Hel*lo*, Lampito dear.
Why, darling, you're simply ravishing! Such a
blemishless complexion—so clean, so out-of-doors!
And will you look at that figure—the pink of
perfection!

KLEONIKE

I'll bet you could strangle a bull.

LAMPITO
I calklate so.[10] Hit's fitness whut done it, fitness and dancin'. You know the step?

Demonstrating.

Foot it out back'ards an' toe yore twitchet.

The women crowd around Lampito.

KLEONIKE
What unbelievably beautiful bosoms!
LAMPITO
Shuckins, whut fer you tweedlin' me up so? I feel like a heifer come fair-time.
LYSISTRATA

Turning to Ismenia.

And who is this young lady here?
LAMPITO
Her kin's purt-near the bluebloodiest folk in Thebes—the First Fam'lies of Boiotia.
LYSISTRATA

As they inspect Ismenia.

Ah, picturesque Boiotia: her verdant meadows, her fruited plain . . .
KLEONIKE

Peering more closely.

Her sunken garden where no grass grows. A cultivated country.

---

[10]To Aristophanes' Athenian audience, the Spartans were not only their military enemies but also their cultural inferiors. Thus, the American translator has given a hillbilly dialect to Lampito and to other Spartans.

LYSISTRATA

Gaping at the gawking Korinthian.

> And who is *this*—er—little thing?

LAMPITO

> She hails from over by Korinth, but her kinfolk's quality—mighty big back there.

KLEONIKE

On her tour of inspection.

> She's mighty big back *here.*

LAMPITO

The womenfolk's all assemblied. Who-all's notion was this-hyer confabulation?

LYSISTRATA

> Mine.

LAMPITO

> Git on with the give-out. I'm hankerin' to hear.

MYRRHINE

> Me, too! I can't imagine what could be so important. Tell us about it!

LYSISTRATA

Right away.—But first, a question. It's not an involved one. Answer yes or no.

A pause.

MYRRHINE

> Well, ASK it!

LYSISTRATA

It concerns the fathers of your children—your husbands, absent on active service. I know you all have men abroad.

> —Wouldn't you like to have them home?

KLEONIKE

> My husband's been gone for the last five months! Way up to Thrace, watchdogging military waste. It's horrible!

MYRRHINE

Mine's been posted to Pylos for seven whole months!

LAMPITO

My man's no sooner rotated out of the line than he's plugged back in. Hain't no discharge in this war!

KLEONIKE

And lovers can't be had for love or money, not even synthetics. Why, since those beastly Milesians revolted and cut off the leather trade, that handy do-it-yourself kit's *vanished* from the open market![11]

LYSISTRATA

If I can devise a scheme for ending the war, I gather I have your support?

KLEONIKE

You can count on me! If you need money, I'll pawn the shift off my back—

Aside.

and drink up the cash before the sun goes down.

MYRRHINE

Me, too! I'm ready to split myself right up the middle like a mackerel, and give you half!

LAMPITO

Me, too! I'd climb Taygetos Mountain plumb to the top to git the leastes' peek at Peace!

LYSISTRATA

Very well, I'll tell you. No reason to keep a secret.

Importantly, as the women cluster around her.

We can force our husbands to negotiate Peace, Ladies, by

---

[11]Miletus, apparently the source of artificial phalluses made from leather, had left its Athenian alliance and joined the Spartan alliance in the preceding year.

exercising steadfast Self-Control—By Total
Abstinence . . .

A pause.

KLEONIKE
                   From WHAT?

MYRRHINE
                        Yes, what?

LYSISTRATA
                             You'll do it?

KLEONIKE
Of course we'll do it! We'd even *die!*

LYSISTRATA
                        Very well,
then here's the program:
                   Total Abstinence
                        from SEX!

The cluster of women dissolves.

—Why are you turning away? Where are you going?

Moving among the women.

—What's this? Such stricken expressions! Such
gloomy gestures!—Why so pale?
                        —Whence these
tears?
     —What IS this?
                   Will you do it or won't you?
Cat got your tongue?

KLEONIKE
                   Afraid I can't make it. Sorry.

On with the War!

MYRRHINE
                   Me neither. Sorry.
                        On with the War!

LYSISTRATA
This from my little mackerel? The girl who
was ready, a minute ago, to split herself right up
the middle?

KLEONIKE

Breaking in between Lysistrata and Myrrhine.

Try something else. Try anything. If you
say so, I'm willing to walk through fire barefoot.
But not to give up SEX—there's nothing like it,
Lysistrata!

LYSISTRATA

To Myrrhine.

And you?

MYRRHINE

Me, too! I'll walk through fire.

LYSISTRATA
Women!

Utter sluts, the entire sex! Will-power, nil.
We're perfect raw material for Tragedy, the stuff of
heroic lays. "Go to bed with a god and then get rid
of the baby"—that sums us up!

Turning to Lampito.

—Oh, Spartan, be a
dear. If *you* stick by me, just you, we still may have
a chance to win. Give me your vote.

LAMPITO

Hit's right
onsettlin' fer gals to sleep all lonely-like, withouten
no humpin'. But I'm on yore side. We shore need
Peace, too.

LYSISTRATA

You're a darling—the only woman here
worthy of the name!

KLEONIKE

Well, just suppose we *did*,
as much as possible, abstain from . . . what you said,
you know—not that we *would*—could something
like that bring Peace any sooner?

LYSISTRATA

Certainly. Here's
how it works: We'll paint, powder, and pluck
ourselves to the last detail, and stay inside,
wearing those filmy tunics that set off
everything we *have*—

and then
slink up to the men. They'll snap to attention, go
absolutely *mad* to love us—

but we won't let them.
We'll Abstain.—I imagine they'll conclude a treaty
rather quickly.

LAMPITO

Nodding.

Menelaos he tuck one squint at
Helen's bubbies all nekkid, and plumb throwed up.

Pause for thought.

Throwed up his sword.[12]

KLEONIKE

Suppose the men just leave
us flat?

LYSISTRATA

In that case, we'll have to take things into our
own hands.

KLEONIKE

There simply isn't any reasonable
facsimile!—Suppose they take up by force and
drag us off to the bedroom against our wills?

LYSISTRATA

Hang on to the door.

KLEONIKE

Suppose they beat us?

---

[12]Menelaos [Menelaus] was a mythical king of Sparta. His wife, Helen, ran away with
Paris, a prince of Troy, thus causing the famous Trojan War. (See selection 1, *The Iliad*,
p. 1.) As the Greek forces were destroying Troy, Menelaos changed his mind about his
personal revenge against Helen when, once again, he saw her beauty.

LYSISTRATA

Give in—
but be bad sports. Be nasty about it—they don't
enjoy these forced affairs. So make them suffer.
Don't worry; they'll stop soon enough. A married
man wants harmony—cooperation, not rape.

KLEONIKE

Well, I suppose so . . .

Looking from Lysistrata to Lampito

If *both* of you approve this,
then so do we.

LAMPITO

Hain't worried over our menfolk
none. We'll bring 'em round to makin' a fair,
straightfor'ard Peace withouten no nonsense
about it. But take this rackety passel in Athens;
I misdoubt no one could make 'em give over thet
blabber of theirn.

LYSISTRATA

They're our concern. Don't
worry. We'll bring them around.

LAMPITO

Not likely. Not
long as they got ships kin still sail straight, an' thet
fountain of money up thar in Athene's temple.[13]

LYSISTRATA

That point is quite well covered:
We're taking over
the Akropolis, including Athene's temple, today.
It's set: Our oldest women have their orders. They're
up there now, pretending to sacrifice, waiting for us
to reach an agreement. As soon as we do, they seize
the Akropolis.

LAMPITO

They way you put them thengs, I
swear I can't see how we kin possibly lose!

---

[13]The Parthenon, the temple of Athene Parthenos ("the Maiden").

LYSISTRATA
Well, now that it's settled, Lampito, let's not lose
any time. Let's take the Oath to make this binding.[14]
LAMPITO
Just trot out thet-thar Oath. We'll swear it.
LYSISTRATA
                                                    Excellent.

    —Where's a policewoman?

*A huge girl, dressed as a Skythian archer (the Athenian police) with bow and circular
shield, lumbers up and gawks.*
                                —What are

        you looking for?

Pointing to a spot in front of the women.
                                Put your shield down here.

The girl obeys.
        No, hollow *up!*

The girl reverses the shield. Lysistrata looks about brightly.
                                —Someone give me the entrails.

A dubious silence.
KLEONIKE
Lysistrata, what kind of an Oath are we supposed
to swear?
LYSISTRATA
                The Standard. Aischylos used it in a play,
they say—the one where you slaughter a sheep and
swear on a shield.
KLEONIKE
                        Lysistrata, you *do not* swear an
Oath for *Peace* on a *shield!*
LYSISTRATA
                                What Oath do you want?

[14]The oath that follows is a parody (takeoff) of a standard ritual animal sacrifice and an
oath of loyalty.

Exasperated.

Something bizzare and expensive? A fancier
victim—"Take one white horse and disembowel"?
KLEONIKE
White horse? The symbolism's too obscure.
LYSISTRATA

                                    *Then how
do we swear this oath?*
KLEONIKE

                        Oh, *I* can tell you *that*, if
you'll let me.
            First, we put an enormous black cup
right here—hollow up, of course. Next, into the
cup we slaughter a jar of Thasian wine, and swear
a mighty Oath that we won't . . . dilute it with
water.
LAMPITO

To Kleonike.

            Let me corngratulate you—that were the
beatenes' Oath I ever heerd on!
LYSISTRATA

Calling inside.

                            Bring out a cup
and a jug of wine!

*Two women emerge, the first staggering under the weight of a huge black cup, the
second even more burdened with a tremendous wine jar. Kleonike addresses them.*

            KLEONIKE
                        You darlings! What a tremendous
display of pottery!

Fingering the cup.

                        A girl could get a glow just
holding a cup like this!

She grabs it away from the first woman, who exits.

LYSISTRATA

Taking the wine jar from the second serving woman (who exits), she barks at Kleonike.

> Put that down and help me
butcher this boar!

Kleonike puts down the cup, over which she and Lysistrata together hold the jar of wine (the "boar"). Lysistrata prays.

> O Mistress Persuasion,
> O Cup of Devotion,
> Attend our invocation:
> Accept this oblation,
> Grant our petition,
> Favor our mission.

Lysistrata and Kleonike tip up the jar and pour the gurgling wine into the cup. Myrrhine, Lampito, and the others watch closely.

MYRRHINE
Such an attractive shade of blood. And the spurt—
pure Art!
LAMPITO
> Hit shore do smell mighty purty!

Lysistrata and Kleonike put down the empty wine jar.

KLEONIKE
Girls, let me be the first

Launching herself at the cup.

> to take the Oath!

LYSISTRATA

Hauling Kleonike back.

> You'll have
to wait your turn like everyone else.—Lampito,
how do we manage with this mob?
> Cumbersome.—
Everyone place her right hand on the cup.

The women surround the cup and obey.

> I need a
> spokeswoman. One of you to take the Oath in behalf
> of the rest.

The women edge away from Kleonike, who reluctantly finds herself elected.

> The rite will conclude with a General
> Pledge of Assent by all of you, thus confirming the
> Oath. Understood?

Nods from the women. Lysistrata addresses Kleonike.

> Repeat after me:

LYSISTRATA
I will withhold all rights of access or entrance
KLEONIKE
I will withhold all rights of access or entrance
LYSISTRATA
**From every husband, lover, or casual
acquaintance**
KLEONIKE
from every husband, lover, or casual acquaintance
LYSISTRATA
Who moves in my direction in erection.
—Go on.
KLEONIKE
who m-moves in my direction in erection.

> Ohhhhh!
—Lysistrata, my knees are shaky. Maybe I'd better. . .
LYSISTRATA
I will create, imperforate in cloistered chastity,
KLEONIKE
I will create, imperforate in cloistered chastity,
LYSISTRATA
**A newer, more glamorous, supremely seductive
me**
KLEONIKE
a newer, more glamorous, supremely seductive me

LYSISTRATA
And fire my husband's desire with my molten allure—

KLEONIKE
and fire my husband's desire with my molten allure—

LYSISTRATA
But remain, to his panting advances, icily pure.

KLEONIKE
but remain, to his panting advances, icily pure.

LYSISTRATA
If he should force me to share the connubial couch,

KLEONIKE
If he should force me to share the connubial couch,

LYSISTRATA
I refuse to return his stroke with the teeniest twitch.

KLEONIKE
I refuse to return his stroke with the teeniest twitch.

LYSISTRATA
I will not lift my slippers to touch the thatch

KLEONIKE
I will not lift my slippers to touch the thatch

LYSISTRATA
Or submit sloping prone in a hangdog crouch.

KLEONIKE
or submit sloping prone in a hangdog crouch.

LYSISTRATA
      If I this oath maintain,
      may I drink this glorious wine.

KLEONIKE
      If I this oath maintain,
      may I drink this glorious wine.

LYSISTRATA
      But if I slip or falter,
      let me drink water.

KLEONIKE
      But if I slip or falter,
      let me drink water.

LYSISTRATA
—And now the General Pledge of Assent:

WOMEN

A-MEN!

LYSISTRATA
Good. I'll dedicate the oblation.

She drinks deeply.

KLEONIKE

Not too much,
darling. You know how anxious we are to become
allies and friends.

Not to mention *staying* friends.

She pushes Lysistrata away and drinks. As the women take their turns at the cup, loud cries and alarums are heard offstage.

LAMPITO
What-all's that bodacious ruckus?

LYSISTRATA

Just what I told
you: It means the women have taken the Akropolis.
Athene's Citadel is ours!

It's time for you to go,
Lampito, and set your affairs in order in Sparta.

Indicating the other women in Lampito's group.

Leave these girls here as hostages.

Lampito exits left. Lysistrata turns to the others.

Let's hurry inside
the Akropolis and help the others shoot the bolts.

KLEONIKE
Don't you think the men will send reinforcements
against us as soon as they can?

LYSISTRATA

So where's the worry?
The men can't burn their way in or frighten us out.
The Gates are ours—they're proof against fire and
fear—and they open only on our conditions.

KLEONIKE

Yes!

That's the spirit—let's deserve our reputations:

As the women hurry off into the Akropolis.

UP THE SLUTS!
WAY FOR THE OLD
IMPREGNABLES!

The door shuts behind the women, and the stage is empty.

A pause, and the Chorus of Men shuffles on from the left in two groups, led by their Koryphaios [Chorus Leader]. They are incredibly aged Athenians; though they may acquire spryness later in the play, at this point they are sheer decrepitude. Their normally shaky progress is impeded by their burdens; each man not only staggers under a load of wood across his shoulders, but has his hands full as well—in one, an earthen pot containing fire (which is in constant danger of going out); in the other, a dried vinewood torch, not yet lit. Their progress toward the Akropolis is very slow.

KORYPHAIOS OF MEN

To the right guide of the First Semichorus, who is stumbling along in mild agony.

Forward, Swifty, keep 'em in
step! Forget your shoulder. I know these logs are
green and heavy—but duty, boy, duty!

SWIFTY

Somewhat inspired, he quavers into slow song to set a pace for his group.

I'm never surprised. At my age, life
is just one damned thing after another.
And yet, I never thought my wife
was anything more than a home-grown bother.
But now, dadblast her,
she's a National Disaster!

FIRST SEMICHORUS OF MEN

What a catastrophe—
MATRIARCHY!
They've brought Athene's statue to heel,

> they've put the Akropolis under a seal,
> they've copped the whole damned
>> commonweal . . .
> What is there left for them to steal?
KORYPHAIOS OF MEN

To the right guide of the Second Semichorus—a slower soul, if possible, than Swifty.

> Now, Chipper, speed's the word. The Akropolis, on
> the double! Once we're there, we'll pile these logs
> around them, and convene a circuit court for a
> truncated trial. Strictly impartial: With a show of
> hands, we'll light a spark of justice under every
> woman who brewed this scheme. We'll burn them
> all on the first ballot—and the first to go is Ly . . .

Pause for thought.

> is Ly . . .

Remembering and pointing at a spot in the audience.

> is *Lykon's* wife—and there she is, right over
> there![15]
CHIPPER

Taking up the song again.

> I won't be twitted, I won't be guyed,
> I'll teach these women not to trouble us!
> Kleomenes the Spartan tried
> expropriating our Akropolis[16]
>> some time ago—
>> ninety-five years or so—
SECOND SEMICHORUS OF MEN
>> but he suffered damaging losses
>> when he ran across US!

---

[15]At this moment the Koryphaios breaks the dramatic illusion in order to ridicule some-one in the audience—Rhodia, wife of the politician Lykon, a woman often criticized for her loose morals.

[16]Kleomenes, a king of Sparta, had occupied the Akropolis in 508 B.C. for a couple of days—not the six years the senile men's chorus "remembers."

He breathed defiance—and more as well:
No bath for six years—you could tell.
We fished him out of the Citadel
and quelled his spirit—but not his smell.

KORYPHAIOS OF MEN

That's how I took him. A savage siege:

                       Seventeen

ranks of shields were massed at that gate, with
blanket infantry cover. I slept like a baby.

                        So when

mere women (who gall the gods and make Euripides
sick)[17] try the same trick, should I sit idly by?

                        Then

demolish the monument I won at Marathon![18]

FIRST SEMICHORUS OF MEN

Singly.

     —The last lap of our journey!
     —I greet it with some dismay.
     —The danger doesn't deter me,

                    —but

it's uphill

        —all the way.
—Please, somebody,

            —find a jackass

to drag these logs

               —to the top.
   —I ache to join the fracas

               —but

my shoulder's aching

            —to stop.

SWIFTY

Backward there's no turning.
Upward and onward, men!

---

[17]Euripides, the tragic dramatist, is always presented in Aristophanes' comedies as a woman-hater.

[18]In 490 B.C. on the plain of Marathon, the Athenians defeated the first Persian invasion of Greece. The "monument" is a mound of earth, still to be seen, erected over the Athenian dead. Obviously, Aristophanes is joking about the decrepitude of the old men's chorus, since they would have had to be over a century old to actually remember Kleomenes and Marathon.

And keep those firepots burning, or
we make this trip again.
CHORUS OF MEN

Blowing into their firepots, which promptly send forth clouds of smoke.

With a puff (pfffff) . . . .
and a cough (hhhhhh) . . . .
The smoke! I'll choke! Turn it off!
SECOND SEMICHORUS OF MEN

Singly.

—Damned embers.
—Should be muzzled.
—There oughta be a law.
—They jumped me
—when I whistled
—and then they gnawed my eyeballs
—raw.
—There's lava in my lashes.
—My lids are oxidized.
—My brows are braised.
—These ashes are
volcanoes
—in disguise.
CHIPPER
This way, men. And remember,
the Goddess needs our aid.
So don't be stopped by cinders. Let's
press on to the stockade!
CHORUS OF MEN

Blowing again into their firepots, which erupt as before.

With a huff (hfffff) . . . .
and a chuff (chffff) . . . .
Drat that smoke. Enough is enough!
KORYPHAIOS OF MEN

Signalling the Chorus, which has now tottered into position before the Akropolis gate, to stop, and peering into his firepot.

Praise be to the gods, it's awake. There's fire in the
old fire yet.—Now the directions. See how they
strike you:

First, we deposit these logs at the
entrance and light our torches. Next, we crash
the gate. When that doesn't work, we request
admission. Politely. When *that* doesn't work,
we burn the damned door down, and
smoke
these women into submission.

That seem acceptable?
Good.

Down with the load . . . ouch, that smoke!
Sonofabitch!

*A horrible tangle results as the Chorus attempts to deposit the logs. The Koryphaios
turns to the audience.*

Is there a general in the house? We have
a logistical problem. . . .

No answer. He shrugs.

Same old story. Still at
loggerheads over in Samos.[19]

With great confusion, the logs are placed somehow.

That's better. The
pressure's off. I've got my backbone back.

To his firepot.

What, pot? You forgot your part in the plot?
Urge that smudge
to be hot on the dot and scorch my torch.
Got it, pot?

[19]At the time of the play's production, the headquarters of the Athenian military forces
was on the distant island of Samos.

Praying.

> Queen Athene, let these strumpets
> crumple before our attack.
> Grant us victory, male supremacy . . .
> and a testimonial plaque.

The men plunge their torches into firepots and arrange themselves purposefully before the gate. Engaged in their preparations, they do not see the sudden entrance, from the right, of the Chorus of Women, led by their Koryphaios. These wear long cloaks and carry pitchers of water. They are very old—though not so old as the men—but quite spry. In their turn, they do not perceive the Chorus of Men.

KORYPHAIOS OF WOMEN

Stopping suddenly.

> What's this—soot? And smoke as well? I may be all
> wet, but this might mean fire. Things look dark,
> girls; we'll have to dash.

They move ahead, at a considerably faster pace than the men.

FIRST SEMICHORUS OF WOMEN

Singly.

> Speed! Celerity!   Save our sorority
> from arson. Combustion.   And heat exhaustion.
> Don't let our sisterhood   shrivel to blisterhood.
>   Fanned into slag by hoary typhoons.
>   By flatulent, nasty, gusty baboons.
>   We're late! Run!
>   The girls might be done!

Tutte. [All together]

> Filling my pitcher   was absolute torture;
> The fountains in town   are so *crowded* at dawn,
> glutted with masses   of the lower classes
> blatting and battering,   shoving, and shattering
> jugs. But I juggled   my burden, and wriggled
> away to extinguish   the igneous anguish
>   of neighbor, and sister, and daughter—
>   Here's Water!

SECOND SEMICHORUS OF WOMEN

Singly.

Get wind of the news? The gaffers are loose.
The blowhards are off with fuel enough
to furnish a bathhouse. But the finish is pathos:
 They're scaling the heights with a horrid
  proposal.
 They're threatening women with rubbish
  disposal!
  How ghastly—how gauche!
  burned up with the trash!

Tutte.

Preserve me, Athene, from gazing on any
matron or maid auto-da-fé'd.[20]
Cover with grace these redeemers of Greece
from battles, insanity, Man's inhumanity.
Gold-browed goddess, hither to aid us!
Fight as our ally, join in our sally
 against pyromaniac slaughter—
  Haul Water!

KORYPHAIOS OF WOMEN

Noticing for the first time the Chorus of Men, still busy at their firepots, she cuts off a member of her Chorus who seems about to continue the song.

Hold it. What have we here? You don't catch true-
blue patriots red-handed. These are authentic
degenerates, male, taken *in flagrante*.[21]

KORYPHAIOS OF MEN

      Oops. Female
troops. This could be upsetting. I didn't expect such
a flood of reserves.

KORYPHAIOS OF WOMEN

     Merely a spearhead. If our
numbers stun you, watch that yellow streak spread.

---

[20]That is, burned to death.

[21]Part of a Latin legal term indicating that the person has been caught in the act of committing the offense.

We represent just one percent of one percent of This
Woman's Army.
KORYPHAIOS OF MEN
                        Never been confronted with such
backtalk. Can't allow it. Somebody pick up a log
and pulverize that brass.
                        Any volunteers?

There are none among the male chorus

KORYPHAIOS OF WOMEN
                                    Put down
the pitchers, girls. If they start waving that lumber,
we don't want to be encumbered.
KORYPHAIOS OF MEN
                            Look, men, a few
sharp jabs will stop that jawing. It never fails.
                                        The
poet Hipponax swears by it. [22]

Still no volunteers. The Koryphaios of Women advances.

KORYPHAIOS OF WOMEN
                            Then step right up.
Have a jab at me. Free shot.
KORYPHAIOS OF MEN

Advancing reluctantly to meet her.

                            Shut up! I'll peel your
pelt. I'll pit your pod.
KORYPHAIOS OF WOMEN
                        The name is Stratyllis. I dare
you to lay one finger on me.
KORYPHAIOS OF MEN
                        I'll lay on you with a
fistful. Er—any specific threats?

---

[22]Hipponax was a satirical poet who threatened, in one of his verses, to "sock [the
sculptor] Boupalos in the jaw" for having made an ugly statue of him.

KORYPHAIOS OF WOMEN

Earnestly.

I'll crop your lungs
and reap your bowels, bite by bite, and leave no balls
on the body for other bitches to gnaw.

KORYPHAIOS OF MEN

Retreating hurriedly.

Can't beat
Euripides for insight. And I quote:
*No creature's found
so lost to shame as Woman.*
Talk about realist
playwrights!

KORYPHAIOS OF WOMEN

Up with the water, ladies. Pitchers at
the ready, place!

KORYPHAIOS OF MEN

Why the water, you sink of iniquity?
More sedition?

KORYPHAIOS OF WOMEN

Why the fire, you walking boneyard?
Self-cremation?

KORYPHAIOS OF MEN

I brought this fire to ignite a pyre and
fricassee your friends.

KORYPHAIOS OF WOMEN

I brought this water to douse
your pyre. Tit for tat.

KORYPHAIOS OF MEN

You'll douse my fire?
Nonsense!

KORYPHAIOS OF WOMEN

You'll see, when the facts soak in.

KORYPHAIOS OF MEN

I have
the torch right here. Perhaps I should barbecue *you*.

KORYPHAIOS OF WOMEN

If you have any soap, I could give you a bath.

KORYPHAIOS OF MEN

A bath

from those polluted hands?

KORYPHAIOS OF WOMEN

Pure enough for a
blushing young bridegroom.

KORYPHAIOS OF MEN

Enough of that insolent
lip.

KORYPHAIOS OF WOMEN

It's merely freedom of speech.

KORYPHAIOS OF MEN

I'll stop that
screeching!

KORYPHAIOS OF WOMEN

You're helpless outside of the jury-box.[23]

KORYPHAIOS OF MEN

Urging his men, torches at the ready, into a charge.

Burn, fire, burn!

KORYPHAIOS OF WOMEN

As the women empty their pitchers over the men.

And cauldron bubble.

KORYPHAIOS OF MEN

Like his troops, soaked and routed.

Arrgh!

KORYPHAIOS OF WOMEN

Goodness.
What seems to be the trouble? Too hot?

KORYPHAIOS OF MEN

Hot, hell!
Stop it! What do you think you're doing?

KORYPHAIOS OF WOMEN

If you must
know, I'm gardening. Perhaps you'll bloom.

---

[23]Jury duty was a frequent—sometimes the only—source of income for older male
Athenians.

KORYPHAIOS OF MEN

Perhaps

I'll fall right off the vine! I'm withered, frozen,
shaking . . .

KORYPHAIOS OF WOMEN

Of course. But, providentially,
you brought along your smudgepot.

The sap should

rise eventually.

Shivering, the Chorus of Men retreats in utter defeat.
A Commissioner of Public Safety enters from the left, followed quite reluctantly by a
squad of police—four Skythian archers [from a region north of Greece]. He surveys
the situation with disapproval.

COMMISSIONER

Fire, eh? Females again—spontaneous
combustion of lust. Suspected as much.

Rubadubdubbing,

incessant incontinent keening for wine, damnable
funeral foofaraw for Adonis resounding from roof to
roof—heard it all before . . .[24]

Savagely, as the Koryphaios of Men tries to interpose a remark.

and WHERE?

The ASSEMBLY!

Recall, if you can, the debate on
the Sicilian Question: That bullbrained demagogue
Demostratos[25] (who will rot, I trust) rose to propose
a naval task force.

His wife, writhing with religion
on a handy roof, bleated a dirge:

"BEREFT! OH

WOE OH WOE FOR ADONIS!"

---

[24] At the time when the disastrous Athenian expedition to Sicily was setting forth, the
female followers of the cult of Adonis were ritually—publicly—lamenting their hero's
death. The expedition to Sicily was aimed against the city of Syracuse, an ally of Sparta.
Later, the women's wailing was seen as having put ill-luck upon the expedition.

[25] One of the most enthusiastic initiators of the Sicilian expedition. Demostratos had also
proposed drafting soldiers into the Athenian forces from the island of Zakynthos (an
allied state) on their way to Sicily.

And so of course Demostratos, taking his cue,
outblatted her:
>   "A DRAFT! ENROLL THE
> WHOLE OF ZAKYNTHOS!"

His wife, a smidgin stewed, renewed her yowling:
> "OH GNASH YOUR TEETH AND BEAT
> YOUR BREASTS FOR ADONIS!"

And so of course Demostratos (that god-detested
blot, that foul-lunged son of an ulcer) gnashed tooth
and nail and voice, and bashed and rammed his
program through. And THERE is the Gift of
Women:
>   MORAL CHAOS!

KORYPHAIOS OF MEN

Save your breath for actual felonies, Commissioner;
see what's happened to us! Insolence, insults, these
we pass over, but not lese-majesty:[26]

>   We're flooded

with indignity from those bitches' pitchers—like a
bunch of weak-bladdered brats. Our cloaks are
sopped. We'll sue!

COMMISSIONER

>   Useless. Your suit won't hold

water. Right's on their side. For female depravity,
gentlemen, WE stand guilty—we, their teachers,
preceptors of prurience, accomplices before the fact
of fornication. We sowed them in sexual license, and
now we reap rebellion.

>   The proof?

Consider. Off we trip to the goldsmith's to leave
an order:

> "That bangle you fashioned last spring
> for my wife is sprung. She was thrashing
> around last night, and the prong popped out
> of the bracket. I'll be tied up all day—I'm
> boarding the ferry right now—but my wife'll
> be home. If you get the time, please stop by
> the house in a bit and see if you can't do

---

[26]An attack against the dignity of a ruler or a revered group (like the senior male citizens
of Athens).

something—anything—to fit a new prong into
the bracket of her bangle."

>   And bang.

Another one ups to a cobbler—young, but no
apprentice, full kit of tools, ready to give his awl—
and delivers this gem:

> "My wife's new sandals are
> tight. The cinch pinches her pinkie right where
> she's sensitive. Drop in at noon with
> something to stretch her cinch and give it
> a little play."

>   And a cinch it is.

Such hanky-panky we have to thank for today's
Utter Anarchy: I, a Commissioner of Public Safety,
duly invested with extraordinary powers to protect
the State in the Present Emergency, have secured a
source of timber to outfit our fleet and solve the
shortage of oarage. I need the money immediately
. . . and WOMEN, no less, have locked me out of
the Treasury!

Pulling himself together.

>   —Well, no profit in standing around.

To one of the archers.

> Bring the crowbars. I'll jack these women back on
> their pedestals!—WELL, you slack-jawed jackass?
> What's the attraction? Wipe that thirst off your face.
> I said *crow*bar, not saloon!—All right, men, all
> together. Shove those bars underneath the gate and
> HEAVE!

Grabbing up a crowbar.

>   I'll take this side. And now let's root them
> out, men, ROOT them out. One, Two . . .

*The gates to the Akropolis burst open suddenly, disclosing Lysistrata. She is perfectly
composed and bears a large spindle. The Commissioner and the Police fall back in
consternation.*

LYSISTRATA
Why the moving equipment? I'm quite well
motivated, thank you, and here I am. Frankly, you
don't need crowbars nearly so much as brains.

COMMISSIONER
Brains? O name of infamy! Where's a policeman?

He grabs wildly for the First Archer and shoves him toward Lysistrata.

Arrest that woman!
                                    Better tie her hands behind her.

LYSISTRATA
By Artemis,[27] goddess of the hunt, if he lays a finger
on me, he'll rue the day he joined the force!

*She jabs the spindle viciously at the First Archer, who leaps, terrified, back to his
comrades.*

COMMISSIONER
What's this—retreat? Never! Take her on the flank.

The First Archer hangs back. The Commissioner grabs the Second Archer.

—Help him.
                                    —Will the two of you kindly
TIE HER UP?

*He shoves them toward Lysistrata. Kleonike, carrying a large chamber pot, springs
out of the entrance and advances on the Second Archer.*

KLEONIKE
                    By Artemis, goddess of the dew, if
you so much as touch her, I'll stomp the shit right
out of you!

The two Archers run back to their group.

COMMISSIONER
                    Shit? Shameless! Where's another
policeman?

He grabs the Third Archer and propels him toward Kleonike.

[27]Virgin goddess of the hunt, the moon, and childbirth; twin sister of Apollo.

Handcuff *her* first. Can't stand a foul-mouthed female.

Myrrhine, carrying a large, blazing lamp, appears at the entrance and advances on the Third Archer.

MYRRHINE

By Artemis, bringer of light, if you lay a finger on her, you won't be able to stop the swelling!

The Third Archer dodges her swing and runs back to the group.

COMMISSIONER

Now what? Where's an officer?

Pushing the Fourth Archer toward Myrrhine.

Apprehend that woman! I'll see that *somebody* stays to take the blame!

Ismenia the Boiotian, carrying a huge pair of pincers, appears at the entrance and advances on the Fourth Archer.

ISMENIA

By Artemis, goddess of [Skythian] Tauris, if you go near that girl, I'll rip the hair right out of your head!

The Fourth Archer retreats hurriedly.

COMMISSIONER

What a colossal mess: Athens' Finest—finished!

Arranging the Archers.

—Now, men, a little *esprit de corps.*
Worsted by women? Drubbed by drabs?
Never!
Regroup,
reform that thin red line.
Ready?

CHARGE!

He pushes them ahead of him.

LYSISTRATA

I warn you. We have four battalions
behind us—full-armed combat infantrywomen,
trained from the cradle . . .

COMMISSIONER

Disarm them, Officers!

Go for the hands!

LYSISTRATA

Calling inside the Akropolis.

MOBILIZE THE RESERVES!

A horde of women, armed with household articles, begins to pour from the Akropolis.

Onward, you ladies from hell!
Forward, you market militia, you battle-hardened
bargain hunters, old sales campaigners, grocery
grenadiers, veterans never bested by an overcharge!
You troops of the breadline, doughgirls—
INTO THE FRAY!

Show them no mercy!

Push!

Jostle!

Shove!

Call them nasty names!

Don't be ladylike.

The women charge and rout the Archers in short order.

Fall back—don't strip the enemy!

The day is ours!

The women obey, and the Archers run off left. The Commissioner, dazed, is left muttering to himself.

COMMISSIONER

Gross ineptitude. A sorry day for
the Force.

LYSISTRATA

Of course. What did you expect? We're
not slaves; we're freeborn Women, and when we're

scorned, we're full of fury. Never Underestimate
the Power of a Woman.

COMMISSIONER

Power? You mean Capacity.
I should have remembered the proverb: *The lower
the tavern, the higher the dudgeon.*[28]

KORYPHAIOS OF MEN

Why cast your
pearls before swine, Commissioner? I know you're
a civil
servant, but don't overdo it. Have you forgotten
the bath they gave us—in public,

fully dressed,
totally soapless? Keep rational discourse for *people!*

He aims a blow at the Koryphaios of Women, who dodges and raises her pitcher.

KORYPHAIOS OF WOMEN

I might point out that lifting one's hand against a
neighbor is scarcely civilized behavior—and entails,
for the lifter, a black eye.

I'm really peaceful by
nature, compulsively inoffensive—a perfect doll.
My ideal is a well-bred repose that doesn't even stir
up dust . . .

Swinging at the Koryphaios of Men with the pitcher.

unless some no-good lowlife tries to rifle
my hive and gets my dander up!

*The Koryphaios of Men backs hurriedly away, and the Chorus of Men goes into a
worried dance.*

CHORUS OF MEN

Singly.

O Zeus, what's the use of this constant abuse?
How do we deal with this female zoo?
Is there no solution to Total Immersion?
What can a poor man DO?

[28]That is, the lower the social class, the greater the resentment.

Tutti. [All together]

> Query the Adversary!
> Ferret out their story!
> What end did they have in view,
> to seize the city's sanctuary,
> snatch its legendary eyrie,[29]
> snare an area so very
>   terribly taboo?

KORYPHAIOS OF MEN

To the Commissioner.

> Scrutinize those women! Scour their depositions—
>   assess their rebuttals!
> Masculine honor demands this affair be probed to
>   the bottom!

COMMISSIONER

Turning to the women from the Akropolis.

> All right, you. Kindly inform me, dammit, in your
> own words: What possible object could you have had
>   in blockading the Treasury?

LYSISTRATA

> We thought we'd deposit the money in escrow and
>   withdraw
> you men from the war.

COMMISSIONER

>   The money's the cause
> of the war?

LYSISTRATA

>   And all our internal disorders—
> the Body Politic's chronic bellyaches: What causes
> Peisandros' frantic rantings, or the raucous
> caucuses of the Friends of Oligarchy?[30] The
> chance for graft.

---

[29]Lofty nest (Athene's chamber in the Parthenon).

[30]A corrupt politician and his party, which would shortly overthrow the democratic constitution of Athens (in May, 411 B.C.).

But now, with the money up there, they can't upset the City's equilibrium—or lower its balance.

COMMISSIONER

And what's your next step?

LYSISTRATA

Stupid question. We'll budget the money.

COMMISSIONER

You'll budget the money?

LYSISTRATA

Why should you find that so shocking? We budget the household accounts, and you don't object at all.

COMMISSIONER

That's different.

LYSISTRATA

Different? How?

COMMISSIONER

The War Effort needs this money!

LYSISTRATA

Who needs the War Effort?

COMMISSIONER

Every patriot who pulses to save all that Athens holds near and dear . . .

LYSISTRATA

Oh, *that*. Don't worry. We'll save you.

COMMISSIONER

You will save us?

LYSISTRATA

Who else?

COMMISSIONER

But this is unscrupulous!

LYSISTRATA

We'll save you. You can't deter us.

COMMISSIONER

Scurrilous!

LYSISTRATA

You seem disturbed. This makes it difficult. But, still—we'll save you.

COMMISSIONER

Doubtless illegal!

LYSISTRATA

We deem it a
duty. For friendship's sake.

COMMISSIONER

Well, forsake this, friend:
I DO NOT WANT TO BE SAVED, DAMMIT!

LYSISTRATA

All the more reason. It's not only Sparta; now we'll
have to save you from *you*.

COMMISSIONER

Might I ask where you
women conceived this concern about War and Peace?

LYSISTRATA

Loftily.

We shall explain.

COMMISSIONER

Making a fist.

Hurry up, and you won't get hurt.

LYSISTRATA

Then *listen*. And do try to keep your hands to
yourself.

COMMISSIONER

Moving threateningly toward her.

I can't. Righteous anger forbids restraint,
and decrees . . .

KLEONIKE

Brandishing her chamber pot.

Multiple fractures?

COMMISSIONER

Retreating.

Keep those
croaks for yourself, you old crow!

To Lysistrata.

All right, lady, I'm
ready. Speak.

LYSISTRATA

I shall proceed:
When the War began, like the prudent, dutiful
wives that we are, we tolerated you men, and
endured your actions in silence. (Small
      wonder—
you wouldn't let us say boo.)

You were not precisely
the answer to a matron's prayer—we knew you
too well, and found out more. Too many times,
as we sat in the house, we'd hear that you'd done
it again—manhandled another affair of state
with your usual staggering incompetence.
Then, masking our worry with a nervous
      laugh,
we'd ask you, brightly, "How was the Assembly
      today, dear?
Anything in the minutes about Peace?" And my
husband would give his stock reply.
"What's that to you? Shut up!" And I did.

KLEONIKE

Proudly.

I never shut up!

COMMISSIONER

I trust you were shut up. Soundly.

LYSISTRATA

Regardless, *I* shut up.

And then we'd learn that
you'd passed another decree, fouler than the first,
and we'd ask again: "Darling, how *did* you manage
anything so idiotic?" And my husband, with his
customary glare, would tell me to spin my thread, or
else get a clout on the head. And of course he'd quote
from Homer:
      The menne must husband the warre.[31]

---

[31]That is, the men must manage the war.

COMMISSIONER
Apt and irrefutably right.

LYSISTRATA

Right, you miserable misfit?

To keep us from giving advice while you fumbled the City away in the Senate? Right, indeed!

But this time was really too much: Wherever we went, we'd hear you engaged in the same conversation:

"What Athens needs is a Man."
"But there isn't a Man in the country."
"You can say that again."

There was obviously no time to lose. We women met in immediate convention and passed a unanimous resolution: To work in concert for safety and Peace in Greece. We have valuable advice to impart, and if you can possibly deign to emulate our silence, and take your turn as audience, we'll rectify you—we'll straighten you out and set you right.

COMMISSIONER

You'll set *us* right? You go too far. I cannot permit such a statement to . . .

LYSISTRATA
Shush.

COMMISSIONER

I categorically decline to shush for some confounded woman, who wears—as a constant reminder of congenital inferiority, an injunction to public silence—a veil! Death before such dishonor!

LYSISTRATA

Removing her veil.

If that's the only obstacle . . .
I feel you need a new panache,
so take the veil, my dear Commissioner, and drape it thus—

and SHUSH!

As she winds the veil around the startled Commissioner's head, Kleonike and Myrrhine, with carding-comb and wool-basket, rush forward and assist in transforming him into a woman.

KLEONIKE
> Accept, I pray, this humble comb.

MYRRHINE
> Receive this basket of fleece as well.

LYSISTRATA
> Hike up your skirts, and card your wool,
> and gnaw your beans—and stay at home!
> > While we rewrite Homer:
> > *The WOMEN must WIVE the warre!*

To the chorus of Women, as the Commissioner struggles to remove his new outfit.

> Women, weaker vessels, arise!
> > > Put down your
> pitchers. It's our turn, now. Let's supply our friends
> with some moral support.

The Chorus of Women dances to the same tune as the Men, but with much more confidence.

CHORUS OF WOMEN

Singly.

> > Oh, yes! I'll dance to bless their success.
> > Fatigue won't weaken my will. Or my
> > > knees.
> > I'm ready to join in any jeopardy,
> > > with girls as good as *these!*

Tutte.

> > A tally of their talents
> > convinces me they're giants
> > of excellence. To commence:
> > there's Beauty, Duty, Prudence,
> > Science, Self-Reliance, Compliance,
> > > Defiance,
> > and Love of Athens in balanced alliance
> > > with Common Sense!

KORYPHAIOS OF WOMEN

To the women from the Akropolis.

> Autochthonous[32] daughters of Attika,[33] sprung from
> the soil that bore your mothers, the spiniest, spikiest
> nettles known to man, prove your mettle and attack!
> Now is no time to dilute your anger. You're running
> ahead of the wind!

LYSISTRATA

> We'll wait for the wind from
> heaven. The gentle breath of Love and his Kyprian
> mother[34] will imbue our bodies with desire, and raise
> a storm to tense and tauten these blasted men until
> they crack. And soon we'll be on every tongue in
> Greece—the *Pacifiers*.[35]

COMMISSIONER

> That's quite a mouthful.
> How will you win it?

LYSISTRATA

> First, we intend to withdraw
> that crazy Army of Occupation from the downtown
> shopping section.

KLEONIKE

> Aphrodite be praised!

LYSISTRATA

> The pottery
> shop and the grocery stall are overstocked with
> soldiers, clanking around like those maniac
> Korybants,[36] armed
> to the teeth for a battle.

COMMISSIONER

> A Hero is Always Prepared!

[32] Native.

[33] The region of which Athens was the dominant city.

[34] Aphrodite, goddess of feminine beauty and love, was associated with the island of
Kypros (Cyprus); her son was "Love" (Eros, Cupid).

[35] A play upon the meaning of Lysistrata's name.

[36] The armed priests of the goddess Cybele, whose rites included frenzied dances and
music.

LYSISTRATA
I suppose he is. But it does look silly to shop for
sardines from behind a shield.

KLEONIKE

                  I'll second that. I saw a
cavalry captain buy vegetable soup on horseback. He
carried the whole mess home in his helmet.

                            And then
that fellow from Thrace, shaking his buckler and
spear—a menace straight from the stage. The
saleslady was stiff with fright. He was hogging her
   ripe figs—free.

COMMISSIONER
I admit, for the moment, that Hellas'[37]affairs are in
one hell of a snarl. But how can you set them
straight?

LYSISTRATA
          Simplicity itself.

COMMISSIONER
                  Pray demonstrate.

LYSISTRATA
It's rather like yarn. When a hank's in a tangle, we
lift it—*so*—and work out the snarls by winding it up
on spindles, now this way, now that way.

                     That's how
we'll wind up the War, if allowed; We'll work out the
snarls by sending Special Commissions—

                     back and
forth, now this way, now that way—to ravel these
tense international kinks.

COMMISSIONER
               I lost your thread, but I
know there's a hitch. Spruce up the world's disasters
with spindles—typically wooly female logic.

LYSISTRATA
                     If *you*
had a scrap of logic, you'd adopt our wool as a
master plan for Athens.

---

[37]Hellas was the name the Greeks gave to their own civilization. The name, Greece, was
applied to Hellas later by the Romans.

COMMISSIONER

What course of action does the wool advise?

LYSISTRATA

Consider the City as fleece, recently shorn.[38] The first step is Cleansing: Scrub it in a public bath, and remove all corruption, offal, and sheepdip.

Next, to the couch for Scutching and Plucking: Cudgel the leeches and similar vermin loose with a club, then pick the prickles and cockleburs out. As for the clots—those lumps that clump and cluster in knots and snarls to snag important posts—you comb these out, twist off their heads, and discard.

Next, to raise the City's nap, you card the citizens together in a single basket of common weal and general welfare. Fold in our loyal Resident Aliens, all Foreigners of proven and tested friendship, and any Disenfranchised Debtors. Combine these closely with the rest.

Lastly, cull the colonies settled by our own people: these are nothing but flocks of wool from the City's fleece, scattered throughout the world. So gather home these far-flung flocks, amalgamate them with the others.

Then, drawing this blend of stable fibers into one fine staple, you spin a mighty bobbin of yarn—and weave, without bias or seam, a cloak to clothe the City of Athens!

COMMISSIONER

This is too much! The City's died in the wool, worsted by the distaff side— by women who bore no share in the War. . . .

LYSISTRATA

None, you hopeless hypocrite? The quota we bear is double. First, we delivered our sons to fill out the front lines in Sicily . . .

[38]Lysistrata's response is actually a conservative political allegory.

COMMISSIONER

Don't tax me with that
memory.

LYSISTRATA

Next, the best years of our lives were
levied. Top-level strategy attached our joy, and we
sleep alone.

But it's not the matrons like us who
matter. I mourn for the virgins, bedded in single
blessedness, with nothing to do but grow old.

COMMISSIONER

Men *have* been known to age, as well as women.

LYSISTRATA

No, not as well as—better.

A man, an absolute
antique, comes back from the war, and he's
    barely
doddered into town before he's married the veriest
nymphet. But a woman's season is brief; it slips, and
she'll have no husband, but sit out her life groping at
omens—and finding no men.

COMMISSIONER

Lamentable state of
affairs. Perhaps we can rectify matters:

To the audience.

TO EVERY
MAN JACK, A CHALLENGE:
                    ARISE!

Provided you can . . .

LYSISTRATA

Instead, Commissioner, why
not simply curl up and *die?*

Just buy a coffin; here's the place.

Banging him on the head with her spindle.

I'll knead you a cake for the wake—and *these*

Winding the threads from the spindle around him.

> make excellent wreaths. So Rest In Peace.
> KLEONIKE

Emptying the chamber pot over him.

> Accept these tokens of deepest grief.
> MYRRHINE

Breaking her lamp over his head.

> A final garland for the dear deceased.
> LYSISTRATA
> May I supply any last request?
> Then run along. You're due at the wharf:
>   Charon's anxious to sail—
>   you're holding up the boat for Hell![39]
> COMMISSIONER
> This is monstrous—maltreatment of a public
> official—maltreatment of ME!
>   I must repair directly
> to the Board of Commissioners, and present my
> colleagues concrete evidence of the sorry specifics
> of this shocking attack!

He staggers off left. Lysistrata calls after him.

> LYSISTRATA
>   You won't haul us into
> court on a charge of neglecting the dead, will you?
> (How like a man to insist on his rights—even his
> last ones.) Two days between death and funeral,
> that's the rule.
>   Come back here early day after
> tomorrow, Commissioner:
>   We'll lay you out.

Lysistrata and her women re-enter the Akropolis. The Koryphaios of Men advances to address the audience.

[39]In Greek mythology, Charon was the god whose boat ferried the dead souls across the River Styx to Hades (the underworld). Lysistrata's earlier "cake for the wake" is a reference to the honey cake needed by the dead souls to please Cerberus, the three-headed dog who guarded the entrance to Hades.

KORYPHAIOS OF MEN
Wake up, Athenians! Preserve your freedom—the
time is Now!

To the Chorus of Men.

Strip for action, men. Let's cope with
the current mess.

*The men put off their long mantles, disclosing short tunics underneath, and advance
toward the audience.*

CHORUS OF MEN
This trouble may be terminal; it has a loaded odor,
    an ominous aroma of constitutional rot.
My nose gives a prognosis of radical disorder—
    it's just the first installment of an absolutist plot!
      The Spartans are behind it:
      they must have masterminded
some morbid local contacts (engineered by
Kleisthenes).[40]
      Predictably infected,
      these women straightway acted
to commandeer the City's cash. They're feverish to
freeze
      my be-all,
      my end-all . . .
      my *payroll!*
KORYPHAIOS OF MEN
The symptoms are clear. Our birthright's already
    nibbled. And oh, so
daintily: WOMEN ticking off troops for improper
    etiquette.
WOMEN propounding their featherweight views
    on the fashionable use
and abuse of the shield. And (if any more proof were
    needed) WOMEN
nagging us to trust the Nice Spartan, and put our

[40]A notoriously effeminate bisexual—and one of Aristophanes' favorite targets of ridicule.

heads in his toothy maw—to make a dessert and call
it Peace.
They've woven the City a seamless shroud,
bedecked with the legend
DICTATORSHIP.
But I won't be hemmed in.
I'll use their weapon against them, and uphold the
right by sneakiness.
With knyf under cloke, gauntlet
in glove, sword in olivebranch,

Slipping slowly toward the Koryphaios of Women.

I'll take up my
post in Statuary Row, beside our honored
National Heroes, the natural foes of tyranny:
Harmodios,
Aristogeiton,[41]
and Me.

Next to her.

Striking an epic pose, so, with the full approval
of the immortal gods,
I'll bash this loathesome
hag in the jaw!

He does, and runs cackling back to the Men. She shakes a fist after him.

KORYPHAIOS OF WOMEN
Mama won't know her little boy
when he gets home!

To the Women, who are eager to launch a full-scale attack.

Let's not be hasty, fellow . . .
hags. Cloaks off first.

*The Women remove their mantles, disclosing tunics very like those of the Men, and
advance toward the audience.*

[41]A reference to a famous statuary group in the Athenian marketplace representing two
young men who, in 514 B.C., had killed a **tyrant**.

CHORUS OF WOMEN
We'll address you, citizens, in beneficial, candid,
    patriotic accents, as our breeding says we must,
since, from the age of seven, Athens graced me with
    a splendid string of civic triumphs to signalize her
    trust:
        I was a Relic-Girl quite early,
        then advanced to Maid of Barley;
in Artemis' "Pageant of the Bear" I played the lead.
        To cap this proud progression,[42]
        I led the whole procession
at Athene's Celebration, certified and pedigreed
        —that cachet
        so distingué—
        a *Lady!*
KORYPHAIOS OF WOMEN

To the audience.

I trust this establishes my qualifications. I may, I take
it, address the City to its profit? Thank you.
                        I admit
to being a woman—but don't sell my contribution
short on that account. It's better than the present
panic. And my word is as good as my bond, because
I hold stock in Athens—stock I paid for in sons.

To the Chorus of Men.

    —But you, you doddering bankrupts, where are
        your shares in the State?

Slipping slowly toward the Koryphaios of Men

    Your grandfathers willed you the Mutual Funds
        from the Persian War—
    and where are they?[43]

---

[42]The chorus mentions four past public festivals in which, as upper class Athenian girls,
they had each played a part.

[43]The original treasury of the Delian League had been on the island of Delos. The League
was an alliance of most Greek states, organized in 477 B.C. for the purpose of maintaining the common defense against any Persian attack. The treasury was transferred by

Nearer.

> You dipped into capital, then
> lost interest . . . and now a pool of your assets won't
> fill a hole in the ground. All that remains is one last
> potential killing—Athens. Is there any rebuttal?

The Koryphaios of Men gestures menacingly. She ducks down, as if to ward off a blow, and removes a slipper.

> Force is a footling resort. I'll take my very sensible
> shoe, and paste you in the jaw!

She does so, and runs back to the women.

CHORUS OF MEN

> Their native respect for our manhood is small,
>   and keeps getting smaller. Let's bottle their
>   gall.
> The man who won't battle has no balls at all!

KORYPHAIOS OF MEN

All right, men, skin out of the skivvies. Let's give
them a whiff of Man, full strength. No point in
muffling the essential Us.

The men remove their tunics.

CHORUS OF MEN

> A century back, we soared to the Heights
>   and beat down Tyranny there.
> Now's the time to shed our moults
>   and fledge our wings once more,
> to rise to the skies in our reborn force,
>   and beat back Tyranny here!

KORYPHAIOS OF MEN

No fancy grappling with these grannies;
    straightforward strength.

the Athenians to their Akropolis in 454 and, thereafter, was turned mainly to Athenian purposes. Obviously, this misuse of the common treasury was a contributing cause of the Peloponnesian War. After the heavy expenses of the Sicilian expedition, the women's question is very embarrassing to the men.

The tiniest toehold, and those nimble, fiddling
fingers will have their foot in the door, and we're
done for.
                    No amount of know-how can lick a
woman's knack.
                    They'll want to build ships . . .
    next thing we know,
we're all at sea, fending off female boarding parties.
(Artemisia fought us at Salamis.[44]Tell me, has
anyone caught her yet?)
                    But we're *really* sunk if they
take up horses. Scratch the Cavalry:
                              A woman is an
easy rider with a natural seat.
                              Take her over the
jumps bareback, and she'll never slip her mount.
(That's how the Amazons nearly took Athens. On
    horseback.
Check on Mikon's mural down in the Stoa.)[45]
Anyway,
            the solution is obvious. Put every woman
in her place—stick her in the stocks.
                              To do this, first
snare your woman around the neck.

He attempts to demonstrate on the Koryphaios of Women. After a brief tussle, she
works loose and chases him back to the Men.

CHORUS OF WOMEN
            The beast in me's eager and fit for a brawl.
            Just rile me a bit and she'll kick down the wall.
            You'll bawl to your friends that you've no balls
                at all.

[44]Artemisia was a queen of Halikarnassos in Asia Minor. She was allied with the Persian
King Xerxes in his invasion of Greece in 480 B.C. and fought bravely at the naval battle
of Salamis.

[45]A Stoa was a roofed colonnade, with a wall on one side, often serving the same purpose
as a modern shopping mall. The wall was usually decorated with paintings; the subject
of the painting referred to here was a common one: an attack by Amazons, a mythical
race of warrior-women.

KORYPHAIOS OF WOMEN

All right, ladies, strip for action. Let's give them a whiff of *Femme Enragée*—piercing and pungent, but not at all tart.

The women remove their tunics.

CHORUS OF WOMEN

We're angry. The brainless bird who tangles
    with *us* has gummed his last mush.
In fact, the coot who even heckles
    is being daringly rash.
So look to your nests, you reclaimed eagles—
    whatever you lay, we'll squash!

KORYPHAIOS OF WOMEN

Frankly, you don't faze me. *With* me, I have my friends—Lampito from Sparta; that genteel girl from Thebes, Ismenia—committed to me forever. *Against* me, *you*—permanently out of commission. So do your damnedest.

             Pass a law.

                    Pass seven. Continue the winning ways that have made your name a short and ugly household word.

                  Like yesterday:
I was giving a little party, nothing fussy, to honor the goddess Hekate. Simply to please my daughters, I'd invited a sweet little thing from the neighborhood—flawless pedigree,
    perfect
taste, a credit to any gathering—a Boiotian eel.
But she had to decline. Couldn't pass the border.
    You'd passed a law.
Not that you care for my party. You'll overwork
    your right of passage
till your august body is overturned,

                    and you break
your silly neck!

She deftly grabs the Koryphaios of Men by the ankle and upsets him. He scuttles back to the Men, who retire in confusion.

Lysistrata emerges from the citadel, obviously distraught.

KORYPHAIOS OF WOMEN

Mock-tragic.

> *Mistress, queen of this our subtle scheme,*
> *why burst you from the hall with brangled brow?*
>
> LYSISTRATA
> *Oh, wickedness of woman! The female mind does*
> *sap my soul and set my wits a-totter.*
>
> KORYPHAIOS OF WOMEN
> *What drear accents are these?*
>
> LYSISTRATA
>   *The merest truth.*
>
> KORYPHAIOS OF WOMEN
> *Be nothing loath to tell the tale to friends.*
>
> LYSISTRATA
> *'Twere shame to utter, pain to hold unsaid.*
>
> KORYPHAIOS OF WOMEN
> *Hide not from me affliction which we share.*
>
> LYSISTRATA
> *In briefest compass,*

Dropping the paratragedy.

>   we want to get laid.
>
> KORYPHAIOS OF WOMEN
>   By Zeus!
>
> LYSISTRATA
> No, no, not HIM!
>   Well, that's the way things are.
> I've lost my grip on the girls—they're mad for men!
> But sly—they slip out in droves.
>   A minute ago,
> I caught one scooping out the little hole that breaks
> through just below Pan's grotto.[46]
>   One had
> jerry-rigged some block-and-tackle business and was
> wriggling away on a rope.

---

[46] A cave just outside the defensive wall that surrounded the top (the Citadel) of the Akropolis.

Another just flat deserted.
Last night I spied one mounting a sparrow, all set to
take off for the nearest bawdyhouse. I hauled her
back by the hair.

And excuses, pretexts for overnight
passes? I've heard them all.

Here comes one. Watch.

To the First Woman, as she runs out of the Akropolis.

—You, there! What's your hurry?

FIRST WOMAN

I have to get home.
I've got all this lovely Milesian wool in the house,
and the moths will simply batter it to bits!

LYSISTRATA

I'll bet.

Get back inside.

FIRST WOMAN

I swear I'll hurry right back!
—Just time enough to spread it out on the couch?

LYSISTRATA

Your wool will stay unspread. And you'll stay here.

FIRST WOMAN

Do I have to let my piecework *rot?*

LYSISTRATA

Possibly.

The Second Woman runs on.

SECOND WOMAN

Oh dear, oh goodness, what shall I do—my flax!
I left and forgot to peel it!

LYSISTRATA

Another one.
She suffers from unpeeled flax.

—Get back inside!

SECOND WOMAN

I'll be right back. I just have to pluck the fibers.

LYSISTRATA

No. No plucking. You start it, and everyone else
will want to go and do their plucking, too.

The Third Woman, swelling conspicuously, hurries on, praying loudly.

THIRD WOMAN
O Goddess of Childbirth, grant that I not deliver until I get me from out this sacred precinct!
LYSISTRATA
What sort of nonsense is *this?*
THIRD WOMAN

                         I'm due—any second!

LYSISTRATA
You weren't pregnant yesterday.
THIRD WOMAN

                      Today I am—a

miracle!
     Let me go home for a midwife, *please!* I may
not make it!
LYSISTRATA

Restraining her.

          You can do better than that.

Tapping the woman's stomach and receiving a metallic clang.

What's this? It's hard.
THIRD WOMAN

               I'm going to have a boy.

LYSISTRATA
Not unless he's made of bronze. Let's see.

She throws open the Third Woman's cloak, exposing a huge bronze helmet.

Of all the brazen . . . You've stolen the helmet from
Athene's statue! Pregnant, indeed!
THIRD WOMAN

                I am *so* pregnant!

LYSISTRATA
Then why the helmet?
THIRD WOMAN

             I thought my time might
come while I was still on forbidden ground.[47] If it

[47]Childbirth was taboo on the holy ground of the Akropolis.

did, I could climb inside Athene's helmet and have
my baby there.
                              The pigeons do it all the time.
LYSISTRATA
Nothing but excuses!

Taking the helmet.

                              This is your baby. I'm afraid
you'll have to stay until we give it a name.
THIRD WOMAN
But the Akropolis is *awful*. I can't even sleep! I saw
the snake that guards the temple.
LYSISTRATA
                              That snake's a
fabrication.[48]
THIRD WOMAN
I don't care *what* kind it is—I'm *scared!*

The other women, who have emerged from the citadel, crowd around.

KLEONIKE
And those goddamned holy owls![49]All night long,
tu-wit, tu-wu—they're hooting me into my grave!
LYSISTRATA
Darlings, let's call a halt to this hocus-pocus. You
miss your men—now isn't that the trouble?

Shamefaced nods from the group.

Don't you think they miss you just as much?
I can assure you, their nights are every bit
as hard as yours. So be good girls; endure!
Persist a few days more, and Victory is ours.
It's fated: a current prophecy declares that the men
will go down to defeat before us, provided that *we*
maintain a United Front.

[48]A snake, never actually seen, was mythically associated with the cult of Athene as guardian of the Akropolis.
[49]Birds sacred to Athene.

Producing a scroll.

I happen to have a copy of
the prophecy.

KLEONIKE

Read it!

LYSISTRATA

Silence, *please*:

Reading from the scroll.

But when the swallows, in flight from the
    hoopoes,[50] have flocked to a hole
on high, and stoutly eschew their
    accustomed perch on the pole,
yea, then shall Thunderer Zeus to
    their suff'ring establish a stop,
by making the lower the upper . . .

KLEONIKE

Then *we'll* be lying on top?

LYSISTRATA

But should these swallows, indulging their
    lust for the perch, lose heart,
dissolve their flocks in winged dissension,
    and singly depart
the sacred stronghold, breaking the
    bands that bind them together—
then know them as lewd, the pervertedest
    birds that ever wore feather.

KLEONIKE

There's nothing obscure about *that* oracle. Ye gods!

LYSISTRATA

Sorely beset as we are, we must not flag or falter. So
back to the citadel!

As the women troop inside.

And if we fail that oracle,
darlings, our image is absolutely *mud!*

[50]A family of birds, here identified with the male sex.

She follows them in. A pause, and the Choruses assemble.

CHORUS OF MEN

I have a simple
tale to relate you
a sterling example
of masculine virtue:

The huntsman bold Melanion
was once a harried quarry.
The women in town tracked him down
and badgered him to marry.

Melanion knew the cornered male
eventually cohabits.
Assessing the odds, he took to the woods
and lived by trapping rabbits.

He stuck to the virgin stand, sustained
by rabbit meat and hate,
and never returned, but ever remained
an alfresco celibate.

Melanion is our ideal;
his loathing makes us free.
Our dearest aim is the gemlike flame
of his misogyny.[51]

OLD MAN

Let me kiss that wizened cheek. . . .

OLD WOMAN

Threatening with a fist.

A wish too rash for that withered flesh.

OLD MAN

and lay you low with a highflying kick.

He tries one and misses.

[51]Hatred for women.

OLD WOMAN

       Exposing an overgrown underbrush.

OLD MAN

A hairy behind, historically, means
    masculine force: Myronides
harassed the foe with his mighty mane,
    and furry Phormion swept the seas
       of enemy ships, never meeting his match—
        such was the nature of his thatch.

CHORUS OF WOMEN

            I offer an anecdote
            for your opinion,
            an adequate antidote
            for your Melanion:

            Timon, the noted local grouch,
            put rusticating hermits
out of style by building his wilds
            inside the city limits.

            He shooed away society
            with natural battlements:
his tongue was edgèd; his shoulder, frigid;
            his beard, a picket fence.

            When random contacts overtaxed him,
            he didn't stop to pack,
but loaded curses on the male of the species,
            left town, and never came back.

            Timon, you see, was a misanthrope[52]
            in a properly narrow sense:
his spleen was vented only on men . . .
            we were his dearest friends.

OLD WOMAN

Making a fist.

            Enjoy a chop to that juiceless chin?

[52]Hater of men.

OLD MAN

Backing away.

>   I'm jolted already. Thank you, no.

OLD WOMAN
>   Perhaps a trip from a well-turned shin?

She tries a kick and misses.

OLD MAN
>   Brazenly baring the mantrap below.

OLD WOMAN
At least it's *neat*. I'm not too sorry
>   to have you see my daintiness.
My habits are still depilatory;
>   age hasn't made me a bristly mess.
>   Secure in my smoothness, I'm never in
doubt—
>   though even down is out.

Lysistrata mounts the platform and scans the horizon. When her gaze reaches the left, she stops suddenly.

LYSISTRATA
Ladies, attention! Battle stations, please!
And quickly!

A general rush of women to the battlements.

KLEONIKE
>   What is it?

MYRRHINE
>   What's all the shouting for?

LYSISTRATA
A MAN!

Consternation.

>   Yes, it's a man. And he's coming this way!
Hmm. Seems to have suffered a seizure. Broken out
with a nasty attack of love.

Prayer, aside

> O Aphrodite,
> Mistress all-victorious,
> mysterious, voluptuous,
> you who make the crooked straight . . .
> don't let this happen to US!

KLEONIKE
I don't care who he is—*where is he?*
LYSISTRATA

Pointing.

> Down there—
> just flanking that temple—Demeter the Fruitful.

KLEONIKE

> My.

Definitely a man.
MYRRHINE

Craning for a look.

> I wonder who it can be?

LYSISTRATA
See for yourselves.—Can anyone identify him?
MYRRHINE
Oh lord, I can.

> *That* is my husband—Kinesias.

LYSISTRATA

To Myrrhine.

> Your duty is clear.
> Pop him on the griddle, twist the
spit, braize him, baste him, stew him in his own
juice, do him to a turn. Sear him with kisses,
coyness, caresses, *everything*—
> but stop where Our
Oath begins.

MYRRHINE
> Relax. I can take care of this.

LYSISTRATA

Of course
you can, dear. Still, a little help can't hurt, now can
it? I'll just stay around for a bit and—er—poke up
the fire.

—Everyone else inside!

*Exit all the women but Lysistrata, on the platform, and Myrrhine, who stands near
the Akropolis entrance, hidden from her husband's view. Kinesias staggers on, in
erection and considerable pain, followed by a male slave who carries a baby boy.*

KINESIAS
OUCH!

Omigod.
Hypertension, twinges. . . . I can't hold out much
more. I'd rather be dismembered.

How long, ye gods,

how long?
LYSISTRATA

Officially.

WHO GOES THERE?

WHO PENETRATES OUR
POSITIONS?
KINESIAS
Me.
LYSISTRATA
A Man?
KINESEAS
Every inch.
LYSISTRATA
Then inch yourself out of
here. Off Limits to Men.
KINESIAS
This *is* the limit.
Just who are *you* to throw me out?
LYSISTRATA
The Lookout.
KINESIAS
Well, look here, Lookout. I'd like to see Myrrhine.
How's the outlook?

LYSISTRATA

                    Unlikely. Bring Myrrhine to
you? The idea!

                    Just by the by, who are you?

KINESIAS

A private citizen. Her husband, Kinesias.

LYSISTRATA

                                        No!
Meeting you—I'm overcome!

                    Your name, you
know, is not without its fame among us girls.

Aside.

—Matter of fact, we have a name for *it*.—
I swear, you're never out of Myrrhine's mouth.
She won't even nibble a quince, or swallow an egg,
without reciting, "Here's to Kinesias!"

KINESIAS

                            For god's

sake,
will you . . .

LYSISTRATA

Sweeping on over his agony.

                    Word of honor, it's true. Why, when we
discuss our husbands (you know how women are),
Myrrhine refuses to argue. She simply insists:
"Compared with Kinesias, the rest have *nothing!*"
Imagine!

KINESIAS

Bring her out here!

LYSISTRATA

                    Really? And what would I get out
of this?

KINESIAS

        You see my situation. I'll raise whatever I can.
This can all be yours.

LYSISTRATA

                    Goodness.
It's really her place. I'll go and get her.

She descends from the platform and moves to Myrrhine, out of Kinesias' sight.

KINESIAS

                              Speed!
—Life is a husk. She left our home, and happiness
went with her. Now pain is the tenant. Oh, to enter
that wifeless house, to sense that awful emptiness, to
eat that tasteless, joyless food—it makes it hard, I tell
you.

          Harder all the time.

MYRRHINE

Still out of his sight, in a voice to be overheard.

Oh, I *do* love him! I'm mad about him! But he
doesn't want my love. Please don't make me see
him.

KINESIAS

Myrrhine darling, why do you *act* this way? Come
down here!

MYRRHINE

Appearing at the wall.

                    Down there? Certainly not!

KINESIAS

It's me, Myrrhine. I'm begging you. Please come
down.

MYRRHINE

I don't see why you're begging me. You don't need
me.

KINESIAS

I don't need you? I'm at the end **of** my rope!

MYRRHINE

I'm leaving.

She turns. Kinesias grabs the boy from the slave.

KINESIAS

                    No! Wait! At least you'll have to listen to
the voice of your child.

To the boy, in a fierce undertone.

—(Call your mother!)

Silence.

. . . to
the voice of your very own child . . .

—(Call your
mother, brat!)

CHILD
MOMMYMOMMYMOMMY!

KINESIAS
Where's your maternal instinct? He hasn't been
washed or fed for a week. How can you be so
pitiless?

MYRRHINE
Him I pity. Of all the pitiful excuses
for a father. . . .

KINESIAS
Come down here, dear. For the
baby's sake.

MYRRHINE
Motherhood! I'll have to come. I've got no choice.

KINESIAS

Soliloquizing as she descends.

It may be me, but I'll swear she looks years
younger—and gentler—her eyes caress me. And
then they flash: that anger, that verve, that high-and-
mighty air! She's fire, she's ice—and I'm stuck right
in the middle.

MYRRHINE

Taking the baby.

Sweet babykins with such a nasty daddy!
Here, let Mummy kissums. Mummy's little darling.

KINESIAS

The injured husband.

You should be ashamed of yourself, letting those women lead you around. Why do you DO these things? You only make me suffer and hurt your poor, sweet self.

MYRRHINE

Keep your hands away from me!

KINESIAS

But the house, the furniture, everything we own— you're letting it go to hell!

MYRRHINE

Frankly, I couldn't care less.

KINESIAS

But your weaving's unraveled—the loom is full of chickens! You couldn't care less about *that?*

MYRRHINE

I certainly couldn't.

KINESIAS

And the holy rites of Aphrodite?[53] Think how long that's been.

Come on, darling, let's go home.

MYRRHINE

I absolutely refuse!

Unless you agree to a truce to stop the war.

KINESIAS

Well, then, if that's your decision, we'll STOP the war.

MYRRHINE

Well, then, if that's your decision, I'll come back—*after* it's done.

But, for the present, I've sworn off.

KINESIAS

At least lie down for a minute. We'll talk.

[53]That is, the act of lovemaking.

MYRRHINE

       I know what you're up to—NO!
—And yet . . . I really can't say I don't love you . . .

KINESIAS

                        You

love me?
So what's the trouble? *Lie down.*

MYRRHINE

                Don't be disgusting.

In front of the baby?

KINESIAS

            Er . . . no. Heaven Forfend.

Taking the baby and pushing it at the slave.

       —Take this home.

The slave obeys.

            —Well, darling, we're rid of the
kid . . . let's go to bed!

MYRRHINE

          Poor dear.
                 But where does one
do this sort of thing?

KINESIAS

            Where? All we need is a little
nook. . . . We'll try Pan's grotto. Excellent spot.

MYRRHINE

With a nod at the Akropolis.

       I'll have to be pure to get back in *there*. How can I
expunge my pollution?

KINESIAS

             Sponge off in the pool next
door.

MYRRHINE

I did swear an Oath. I'm supposed to perjure myself?

KINESIAS

Bother the Oath. Forget it—I'll take the blame.

A pause.

> **MYRRHINE**
> Now I'll go get us a cot.
> **KINESIAS**
>   No! Not a cot!
> The ground's enough for us.
> **MYRRHINE**
>   *I'll get the cot.*
> For all your faults, I refuse to put you to bed in the
> dirt.

She exits to the Akropolis.

> **KINESIAS**
>   She certainly loves me. That's nice to know.
> **MYRRHINE**

Returning with a rope-tied cot.

> Here. You hurry to bed while I undress.

Kinesias lies down.

> Gracious me—I forgot. We need a mattress.
> **KINESIAS**
> Who wants a mattress? Not me!
> **MYRRHINE**
>   Oh, yes, you do.
> It's perfectly squalid on the ropes.
> **KINESIAS**
>   Well, give me a
> kiss to tide me over.
> **MYRRHINE**
>   *Voilà.*

She pecks at him and leaves.

> **KINESIAS**
>   OoolaLAlala!
> —Make it a quick trip, dear.

MYRRHINE

Entering with the mattress, she waves Kinesias off the cot and lays the mattress on it.

Here we are.
Our mattress. Now hurry to bed while I undress.

Kinesias lies down again.

Gracious me—I forgot. You don't have a pillow.
KINESIAS
I do *not* need a pillow.
MYRRHINE

I know, but *I* do.

She leaves.

KINESIAS
What a lovefeast! Only the table gets laid.
MYRRHINE

Returning with a pillow.

Rise and shine!

Kinesias jumps up. She places the pillow.

And now I have everything I need.
KINESIAS

Lying down again.

You certainly do.
Come here, my little jewelbox!
MYRRHINE
Just taking off my bra.
Don't break your promise: no
cheating about the Peace.
KINESIAS
I swear to god, I'll die first!
MYRRHINE

Coming to him.

Just
look. You don't have a blanket.

KINESIAS
I didn't plan to go camping—I want to make love!
MYRRHINE
Relax. You'll get your love. I'll be right back.

She leaves.

KINESIAS
Relax? I'm dying a slow death by dry goods!
MYRRHINE

Returning with the blanket.

Get up!

KINESIAS

Getting out of bed.

I've been up for hours. I was up before I was up.

Myrrhine spreads the blanket on the mattress, and he lies down again.

MYRRHINE
I presume you want perfume?
KINESIAS
Positively NO!
MYRRHINE
Absolutely yes—whether you want it or not.

She leaves.

KINESIAS
Dear Zeus, I don't ask for much—but please let her
spill it.
MYRRHINE

Returning with a bottle.

Hold out your hand like a good boy.
Now rub it in.

KINESIAS

Obeying and sniffing.

> *This* is to quicken desire? Too strong. It grabs your
> nose and bawls out: *Try again tomorrow.*
> MYRRHINE
> I'm *awful!* I brought you that rancid Rhodian brand.

She starts off with the bottle.

> KINESIAS
> This is just *lovely*. Leave it, woman!
> MYRRHINE
> > > Silly!

She leaves.

> KINESIAS
> God damn the clod who first concocted perfume!
> MYRRHINE

Returning with another bottle.

> Here, try this flask.
> KINESIAS
> > > Thanks—but you try mine.
> Come to bed, you witch—
> > > *and please stop bringing*
> *things!*
> MYRRHINE
> > *That* is exactly what I'll do.
> There go my shoes.
> > > Incidentally, darling, you *will*
> remember to vote for the truce?
> KINESIAS
> > > I'LL THINK IT
> OVER!

Myrrhine runs off for good.

> That woman's laid me waste—destroyed me, root
> and branch!

I'm scuttled,
                    gutted,
                              up the spout!
And Myrrhine's gone!

In a parody of tragic style

Out upon't! But how? But where?
Now I have lost the fairest fair,
how screw my courage to yet another
sticking-place? Aye, there's the rub—
And yet, this wagging, wanton babe
must soon be laid to rest, or else . . .
Ho Pandar![54]
                         Pandar!

I'd hire a nurse.

KORYPHAIOS OF MEN

Grievous your bereavement, cruel
the slow tabescence[55]of your soul.
I bid my liquid pity mingle.

Oh, where the soul, and where, alack!
the cod to stand the taut attack
of swollen prides, the scorching tensions
that ravine up the lumbar regions?
         His morning lay
         has gone astray.

KINESIAS

In agony.

O Zeus, reduce the throbs, the throes!

KORYPHAIOS OF MEN

I turn my tongue to curse the cause
of your affliction—that jade, that slut,
that hag, that ogress . . .

---

[54]The translator has here adapted the common Greek name Pandaros whose English form ("pander") means "pimp."

[55]Wasting away.

KINESIAS

No! Slight not
my light-o'-love, my dove, my sweet!

KORYPHAIOS OF MEN

Sweet!

O Zeus who rul'st the sky,
snatch that slattern up on high,
crack thy winds, unleash thy thunder,
tumble her over, trundle her under,
juggle her from hand to hand;
twirl her ever near the ground—
drop her in a well-aimed fall
on our comrade's tool!

That's all.

Kinesias exits left.
A Spartan herald enters from the right, holding his cloak together in a futile attempt to conceal his condition.

HERALD

This Athens? Where-all kin I find the Council of
Elders or else the Executive Board? I brung some
news.

The Commissioner, swathed in his cloak, enters from the left.

COMMISSIONER

And what are you—a man? a signpost? a joint-stock
company?

HERALD

A herald, sonny, a honest-to-Kastor[56]
herald. I come to chat 'bout thet-there truce.

COMMISSIONER

. . . carrying a concealed weapon? Pretty
underhanded.

HERALD

Twisting to avoid the Commissioner's direct gaze.

[56]A son of Zeus.

Hain't done no sech a thang!
COMMISSIONER

                                Very well, stand
still. Your cloak's out of crease—hernia? Are the
roads that bad?
SPARTAN
I swear this feller's plumb tetched in the haid!
COMMISSIONER

Throwing open the Spartan's cloak, exposing the phallus.

                                                    You
clown, you've got an erection!
SPARTAN

Wildly embarrassed.

                                Hain't got no sech a
thang!
You stop this–hyer foolishment!
COMMISSIONER

                                What *have* you got
there, then?
SPARTAN
Thet-thur's a Spartan epistle. In code.[57]
COMMISSIONER

                                                I have the
key.

Throwing open his cloak.

Behold another Spartan epistle. In code.

Tiring of teasing.

Let's get down to cases. I know the score, so tell me
the truth.
                    How are things with you in Sparta?

---

[57]For their coded communications the Spartans inscribed their messages on a leather strip
wound around a slender rod. When the strip was delivered, it had to be wound around
a rod identical in size and shape—or else the message would appear to be a meaningless
collection of letters.

HERALD

Thangs is up in the air. The whole Alliance is purt-
near 'bout to explode. We-uns'll need barrels, 'stead
of women.

COMMISSIONER

What was the cause of this outburst?
The great god Pan?[58]

HERALD

Nope. I'll lay 'twere Lampito,
most likely. She begun, and then they was off and
runnin' at the post in a bunch, every last little gal in
Sparta, drivin' their menfolk away from the winner's
circle.

COMMISSIONER

How are you taking this?

HERALD

Painful-like.
Everyone's doubled up worse as a midget nursin' a
wick in a midnight wind come moon-dark time.
Cain't even tetch them little old gals on the moosey
without we all agree to a Greece-wide Peace.

COMMISSIONER

Of course!
A universal female plot—all Hellas risen
in rebellion—I should have known!
Return
to Sparta with this request:
Have them despatch us a
Plenipotentiary Commission, fully empowered to
conclude an armistice. I have full confidence that I
can persuade our Senate to do the same, without
extending myself. The evidence is at hand.

HERALD

I'm a-flyin', Sir! I hev never heered your equal!

Exeunt hurriedly, the Commissioner to the left, the Herald to the right.

KORYPHAIOS OF MEN

The most unnerving work of nature,

[58]The woodland god, Pan, sometimes caused fits of madness or "panic"—which might
also be expressed as fits of sexual excess.

the pride of applied immorality,
is the common female human.
No fire can match, no beast can best her.
O Unsurmountability,
thy name—worse luck—is Woman.

KORYPHAIOS OF WOMEN

After such knowledge, why persist
in wearing out this feckless
war between the sexes?
When can I apply for the post
of ally, partner, and general friend?

KORYPHAIOS OF MEN

I won't be ployed to revise, re-do,
amend, extend, or bring to an end
my irreversible credo:
Misogyny Forever!
—The answer's never.

KORYPHAIOS OF WOMEN

All right. Whenever you choose.
But, for the present, I refuse
to let you look your absolute worst,
parading around like an unfrocked freak:
I'm coming over and get you dressed.

She dresses him in his tunic, an action (like others in this scene) imitated by the members of the Chorus of Women toward their opposite members in the Chorus of Men.

KORYPHAIOS OF MEN

This seems sincere. It's not a trick.
Recalling the rancor with which I stripped,
I'm overlaid with chagrin.

KORYPHAIOS OF WOMEN

Now you resemble a man,
not some ghastly practical joke.
And if you show me a little respect
(and promise not to kick), I'll extract
the beast in you.

KORYPHAIOS OF MEN

Searching himself.

>   What beast in me?

KORYPHAIOS OF WOMEN
>   That insect. There. The bug that's stuck in your
>   eye.

KORYPHAIOS OF MEN

Playing along dubiously.

>   This gnat?

KORYPHAIOS OF WOMEN
>   Yes, nitwit!

KORYPHAIOS OF MEN
>   Of course.
>   That steady, festering agony. . . .
>   You've put your finger on the source
>   of all my lousy troubles. Please
>   roll back the lid and scoop it out.
>   I'd like to see it.

KORYPHAIOS OF WOMEN
>   All right, I'll do it.

Removing the imaginary insect.

>   Although, of all the impossible cranks. . . .
>   Do you sleep in a swamp? Just look at this.
>   I've never seen a bigger chigger.

KORYPHAIOS OF MEN
>   Thanks.
>   Your kindness touches me deeply. For years,
>   that thing's been sinking wells in my eye.
>   Now you've unplugged me. Here come the tears.

KORYPHAIOS OF WOMEN
>   I'll dry your tears, though I can't say why.

Wiping away the tears.

>   Of all the irresponsible boys. . . .
>   *And* I'll kiss you.

KORYPHAIOS OF MEN

Don't you kiss me!

KORYPHAIOS OF WOMEN

What made you think you had a choice?

She kisses him.

KORYPHAIOS OF MEN

All right, damn you, that's enough of that ingrained
palaver.
I can't dispute the truth or logic of the pithy old
proverb:

Life with women is hell.
Life without women is hell, too.

And so we conclude a truce with you, on the
following terms: in future, a mutual moratorium on
mischief in all its forms. Agreed?—Let's make a
single chorus and start our song.

The two Choruses unite and face the audience.

CHORUS OF MEN

We're not about to introduce
the standard personal abuse—
    the Choral Smear
Of Present Persons (usually,
in every well-made comedy,
    inserted here).
Instead, in deed and utterance, we
shall now indulge in philanthropy
    because we feel
that members of the audience
endure, in the course of current events,
    sufficient hell.
Therefore, friends, be rich! Be flush!
Apply to us, and borrow cash
    in large amounts.
The Treasury stands behind us—there—
and we can personally take care
    of small accounts.

Drop up today. Your credit's good.
Your loan won't have to be repaid
    in full until
the war is over. And then, your debt
is only the money you actually get—
    nothing at all.

CHORUS OF WOMEN

Just when we meant to entertain
some madcap gourmets from out of town
    —such flawless taste!—
the present unpleasantness intervened,
and now we fear the feast we planned
    will go to waste.
The soup is waiting, rich and thick;
I've sacrificed a suckling pig
    —the pièce de résistance—
whose toothsome cracklings should amaze
the most fastidious gourmets—
    you, for instance.
To everybody here, I say
take potluck at my house today
    with me and mine.
Bathe and change as fast as you can,
bring the children, hurry down,
    and walk right in.
Don't bother to knock. No need at all.
My house is yours. Liberty Hall.
    What are friends for?
Act self-possessed when you come over;
it may help out when you discover
    I've locked the door.

A delegation of Spartans enters from the right, with difficulty. They have removed their cloaks, but hold them before themselves in an effort to conceal their condition.

KORYPHAIOS OF MEN

What's this? Behold the Spartan ambassadors,
    dragging their beards,
pussy-footing along. It appears they've developed
    a hitch in the crotch.

Advancing to greet them.

> Men of Sparta, I bid you welcome!
>   And now
> to the point: What predicament brings you among
> us?
> SPARTAN
> We-uns is up a stump. Hain't fit fer chatter.

Flipping aside his cloak.

> Here's our predicament. Take a look for yourselfs.
> KORYPHAIOS OF MEN
> Well, I'll be damned—a regular disaster area.
> Inflamed. I imagine the temperature's rather intense?
> SPARTAN
> Hit ain't the heat, hit's the tumidity.
>   But words
> won't help what ails us. We-uns come after Peace.
> Peace from any person, at any price.

*Enter the Athenian delegation from the left, led by Kinesias. They are wearing
cloaks, but are obviously in as much travail as the Spartans.*

> KORYPHAIOS OF MEN
> Behold our local Sons of the Soil, stretching their
> garments away from their groins, like wrestlers.
> Grappling with their plight. Some sort of athlete's
> disease, no doubt. An outbreak of epic proportions.
>   Athlete's foot?
> No. Could it be athlete's . . . ?
> KINESIAS

Breaking in.

>   Who can tell us how
> to get hold of Lysistrata? We've come as delegates to
> the Sexual Congress.

Opening his cloak.

>   Here are our credentials.

KORYPHAIOS OF MEN

Ever the scientist, looking from the Athenians to the Spartans and back again.

>The words are different, but the malady seems the same.

To Kinesias.

>Dreadful disease. When the crisis reaches its height, what do you take for it?

KINESIAS

>   Whatever comes to hand.
>But now we've reached the bitter end. It's Peace or we fall back on Kleisthenes.
>   And he's got a waiting list.

KORYPHAIOS OF MEN

To the Spartans.

>Take my advice and put your clothes on. If someone from that self-appointed Purity League comes by, you may be docked. They do it to the statues of Hermes, they'll do it to you.[59]

KINESIAS

Since he has not yet noticed the Spartans, he interprets the warning as meant for him, and hurriedly pulls his cloak together, as do the other Athenians.

>Excellent advice.

SPARTAN

>   Hit shorely is.
>Hain't nothing to argue after. Let's git dressed.

As they put on their cloaks, the Spartans are finally noticed by Kinesias.

---

[59]Squared stone posts with the head and phallus of Hermes, messenger of the gods, were set up at Athenian street intersections and in front of houses. The sacrilegious mutilation of these statues by unknown persons, just before the sailing of the Sicilian expedition, had caused great consternation among the citizens and disruption among the leadership.

KINESIAS

Welcome, men of Sparta! This is a shameful disgrace to masculine honor.

SPARTAN

Hit could be worser.

Ef them Herm–choppers seed us all fired up, they'd *really* take us down a peg or two.

KINESIAS

Gentlemen, let's descend to details. Specifically, why are you here?

SPARTAN

Ambassadors. We come to dicker 'bout thet-thur Peace.

KINESIAS

Perfect! Precisely our purpose. Let's send for Lysistrata. Only she can reconcile our differences. There'll be no Peace for us without her.

SPARTAN

We-uns ain't fussy. Call Lysistratos, too, if you want.

The gates to the Akropolis open, and Lysistrata emerges, accompanied by her handmaid, Peace—a beautiful girl without a stitch on. Peace remains out of sight by the gates until summoned.

KORYPHAIOS OF MEN

Hail, most virile of women! Summon up all your experience:

Be terrible and tender,

lofty and lowbrow,

severe and

demure.

Here stand the Leaders of Greece, enthralled by your charm.

They yield the floor to you and submit their claims for your

arbitration.

LYSISTRATA

Really, it shouldn't be difficult, if I can catch them all bothered, before they start to solicit each other. I'll find out soon enough. Where's Peace?

—Come here.

Peace moves from her place by the gates to Lysistrata. The delegations goggle at her.

> Now, dear, first get those Spartans and bring them to
> me. Take them by the hand, but don't be pushy
> about it, not like our husbands (no savoir-faire[60] at
> all!).
> Be a lady, be proper, do just what you'd do at home:
> if hands are refused, conduct them by the handle.

Peace leads the Spartans to a position near Lysistrata.

> And now a hand to the Athenians—it doesn't matter
> where; accept any offer—and bring *them* over.

Peace conducts the Athenians to a position near Lysistrata, opposite the Spartans.

> You Spartans move up closer—right *here*—

To the Athenians.

>   and *you*
> stand over *here*.
>   —And now attend my speech.

This the delegations do with some difficulty, because of the conflicting attractions of Peace, who is standing beside her mistress.

> I am a woman—but not without some wisdom:
> my native wit is not completely negligible,
> and I've listened long and hard to the discourse of
> my elders—my education is not entirely despicable.
>   Well,
> now that I've got you, I intend to give you hell,
> and I'm perfectly right. Consider your actions:
>   At
> festivals, in Pan-Hellenic harmony, like true blood-
> brothers, you share the selfsame basin of holy water,
> and sprinkle altars all over Greece—Olympia,
> Delphoi, Thermopylai . . . (I could go on and on, if
> length were my only object.)
>   But now, when the
> Persians sit by and wait, in the very presence of your

[60]Sophistication (literally, in French, "knowing how to do").

enemies, you fight each other, destroy *Greek* men,
destroy *Greek* cities!
—Point One of my address is now concluded.
KINESIAS

Gazing at Peace.

I'm destroyed, if this is drawn out much longer!
LYSISTRATA

Serenely unconscious of the interruption.

—Men of Sparta, I direct these remarks to you. Have
you forgotten that a Spartan suppliant once came
to beg assistance from Athens? Recall Perikleidas:
Fifty years ago, he clung to our altar,
his face dead-white above his crimson robe, and
pleaded for an army. Messene was pressing you hard
in revolt, and to this upheaval, Poseidon, the
Earthshaker, added another.
       But Kimon took four thousand troops from
Athens—an army which saved the state of Sparta.
Such treatment have you received at the hands of
Athens, you who devastate the country that came to
your aid!
KINESIAS

Stoutly; the condemnation of his enemy has made him forget the girl momentarily.

You're right, Lysistrata. The Spartans are clearly in
the wrong!
SPARTAN

Guiltily backing away from Peace, whom he has attempted to pat.

Hit's wrong, I reckon, but that's the purtiest
behind . . .
LYSISTRATA

Turning to the Athenians.

—Men of Athens, do you think I'll let *you* off?

Have you forgotten the Tyrant's days, [61]when you wore the smock of slavery, when the Spartans turned to the spear, cut down the pride of Thessaly, despatched the friends of tyranny, and dispossessed your oppressors?

Recall:

On that great day, your only allies were Spartans; your liberty came at their hands, which stripped away your servile garb and clothed you again in Freedom!

SPARTAN

Indicating Lysistrata.

Hain't never seed no higher type of woman.

KINESIAS

Indicating Peace.

Never saw one I wanted so much to top.

LYSISTRATA

Oblivious to the byplay, addressing both groups.

With such a history of mutual benefits conferred and received, why are you fighting? Stop this wickedness! Come to terms with each other! What prevents you?

SPARTAN

We'd a heap sight druther make Peace, if we was indemnified with a plumb strategic location.

Pointing at Peace's rear.

We'll

take thet butte.

LYSISTRATA

Butte?

---

[61]The reign of the tyrant Hippias; he was expelled by the Athenians in 510 B.C. with the help of the Spartans who defeated Hippias' Thessalian allies.

SPARTAN

> The Promontory of Pylos[62]—Sparta's Back Door. We've missed it fer a turrible spell.

Reaching.

> Hev to keep our hand in.

KINESIAS

Pushing him away.

> The price is too high—you'll never take that!

LYSISTRATA

Oh, let them have it.

KINESIAS

> What room will we have left for maneuvers?

LYSISTRATA

> Demand another spot in exchange.

KINESIAS

Surveying Peace like a map as he addresses the Spartan.

> Then you hand over to us—uh, let me see—let's try Thessaly—

Indicating the relevant portions of Peace.

> First of all, Easy Mountain . . . then the Maniac Gulf behind it . . .
>
> and down to Megara for the legs . . .

SPARTAN

> You cain't take all of thet! Yore plumb out of yore mind!

---

[62]Pylos was once Spartan territory, held during the war by the Athenians. (The geographical references in this exchange correspond to portions of the anatomy of the young lady, Peace.)

LYSISTRATA

To Kinesias.

> Don't argue. Let the legs go.

Kinesias nods. A pause. General smiles of agreement.

KINESIAS

Doffing his cloak.

> I feel an urgent desire to plow a few furrows.

SPARTAN

Doffing his cloak.

> Hit's time to work a few loads of fertilizer in.

LYSISTRATA

Conclude the treaty and the simple life is yours. If such is your decision, convene your councils, and then deliberate the matter with your allies.

KINESIAS

Deliberate? Allies?

> We're over-extended already! Wouldn't every ally approve of our position—*Union Now?*

SPARTAN

> I know I kin speak for ourn.

KINESIAS

And I for ours.

> They're just a bunch of gigolos.

LYSISTRATA

I heartily approve.

> Now first attend to your purification, then we, the women, will welcome you to the Citadel and treat you to all the delights of a home-cooked banquet. Then you'll exchange your oaths and pledge your faith, and every man of you will take his wife and depart for home.

Lysistrata and Peace enter the Akropolis.

KINESIAS

> Let's hurry!

SPARTAN

Lead

on, everwhich way's yore pleasure.

KINESIAS

This way, then—

and HURRY!

The delegations exeunt at a run.

CHORUS OF WOMEN

I'd never stint on anybody.
And now I include, in my boundless bounty,
    the younger set.
Attention, you parents of teenage girls
about to debut in the social whirl.
    Here's what you get:
Embroidered linens, lush brocades,
a huge assortment of ready-mades,
    from mantles to shifts;
plus bracelets and bangles of solid gold—
every item my wardrobe holds—
    absolute gifts!
Don't miss this offer. Come to my place,
barge right in, and make your choice.
    You can't refuse.
Everything there must go today.
Finders keepers—cart it away!
    How can you lose?
Don't spare me. Open all the locks.
Break every seal. Empty every box.
    Keep ferreting—
And your sight's considerably better than mine
if you should possibly chance to find
    a single thing.

CHORUS OF MEN

Troubles, friend? Too many mouths
to feed, and not a scrap in the house
    to see you through?
Faced with starvation? Don't give it a thought
Pay attention; I'll tell you what
    I'm gonna do.

I overbought. I'm overstocked.
Every room in my house is clogged
   with flour (best ever),
glutted with luscious loaves whose size you
wouldn't believe. I need the space;
   do me a favor:
Bring gripsacks, knapsacks, duffle bags,
pitchers, cisterns, buckets, and kegs
   around to me.
A courteous servant will see to your needs;
he'll fill them up with A-1 wheat—
   and all for free!
—Oh. Just one final word before
you turn your steps to my front door:
   I happen to own
a dog. Tremendous animal.
Can't stand a leash. And bites like hell—
   better stay home.

The united Chorus flocks to the door of the Akropolis.

KORYPHAIOS OF MEN

Banging at the door.

      Hey, open up in there!

The door opens, and the Commissioner appears. He wears a wreath, carries a torch, and is slightly drunk. He addresses the Koryphaios.

COMMISSIONER
                    You know the Regulations.
Move along!

He sees the entire Chorus.

            —And why are YOU lounging around?
I'll wield my trusty torch and scorch the lot!

The Chorus backs away in mock horror. He stops and looks at his torch.

      —*This* is the bottom of the barrel. A cheap
burlesque bit. I refuse to do it. I have my pride.

With a start, he looks at the audience, as though hearing a protest. He shrugs and addresses the audience.

—No choice, eh?
Well, if that's the way it is, we'll take the trouble.
Anything to keep you happy.

The Chorus advances eagerly

KORYPHAIOS OF MEN

Don't forget us!
We're in this, too. Your trouble is ours!

COMMISSIONER

Resuming his character and jabbing with his torch at the Chorus.

Keep
moving!
Last man out of the way goes home without hair!
Don't block the exit. Give the Spartans some room.
They've dined in comfort; let them go home in
peace.

The Chorus shrinks back from the door. Kinesias, wreathed and quite drunk, appears at the door. He speaks his first speech in Spartan.

KINESIAS
Hain't never seed sech a spread! Hit were
splendiferous!

COMMISSIONER
I gather the Spartans won friends and influenced
people?

KINESIAS
And *we've* never been so brilliant. It was the wine.

COMMISSIONER
Precisely.
The reason? A sober Athenian is just *non
compos.*[63] If I can carry a little proposal I have in

---

[63]Latin: *non compos mentis*: "not of sound mind."

mind, our Foreign Service will flourish, guided by this rational rule:

No Ambassador Without a Skinful [*of wine*].

Reflect on our past performance:
Down to a Spartan parley we troop, in a state of disgusting sobriety, looking for trouble. It muddles our senses: we read between the lines; we hear, not what the Spartans say, but what we suspect they might have been about to be going to say. We bring back paranoid reports—cheap fiction, the fruit of temperance. Cold-water diplomacy, pah!

Contrast this evening's total pleasure, the free-and-easy give-and-take of friendship: If we were singing,

Just Kleitagora and me,
Alone in Thessaly,

and someone missed his cue and cut in loudly,

Ajax, son of Telamon,
He was one hell of a man—

no one took it amiss, or started a war;
we clapped him on the back and gave three cheers.

During this recital, the Chorus has sidled up to the door.

—Dammit, are you back here again?

Waving his torch

Scatter!
Get out of the road! Gangway, you gallowsbait!
KINESIAS
Yes, everyone out of the way. They're coming out.

Through the door emerge the Spartan delegation, a flutist, the Athenian delegation, Lysistrata, Kleonike, Myrrhine, and the rest of the women from the citadel, both Athenian and Peloponnesian. The Chorus splits into its male and female components and draws to the sides to give the procession room.

SPARTAN

To the flutist.

Friend and kinsman, take up them pipes a yourn. I'd
like fer to shuffle a bit and sing a right sweet song in
honor of Athens and us'uns, too.

COMMISSIONER

To the flutist.

Marvelous, marvelous—come, take up your pipes!

To the Spartan.

I certainly love to see you Spartans dance.

The flutist plays, and the Spartan begins a slow dance.

SPARTAN

Memory
send me
your Muse,
who knows
our glory,
knows Athens'—
Tell the story:
At Artemision[64]
like gods, they stampeded
the hulks of the Medes, and
beat them.

And Leonidas[65]
leading us—
the wild boars
whetting their tusks.
And the foam flowered,
flowered and flowed,
down our cheeks
to our knees below.

[64]Site of a sea battle in 480 B.C. in which the Athenians defeated the invading Persians.

[65]Spartan king and general who, with 300 of his infantry, fought to the death to hold the
pass at Thermopylae (in central Greece) against a vast Persian army. (See pp. 141–48.)

The Persians there
like the sands of the sea—

Hither, huntress,
virgin, goddess,[66]
tracker, slayer,
to our truce!
Hold us ever
fast together;
bring our pledges
love and increase;
wean us from the
fox's wiles—

Hither, huntress!
Virgin, hither!

LYSISTRATA

Surveying the assemblage with a proprietary air.

Well, the preliminaries are over—very nicely, too.
So, Spartans,

Indicating the Peloponnesian women who have been hostages.

take these girls back home. And *you*

To the Athenian delegation, indicating the women from the Akropolis.

take *these* girls. Each man stand by his wife, each
wife by her husband. Dance to the gods' glory, and
thank them for the happy ending. And, from now
on, please be careful. Let's not make the same
mistakes again.

The delegations obey; the men and women of the chorus join again for a rapid ode.

CHORUS

Start the chorus dancing,
Summon all the Graces,

[66]Artemis.

Send a shout to Artemis in invocation.
>Call upon her brother,
>healer, chorus master,
Call the blazing Bacchos, with his maddened
>muster.

Call the flashing, fiery Zeus, and
call his mighty, blessed spouse, and
call the gods, call all the gods,
to witness now and not forget
our gentle, blissful Peace—the gift,
>the deed of Aphrodite,
>>Ai!
>Alalai!   Paion!
>Leap you!   Paion!
>Victory!   Alalai!
Hail!   Hail!   Hail!

LYSISTRATA
Spartan, let's have another song from you, a new
one.

SPARTAN

>Leave darlin' Taygetos,[67]
>Spartan Muse! Come to us
>once more, flyin'
>and glorifyin'
>*Spartan* themes:
>the god at Amyklai,
>bronze-house Athene,[68]
>Tyndaros' twins,[69]
>the valiant ones,
>playin' still by Eurotas' streams.

>>Up! Advance!
>>Leap to the dance!

---

[67]A high mountain near Sparta. (All of the references in the following passage are to personages and places sacred to the Spartans.)

[68]The bronze-plated temple of Athene in Sparta.

[69]Leda, wife of Tyndaros the Spartan, was raped by Zeus, chief of the gods, in the form of a swan. Born from that union were the heroic twins, Kastor and Polydeukes, as well as Helen (whose abduction caused the Trojan War).

Help us hymn Sparta,
lover of dancin',
lover of foot-pats,
where girls go prancin'
like fillies along Eurotas' banks,
whirlin' the dust, twinklin' their shanks,
shakin' their hair
like Maenads[70]playin'
and jugglin' the thyrsis,
in frenzy obeyin'
Leda's daughter, the fair, the pure
Helen, the mistress of the choir.

Here, Muse, here!
Bind up your hair!
Stamp like a deer! Pound your feet!
Clap your hands! Give us a beat!
Sing the greatest,
sing the mightiest,
sing the conqueror,
sing to honor her—

Athene of the Bronze House!
Sing Athene!

Exeunt omnes[71]*dancing and singing.*

---

[70]Literally "mad women": intoxicated, dancing followers of the god Bacchos. They sometimes carried a thyrsis, a staff topped with a pine cone and twined with vines.

[71]Latin: *All leave.*

8

Plato

Apology

NEITHER *Socrates nor Jesus, the most famous and most beloved teachers of the ancient world, are known through their own writings. For our knowledge of both we must depend mainly upon the works of disciples. In the case of Socrates, our primary source is Plato, in whose written dialogues (discussions) the Athenian sage is the dominant figure.*

Socrates (469–399 B.C.) was born and raised in Athens during the "Golden Age" and, later in his life, fought bravely in the Peloponnesian War that ended the glory of his city. He lived in an age that was, like our own, one of intellectual and moral unrest. In Athens many time-honored values and opinions were being subjected to radical criticism and re-evaluation, especially by a group of skeptical teachers known as the Sophists. Socrates, although not a Sophist himself, contributed to the shaking of popular beliefs by challenging them with everyone he met; this questioning of tradition was largely responsible for his being brought to trial and put to death.

Socrates' place in history does not come from this negative influence. Unlike the Sophists he had no doubt at all that absolute, unchanging truth exists. Truth, he maintained, is already in the possession of everyone, hidden under smug self-satisfaction and narrow prejudices, and needs only to be liberated by the rigorous examination and testing of opinion. His "Socratic method" was aimed at revealing the eternal principles of human conduct, upon which personal happiness and social stability depend. This means of truth-seeking, the action of mind upon mind, is called dialectic. *It assumes that real truth is there to be found through honest and systematic intellectual* argument.

In the following selection, the Apology, *we see Socrates defending himself in court, at the age of seventy, before a typically large jury of 501 male citizens.*

APOLOGY   Plato, *Apology,* in *The Dialogues of Plato,* trans. Benjamin Jowett (Oxford: Clarendon Press, 1953), 341–356, 360–366. Adapted by the editor.

(Athenian legal custom required that the trial take only a single day and that the accused person act as his own defense lawyer.) Plato was present and, therefore, we may trust that his account of the speech gives a clear picture of the genuine Socrates—perhaps somewhat idealized by Plato's own admiration.

The accusers had charged that Socrates did not believe in the official gods of the city but rather invented his own gods, and that he had corrupted the Athenian youth to believe as he did. Socrates, with calm defiance, not only dealt with the charges but also used the trial as yet another opportunity to explain the truth-seeking mission to which his life had been devoted. (The meaning in Greek of the root word for "apology" does not carry the word's modern meaning of an expression of regret; it means, rather, an explanation and justification of one's actions.)

[To the jury:]

How you, O Athenians, have been affected by my accusers, I cannot tell; but I know that they almost made me forget who I was—so persuasively did they speak; and yet they have hardly uttered a word of truth. But of the many falsehoods told by them, there was one which quite amazed me;—I mean when they said that you should be upon your guard and not allow yourselves to be deceived by the force of my eloquence. To say this, when they were certain to be detected as soon as I opened my lips and proved myself to be anything but a great speaker, did indeed appear to me most shameless—unless by the force of eloquence they mean the force of truth; for if such is their meaning, I admit that I am eloquent. But in how different a way from theirs! Well, as I was saying, they have scarcely spoken the truth at all; from me you shall hear the whole truth, but not delivered after their manner in a set oration duly ornamented with fine words and phrases. No, by heaven! I shall use the words and arguments which occur to me at the moment, for I am confident in the justice of my cause: at my time of life I ought not to be appearing before you, O men of Athens, in the character of a boy inventing falsehoods—let no one expect it of me. And I must particularly beg of you to grant me this favour:—If I defend myself in my accustomed manner, and you hear me using the words which many of you have heard me using habitually in the agora,[1] at the tables of the money-changers, and elsewhere, I would ask you not

---

[1] The market place, a favorite social center of the citizens.

to be surprised, and not to interrupt me on this account. For I am more than seventy years of age, and appearing now for the first time before a court of law, I am quite a stranger to the language of the place; and therefore I would have you regard me as if I were really a stranger, whom you would excuse if he spoke in his native tongue, and after the fashion of his country:—Am I making an unfair request of you? Never mind the manner, which may or may not be good; but think only of the truth of my words, and give heed to that: let the speaker speak truly and the judge decide justly.

And first, I have to reply to the older charges and to my first accusers,[2] and then I will go on to the later ones. For of old I have had many accusers, who have accused me falsely to you during many years; and I am more afraid of them than of Anytus[3] and his associates, who are dangerous, too, in their own way. But far more dangerous are the others, who began when most of you were children, and took possession of your minds with their falsehoods, telling of one Socrates, a wise man, who speculated about the heaven above, and searched into the earth beneath, and made the worse appear the better cause.[4] The men who have besmeared me with this tale are the accusers whom I dread; for their hearers are apt to fancy that such inquirers do not believe in the existence of the gods. And they are many, and their charges against me are of ancient date, and they were made by them in the days when some of you were more impressible than you are now—in childhood, or it may have been in youth—and the cause went by default, for there was none to answer. And hardest of all, I do not know and cannot tell the names of my accusers; unless in the chance case of a comic poet.[5] All who from envy and malice have persuaded you—some of them having first convinced themselves—all this class

[2]Socrates had been much criticized for many years before his trial; here, he states that he will deal first with the old falsehoods that created the prejudices that are the real cause of the current charges against him.

[3]Anytus, Meletus, and Lycon were the three men pressing charges against Socrates. (Anytus was a wealthy merchant whose son was intellectually gifted and wished to be a follower of Socrates; Anytus had angrily refused and insisted his son go into the family's business; the young man—according to tradition—became an alcoholic.)

[4]Socrates was accused by some of being a natural philosopher (physical scientist) who speculated, or theorized, about the material nature of the universe—and was thought, therefore, to be an atheist. He was also accused of being a Sophist, a teacher of public speaking who taught people to argue their law cases without regard for truth. Actually, he had lost interest in natural philosophy decades earlier and had never been a Sophist.

[5]Aristophanes (see selection 7), whose satirical comedy, *The Clouds* (423 B.C.), portrayed Socrates as a ridiculous fake who had contempt for religion and tradition.

of men are most difficult to deal with; for I cannot have them up here, and cross-examine them, and therefore I must simply fight with shadows in my own defence, and argue when there is no one who answers. I will ask you then to take it from me that my opponents are of two kinds; one recent, the other ancient: and I hope that you will see the propriety of my answering the latter first, for these accusations you heard long before the others, and much oftener.

Well, then, I must make my defence, and endeavour to remove from your minds in a short time, a slander which you have had a long time to take in. May I succeed, if to succeed be for my good and yours, or likely to avail me in my cause! The task is not an easy one; I quite understand the nature of it. And so leaving the event with God, in obedience to the law I will now make my defence.

I will begin at the beginning, and ask what is the accusation which has given rise to the slander of me, and in fact has encouraged Meletus to prefer this charge against me. Well, what do the slanderers say? They shall be my prosecutors, and this is the information they swear against me: 'Socrates is an evil-doer; a meddler who searches into things under the earth and in heaven, and makes the worse appear the better cause, and teaches the aforesaid practices to others.' Such is the nature of the accusation: it is just what you have yourselves seen in the comedy of Aristophanes, who has introduced a man whom he calls Socrates, swinging about and saying that he walks on air, and talking a deal of nonsense concerning matters of which I do not pretend to know either much or little—not that I mean to speak disparagingly of anyone who is a student of natural philosophy. May Meletus never bring so many charges against me as to make me do that! But the simple truth is, O Athenians, that I have nothing to do with physical speculations. Most of those here present are witnesses to the truth of this, and to them I appeal. Speak then, you who have heard me, and tell your neighbours whether any of you have ever known me hold forth in few words or in many upon such matters. . . . You hear their answer. And from what they say of this part of the charge you will be able to judge of the truth of the rest.

As little foundation is there for the report that I am a teacher, and take money;[6] this accusation has no more truth in it than the other. Although, if a man were really able to instruct mankind, this too would, in my opinion, be an honour to him. . . .

[6] The Sophists often charged high fees. Socrates, on the other hand, charged no fees at all for his philosophical questioning.

I dare say, Athenians, that someone among you will reply, 'Yes, Socrates, but what *is* your occupation? What is the origin of these accusations which are brought against you; there must have been something strange which you have been doing? All these rumours and this talk about you would never have arisen if you had been like other men: tell us, then, what is the cause of them, for we should be sorry to judge hastily of you.' Now I regard this as a fair challenge, and I will endeavour to explain to you the reason why I am called wise and have such an evil fame. Please to attend then. And although some of you may think that I am joking, I declare that I will tell you the entire truth. Men of Athens, this reputation of mine has come of a certain sort of wisdom which I possess. If you ask me what kind of wisdom, I reply, wisdom such as may perhaps be attained by man, for to that extent I am inclined to believe that I am wise; whereas the persons of whom I was speaking have a kind of superhuman wisdom,[7] which I know not how to describe, because I have it not myself; and he who says that I have, speaks falsely, and is taking away my character. And here, O men of Athens, I must beg you not to interrupt me, even if I seem to say something extravagant. For the word which I will speak is not mine. I will refer you to a witness who is worthy of credit; that witness shall be the god of Delphi[8]—he will tell you about my wisdom, if I have any, and of what sort it is. You must have known Chaerephon; he was early a friend of mine, and also a friend of yours, for he shared in the recent exile of the people, and returned with you.[9] Well, Chaerephon, as you know, was very impetuous in all his doings, and he went to Delphi and boldly asked the oracle to tell him whether—as I was saying, I must beg you not to interrupt—he actually asked the oracle to tell him whether anyone was wiser than I was, and the Pythian prophetess answered that there was no man wiser. Chaerephon is dead himself; but his brother, who is in court, will confirm the truth of what I am saying.

Why do I mention this? Because I am going to explain to you why I have such an evil name. When I heard the answer, I said to myself,

---

[7]Socrates, with his customary ironic (sarcastic) humor, is speaking here of the Sophists.

[8]Apollo's most famous temple was at Delphi, about seventy-five miles northwest of Athens; the Pythia, Apollo's priestess, there uttered the god's oracles (divine statements).

[9]Five years before Socrates' trial, after the defeat of Athens ended the Peloponnesian War in 404 B.C., the "Thirty Tyrants" drove the democratic leadership of Athens (including Socrates' friend Chaerephon) into exile. The democracy was restored in 403.

What can the god mean? and what is the interpretation of his riddle? for I know that I have no wisdom, small or great. What then can he mean when he says that I am the wisest of men? And yet he is a god, and cannot lie; that would be against his nature. After long perplexity, I thought of a method of trying the question. I reflected that if I could only find a man wiser than myself, then I might go to the god with a refutation in my hand. I should say to him, 'Here is a man who is wiser than I am; but you said that I was the wisest.' Accordingly I went to one who had the reputation of wisdom, and observed him—his name I need not mention, he was a politician; and in the process of examining him and talking with him, this, men of Athens, was what I found. I could not help thinking that he was not really wise, although he was thought wise by many, and still wiser by himself; and thereupon I tried to explain to him that he thought himself wise, but was not really wise; and the consequence was that he hated me, and his enmity was shared by several who were present and heard me. So I left him, saying to myself as I went away: Well, although I do not suppose that either of us knows anything really worth knowing, I am at least wiser than this fellow—for he knows nothing, and thinks that he knows; I neither know nor think that I know. In this one little point, then, I seem to have the advantage of him. Then I went to another who had still higher pretensions to wisdom, and my conclusion was exactly the same. Whereupon I made another enemy of him, and of many others besides him.

Then I went to one man after another, being not unconscious of the enmity which I provoked, and I lamented and feared this: but necessity was laid upon me,—the word of God [Apollo], I thought, ought to be considered first. And I said to myself, Go I must to all who appear to know, and find out the meaning of the oracle. And I swear to you, Athenians,—for I must tell you the truth—the result of my mission was just this: I found that the men most in repute were nearly the most foolish; and that others less esteemed were really closer to wisdom. I will tell you the tale of my wanderings and of the 'Herculean' labours, as I may call them, which I endured only to find at last the oracle irrefutable. After the politicians, I went to the poets; tragic, dithyrambic, and all sorts. And there, I said to myself, you will be instantly detected; now you will find out that you are more ignorant than they are. Accordingly, I took them some of the most elaborate passages in their own writings, and asked what was the meaning of them—thinking that they would teach me something. Will you believe me? I am ashamed to confess the truth, but I must say that there is hardly a person present who would not have talked better about their poetry than they did themselves. So I learnt that not by wisdom do poets write poetry, but by a sort of genius and inspiration; they are like diviners or soothsayers who also say many fine things, but do not understand the meaning of them. The poets appeared to me to be much in the same case; and I further observed that upon the strength of their poetry they believed themselves to be the wisest of men in other things in which they were not wise. So I departed, conceiving myself to be superior to them for the same reason that I was superior to the politicians.

At last I went to the skilled craftsmen for I was conscious that I knew nothing at all, as I may say, and I was sure that they knew many fine things; and here I was not mistaken, for they did know many things of which I was ignorant, and in this they certainly were wiser than I was. But I observed that even the good craftsmen fell into the same error as the poets;—because they were good workmen they thought that they also knew all sorts of high matters, and this defect in them overshadowed their wisdom; and therefore I asked myself on behalf of the oracle, whether I would like to be as I was, neither having their knowledge nor their ignorance, or like them in both; and I made answer to myself and to the oracle that I was better off as I was.

This inquiry has led to my having many enemies of the worst and most dangerous kind, and has given rise also to many imputations, including the name of 'wise'; for my hearers always imagine that I myself possess the wisdom which I find wanting in others. But the truth is, O men of Athens, that God only is wise; and by his answer he intends to show that the wisdom of men is worth little or nothing; although speaking of Socrates, he is only using my name by way of illustration, as if he said, He, O men, is the wisest, who, like Socrates, knows that his wisdom is in truth worth nothing. And so I go about the world, obedient to the god, and search and make inquiry into the wisdom of anyone, whether citizen or stranger, who appears to be wise; and if he is not wise, then in vindication of the oracle I show him that he is not wise; and my occupation quite absorbs me, and I have had no time to do anything useful either in public affairs or in any concern of my own, but I am in utter poverty by reason of my devotion to the god.

There is another thing:—young men of the richer classes, who have not much to do, come about me of their own accord; they like to hear people examined, and they often imitate me, and proceed to do some examining themselves; there are plenty of persons, as they quickly discover, who think that they know something, but really know little or nothing; and then those who are examined by them instead of being angry with themselves are angry with me: This confounded Socrates, they say; this villainous misleader of youth!—and then if somebody asks them, Why, what evil does he practise or teach? they do not know, and cannot tell; but in order that they may not appear to be at a loss, they repeat the ready-made charges which are used against all philosophers about teaching things up in the clouds and under the earth, and having no gods, and making the worse appear the better cause; for they do not like to confess that their pretence of knowledge has been detected—which is the truth; and as they are numerous and ambitious and energetic, and speak vehemently with persuasive tongues, they have filled your ears with their loud and inveterate slanders. And this is the reason why my three accusers, Meletus and Anytus and Lycon, have set upon me. . . .

I have said enough in my defence against the first class of my accusers; I turn to the second class. They are headed by Meletus, that good man and true lover of his country, as he calls himself. Against these, too, I must try to make a defence:—Let their affidavit be read: it contains something of this kind: It says that Socrates is a doer of evil, inasmuch as he corrupts the youth, and does not receive the gods whom the state receives, but has a new religion of his own. Such is the charge; and now let us examine the particular counts. He says that I am a doer of evil, and corrupt the youth; but I say, O men of Athens, that Meletus is a doer of evil, in that he is playing a solemn farce, recklessly bringing men to trial from a pretended zeal and interest about matters in which he really never had the smallest interest. And the truth of this I will endeavor to prove to you.

Come hither, Meletus, and let me ask a question of you. You attach great importance to the improvement of youth?

Yes, I do.

Tell the judges, then, who is their improver; for you must know, as you take such interest in the subject, and have discovered their corrupter, and are citing and accusing me in this court. Speak, then, and tell the judges who is the improver of youth:—Observe, Meletus, that you are silent, and have nothing to say. But is this not rather disgraceful, and a very considerable proof of what I was saying, that you have no interest in the matter? Speak up, friend, and tell us who their improver is.

The laws.

But that, my good sir, is not my question: Can you not name some person—whose first qualification will be that he knows the laws?[10]

The judges, Socrates, who are present in court.

What, do you mean to say, Meletus, that they are able to instruct and improve youth?

Certainly they are.

What, all of them, or some only and not others?

All of them.

Truly, that is good news! There are plenty of improvers, then. And what do you say of the audience,—do they improve them?

Yes, they do.

And the senators?

Yes, the senators improve them.

But perhaps the members of the assembly corrupt them?—or do they too improve them?

They improve them.

Then every Athenian improves and elevates them; all with the exception of myself; and I alone am their corrupter? Is that what you affirm?

That is what I stoutly affirm.

I am very unfortunate if you are right. But suppose I ask you a question: Is it the same with horses? Does one man do them harm and all the world good? Is not the exact opposite the truth? One man is able to do them good, or at least very few;—the trainer of horses, that is to say, does them good, but the ordinary man does them harm if he has to do with them? Is not that true, Meletus, of horses, or of any other animals? Most assuredly it is; whether you and Anytus say yes or no. Happy indeed would be the condition of youth if they had one corrupter only, and all the rest of the world were their benefactors. But you, Meletus, have sufficiently shown that you never had a thought about

[10]In the following series of questions Socrates, as part of his right to cross-examine his accuser, playfully uses his logical method *(dialectic)* to make the angrily squirming Meletus look foolish. Meletus is first forced, by Socrates' questions, to define the "improver of youth" as all the "judges" (the entire jury of 501); then as the non-voting "audience"; then as the "senators" (the Council of 500 which drafted the laws and supervised their carrying out); and finally, as the "assembly" (all the adult male citizens, who voted approval of the laws of Athens).

the young: your carelessness is plainly seen in your not caring about the very things which you bring against me. . . .

It will be very clear to you, Athenians, as I was saying, that Meletus has never had any care, great or small, about the matter. But still I should like to know, Meletus, in what I am affirmed to corrupt the young. I suppose you mean, as I infer from your indictment, that I teach them not to acknowledge the gods which the state acknowledges, but some other new divinities or spiritual agencies in their stead. These are the lessons by which I corrupt the youth, as you say.

Yes, that I say emphatically.

Then, by the gods, Meletus, of whom we are speaking, tell me and the court, in somewhat plainer terms, what you mean! for I do not as yet understand whether you affirm that I teach other men to acknowledge some gods, and therefore that I do believe in gods, and am not an entire atheist—this you do not lay to my charge,—but only you say that they are not the same gods which the city recognizes—the charge is that they are different gods. Or, do you mean that I am an atheist simply, and a teacher of atheism?

I mean the latter—that you are a complete atheist.

What an extraordinary statement! Why do you think so, Meletus? Do you mean that I do not believe in the god-head of the sun or moon, like the rest of mankind?[11]

I assure you, judges, that he does not: for he says that the sun is stone, and the moon earth.

Friend Meletus, do you think that you are accusing Anaxagoras?[12] Have you such a low opinion of the judges, that you fancy them so illiterate as not to know that these doctrines are found in the books of Anaxagoras the Clazomenian, which are full of them? And so, forsooth, the youth are said to be taught them by Socrates, when they can be bought in the book-market for one drachma[13] at the most; and they might pay their money, and laugh at Socrates if he pretends to father these extraordinary views. And so, Meletus, you really think that I do not believe in any god?

---

[11]Apollo was the sun god, Artemis the moon goddess. Whether or not those two divine personalities were meant in Socrates' question, reverence for the sun and moon themselves was expected of all Greeks.

[12]A natural philosopher from Clazomenae, a town in Asia Minor. Condemned for impiety, he was forced to leave Athens partly because of his materialist, anti-supernatural views of the sun and moon.

[13]A Greek coin of small value.

I swear by Zeus that you verily believe in none at all.

Nobody will believe you, Meletus, and I am pretty sure that you do not believe yourself. I cannot help thinking, men of Athens, that Meletus is reckless and impudent, and that he has brought this indictment in a spirit of mere wantonness and youthful bravado. Has he not compounded a riddle, thinking to try me? He said to himself:—I shall see whether the wise Socrates will discover my facetious self-contradiction, or whether I shall be able to deceive him and the rest of them. For he certainly does appear to me to contradict himself in the indictment as much as if he said that Socrates is guilty of not believing in the gods, and yet of believing in them—but this is not like a person who is in earnest.

I should like you, O men of Athens, to join me in examining what I conceive to be his inconsistency; and do you, Meletus, answer. And I must remind the audience of my request that they would not make a disturbance if I speak in my accustomed manner:

Did ever man, Meletus, believe in the existence of human things, and not of human beings? . . . I wish, men of Athens, that he would answer, and not be always trying to get up an interruption. Did ever any man believe in horsemanship, and not in horses? or in flute-playing, and not in flute-players? My friend, no man ever did; I answer to you and to the court, as you refuse to answer for yourself. But now please to answer the next question: Can a man believe in the existence of things spiritual and divine, and not in spirits or demigods?

He cannot.

How lucky I am to have extracted that answer, by the assistance of the court! But then you swear in the indictment that I teach and believe in divine or spiritual things (new or old, no matter for that); at any rate, I believe in spiritual things,—so you say and swear in the affidavit; and yet if I believe in them, how can I help believing in spirits or demigods;—must I not? To be sure I must; your silence gives consent. Now what are spirits or demigods? are they not either gods or the sons of gods?

Certainly they are.

But this is what I call the facetious riddle invented by you: the demigods or spirits are gods, and you say first that I do not believe in gods, and then again that I do believe in gods; that is, if I believe in demigods. For if the demigods are the illegitimate sons of gods, whether by nymphs, or by other mothers, as some are said to be—what human being will ever believe that there are no gods when there are sons of gods? You might as well affirm the existence of mules, and deny that of horses and asses.[14] Such nonsense, Meletus, could only have been intended by you to make trial of me. You have put this into the indictment because you could think of nothing real of which to accuse me. But no one who has a particle of understanding will ever be convinced by you that a man can believe in the existence of things divine and superhuman, and the same man refuse to believe in gods and demigods and heroes.

I have said enough in answer to the charge of Meletus: any elaborate defence is unnecessary. You know well the truth of my statement that I have incurred many violent enmities; and this is what will be my destruction if I am destroyed;—not Meletus, nor yet Anytus, but the envy and detraction of the world, which has been the death of many good men, and will probably be the death of many more; there is no danger of my being the last of them.

Someone will say: And are you not ashamed, Socrates, of a course of life which is likely to bring you to an untimely end? To him I may fairly answer: There you are mistaken: a man who is good for anything ought not to calculate the chance of living or dying; he ought only to consider whether in doing anything he is doing right or wrong—acting the part of a good man or of a bad. . . .

Strange, indeed, would be my conduct, O men of Athens, if I who, when I was ordered by the generals whom you chose to command me at Potidaea and Amphipolis and Delium,[15] remained where they placed me, like any other man, facing death—if now, when, as I conceive and imagine, God orders me to fulfil the philosopher's mission of searching into myself and other men, I were to desert my post through fear of death, or any other fear; that would indeed be strange, and I might justly be arraigned in court for denying the existence of the gods, if I disobeyed the oracle because I was afraid of death, fancying that I was wise when I was not wise. For the fear of death is indeed the pretence of wisdom, and not real wisdom, being a pretence of knowing the unknown; and no one knows whether death, of which men are afraid because they apprehend it to be the greatest evil, may not be the greatest good. Is not this ignorance of a disgraceful sort, the ignorance which is the conceit that a man knows what he does not know? And in

[14]A mule is a sterile work animal produced by the mating of a mare with a male donkey (jackass).

[15]Sites of battles during the Peloponnesian War where Socrates had fought as an Athenian infantryman.

this respect only I believe myself to differ from men in general, and may perhaps claim to be wiser than they are:—that whereas I know but little of the world below,[16] I do not suppose that I know: but I do know that injustice and disobedience to a better, whether God or man, is evil and dishonourable, and I will never fear or avoid a possible good rather than a certain evil. And therefore if you let me go now, and . . . if you say to me, Socrates, this time we will not mind Anytus, and you shall be let off, but upon one condition: that you are not to inquire and speculate in this way any more, and that if you are caught doing so again you shall die. If this was the condition on which you let me go, I should reply: Men of Athens, I honour and love you; but I shall obey God rather than you, and while I have life and strength I shall never cease from the practice and teaching of philosophy, exhorting any one of you whom I meet and saying to him after my manner: You, my friend,—a citizen of the great and mighty and wise city of Athens,— are you not ashamed of heaping up the largest amount of money and honour and reputation, and caring so little about wisdom and truth and the greatest improvement of the soul, which you never regard nor heed at all? And if the person with whom I am arguing, says; Yes, but I do care; then I shall not leave him nor let him go at once, but proceed to interrogate and examine and cross-examine him, and if I think that he has no virtue in him but only says that he has, I shall reproach him with undervaluing the most precious, and overvaluing the less. And I shall repeat the same words to everyone whom I meet, young and old, citizen and alien, but especially to you citizens, inasmuch as you are my brethren. . . . This is my teaching, and if it corrupts the young, it is mischievous; but if anyone says that this is not my teaching, he is speaking an untruth. Wherefore, O men of Athens, I say to you, do as Anytus bids or not as Anytus bids, and either acquit me or not; but whichever you do, understand that I shall never alter my ways, not even if I have to die many times.

Men of Athens, do not interrupt,[17] but hear me; I begged you before to listen to me without interruption, and I beg you now to hear me to the end. I have something more to say, at which you may be inclined to cry out; but I believe that to hear me will be good for you, and therefore I beseech you to restrain yourselves. I would have you know, that if you kill such an one as I am, you will injure yourselves more

[16]The afterlife, thought by the Greeks to be in an underground place called Hades.

[17]Apparently, Socrates is now speaking over noises from the crowd, as he directly defies the city's power in stating that he will never alter his ways.

than you will injure me. Nothing will injure me, not Meletus nor yet Anytus—they cannot, for a bad man is not permitted to injure a better than himself. I do not deny that Anytus may, perhaps, kill him, or drive him into exile, or deprive him of civil rights; and he may imagine, and others may imagine, that he is inflicting a great injury upon him: but there I do not agree. For the evil of doing as he is doing—the evil of seeking unjustly to take the life of another—is far greater.

And now, Athenians, I am not going to argue for my own sake, as you may think, but for yours, that you may not sin against God by condemning me, who am his gift to you. For if you kill me you will not easily find a successor to me, who, if I may use such a ludicrous figure of speech, am a sort of gadfly,[18] given to the state by God; and the state is a great and noble horse who is tardy in his motions owing to his very size, and requires to be stirred into life. I am that gadfly which God has attached to the state, and all day long and in all places am always fastening upon you, arousing and persuading and reproaching you. You will not easily find another like me, and therefore I would advise you to spare me. I dare say that you may feel out of temper (like a person who is suddenly awakened from sleep), and you think that you might easily strike me dead as Anytus advises, and then you would sleep on for the remainder of your lives, unless God in his care of you sent you another gadfly. When I say that I am given to you by God, the proof of my mission is this:—if I had been like other men, I should not have neglected all my own concerns or patiently seen the neglect of them during all these years, and have been doing yours, coming to you individually like a father or elder brother, exhorting you to regard virtue; such conduct, I say, would be unlike human nature. . . .

Someone may wonder why I go about in private giving advice and busying myself with the concerns of others, but do not venture to come forward in public and advise the state. I will tell you why. You have heard me speak at different times and places of a superhuman oracle or sign which comes to me, and is the divinity which Meletus ridicules in the indictment. This sign, which is a kind of voice, first began to come to me when I was a child; from time to time it forbids me to do something which I am going to do, but never commands anything. This is what deters me from being a politician. And rightly, as I think. For I am certain, O men of Athens, that if I had engaged in politics, I should have perished long ago, and done no good either to

---

[18]A fly that bites and annoys horses and livestock.

you or to myself. And do not be offended at my telling you the truth: for the truth is, that no man who sets himself firmly against you or any other multitude, honestly striving to keep the state from many lawless and unrighteous deeds, will save his life; he who will fight for the right, if he would live even for a brief space, must have a private station and not a public one. . . .

[Editor's note: At the end of his defense, in which—contrary to accepted custom—Socrates refused to appeal to the sympathetic emotions of the jury, he was found guilty. The vote was 280 to 221. In the next phase of the trial, the prosecution and the convicted person each propose a *penalty*. The jury must then vote for one or the other penalty.]

There are many reasons why I am not grieved, O men of Athens, at the vote of condemnation. I expected it, and am only surprised that the votes are so nearly equal; for I had thought that the majority against me would have been far larger; but now, had thirty votes gone over to the other side, I should have been acquitted. . . .

And so he [Meletus] proposes death as the penalty. And what shall I propose on my part, O men of Athens? Clearly that which is my due. And what is my due? What ought I to have done to me, or to pay—a man who has never had the wit to keep quiet during his whole life; but has been careless of what the many care for—wealth, and family interests, and military offices, and speaking in the assembly, and magistracies, and plots, and parties. Reflecting that I was really too honest a man to be a politician and live, I did not go where I could do no good to you or to myself; but where I could do privately the greatest good (as I affirm it to be) to everyone of you, thither I went, and sought to persuade every man among you that he must look to himself, and seek virtue and wisdom before he looks to his private interests, and look to the state before he looks to the interests of the state; and that this should be the order which he observes in all his actions. What shall be done to such an one? Doubtless some good thing, O men of Athens, if he has his reward; and the good should be of a kind suitable to him. What would be a reward suitable to a poor man who is your benefactor, and who desires leisure that he may instruct you? There can be no reward so fitting as a full pension in the Prytaneum,[19] O men of Athens, a reward which he deserves far more than the citizen who has won the

---

[19] The place where benefactors of Athens and winners of the athletic contests at Olympia were entertained as guests.

prize at Olympia in the horse or chariot race, whether the chariots were drawn by two horses or by many. For I am in want, and he has enough; and he only gives you the appearance of happiness, and I give you the reality. And if I am to estimate the penalty fairly, I should say that maintenance in the Prytaneum is the just return.

Perhaps you think that I am braving you in what I am saying now, as in what I said before about the tears and prayers. But this is not so. I speak rather because I am convinced that I never intentionally wronged anyone, although I cannot convince you—the time has been too short; if there were a law at Athens, as there is in other cities, that a capital cause should not be decided in one day, then I believe that I should have convinced you. But I cannot in a moment refute great slanders; and, as I am convinced that I never wronged another, I will assuredly not wrong myself. I will not say of myself that I deserve any evil, nor propose any penalty. Why should I? Because I am afraid of the penalty of death which Meletus proposes? When I do not know whether death is a good or an evil, why should I propose a penalty which would certainly be an evil? Shall I say imprisonment? And why should I live in prison, and be the slave of the magistrates of the year? . . . Or shall the penalty be a fine, and imprisonment until the fine is paid? There is the same objection. I should have to lie in prison, for money I have none, and cannot pay. And if I say exile (and this may possibly be the penalty which you will affix), I must indeed be blinded by the love of life, if I am so irrational as to expect that when you, who are my own citizens, cannot endure my discourses and arguments, and have found them so grievous and odious that you will have no more of them, others are likely to endure them. No indeed, men of Athens, that is not very likely. And what a life should I lead, at my age, wandering from city to city, ever changing my place of exile, and always being driven out! For I am quite sure that wherever I go, there, as here, the young men will flock to listen to me; and if I drive them away, their elders will drive me out at their request; and if I let them come, their fathers and friends will drive me out for their sakes.

Someone will say: Yes, Socrates, but cannot you hold your tongue, and then you may go into a foreign city, and no one will interfere with you? Now I have great difficulty in making you understand my answer to this. For if I tell you that to do as you say would be a disobedience to God, and therefore that I cannot hold my tongue, you will not believe that I am serious; and if I say again that daily to discourse about virtue, and of those other things about which you hear me examining myself and others, is the greatest good of man, and that the unexamined life is no life for a human being, you are still less likely to believe me. Yet I say what is true, although a thing of which it is hard for me to persuade you. Also, I have never been accustomed to think that I deserve to suffer any harm. Had I money I might have estimated the offence at what I was able to pay, and not have been much the worse. But I have none, and therefore I must ask you to proportion the fine to my means. Well, perhaps I could afford a mina,[20] and therefore I propose that penalty: Plato, Crito, Critobulus, and Apollodorus, my friends here, bid me say thirty minas, and they will be the sureties. Let thirty minas be the penalty; for which sum they will be ample security to you.

[Editor's note: The jury, insulted by Socrates' suggestion that he be rewarded for his service to Athens, voted for the death penalty, 360 to 141.]

Not much time will be gained, O Athenians, in return for the evil name which you will get from the detractors of the city, who will say that you killed Socrates, a wise man; for they will call me wise, even though I am not wise, when they want to reproach you. If you had waited a little while, your desire would have been fulfilled in the course of nature. For I am far advanced in years, as you may perceive, and not far from death. I am speaking now not to all of you, but only to those who have condemned me to death. And I have another thing to say to them: You think that I was convicted because I had no words of the sort which would have procured my acquittal—I mean, if I had thought fit to leave nothing undone or unsaid. Not so; the deficiency which led to my conviction was not of words—certainly not. But I had not the boldness nor impudence nor inclination to address you as you would have liked me to do, weeping and wailing and lamenting, and saying and doing many things, such indeed as you have been accustomed to hear from others, but I maintain to be unworthy of myself. I thought at the time that I ought not to do anything common or mean when in danger: nor do I now repent the style of my defence; I would rather die having spoken after my manner, than speak in your manner and live. For neither in war nor yet at law ought I or any man to use every way of escaping death. Often in battle there can be no doubt that if a man will throw away his arms, and fall on his knees before his pursuers, he may escape death; and in other dangers there

[20]A valuable coin, probably equal to 100 drachmas.

are other ways of escaping death, if a man has the hardihood to say and do anything. The difficulty, my friends, is not to avoid death, but to avoid unrighteousness; for that runs faster than death. I am old and move slowly, and the slower runner has overtaken me; my accusers are keen and quick, and the faster runner, who is wickedness, has overtaken them. And now I depart hence condemned by you to suffer the penalty of death,—they too go their ways condemned by the truth to suffer the penalty of villainy and wrong; and I must abide by my award—let them abide by theirs. I suppose that these things may be regarded as fated,—and I think that they are well.

And now, O men who have condemned me, I would fain prophesy to you; for I am about to die, and in the hour of death men are gifted with prophetic power. And I prophesy to you who are my murderers, that immediately after my departure punishment far heavier than you have inflicted on me surely awaits you. Me you have killed because you wanted to escape the accuser, and not to give an account of your lives. But that will not be as you suppose: far otherwise. For I say that there will be more accusers of you than there are now; accusers whom hitherto I have restrained: and as they are younger they will be more severe with you, and you will be more offended at them. If you think that by killing men you will stop all censure of your evil lives, you are mistaken; that is not a way of escape which is either very possible, or honourable; the easiest and the noblest way is not to be disabling others, but to be improving yourselves. This is the prophecy which I utter before my departure to the judges who have condemned me.

Friends, who would have acquitted me, I would like also to talk with you about the thing which has come to pass, while the magistrates are busy, and before I go to the place at which I must die. Stay then a little, for we may as well talk with one another while there is time. You are my friends, and I should like to show you the meaning of this event which has happened to me. O my judges—for you I may truly call judges—I should like to tell you of a wonderful circumstance. Hitherto the divine faculty of which my inner voice is the source has constantly been in the habit of opposing me even about trifles, if I was going to make a slip or error in any matter; and now as you see there has come upon me that which may be thought, and is generally believed to be, the last and worst evil. But the oracle made no sign of opposition, either when I was leaving my house in the morning, or when I was on my way to the court, or while I was speaking, at anything which I was going to say; and yet I have often been stopped in the middle of a speech, but now in nothing I either said or did touching the matter in hand has the oracle opposed me. What do I take to be the explanation of this silence? I will tell you. It is an intimation that what has happened to me is a good, and therefore those of us who think that death is an evil must be in error. I have this conclusive proof; the customary sign would surely have opposed me had I been going to evil and not to good.

Let us reflect in another way, and we shall see that there is great reason to hope that death is a good; for one of two things—either death is a state of nothingness and utter unconsciousness, or, as men say, there is a change and migration of the soul from this world to another. Now if you suppose that there is no consciousness, but a sleep like the sleep of him who is undisturbed even by dreams, death will be an unspeakable gain. For if a person were to select the night in which his sleep was undisturbed even by dreams, and were to compare with this the other days and nights of his life, and then were to tell us how many days and nights he had passed in the course of his life better and more pleasantly than this one, I think that any man, I will not say a private man, but even the great king will not find many such days or nights, when compared with the others. Now if death be of such a nature, I say that to die is gain; for eternity is then only a single night. But if death is the journey to another place, and there, as men say, all the dead abide, what good, O my friends and judges, can be greater than this? If indeed when the pilgrim arrives in the world below, he is delivered from our earthly professors of justice, and finds the true judges who are said to give judgement there . . . and other sons of God who were righteous in their own life, that pilgrimage will be worth making. What would not a man give if he might converse with Orpheus and Musaeus and Hesiod and Homer?[21] Nay, if this be true, let me die again and again. . . . Above all, I shall then be able to continue my search into true and false knowledge, as in this world, so also in the next; and I shall find out who is wise, and who pretends to be wise, and is not. . . . In another world they do not put a man to death for asking questions: assuredly not. For besides being happier than we are, they will be immortal, if what is said is true.

Wherefore, O judges, be of good cheer about death, and know of a certainty that no evil can happen to a good man, either in life or after death, and that he and his are not neglected by the gods. Nor has my

---

[21]Orpheus and Musaeus were poets in ancient mythological accounts; Hesiod and Homer were historical figures—Greek poets of the eighth century B.C.

own approaching end happened by mere chance; I see clearly that the time had arrived when it was better for me to die and be released from trouble; therefore the oracle gave no sign, and therefore also I am not at all angry with my condemners, or with my accusers. But although they have done me no harm, they intended it; and for this I may properly blame them.

Still I have a favour to ask of them. When my sons are grown up, I would ask you, O my friends, to punish them; I would have you trouble them, as I have troubled you, if they seem to care about riches, or anything, more than about virtue; or if they pretend to be something when they are really nothing,—then reprove them, as I have reproved you, for not caring about that for which they ought to care, and thinking that they are something when they are really nothing. And if you do this, I shall have received justice at your hands, and so will my sons.

The hour of departure has arrived, and we go our ways—I to die, and you to live. Which is better God only knows.

9

Plato

Phaedo

*A*FTER *his conviction and sentence of death (see selection 8), the philosopher Socrates (469–399 B.C.) was confined to prison for a month awaiting the carrying out of his sentence. (It was a period of religious purification in Athens and, during that time, no executions were allowed to pollute the city.) Socrates refused an opportunity to escape, when it had been arranged by his friends, out of his respect for the laws of Athens (even though, in his case, they had been maliciously applied).*

In the following selection from Plato's dialogue Phaedo, *we see Socrates, in prison, comforting his friends in the last hours before his death. The dialogue is reported by Socrates' friend Phaedo, who had been present; the discussion takes place in the Greek town of Phlius, where Phaedo recounts the moving event to another friend, Echecrates. As Phaedo recalls it, Socrates—even at his mortal end—persisted in his outlook and method. Socrates tells his friends that behind the present world of appearances lies the unseen eternal order. It is for this, the world of pure Forms or Ideas, that people should live; when freed through death, the souls of those who have lived wisely will return to that eternal world. The philosopher, therefore, has no reason to fear death; for "after death he may hope to obtain the greatest good in the other world."*

Centuries later this philosophy would contribute mightily to the intellectual capital of Christianity. In addition, since he subjected everything to the test of reason, and based morality upon humanly understood values—rather than the wills of the many gods—Socrates is regarded as a leading spirit in the rationalist and humanist *traditions.*

PHAEDO   Plato, *Phaedo*, in *The Dialogues of Plato*, trans. Benjamin Jowett (Oxford: Clarendon Press, 1953), 414–420, 435–439, 475–477. Adapted by the editor.

Now, O my judges,[1] I desire to prove to you that the real philosopher has reason to be of good cheer when he is about to die, and that after death he may hope to obtain the greatest good in the other world. And how this may be, Simmias and Cebes,[2] I will endeavour to explain. For I deem that the true believer in philosophy is likely to be misunderstood by other men; they do not perceive that he is always pursuing death and dying; and if this be so, and he has had the desire of death all his life long, why when his time comes should he regret that which he has been always pursuing and desiring?

Simmias said laughingly: Though not in a laughing humour, you have made me laugh, Socrates; for I cannot help thinking that the many when they hear your words will say how truly you have described philosophers, and our people at home will likewise say that the life which philosophers desire is in reality death, and that they have found them out to be deserving of the death which they desire.

And they are right, Simmias, in thinking so, with the exception of the words 'they have found them out'; for they have not found out either what is the nature of that death which the true philosopher deserves, or how he deserves or desires death. But enough of them:—let us discuss the matter among ourselves. Do we believe that there is such a thing as death?

To be sure, replied Simmias.

Is it not the separation of soul and body? And to be dead is the completion of this; when the soul exists in herself, and is released from the body and the body is released from the soul, what is this but death?

Just so, he replied.

There is another question, which will probably throw light on our present enquiry if you and I can agree about it:—Ought the philosopher to care about the pleasures—if they are to be called pleasures—of eating and drinking?

Certainly not, answered Simmias.

And what about the pleasures of love—should he care for them?

By no means.

And will he think much of the other ways of indulging the body, for example, the acquisition of costly raiment, or sandals, or other adornments of the body? Instead of caring about them, does he not rather despise anything more than nature needs? What do you say?

[1] Socrates is speaking to the friends and fellow-philosophers who are visiting him during his final hours. He is asking them to "judge" his arguments for the immortality of the soul; he will "prove" his case through his "question and answer" method.

[2] Two philosophers visiting Socrates from the Greek city of Thebes.

I should say that the true philosopher would despise them.

Would you not say that he is entirely concerned with the soul and not with the body? He would like, as far as he can, to get away from the body and to turn to the soul.

Quite true.

In matters of this sort philosophers, above all other men, may be observed in every sort of way to separate the soul from the communion of the body.

Very true.

Whereas, Simmias, the rest of the world are of opinion that to him who has no sense of pleasure and no part in bodily pleasure, life is not worth having; and that he who is indifferent about them is as good as dead.

That is also true.

What again shall we say of the actual acquirement of knowledge?—is the body, if invited to share in the enquiry, a hinderer or a helper? I mean to say, have sight and hearing any truth in them? Are they not, as the poets are always telling us, inaccurate witnesses? and yet, if even they are inaccurate and indistinct, what is to be said of the other senses—for you will allow that they are the best of them?

Certainly, he replied.

Then when does the soul attain truth?—for in attempting to consider anything in company with the body she is obviously deceived.

True.

Then must not true existence be revealed to her in thought, if at all?

Yes.

And thought is best when the mind is gathered into herself and none of these things trouble her—neither sounds nor sights nor pain nor any pleasure,—when she takes leave of the body, and has as little as possible to do with it, when she has no bodily sense or desire, but is aspiring after true being?

Certainly.

And in this the philosopher dishonours the body; his soul runs away from his body and desires to be alone and by herself?

That is true.

Well, but there is another thing, Simmias: Is there or is there not an absolute justice?

Assuredly there is.

And an absolute beauty and absolute good?

Of course.

But did you ever behold any of them with your eyes?

Certainly not.

Or did you ever reach them with any other bodily sense?—and I speak not of these alone, but of absolute greatness, and health, and strength, and of the essence or true nature of everything. Has the reality of them ever been perceived by you through the bodily organs? or rather, is not the nearest approach to the knowledge of their several natures made by him who so orders his intellectual vision as to have the most exact conception of the essence of each thing which he considers?

Certainly.

And he attains to the purest knowledge of them who goes to each with the mind alone, not introducing or intruding in the act of thought, sight, or any other sense together with reason, but with the very light of the mind in her own clearness searches into the very truth of each; he who has got rid, as far as he can, of eyes and ears and, so to speak, of the whole body, these being in his opinion distracting elements which when they infect the soul hinder her from acquiring truth and knowledge—who, if not he, is likely to attain to the knowledge of true being?

What you say has a wonderful truth in it, Socrates, replied Simmias.

And when real philosophers consider all these things, will they not be led to make a reflection which they will express in words something like the following? 'Have we not found,' they will say, 'a path of thought which seems to bring us and our argument to the conclusion, that while we are in the body, and while the soul is infected with the evils of the body, our desire will not be satisfied? and our desire is of the truth. For the body is a source of endless trouble to us by reason of the mere requirement of food; and is subject also to diseases which overtake and impede us in the search after true being: it fills us full of loves, and lusts, and fears, and fancies of all kinds, and endless foolery, and in fact, as men say, takes away from us the power of thinking at all. From where come wars, and fightings, and rival cliques? except from the body and the lusts of the body? Wars are occasioned by the love of money, and money has to be acquired for the sake and in the service of the body; and by reason of all these impediments we have no time to give to philosophy; and, last and worst of all, even if we are at leisure and exercise thought, the body is always breaking in upon us, causing turmoil and confusion in our enquiries, and so amazing us that we are prevented from seeking the truth. It has been proved to us by experience that if we would have pure knowledge of anything we must be quit of the body—the soul in herself must behold things in themselves; and then we shall attain the wisdom which we desire, and of which we say that we are lovers; not while we live, but after death; for if while in company with the body, the soul cannot have pure knowledge, one of two things follows—either knowledge is not to be attained at all, or, if at all, after death. For then, and not till then, the soul will be parted from the body and exist in herself alone. In this present life, I believe that we make the nearest approach to knowledge when we have the least possible communion with the body, and are not totally absorbed in our bodily nature, but keep ourselves pure until the hour when God himself is pleased to release us. And thus having got rid of the foolishness of the body we shall be pure and associate with the pure, and know of ourselves the clear light everywhere, which is no other than the light of truth.' For the impure are not permitted to approach the pure. These are the sort of words, Simmias, which the true lovers of knowledge cannot help saying to one another and thinking. You would agree; would you not?

Undoubtedly, Socrates.

But, O my friend, if this be true, there is great reason to hope that, going where I go, when I have come to the end of my journey, I shall attain that which has been the pursuit of my life. And therefore I go on my way rejoicing, and not I only, but every other man who believes that his mind has been made ready and that he is in a manner purified.

Certainly, replied Simmias.

And what is purification but the separation of the soul from the body, as I was saying before; the habit of the soul gathering and collecting herself into herself from all sides out of the body; the dwelling in her own place alone, as in another life, so also in this, as far as she can;—the release of the soul from the chains of the body?

Very true, he said.

And this separation and release of the soul from the body is termed death?

To be sure, he said.

And the true philosophers, and they only, are ever seeking to release the soul. Is not the separation and release of the soul from the body their especial study?

That is true.

And, as I was saying at first, there would be a ridiculous contradiction in men studying to live as nearly as they can in a state of death, and yet feeling regret when it comes upon them.

Clearly.

And the true philosophers, Simmias, are always occupied in the practice of dying; therefore, to them least of all men is death terrible. Look at the matter thus:—if they have been in every way the enemies of the body, and are wanting to be alone with the soul, when this desire of theirs is granted, how inconsistent would they be if they trembled and repined, instead of rejoicing at their departure to that place where, when they arrive, they hope to gain that which in life they desired—and this was wisdom—and at the same time to be rid of the company of their enemy. Many a man has been willing to go to the world below in the hope of seeing there an earthly love, or wife, or son, and conversing with them. And will he who is a true lover of wisdom, and is strongly persuaded in like manner that only in the world below he can worthily enjoy her, still be sad at death? Will he not depart with joy? Surely he will, O my friend, if he be a true philosopher. For he will have a firm conviction that there, and there only, he can find wisdom in her purity. And if this be true, he would be very absurd, as I was saying, if he were afraid of death.

He would indeed, replied Simmias.

And when you see a man who is holding back at the approach of death, is not his reluctance a sufficient proof that he is not a lover of wisdom, but a lover of the body, and probably at the same time a lover of either money or power, or both?

Quite so, he replied.

And is not courage, Simmias, a quality which is specially characteristic of the philosopher?

Certainly.

There is temperance again, which even in the popular view is supposed to consist in the control and regulation of the passions, and in the sense of superiority to them—is not temperance a virtue belonging to those only who despise the body, and who pass their lives in philosophy?

Most assuredly.

For the courage and temperance of other men, if you will consider them, are really a contradiction.

How so?

Well, he said, you are aware that death is regarded by men in general as a great evil.

Very true, he said.

And do not courageous men face death because they are afraid of yet greater evils?

That is quite true.

Then all but the philosophers are courageous only from fear, and because they are afraid; and yet that a man should be courageous from fear, and because he is a coward, is surely a strange thing.

Very true.

And are not the temperate exactly in the same case? They are temperate because they are intemperate—which might seem to be a contradiction, but is nevertheless the sort of thing which happens with this foolish temperance. For there are pleasures which they are afraid of losing; and in their desire to keep them, they abstain from some pleasures, because they are overcome by others; and although to be conquered by pleasure is called by men intemperance, to them the conquest of pleasure consists in being conquered by pleasure. And that is what I mean by saying that, in a sense, they are made temperate through intemperance.

Such appears to be the case.

Yet the exchange of one fear or pleasure or pain for another fear or pleasure or pain, and of the greater for the less, as if they were coins, is not the exchange of virtue. O my blessed Simmias, is there not one true coin for which all things ought to be exchanged?—and that is wisdom; and only in exchange for this, and in company with this, is anything truly bought or sold, whether courage or temperance or justice. And is not all true virtue the companion of wisdom, no matter what fears or pleasures or other similar goods or evils may or may not accompany her? But the virtue which is made up of these goods, when they are severed from wisdom and exchanged with one another, is a shadow of virtue only, nor is there any freedom or health or truth in her; but in the true exchange there is a purging away of all these things, and temperance, and justice, and courage, and wisdom herself are the purgation of them.

• • •

The soul, I say, herself invisible, departs to the invisible world—to the divine and immortal and rational. Arriving there, she is secure of bliss and is released from the error and folly of men, their fears and wild passions and all other human ills, and for ever dwells, as they say of the initiated, in company with the gods. Is not this true, Cebes?

Yes, said Cebes, beyond a doubt.

But the soul which has been polluted, and is impure at the time of her departure, and is the companion and servant of the body always, and is in love with and fascinated by the body and by the desires and pleasures of the body, until she is led to believe that the truth only exists in a bodily form, which a man may touch and see and taste, and use for the purposes of his lusts . . . do you suppose that such a soul will depart pure and unalloyed?

Impossible, he replied.

She is held fast by the corporeal, which the continual association and constant care of the body have worked into her nature.

Very true.

And this bodily element, my friend, is heavy and weighty and earthy, and is that element of sight by which a soul is depressed and dragged again into the visible world, because she is afraid of the invisible and of the world below[3]—prowling about tombs and graves near which, as they tell us, are seen certain ghostly appearances of souls which have not departed pure, but are filled with sight and therefore visible.

That is very likely, Socrates.

Yes, that is very likely, Cebes; and these must be the souls, not of the good, but of the evil, which are compelled to wander about such places in payment of the penalty of their former evil way of life; and they continue to wander until through the craving after the corporeal which never leaves them, they are imprisoned finally in another body. And they may be supposed to find their prisons in the same natures which they have had in their former lives.

What natures do you mean, Socrates?

What I mean is that men who have followed after gluttony, and lewdness, and drunkenness, and have had no thought of avoiding them, would pass into asses and animals of that sort. What do you think?

I think such an opinion to be exceedingly probable.

And those who have chosen the portion of injustice, and tyranny, and violence, will pass into wolves, or into birds of prey—where else can we suppose them to go?

Yes, said Cebes; with such natures, beyond question.

And there is no difficulty, he said, in assigning to all of them places answering to their several natures?

[3]The afterlife, thought by the Greeks to be in an underground place called Hades.

There is not, he said.

Some are happier than others; and the happiest both in themselves and in the place to which they go are those who have practised the civil and social virtues which are called temperance and justice, and are acquired by habit and attention without philosophy and mind.

Why are they the happiest?

Because they may be expected to pass into some gentle and social kind which is like their own, such as bees or wasps or ants, or back again into the form of man, and just and moderate men may be supposed to spring from them.

Very likely.

No one who has not studied philosophy and who is not entirely pure at the time of his departure is allowed to enter the company of the Gods, but the lover of knowledge only. And this is the reason, Simmias and Cebes, why the true believers in philosophy abstain from all fleshly lusts, and hold out against them and refuse to give themselves up to them,—not because they fear poverty or the ruin of their families, like the lovers of money, and the world in general; nor like the lovers of power and honour, because they dread the dishonour or disgrace of evil deeds.

No, Socrates, that would not become them, said Cebes.

No indeed, he replied; and therefore they who have any care of their own souls, and do not merely live moulding and fashioning the body, say farewell to all this; they will not walk in the ways of the blind: and when philosophy offers them purification and release from evil, they feel that they ought not to resist her influence, and where she leads they turn and follow.

What do you mean, Socrates?

I will tell you, he said. The lovers of knowledge are conscious that the soul was simply fastened and glued to the body—until philosophy received her. She could only view real existence through the bars of a prison, not in and through herself; she was wallowing in the mire of every sort of ignorance, and by reason of lust had become the principal accomplice in her own captivity. This was her original state; and then, as I was saying, and as the lovers of knowledge are well aware, philosophy, seeing how terrible was her confinement, of which she was to herself the cause, received and gently comforted her and sought to release her. Philosophy pointed out that the eye and the ear and the other senses are full of deception, and persuaded her to retire from them, and abstain from all but the necessary use of them, and be gathered up and collected into herself. . . . And the soul of the true philosopher thinks that she ought not to resist this deliverance, and therefore abstains from pleasures and desires and pains and fears, as far as she is able. She reflects that when a man has great joys or sorrows or fears or desires, he suffers from them, not merely the sort of evil which might be anticipated—as for example, the loss of his health or property which he has sacrificed to his lusts—but an evil greater far, which is the greatest and worst of all evils, and one of which he never thinks.

What is it, Socrates? said Cebes.

The evil is that when the feeling of pleasure or pain is most intense, every soul of man imagines the objects of this intense feeling to be then plainest and truest: but this is not so, they are really the things of sight.

Very true.

And is not this the state in which the soul is most overcome by the body?

How so?

Why, because each pleasure and pain is a sort of nail which nails and rivets the soul to the body, until she becomes like the body, and believes that to be true which the body affirms to be true; and from agreeing with the body and having the same delights she is obliged to have the same habits, and is not likely ever to be pure at her departure to the world below. She is always infected by the body; and so she sinks into another body and there germinates and grows, and has therefore no part in the communion of the divine and pure and simple.

Most true, Socrates, answered Cebes.

And this, Cebes, is the reason why the true lovers of knowledge are temperate and brave; and not for the reason which the world gives.

Certainly not.

Certainly not! The soul of a philosopher will reason in quite another way; she will not ask philosophy to release her in order that when released she may deliver herself up again to the slavery of pleasures and pains, doing a work only to be undone again. . . . But she will calm passion, and follow reason, and dwell in thought beholding the true and divine (which is not a matter of opinion), and so deriving nourishment. Thus she seeks to live while she lives, and after death she hopes to go to her own kindred and to that which is like her, and to be freed from human ills. Never fear, Simmias and Cebes, that a soul which has been thus nurtured and has had these pursuits, will at her departure from the body be scattered and blown away by the winds and be nowhere and nothing.

• • •

When he had spoken these words, he arose and went into a chamber to bathe; Crito⁴ followed him, and told us to wait. So we remained behind, talking and thinking of the subject of the discussion, and also of the greatness of our sorrow; he was like a father of whom we were being bereaved, and we were about to pass the rest of our lives as orphans. When he had taken the bath his children were brought to him—(he had two young sons and an elder one); and the women of the family also came, and he talked to them and gave them a few directions in the presence of Crito; then he dismissed them and returned to us.

Now the hour of sunset was near, for a good deal of time had passed while he was within. When he came out, he sat down with us again after his bath, but not much was said. Soon the jailer, who was the servant of the Eleven,⁵ entered and stood by him, saying:—To you, Socrates, whom I know to be the noblest and gentlest and best of all who ever came to this place, I will not impute the angry feelings of other men, who rage and swear at me, when, in obedience to the authorities, I bid them drink the poison—indeed, I am sure that you will not be angry with me; for others, as you are aware, and not I, are to blame. And so fare you well, and try to bear lightly what must needs be—you know my errand. Then bursting into tears he turned away and went out.

Socrates looked at him, and said: I return your good wishes, and will do as you bid. Then turning to us, he said, How charming the man is: since I have been in prison he has always been coming to see me, and at times he would talk to me, and was as good to me as could be, and now see how generously he sorrows on my account. We must do as he says, Crito; and therefore let the cup be brought, if the poison is prepared: if not, let the attendant prepare some.

Yet, said Crito, the sun is still upon the hill-tops, and I know that many a one has taken the cup late, and after the announcement has

---

⁴A friend who had arranged an escape from prison, which Socrates had refused.

⁵A government committee in charge of administering prisons and penalties, including executions.

been made to him, he has eaten and drunk, and enjoyed the society of his beloved; do not hurry—there is time enough.

Socrates said: Yes, Crito, and they of whom you speak are right in so acting, for they think that they will be gainers by the delay; but I am right in not following their example, for I do not think that I should gain anything by drinking the poison a little later; I should only be ridiculous in my own eyes for sparing and saving a life which is already forfeit. Please then to do as I say, and not to refuse me.

Crito made a sign to the servant, who was standing by; and he went out, and having been absent for some time, returned with the jailer carrying the cup of poison. Socrates said: You, my good friend, who are experienced in these matters, shall give me directions how I am to proceed. The man answered: You have only to walk about until your legs are heavy, and then to lie down, and the poison will act. At the same time he handed the cup to Socrates, who in the easiest and gentlest manner, without the least fear or change of colour or feature, looking at the man with all his eyes, Echecrates, as his manner was, took the cup and said: What do you say about making a libation out of this cup to any god?[6] May I, or not? The man answered: We only prepare, Socrates, just so much as we deem enough. I understand, he said: but I may and must ask the gods to prosper my journey from this to the other world—even so—and so be it according to my prayer. Then raising the cup to his lips, quite readily and cheerfully he drank off the poison. And hitherto most of us had been able to control our sorrow; but now when we saw him drinking, and saw too that he had finished the cup, we could no longer hold back, and in spite of myself my own tears were flowing fast; so that I covered my face and wept, not for him, but at the thought of my own calamity in having to part from such a friend. Nor was I the first; for Crito, when he found himself unable to restrain his tears, had got up, and I followed; and at that moment, Apollodorus, who had been weeping all the time, broke out in a loud and passionate cry which made cowards of us all. Socrates alone retained his calmness: What is this strange outcry? he said. I sent away the women mainly in order that they might not misbehave in this way, for I have been told that a man should die in peace. Be quiet then, and have patience. When we heard his words we were ashamed, and refrained our tears; and he walked about until, as he said, his legs began

[6]As an offering (libation) to a god it was customary, before drinking, to pour a few drops of wine or other liquid on the ground.

to fail, and then he lay on his back, according to the directions, and the man who gave him the poison now and then looked at his feet and legs; and after a while he pressed his foot hard, and asked him if he could feel; and he said, No; and then his leg, and so upwards and upwards, and showed us that he was cold and stiff. And he felt them himself, and said: When the poison reaches the heart, that will be the end. He was beginning to grow cold about the groin, when he uncovered his face, for he had covered himself up, and said—they were his last words—he said: Crito, I owe a cock to Asclepius;[7] will you remember to pay the debt? The debt shall be paid, said Crito; is there anything else? There was no answer to this question; but in a minute or two a movement was heard, and the attendants uncovered him; his eyes were set, and Crito closed his eyes and mouth.

Such was the end, Echecrates, of our friend; concerning whom I may truly say, that of all the men of his time whom I have known, he was the wisest, most just, and best.

---

[7]The god of healing. Socrates is referring to the sacrifice of a bird that he had promised the deity.

10

Plato

Republic

*T*O Plato (ca. 429–347 B.C.), Socra-
tes' most brilliant disciple, the trial and death of the master came as a profound
shock (see selections 8 and 9). Born a member of the Athenian ruling class,
Plato had grown up in an atmosphere of war and revolution. In 404 B.C. he
had seen the discredited Athenian democracy go down in ruin at the end of the
Peloponnesian War. He had looked to a government by chosen aristocrats to
restore order and justice, only to be disillusioned by the incompetence of those
installed (with Spartan support)—who came to be known as the "Thirty
Tyrants." The death of his revered master turned Plato from a life of prospective public service, normal for an aristocrat, to the teaching and application of
the Socratic ideals. About 387 B.C., after a prolonged absence following Socrates' death, he returned to Athens and began to gather about himself a community of young disciples, teaching them the principles of his beloved teacher.

The basic human problem, it seemed to Plato, was this: How can society be
reconstituted so that all individuals may know happiness and justice? To guide
a careful inquiry into this problem, Plato established a school, known as the
Academy, in a grove of olive trees on the outskirts of Athens. (The school's
name came from the fact that the grove was sacred to a mythological hero,
Academus.) The Academy was to be used to train philosopher-statesmen who,
Plato hoped, would one day govern Athens; for he believed that only a city-
state governed by such men would achieve justice. Soon, however, the Academy
became not only a pan-Hellenic center for study and research, but a magnet for
philosophers throughout the Western world; it was to remain such for almost a
thousand years.

REPUBLIC   Reprinted from *The Republic of Plato* translated by F. M. Cornford (1941)
by permission of Oxford University Press. Pp. 103–111, 148–50, 152–58, 163–64, 176–
79, 227–31, 234.

There, until his death, Plato taught and developed the thought of Socrates and continued to write the dialogues (discussions), in which Socrates is almost always portrayed as the principal speaker. Among these dialogues are the Apology, *the* Phaedo *(selections 8 and 9), and the* Republic, *from which the following passages are taken. Although the Spartan laws and customs are taken as an imperfect working model, the central thesis of the* Republic *is that government is a task only for those qualified; that the impartial lover of truth, the philosopher, alone is qualified to govern; and that until philosophy and political power meet in one authority, there will be no end to human misery.*

The Republic *is a discussion of great intellectual richness and breadth; and as Plato's most widely read work, it has exercised a profound influence upon Western thought. To many it is known only as a utopian or visionary program, the first of its kind in the literature of the West. But to others—perhaps reflecting upon the social disturbances, political stupidities, and mass sufferings of the twentieth century—it is regarded as the greatest work of political philosophy ever written.*

The dialogue as a whole is concerned with the nature of justice and how a just social order may be realized. Socrates (the "I" of the dialogue) develops the true meaning of justice and describes an ideal society in which justice has been made real. The passages included here deal with the proposed ruling elite (called Guardians); the roles and relationships of men, women, and children; the central place of philosophy in human affairs; and, in the famous "Allegory of the Cave," with the key function of philosophers as educators and governors. The persons who participate in the imaginary dialogue are, besides Socrates himself, Glaucon and Adeimantus, the brothers of Plato. The setting is the house of a mutual friend in the Piraeus, a port about four miles southwest of Athens.

[Editor's note: Earlier in the dialogue, the discussion has turned about the preliminary education of the Guardians,[1] ending at the age of twenty, intended to develop a harmony of mental, physical, and "philosophic" elements in their character. As we begin the selected passage, Socrates moves on to a higher level of training: to the "kingly science" that prepares the best individuals for rule.]

[1]The Guardians were authoritarian, but their function was custodianship, not leadership. Unlike some twentieth-century dictators, they would work to preserve values, not to bring about change.

Good, said Socrates; and what is the next point to be settled? Is it not the question, which of these Guardians are to be rulers and which are to obey?

No doubt, said Glaucon.

Well, it is obvious that the elder must have authority over the young, and that the rulers must be the best.

Yes.

And as among farmers the best are those with a natural turn for farming, so, if we want the best among our Guardians, we must take those naturally fitted to watch over a commonwealth. They must have the right sort of intelligence and ability; and also they must look upon the commonwealth as their special concern—the sort of concern that is felt for something so closely bound up with oneself that its interests and fortunes, for good or ill, are held to be identical with one's own.

Exactly.

So the kind of men we must choose from among the Guardians will be those who, when we look at the whole course of their lives, are found to be full of zeal to do whatever they believe is for the good of the commonwealth and never willing to act against its interest.

Yes, they will be the men we want.

We must watch them, I think, at every age and see whether they are capable of preserving this conviction that they must do what is best for the community, never forgetting it or allowing themselves to be either forced or bewitched into throwing it over.

How does this throwing over come about?

I will explain. When a belief passes out of the mind, a man may be willing to part with it, if it is false and he has learnt better, or unwilling, if it is true.

I see how he might be willing to let it go; but you must explain how he can be unwilling.

Where is your difficulty? Don't you agree that men are unwilling to be deprived of good, though ready enough to part with evil? Or that to be deceived about the truth is evil, to possess it good? Or don't you think that possessing truth means thinking of things as they really are?

You are right. I do agree that men are unwilling to be robbed of a true belief.

When that happens to them, then, it must be by theft, or violence, or bewitchment.

Again I do not understand.

Perhaps my metaphors are too high-flown. I call it theft when one is persuaded out of one's belief or forgets it. Argument in the one case, and time in the other, steal it away without one's knowing what is happening. You understand now?

Yes.

And by violence I mean being driven to change one's mind by pain or suffering.

That too I understand, and you are right.

And bewitchment, as I think you would agree, occurs when a man is beguiled out of his opinion by the allurements of pleasure or scared out of it under the spell of panic.

Yes, all delusions are like a sort of bewitchment.

As I said just now, then, we must find out who are the best guardians of this inward conviction that they must always do what they believe to be best for the commonwealth. We shall have to watch them from earliest childhood and set them tasks in which they would be most likely to forget or to be beguiled out of this duty. We shall then choose only those whose memory holds firm and who are proof against delusion.

Yes.

We must also subject them to ordeals of toil and pain and watch for the same qualities there. And we must observe them when exposed to the test of yet a third kind of bewitchment. As people lead colts up to alarming noises to see whether they are timid, so these young men must be brought into terrifying situations and then into scenes of pleasure, which will put them to severer proof than gold tried in the furnace. If we find one bearing himself well in all these trials and resisting every enchantment, a true guardian of himself, preserving always that perfect rhythm and harmony of being which he has acquired from his training in music and poetry, such a one will be of the greatest service to the commonwealth as well as to himself. Whenever we find one who has come unscathed through every test in childhood, youth, and manhood, we shall set him as a Ruler to watch over the commonwealth; he will be honoured in life, and after death receive the highest tribute of funeral rites and other memorials. All who do not reach this standard we must reject. And that, I think, my dear Glaucon, may be taken as an outline of the way in which we shall select Guardians to be set in authority as Rulers.

I am very much of your mind.

These, then, may properly be called Guardians in the fullest sense, who will ensure that neither foes without shall have the power, nor friends within the wish, to do harm. Those young men whom up to now we have been speaking of as Guardians, will be better described as Auxiliaries, who will enforce the decisions of the Rulers.

I agree.

Now, said I, can we devise something in the way of those convenient fictions we spoke of earlier, a single bold flight of invention,[2] which we may induce the community in general, and if possible the Rulers themselves, to accept?

What kind of fiction?

Nothing new; something like an Eastern tale of what, according to the poets, has happened before now in more than one part of the world. The poets have been believed; but the thing has not happened in our day, and it would be hard to persuade anyone that it could ever happen again.

You seem rather shy of telling this story of yours.

With good reason, as you will see when I have told it.

Out with it; don't be afraid.

Well, here it is; though I hardly know how to find the courage or the words to express it. I shall try to convince, first the Rulers and the soldiers, and then the whole community, that all that nurture and education which we gave them was only something they seemed to experience as it were in a dream. In reality they were the whole time down inside the earth, being moulded and fostered while their arms and all their equipment were being fashioned also; and at last, when they were complete, the earth sent them up from her womb into the light of day. So now they must think of the land they dwell in as a mother and nurse, whom they must take thought for and defend against any attack, and of their fellow citizens as brothers born of the same soil.

You might well be bashful about coming out with your fiction.

No doubt; but still you must hear the rest of the story. It is true, we shall tell our people in this fable, that all of you in this land are brothers; but the god who fashioned you mixed gold in the composition of those among you who are fit to rule, so that they are of the most precious quality; and he put silver in the Auxiliaries, and iron and brass in the farmers and craftsmen. Now, since you are all of one stock, although your children will generally be like their parents, sometimes a golden parent may have a silver child or a silver parent a golden one, and so

---

[2]Sometimes translated as "the noble lie"; but, although a fiction, it was "true in spirit" and intended for the good of all. The Guardians themselves were to accept it.

on with all the other combinations. So the first and chief injunction laid by heaven upon the Rulers is that, among all the things of which they must show themselves good guardians, there is none that needs to be so carefully watched as the mixture of metals in the souls of the children. If a child of their own is born with an alloy of iron or brass, they must, without the smallest pity, assign him the station proper to his nature and thrust him out among the craftsmen or the farmers. If, on the contrary, these classes produce a child with gold or silver in his composition, they will promote him, according to his value, to be a Guardian or an Auxiliary. They will appeal to a prophecy that ruin will come upon the state when it passes into the keeping of a man of iron or brass. Such is the story; can you think of any device to make them believe it?

Not in the first generation; but their sons and descendants might believe it, and finally the rest of mankind.

Well, said I, even so it might have a good effect in making them care more for the commonwealth and for one another; for I think I see what you mean.

So, I continued, we will leave the success of our story to the care of popular tradition; and now let us arm these sons of Earth and lead them, under the command of their Rulers, to the site of our city. There let them look round for the best place to fix their camp, from which they will be able to control any rebellion against the laws from within and to beat off enemies who may come from without like wolves to attack the fold. When they have pitched their camp and offered sacrifice to the proper divinities, they must arrange their sleeping quarters; and these must be sufficient to shelter them from winter cold and summer heat.

Naturally. You mean they are going to live there?

Yes, said I; but live like soldiers, not like men of business.

What is the difference?

I will try to explain. It would be very strange if a shepherd were to disgrace himself by keeping, for the protection of his flock, dogs who were so ill-bred and badly trained that hunger or unruliness or some bad habit or other would set them worrying the sheep and behaving no better than wolves. We must take every precaution against our Auxiliaries treating the citizens in any such way and, because they are stronger, turning into savage tyrants instead of friendly allies; and they will have been furnished with the best of safeguards, if they have really been educated in the right way.

But surely there is nothing wrong with their education.

We must not be too positive about that, my dear Glaucon; but we can be sure of what we said not long ago, that if they are to have the best chance of being gentle and humane to one another and to their charges, they must have the right education, whatever that may be.

We were certainly right there.

Then besides that education, it is only common sense to say that the dwellings and other belongings provided for them must be such as will neither make them less perfect Guardians nor encourage them to maltreat their fellow citizens.

True.

With that end in view, let us consider how they should live and be housed. First, none of them must possess any private property beyond the barest necessaries. Next, no one is to have any dwelling or storehouse that is not open for all to enter at will. Their food, in the quantities required by men of temperance and courage who are in training for war, they will receive from the other citizens as the wages of their guardianship, fixed so that there shall be just enough for the year with nothing over; and they will have meals in common and all live together like soldiers in a camp. Gold and silver, we shall tell them, they will not need, having the divine counterparts of those metals always in their souls as a god-given possession, whose purity it is not lawful to sully by the acquisition of that mortal dross, current among mankind, which has been the occasion of so many unholy deeds. They alone of all the citizens are forbidden to touch and handle silver or gold, or to come under the same roof with them, or wear them as ornaments, or drink from vessels made of them. This manner of life will be their salvation and make them the saviours of the commonwealth. If ever they should come to possess land of their own and houses and money, they will give up their guardianship for the management of their farms and households and become tyrants at enmity with their fellow citizens instead of allies. And so they will pass all their lives in hating and being hated, plotting and being plotted against, in much greater fear of their enemies at home than of any foreign foe, and fast heading for the destruction that will soon overwhelm their country with themselves. For all these reasons let us say that this is how our Guardians are to be housed and otherwise provided for, and let us make laws accordingly.

By all means, said Glaucon.

Here Adeimantus interposed. Socrates, he said, how would you meet the objection that you are not making these people particularly happy? It is their own fault too, if they are not; for they are really masters of the state, and yet they get no good out of it as other rulers do, who own lands, build themselves fine houses with handsome furniture, offer private sacrifices to the gods, and entertain visitors from abroad; who possess, in fact, that gold and silver you spoke of, with everything else that is usually thought necessary for happiness. These people seem like nothing so much as a garrison of mercenaries posted in the city and perpetually mounting guard.

Yes, I said, and what is more they will serve for their food only without getting a mercenary's pay, so that they will not be able to travel on their own account or to make presents to a mistress or to spend as they please in other ways, like the people who are commonly thought happy. You have forgotten to include these counts in your indictment, and many more to the same effect.

Well, take them as included now.

And you want to hear the answer?

Yes.

We shall find one, I think, by keeping to the line we have followed so far. We shall say that, though it would not be surprising if even these people were perfectly happy under such conditions, our aim in founding the commonwealth was not to make any one class specially happy, but to secure the greatest possible happiness for the community as a whole. We thought we should have the best chance of finding justice in a state so constituted, just as we should find injustice where the constitution was of the worst possible type; we could then decide the question which has been before us all this time. For the moment, we are constructing, as we believe, the state which will be happy as a whole, not trying to secure the well-being of a select few; we shall study a state of the opposite kind presently. It is as if we were colouring a statue[3] and someone came up and blamed us for not putting the most beautiful colours on the noblest parts of the figure; the eyes, for instance, should be painted crimson, but we had made them black. We should think it a fair answer to say: Really, you must not expect us to paint eyes so handsome as not to look like eyes at all. This applies to all the parts: the question is whether, by giving each its proper colour, we make the whole beautiful. So too, in the present case, you must not press us to endow our Guardians with a happiness that will make them anything rather than guardians. We could quite easily clothe our farm-

[3]Greek sculpture was usually painted.

ers in gorgeous robes, crown them with gold, and invite them to till the soil at their pleasure; or we might set our potters to lie on couches by their fire, passing round the wine and making merry, with their wheel at hand to work at whenever they felt so inclined. We could make all the rest happy in the same sort of way, and so spread this well-being through the whole community. But you must not put that idea into our heads; if we take your advice, the farmer will be no farmer, the potter no longer a potter; none of the elements that make up the community will keep its character. In many cases this does not matter so much: if a cobbler goes to the bad and pretends to be what he is not, he is not a danger to the state; but, as you must surely see, men who make only a vain show of being guardians of the laws and of the commonwealth bring the whole state to utter ruin, just as, on the other hand, its good government and well-being depend entirely on them. We, in fact, are making genuine Guardians who will be the last to bring harm upon the commonwealth; if our critic aims rather at producing a happiness like that of a party of peasants feasting at a fair, what he has in mind is something other than a civic community. So we must consider whether our aim in establishing Guardians is to secure the greatest possible happiness for them, or happiness is something of which we should watch the development in the whole commonwealth. If so, we must compel these Guardians and Auxiliaries of ours to second our efforts; and they, and all the rest with them, must be induced to make themselves perfect masters each of his own craft. In that way, as the community grows into a well-ordered whole, the several classes may be allowed such measure of happiness as their nature will compass.

I think that is an admirable reply.

•   •   •

We must go back, then, said Socrates, to a subject which ought, perhaps, to have been treated earlier in its proper place; though, after all, it may be suitable that the women should have their turn on the stage when the men have quite finished their performance, especially since you are so insistent. In my judgement, then, the question under what conditions people born and educated as we have described should possess wives and children, and how they should treat them, can be rightly settled only by keeping to the course on which we started them at the outset. We undertook to put these men in the position of watchdogs guarding a flock. Suppose we follow up the analogy and imagine them bred and reared in the same sort of way. We can then see if that plan will suit our purpose.

How will that be?

In this way. Which do we think right for watch-dogs: should the females guard the flock and hunt with the males and take a share in all they do, or should they be kept within doors as fit for no more than bearing and feeding their puppies, while all the hard work of looking after the flock is left to the males?

They are expected to take their full share, except that we treat them as not quite so strong.

Can you employ any creature for the same work as another, if you do not give them both the same upbringing and education?

No.

Then, if we are to set women to the same tasks as men, we must teach them the same things. They must have the same two branches of training for mind and body and also be taught the art of war, and they must receive the same treatment.

That seems to follow.

Possibly, if these proposals were carried out, they might be ridiculed as involving a good many breaches of custom.

They might indeed.

The most ridiculous—don't you think?—being the notion of women exercising naked along with the men in the wrestling-schools; some of them elderly women too, like the old men who still have a passion for exercise when they are wrinkled and not very agreeable to look at.

Yes that would be thought laughable, according to our present notions.

Now we have started on this subject, we must not be frightened of the many witticisms that might be aimed at such a revolution, not only in the matter of bodily exercise but in the training of women's minds, and not least when it comes to their bearing arms and riding on horseback. Having begun upon these rules, we must not draw back from the harsher provisions. The wits may be asked to stop being witty and try to be serious; and we may remind them that it is not so long since the Greeks, like most foreign nations of the present day, thought it ridiculous and shameful for men to be seen naked. When gymnastic exercises were first introduced in Crete and later at Sparta, the humorists had their chance to make fun of them; but when experience had shown that nakedness is better uncovered than muffled up, the laughter died down and a practice which the reason approved ceased to look ridiculous to the eye. This shows how idle it is to think anything ludicrous but what is base. One who tries to raise a laugh at any spectacle save that of baseness and folly will also, in his serious moments, set before himself some other standard than goodness of what deserves to be held in honour.

Most assuredly.

The first thing to be settled, then, is whether these proposals are feasible; and it must be open to anyone, whether a humorist or serious-minded, to raise the question whether, in the case of mankind, the feminine nature is capable of taking part with the other sex in all occupations, or in none at all, or in some only; and in particular under which of these heads this business of military service falls. Well begun is half done, and would not this be the best way to begin?

Yes.

Shall we take the other side in this debate and argue against ourselves? We do not want the adversary's position to be taken by storm for lack of defenders.

I have no objection.

Let us state his case for him. "Socrates and Glaucon," he will say, "there is no need for others to dispute your position; you yourselves, at the very outset of founding your commonwealth, agreed that everyone should do the one work for which nature fits him." Yes, of course; I suppose we did. "And isn't there a very great difference in nature between man and woman?" Yes, surely. "Does not that natural difference imply a corresponding difference in the work to be given to each?" Yes. . . .

If, then, we find that either the male sex or the female is specially qualified for any particular form of occupation, then that occupation, we shall say, ought to be assigned to one sex or the other. But if the only difference appears to be that the male begets and the female brings forth, we shall conclude that no difference between man and woman has yet been produced that is relevant to our purpose. We shall continue to think it proper for our Guardians and their wives to share in the same pursuits.

And quite rightly.

The next thing will be to ask our opponent to name any profession or occupation in civic life for the purposes of which woman's nature is different from man's.

That is a fair question.

He might reply, as you did just now, that it is not easy to find a satisfactory answer on the spur of the moment, but that there would be no difficulty after a little reflection.

Perhaps.

Suppose, then, we invite him to follow us and see if we can convince him that there is no occupation concerned with the management of social affairs that is peculiar to women. We will confront him with a question: When you speak of a man having a natural talent for something, do you mean that he finds it easy to learn, and after a little instruction can find out much more for himself; whereas a man who is not so gifted learns with difficulty and no amount of instruction and practice will make him even remember what he has been taught? Is the talented man one whose bodily powers are readily at the service of his mind, instead of being a hindrance? Are not these the marks by which you distinguish the presence of a natural gift for any pursuit?

Yes, precisely.

Now do you know of any human occupation in which the male sex is not superior to the female in all these respects? Need I waste time over exceptions like weaving and watching over saucepans and batches of cakes, though women are supposed to be good at such things and get laughed at when a man does them better?

It is true, he replied, in almost everything one sex is easily beaten by the other. No doubt many women are better at many things than many men; but taking the sexes as a whole, it is as you say.

To conclude, then, there is no occupation concerned with the management of social affairs which belongs either to woman or to man, as such. Natural gifts are to be found here and there in both creatures alike; and every occupation is open to both, so far as their natures are concerned, though woman is for all purposes the weaker.

Certainly. . . .

It follows that one woman will be fitted by nature to be a Guardian, another will not; because these were the qualities for which we selected our men Guardians. So for the purpose of keeping watch over the commonwealth, woman has the same nature as man, save in so far as she is weaker.

So it appears.

It follows that women of this type must be selected to share the life and duties of Guardians with men of the same type, since they are competent and of a like nature, and the same natures must be allowed the same pursuits.

Yes.

We come round, then, to our former position, that there is nothing contrary to nature in giving our Guardians' wives the same training for mind and body. The practice we proposed to establish was not impossible or visionary, since it was in accordance with nature. Rather, the contrary practice which now prevails turns out to be unnatural.

So it appears.

Well, we set out to inquire whether the plan we proposed was feasible and also the best. That it is feasible is now agreed; we must next settle whether it is the best.

Obviously.

Now, for the purpose of producing a woman fit to be a Guardian, we shall not have one education for men and another for women, precisely because the nature to be taken in hand is the same.

True.

What is your opinion on the question of one man being better than another? Do you think there is no such difference?

Certainly I do not.

And in this commonwealth of ours which will prove the better men—the Guardians who have received the education we described, or the shoemakers who have been trained to make shoes?

It is absurd to ask such a question.

Very well. So these Guardians will be the best of all the citizens?

By far.

And these women the best of all the women?

Yes.

Can anything be better for a commonwealth than to produce in it men and women of the best possible type?

No.

And that result will be brought about by such a system of mental and bodily training as we have described?

Surely.

We may conclude that the institution we proposed was not only practicable, but also the best for the commonwealth.

Yes.

The wives of our Guardians, then, must strip for exercise, since they will be clothed with virtue, and they must take their share in war and in the other social duties of guardianship. They are to have no other occupation; and in these duties the lighter part must fall to the women, because of the weakness of their sex. The man who laughs at naked women, exercising their bodies for the best of reasons, is like one that "gathers fruit unripe," for he does not know what it is that he is laughing at or what he is doing. There will never be a finer saying than the one which declares that whatever does good should be held in honour, and the only shame is in doing harm.

That is perfectly true. . . . So far, then, in regulating the position of women, we may claim to have come safely through with one hazardous proposal, that male and female Guardians shall have all occupations in common. The consistency of the argument is an assurance that the plan is a good one and also feasible. We are like swimmers who have breasted the first wave without being swallowed up.

Not such a small wave either.

You will not call it large when you see the next.

Let me have a look at the next one, then.

Here it is: a law which follows from that principle and all that has gone before, namely that, of these Guardians, no one man and one woman are to set up house together privately: wives are to be held in common by all; so too are the children, and no parent is to know his own child, nor any child his parent.

It will be much harder to convince people that that is either a feasible plan or a good one.

As to its being a good plan, I imagine no one would deny the immense advantage of wives and children being held in common, provided it can be done. I should expect dispute to arise chiefly over the question whether it is possible.

There may well be a good deal of dispute over both points.

You mean, I must meet attacks on two fronts. I was hoping to escape one by running away: if you agreed it was a good plan, then I should only have had to inquire whether it was feasible.

No, we have seen through that maneuver. You will have to defend both positions.

Well, I must pay the penalty for my cowardice. But grant me one favour. Let me indulge my fancy, like one who entertains himself with idle day-dreams on a solitary walk. Before he has any notion how his desires can be realized, he will set aside that question, to save himself the trouble of reckoning what may or may not be possible. He will assume that his wish has come true, and amuse himself with settling all the details of what he means to do then. So a lazy mind encourages itself to be lazier than ever; and I am giving way to the same weakness myself. I want to put off till later that question, how the thing can be done. For the moment, with your leave, I shall assume it to be possible, and ask how the Rulers will work out the details in practice; and I shall argue that the plan, once carried into effect, would be the best thing in the world for our commonwealth and for its Guardians. That is what I shall now try to make out with your help, if you will allow me to postpone the other question.

Very good; I have no objection.

Well, if our Rulers are worthy of the name, and their Auxiliaries likewise, these latter will be ready to do what they are told, and the Rulers, in giving their commands, will themselves obey our laws and will be faithful to their spirit in any details we leave to their discretion.

No doubt.

It is for you, then, as their lawgiver, who have already selected the men, to select for association with them women who are so far as possible of the same natural capacity. Now since none of them will have any private home of his own, but they will share the same dwelling and eat at common tables, the two sexes will be together; and meeting without restriction for exercise and all through their upbringing, they will surely be drawn towards union with one another by a necessity of their nature—necessity is not too strong a word, I think?

Not too strong for the constraint of love, which for the mass of mankind is more persuasive and compelling than even the necessity of mathematical proof.

Exactly. But in the next place, Glaucon, anything like unregulated unions would be a profanation in a state whose citizens lead the good life. The Rulers will not allow such a thing.

No, it would not be right.

Clearly, then, we must have marriages, as sacred as we can make them; and this sanctity will attach to those which yield the best results.

Certainly. . . .

This, then, Glaucon, is the manner in which the Guardians of your commonwealth are to hold their wives and children in common. Must we not next find arguments to establish that it is consistent with our other institutions and also by far the best plan?

Yes, surely.

We had better begin by asking what is the greatest good at which the lawgiver should aim in laying down the constitution of a state, and what is the worst evil. We can then consider whether our proposals are in keeping with that good and irreconcilable with the evil.

By all means.

Does not the worst evil for a state arise from anything that tends to rend it asunder and destroy its unity, while nothing does it more good than whatever tends to bind it together and make it one?

That is true.

And are not citizens bound together by sharing in the same pleasures and pains, all feeling glad or grieved on the same occasions of gain or loss; whereas the bond is broken when such feelings are no longer universal, but any event of public or personal concern fills some with joy and others with distress?

Certainly.

And this disunion comes about when the words "mine" and "not mine," "another's" and "not another's" are not applied to the same things throughout the community. The best ordered state will be the one in which the largest number of persons use these terms in the same sense, and which accordingly most nearly resembles a single person. When one of us hurts his finger, the whole extent of those bodily connexions which are gathered up in the soul and unified by its ruling element is made aware and it all shares as a whole in the pain of the suffering part; hence we say that the man has a pain in his finger. The same thing is true of the pain or pleasure felt when any other part of the person suffers or is relieved.

Yes; I agree that the best organized community comes nearest to that condition.

And so it will recognize as a part of itself the individual citizen to whom good or evil happens, and will share as a whole in his joy or sorrow.

•   •   •

But really, Socrates, Glaucon continued, if you are allowed to go on like this, I am afraid you will forget all about the question you thrust aside some time ago: whether a society so constituted can ever come into existence, and if so, how. No doubt, if it did exist, all manner of good things would come about. I can even add some that you have passed over. Men who acknowledged one another as fathers, sons, or brothers and always used those names among themselves would never desert one another; so they would fight with unequalled bravery. And if their womenfolk went out with them to war, either in the ranks or drawn up in the rear to intimidate the enemy and act as a reserve in case of need, I am sure all this would make them invincible. At home, too, I can see many advantages you have not mentioned. But, since I admit that our commonwealth would have all these merits and any number more, if once it came into existence, you need not describe it in further detail. All we have now to do is to convince ourselves that it can be brought into being and how.

This is a very sudden onslaught, said I; you have no mercy on my shilly-shallying. Perhaps you do not realize that, after I have barely escaped the first two waves,[4] the third, which you are now bringing down upon me, is the most formidable of all. When you have seen what it is like and heard my reply, you will be ready to excuse the very natural fears which made me shrink from putting forward such a paradox for discussion.

The more you talk like that, he said, the less we shall be willing to let you off from telling us how this constitution can come into existence; so you had better waste no more time.

Well, said I, let me begin by reminding you that what brought us to this point was our inquiry into the nature of justice and injustice.

True; but what of that?

Merely this: suppose we do find out what justice is, are we going to demand that a man who is just shall have a character which exactly corresponds in every respect to the ideal of justice? Or shall we be satisfied if he comes as near to the ideal as possible and has in him a larger measure of that quality than the rest of the world?

That will satisfy me.

If so, when we set out to discover the essential nature of justice and injustice and what a perfectly just and a perfectly unjust man would be like, supposing them to exist, our purpose was to use them as ideal patterns: we were to observe the degree of happiness or unhappiness that each exhibited, and to draw the necessary inference that our own destiny would be like that of the one we most resembled. We did not set out to show that these ideals could exist in fact.

That is true.

Then suppose a painter had drawn an ideally beautiful figure complete to the last touch, would you think any the worse of him, if he could not show that a person as beautiful as that could exist?

No, I should not.

Well, we have been constructing in discourse the pattern of an ideal state. Is our theory any the worse, if we cannot prove it possible that a state so organized could be actually founded?

[4] Socrates is referring to the difficulties ("waves" of public opinion) he has overcome in proposing equality for women and an end to the traditional family unit.

Surely not.

That, then, is the truth of the matter. But if, for your satisfaction, I am to do my best to show under what conditions our ideal would have the best chance of being realized, I must ask you once more to admit that the same principle applies here. Can theory ever be fully realized in practice? Is it not in the nature of things that action should come less close to truth than thought? People may not think so; but do you agree or not?

I do.

Then you must not insist upon my showing that this construction we have traced in thought could be reproduced in fact down to the last detail. You must admit that we shall have found a way to meet your demand for realization, if we can discover how a state might be constituted in the closest accordance with our description. Will not that content you? It would be enough for me.

And for me too.

Then our next attempt, it seems, must be to point out what defect in the working of existing states prevents them from being so organized, and what is the least change that would effect a transformation into this type of government—a single change if possible, or perhaps two; at any rate let us make the changes as few and insignificant as may be.

By all means.

Well, there is one change which, as I believe we can show, would bring about this revolution—not a small change, certainly, nor an easy one, but possible.

What is it?

I have now to confront what we called the third and greatest wave. But I must state my paradox, even though the wave should break in laughter over my head and drown me in ignominy. Now mark what I am going to say.

Go on.

Unless either philosophers become kings in their countries or those who are now called kings and rulers come to be sufficiently inspired with a genuine desire for wisdom; unless, that is to say, political power and philosophy meet together, while the many natures who now go their several ways in the one or the other direction are forcibly debarred from doing so, there can be no rest from troubles, my dear Glaucon, for states, nor yet, as I believe, for all mankind; nor can this commonwealth which we have imagined ever till then see the light of day and grow to its full stature. This it was that I have so long hung back from saying; I knew what a paradox it would be, because it is hard to see that there is no other way of happiness either for the state or for the individual.

• • •

Next, said I, here is a parable[5] to illustrate the degrees in which our nature may be enlightened or unenlightened. Imagine the condition of men living in a sort of cavernous chamber underground, with an entrance open to the light and a long passage all down the cave. Here they have been from childhood, chained by the leg and also by the neck, so that they cannot move and can see only what is in front of them, because the chains will not let them turn their heads. At some distance higher up is the light of a fire burning behind them; and between the prisoners and the fire is a track with a parapet built along it, like the screen at a puppetshow, which hides the performers while they show their puppets over the top.

I see, said he.

Now behind this parapet imagine persons carrying along various artificial objects, including figures of men and animals in wood or stone or other materials, which project above the parapet. Naturally, some of these persons will be talking, others silent.

It is a strange picture, he said, and a strange sort of prisoners.

Like ourselves, I replied; for in the first place prisoners so confined would have seen nothing of themselves or of one another, except the shadows thrown by the fire-light on the wall of the Cave facing them, would they?

Not if all their lives they had been prevented from moving their heads.

And they would have seen as little of the objects carried past.

Of course.

Now, if they could talk to one another, would they not suppose that their words referred only to those passing shadows which they saw?

Necessarily.

And suppose their prison had an echo from the wall facing them? When one of the people crossing behind them spoke, they could only suppose that the sound came from the shadow passing before their eyes.

[5]What follows is Plato's view of human alienation—not from a personal God or from society, but from Plato's concept of Reality. This parable, or fable, is often referred to as the "Allegory of the Cave."

No doubt.

In every way, then, such prisoners would recognize as reality nothing but the shadows of those artificial objects.

Inevitably.

Now consider what would happen if their release from the chains and the healing of their unwisdom should come about in this way. Suppose one of them set free and forced suddenly to stand up, turn his head, and walk with eyes lifted to the light; all these movements would be painful, and he would be too dazzled to make out the objects whose shadows he had been used to see. What do you think he would say, if someone told him that what he had formerly seen was meaningless illusion, but now, being somewhat nearer to reality and turned towards more real objects, he was getting a truer view? Suppose further that he were shown the various objects being carried by and were made to say, in reply to questions, what each of them was. Would he not be perplexed and believe the objects now shown him to be not so real as what he formerly saw?

Yes, not nearly so real.

And if he were forced to look at the fire-light itself, would not his eyes ache, so that he would try to escape and turn back to the things which he could see distinctly, convinced that they really were clearer than these other objects now being shown to him?

Yes.

And suppose someone were to drag him away forcibly up the steep and rugged ascent and not let him go until he had hauled him out into the sunlight, would he not suffer pain and vexation at such treatment, and, when he had come out into the light, find his eyes so full of its radiance that he could not see a single one of the things that he was now told were real?

Certainly he would not see them all at once.

He would need, then, to grow accustomed before he could see things in that upper world. At first it would be easiest to make out shadows, and then the images of men and things reflected in water, and later on the things themselves. After that, it would be easier to watch the heavenly bodies and the sky itself by night, looking at the light of the moon and stars rather than the Sun and the Sun's light in the daytime.

Yes, surely.

Last of all, he would be able to look at the Sun and contemplate its nature, not as it appears when reflected in water or any alien medium, but as it is in itself in its own domain.

No doubt.

And now he would begin to draw the conclusion that it is the Sun that produces the seasons and the course of the year and controls everything in the visible world, and moreover is in a way the cause of all that he and his companions used to see.

Clearly he would come at last to that conclusion.

Then if he called to mind his fellow prisoners and what passed for wisdom in his former dwelling-place, he would surely think himself happy in the change and be sorry for them. They may have had a practice of honouring and commending one another, with prizes for the man who had the keenest eye for the passing shadows and the best memory for the order in which they followed or accompanied one another, so that he could make a good guess as to which was going to come next. Would our released prisoner be likely to covet those prizes or to envy the men exalted to honour and power in the Cave? Would he not feel like Homer's Achilles, that he would far sooner "be on earth as a hired servant in the house of a landless man"[6] or endure anything rather than go back to his old beliefs and live in the old way?

Yes, he would prefer any fate to such a life.

Now imagine what would happen if he went down again to take his former seat in the Cave. Coming suddenly out of the sunlight, his eyes would be filled with darkness. He might be required once more to deliver his opinion on those shadows, in competition with the prisoners who had never been released, while his eyesight was still dim and unsteady; and it might take some time to become used to the darkness. They would laugh at him and say that he had gone up only to come back with his sight ruined; it was worth no one's while even to attempt the ascent. If they could lay hands on the man who was trying to set them free and lead them up, they would kill him.[7]

Yes, they would.

Every feature in this parable, my dear Glaucon, is meant to fit our earlier analysis. The prison dwelling corresponds to the region revealed to us through the sense of sight, and the fire-light within it to the power of the Sun. The ascent to see the things in the upper world you may take as standing for the upward journey of the soul into the region of the intelligible; then you will be in possession of what I

---

[6]Achilles was the mightiest of the warriors who had died at Troy (see selection 1). In Homer's epic poem *The Odyssey*, the soul of the dead Achilles states that he would rather be the lowliest slave up on earth than the king of the departed souls in the underworld of Hades.

[7]As happened to Socrates (selection 9).

surmise, since that is what you wish to be told. Heaven knows whether it is true; but this, at any rate, is how it appears to me. In the world of knowledge, the last thing to be perceived and only with great difficulty is the essential Form of Goodness. Once it is perceived, the conclusion must follow that, for all things, this is the cause of whatever is right and good; in the visible world it gives birth to light and to the lord of light, while it is itself sovereign in the intelligible world and the parent of intelligence and truth. Without having had a vision of this Form no one can act with wisdom, either in his own life or in matters of state.

So far as I can understand, I share your belief. . . .

You will see, then, Glaucon, that there will be no real injustice in compelling our philosophers to watch over and care for the other citizens. We can fairly tell them that their peers in other states may quite reasonably refuse to collaborate: there they have sprung up, like a self-sown plant, in despite of their country's institutions; no one has fostered their growth, and they cannot be expected to show gratitude for a care they have never received. "But," we shall say, "it is not so with you. We have brought you into existence for your country's sake as well as for your own, to be like leaders and king-bees in a hive; you have been better and more thoroughly educated than those others and hence you are more capable of playing your part both as men of thought and as men of action. You must go down, then, each in his turn, to live with the rest and let your eyes grow accustomed to the darkness. You will then see a thousand times better than those who live there always; you will recognize every image for what it is and know what it represents, because you have seen justice, beauty, and goodness in their reality; and so you and we shall find life in our commonwealth no mere dream, as it is in most existing states, where men live fighting one another about shadows and quarrelling for power, as if that were a great prize; whereas in truth government can be at its best and free from dissension only where the destined rulers are least desirous of holding office."

11

Aristotle

Ethics

*T*ODAY, *many people accept the idea that morals are relative—to the cultural environment or to the individual's point of view; but most influential thinkers among the ancient Greeks rejected this position. They believed it possible to arrive, rationally, at values true for all times and places. That their rigorous pursuit of such values was carried on so brilliantly is one of the marvels of Western culture.*

In this achievement no one took a greater part than Aristotle (384–322 B.C.). He was born at Stagira in Macedonia, north of Greece, and his father was physician to the king of Macedonia. From the age of seventeen to the death of Plato, twenty years later, Aristotle studied in Athens under the master at the Academy; later, he spent three years as tutor to the young Alexander, who would inherit the Macedonian throne. In 335, after Alexander had become king and begun his vast conquests (in Greece and the Middle East), Aristotle established a rival school to Plato's Academy, his famous Lyceum. During the next dozen years he taught there, while producing a wealth of writings. Upon Alexander's death in 323 B.C. Aristotle was forced by the anti-Macedonian party to flee from Athens and died in exile a year later.

Throughout his works, which systematically covered all the fields of human knowledge—both theoretical and practical—Aristotle was concerned (as was his teacher Plato) with the search for reality, for objective truth. (Aristotle's surviving writings consist mainly of notes or summaries of his lectures, intended for the use of students at the Lyceum. Unfortunately, none of his highly polished "Platonic style" dialogues, or other works intended for a general readership, survives.) In substance, Aristotle was more down-to-earth than

ETHICS   Aristotle, *The Nichomachean Ethics,* trans. F. H. Peters, 3rd edition (London: Kegan Paul, Trench, Truebner, 1886), 1–4, 12–17, 23–27, 36–38, 41–55, 113–119. Adapted by the editor.

Plato; he tried to show that material objects are no less real than Plato's world of "Forms" or "Ideas." Thus, in the Ethics *(originally Aristotle's lectures edited by his son Nicomachus), in which he deals with the problem of achieving the good life, Aristotle tests his value-judgments by comparing them to things as they are, rather than by describing a vision of the "ideal" as did Plato.*

Although Aristotle constantly strove for permanent and universal values, the Ethics *(ca. 332 B.C.) reflects conditions unique to Greek life in the ancient city-state. Its values are aristocratic—concerned with the good life for the cultivated few, not for the indifferent masses, with the highest form of happiness being the contemplative (thoughtful) life. Thus, after many centuries of Christian and democratic influences, it is a challenge for most modern readers to appreciate the following selection, which describes the Aristotelian "high-minded man" and the virtues he stands for. Nevertheless, the concept has made a lasting impression on Western thought and conduct. To this day, wherever the all-round amateur is prized, wherever manners are admired, and wherever narrow professionalism is deplored, the spirit of the* Ethics *still lives.*

[DEFINITION OF THE GOOD]

Every art and every kind of inquiry, and likewise every act and purpose, seems to aim at some good: and so it has been well said that the good is that at which everything aims.

But a difference is observable among these aims or ends. What is aimed at is sometimes the exercise of a faculty, sometimes a certain result beyond that exercise. And where there is an end beyond the act, there the result is better than the exercise of the faculty.

Now since there are many kinds of actions and many arts and sciences, it follows that there are many ends also; for example, health is the end of medicine, ships of shipbuilding, victory of the art of war, and wealth of economy.

But when several of these are subordinated to some one art or science—as the making of bridles and other trappings to the art of horsemanship, and this in turn, along with all else that the soldier does, to the art of war, and so on—then the end of the master-art is always more desired than the ends of the subordinate arts, since these are pursued for its sake. And this is equally true whether the end in view be the mere exercise of a faculty or something beyond that, as in the above instances.

If then in what we do there be some end which we wish for on its own account, choosing all the others as means to this, but not every end without exception as a means to something else (for if so we should go on *ad infinitum,* and desire would be left void and objectless)—this evidently will be the good or the best of all things.

And surely from a practical point of view it much concerns us to know this good; for then, like archers shooting at a definite mark, we shall be more likely to attain what we want.

[POLITICS AS THE MASTER-ART]

If this be so, we must try to indicate roughly what it is, and first of all to which of the arts or sciences it belongs.

It would seem to belong to the supreme art or science, that one which most of all deserves the name of master-art or master-science.

Now Politics seems to answer to this description. For it prescribes which of the sciences a state needs, and which each man shall study, and up to what point; and to it we see subordinated even the highest arts, such as economy, rhetoric, and the art of war.

Since then it makes use of the other practical sciences, and since it further ordains what men are to do and from what to refrain, its end must include the ends of the others, and must be the proper good of man.

For though this good is the same for the individual and the state, yet the good of the state seems a grander and more perfect thing both to attain and to secure; and glad as one would be to do this service for a single individual, to do it for a people and for a number of states is nobler and more divine.

This then is the aim of the present inquiry, which is a sort of political inquiry.

We must be content if we can attain to so much precision in our statement as the subject before us admits of; for the same degree of accuracy is no more to be expected in all kinds of reasoning than in all kinds of manufacture.

Now what is noble and just (with which Politics deals) is so various and so uncertain, that some think these are merely conventional and not natural distinctions.

There is a similar uncertainty also about what is good, because good things often do people harm: men have before now been ruined by wealth, and have lost their lives through courage.

Our subject, then, and our data being of this nature, we must be content if we can indicate the truth roughly and in outline, and if, in dealing with matters that are not amenable to immutable laws, and reasoning from premises that are but probable, we can arrive at probable conclusions.

• • •

[FUNCTIONAL DEFINITION OF MAN'S HIGHEST GOOD: ACTING IN ACCORDANCE WITH REASON]

Leaving these matters, then, let us return once more to the question, what this good can be of which we are in search.

It seems to be different in different kinds of action and in different arts—one good in medicine and another in war, and so on. What then is the good in each of these cases? Surely that for the sake of which all else is done. And that in medicine is health, in war is victory, in building is a house—a different thing in each different case, but always, in whatever we do and in whatever we choose, the end. For it is always for the sake of the end that all else is done.

If then there be one end of all that man does, this end will be the realizable good—or these ends, if there be more than one.

Our argument has thus come round by a different path to the same point as before. This point we must try to explain more clearly.

We see that there are many ends. But some of these are chosen only as means, as wealth, flutes, and the whole class of instruments. And so it is plain that not all ends are final.

But the best of all things must, we conceive, be something final.

If then there be only one final end, this will be what we are seeking—or if there be more than one, then the most final of them.

Now that which is pursued as an end in itself is more final than that which is pursued as means to something else, and that which is never chosen as means than that which is chosen both as an end in itself and as means, and that is strictly final which is always chosen as an end in itself and never as means.

Happiness seems more than anything else to answer to this description: for we always choose it for itself, and never for the sake of something else; while honour and pleasure and reason, and all virtue or excellence, we choose partly indeed for themselves (for, apart from any result, we should choose each of them), but partly also for the sake of happiness, supposing that they will help to make us happy. But no one chooses happiness for the sake of these things, or as a means to anything else at all.

We seem to be led to the same conclusion when we start from the notion of self-sufficiency.

The final good is thought to be self-sufficing [or all-sufficing]. In applying this term we do not regard a man as an individual leading a solitary life, but we also take account of parents, children, wife, and, in short, friends and fellow-citizens generally, since man is naturally a social being. Some limit must indeed be set to this; for if you go on to parents and descendants and friends of friends, you will never come to a stop. But this we will consider further on: for the present we will take self-sufficing to mean what by itself makes life desirable and in want of nothing. And happiness is believed to answer to this description.

And further, happiness is believed to be the most desirable thing in the world, and that not merely as one among other good things: if it were merely one among other good things [so that other things could be added to it], it is plain that the addition of the least of other goods must make it more desirable; for the addition becomes a surplus of good, and of two goods the greater is always more desirable.

Thus it seems that happiness is something final and self-sufficing, and is the end of all that man does.

But perhaps the reader thinks that though no one will dispute the statement that happiness is the best thing in the world, yet a still more precise definition of it is needed.

This will best be gained, I think, by asking, What is the function of man? For as the goodness and the excellence of a piper or a sculptor, or the practiser of any art, and generally of those who have any function or business to do, lies in that function, so man's good would seem to lie in his function, if he has one.

But can we suppose that, while a carpenter and a cobbler has a function and a business of his own, man has no business and no function assigned him by nature? Nay, surely as his several members, eye and hand and foot, plainly have each his own function, so we must suppose that man also has some function over and above all these.

What then is it?

Life evidently he has in common even with the plants, but we want that which is peculiar to him. We must exclude, therefore, the life of mere nutrition and growth.

Next to this comes the life of sense; but this too he plainly shares with horses and cattle and all kinds of animals.

There remains then the life whereby he acts—the life of his rational nature, with its two sides or divisions, one rational as obeying reason, the other rational as having and exercising reason.

But as this expression is ambiguous, we must be understood to mean thereby the life that consists in the exercise of the faculties; for this seems to be more properly entitled to the name.

The function of man, then, is exercise of his vital faculties [or soul] on one side in obedience to reason, and on the other side with reason.

But what is called the function of a man of any profession and the function of a man who is good in that profession are generically the same, for example, of a harper and of a good harper; and this holds in all cases without exception, only that in the case of the latter his superior excellence at his work is added; for we say a harper's function is to harp, and a good harper's to harp well.

Man's function then being, as we say, a kind of life—that is to say, exercise of his faculties and action of various kinds with reason—the good man's function is to do this well and beautifully [or nobly].

But the function of anything is done well when it is done in accordance with the proper excellence of that thing.

Putting all this together, then, we find that the good of man is exercise of his faculties in accordance with excellence or virtue, or, if there be more than one, in accordance with the best and most complete virtue.

But there must also be a full term of years for this exercise; for one swallow or one fine day does not make a spring, nor does one day or any small space of time make a blessed or happy man.

This, then, may be taken as a rough outline of the good; for this, I think, is the proper method—first to sketch the outline, and then to fill in the details.

•   •   •

[HAPPINESS AND THE CHANGES OF FORTUNE]

Are we, then, to call no man happy as long as he lives, but to wait for the end, as Solon[1] said?

And, supposing we have to allow this, do we mean that he actually is happy after he is dead? Surely that is absurd, especially for us who say that happiness is a kind of activity or life.

But if we do not call the dead man happy, and if Solon meant not this, but that only then could we safely apply the term to a man, as being now beyond the reach of evil and calamity, then here too we find

---

[1]A sixth-century Athenian sage and lawgiver. (See the "Croesus-Solon Story" in the excerpt from Herodotus' *History*, selection 4.)

some ground for objection. For it is thought that both good and evil may in some sort befall a dead man (just as they may befall a living man, although he is unconscious of them), for example, honours rendered to him, or the reverse of these, and again the prosperity or the misfortune of his children and all his descendants.

But this, too, has its difficulties; for after a man has lived happily to a good old age, and ended as he lived, it is possible that many changes may befall him in the persons of his descendants, and that some of them may turn out good and meet with the good fortune they deserve, and others the reverse. It is evident too that the degree in which the descendants are related to their ancestors may vary to any extent. And it would be a strange thing if the dead man were to change with these changes and become happy and miserable by turns. But it would also be strange to suppose that the dead are not affected at all, even for a limited time, by the fortunes of their posterity.

But let us return to our former question; for its solution will, perhaps, clear up this other difficulty.

The saying of Solon may mean that we ought to look for the end and then call a man happy, not because he now is, but because he once was happy.

But surely it is strange that when he is happy we should refuse to say what is true of him, because we do not like to apply the term to living men in view of the changes to which they are liable, and because we hold happiness to be something that endures and is little liable to change, while the fortunes of one and the same man often undergo many revolutions: for, it is argued, it is plain that, if we follow the changes of fortune, we shall call the same man happy and miserable many times over, making the happy man "a sort of chameleon and one who rests on no sound foundation."

We reply that it cannot be right thus to follow fortune. For it is not in this that our weal or woe lies; but, as we said, though the life of man needs these gifts of fortune, yet it is the excellent employment of his powers that constitutes his happiness, as the reverse of this constitutes his misery.

But the discussion of this difficulty leads to a further confirmation of our account. For nothing human is so constant as the excellent exercise of our faculties. (Knowledge of the sciences themselves seems to be less abiding.) And the highest of these exercises are the most abiding, because the happy are occupied with them most of all and most continuously (for this seems to be the reason why we do not forget how to do them).

The happy man, then, as we define him, will have this required property of permanence, and all through life will preserve his character; for he will be occupied continually, or with the least possible interruption, in excellent deeds and excellent speculations; and, whatever his fortune be, he will take it in the noblest fashion, and bear himself always and in all things suitably, since he is truly good and "foursquare without a flaw."

But the dispensations of fortune are many, some great, some small. The small ones, whether good or evil, plainly are of no weight in the scale; but the great ones, when numerous, will make life happier if they be good; for they help to give a grace to life themselves, and their use is noble and good; but, if they be evil, will enfeeble and spoil happiness; for they bring pain, and often impede the exercise of our faculties.

But nevertheless true worth shines out even here, in the calm endurance of many great misfortunes, not through insensibility, but through nobility and greatness of soul. And if it is what man does that determines the character of his life, as we said, then no happy man will become miserable, for he will never do what is hateful and base. For we hold that the man who is truly good and wise will bear with dignity whatever fortune sends, and will always make the best of his circumstances, as a good general will turn the forces at his command to the best account, and a good shoemaker will make the best shoe that can be made out of a given piece of leather, and so on with all other crafts.

If this be so, the happy man will never become miserable, though he will not be truly happy if he meets with the fate of Priam.[2]

But yet he is not unstable and lightly changed: he will not be moved from his happiness easily, nor by any ordinary misfortunes, but only by many heavy ones; and after such, he will not recover his happiness again in short time, but if at all, only in a considerable period, which has a certain completeness, and in which he attains to great and noble things.

We shall meet all objections, then, if we say that a happy man is "one who exercises his faculties in accordance with perfect excellence, being duly furnished with external goods, not for any chance time, but for a full term of years": to which perhaps we should add, "and who shall continue to live so, and shall die as he lived," since the future is veiled to us, but happiness we take to be the end and in all ways perfectly final or complete.

[2]King of ancient Troy, slain by Achilles' son upon the fall of the city.

If this be so, we may say that those living men are blessed or perfectly happy who both have and shall continue to have these characteristics, but happy as men only.

• • •

[ON THE RIGHT KINDS OF ACTIONS]

But our present inquiry has not, like the rest, a merely speculative aim; we are not inquiring merely in order to know what excellence or virtue is, but in order to become good; for otherwise it would profit us nothing. We must ask therefore about these acts, and see of what kind they are to be; for, as we said, it is they that determine our habits or character.

These acts, of course, must be in accordance with right reason. . . . But let it be understood, before we go on, that all reasoning on matters of practice must be only general, and not scientifically exact; . . . in practical matters and questions of expediency there are no invariable laws. . . .

First of all, we must observe that, in matters of this sort, to fall short and to exceed are alike fatal. This is plain (to illustrate what we cannot see by what we can see) in the case of strength and health. Too much and too little exercise alike destroy strength, and to take too much meat and drink, or to take too little, is equally ruinous to health, but the fitting amount produces and increases and preserves them. Just so, then, is it with temperance also, and courage, and the other virtues. The man who shuns and fears everything and never makes a stand, becomes a coward; while the man who fears nothing at all, but will face anything, becomes foolhardy. So, too, the man who takes his fill of any kind of pleasure, and abstains from none, is a profligate, but the man who shuns all (like him whom we call a "boor") is lacking in feelings. For temperance and courage are destroyed both by excess and defect, but preserved by moderation.

• • •

[VIRTUE AND VIRTUOUS ACTION]

But here we may be asked what we mean by saying that men can become just and temperate only by doing what is just and temperate: surely, it may be said, if their acts are just and temperate, they themselves are already just and temperate, as they are grammarians and musicians if they do what is grammatical and musical.

We may answer, I think, firstly, that this is not quite the case even with the arts. A man may do something grammatical [or write something correctly] by chance, or at the prompting of another person: he will not be grammatical till he not only does something grammatical, but also does it grammatically [or like a grammatical person], that is, in virtue of his own knowledge of grammar.

But, secondly, the [moral] virtues are not in this point analogous to the arts. The products of art have their excellence in themselves, and so it is enough if when produced they are of a certain quality; but in the case of the virtues, a man is not said to act justly or temperately [or like a just or temperate man] if what he does merely be of a certain sort—he must also be in a certain state of mind when he does it, *i.e.,* first of all, he must know what he is doing; secondly, he must choose it, and choose it for itself; and thirdly, his act must be the expression of a formed and stable character. Now, of these conditions, only one, the knowledge, is necessary for the possession of any art; but for the possession of the virtues knowledge is of little or no avail, while the other conditions that result from repeatedly doing what is just and temperate are not a little important, but all-important.

The thing that is done, therefore, is called just or temperate when it is such as the just or temperate man would do; but the man who does it is not just or temperate, unless he also does it in the spirit of the just or the temperate man.

It is right, then, to say that by doing what is just a man becomes just, and temperate by doing what is temperate, while without doing thus he has no chance of ever becoming good.

But most men, instead of doing thus, fly to theories, and fancy that they are philosophizing and that this will make them good, like a sick man who listens attentively to what the doctor says and then disobeys all his orders. This sort of philosophizing will no more produce a healthy habit of mind than this sort of treatment will produce a healthy habit of body.

•   •   •

[MORAL VIRTUE: THE DOCTRINE OF THE MEAN]

If, then, the virtues be neither emotions nor faculties [capacities or aptitudes], it only remains for them to be habits or practiced traits of character. We have thus found the category to which virtue belongs; but we want to know, not only that it is a trait of character, but also what kind of trait it is.

We may safely assert that the virtue or excellence of a thing causes that thing both to be itself in good condition and to perform its function well. The excellence of the eye, for instance, makes both the eye and its work good; for it is by the excellence of the eye that we see well. So the proper excellence of the horse makes a horse what he should be, and makes him good at running, and carrying his rider, and standing a charge.

If, then, this holds good in all cases, the proper excellence or virtue of man will be a habit or trained faculty that makes a man good and makes him perform his function well.

How this is to be done we have already said, but we may exhibit the same conclusion in another way, by inquiring what the nature of this virtue is.

Now, if we have any quantity, whether continuous or discrete, it is possible to take either a larger [or too large], or a smaller [or too small], or an equal [or fair] amount, and that either absolutely or relatively to our own needs.

By an equal or fair amount I understand a *mean* amount, or one that lies between excess and deficiency.

By the absolute mean, or mean relatively to the thing itself, I understand that which is equidistant from both extremes, and this is one and the same for all.

By the mean relatively to us I understand that which is neither too much nor too little for us; and this is not one and the same for all.

For instance, if ten be larger [or too large] and two be smaller [or too small], if we take six we take the mean relatively to the thing itself [or the arithmetical mean]; for it exceeds one extreme by the same amount by which it is exceeded by the other extreme: and this is the mean in arithmetical proportion.

But the mean relatively to us cannot be found in this way. If ten pounds of food is too much for a given man to eat, and two pounds too little, it does not follow that the trainer will order him six pounds: for that also may perhaps be too much for the man in question, or too little; too little for Milo,[3] too much for the beginner. The same holds true in running and wrestling.

[3]A famous Greek wrestler.

And so we may say generally that a master in any art avoids what is too much and what is too little, and seeks for the mean and chooses it—not the absolute but the relative mean.

Every art or science, then, perfects its work in this way, looking to the mean and bringing its work up to this standard; so that people say of a good work that nothing could be taken from it or added to it, implying that excellence is destroyed by excess or deficiency, but secured by observing the mean. And good artists, as we say, do in fact keep their eyes fixed on this in all that they do.

Virtue, therefore, since like nature it is more exact and better than any art, must also aim at the mean—virtue of course meaning moral virtue or excellence; for it has to do with passions and actions, and it is these that admit of excess and deficiency and the mean. For instance, it is possible to feel fear, confidence, desire, anger, pity, and generally to be affected pleasantly and painfully, either too much or too little, in either case wrongly; but to be thus affected at the right times, and on the right occasions, and towards the right persons, and with the right object, and in the right fashion, is the mean course and the best course, and these are characteristics of virtue. And in the same way our outward acts also admit of excess and deficiency, and the mean or due amount.

Virtue, then, has to deal with feelings or passions and with outward acts, in which excess is wrong and deficiency also is blamed, but the mean amount is praised and is right—both of which are characteristics of virtue.

Virtue, then, is a kind of moderation inasmuch as it aims at the mean or moderate amount.

Again, there are many ways of going wrong (for evil is infinite in nature, while good is finite), but only one way of going right; so that the one is easy and the other hard—easy to miss the mark and hard to hit. On this account also, then, excess and deficiency are characteristic of vice, hitting the mean is characteristic of virtue:

"Goodness is simple, ill takes any shape."

Virtue, then, is a habit or practiced trait of choice, the characteristic of which lies in observing the mean relatively to the persons concerned, and which is guided by reason, that is, by the judgment of the prudent man. . . .

Regarded in its essence, therefore, or according to the definition of its nature, virtue is a moderation or middle state, but viewed in its relation to what is best and right it is the extreme of perfection.

But it is not all actions nor all passions that admit of moderation; there are some whose very names imply badness, as malevolence, shamelessness, envy, and, among acts, adultery, theft, murder. These and all other like things are blamed as being bad in themselves, and not merely in their excess or deficiency. It is impossible therefore to go right in them; they are always wrong: rightness and wrongness in such things (for example, in adultery) does not depend upon whether it is the right person and occasion and manner, but the mere doing of any one of them is wrong.

It would be equally absurd to look for moderation or excess or deficiency in unjust, cowardly, or profligate conduct; for then there would be moderation in excess or deficiency, and excess in excess, and deficiency in deficiency.

The fact is that just as there can be no excess or deficiency in temperance or courage because the mean or moderate amount is, in a sense, an extreme, so in these kinds of conduct also there can be no moderation or excess or deficiency, but the acts are wrong however they be done. For, to put it generally, there cannot be moderation in excess or deficiency, nor excess or deficiency in moderation.

But it is not enough to make these general statements [about virtue and vice]: we must go on and apply them to particulars [that is, to the several virtues and vices]. For in reasoning about matters of conduct general statements are too vague, and do not convey so much truth as particular propositions. It is with particulars that conduct is concerned: our statements, therefore, when applied to these particulars, should be found to hold good.

These particulars then [for example, the several virtues and vices and the several acts and affections with which they deal], we will take from the following list:

Moderation in the feelings of fear and confidence is courage; of those that exceed, he that exceeds in fearlessness has no name (as often happens), but he that exceeds in confidence is foolhardy, while he that exceeds in fear, but is deficient in confidence, is cowardly.

Moderation in respect to certain pleasures and also (though to a less extent) certain pains is temperance, while excess is over-indulgence. But defectiveness in the matter of these pleasures is hardly ever found, and so this sort of people also have as yet received no name: let us put them down as lacking in feelings.

In the matter of giving and taking money, moderation is liberality, excess and deficiency are extravagance and stinginess. But these two vices exceed and fall short in contrary ways: the extravagant person exceeds in spending, but falls short in taking; while the stingy man exceeds in taking, but falls short in spending. . . .

But, besides these, there are other dispositions in the matter of money: there is a moderation which is called magnificence (for the magnificent is not the same as the liberal man: the former deals with large sums, the latter with small), and an excess which is called bad taste or vulgarity, and a deficiency which is called meanness; and these vices differ from those which are opposed to liberality: how they differ will be explained later.

With respect to honour and disgrace, there is a moderation which is high-mindedness, an excess which may be called vanity, and a deficiency which is small-mindedness. . . .

In the matter of anger also we find excess and deficiency and moderation. The characters themselves hardly have recognized names, but as the moderate man is here called gentle, we will call his character gentleness; of those who go into extremes, we may take the term wrathful for him who exceeds, with wrathfulness for the vice, and apathetic for him who is deficient, with apathy for his character. . . .

Righteous indignation, again, hits the mean between envy and malevolence. These have to do with feelings of pleasure and pain at what happens to our neighbors. A man is called righteously indignant when he feels pain at the sight of undeserved prosperity, but your envious man goes beyond him and is pained by the sight of any one in prosperity, while the malevolent man is so far from being pained that he actually exults in the sight of prosperous iniquity. . . .

There are, as we said, three classes of disposition: two kinds of vice, one marked by excess, the other by deficiency; and one kind of virtue, the observance of the mean.

Now, the extreme dispositions are opposed both to the mean or moderate disposition and to one another, while the moderate disposition is opposed to both the extremes. Just as a quantity which is equal to a given quantity is also greater when compared with a less, and less when compared with a greater quantity, so the mean or moderate dispositions exceed as compared with the defective dispositions, and fall short as compared with the excessive dispositions, both in feeling and in action; for example, the courageous man seems foolhardy as compared with the coward, and cowardly as compared with the foolhardy . . . and the liberal man appears extravagant by the side of the stingy man, and stingy by the side of the extravagant man.

And so the extreme characters try to displace the mean or moderate character, and each represents him as falling into the opposite extreme, the coward calling the courageous man foolhardy, the foolhardy calling him coward, and so on in other cases.

But while the mean and the extremes are thus opposed to one another, the extremes are still more contrary to each other than to the mean; for they are further removed from one another than from the mean. . . .

Sometimes, again, an extreme, when compared with the mean, has a sort of resemblance to it, as foolhardiness to courage, or prodigality to liberality; but there is the greatest possible dissimilarity between the extremes.

Again, "things that are as far as possible removed from each other" is the accepted definition of contraries, so that the further things are removed from each other the more contrary they are.

In comparison with the mean, however, it is sometimes the deficiency that is the more opposed, and sometimes the excess; for example, foolhardiness, which is excess, is not so much opposed to courage as cowardice, which is deficiency; but lack of feeling, is not so much opposed to temperance as overindulgence, which is excess. . . .

We have sufficiently explained, then, that moral virtue is moderation or observance of the mean, and in what sense, namely (1) as holding a middle position between two vices, one on the side of excess, and the other on the side of deficiency, and (2) as aiming at the mean or moderate amount both in feeling and in action.

And on this account it is a hard thing to be good; for finding the middle or the mean in each case is a hard thing, just as finding the middle or centre of a circle is a thing that is not within the power of everybody, but only of him who has the requisite knowledge.

Thus anyone can be angry—that is quite easy; anyone can give money away or spend it: but to do these things to the right person, to the right extent, at the right time, with the right motive, and in the right manner, is not what everybody can do, and is by no means easy. And that is the reason why right doing is rare and praiseworthy and noble.

• • •

[HIGH MINDEDNESS: GREATNESS OF SOUL: ARISTOCRATIC PRIDE]

High-mindedness would seem from its very name to have to do with great things; let us first ascertain what these are.

It will make no difference whether we consider the quality itself, or the man who exhibits the quality.

By a high-minded man we seem to mean one who claims much and deserves much: for he who claims much without deserving it is a fool; but the possessor of a virtue is never foolish or silly. The man we have described, then, is high-minded.

He who deserves little and claims little is temperate [or modest], but not high-minded: for high-mindedness [or greatness of soul] implies greatness, just as beauty implies stature; small men may be neat and well proportioned, but cannot be called beautiful. . . .

He who claims less than he deserves is small-minded, whether his rewards be great or moderate, or whether they be small and he claims still less: but this small-mindedness is most conspicuous in him whose rewards are great; for what would he do if his rewards were less than they are?

The high-minded man, then, in respect to the greatness of his rewards occupies an extreme position, but in that he behaves as he ought, observes the mean; for he claims that which he deserves, while all the others claim too much or too little.

But now if he deserves much and claims much, and most of all deserves and claims the greatest things, there will be one thing with which he will be especially concerned. For reward has reference to external good things. Now, the greatest of external good things we may assume to be that which we render to the Gods as their due, and that which people in high stations most desire, and which is the prize appointed for the noblest deeds. But the thing that answers to this description is honour, which, we may safely say, is the greatest of all external goods. Honours and dishonours, therefore, are the field in which the high-minded man behaves as he ought.

And indeed we may see, without going about to prove it, that honour is what high-minded men are concerned with; for it is honour that great men claim and deserve.

The small-minded man falls short, whether we compare his claims with his own rewards or with what the high-minded man claims for himself.

The vain or conceited man exceeds what is due to himself, though he does not exceed the high-minded man in his claims.

But the high-minded man, as he deserves the greatest things, must be a perfectly good or excellent man; for the better man always deserves the greater things, and the best possible man the greatest possible things. The really high-minded man, therefore, must be a good or excellent man. And indeed greatness in every virtue or excellence would seem to be necessarily implied in being a high-minded or great-souled man.

It would be equally inconsistent with the high-minded man's character to run along swinging his arms, and to commit an act of injustice; for what thing is there for love of which he would do anything unseemly, seeing that all things are of little account to him? . . .

High-mindedness, then, seems to be the crowning grace, as it were, of the virtues; it makes them greater, and cannot exist without them. And on this account it is a hard thing to be truly high-minded; for it is impossible without the union of all the virtues.

The high-minded man, then, exhibits his character especially in the matter of honours and dishonours and at great honour from good men he will be moderately pleased, as getting nothing more than his due, or even less; for no honour can be adequate to complete virtue; but nevertheless he will accept it, as they have nothing greater to offer him. But honour from ordinary men and on trivial grounds he will utterly despise; for that is not what he deserves. And dishonour likewise he will make light of; for he will never merit it.

But though it is especially in the matter of honours, as we have said, that the high-minded man displays his character, yet he will also observe the mean in his feelings with regard to wealth and power and all kinds of good and evil fortune, whatever may befall him, and will neither be very much exalted by prosperity, nor very much cast down by adversity; seeing that not even honour affects him as if it were a very important thing. For power and wealth are desirable for honour's sake (at least, those who have them wish to gain honour by them). He then who thinks lightly of honour must think lightly of them also.

And so high-minded men seem to look down upon everything.

But the gifts of fortune also are commonly thought to contribute to high-mindedness. For those who are well born are thought worthy of honour, and those who are powerful or wealthy; for they are in a position of superiority, and that which is superior in any good thing is always held in greater honour. And so these things do make people more high-minded in a sense; for such people find honour from some. But in strictness it is only the good man that is worthy of honour, though he that has both goodness and good fortune is commonly thought to be more worthy of honour. Those, however, who have good fortune without virtue, neither have any just claim to great things, nor are properly to be called high-minded; for neither is possible without complete virtue. . . .

The high-minded man is not quick to run into petty dangers, and indeed does not love danger, since there are few things that he much values; but he is ready to incur a great danger, and whenever he does so is unsparing of his life, as a thing that is not worth keeping at the cost of honour.

It is his nature to confer benefits, but he is ashamed to receive them; for the former is the part of a superior, the latter of an inferior. And when he has received a benefit, he is apt to confer a greater in return; for thus his creditor will become his debtor and be in the position of a recipient of his favour.

It is thought, moreover, that such men remember those on whom they have conferred favours better than those from whom they have received them; for the recipient of a benefit is inferior to the benefactor, but such a man wishes to be in the position of a superior. So he likes to be reminded of the one, but dislikes to be reminded of the other; and this is the reason why we read that Thetis[4] would not mention to Zeus[5] the services she had done him, and why the Spartans in treating with the Athenians, reminded them of the benefits received by Sparta rather than of those conferred by her.

It is characteristic of the high-minded man, again, never or reluctantly to ask favours, but to be ready to confer them, and to be haughty in his behaviour to those who are high in station and favoured by fortune, but unassuming to those of the middle ranks; for it is a difficult thing and a dignified thing to assert superiority over the former, but easy to assert it over the latter. A haughty demeanour in dealing with the great is quite consistent with good breeding, but in dealing with those of low estate is brutal, like showing off one's strength upon a cripple.

Another of his characteristics is not to rush in wherever honour is to be won, nor to go where others take the lead, but to hold aloof and to shun an enterprise, except when great honour is to be gained, or a great work to be done—not to do many things, but great things and notable.

Again, he must be open in his hate and in his love; for concealment shows fear.

---

[4]A minor goddess and sea nymph who pleaded on behalf of her son, the Greek hero Achilles. (See selection 1, Homer's *Iliad*, p. 14.)

[5]The principal Greek god.

He must care for truth more than for what men will think of him, and speak and act openly; he will not hesitate to say all that he thinks, as he looks down upon humankind. So he will speak the truth, except when he speaks ironically; and irony he will employ in speaking to the ordinary people.

Another of his characteristics is that he cannot fashion his life to suit another, except if he be a friend; for that is servile; and so all flatterers or hangers on of great men are of a slavish nature, and men of low natures become flatterers.

Nor is he easily moved to admiration; for nothing is great to him.

He readily forgets injuries; for it is not consistent with his character to brood on the past, especially on past injuries, but rather to overlook them.

He is no gossip; he will neither talk about himself nor about others; for he cares not that men should praise him, nor that others should be blamed (though, on the other hand, he is not very ready to bestow praise); and so he is not apt to speak evil of others, not even of his enemies, except with the express purpose of deliberately insulting them.

When an unfortunate event happens that cannot be helped or is of slight importance, he is the last man in the world to cry out or to beg for help; for that is the conduct of a man who thinks these events very important.

He loves to possess beautiful things that bring no profit, rather than useful things that pay; for this is characteristic of the man whose resources are in himself.

Further, the character of the high-minded man seems to require that his walk should be slow, his voice deep, his speech measured; for a man is not likely to be in a hurry when there are few things in which he is deeply interested; nor excited when he holds nothing to be of very great importance; and these are the causes of a high voice and rapid movements.

This, then, is the character of the high-minded man.

12

Aristotle

Politics

*T*HE Greek polis (city-state) and its culture were the affair of a small minority of privileged citizens who, ideally, placed honor and the esteem of their fellow citizens above power and profit. This fact is abundantly reflected in the writings of Xenophon and Plato, who held anti-democratic views (see selections 5 and 10). Aristotle, growing up as he did in Macedonian court circles, also had no democratic sympathies, as clearly shown in his Ethics (see selection 11).

Aristotle held that ethics and politics were complementary ways of going about the same thing: attainment of the good life for those individuals capable of attaining it. This practical aspiration, therefore, is the subject of his Politics (ca. 330 B.C.), as well as of the Ethics.

Aristotle believed that human beings are "political [social] animals" and that their moral character could be perfected only in the community life of the polis. But what kind of polis? The selection that follows gives a portion of Aristotle's idea of the "best form of the state." Its purpose would not be rule by the many, equality for all, or a high material standard of life, but rather promotion of the good life for its "high-minded" citizens. In fact, his model political community, like all Greek city-states, rested upon the institution of slave-labor. Aristotle believed that many individuals were not capable of governing themselves through reason and, therefore, were "slaves by nature."

Nowhere are the limits of Greek political theory better demonstrated than in Aristotle's inability to elevate his thinking beyond the actualities of his own time and place. (Indeed, he is supposed to have studied the constitutions of 158 Greek city-states before composing the Politics.) Despite his learning and powers of logic, he did not realize that the day of the small city-state was past.

POLITICS   *The Politics of Aristotle*, trans. Benjamin Jowett, 2 vols. (Oxford, 1885), Book VII, chaps. 4–9. Adapted by the editor.

Aristotle lacked the wide-ranging imagination and practical political skills of his pupil Alexander, whose career and policy pointed dramatically to the emergence of the great leader *and the* imperial state.

———————

In what has preceded I have discussed other forms of government; in what remains the first point to be considered is what should be the conditions of the ideal or perfect state; for the perfect state cannot exist without a due supply of the means of life. And therefore we must presuppose many purely imaginary conditions, but nothing impossible. There will be a certain number of citizens, a country in which to place them, and the like. As the weaver or shipbuilder or any other skilled craftsman must have the material proper for his work (and in proportion as this is better prepared, so will the result of his art be nobler), so the statesman or legislator must also have the materials suited to him.

First among the materials required by the statesman is population: he will consider what should be the number and characer of the citizens, and then what should be the size and character of the country. Most persons think that a state in order to be happy ought to be large; but even if they are right, they have no idea what is a large and what a small state. For they judge of the size of the city by the number of the inhabitants; whereas they ought to regard, not their number, but their power. A city too, like an individual, has a work to do; and that city which is best adapted to the fulfillment of its work is to be deemed greatest, in the same sense of the word great in which Hippocrates[1] might be called greater, not as a man, but as a physician, than some one else who was taller. And even if we reckon greatness by numbers, we ought not to include everybody, for there must always be in cities a multitude of slaves and foreigners; but we should include those only who are members of the state, and who form an essential part of it. The number of the latter is a proof of the greatness of a city; but a city which produces numerous craftsmen and comparatively few soldiers cannot be great, for a great city is not to be confused with a populous one. Moreover, experience shows that a very populous city can rarely, if ever, be well governed; since all cities which have a reputation for good government have a limit of population. We may argue on

[1] A noted Greek physician of the fifth century B.C.

grounds of reason, and the same result will follow. For law is order, and good law is good order; but a very great multitude cannot be orderly: to introduce order into the unlimited is the work of a divine power—of such a power as holds together the universe. Beauty is realized in number and magnitude, and the state which combines magnitude with good order must necessarily be the most beautiful. To the size of states there is a limit, as there is to other things, plants, animals, implements; for none of these retain their natural power when they are too large or too small, but they either wholly lose their nature, or are spoiled. For example, a ship which is only a span long will not be a ship at all, nor a ship a quarter of a mile long; yet there may be a ship of a certain size, either too large or too small, which will still be a ship, but bad for sailing. In like manner a state when composed of too few is not, as a state ought to be, self-sufficing; when of too many, though self-sufficing in all mere necessities, as a nation may be, it is not a state, being almost incapable of constitutional government. For who can be the general of such a vast multitude, or who the herald, unless he have the voice of a Stentor?[2]

A state, then, only begins to exist when it has attained a population sufficient for a good life in the political community: it may indeed, if it somewhat exceed this number, be a greater state. But, as I was saying, there must be a limit. What should be the limit will be easily ascertained by experience. For both governors and governed have duties to perform; the special functions of a governor are to command and to judge. But if the citizens of a state are to judge and to distribute offices according to merit, then they must know each other's characters; where they do not possess this knowledge, both the election to offices and the decision of lawsuits will go wrong. When the population is very large they are settled randomly, which clearly ought not to be. Besides, in an over-populous state foreigners and resident aliens will readily acquire the rights of citizens, for who will find them out? Clearly then the best limit of the population of a state is the largest number which suffices for the purposes of life, and can be taken in at a single view. Enough concerning the size of a state.

Much the same principle will apply to the territory of the state: every one would agree in praising the territory which is most entirely self-sufficing; and that must be the territory which is all-producing, for to have all things and to want nothing is sufficiency. In size and

---

[2]A herald in Homer's *Iliad,* known for his powerful voice.

extent it should be such as may enable the inhabitants to live at once temperately and liberally in the enjoyment of leisure. Whether we are right or wrong in laying down this limit we will inquire more precisely hereafter, when we have occasion to consider what is the right use of property and wealth: a matter which is much disputed, because men are inclined to rush into one of two extremes, some into stinginess, others into luxury.

It is not difficult to determine the general character of the territory which is required (there are, however, some points on which military authorities should be heard); it should be difficult of access to the enemy, and easy of escape to the inhabitants. Further, we require that the land as well as the inhabitants of whom we were just now speaking should be taken in at a single view, for a country which is easily seen can be easily protected. As to the position of the city, if we could have what we wish, it should be well situated in regard both to sea and land. This then is one principle, that it should be a convenient centre for the protection of the whole country; the other is, that it should be suitable for receiving the fruits of the soil, and also for the bringing in of timber and any other products that are easily transported.

Whether a communication with the sea is beneficial to a well-ordered state or not is a question which has often been asked. It is argued that the introduction of strangers brought up under other laws, and the increase of population, will be adverse to good order; the increase arises from their using the sea and having a crowd of merchants coming and going, and is harmful to good government. Apart from these considerations, it would be undoubtedly better, both with a view to safety and to the provision of necessaries, that the city and territory should be connected with the sea; the defenders of a country, if they are to maintain themselves against an enemy, should be easily relieved both by land and by sea. . . . Moreover, it is necessary that they should import from abroad what is not found in their own country, and that they should export what they have in excess; for a city ought to be a market, not indeed for the interest of others, but for her own interest.

Those who make themselves a market for the world only do so for the sake of revenue, and if a state ought not to desire profit of this kind it ought not to have such a trading center. Nowadays we often see in countries and cities dockyards and harbours very conveniently placed outside the city, but not too far off; and they are kept in dependence by walls and similar fortifications. Cities thus situated reap the benefits from their ports; and any harm which is likely to accrue may be easily guarded against by the laws, which will pronounce and determine who may hold communication with one another, and who may not.

There can be no doubt that the possession of a moderate naval force is advantageous to a city; the city should be formidable not only to its own citizens but to some of its neighbours, or, if necessary, able to assist them by sea as well as by land. The proper number or magnitude of this naval force is relative to the character of the state; for if her function is to take a leading part in politics, her naval power should be commensurate with the scale of her enterprises. The population of the state need not be much increased, since there is no necessity that the sailors should be citizens. The marines who have the control and command will be freemen, and belong also to the infantry; and wherever there is a dense population of resident aliens and farmers, there will always be sailors more than enough. Of this we see instances at the present day. The city of Heraclea,[3] for example, although small in comparison with many others, can furnish a considerable fleet. Such are our conclusions respecting the territory of the state, its harbours, its towns, its relations to the sea, and its maritime power.

Having spoken of the number of the citizens, we will proceed to speak of what should be their character. This is a subject which can be easily understood by any one who casts his eye on the more celebrated states of Hellas,[4] and generally on the distribution of races in the habitable world. Those who live in a cold climate and in Europe are full of spirit, but lacking in intelligence and skill; and therefore they retain comparative freedom, but have no political organization, and are incapable of ruling over others. The natives of Asia [the Middle East] are intelligent and inventive, but they are lacking in spirit, and therefore they are always in a state of subjection and slavery. But the Hellenic nation, which is situated between them, is likewise intermediate in character, being high-spirited and also intelligent. Hence it continues free, and is the best-governed of any nation, and, if it could be formed into one state, would be able to rule the world.[5] There are also similar differences in the different tribes of Hellas; for some of them are of a one-sided nature, and are intelligent or courageous only, while in oth-

[3]A small Greek city in southern Italy.

[4]The Greek world.

[5]Aristotle's most famous pupil, Alexander of Macedonia, organized a Hellenic army that conquered a vast territory, stretching from Greece into India. Alexander's mixing of nations in his empire was criticized by Aristotle. (After Alexander's death his empire was divided among his generals.)

ers there is a happy combination of both qualities. And clearly those whom the legislator will most easily lead to virtue may be expected to be both intelligent and courageous. Some say that the protectors of the state should be friendly towards those whom they know, fierce towards those whom they do not know. Now, passion is the quality of the soul which produces friendship and enables us to love; notably the spirit within us is more stirred against our friends and acquaintances than against those who are unknown to us, when we think that we are despised by them—for which reason Archilochus,[6] complaining of his friends, very naturally addresses his soul in these words,

> 'For surely thou art plagued on account of friends.'

The power of command and the love of freedom are in all men based upon this quality, for passion is commanding and invincible. Nor is it right to say that the protectors should be fierce towards those whom they do not know, for we ought not to be out of temper with any one; and a lofty spirit is not fierce by nature, but only when excited against evil-doers. And this, as I was saying before, is a feeling which men show most strongly towards their friends if they think they have received a wrong at their hands: as indeed is reasonable; for, besides the actual injury, they seem to be deprived of a benefit by those who owe them one. Hence the saying,

> 'Cruel is the strife of brethren,'

and again,

> 'They who love in excess also hate in excess.'

Thus we have nearly determined the number and character of the citizens of our state, and also the size and nature of their territory. I say 'nearly,' for we ought not to require the same minuteness in theory as in the facts that come to us through sense-perceptions. . . .

Now, whereas happiness is the highest good, being a realization and perfect practice of virtue, which some can attain, while others have little or none of it, the various qualities of men are clearly the reason why there are various kinds of states and many forms of government. For different men seek after happiness in different ways and by different means, and so make for themselves different modes of life and forms of government. We must see also how many things are indispensable to the existence of a state, for what we call the parts of a state

[6]Greek poet of the seventh century B.C..

will be found among the indispensables. Let us then enumerate the functions of a state, and we shall easily find what we want:

First, there must be food; secondly, arts, for life requires many instruments; thirdly, there must be arms, for the members of a community have need of them, and in their own hands, too, in order to maintain authority both against disobedient subjects and against external assailants; fourthly, there must be a certain amount of revenue, both for internal needs, and for the purposes of war; fifthly, or rather first, there must be a care of religion, which is commonly called worship; sixthly, and most necessary of all, there must be a power of deciding what is for the public interest, and what is just in men's dealings with one another.

These are the services which every state may be said to need. For a state is not a mere aggregate of persons, but a union of them sufficing for the purposes of life; and if any of these things be lacking, it is as we maintain impossible that the community can be absolutely self-sufficing. A state then should be framed with a view to the fulfillment of these functions. There must be farmers to procure food, and skilled craftsmen, and a warlike and a wealthy class, and priests, and judges to decide what is necessary and expedient.

Having determined these points, we have in the next place to consider whether all ought to share in every sort of occupation. Shall every man be at once farmer, craftsman, legislator, judge, or shall we suppose the several occupations just mentioned assigned to different persons? or, thirdly, shall some employments be assigned to individuals and others common to all? The same arrangement, however, does not occur in every constitution; as we were saying, all may be shared by all, or not all by all, but only by some. From this arises the differences of constitutions, for in democracies all share in all, in oligarchies the opposite practice prevails. Now, since we are here speaking of the best form of government, that is, that under which the state will be most happy (and happiness, as has been already said, cannot exist without virtue), it clearly follows that in the state which is best governed and possesses men who are just absolutely, and not merely relatively to the principle of the constitution, the citizens[7] must not lead the life of mechanics or tradesmen, for such a life is ignoble, and harmful to virtue. Neither must they be farmers, since leisure is necessary both for the development of virtue and the performance of political duties.

[7]Male citizens alone exercise political power; citizenship in Greece was normally limited to those individuals born of citizens.

Again, there is in a state a class of warriors, and another of legislators who advise and determine matters of law, and these seem in a special manner parts of a state. Now, should these two classes be distinguished, or are both functions to be assigned to the same persons? Here again there is no difficulty in seeing that both functions will in one way belong to the same, in another, to different persons. To different persons in so far as these employments are suited to different times of life, for the one requires wisdom and the other strength. But on the other hand, since it is an impossible thing that those who are able to use or to resist force should be willing to remain always in subjection, from this point of view the persons are the same; for those who carry arms can always determine the fate of the constitution. It remains therefore that both functions should be entrusted by the ideal constitution to the same persons—not, however, at the same time, but in the order prescribed by nature, who has given to young men strength and to older men wisdom. Such a distribution of duties will be practical and also just, and is founded upon a principle of conformity to merit. Besides, the ruling class should be the owners of property, for they are citizens, and the citizens of a state should be in good circumstances; whereas mechanics or any other class which is not a producer of virtue have no power in the state. This follows from our first principle, for happiness cannot exist without virtue, and a city is not to be termed happy in regard to a portion of the citizens, but in regard to them all. . . .

Of the classes enumerated there remain only the priests, and the manner in which their office is to be regulated is obvious. No farmer or mechanic should be appointed to it; for the Gods should receive honour from the citizens only. Now since the body of the citizens is divided into two classes, the warriors and the legislators, and it is fitting that the worship of the Gods should be duly performed, and also a rest provided in their service for those who from age have given up active life, to the old men of these two classes should be assigned the duties of priesthood.

We have shown what are the necessary conditions, and what the parts of a state: farmers, craftsmen, and labourers of all kinds are necessary to the existence of states, but the essential parts[8] of the state are the warriors and legislators. And these are distinguished severally from one another, the distinction being in some cases permanent, in others not.

---

[8]The active *citizen* elements that, strictly speaking, constitute the state.

13

Aristotle

Poetics

*A*LTHOUGH *Aristotle's surviving writings resemble lecture notes and are not generally valued as* literature, *Aristotle was, nevertheless, the author of the earliest book of literary criticism. Literature was a major subject of the curriculum at his Lyceum, and Aristotle tried to analyze it in the same methodical way found in his* Ethics *and* Politics.

The Greeks had a profound sense of form; as the citizens of Aristotle's time looked back a century or more, they marvelled at the masterful integration of form and content shown by the leading tragic playwrights of the fifth century B.C. *They thought that if their techniques could be analyzed and a formula drawn from them, great tragedies might then be produced at will. The origin of this theory of poetic art as deliberate imitation of life rather than as unconscious inspiration, had its roots in traditional Greek ways of thinking and doing—ways which both Plato and Aristotle tried to present as "universal" and "true." In this theory of dramatic poetry the explanation was linguistic: the Greek word for* poet *is* poietes, *which means* maker. *Aristotle reasoned that since Sophocles had not made Oedipus' tragic reversal (in the sense of causing it), he must have made an imitation of it. Other playwrights might do the same. In his* Poetics *Aristotle explains why men take pleasure in such imitations—even of tragic events.*

In the portion that survives, the Poetics *(ca. 330 B.C.) deals mainly with such matters as the definition of Tragedy and the Tragic Hero, and an analysis of what makes certain tragedies dramatically and emotionally effective. By clarifying all the dramatic elements—language, plot, and character—the* Poetics *established a standard of literary criticism and dramatic composition that*

POETICS   S. H. Butcher, *Aristotle's Theory of Poetry and Fine Art, with a Critical Text and Translation of the Poetics,* fourth edition (London: Macmillan, 1907), pp. 23, 25, 27, 31, 33, 35, 37, 39, 41, 45, 47, 49, 51, 53, 55, 57. Adapted by the editor.

has endured until modern times. And, in numerous other areas of learning, the authority of Aristotle carried enormous weight for many centuries. Literary critics regarded his comments as "classic" rules, laid down for all time; unlike Aristotle, therefore, their own originality as critics was inhibited by his authority.

Tragedy, then, is an imitation of an action that is serious, complete, and of a certain magnitude; in language embellished with each kind of artistic ornament, the several kinds being found in separate parts of the play; in the form of action, not of narrative; through pity and fear effecting the proper purgation of these emotions.[1] By 'language embellished,' I mean language into which rhythm, 'harmony,' and song enter. By 'the several kinds in separate parts,' I mean, that some parts are rendered through the medium of verse alone, others again with the aid of song.

Now as tragic imitation implies persons acting, it necessarily follows, in the first place, that stage Scenery will be a part of Tragedy. Next, Song and Diction, for these are the medium of imitation. By 'Diction' I mean the mere metrical arrangement of the words: as for 'Song,' it is a term whose sense every one understands.

Again, Tragedy is the imitation of an action; and an action implies persons, who necessarily possess certain distinctive qualities both of character and thought; for it is by these that we qualify actions themselves, and these—thought and character—are the two natural causes from which actions spring, and on actions again all success or failure depends. Hence, the Plot is the imitation of the action—for by plot I here mean the arrangement of the incidents. By Character I mean that in virtue of which we ascribe certain qualities to the persons. Thought is required wherever a statement is proved, or, it may be, a general truth enunciated. Every Tragedy, therefore, must have six parts, which parts determine its quality—namely, Plot, Character, Diction, Thought, Scenery, Song. Two of the parts [Diction and Song] constitute the medium of imitation, one [Scenery] the manner, and three

---

[1]Purgation (Greek *katharsis*) is a cleansing or washing out of impurities. Although Aristotle's precise meaning for the term has been much disputed, clearly he believes that a person is made somehow healthier, even derives a form of pleasure, from the calling up of the emotions of pity and fear.

[Plot, Character, Thought] the objects of imitation. And these complete the list. These elements have been employed, we may say, by the poets to a man; in fact, every play contains stage Scenery elements as well as Character, Plot, Diction, Song, and Thought.

But most important of all is the structure of the incidents. For Tragedy is an imitation, not of men, but of an action and of life, and life consists in action, and its aim is a mode of action, not a quality. Now character determines men's qualities, but it is by their actions that they are happy or the reverse. Dramatic action, therefore, is not with a view to the representation of character; character comes in as subsidiary to the actions. Hence the incidents and the plot are the aim of a tragedy; and the aim is the chief thing of all. . . .

These principles being established, let us now discuss the proper structure of the Plot, since this is the first and most important thing in Tragedy.

Now, according to our definition, Tragedy is an imitation of an action that is complete, and whole, and of a certain magnitude; for there may be a whole that is wanting in magnitude. A whole is that which has a beginning, a middle, and an end. A beginning is that which does not itself follow anything by causal necessity, but after which something naturally is or comes to be. An end, on the contrary, is that which itself naturally follows some other thing, either by necessity, or as a rule, but has nothing following it. A middle is that which follows something as some other thing follows it. A well constructed plot, therefore, must neither begin nor end at haphazard, but conform to these principles. . . .

Unity of plot does not, as some persons think, consist in the unity of the hero. For infinitely various are the incidents in one man's life which cannot be reduced to unity; and so, too, there are many actions of one man out of which we cannot make one action. Hence the error, as it appears, of all poets who have composed a *Heracleid,* a *Theseid,* or other poems of the kind.[2] They imagine that as Heracles was one man, the story of Heracles must also be a unity. But Homer, as in all else he is of surpassing merit, here too—whether from art or natural genius— seems to have happily discerned the truth. In composing the *Odyssey* he did not include all the adventures of Odysseus—such as his wound on Mt. Parnassus, or his pretended madness at the mustering of the

[2]That is, the sort of long narrative poems that tell *all* of the adventures of a great hero like Heracles or Theseus.

Greek expeditionary force[3]—incidents between which there was no necessary or probable connexion: but he made the *Odyssey,* and likewise the *Iliad,* to centre round an action that in our sense of the word is one. As therefore, in the other imitative arts, the imitation is one when the object imitated is one, so the plot, being an imitation of an action, must imitate one action and that a whole—the structural union of the parts being such that, if any one of them is displaced or removed, the whole will be disjointed and disturbed. For a thing whose presence or absence makes no visible difference, is not an organic part of the whole.

It is, moreover, evident from what has been said, that it is not the function of the poet to relate what has happened, but what may have happened—what is possible according to the law of probability or necessity. The poet differs from the historian not by writing in verse rather than in prose. The work of Herodotus[4] might be put into verse, and it would still be history, with metre no less than without it. The true difference is that one relates what has happened, the other what may have happened. Poetry, therefore, is a more philosophical and a higher thing than history; for poetry tends to express the universal, history the particular. By the universal I mean how a person of a certain type will on occasion speak or act, according to the law of probability or necessity; and it is this universality at which poetry aims in the names she attaches to the personages. . . .

Of all plots and actions the episodic are the worst. I call a plot 'episodic' in which the episodes or acts succeed one another without probable or necessary sequence. Bad poets compose such pieces by their own fault, good poets, to please the players; for, as they write show pieces for competition, they stretch the plot beyond its capacity, and are often forced to break the natural continuity.

But again, Tragedy is an imitation not only of a complete action, but of events inspiring fear or pity. Such an effect is best produced when the events come on us by surprise; and the effect is heightened when, at the same time, they follow as cause and effect. The tragic wonder will then be greater than if they happened of themselves or by accident; for even coincidences are most striking when they have an air of design. We may instance the statue of Mitys at Argos, which fell

---

[3]Exploits of Odysseus which occurred before the events recounted in Homer's epic poems, *The Iliad* and *The Odyssey* (see selection 1).

[4]The historian of the Persian wars (see selection 4).

upon his murderer while he was a spectator at a festival, and killed him. Such events seem not to be due to mere chance. Plots, therefore, constructed on these principles are necessarily the best.

Plots are either simple or complex, for the actions in real life, of which the plots are an imitation, obviously show a similar distinction. An action which is one and continuous in the sense above defined, I call simple, when the change of fortune takes place without reversal of the situation and without recognition.

A complex action is one in which the change is accompanied by such reversal, or by recognition, or by both. These last should arise from the internal structure of the plot, so that what follows should be the necessary or probable result of the preceding action. It makes all the difference whether any given event is caused by or simply happens after the previous action.

Reversal of the situation is a change by which the action veers round to its opposite, subject always to our rule of probability or necessity. Thus in the *Oedipus,* the messenger comes to cheer Oedipus and free him from his alarms about his mother, but by revealing who he is, he produces the opposite effect.[5] . . .

Recognition, as the name indicates, is a change from ignorance to knowledge, producing love or hate between the persons destined by the poet for good or bad fortune. The best form of recognition is coincident with a reversal of the situation, as in the *Oedipus*. There are indeed other forms. Even inanimate things of the most trivial kind may in a sense be objects of recognition. Again, we may recognise or discover whether a person has done a thing or not. But the recognition which is most intimately connected with the plot and action is, as we have said, the recognition of persons. This recognition, combined with reversal, will produce either pity or fear; and actions producing these effects are those which, by our definition, Tragedy represents. Moreover, it is upon such situations that the issues of good or bad fortune will depend. . . .

As the sequel to what has already been said, we must proceed to consider what the poet should aim at, and what he should avoid, in constructing his plots; and by what means the specific effect of Tragedy will be produced.

A perfect tragedy should, as we have seen, be arranged not on the

[5]The scene in which the messenger from Corinth unknowingly reveals the fulfillment of Oedipus' tragic fate, that he has killed his father and married his mother, in Sophocles' tragedy, *Oedipus the King* (selection 3, pp. 96–115).

simple but on the complex plan. It should, moreover, imitate actions which excite pity and fear, this being the distinctive mark of tragic imitation. It follows plainly, in the first place, that the change of fortune presented must not be the spectacle of a virtuous man brought from prosperity to adversity; for this moves neither pity nor fear. It merely shocks us. Nor, again, that of a bad man passing from adversity to prosperity, for nothing can be more alien to the spirit of Tragedy. It possesses no single tragic quality; it neither satisfies the moral sense nor calls forth pity or fear. Nor, again, should the downfall of the utter villain be exhibited. A plot of this kind would, doubtless, satisfy the moral sense, but it would inspire neither pity nor fear; for pity is aroused by unmerited misfortune, fear by the misfortune of a man like ourselves. Such an event, therefore, will be neither pitiful nor terrible. There remains, then, the character between these two extremes—that of a man who is not eminently good and just, yet whose misfortune is brought about not by vice or depravity, but by some error or frailty. He must be one who is highly renowned and prosperous—a personage like Oedipus, Thyestes, or other famous men of great families.

A well constructed plot should, therefore, be single in its issue, rather than double as some maintain. The change of fortune should be not from bad to good, but, reversely, from good to bad. It should come about as the result not of vice, but of some great error or frailty, in a character either such as we have described, or better rather than worse. . . . A tragedy, then, to be perfect according to the rules of art should be of this construction. . . .

In the second rank comes the kind of tragedy which some place first. Like the *Odyssey*, it has a double thread of plot, and also an opposite ending for the good and for the bad characters. It is accounted the best because of the weakness of the spectators; for the poet is guided in what he writes by the wishes of his audience. The pleasure, however, thence derived is not the true tragic pleasure. It is proper rather to comedy, where those who, in the piece, are the deadliest enemies— quit the stage as friends at the close, and no one slays or is slain.

Fear and pity may be aroused by spectacular stage-effects; but they may also result from the inner structure of the piece, which is the better way, and indicates a superior poet. For the plot ought to be so con- structed that, even without the aid of the eye, he who hears the tale told will thrill with horror and melt to pity at what takes place. This is the impression we should receive from hearing the story of Oedipus. But to produce this effect by the mere spectacle is a less artistic method, and dependent on external aids. Those who employ spectacular means to create a sense not of the terrible but only of the monstrous, are strangers to the purpose of Tragedy; for we must not demand of Tragedy any and every kind of pleasure, but only that which is proper to it. And since the pleasure which the poet should afford is that which comes from pity and fear through imitation, it is evident that this quality must be impressed upon the incidents.

Let us then determine what are the circumstances which strike us as terrible or pitiful.

Actions capable of this effect may happen between persons who are either friends or enemies or indifferent to one another. If an enemy kills an enemy, there is nothing to excite pity either in the act or the intention—except so far as the suffering in itself is pitiful. So again with indifferent persons. But when the tragic incident occurs between those who are near or dear to one another—if, for example, a brother kills, or intends to kill, a brother, a son his father, a mother her son, a son his mother, or any other deed of the kind is done—these are the situations to be looked for by the poet. He may not indeed destroy the framework of the accepted legends . . . but he ought to show invention of his own, and skillfully handle the traditional material. Let us explain more clearly what is meant by skillful handling.

The action may be done consciously and with knowledge of the persons, in the manner of the older poets. It is thus too that Euripides makes Medea slay her children. Or, again, the deed of horror may be done, but done in ignorance, and the tie of kinship or friendship be discovered afterwards. The *Oedipus* of Sophocles is an example. Here, indeed, the incident is outside the drama proper; but cases occur where it falls within the action of the play. . . . Again, there is a third case,— to be about to act with knowledge of the persons and then not to act. The fourth case is when some one is about to do an irreparable deed through ignorance, and makes the discovery before it is done. These are the only possible ways. For the deed must either be done or not done—and that knowingly or unknowingly. But of all these ways, to be about to act knowing the persons, and then not to act, is the worst. It is shocking without being tragic, for no disaster follows. It is, therefore, never, or very rarely, found in poetry. . . . And this is why a few families only, as has been already observed, furnish the subjects of tragedy. It was not art, but happy chance, that led the poets in search of subjects to impress the tragic quality upon their plots. They are compelled, therefore, to have recourse to those houses whose history contains moving incidents like these.

Enough has now been said concerning the structure of the incidents, and the right kind of plot.

In respect to Character there are four things to be aimed at. First, and most important, it must be good. Now any speech or action that shows moral purpose of any kind will be expressive of character; the character will be good if the purpose is good. This rule is relative to each class. Even a woman may be good, and also a slave; though the woman may be said to be an inferior being, and the slave quite worthless. The second thing to aim at is appropriateness. There is a type of manly valour; but valour in a woman, or vicious cleverness, is inappropriate. Thirdly, character must be true to life; for this is a different thing from goodness and appropriateness, as here described. The fourth point is consistency; for even though the subject of the imitation, who suggested the type, be inconsistent, still he must be consistently inconsistent. . . .

As in the structure of the plot, so too in the portraiture of character, the poet should always aim either at the necessary or the probable. Thus a person of a given character should speak or act in a given way, by the rule either of necessity or of probability—just as events should follow one another by necessary or probable sequence. It is therefore evident that the unravelling of the plot, no less than the complication, must arise out of the plot itself; it should not be brought about by supernatural intervention. The supernatural could be employed only for events external to the drama—for past or future events, which lie beyond the range of human knowledge, and which need to be reported or foretold; for to the gods we ascribe the power of seeing all things. Within the action there must be nothing improbable. . . .

Again, since Tragedy is an imitation of persons who are above the common level, the example of good portrait-painters should be followed. They, while reproducing the distinctive form of the original, make a likeness which is true to life and yet more beautiful. So too the poet, in representing men who are hot-tempered or lazy, or have other defects of character, should preserve the type and yet ennoble it. In this way Achilles is portrayed by . . . Homer.

These then are rules the poet should observe. . . .

14
Livy

The History of Rome from its Foundation

*N*EITHER *Herodotus nor Thucydides wrote primarily to encourage patriotism and ancestral ways. The greatness of the Greek founders of history lay in their emphasis upon* impartial inquiry.

Quite the opposite was true, however, of the Roman historian, Titus Livius (ca. 59 B.C.–A.D. 17). Livy was born at Patavium (the modern Padua) in northern Italy. Apparently of aristocratic stock, he seems to have had sufficient income to enable him to devote his long life to the writing of The History of Rome from its Foundation. *This prose epic traces the story of Rome from the mythical hero Aeneas, survivor of ancient Troy, to Livy's time. It was an enormous undertaking, covering a span of over seven hundred years; unfortunately, only 35 of his 142 volumes have come down to us.*

His upbringing in an old-fashioned country town seems to have given Livy an enduring love of the simple life and traditional moral discipline—a rare virtue in Rome during the ugly last years of the Republic. Thus equipped, Livy was thoroughly in harmony with the official moral and religious revival promoted by the first Roman emperor, Augustus, and the two men became close friends.

Livy's History, *then, is a long glorification of the Roman Republic; of its heroes, such as King Romulus, Lucius Junius Brutus, and Titus Manlius; and of its heroines, such as Lucretia, whose character and deeds are celebrated in the following selection. Livy's picture of Rome's distant past is often myth-*

THE HISTORY OF ROME FROM ITS FOUNDATION   Livy, *The Early History of Rome: Books I–V of the History of Rome from its Foundation,* trans. Aubrey De Selincourt (London: Penguin Books, 1960), pp. 17–18, 21–24, 26–28. 72–73, 78–85. Copyright ©the Estate of Aubrey de Selincourt, 1960. Reproduced by permission of Penguin Books Ltd. Livy, *Rome and Italy: Books VI–X of The History of Rome from its Foundation,* trans. Betty Radice (London: Penguin Books, 1982), pp. 164–167. Copyright ©Betty Radice, 1982. Reproduced by permission of Penguin Books Ltd.

ical, as he openly admits, and always idealized; and his use of source material is uncritical. He lacked the practical knowledge of war and politics necessary to describe the rise of a community of soldier-farmers to world domination. But a scholarly account was not what he intended; rather, he wanted to create a morally uplifting work of literature. Livy hoped that its style and content would inspire his countrymen to imitate the simple and soldierly old Roman virtues, avoid the self-indulgent luxuries and immoralities of their recent past, renew their sense of common destiny, and seal their determination to rule the world.

Livy's influence has remained, for many, as the principal guide to the history of the Roman Republic. For example, Machiavelli, the Renaissance political thinker, wrote his admiring Discourses on Livy, *and the French revolutionaries of the eighteenth century took Livy as their favorite sourcebook in planning their "new" Roman Republic.*

The task of writing a history of our nation from Rome's earliest days fills me, I confess, with some misgiving, and even were I confident in the value of my work, I should hesitate to say so. I am aware that for historians to make extravagant claims is, and always has been, all too common: every writer on history tends to look down his nose at his less cultivated predecessors, happily persuaded that he will better them in point of style, or bring new facts to light. But however that may be, I shall find satisfaction in contributing—not, I hope, ignobly—to the labour of putting on record the story of the greatest nation in the world. Countless others have written on this theme and it may be that I shall pass unnoticed amongst them; if so, I must comfort myself with the greatness and splendour of my rivals, whose work will rob my own of recognition.

My task, moreover, is an immensely laborious one. I shall have to go back more than seven hundred years, and trace my story from its small beginning up to these recent times when its ramifications are so vast that any adequate treatment is hardly possible. I am aware, too, that most readers will take less pleasure in my account of how Rome began and in her early history; they will wish to hurry on to more modern times and to read of the period, already a long one, in which the might of an imperial people is beginning to work its own ruin. My own feeling is different; I shall find antiquity a rewarding study, if only because, while I am absorbed in it, I shall be able to turn my eyes from the troubles which for so long have tormented the modern world, and to write without any of that over-anxious consideration which may well plague a writer on contemporary life, even if it does not lead him to conceal the truth.

Events before Rome was born or thought of have come to us in old tales with more of the charm of poetry than of a sound historical record, and such traditions I propose neither to affirm nor refute. There is no reason, I feel, to object when antiquity draws no hard line between the human and the supernatural; it adds dignity to the past, and, if any nation deserves the privilege of claiming a divine ancestry, that nation is our own. And so great is the glory won by the Roman people in their wars that, when they declare that Mars himself was their first parent and father of the man who founded their city,[1] all the nations of the world might well allow the claim as readily as they accept Rome's imperial dominion.

These, however, are comparatively trivial matters and I set little store by them. I invite the reader's attention to the much more serious consideration of the kind of lives our ancestors lived, of who were the men, and what the means both in politics and war by which Rome's power was first acquired and subsequently expanded; I would then have him trace the process of our moral decline, to watch, first, the sinking of the foundations of morality as the old teaching was allowed to lapse, then the rapidly increasing disintegration, then the final collapse of the whole edifice, and the dark dawning of our modern day when we can neither endure our vices nor face the remedies needed to cure them. The study of history is the best medicine for a sick mind; for in history you have a record of the infinite variety of human experience plainly set out for all to see; and in that record you can find for yourself and your country both examples and warnings: fine things to take as models, base things, rotten through and through, to avoid.

I hope my passion for Rome's past has not impaired my judgement; for I do honestly believe that no country has ever been greater or purer than ours or richer in good citizens and noble deeds; none has been free for so many generations from the vices of avarice and luxury; nowhere have thrift and plain living been for so long held in such esteem.

---

[1] Romulus was the legendary founder and first king of Rome in 753 B.C.; his mother claimed that his father was Mars (called Ares by the Greeks), god of war, gladiators, hunting, and other warlike pursuits. Mars was worshipped extensively in Rome as a patron god of the city.

Indeed, poverty, with us, went hand in hand with contentment. Of late years wealth has made us greedy, and self-indulgence has brought us, through every form of sensual excess, to be, if I may so put it, in love with death both individual and collective.

But bitter comments of this sort are not likely to find favour, even when they have to be made. Let us have no more of them, at least at the beginning of our great story. On the contrary, I should prefer to borrow from the poets and begin with good omens and with prayers to all the host of heaven to grant a successful issue to the work which lies before me.

•   •   •

But (I must believe) it was already written in the book of fate that this great city of ours should arise, and the first steps be taken to the founding of the mightiest empire the world has known—next to [that of the gods]. The Vestal Virgin was raped and gave birth to twin boys.[2] Mars, she declared, was their father—perhaps she believed it, perhaps she was merely hoping by the pretence to palliate her guilt. Whatever the truth of the matter, neither gods nor men could save her or her babes from the savage hands of [King Amulius]. The mother was bound and flung into prison; the boys, by the king's order, were condemned to be drowned in the river. Destiny, however, intervened; the Tiber had overflowed its banks; because of the flooded ground it was impossible to get to the actual river, and the men entrusted to do the deed thought that the flood-water, sluggish though it was, would serve their purpose. Accordingly they made shift to carry out the king's orders by leaving the infants on the edge of the first flood-water they came to, at the spot where now stands the Ruminal fig-tree—said to have once been known as the fig-tree of Romulus. In those days the country thereabouts was all wild and uncultivated, and the story goes that when the basket in which the infants had been exposed was left high and dry by the receding water, a she-wolf, coming down from

[2]The Vestals were virgin priestesss selected from noble families for terms of thirty years; they were expected to remain chaste and to tend the sacred fire in the temple of Vesta (Roman goddess of the family hearth). Rhea Silvia, a Vestal Virgin and King Numitor's daughter, gave birth to twin boys, Romulus and Remus, supposedly after having been raped by Mars. Her uncle, King Amulius, usurper of his brother Numitor's crown, had consecrated Rhea Silvia to the service of Vesta so that she would not have children who might threaten his royal position.

the neighbouring hills to quench her thirst, heard the children crying and made her way to where they were. She offered them her teats to suck and treated them with such gentleness that Faustulus, the king's herdsman, found her licking them with her tongue. Faustulus took them to his hut and gave them to his wife Larentia to nurse. Some think that the origin of this fable was the fact that Larentia was a common whore and was called Wolf by the shepherds.

Such, then, was the birth and upbringing of the twins. By the time they were grown boys, they employed themselves actively on the farm and with the flocks and began to go hunting in the woods; their strength grew with their resolution, until not content only with the chase they took to attacking robbers and sharing their stolen goods with their friends the shepherds. Other young fellows joined them, and they and the shepherds would fleet the time together, now in serious talk, now in jollity.

Even in that remote age the Palatine hill[3](which got its name from the Arcadian settlement Pallanteum) is supposed to have been the scene of the gay festival of the Lupercalia. The Arcadian Evander,[4] who many years before held that region, is said to have instituted there the old Arcadian practice of holding an annual festival in honour of Lycean Pan (afterwards called Inuus by the Romans), in which young men ran about naked and disported themselves in various pranks and fooleries. The day of the festival was common knowledge, and on one occasion when it was in full swing some brigands, incensed at the loss of their ill-gotten gains, laid a trap for Romulus and Remus. Romulus successfully defended himself, but Remus was caught and handed over to Amulius. The brigands laid a complaint against their prisoner, the main charge being that he and his brother were in the habit of raiding Numitor's land with an organized gang of ruffians and stealing the cattle. Thereupon Remus was handed over for punishment to Numitor.

Now Faustulus had suspected all along that the boys he was bringing up were of royal blood. He knew that two infants had been exposed by the king's orders, and the rescue of his own two fitted perfectly in point of time. Hitherto, however, he had been unwilling to declare what he knew, until either a suitable opportunity occurred or circumstances compelled him. Now the truth could no longer be concealed,

[3]One of the famed Seven Hills of Rome.

[4]Arcadia is in Greece; thus, one of the many legendary ways that the origin of Rome was connected to Greece was through the story of Evander, who transmitted the worship of the Greek woodland god Pan to the site that would become Rome.

so in his alarm he told Romulus the whole story; Numitor, too, when he had Remus in custody and was told that the two brothers were twins, was set thinking about his grandsons; the young men's age and character, so different from the lowly born, confirmed his supicions; and further inquiries led him to the same conclusion, until he was on the point of acknowledging Remus. The net was closing in, and Romulus acted. He was not strong enough for open hostilities, so he instructed a number of the herdsmen to meet at the king's house by different routes at a preordained time; this was done, and with the help of Remus, at the head of another body of men, the king [Amulius]was surprised and killed. Before the first blows were struck, Numitor gave it out that an enemy had broken into the town and attacked the palace; he then drew off all the men of military age to garrison the inner fortress, and, as soon as he saw Romulus and Remus, their purpose accomplished, coming to congratulate him, he summoned a meeting of the people and laid the facts before it: Amulius's crime against himself, the birth of his grandsons, and the circumstances attending it, how they were brought up and ultimately recognized, and, finally, the murder of the king [Amulius]for which he himself assumed responsibility. The two brothers marched through the crowd at the head of their men and saluted their grandfather as king, and by a shout of unanimous consent his royal title was confirmed.

Romulus and Remus, after the control of Alba had passed to Numitor in the way I have described, were suddenly seized by an urge to found a new settlement on the spot where they had been left to drown as infants and had been subsequently brought up. There was, in point of fact, already an excess of population at Alba, what with the Albans themselves, the Latins, and the addition of the herdsmen—enough, indeed, to justify the hope that Alba and Lavinium would one day be small places compared with the proposed new settlement. Unhappily the brothers' plans for the future were marred by the same curse which had divided their grandfather and Amulius—jealousy and ambition. A disgraceful quarrel arose from a matter in itself trivial. As the brothers were twins and all question of seniority was thereby precluded, they determined to ask the tutelary [guardian] gods of the countryside to declare by augury [prophecy] which of them should govern the new town once it was founded, and give his name to it. For this purpose Romulus took the Palatine hill and Remus the Aventine as their respective stations from which to observe the [bird signs]. Remus, the story goes, was the first to receive a sign—six vultures; and no sooner was this made known to the people than double the number of birds appeared to Romulus. The followers of each promptly saluted their master as king, one side basing its claim upon priority, the other upon number. Angry words ensued, followed all too soon by blows, and in the course of the affray Remus was killed. There is another story, a commoner one, according to which Remus, by way of jeering at his brother, jumped over the half-built walls of the new settlement, whereupon Romulus killed him in a fit of rage, adding the threat, 'So perish whoever else shall overleap my battlements.'

This, then, was how Romulus obtained the sole power. The newly built city was called by its founder's name.

•   •   •

Meanwhile Rome was growing. More and more ground was coming within the circuit of its walls. Indeed, the rapid expansion of the enclosed area was out of proportion to the actual population, and evidently indicated an eye to the future. In antiquity the founder of a new settlement, in order to increase its population, would as a matter of course shark up a lot of homeless and destitute folk and pretend that they were 'born of earth' to be his progeny [descendants]; Romulus now followed a similar course: to help fill his big new town, he threw open, in the ground—now enclosed—between the two copses as you go up the Capitoline hill, a place of asylum for fugitives. Hither fled for refuge all the rag-tag-and-bobtail from the neighbouring peoples: some free, some slaves, and all of them wanting nothing but a fresh start. That mob was the first real addition to the City's strength, the first step to her future greatness.

Having now adequate numbers, Romulus proceeded to temper strength with policy and turned his attention to social organization. He created a hundred senators—fixing that number either because it was enough for his purpose, or because there were no more than a hundred who were in a position to be made 'Fathers,' as they were called, or Heads of Clans. The title of 'fathers' (*patres*) undoubtedly was derived from their rank, and their descendants were called 'patricians.'

Rome was now strong enough to challenge any of her neighbours; but, great though she was, her greatness seemed likely to last only for a single generation. There were not enough women, and that, added to the fact that there was no intermarriage with neighbouring communities, ruled out any hope of maintaining the level of population. Romulus accordingly, on the advice of his senators, sent representatives to the various peoples across his borders to negotiate alliances and the right of intermarriage for the newly established state. The envoys were instructed to point out that cities, like everything else, have to begin small; in course of time, helped by their own worth and the favour of heaven, some, at least, grow rich and famous, and of these Rome would assuredly be one. Gods had blessed her birth, and the valour of her people would not fail in the days to come. The Romans were men, as they were; why, then, be reluctant to intermarry with them?

Romulus's overtures were nowhere favourably received; it was clear that everyone despised the new community, and at the same time feared, both for themselves and for posterity, the growth of this new power in their midst. More often than not his envoys were dismissed with the question of whether Rome had thrown open her doors to female, as well as to male, runaways and vagabonds, as that would evidently be the most suitable way for Romans to get wives. The young Romans naturally resented this jibe, and a clash seemed inevitable. Romulus, seeing it must come, set the scene for it with elaborate care. Deliberately hiding his resentment, he prepared to celebrate the Consualia, a solemn festival in honour of Neptune,[5] patron of the horse, and sent notice of his intention all over the neighbouring countryside. The better to advertise it, his people lavished upon their preparations for the spectacle all the resources—such as they were in those days—at their command. On the appointed day crowds flocked to Rome, partly, no doubt, out of sheer curiosity to see the new town. The majority were from the neighbouring settlements of Caenina, Crustumium, and Antemnae, but all the Sabines were there too, with their wives and children. Many houses offered hospitable entertainment to the visitors; they were invited to inspect the fortifications, layout, and numerous buildings of the town, and expressed their surprise at the rapidity of its growth. Then the great moment came; the show began, and nobody had eyes or thoughts for anything else. This was the Romans' opportunity: at a given signal all the able-bodied men burst through the crowd and seized the young women. Most of the girls were the prize of whoever got hold of them first, but a few conspicuously handsome ones had been previously marked down for leading senators, and these were brought to their houses by special gangs. . . .

[5]Neptune (Poseidon to the Greeks) was also god of the sea.

By this act of violence the fun of the festival broke up in panic. The girls' unfortunate parents made good their escape, not without bitter comments on the treachery of their hosts and heartfelt prayers to the God to whose festival they had come in all good faith in the solemnity of the occasion, only to be grossly deceived. The young women were no less indignant and as full of foreboding for the future.

Romulus, however, reassured them. Going from one to another he declared that their own parents were really to blame, in that they had been too proud to allow intermarriage with their neighbours; nevertheless, they need not fear; as married women they would share all the fortunes of Rome, all the privileges of the community, and they would be bound to their husbands by the dearest bond of all, their children. He urged them to forget their wrath and give their hearts to those to whom chance had given their bodies. Often, he said, a sense of injury yields in the end to affection, and their husbands would treat them all the more kindly in that they would try, each one of them, not only to fulfill their own part of the bargain but also to make up to their wives for the homes and parents they had lost. The men, too, played their part; they spoke honied words and vowed that it was passionate love which had prompted their offence. No plea can better touch a woman's heart.

•   •   •

Now began the reign of [Lucius]Tarquinius Superbus—Tarquin the Proud.[6] His conduct merited the name. . . . He executed the leading senators who he thought had supported Servius.[7] Well aware that his treachery and violence might form a precedent to his own disadvantage, he employed a bodyguard. His anxiety was justified; for he had usurped by force the throne to which he had no title whatever; the people had not elected him, the Senate had not sanctioned his accession. Without hope of his subjects' affection, he could rule only by fear; and to make himself feared as widely as possible he began the

---

[6]The last king of Rome. After the citizens expelled him in 510 B.C., they formed a republic.

[7]Servius Tullius was the previous mild and moderate king, Tarquin's father-in-law. According to Livy he was murdered by the plotting of his own daughter, Tullia, and her husband, Tarquin.

practice of trying capital causes without consultation and by his own sole authority. He was thus enabled to punish with death, exile, or confiscation of property not only such men as he happened to suspect or dislike, but also innocent people from whose conviction he had nothing to gain but their money. Those of senatorial rank were the worst sufferers from this procedure; their numbers were reduced, and no new appointments made, in the hope, no doubt, that sheer numerical weakness might bring the [senatorial] order into contempt, and the surviving members be readier to acquiesce in political impotence. Tarquin was the first king to break the established tradition of consulting the Senate on all matters of public business, and to govern by the mere authority of himself and his household. In questions of war and peace he was his own sole master; he made and unmade treaties and alliances with whom he pleased without any reference whatever either to the [people] or to the Senate. He made particular efforts to win the friendship of the Latins,[8] in the hope that any power or influence he could obtain abroad might give him greater security at home. With this in view he went beyond mere official friendly relations with the Latin nobility, and married his daughter to Octavius Mamilius of Tusculum [a town in Latium], by far the most distinguished bearer of the Latin name. . . . By this marriage he attached to his interest Mamilius's numerous relatives and friends.

•   •   •

Tarquin next turned his attention to home affairs. His first concern was the temple of Jupiter[9] on the Capitoline,[10] which he hoped to leave as a memorial of the royal house of the Tarquins—of the father who had made the vow, and of the son who had fulfilled it. . . . The new work was hardly begun, when, we are told, heaven itself was moved to give a sign of the future greatness of Rome's dominion. . . . A man's head with the features intact was discovered by the workmen who were digging the foundations of the temple [of Jupiter]. This meant without any doubt that on this spot would stand the imperial citadel of the capital city of the world. Nothing could be plainer—and such was

[8]Inhabitants of Latium, a coastal strip extending south of Rome.
[9]The most powerful of the ancient gods (known to the Greeks as Zeus).
[10]Chief of the Seven Hills of Rome.

the interpretation put upon the discovery not only by the Roman soothsayers but also by those who were specially brought from Etruria[11] for consultation.

In view of all this, Tarquin became more extravagant in his ideas. . . . Tarquin's chief interest was now the completion of the temple. Builders and engineers were brought in from all over Etruria, and the project involved the use not only of public funds but also of a large number of labourers from the poorer classes. The work was hard in itself, and came as an addition to their regular military duties; but it was an honourable burden with a solemn and religious significance, and they were not, on the whole, unwilling to bear it; but it was a very different matter when they were put on to other tasks less spectacular but more laborious still, such as the construction of the tiers of seats in the Circus[12] and the excavation of the . . . Great Sewer, designed to carry off the sewage of the entire city by an underground pipe-line. The magnitude of both these projects could hardly be equalled by any work even of modern times. It was Tarquin's view that an idle proletariat was a burden on the state, so in addition to the major works I have mentioned he made use of some of the surplus population by sending settlers out to [nearby towns]. This had the further advantages of increasing the extent of Roman territory and of providing points of resistance against future attack either by land or sea.

About this time an alarming and ominous event occurred: a snake slid out from a crack in a wooden pillar in the palace. Everyone ran from it in fright; even the king was scared, though in his case it was not fear so much as foreboding. About signs and omens of public import the custom had always been to consult only Etruscan soothsayers; this, however, was a different matter. It was in the king's own house that the portentous sight had been seen; and that, Tarquin felt, justified the unusual step of sending to Delphi, to consult the most famous oracle in the world. Unwilling to entrust the answer of the oracle to anybody else, he sent on the mission two of his sons, Titus and Arruns, who accordingly set out for Greece through country which Roman feet had seldom trod and over seas which Roman ships had never sailed. With them went Lucius Junius Brutus, son of the king's sister Tarquinia.

Now Brutus had deliberately assumed a mask to hide his true char-

---

[11]An area of Italy north of Rome, occupied by the once-dominating Etruscans.

[12]A circular, open-air arena, for races and other spectacles.

acter. When he learned of the murder by Tarquin of the Roman aristocrats, one of the victims being his own brother, he had come to the conclusion that the only way of saving himself was to appear in the king's eyes as a person of no account. If there were nothing in his character for Tarquin to fear, and nothing in his fortune to covet, then the sheer contempt in which he was held would be a better protection than his own rights could ever be. Accordingly he pretended to be a half-wit and made no protest at the seizure by Tarquin of everything he possessed. He even submitted to being known publicly as the 'Dullard' (which is what his name signifies), that under cover of that [degrading] title the great spirit which gave Rome her freedom might be able to bide its time. On this occasion he was taken by Arruns and Titus to Delphi less as a companion than as a butt for their amusement; and he is said to have carried with him, as his gift to Apollo, a rod of gold inserted into a hollow stick of cornel-wood—symbolic, it may be, of his own character.

The three young men reached Delphi, and carried out the king's instructions. That done, Titus and Arruns found themseves unable to resist putting a further question to the oracle. Which of them, they asked, would be the next king of Rome? From the depths of the cavern came the mysterious answer: 'He who shall be the first to kiss his mother shall hold in Rome supreme authority.' Titus and Arruns were determined to keep the prophecy absolutely secret, to prevent their other brother, Tarquin, who had been left in Rome, from knowing anything about it. Thus he, at any rate, would be out of the running. For themselves, they drew lots to determine which of them, on their return, should kiss his mother first.

Brutus, however, interpreted the words of Apollo's priestess in a different way. Pretending to trip, he fell flat on his face, and his lips touched the Earth—the mother of all living things.

Back in Rome, they found vigorous preparations in progress for war with the Rutuli.[13] The chief town of the Rutuli was Ardea, and they were a people, for that place and period, of very considerable wealth. Their wealth was, indeed, the reason for Tarquin's preparations; he needed money to repair the drain on his resources resulting from his ambitious schemes of public building and he knew, moreover, that the [common people] were growing ever more restive, not only in view of his tyrannical behaviour generally but also, and especially,

[13]Close neighbors of the Romans.

because they had been so long employed in manual labour such as belonged properly to slaves, and the distribution of plunder from a captured town would do much to soften their resentment.

The attempt was made to take Ardea by assault. It failed; siege operations were begun, and the army settled down into permanent quarters. With little prospect of any decisive action, the war looked like being a long one, and in these circumstances leave was granted, quite naturally, with considerable freedom, especially to officers. Indeed, the young princes, at any rate, spent most of their leisure enjoying themselves in entertainments on the most lavish scale. They were drinking one day in the quarters of Sextus Tarquinius[14]—Collatinus, son of Egerius, was also present—when someone chanced to mention the subject of wives. Each of them, of course, extravagantly praised his own; and the rivalry got hotter and hotter, until Collatinus suddenly cried: 'Stop! What need is there of words, when in a few hours we can prove beyond doubt the incomparable superiority of my Lucretia? We are all young and strong: why shouldn't we ride to Rome and see with our own eyes what kind of women our wives are? There is no better evidence, I assure you, than what a man finds when he enters his wife's room unexpectedly.'

They had all drunk a good deal, and the proposal appealed to them; so they mounted their horses and galloped off to Rome. They reached the city as dusk was falling; and there the wives of the royal princes were found enjoying themselves with a group of young friends at a dinner-party, in the greatest of luxury. The riders then went on to Collatia, where they found Lucretia very differently employed: it was already late at night, but there, in the hall of her house, surrounded by her busy maid-servants, she was still hard at work by lamplight upon her spinning. Which wife had won the contest in womanly virtue was no longer in doubt.

With all courtesy Lucretia rose to bid her husband and the princes welcome, and Collatinus, pleased with his success, invited his friends to sup with him. It was at that fatal supper that Lucretia's beauty, and proven chastity, kindled in Sextus Tarquinius the flame of lust, and determined him to [degrade] her.

Nothing further occurred that night. The little jaunt was over, and the young men rode back to camp.

[14]Son of King Tarquin.

A few days later Sextus, without Collatinus's knowledge, returned with one companion to Collatia, where he was hospitably welcomed in Lucretia's house, and, after supper, escorted, like the honoured visitor he was thought to be, to the guest-chamber. Here he waited till the house was asleep, and then, when all was quiet, he drew his sword and made his way to Lucretia's room determined to rape her. She was asleep. Laying his left hand on her breast, 'Lucretia,' he whispered, 'not a sound! I am Sextus Tarquinius. I am armed—if you utter a word, I will kill you.' Lucretia opened her eyes in terror; death was imminent, no help at hand. Sextus urged his love, begged her to submit, pleaded, threatened, used every weapon that might conquer a woman's heart. But all in vain; not even the fear of death could bend her will. 'If death will not move you,' Sextus cried, 'dishonour shall. I will kill you first, then cut the throat of a slave and lay his naked body by your side. Will they not believe that you have been caught in adultery with a servant— and paid the price?' Even the most resolute chastity could not have stood against this dreadful threat.

Lucretia yielded. Sextus enjoyed her, and rode away, proud of his success.

The unhappy girl wrote to her father in Rome and to her husband in Ardea, urging them both to come at once with a trusted friend— and quickly, for a frightful thing had happened. Her father came with Valerius, Volesus's son, her husband with Brutus, with whom he was returning to Rome when he was met by the messenger. They found Lucretia sitting in her room, in deep distress. Tears rose to her eyes as they entered, and to her husband's question, 'Is it well with you?' she answered, 'No. What can be well with a woman who has lost her honour? In your bed, Collatinus, is the impress of another man. My body only has been violated. My heart is innocent, and death will be my witness. Give me your solemn promise that the adulterer shall be punished—he is Sextus Tarquinius. He it is who last night came as my enemy disguised as my guest, and took his pleasure of me. That pleasure will be my death—and his, too, if you are men.'

The promise was given. One after another they tried to comfort her. They told her she was helpless, and therefore innocent; that he alone was guilty. It was the mind, they said, that sinned, not the body; without intention there could never be guilt.

'What is due to *him*,' Lucretia said, 'is for you to decide. As for me I am innocent of fault, but I will take my punishment. Never shall

Lucretia provide a precedent for unchaste women to escape what they deserve.' With these words she drew a knife from under her robe, drove it into her heart, and fell forward, dead.

Her father and husband were overwhelmed with grief. While they stood weeping helplessly, Brutus drew the bloody knife from Lucretia's body, and holding it before him cried: 'By this girl's blood—none more chaste till a tyrant wronged her—and by the gods, I swear that with sword and fire, and whatever else can lend strength to my arm, I will pursue Lucius Tarquinius the Proud, his wicked wife, and all his children, and never again will I let them or any other man be King in Rome.'

He put the knife into Collatinus's hands, then passed it to Lucretius,[15] then to Valerius. All looked at him in astonishment: a miracle had happened—he was a changed man. Obedient to his command, they swore their oath. Grief was forgotten in the sudden surge of anger, and when Brutus called upon them to make war, from that instant, upon the tyrant's throne, they took him for their leader.

Lucretia's body was carried from the house into the public square. Crowds gathered, as crowds will, to gape and wonder—and the sight was unexpected enough, and horrible enough, to attract them. Anger at the criminal brutality of the king's son and sympathy with the father's grief stirred every heart; and when Brutus cried out that it was time for deeds not tears, and urged them, like true Romans, to take up arms against the tyrants who had dared to treat them as a vanquished enemy, not a man amongst them could resist the call. The boldest spirits offered themselves at once for service; the rest soon followed their lead. Lucretia's father was left to hold Collatia; guards were posted to prevent news of the rising from reaching the palace, and with Brutus in command the armed populace began their march on Rome.

In the city the first effect of their appearance was alarm and confusion, but the sight of Brutus, and others of equal distinction, at the head of the mob, soon convinced people that this was, at least, no mere popular demonstration. Moreover the horrible story of Lucretia had had hardly less effect in Rome than in Collatia. In a moment the Forum[16] was packed, and the crowds, by Brutus's order, were immediately summoned to attend the Tribune of Knights—an office held at

---

[15]Father of Lucretia.

[16]The chief public square of the city.

the time by Brutus himself. There, publicly throwing off the mask under which he had hitherto concealed his real character and feelings, he made a speech painting in vivid colours the brutal and unbridled lust of Sextus Tarquinius, the hideous rape of the innocent Lucretia and her pitiful death, and the bereavement of her father, for whom the cause of her death was an even bitterer and more dreadful thing than the death itself. He went on to speak of the king's arrogant and tyrannical behaviour; of the sufferings of the [common people] condemned to labour underground clearing or constructing ditches and sewers; of gallant Romans—soldiers who had beaten in battle all neighbouring peoples—robbed of their swords and turned into stone-cutters and artisans. . . . Doubtless he told them of other, and worse, things, brought to his mind in the heat of the moment and by the sense of this latest outrage, which still lived in his eye and pressed upon his heart; but a mere historian can hardly record them.

The effect of his words was immediate: the populace took fire, and were brought to demand the [removal] of the king's authority and the exile of himself and his family.

With an armed body of volunteers Brutus then marched for Ardea to rouse the army to revolt. Lucretius, who some time previously had been appointed by the king Prefect of the City, was left in command in Rome. [Queen]Tullia fled from the palace during the disturbances; wherever she went she was met with curses; everyone, men and women alike, called down upon her head the vengeance of the furies who punish sinners against the sacred ties of blood.

When news of the rebellion reached Ardea, the king immediately started for Rome, to restore order. Brutus got wind of his approach, and changed his route to avoid meeting him, finally reaching Ardea almost at the same moment as Tarquin arrived at Rome. Tarquin found the city gates shut against him and his exile decreed. Brutus the Liberator was enthusiastically welcomed by the troops, and Tarquin's sons were expelled from the camp. Two of them followed their father into exile at Caere in Etruria. Sextus Tarquinius went to Gabii—his own territory, as he doubtless hoped; but his previous record there of robbery and violence had made him many enemies, who now took their revenge and assassinated him.

Tarquin the Proud reigned for twenty-five years. The whole period of monarchical government, from the founding of Rome to its liberation, was 244 years. After the liberation two consuls were elected by

popular vote. . . . The two consuls were Lucius Junius Brutus and
Lucius Tarquinius Callatinus.

• • •

It was argued in the council that if ever at any time a war had been
conducted under strict command, now was the moment to recall military discipline to its former ways.[17] Their anxiety was more acute
because they had to make war on Latins, who were the same as themselves in language, customs, type of arms, and above all in military
institutions; soldiers had intermingled with soldiers, centurions [offi-
cers] with centurions, tribunes with tribunes as equals and colleagues
in the same garrisons and often in the same maniples.[18] To prevent the
men committing some blunder on account of this, the consuls issued
the order that no one was to leave his position to fight the enemy.

It happened that among the squadron leaders in the cavalry, who
had been sent off to reconnoitre in all directions, was the consul's son,
Titus Manlius.[19] He had managed to ride with his cavalry beyond the
enemy's camp until he was hardly a spear throw from their nearest
outpost. There the Tusculan [Latin] cavalry were stationed under the
command of Geminus Maecius, whose reputation was high amongst
his fellows for his exploits as much as for his noble birth. He recognized the Roman cavalry, and amongst them the conspicuous figure of
the consul's son, riding at their head (for they were all known to each
other, especially the nobility). 'Do you Romans,' he cried, 'intend to
make war on the Latins and their allies with a single squadron? What
will your consuls and your two consular armies be doing meanwhile?'
'They'll be here in good time,' replied Manlius, 'and with them will be
Jupiter himself, who has more power and might than they, as witness
of the treaties violated by you. If we gave you your fill of fighting at
Lake Regillus, here too we shall certainly see that you get little joy out
of our fighting force and a clash with us.' At this Geminus rode out a
little in front of his men: 'Then will you fight me yourself, while
waiting for that great day to come when you all make a mighty effort
to get your armies moving? The outcome of a duel between you and
me will show how much better a Latin cavalryman is than a Roman.'

[17]The following episode occurred, calculating from Livy's chronology, around 340 B.C.

[18]A maniple was a subdivision of a Roman legion, consisting of 60 or 120 heavily armed
foot-soldiers.

[19]The consul's (father's) name was also Titus Manlius.

The young man's bold spirit was roused, whether by anger, by shame at the thought of refusing the challenge, or through the invincible power of destiny. And so, forgetting his father's supreme authority and the consuls' order, he threw himself headlong into a fight where it mattered little whether he won or lost. The rest of the cavalry were made to stand back, as if to watch a riding display, and the two men rode their horses hard at each other across the empty space between them. But when they met with spears levelled for attack, Manlius's spear glanced off his enemy's helmet, while Maecius's passed over the neck of the other's horse. Then when they wheeled their horses round, Manlius was the first to collect himself for a second blow and pricked Maecius's horse between the ears with his spear-point. The horse reared when it felt the wound and shook its head so violently that it threw its rider; and as Maecius was trying to get up after the heavy fall, leaning on his spear and shield, Manlius ran through his throat so that the spear came out between his ribs and pinned him to the ground. Gathering up the spoils, Manlius rode back to his men, and then made for the camp, accompanied by their shouts of triumph. He went straight to his father's headquarters, not knowing what fate and future awaited him, or whether praise or punishment were to be his desert.

'Father,' he said, 'so that all men may proclaim me your true son, I am bringing you these cavalryman's spoils, taken from the enemy I killed after accepting his challenge.' On hearing this, the consul promptly turned away from his son and gave orders for a trumpet to summon an assembly. When this had filled up, he spoke as follows: 'Titus Manlius, you have respected neither consular authority nor your father's dignity; you have left your position to fight the enemy in defiance of my order, and, as far as was in your power, have subverted military discipline, on which the fortune of Rome has rested up to this day; you have made it necessary for me to forget either the republic or myself. We would therefore rather be punished for our own wrong-doing than allow our country to [suffer] our sins at so great a cost to itself; it is a harsh example we shall set, but a salutary one for the young men of the future. As far as my own feelings are concerned, they are stirred by a man's natural love for his children, as well as by the example you have given of your courage, even though this was marred by a false conception of glory. But since consular authority must either be confirmed by your death or annulled for ever by your going unpunished, I believe that you yourself, if you have any drop of my blood in you, would agree that the military discipline which you undermined by your error must be restored by your punishment. Go, lictor,[20] bind him to the stake.'

All were transfixed with horror by this dreadful command; every man saw the axe as if raised against himself, and it was fear, not obedience, which held them in check. So they stood rooted to the spot in silence, as if lost in amazement; then when the blood gushed from the severed neck, suddenly their voices broke out in agonized complaint so unrestrained that they spared neither laments nor curses. They covered the young man's body with his spoils, built a pyre outside the earthworks, and burnt it with all the honours that can attend any military funeral. The 'commands of Manlius' not only caused a shudder at the time but were a grim warning in the future. However, the brutality of the punishment made the soldiers more obedient to their commander, and not only was better attention given everywhere to guard-duties, night watches, and picket-stationing, but in the final struggle too, when the army went into battle, that stern act of discipline did them good.

---

[20]An attendant who walked before certain high Roman officials carrying the *fasces*, a bundle of wooden rods enclosing an axe, a symbol of Roman authority.

15

Plutarch

Lives: Marcus Cato

GREEK *literature did not end with the decline of the Greek city-state in the fourth century* B.C. *The literature continued to grow, and from the fourth century a new form made its appearance: the short biography, presenting a specific person with unique traits. As Greek literature gained new admirers in the early Roman Empire, this sort of biographical writing became widely practiced and may even have provided a pattern for the Christian gospels. Certainly, the form reached its peak in Lucius Mestrius Plutarchus (ca.* A.D. *46–ca. 124).*

Little is known of Plutarch's own life. After student days in Athens, he spent some years lecturing (in Greek) in Rome. An amiable man of wide interests, broad learning, and cultivated taste, he came to be on close terms with the "mighty"; there is, in fact, some evidence that the Emperor Trajan made him a consul and a provincial governor. Plutarch, however, preferred the life of a country gentleman; he returned to his native Chaeronea in Greece, where he happily filled its petty offices and priesthoods. It was then that he composed, in Greek, his best known work, the Lives. *It is a collection of biographical studies of famous Greek soldiers and statesmen, paired—for purposes of comparison—with their Roman counterparts. Twenty-three of these paired studies have come down to us, along with four single* Lives. *In general, Plutarch was more interested in portraying character than in narrating events. While remaining impartial in his comparisons, he intended to show that Greece during its glorious past had produced men as great as the greatest of the now dominant Romans. Plutarch embodies the upper class, conservative, Greco-Roman attitudes of his time.*

LIVES: MARCUS CATO   Plutarch, *Lives*, trans. Bernadotte Perrin, Vol. II, "Marcus Cato" (London, 1914), pp. 303–309, 313–317, 319–321, 333–335, 337, 347–351, 357–373, 379–383. Adapted by the editor.

The following selection from the Lives *is taken from Plutarch's biography of Marcus Porcius Cato (234–149 B.C.), usually known as Cato the Elder, or the Censor. As "social history," it offers a penetrating glimpse into the life of the early Roman Republic. But, foremost, it gives a memorable picture of one of the Republic's influential personalities and patriotic heroes who, throughout his private and public life, sought to stem the foreign cultural tide that was eroding the ancestral ways of the Roman people—once the most puritanical of antiquity. In his moralizing attitude Cato might be compared to the later Roman historian Livy (selection 14). Cato, in any case, remains to this day an admired model for advocates of "free enterprise"; thus, the conservative Cato Institute (of Washington, D.C.) is named for him.*

If only because Plutarch's sources of information have not survived, his Lives *are vital to our knowledge of many Greek and Roman personalities. The wide popularity of the* Lives *across the centuries gives Plutarch first place among the Greek authors who shaped an image of the ancient world for later ages. Among the influential writers who followed, Shakespeare, Montaigne (a sixteenth-century French essayist), Corneille and Racine (seventeenth-century French playwrights) used him as a principal guide in their portrayals of classical characters.*

MARCUS CATO

The family of Marcus Cato, it is said, was of Tusculan[1] origin, though he lived, previous to his career as soldier and statesman, on an inherited estate in the country of the Sabines.[2] His ancestors commonly passed for men of no note whatever, but Cato himself extols his father, Marcus, as a brave man and good soldier. He also says that his grandfather, Cato, often won prizes for soldierly valour, and received from the state treasury, because of his bravery, the price of five horses which had been killed under him in battle. The Romans used to call men who had no family distinction, but were coming into public notice through their own achievements, "new men," and such they called Cato. But he himself used to say that as far as office and distinction went, he was

---

[1]Tusculum was an ancient town about ten miles southeast of Rome.

[2]The Sabines were a tribal group living northeast of Rome in its earliest days. (See the legendary rape of the Sabine women described by Livy, pp. 390–92.) By 268 B.C. the Sabines had become fully Romanized and ceased to be a separate people.

indeed new, but having regard to ancestral deeds of valour, he was oldest of the old. His third name[3] was not Cato at first, but Priscus. Afterwards he got the surname of Cato for his great abilities. The Romans call a man who is wise and prudent, *catus*.

As for his outward appearance, he had reddish hair, and keen grey eyes, as the author of the well-known epigram ill-naturedly gives us to understand:

> Red-haired, snapper and snarler, his grey eyes
> > flashing defiance,
> Cato, come to Hades, will be thrust back
> > by their Queen.[4]

His physical body—since he laboured from the very first with his own hands, held to a temperate way of life, and performed military duties—was very serviceable, vigorous, and healthy. His eloquence—a second body, as it were, and an instrument with which to perform not only necessary, but also high and noble services—he developed and perfected in the villages and towns about Rome. There he served as advocate for all who needed him, and got the reputation of being, first a zealous pleader, and then a capable orator. Thenceforth the weight and dignity of his character revealed themselves more and more to those who had dealings with him; they saw that he was bound to be a man of great affairs, and have a leading place in the state. For he not only gave his services in legal contests without fee of any sort, but did not appear to cherish even the reputation won in such contests. For he was more desirous of high reputation in battles and campaigns against the enemy, and while he was yet a mere youth had his breast covered with honourable wounds. He says himself that he made his first campaign when he was seventeen years old, at the time when Hannibal was consuming Italy with the flames of his successes.[5]

In battle, he showed himself effective in hand combat, sure and steadfast of foot, and with a fierce expression. With threatening speech and harsh cries he would advance upon the foe, for he rightly thought,

[3]Roman men normally had a first, second, and third name.

[4]That is, according to this writer, Cato is so ill-tempered that even the queen of the underworld will not admit him.

[5]Hannibal, pledged to undying hatred of Rome, was the most brilliant general of Carthage in its wars against Rome. His army devastated much of Italy, although he never succeeded in capturing Rome itself. The year was 217 B.C. when Cato fought against Hannibal's army.

and tried to show others, that often-times such action terrifies the enemy more than does the sword. On the march, he carried his own armour on foot, while a single servant followed in charge of his camp provisions. With this man, it is said, he was never angry, and never scolded him when he served up a meal; he actually assisted in most of such preparations, provided he was free from his military duties. Water was what he drank on his campaigns, except that once in a while, in a raging thirst, he would call for vinegar, or, when his strength was failing, would add a little wine.

Near his fields was the cottage which had once belonged to Manius Curius, a hero of three triumphs.[6] To this he would often go, and the sight of the small farm and the simple dwelling led him to think of their former owner, who, though he had become the greatest of the Romans, had subdued the most warlike nations, and driven Pyrrhus[7] out of Italy. Nevertheless, he tilled this little patch of ground with his own hands and occupied this cottage, after three triumphs. Here it was that the ambassadors of the Samnites once found him seated at his hearth cooking turnips, and offered him much gold; but he dismissed them, saying that a man whom such a meal satisfied had no need of gold, and for his part he thought that a more honourable thing than the possession of gold was the conquest of its possessors. Cato would go away with his mind full of these things, and on viewing again his own house and lands and servants and way of life, would increase the labours of his hands and reduce his extravagances.

●　　●　　●

The influence which Cato's oratory won for him increased, and men called him a Roman Demosthenes;[8] but his manner of life was even more talked about and carried abroad. For his oratorical ability set before young men not only a goal which many already were striving eagerly to attain, but a man who worked with his own hands, as his fathers did, and was contented with a cold breakfast, a frugal dinner, simple clothing, and a humble dwelling—one who thought more of

---

[6]When a Roman general had won a great victory against foreign enemies, he was rewarded with a triumphal procession, by the authority of the Senate, at Rome. This elaborate celebration was the highest Roman military honor.

[7]A king of Epirus, northwest of Greece, distant cousin of Alexander the Great. Pyrrhus invaded Italy in 280 B.C.

[8]An Athenian (383–322 B.C.), the most famous Greek orator.

rejecting the extras of life than of possessing them. The Roman commonwealth had now grown too large to keep its earlier integrity. The conquest of many kingdoms and peoples had brought a large mixture of customs, and the adoption of ways of life of every sort. It was natural, therefore, that men should admire Cato, when they saw that, whereas other men were broken down by labors and weakened by pleasures, he was victor over both. And this too, not only while he was still young and ambitious, but even in his old age, after consulship[9] and triumph. Then, like some victorious athlete, he persisted in the regimen of his training, and kept his mind unaltered to the last.

He tells us that he never wore expensive clothing; that he drank the same wine as his slaves; that as for fish and meats, he would buy enough for his dinner from the public stalls—and even this for Rome's sake, that he might strengthen his body for military service. He once inherited an embroidered Babylonian robe, but sold it at once; not a single one of his farm-houses had plastered walls; he never paid much for a slave, since he did not want them to be delicately beautiful, but sturdy workers, such as grooms and herdsmen. And these he thought it his duty to sell when they got old, instead of feeding them when they were useless; and that in general, he thought nothing cheap that one could do without. He said also that he bought lands where crops were raised and cattle herded, not those where lawns were sprinkled and paths swept for pleasure.

These things were thought by some to be the result of the man's stinginess; but others excused them in the belief that he lived in this way only to correct and moderate the extravagance of others. However, for my part, I regard his treatment of his slaves like beasts of burden, using them to the utmost, and then, when they were old, driving them off and selling them, as the mark of a very mean nature, which recognizes no tie between man and man but that of profit. . . . A kindly man will take good care even of his horses when they are worn out with age, and of his dogs, too, not only in their puppyhood, but when their old age needs nursing. . . .

We should not treat living creatures like shoes or pots and pans, casting them aside when they are bruised and worn out with service; but, if for no other reason, than for the sake of practice in kindness to

[9]During the time of the Roman Republic, when Cato lived, two consuls were elected annually by the male citizens. They carried the judicial and military authority that had formerly been wielded by the kings. The Romans of that period even dated the years by the names of their consuls. (Cato was consul in 195 B.C.)

our fellow men, we should accustom ourselves to mildness and gentleness in our dealings with other creatures. I certainly would not sell even an ox that had worked for me, just because he was old, much less an elderly man, removing him from his habitual place and customary life, as it were from his native land, for a paltry price, useless as he is to those who sell him and as he will be to those who buy him. But Cato, boasting of such things, says that he left in Spain even the horse which had carried him through his military campaign, that he might not tax the city with the cost of its transportation home. Whether these things should be set down to greatness of spirit or littleness of mind, is an open question.

But in other matters, his self-restraint was beyond measure admirable. For instance, when he was in command of an army, he took for himself and his staff not more than three bushels of wheat a month, and for his beasts of burden, less than a bushel and a half of barley a day. He received Sardinia to govern as his province; and whereas his predecessors used to charge the public treasury for their tents, couches, and clothing, . . . his simple economy stood out in an incredible contrast. He made no demands whatever upon the public treasury, and made his circuit of the cities on foot, followed by a single public officer, who carried his robe and cup for libations to the gods. And yet, though in such matters he showed himself mild and lenient to those under his authority, in other ways he displayed a dignity and severity proper to the administration of justice. He carried out the edicts of the government in a direct and masterful way so that the Roman power never inspired its subjects with greater fear or affection.

* * *

He dealt with the Athenians through an interpreter. He could have spoken to them directly, but he always clung to his native ways, and mocked at those who were lost in admiration of anything that was Greek.

* * *

Ten years after his consulship, Cato was a candidate for the censorship. This office towered, as it were, above every other civic honour, and was, in a way, the high point of a political career. The variety of its powers was great, including that of examining into the lives and manners of the citizens. Its creators thought that no one should be left to his own ways and desires, without inspection and review, either in his marrying, having children, ordering his daily life, or in the entertainment of his friends. Thinking that these things revealed a man's real character more than did his public and political career, they set men in office to watch, warn, and chastise, that no one should turn to vices and give up his native and customary way of life. They chose to this office one of the so-called patricians,[10] and one of the plebeians.[11] These officers were called censors, and they had authority to degrade a knight, or to expel a senator who led a wild and disorderly life. They also revised the assessments of property, and arranged the citizens in lists [for military service] according to their social and political classes. There were other great powers also connected with the office.

Therefore, when Cato became a candidate, nearly all the best known and most influential men of the senatorial party united to oppose him. The men of noble parentage among them were moved by jealousy, thinking that nobility of birth would be trampled if men of lowly origin forced their way up to the summits of honour and power; while those who were conscious of base practices and of a departure from ancestral customs, feared the severity of the man, which was sure to be harsh and unyielding in the exercise of power. Therefore, after due consultation and preparation, they put up in opposition to Cato seven candidates for the office, who sought the favour of the people with promises of mild conduct in office, supposing that they wanted to be ruled with a lax and indulgent hand. Cato, on the contrary, showed no inclination to be agreeable whatever, but plainly threatened wrong-doers in his speeches, and loudly cried that the city had need of a great purification. He urged the people, if they were wise, not to choose the most agreeable physician, but the one who was most in earnest. He himself, he said, was such a physician, and so was Valerius Flaccus, of the patricians. With him as colleague, and him alone, he thought he could cut the excessive luxury and effeminacy of the time. As for the rest of the candidates, he saw that they were all trying to force their way into the office in order to administer it badly, since they feared those who would administer it well. And so truly great were the Roman voters, and so worthy of great leaders, that they did not fear Cato's rigour and haughty independence, but rejected those candidates

[10]Members of the Roman aristocratic, privileged class.
[11]The majority of citizens, like Cato, who were not patricians.

who, it was believed, would do every thing to please them, and elected Flaccus to the office along with Cato.[12]

• • •

As censor, Cato paid not the slightest heed to his accusers, but grew still more strict. He cut off the pipes by which people conveyed part of the public water supply into their private houses and gardens; he upset and demolished all buildings that enroached on public land; he reduced the cost of public works to the lowest, and forced the rent of public lands to the highest possible figure. All these things brought much hatred upon him. Titus Flamininus headed a party against him which induced the Senate to annul as useless the outlays and payments which he had authorised for temples and public works, and incited the boldest of the tribunes to call him to account before the people and fine him two talents. The Senate also strongly opposed the erection of the basilica [large rectangular public hall] which he built at the public cost below the council-house in the Forum, and which was called the Basilica Porcia.

Still, it appears that the people approved of his censorship to an amazing extent. At any rate, after erecting a statue to his honour in the temple of Health, they commemorated in the inscription upon it, not the military commands nor the triumph of Cato, but, as the inscription may be translated, the fact "that when the Roman state was tottering to its fall, he was made censor, and by helpful guidance, wise restraints, and sound teachings, restored it again." . . .

He heaped high praise upon himself. He tells us that men of self-indulgent lives, when rebuked for it, used to say: "We ought not to be blamed; we are no Catos." Also that those who imitated some of his practices and did it clumsily, were called "left-handed Catos." Also that the Senate looked to him in the most dangerous crises as seafarers to their helmsman, and often, if he was not present, postponed its most serious business. These boasts of his are confirmed by other witnesses, for he had great authority in the city, alike for his life, his eloquence, and his age.

He was also a good father, a considerate husband, and a household

---

[12]In 184 B.C.

manager of no little talent; nor did he give only a fitful attention to this, as a matter of little or no importance. Therefore, I think I ought to give suitable instances of his conduct in these relations. He married a wife who was of higher birth than she was rich, thinking that, although the rich and the high-born may be alike given to pride, still, women of high birth have such a horror of what is disgraceful that they are more obedient to their husbands in all that is honourable. He used to say that the man who struck his wife or child, laid violent hands on the holiest of holy things. Also that he thought it more praiseworthy to be a good husband than a great senator, and there was nothing more to admire in Socrates of old than that he was always kind and gentle with his shrewish wife and stupid sons. After the birth of his own son, no business could be so urgent, unless it had a public character, as to prevent him from being present when his wife bathed and wrapped the babe. For the mother nursed it herself, and often gave her breast also to the infants of her slaves, that so they might come to cherish a brotherly affection for her son. As soon as the boy showed signs of understanding, his father took him under his own charge and taught him to read, although he had an accomplished slave, Chilo by name, who was a school-teacher, and taught many boys. Still, Cato thought it not right, as he tells us himself, that his son should be scolded by a slave, or have his ears tweaked when he was slow to learn, still less that he should be indebted to his slave for such a priceless thing as education. He was therefore himself not only the boy's reading-teacher, but his tutor in law, and his athletic trainer, and he taught his son not merely to hurl the javelin and fight in armour and ride the horse, but also to box, to endure heat and cold, and to swim strongly through the eddies and billows of the Tiber. His "History of Rome," as he tells us himself, he wrote out with his own hand and in large characters, that his son might have in his own home an aid to acquaintance with his country's ancient traditions. He declares that his son's presence put him on guard against making indecencies of speech as if in the presence of the Vestal Virgins,[13] and that he never bathed with him. This, indeed, would seem to have been a general taboo with the Romans, for even fathers-in-law avoided bathing with their sons-in-law, because they were ashamed to uncover their nakedness. Afterwards, however,

[13]The Vestals were virgin priestesses selected from noble families for terms of thirty years; they were expected to remain chaste and to tend the sacred fire in the temple of Vesta (Roman goddess of the family hearth).

when they had learned from the Greeks their freedom in going naked before men, they in their turn infected the Greeks with the practice of doing so even before women.

So Cato worked at the task of molding his son to virtue. But since his body was rather too frail to endure much hardship, he relaxed somewhat the excessive rigidity and austerity of his own way of life. But his son, although frail, made a sturdy soldier, and fought brilliantly under Aemilius Paulus in the battle against Perseus.[14] On that occasion his sword either was knocked from his hand or slipped from his moist grasp. Distressed by this mishap, he turned to some of his companions for aid, and supported by them rushed again into the thick of the enemy. After a long and furious struggle, he succeeded in clearing the place, and found the sword at last among the many heaps of arms and dead bodies where friends and foes alike lay piled upon one another. Paulus, his commander, admired the young man's exploit, and there is still in existence a letter written by Cato himself to his son, in which he heaps extravagant praise upon him for this honourable zeal in recovering his sword. The son afterwards married Tertia, a daughter of Paulus and a sister of Scipio the Younger;[15] his admission into such a family was due no less to himself than to his father. Thus Cato's careful attention to the education of his son bore worthy fruit.

He owned many slaves, and usually bought those prisoners of war who were young and still capable of being reared and trained. Not one of his slaves ever entered another man's house unless sent there by Cato or his wife, and when any of them was asked what Cato was doing, he always answered that he did not know. A slave of his was expected either to be busy about the house, or to be asleep, and he preferred the sleepy ones. He thought these gentler than the wakeful ones, and that those who had enjoyed the gift of sleep were better for any kind of service than those who lacked it. In the belief that his slaves were led into most mischief by their sexual passions, he required that the males should have sex with the female slaves of the house at a fixed price, but should never approach any other woman.

At the outset, when Cato was still poor and in military service, he

[14]Aemilius Paulus was a consul who totally defeated Perseus, the last king of Macedonia, at the battle of Pydna in 168 B.C. Twenty years after that decisive battle, Macedonia became a Roman province.

[15]This Scipio was adopted into the distinguished family of Scipio Africanus, conqueror of Hannibal the Carthaginian general. Scipio the Younger later (146 B.C.) won the *final* victory for Rome against Carthage.

found no fault at all with what was served up to him, declaring that it was shameful for a man to quarrel with a servant over food and drink. But afterwards, when his circumstances were improved and he used to entertain his friends and colleagues at table, no sooner was the dinner over than he would flog those slaves who had been unsatisfactory in preparing or serving it. He was always arranging that his slaves should have feuds and disagreements among themselves; harmony among them made him suspicious and fearful of them. He had those who were suspected of some capital offence brought to trial before all their fellow servants, and, if convicted, put to death.

However, as he applied himself more strenuously to money-getting, he came to regard agriculture as more entertaining than profitable, and invested his money in business that was safe and sure. He bought ponds, hot springs, districts given over to fullers,[16] pitch factories, land with natural pasture and forest, all of which brought him large profits. He used to loan money also on ships, and his method was as follows. He required his borrowers to form a large company, and when there were fifty partners and as many ships for his security, he took one share in the company himself, and was represented by Quintio, a freedman of his, who accompanied his clients in all their ventures. In this way his entire security was not risked, but only a small part of it, and his profits were large. He used to lend money also to those of his slaves who wished it, and they would buy boys with it, and after training and teaching them for a year, at Cato's expense, would sell them again. Many of these boys Cato would retain for himself, counting to the credit of the slave the highest price bid for his boy by outsiders. He tried to persuade his son also to such investments, by saying that it was not the part of a man, but of a widow woman, to lessen his property. But surely Cato was going too far when he said that a man should be admired and glorified like a god if the final inventory of his property showed that he had added to it more than he had inherited.

When he was now well on in years, there came as delegates from Athens to Rome, Carneades the Academic, and Diogenes the Stoic philosopher,[17] to beg the reversal of a certain decision against the Ath-

---

[16]Fuller's earth is an absorbent clay, used especially for removing grease from fabrics, as a filter, and as a dusting powder.

[17]This visit in 155 B.C. became quite famous as it drew the attention of many Romans to the Greek schools of philosophy. Carneades was called "the Academic" because he was head of the Academy founded by Plato. (See introduction to selection 10.) Diogenes was the head of the Stoic school of philosophy.

enian people, which imposed upon them a heavy fine. Upon the arrival of these philosophers, the most studious of the city's youth hastened to wait upon them, and became their devoted and admiring listeners. The charm of Carneades especially, which had boundless power, and a fame not inferior to its power, won large and sympathetic audiences, and filled the city, like a rushing mighty wind, with the noise of his praises. Report spread far and wide that a Greek of amazing talent, who disarmed all opposition by the magic of his eloquence, had infused a tremendous passion into the youth of the city—in consequence of which they gave up their other pleasures and pursuits and were "possessed" about philosophy. The other Romans were pleased at this, and glad to see their young men lay hold of Greek culture and associate with such admirable men. But Cato, at the very outset, when this zeal for discussion came into the city, was distressed—fearing that the young men, by giving this direction to their ambition, should come to love a reputation based on mere words more than one achieved by military deeds. And when the fame of the visiting philosophers rose yet higher in the city, and their first speeches before the Senate were interpreted, at his own instance and request, by so conspicuous a man as Gaius Acilius, Cato determined, on some excuse or other, to rid the city of them all. So he rose in the Senate and condemned the city officials for keeping for so long a time a delegation composed of men who could easily secure anything they wished, so persuasive were they. "We ought," he said, "to make up our minds one way or another, and vote on what the delegation proposes, in order that these men may return to their schools and lecture to the sons of Greece, while the youth of Rome give ear to their laws and officials, as before."

This he did, not, as some think, out of personal hostility to Carneades, but because he was wholly opposed to philosophy, and made mock of all Greek culture and training, out of patriotic Roman zeal. He says, for instance, that Socrates was a mighty talker, who attempted, as best he could, to be his country's tyrant, by abolishing its customs, and by enticing his fellow citizens into opinions contrary to the laws. He made fun of the school of Isocrates,[18] declaring that his pupils kept on studying with him till they were old men, as if they were to practise their arts and plead their cases before Minos[19] in Hades. And seeking to prejudice his son against Greek culture, he

---

[18]A student of Socrates (see selections 8 and 9) and a famous orator, who established his own school in Athens.

[19]In Greco-Roman mythology, the judge of dead souls in the underworld.

declared, in the tone of a prophet or a seer, that Rome would lose her empire when she had become infected with Greek literature. But time has certainly shown the emptiness of this pessimistic declaration, for while the city was at the height of its empire, she made every form of Greek learning and culture her own.

It was not only Greek philosophers that he hated, but he was also suspicious of Greeks who practised medicine at Rome. He had heard, it would seem, of Hippocrates'[20] reply when the Great King of Persia sent for him, with the promise of a large fee, that he would never put his skill at the service of non-Greeks who were enemies of Greece. He said all Greek physicians had taken a similar oath, and urged his son to beware of them all. He himself, he said, had written a book of recipes, which he followed in the treatment of any who were sick in his family. He never required his patients to fast, but fed them on greens, or bits of duck, pigeon, or hare. Such a diet, he said, was light and good for sick people, except that it often causes dreams. By following such treatment he said he had good health himself, and kept his family in good health.

• • •

The last of his public services is supposed to have been the destruction of Carthage.[21] It was Scipio the Younger who actually brought the task to completion, but it was largely in consequence of the advice and counsel of Cato that the Romans undertook the war. Cato first became involved when sent on a mission to the Carthaginians and Masinissa the Numidian,[22] who were at war with one another, to inquire into the grounds of their quarrel. Masinissa had been a friend of the Roman people from the first, and the Carthaginians had entered into treaty relations with Rome only after the defeat which the elder Scipio [Africanus] had given them. The treaty deprived them of their empire, and imposed a heavy money tribute upon them. Cato, however, found the city by no means in a poor and lowly state, as the

[20]A famous Greek physician of the fifth century **B.C.**

[21]The powerful city on the African coast that rivalled Rome for control of the Mediterranean world. The Roman Republic fought three major wars against Carthage, ending in its capture and total destruction by Scipio the Younger in 146 **B.C.**, three years after Cato's death.

[22]Numidia was a country of the African nomads lying immediately west and south of Carthage. Masinissa was the head of one of their tribal alliances.

Romans supposed, but rather teeming with vigorous fighting men, overflowing with enormous wealth, filled with arms of every sort and with military supplies, and not a little puffed up by all this. He therefore thought it no time for the Romans to be straightening out the affairs of Masinissa and the Numidians, but that they should repress the power of Carthage, which was becoming once again a deadly danger. Accordingly, he returned speedily to Rome, and advised the Senate that the former defeats of the Carthaginians had diminished not so much their power as their foolhardiness, and were likely to make them in the end not weaker, but more expert in war. He declared that their present contest with Numidia was but a prelude to a contest with Rome, while peace and treaty were mere names wherewith to cover their postponement of war till a proper occasion arose.

In addition to this, it is said that Cato purposely dropped an African fig in the Senate, as he shook out the folds of his toga; and then, as the senators admired its size and beauty, he said that the country where it grew was only three days' sail from Rome. And in one thing he was even more savage, namely, in adding to any speech of his whatsoever these words: "And, in my opinion, Carthage must be destroyed." . . . He saw, probably, that the Roman public, in its recklessness, was already guilty of many excesses—and in the pride of its prosperity, spurned the control of the Senate, and dragged the whole state with it, wherever its mad desires led it. He wished, therefore, that the fear of Carthage should continue to curb the public, like a bridle, believing Carthage not strong enough to conquer Rome, nor yet weak enough to be despised. What Cato dreaded was that the Roman people, sunk in their follies and excesses, faced a growing and sober external power that had always threatened them. That power ought to be done away with altogether, he thought, so that the Romans might be free to concentrate on a cure for their internal failings.

In this way Cato is said to have brought to pass the third and last war against Carthage. . . .

16

Tacitus

Germania

*T*HE *patriotic pride that Livy (selection 14) expressed in Roman character and achievement gave way in the writings of Tacitus, imperial Rome's greatest historian, to a more critical and factual account, one that goes into psychological motives and philosophizes on the true causes of tragic events. The reader senses in Tacitus' writings a pessimism as to the future of the empire. His narratives are notable for their scope and insights and may be compared with Thucydides' account of Athens' fall from glory (selection 6).*

Publius Cornelius Tacitus (ca. A.D. 56–ca. 118) was not only a historian but also a distinguished orator and public official. After holding—among other positions—the offices of tribune and quaestor, he was admitted to the Senate. He may even have commanded a Roman legion. Around A.D. 97 the Emperor designated him to the consulship. With the accession of the competent Trajan to the imperial throne in 98, Tacitus prosecuted many well-known corrupt officials and eventually was entrusted with the highest administrative post open to a senator, the proconsulate of Asia (western Asia Minor).

Tacitus' major works are the Histories *and the* Annals. *The* Histories *traces major Roman events of his own time (68–96); the* Annals—*his last and greatest masterpiece—reaches back to the death of Augustus (A.D. 14), the first emperor, and ends during the reign of Nero (66). Although much of both texts has been lost, what remains provides us with the best account of Roman history during the first century of the Christian era.*

Tacitus, as a senator, admired the traditions of republican *Rome—gone forever since the reign of Augustus. Although Tacitus expresses gratitude for being able to write during the comparatively enlightened reigns of Nerva and*

GERMANIA   Tacitus, *The Agricola and Germany of Tacitus,* trans. A. J. Church and W.J. Brodribb (London, Macmillan and Co., 1868, rev. 1877).

Trajan, he frequently points out the essential evil of rule by one man. Since the emperor controls everything, his motives and morals deserve the closest scrutiny. The moral characters of the four emperors—Tiberius, Caligula, Claudius, and Nero—whose reigns are described in the Annals were sufficiently odious to have made any historian pessimistic about the future of Roman civilization. Tacitus shared Thucydides' belief that individuals determine historical events. Given the perverse behavior of recent emperors and the impossibility of restoring republican government, political decay was inevitable.

The Germania, perhaps Tacitus' earliest surviving work (A.D. 98), already suggests Tacitus' moral warning. The accumulating luxurious degeneracy of Roman culture contrasts sharply to the simpler vigor of the tribesmen beyond the Rhine River, who were bound to their chiefs by the code of the comitatus, *the warrior band. In the year of* Germania's *publication the newly crowned Emperor Trajan was already engaged in military operations against the Germans. Tacitus shows prophetic insight in describing the people who— despite a far more primitive social organization—would, by the fifth century, take over the decayed Roman Empire in the West.*

As its full title indicates, On the Origin, Geography, Institutions and Tribes of the Germans, *the book is a geographical and socio-cultural study— not a historical narrative. It is the most important source for our knowledge of the ancient Germans. (About half of the book is included in the following excerpt.) In twentieth-century Germany the book has been much studied for its insights into the Germanic "racial character." After the fall of Rome the emerging medieval civilization would be a fusion of Germanic ideas and institutions with those remaining from a Christianized Greco-Roman civilization.*

. . . The name Germany, . . . they say, is modern and newly introduced, from the fact that the tribes which first crossed the Rhine and drove out the Gauls, and are now called Tungrians, were then called Germans. Thus what was the name of a tribe, and not of a race, gradually prevailed, till all called themselves by this self-invented name of Germans, which the conquerors had first employed to inspire terror.

They say that Hercules,[1] too, once visited them; and when going into battle, they sing of him first of all heroes. They have also those

---

[1]Greek Heracles, the most popular of all Greek heroes, renowned for his strength and courage; in Roman literature he was very popular as a defender against evil. After his death Heracles became a god.

songs of theirs, by the recital of which ("baritus," they call it), they rouse their courage, while from the note they augur the result of the approaching conflict. For, as their line shouts, they inspire or feel alarm. It is not so much an articulate sound, as a general cry of valour. They aim chiefly at a harsh note and a confused roar, putting their shields to their mouth, so that, by reverberation, it may swell into a fuller and deeper sound. Ulysses,[2] too, is believed by some, in his long legendary wanderings, to have found his way into this ocean, and, having visited German soil, to have founded and named the town of Asciburgium, which stands on the bank of the Rhine, and is to this day inhabited. They even say that an altar dedicted to Ulysses, with the addition of the name of his father, Laertes, was formerly discovered on this same spot, and that certain monuments and tombs, with Greek inscriptions, still exist on the borders of Germany and Rhætia. These statements I have no intention of sustaining by proofs, or of refuting; every one may believe or disbelieve them as he feels inclined.

For my own part, I agree with those who think that the tribes of Germany are free from all taint of intermarriages with foreign nations, and that they appear as a distinct, unmixed race, like none but themselves. Hence, too, the same physical peculiarities throughout so vast a population. All have fierce blue eyes, red hair, huge frames, fit only for a sudden exertion. They are less able to bear laborious work. Heat and thirst they cannot in the least endure; to cold and hunger their climate and their soil inure them.

Their country, though somewhat various in appearance, yet generally either bristles with forests or reeks with swamps; it is more rainy on the side of Gaul,[3] bleaker on that of Noricum and Pannonia.[4] It is productive of grain, but unfavourable to fruit-bearing trees; it is rich in flocks and herds, but these are for the most part undersized, and even the cattle have not their usual beauty or noble head. It is number that is chiefly valued; they are in fact the most highly prized, indeed the only riches of the people. Silver and gold the gods have refused to them, whether in kindness or in anger I cannot say. I would not, however, affirm that no vein of German soil produces gold or silver, for who has ever made a search? They care but little to possess or use them. You may see among them vessels of silver, which have been

[2]Greek Odysseus, the hero of Homer's epic poem, *The Odyssey,* who fought at Troy and then travelled widely for ten years in order to return to his homeland.

[3]Gaul is the region that begins west of the Rhine River; Germany lies to the east.

[4]Noricum and Pannonia begin west of the Danube River; Germany lies to the northeast.

presented to their envoys and chieftains, held as cheap as those of clay. The border population, however, value gold and silver for their commercial utility, and are familiar with, and show preference for, some of our coins. The tribes of the interior use the simpler and more ancient practice of the barter of commodities. They like the old and well-known money, coins milled, or showing a two-horse chariot. They likewise prefer silver to gold, not from any special liking, but because a large number of silver pieces is more convenient for use among dealers in cheap and common articles.

Even iron is not plentiful with them, as we infer from the character of their weapons. But few use swords or long lances. They carry a spear with a narrow and short head, but so sharp and easy to wield that the same weapon serves, according to circumstances, for close or distant conflict. As for the horse-soldier, he is satisfied with a shield and spear; the foot-soldiers also scatter showers of missiles, each man having several and hurling them to an immense distance, and being naked or lightly clad with a little cloak. There is no display about their equipment: their shields alone are marked with very choice colours. A few only have corslets, and just one or two here and there a metal or leathern helmet. Their horses are remarkable neither for beauty nor for fleetness. Nor are they taught various evolutions after our fashion, but are driven straight forward, or so as to make one wheel to the right in such a compact body that none is left behind another. On the whole, one would say that their chief strength is in their infantry, which fights along with the cavalry; admirably adapted to the action of the latter is the swiftness of certain foot-soldiers, who are picked from the entire youth of their country, and stationed in front of the line. Their number is fixed,—a hundred from each canton; and from this they take their name among their countrymen, so that what was originally a mere number has now become a title of distinction. Their line of battle is drawn up in a wedge-like formation. To give ground, provided you return to the attack, is considered prudence rather than cowardice. The bodies of their slain they carry off even in indecisive engagements. To abandon your shield is the basest of crimes; nor may a man thus disgraced be present at the sacred rites, or enter their council; many, indeed, after escaping from battle, have ended their infamy with the halter.[5]

[5]Hanged themselves.

They choose their kings by birth, their generals for merit. These kings have not unlimited or arbitrary power, and the generals do more by example than by authority. If they are energetic, if they are conspicuous, if they fight in the front, they lead because they are admired. But to reprimand, to imprison, even to flog, is permitted to the priests alone, and that not as a punishment, or at the general's bidding, but, as it were, by the mandate of the god whom they believe to inspire the warrior. They also carry with them into battle certain figures and images taken from their sacred groves. And what most stimulates their courage is, that their squadrons or battalions, instead of being formed by chance or by a fortuitous gathering, are composed of families and clans. Close by them, too, are those dearest to them, so that they hear the shrieks of women, the cries of infants. *They* are to every man the most sacred witnesses of his bravery—*they* are his most generous applauders. The soldier brings his wounds to mother and wife, who shrink not from counting or even demanding them and who administer both food and encouragement to the combatants.

Tradition says that armies already wavering and giving way have been rallied by women who, with earnest entreaties and bosoms laid bare, have vividly represented the horrors of captivity, which the Germans fear with such extreme dread on behalf of their women, that the strongest tie by which a state can be bound is the being required to give, among the number of hostages, maidens of noble birth. They even believe that the sex has a certain sanctity and prescience, and they do not despise their counsels, or make light of their answers. In Vespasian's days[6] we saw Veleda, long regarded by many as a divinity. In former times, too, they venerated Aurinia, and many other women, but not with servile flatteries, or with sham deification.[7]

Mercury[8] is the deity whom they chiefly worship, and on certain days they deem it right to sacrifice to him even with human victims. Hercules and Mars[9] they appease with more lawful offerings. Some of

---

[6]Vespasian was Roman Emperor, A.D. 69–79.

[7]Tacitus is referring scornfully to the occasional Roman practice of exalting female members of the imperial household to the status of goddesses. Examples are Nero's wife, Poppaea, and his infant daughter.

[8]Greek Hermes, divine messenger, patron god of luck, wealth, merchants, and thieves; he conducted the souls of the dead into the underworld.

[9]Greek Ares, god of war; in early Roman religion he was also associated with agriculture.

the Suevi also sacrifice to Isis.[10] Of the occasion and origin of this foreign rite I have discovered nothing, but that the image, which is fashioned like a light galley,[11] indicates an imported worship. The Germans, however, do not consider it consistent with the grandeur of celestial beings to confine the gods within walls, or to liken them to the form of any human countenance. They consecrate woods and groves, and they apply the names of deities to the abstraction which they see only in spiritual worship.

Augury and divination[12] by lot no people practise more diligently. The use of the lots is simple. A little bough is lopped off a fruit-bearing tree, and cut into small pieces; these are distinguished by certain marks, and thrown carelessly and at random over a white garment. In public questions the priest of the particular state, in private the father of the family, invokes the gods, and, with his eyes towards heaven, takes up each piece three times, and finds in them a meaning according to the mark previously impressed on them. If they prove unfavourable, there is no further consultation that day about the matter; if they sanction it, the confirmation of augury is still required. For they are also familiar with the practice of consulting the notes and the flight of birds. It is peculiar to this people to seek omens from horses. Kept at the public expense, in these same woods and groves, are white horses, pure from the taint of earthly labour; these are yoked to a sacred car, and accompanied by the priest and the king, or chief of the tribe, who note their neighings and snortings. No species of augury is more trusted, not only by the people and by the nobility, but also by the priests, who regard themselves as the ministers of the gods, and the horses as acquainted with their will. They have also another method of observing auspices, by which they seek to learn the result of an important war. Having taken, by whatever means, a prisoner from the tribe with whom they are at war, they pit him against a picked man of their own tribe, each combatant using the weapons of their country. The victory of the one or the other is accepted as an indication of the issue.

About minor matters the chiefs deliberate, about the more impor-

[10]An Egyptian goddess whose worship spread throughout the Mediterranean world. (See the conversion episode in selection 23). She represented the female generative force in nature and was also one of the rulers of the underworld. Actually, Tacitus is following typical Roman practice in identifying the foreign gods of the German tribesmen with the gods familiar to the Romans. For example, to Tacitus, Mercury corresponds to the Germanic god Woden; Hercules to Thor; Mars to Tiu; Isis to Ziza.

[11]A boat.

[12]Foretelling events.

tant the whole tribe. Yet even when the final decision rests with the people, the affair is always thoroughly discussed by the chiefs. They assemble, except in the case of a sudden emergency, on certain fixed days, either at new or at full moon; for this they consider the most auspicious season for the transaction of business. Instead of reckoning by days as we do, they reckon by nights, and in this manner fix both their ordinary and their legal appointments. Night they regard as bringing on day. Their freedom has this disadvantage, that they do not meet simultaneously or as they are bidden, but two or three days are wasted in the delays of assembling. When the multitude think proper, they sit down armed. Silence is proclaimed by the priests, who have on these occasions the right of keeping order. Then the king or the chief, according to age, birth, distinction in war, or eloquence, is heard, more because he has influence to persuade than because he has power to command. If his sentiments displease them, they reject them with murmurs; if they are satisfied, they brandish their spears. The most complimentary form of assent is to express approbation with their weapons.

In their councils an accusation may be preferred or a capital crime prosecuted. Penalties are distinguished according to the offence. Traitors and deserters are hanged on trees; the coward, the unwarlike, the man stained with abominable vices, is plunged into the mire of the morass, with a hurdle[13] put over him. This distinction in punishment means that crime, they think, ought, in being punished, to be exposed, while infamy ought to be buried out of sight. Lighter offences, too, have penalties proportioned to them; he who is convicted, is fined in a certain number of horses or of cattle. Half of the fine is paid to the king or to the state, half to the person whose wrongs are avenged and to his relatives. In these same councils they also elect the chief magistrates, who administer law in the cantons and the towns. Each of these has a hundred associates chosen from the people, who support him with their advice and influence.

They transact no public or private business without being armed. It is not, however, usual for anyone to wear arms till the state has recognised his power to use them. Then in the presence of the council one of the chiefs, or the young man's father, or some kinsman, equips him with a shield and a spear. These arms are what the "toga" is with us, the first honour with which youth is invested. Up to this time he is

---

[13]A framework of branches to both conceal and sink the offender.

regarded as a member of a household, afterwards as a member of the commonwealth. Very noble birth or great services rendered by the father secure for lads the rank of a chief; such lads attach themselves to men of mature strength and of long approved valour. It is no shame to be seen among a chief's followers. Even in his escort there are gradations of rank, dependent on the choice of the man to whom they are attached. These followers vie keenly with each other as to who shall rank first with his chief, the chiefs as to who shall have the most numerous and the bravest followers. It is an honour as well as a source of strength to be thus always surrounded by a large body of picked youths; it is an ornament in peace and a defence in war. And not only in his own tribe but also in the neighbouring states it is the renown and glory of a chief to be distinguished for the number and valour of his followers, for such a man is courted by embassies, is honoured with presents, and the very prestige of his name often settles a war.

When they go into battle, it is a disgrace for the chief to be surpassed in valour, a disgrace for his followers not to equal the valour of the chief. And it is an infamy and a reproach for life to have survived the chief, and returned from the field. To defend, to protect him, to ascribe one's own brave deeds to his renown, is the height of loyalty. The chief fights for victory; his vassals fight for their chief. If their native state sinks into the sloth of prolonged peace and repose, many of its noble youths voluntarily seek those tribes which are waging some war, both because inaction is odious to their race, and because they win renown more readily in the midst of peril, and cannot maintain a numerous following except by violence and war. Indeed, men look to the liberality of their chief for their war-horse and their blood-stained and victorious lance. Feasts and entertainments, which, though inelegant, are plentifully furnished, are their only pay. The means of this bounty come from war and rapine. Nor are they as easily persuaded to plough the earth and to wait for the year's produce as to challenge an enemy and earn the honour of wounds. Nay, they actually think it tame and stupid to acquire by the sweat of toil what they might win by their blood.

Whenever they are not fighting, they pass much of their time in the chase, and still more in idleness, giving themselves up to sleep and to feasting, the bravest and the most warlike doing nothing, and surrendering the management of the household, of the home, and of the land, to the women, the old men, and all the weakest members of the family. They themselves lie buried in sloth, a strange combination in their nature that the same men should be so fond of idleness, so averse to peace. It is the custom of the states to bestow by voluntary and individual contribution on the chiefs a present of cattle or of grain, which, while accepted as a compliment, supplies their wants. They are particularly delighted by gifts from neighbouring tribes, which are sent not only by individuals but also by the state, such as choice steeds, heavy armour, trappings, and neckchains. We have now taught them to accept money also.

It is well known that the nations of Germany have no cities, and that they do not even tolerate closely contiguous dwellings. They live scattered and apart, just as a spring, a meadow, or a wood has attracted them. Their villages they do not arrange in our fashion, with the buildings connected and joined together, but every person surrounds his dwelling with an open space, either as a precaution against the disasters of fire, or because they do not know how to build. No use is made by them of stone or tile; they employ timber for all purposes, rude masses without ornament or attractiveness. Some parts of their buildings they stain more carefully with a clay so clear and bright that it resembles painting, or a coloured design. They are wont also to dig out subterranean caves, and pile on them great heaps of dung, as a shelter from winter and as a receptacle for the year's produce, for by such places they mitigate the rigour of the cold. And should an enemy approach, he lays waste the open country, while what is hidden and buried is either not known to exist, or else escapes him from the very fact that it has to be searched for.

They all wrap themselves in a cloak which is fastened with a clasp, or, if this is not forthcoming, with a thorn, leaving the rest of their persons bare. They pass whole days on the hearth by the fire. The wealthiest are distinguished by a dress which is not flowing, like that of the Sarmatae and Parthi,[14] but is tight, and exhibits each limb. They also wear the skins of wild beasts; the tribes on the Rhine and Danube in a careless fashion, those of the interior with more elegance, as not obtaining other clothing by commerce. These select certain animals, the hides of which they strip off and vary them with the spotted skins of beasts, the produce of the outer ocean, and of seas unknown to us. The women have the same dress as the men, except that they generally wrap themselves in linen garments, which they embroider with purple, and do not lengthen out the upper part of their clothing into sleeves. The upper and lower arm is thus bare, and the nearest part of the bosom is also exposed.

---

[14]Non-Germanic peoples of eastern Europe and western Asia.

Their marriage code, however, is strict, and indeed no part of their manners is more praiseworthy. Almost alone among barbarians they are content with one wife, except a very few among them, and these not from sensuality, but because their noble birth procures for them many offers of alliance. The wife does not bring a dower to the husband, but the husband to the wife. The parents and relatives are present, and pass judgment on the marriage-gifts, gifts not meant to suit a woman's taste, nor such as a bride would deck herself with, but oxen, a caparisoned steed, a shield, a lance, and a sword. With these presents the wife is espoused, and she herself in her turn brings her husband a gift of arms. This they count their strongest bond of union, these their sacred mysteries, these their gods of marriage. Lest the woman should think herself to stand apart from aspirations after noble deeds and from the perils of war, she is reminded by the ceremony which inaugurates marriage that she is her husband's partner in toil and danger, destined to suffer and to dare with him alike both in peace and in war. The yoked oxen, the harnessed steed, the gift of arms, proclaim this fact. She must live and die with the feeling that she is receiving what she must hand down to her children neither tarnished nor depreciated, what future daughters-in-law may receive, and may be so passed on to her grand-children.

Thus with their virtue protected they live uncorrupted by the allurements of public shows or the stimulant of feastings. Clandestine correspondence is equally unknown to men and women. Very rare for so numerous a population is adultery, the punishment for which is prompt, and in the husband's power. Having cut off the hair of the adulteress and stripped her naked, he expels her from the house in the presence of her kinsfolk, and then flogs her through the whole village. The loss of chastity meets with no indulgence; neither beauty, youth, nor wealth will procure the culprit a husband. No one in Germany laughs at vice, nor do they call it the fashion to corrupt and to be corrupted. Still better is the condition of those states in which only maidens are given in marriage, and where the hopes and expectations of a bride are then finally terminated. They receive one husband, as having one body and one life, that they may have no thoughts beyond, no further-reaching desires, that they may love not so much the husband as the married state. To limit the number of their children or to destroy any of their subsequent offspring[15] is accounted infamous, and good habits are here more effectual than good laws elsewhere.

[15]Children born after their parents' heirs had been legally specified; among the Romans it was apparently permissible to kill such children if the father so chose.

In every household the children, naked and filthy, grow up with those stout frames and limbs which we so much admire. Every mother suckles her own offspring, and never entrusts it to servants and nurses. The master is not distinguished from the slave by being brought up with greater delicacy. Both live amid the same flocks and lie on the same ground till the freeborn are distinguished by age and recognised by merit. The young men marry late, and their vigour is thus unimpaired. Nor are the maidens hurried into marriage;[16] the same age and a similar stature is required; well-matched and vigorous they wed, and the offspring reproduce the strength of the parents. Sisters' sons are held in as much esteem by their uncles as by their fathers; indeed, some regard the relation as even more sacred and binding, and prefer it in receiving hostages, thinking thus to secure a stronger hold on the affections and a wider bond for the family. But every man's own children are his heirs and successors, and there are no wills. Should there be no issue, the next in succession to the property are his brothers and his uncles on either side. The more relatives he has, the more numerous his connections, the more honoured is his old age; nor are there any advantages in childlessness.[17]

It is a duty among them to adopt the feuds as well as the friendships of a father or a kinsman. These feuds are not implacable; even homicide is expiated by the payment of a certain number of cattle and of sheep, and the satisfaction is accepted by the entire family, greatly to the advantage of the state, since feuds are dangerous in proportion to a people's freedom.

No nation indulges more profusely in entertainments and hospitality. To exclude any human being from their roof is thought impious; every German, according to his means, receives his guest with a well-furnished table. When his supplies are exhausted, he who was but now the host becomes the guide and companion to further hospitality, and without invitation they go to the next house. It matters not; they are entertained with like cordiality. No one distinguishes between an acquaintance and a stranger, as regards the rights of hospitality. It is usual to give the departing guest whatever he may ask for, and a present in return is asked with as little hesitation. They are greatly charmed with gifts, but they expect no return for what they give, nor feel any obligation for what they receive.

---

[16]Tacitus is implying a contrast to the Roman custom in which girls might marry as early as the age of twelve.

[17]A satirical reference to Roman inheritance hunters who courted the rich and childless.

On waking from sleep, which they generally prolong to a late hour of the day, they take a bath, oftenest of warm water, which suits a country where winter is the longest of the seasons. After their bath they take their meal, each having a separate seat and table of his own. Then they go armed to business, or no less often to their festal meetings. To pass an entire day and night in drinking disgraces no one. Their quarrels, as might be expected with intoxicated people, are seldom fought out with mere abuse, but commonly with wounds and bloodshed. Yet it is at their feasts that they generally consult on the reconciliation of enemies, on the forming of matrimonial alliances, on the choice of chiefs, finally even on peace and war, for they think that at no time is the mind more open to simplicity of purpose or more warmed to noble aspirations. A race without either natural or acquired cunning, they disclose their hidden thoughts in the freedom of the festivity. Thus the sentiments of all having been discovered and laid bare, the discussion is renewed on the following day, and from each occasion its own peculiar advantage is derived. They deliberate when they have no power to dissemble; they resolve when error is impossible.

A liquor for drinking is made out of barley or other grain, and fermented into a certain resemblance to wine. The dwellers on the river-bank also buy wine. Their food is of a simple kind, consisting of wild-fruit, fresh game, and curdled milk. They satisfy their hunger without elaborate preparation and without delicacies. In quenching their thirst they are not equally moderate. If you indulge their love of drinking by supplying them with as much as they desire, they will be overcome by their own vices as easily as by the arms of an enemy.

One and the same kind of spectacle is always exhibited at every gathering. Naked youths who practise the sport bound in the dance amid swords and lances that threaten their lives. Experience gives them skill, and skill again gives grace; profit or pay are out of the question; however reckless their pastime, its reward is the pleasure of the spectactors. Strangely enough they make games of hazard a serious occupation even when sober, and so venturesome are they about gaining or losing, that, when every other resource has failed, on the last and final throw they stake the freedom of their own persons. The loser goes into voluntary slavery; though the younger and stronger, he suffers himself to be bound and sold. Such is their stubborn persistency in a bad practice; they themselves call it honour. Slaves of this kind the owners part with in the way of commerce, and also to relieve themselves from the scandal of such a victory.

The other slaves are not employed after our manner with distinct domestic duties assigned to them, but each one has the management of a house and home of his own. The master requires from the slave a certain quantity of grain, of cattle, and of clothing, as he would from a tenant, and this is the limit of subjection. All other household functions are discharged by the wife and children. To strike a slave or to punish him with bonds or with hard labour is a rare occurrence. They often kill them, not in enforcing strict discipline, but on the impulse of passion, as they would an enemy, only it is done with impunity. The freedmen do not rank much above slaves, and are seldom of any weight in the family, never in the state, with the exception of those tribes which are ruled by kings. There indeed they rise above the freedborn and the noble; elsewhere the inferiority of the freedman marks the freedom of the state.

Of lending money on interest and increasing it by compound interest they know nothing—a more effectual safeguard[18] than if it were prohibited.

Land proportioned to the number of inhabitants is occupied by the whole community in turn, and afterwards divided among them according to rank. A wide expanse of plains makes the partition easy. They till fresh fields every year, and they have still more land than enough; with the richness and extent of their soil, they do not laboriously exert themselves in planting orchards, inclosing meadows, and watering gardens. Corn[19] is the only produce required from the earth; hence even the year itself is not divided by them into as many seasons as with us. Winter, spring, and summer have both a meaning and a name; the name and blessings of autumn are alike unknown.

In their funerals there is no pomp; they simply observe the custom of burning the bodies of illustrious men with certain kinds of wood. They do not heap garments or spices on the funeral pile. The weapons of the dead man and in some cases his horse are consigned to the fire. A turf mound forms the tomb. Monuments with their lofty elaborate splendour they reject as oppressive to the dead. Tears and lamentations they soon dismiss; grief and sorrow but slowly. It is thought becoming for women to bewail, for men to remember, the dead.

Such on the whole is the account which I have received of the origin and manners of the entire German people.

---

[18]Against usury (excessively high rates of interest).

[19]A general term for grain.

17

Cicero

On the Laws

MARCUS Tullius Cicero (106–43
B.C.), living through the last years of the Roman Republic, expressed the
highest tradition of Greco-Roman civilization. All his works—speeches, philosophical and political writings, letters, and poems—are marked by a sense of
public interest and duty. We find in them also a constant regard for humanitas,
a word coined by Cicero, meaning the mental and moral qualities that make
for civilized living.

Cicero was born in Arpinum, a small city sixty miles southeast of Rome,
whose inhabitants enjoyed full Roman citizenship. Although his family was
well-respected locally, to the Romans he was a "new man" (novus homo, a
man without any ancestor who had achieved the political rank of consul).
Nevertheless, he rapidly made his way against the initial aristocratic prejudices. After schooling in Rome, Athens, and Rhodes—studying under Platonic
and Stoic philosophers—he rose to leadership in the legal profession and was
recognized as Rome's most compelling public speaker. (As a young man his
success as a lawyer was assured when he successfully prosecuted a corrupt
provincial governor.) He became a consul (the highest elective office of the
Roman Republic) in 63 B.C. and, later, a provincial governor. In 44 B.C.,
after the assassination of Julius Caesar by a group of senators fearful of Caesar's
growing power, Cicero backed the senatorial party. As a consequence, in the
following year when the supporters of Caesar had become dominant, Cicero
was murdered; this was done by order of Mark Antony, whom Cicero had
attacked in speeches aimed at restoring the power of the Senate and the Roman
Republic.

ON THE LAWS   Cicero, *De Legibus [On the Laws]*, trans. Clinton W. Keyes (London:
Loeb Classical Library, 1928), 311, 313, 315, 317, 319, 321, 323, 329, 331, 333, 335, 337,
339, 379, 381, 383, 385, 387, 389, 391. Reprinted by permission of the Harvard University Press.

The writings of Cicero are more numerous than those of any other author of ancient times. He expanded the Latin language's vocabulary so that it could better express his beloved Greek philosophical ideas. His role as selector and transmitter of Greco-Roman thought and values has been of enormous importance to later civilizations. He was also a master of Latin prose style; his stylistic influence (Ciceronianism), especially strong during the Renaissance, has been transmitted to us through many influential English prose works. These include the "King James" Version (1611) of the Bible, Edward Gibbon's Decline and Fall of the Roman Empire, *and the political speeches of Edmund Burke and Winston Churchill.*

On the Laws (De Legibus) *was begun about 52* B.C. *but probably never finished. It is an exposition of the ideal state and takes the form of a dialogue between Cicero (Marcus), his brother Quintus, and his friend Pomponius Atticus; the scene is Cicero's estate at Arpinum. The following selection sets forth the idea (previously advanced by the Stoic philosophers) that divine justice is the source of all law, everywhere. Existing codes and statutes, so-called "positive law," draw whatever validity they have from this "higher" or "natural" law of divine justice, which is also identical with right reason. This doctrine of natural law—with its ideals of universal reason, freedom, and equality— was to have a long and influential life. It became the* jus naturale *of Roman law, shaped the laws of the medieval Church, and reached its peak of influence in the "natural rights" doctrine of the eighteenth-century Enlightenment—the philosophical foundation of the American and French Revolutions.*

ATTICUS. Kindly begin without delay the statement of your opinions on the civil law.

MARCUS. My opinions? Well then, I believe that there have been most eminent men in our State whose customary function it was to interpret the law to the people and answer questions in regard to it, but that these men, though they have made great claims, have spent their time on unimportant details. What subject indeed is so vast as the law of the State? But what is so trivial as the task of those who give legal advice? It is, however, necessary for the people. But, while I do not consider that those who have applied themselves to this profession have lacked a conception of universal law, yet they have carried their studies of this civil law, as it is called, only far enough to accomplish their purpose of being useful to the people. Now all this amounts to little so far as learning is concerned, though for practical purposes it is indispensable. What subject is it, then, that you are asking me to expound? To what task are you urging me? Do you want me to write a treatise on the law of eaves and house-walls? Or to compose formulas for contracts and court procedure? These subjects have been carefully treated by many writers, and are of a humbler character, I believe, than what is expected of me.

ATTICUS. Yet if you ask what I expect of you, I consider it a logical thing that, since you have already written a treatise on the constitution of the ideal State,[1] you should also write one on its laws. For I note that this was done by your beloved Plato,[2] whom you admire, revere above all others, and love above all others.

MARCUS. Is it your wish, then, that, as he discussed the institutions of States and the ideal laws, . . . sometimes walking about, sometimes resting—you recall his description—we, in like manner, strolling or taking our ease among these stately poplars on the green and shady river bank, shall discuss the same subjects along somewhat broader lines than the practice of the courts calls for?

ATTICUS. I should certainly like to hear such a conversation.

MARCUS. What does Quintus say?

QUINTUS. No other subject would suit me better.

MARCUS. And you are wise, for you must understand that in no other kind of discussion can one bring out so clearly what Nature's gifts to man are, what a wealth of most excellent possessions the human mind enjoys, what the purpose is, to strive after and accomplish which we have been born and placed in this world, what it is that unites men, and what natural fellowship there is among them. For it is only after all these things have been made clear that the origin of Law and Justice can be discovered.

ATTICUS. Then you do not think that the science of law is to be derived from the praetor's edict,[3] as the majority do now, or from the

[1]Just before beginning *On the Laws* Cicero had written *On the State*, which takes the Roman Republic as its ideal.

[2]Plato, who inspired Cicero's philosophy, described his political ideal in the *Republic* (see selection 10). Later, in the *Laws*, Plato restated his political theory in more down-to-earth terms.

[3]Praetors were judges of civil law who were elected annually and, during the Roman Republic, given wide powers. Upon taking office, a praetor issued an edict that outlined the principles of law that would guide him. Such edicts became a source of Roman law—even under the emperors.

Twelve Tables,[4] as people used to think, but from the deepest mysteries of philosophy?

MARCUS. Quite right; for in our present conversation, Pomponius, we are not trying to learn how to protect ourselves legally, or how to answer clients' questions. Such problems may be important, and in fact they are; for in former times many eminent men made a specialty of their solution, and at present one person[5] performs this duty with the greatest authority and skill. But in our present investigation we intend to cover the whole range of universal Justice and Law in such a way that our own civil law, as it is called, will be confined to a small and narrow corner. For we must explain the nature of Justice, and this must be sought for in the nature of man; we must also consider the laws by which States ought to be governed; then we must deal with the enactments and decrees of nations which are already formulated and put in writing; and among these the civil law, as it is called, of the Roman people will not fail to find a place.

QUINTUS. You probe deep, and seek, as you should, the very fountain-head, to find what we are after, brother. And those who teach the civil law in any other way are teaching not so much the path of justice as of litigation.

MARCUS. There you are mistaken, Quintus, for it is rather ignorance of the law than knowledge of it that leads to litigation. But that will come later; now let us investigate the origins of Justice.

Well then, the most learned men have determined to begin with Law, and it would seem that they are right, if, according to their definition, Law is the highest reason, implanted in Nature, which commands what ought to be done and forbids the opposite. This reason, when firmly fixed and fully developed in the human mind, is Law. And so they believe that Law is intelligence, whose natural function it is to command right conduct and forbid wrongdoing. . . . Now if this is correct, as I think it to be in general, then the origin of Justice is to be found in Law, for Law is a natural force; it is the mind and reason of the intelligent man, the standard by which Justice and Injustice are measured. But since our whole discussion has to do with the reasoning

---

[4]The first *written* code of Roman law. The name of the code came from the fact that they were first set down (450 B.C.) on twelve bronze tablets. The law of the Twelve Tables was still taught to Roman schoolboys in Cicero's time and considered authoritative, at least in part, into the second century A.D.

[5]Servius Sulpicius Rufus, Cicero's friend and professional rival, author of a large number of legal studies.

of the populace, it will sometimes be necessary to speak in the popular manner, and give the name of law to that which in written form decrees whatever it wishes, either by command or prohibition. For such is the crowd's definition of law. But in determining what Justice is, let us begin with that supreme Law which had its origin ages before any written law existed or any State had been established.

QUINTUS. Indeed that will be preferable and more suitable to the character of the conversation we have begun.

MARCUS. Well, then, shall we seek the origin of Justice itself at its fountain-head? For when that is discovered we shall undoubtedly have a standard by which the things we are seeking may be tested.

QUINTUS. I think that is certainly what we must do.

* * *

MARCUS. I will not make the argument long. Your admission leads us to this: that animal which we call man, endowed with foresight and quick intelligence, complex, keen, possessing memory, full of reason and prudence, has been given a certain distinguished status by the supreme God who created him; for he is the only one among so many different kinds and varieties of living beings who has a share in reason and thought, while all the rest are deprived of it. But what is more divine, I will not say in man only, but in all heaven and earth, than reason? And reason, when it is full grown and perfected, is rightly called wisdom. Therefore, since there is nothing better than reason, and since it exists both in man and God, the first common possession of man and God is reason. But those who have reason in common must also have right reason in common. And since right reason is Law, we must believe that men have Law also in common with the gods. Further, those who share Law must also share Justice; and those who share these are to be regarded as members of the same commonwealth. If indeed they obey the same authorities and powers, this is true in a far greater degree; but as a matter of fact they do obey this celestial system, the divine mind, and the God of transcendent power. Hence we must now conceive of this whole universe as one commonwealth of which both gods and men are members.

* * *

MARCUS. The points which are now being briefly touched upon are certainly important; but out of all the material of the philosophers' discussions, surely there comes nothing more valuable than the full realization that we are born for Justice, and that right is based, not upon men's opinions, but upon Nature. This fact will immediately be plain if you once get a clear conception of man's fellowship and union with his fellow-men. For no single thing is so like another, so exactly its counterpart, as all of us are to one another. Nay, if bad habits and false beliefs did not twist the weaker minds and turn them in whatever direction they are inclined, no one would be so like his own self as all men would be like all others.[6] And so, however we may define man, a single definition will apply to all. This is a sufficient proof that there is no difference in kind between man and man; for if there were, one definition could not be applicable to all men; and indeed reason, which alone raises us above the level of the beasts and enables us to draw inferences, to prove and disprove, to discuss and solve problems, and to come to conclusions, is certainly common to us all, and, though varying in what it learns, at least in the capacity to learn it is invariable. For the same things are invariably perceived by the senses, and those things which stimulate the senses, stimulate them in the same way in all men; and those rudimentary beginnings of intelligence to which I have referred, which are imprinted on our minds, are imprinted on all minds alike; and speech, the mind's interpreter, though differing in the choice of words, agrees in the sentiments expressed. In fact, there is no human being of any race who, if he finds a guide, cannot attain to virtue.

● ● ●

MARCUS. The next point, then, is that we are so constituted by Nature as to share the sense of Justice with one another and to pass it on to all men. And in this whole discussion I want it understood that what I shall call Nature is that which is implanted in us by Nature; that, however, the corruption caused by bad habits is so great that the sparks of fire, so to speak, which Nature has kindled in us are extinguished by this corruption, and the vices which are their opposites spring up and are established. But if the judgments of men were in agreement with Nature, so that . . . they considered "nothing alien to them which concerns mankind," then Justice would be equally observed by all. For those creatures who have received the gift of reason from Nature have also received right reason, and therefore they have also received the

---

[6]That is, if not for bad habits and false beliefs, humans would all be exactly alike.

gift of Law, which is right reason applied to command and prohibition. And if they have received Law, they have received Justice also. Now all men have received reason; therefore all men have received Justice. . . .

Now all this is really a preface to what remains to be said in our discussion, and its purpose is to make it more easily understood that Justice is inherent in Nature. After I have said a few words more on this topic, I shall go on to the civil law, the subject which gives rise to all this discourse. . . .

But you see the direction this conversation is to take; our whole discourse is intended to promote the firm foundation of States, the strengthening of cities, and the curing of the ills of peoples. For that reason I want to be especially careful not to lay down first principles that have not been wisely considered and thoroughly investigated. Of course I cannot expect that they will be universally accepted, for that is impossible; but I do look for the approval of all who believe that everything which is right and honourable is to be desired for its own sake, and that nothing whatever is to be accounted a good unless it is praiseworthy in itself, or at least that nothing should be considered a great good unless it can rightly be praised for its own sake.

• • •

MARCUS. Once more, then, before we come to the individual laws, let us look at the character and nature of Law, for fear that, though it must be the standard to which we refer everything, we may now and then be led astray by an incorrect use of terms, and forget the rational principles on which our laws must be based.

QUINTUS. Quite so, that is the correct method of exposition.

MARCUS. Well, then, I find that it has been the opinion of the wisest men that Law is not a product of human thought, nor is it any enactment of peoples, but something eternal which rules the whole universe by its wisdom in command and prohibition. Thus they have been accustomed to say that Law is the primal and ultimate mind of God [Jupiter], whose reason directs all things either by compulsion or restraint. Wherefore that Law which the gods have given to the human race has been justly praised; for it is the reason and mind of a wise lawgiver applied to command and prohibition.

QUINTUS. You have touched upon this subject several times before. But before you come to the laws of peoples, please make the character of this heavenly Law clear to us, so that the waves of habit may not carry us away and sweep us into the common mode of speech on such subjects.

MARCUS. Ever since we were children, Quintus, we have learned to call, "If one summon another to court,"[7] and other rules of the same kind, laws. But we must come to the true understanding of the matter, which is as follows: this and other commands and prohibitions of nations have the power to summon to righteousness and away from wrong-doing; but this power is not merely older than the existence of nations and states, it is coeval [of the same age] with that God who guards and rules heaven and earth. For the divine mind cannot exist without reason, and divine reason cannot but have this power to establish right and wrong. . . . Even if there was no written law against rape at Rome in the reign of Lucius Tarquinius, we cannot say on that account that Sextus Tarquinius did not break that eternal Law by violating Lucretia, the daughter of Lucretius![8] For reason did exist, derived from the Nature of the universe, urging men to right conduct and diverting them from wrongdoing, and this reason did not first become Law when it was written down, but when it first came into existence; and it came into existence simultaneously with the divine mind. Wherefore the true and primal Law, applied to command and prohibition, is the right reason of supreme Jupiter.

QUINTUS. I agree with you, brother, that what is right and true is also eternal, and does not begin or end with written statutes.

MARCUS. Therefore, just as that divine mind is the supreme Law, so, when reason is perfected in man, that also is Law; and this perfected reason exists in the mind of the wise man; but those rules which, in varying forms and for the need of the moment, have been formulated for the guidance of nations, bear the title of laws rather by favour than because they are really such. . . . It is agreed, of course, that laws were invented for the safety of citizens, the preservation of States, and the tranquillity and happiness of human life, and that those who first put statutes of this kind in force convinced their people that it was their intention to write down and put into effect such rules as, once accepted and adopted, would make possible for them an honourable and happy life; and when such rules were drawn up and put in force, it is clear that men called them "laws." From this point of view it can be readily

---

[7] A quotation from the law code of the Twelve Tables.

[8] See the story of the rape of Lucretia in Livy's *History of Rome* (selection 14, pp. 396–400).

understood that those who formulated wicked and unjust statutes for nations, thereby breaking their promises and agreements, put into effect anything but "laws." It may thus be clear that in the very definition of the term "law" there inheres the idea and principle of choosing what is just and true.[9] I ask you then, Quintus, according to the custom of the philosophers:[10] if there is a certain thing, the lack of which in a State compels us to consider it no State at all, must we consider this thing a good?

QUINTUS. One of the greatest goods, certainly.

MARCUS. And if a State lacks Law, must it for that reason be considered no State at all?

QUINTUS. It cannot be denied.

MARCUS. Then Law must necessarily be considered one of the greatest goods.

QUINTUS. I agree with you entirely.

MARCUS. What of the many deadly, the many pestilential statutes which nations put in force? These no more deserve to be called laws than the rules a band of robbers might pass in their assembly. For if ignorant and unskilful men have prescribed deadly poisons instead of healing drugs, these cannot possibly be called physicians' prescriptions; neither in a nation can a statute of any sort be called a law, even though the nation, in spite of its being a ruinous regulation, has accepted it. Therefore Law is the distinction between things just and unjust, made in agreement with that primal and most ancient of all things, Nature; and in conformity to Nature's standard are framed those human laws which inflict punishment upon the wicked but defend and protect the good.

•   •   •

MARCUS. So in the very beginning we must persuade our citizens that the gods are the lords and rulers of all things, and that what is done, is done by their will and authority; that they are likewise great benefactors of man, observing the character of every individual, what he does, of what wrong he is guilty, and with what intentions and with what piety he fulfils his religious duties; and that they take note of the pious

[9]According to Cicero the Latin word for "law" (*lex*) comes from the word for "to choose" (*legere*).

[10]Cicero here begins to question Quintus, using a bit of the *dialectical* style from the "Socratic method" (see the introduction to selection 8).

and the impious. For surely minds which are imbued with such ideas will not fail to form true and useful opinions. Indeed, what is more true than that no one ought to be so foolishly proud as to think that, though reason and intellect exist in himself, they do not exist in the heavens and the universe, or that those things which can hardly be understood by the highest reasoning powers of the human intellect are guided by no reason at all? In truth, the man that is not driven to gratitude by the orderly courses of the stars, the regular alternation of day and night, the gentle progress of the seasons, and the produce of the earth brought forth for our sustenance—how can such an one be accounted a man at all? And since all things that possess reason stand above those things which are without reason, and since it would be sacrilege to say that anything stands above universal Nature, we must admit that reason is inherent in Nature. Who will deny that such beliefs are useful when he remembers how often oaths are used to confirm agreements, how important to our well-being is the sanctity of treaties, how many persons are deterred from crime by the fear of divine punishment, and how sacred an association of citizens becomes when the immortal gods are made members of it, either as judges or as witnesses?

18

Horace

Odes

*I*N 27 B.C. *Octavian, adopted son and grandnephew of the murdered Julius Caesar, took the title of "Augustus" and—having triumphed in the Civil War against Caesar's murderers—became the first of the Roman emperors. Propaganda contributed as much as military power to the success of the Emperor Augustus. Once he was master of the Western world he centralized and systematized the influencing of opinion. Augustus spared no effort in reconciling all to his new order and in proclaiming the mission of a morally reformed Rome. Fortunately for him and for the world, among those who lent themselves to his purposes were several writers of genius.*

One of these literary forces was Quintus Horatius Flaccus (65–8 B.C.), born at Venusia in southeastern Italy, the son of a freed slave who gave him the education of a gentleman. Horace studied, under famous teachers, in Rome and Athens. While in Athens he joined the losing cause of Brutus, one of Julius Caesar's murderers, in the Civil War. After Brutus's defeat, Horace returned home to poverty and made his peace with the new authority. His bitter early verses brought him to the attention of the distinguished epic poet Virgil, who helped him to meet some influential people. In 33 B.C. the gift of a farm from Maecenas, wealthy patron of poets and trusted counsellor to

ODES   Odes I:5, I:20, II:15, II:16, III:6 reprinted from *The Odes and Epodes of Horace: A Modern Verse Translation*, by Joseph P. Clancy, by permission of the University of Chicago Press. Copyright © 1960 by the University of Chicago. [Pp. 30, 51, 94, 95–96, 117–118.] Odes I:11 and IV:15 reprinted from *The Odes of Horace*, trans. Edward Marsh (London: Macmillan & Co., Ltd., 1941), pp. 19, 181–182. Reprinted by permission of the publisher. Ode I:25 reprinted from *The Complete Works of Horace*, trans. and ed. Charles E. Passage (New York: Frederick Ungar Publishing Co., 1983), pp. 163–164. Copyright © 1983 by Frederick Ungar Publishing Co. Reprinted by permission of the publisher.

Octavian, made Horace financially independent and showed that he had accepted the new order—to be known, later, as the "Augustan Age."

The 103 lyrics called the Odes, *his finest work, should not be regarded as a mere product of patronage—even though the last fifteen of the* Odes *(Book IV) were written at the request of Augustus himself. They are the voice of true Roman feeling, devoted to the ideals of the Augustan Age: love of the soil, military prowess, and old-fashioned religious and moral values. Not all the* Odes, *however, are grave in tone; some are graceful, witty, or trivial expressions of Horace's personality—giving first place to the values of friendship, good wines, and a life of leisure on his beloved farm. There are frequent satirical references to the emotional dangers of sexual "affairs" between men and women. Horace also, as a true pagan, advises his readers to "enjoy the pleasures of each day." Though showing the same imitation of Greek models that marks Latin literature in general, the* Odes *strike a distinctive Roman note of their own. Although his poetic style is somewhat difficult, Horace has long been among the most popular of Roman poets, mainly, perhaps, because of his quotability and common sense.*

———

I: 5

What slim and sweetly scented boy
presses you to the roses, Pyrrha,[1]
   in your favorite grotto?
     For whom is your blond hair styled,

deceptively simple? Ah, how often he'll sob
over your faithless conversions,[2] staring
   stupidly at the black
     winds and wild seas. He has you

now, for him you have a golden glow,
ever contented, ever loving

---

[1] In ancient Greek mythology Pyrrha and her husband were the only survivors of the great flood sent by Zeus. (The poet has survived the great flood of passion he had earlier experienced with his own "Pyrrha.")

[2] That is, complete changes from Pyrrha's previous vows of love, based on her wild and changeable moods.

he hopes, unaware of the
tricky breeze. Poor things, for whom

you glitter before you're tried. The temple
wall with its plaque serves notice: I
have hung my wet clothes up
and bowed to the sea god's power.[3]

I: 11

Both you and I must surely die, Leuconoe![4] but
never pry
In Heaven's guarded calendars among the riddles
of the stars
With Babylonian charts[5] to date the secret purposes
of Fate.
Whether this winter be our last, that now with
overweening blast[6]
Shatters his waves against the shore, or Jove[7] has
many a year in store
For us to savour, let it be: not ours to question
his decree!
So take your ease with flowers and wine, and in
brief span long hopes confine.
—Before my next quick word is said, a precious
second will have fled—
Be wise, drown sorrow, enjoy today, and leave
tomorrow its yea or nay.

I: 20

Cheap Sabine wine will be your drink, in plain
tankards; from a Greek jar, though, where I stored

---

[3]It was traditional for those who had survived a shipwreck to dedicate a plaque in the temple of Neptune, god of the sea, together with the clothes in which they had survived.

[4]Probably a woman of fair complexion, since the Greek word *leukos* means "white."

[5]Fortune-telling, based on astronomical charts, was much practiced by the ancient Babylonians.

[6]Extreme force.

[7]Also called Jupiter, the chief of the Roman gods.

and sealed it myself, that day they filled the theater
   with applause for you,

dear lord Maecenas,[8] and the banks of Tiber,
the river of your homeland, and the playful
echo from Mount Vatican[9] answered
   the sounds of your praise.

The best vintages, Caecuban, Calenian,
you may drink when you wish; my goblets hold
no flavor of wine from the vines of Falernus
   or Formia's hills.[10]

I:25

Lively lads less often besiege your bolted
Windows now with fistfuls of high-flung pebbles,
Rob you less of sleep, and the entrance door finds
   Rest on its threshold,

Where before it readily swung upon its
Hinges; less and less do you hear them calling:
"Must I perish, Lydia, through the nights while
   You go on sleeping?"

Now, old crone, it's *your* turn to sit alone on
Back stairs, grieved by lovers that will not take you,
Raising louder rumpus than Thracian gales that
   Bluster at new-moon

While a searing lust and tormenting passion
Such as drives a mother of horses frantic[11]
Rages through your heart where the love-wounds fester,
   Railing for spite that

[8]Horace's wealthy patron. The poet is referring to an occasion in 30 B.C. when Maecenas had been given an ovation from the audience as he arrived at the Roman theater. It was his first public appearance after recovering from severe illness.

[9]One of the hills of ancient Rome, on the west bank of the Tiber River. Today, that area contains the palace of the Pope.

[10]The four locations mentioned in the last stanza were some of the very best Italian wine-producing areas.

[11]That is, Lydia craves a stallion-like partner.

All the lusty partners–in–bed delight in
Gloss of verdant ivy and dusky myrtle,—
Withered boughs[12] consigning to fellowship with
    Winds of the winter.

II: 15

There will soon be few acres left for a plow
by these splendid heaps; all around you will see
    ponds for fish stretching wider than Lake
        Lucrine,[13] and the solitary plane tree

will oust the ivied elms:[14] then violet-beds
and myrtles and all that enriches the nose
    will spread their perfumes where olive groves
        grew richly once for the former owner.

Then the dense branches of laurel will cut off
the sun's hot rays. When Romulus and long-haired
    Cato[15] and ancestral tradition
        ruled over us, things like this were not done.

In their days the private holdings were little,
the public large: no portico with northern
    exposure, measured in ten-foot lengths,
        was possessed by a private citizen;

their way of life did not let them disdain the
sod when it came in handy,[16] but it made them
    beautify at public cost their towns
        and temples to the gods with rare marble.

[12]Lydia is now like "withered boughs," dried old branches.

[13]A small coastal lake located in a fashionable area near Naples.

[14]Elms were often used to support grapevines; plane trees, in contrast, were "solitary," because their decorative broad leaves would not allow grapes to ripen.

[15]Romulus was the legendary founder and first king of Rome (see selection 14). Cato was a Roman senator, a century before Horace, known for his hard work, thrift, and dedication to the public good (see selection 15).

[16]Sod was used as inexpensive material for the roof of a house.

II: 16

Peace, he begs of the gods, caught on the open
Aegean, with black clouds holding the moon in
hiding, and the stars no longer steadily
    shining for sailors;

peace is the prayer of battle-maddened Thrace;[17]
peace, beg Parthians[18] with their painted quivers:
it is not bought, Grosphus,[19] with purple cloths, with
    jewels or with gold.

No, neither royal treasures nor a consul's
lictor[20] can clear the crowd of worries away
from the mind, and the troubles that flutter near
    the paneled ceilings.

He lives well with little, the man whose fathers'
salt dish shines on his impoverished table,
and whose easy sleep is not stolen by fear
    or by filthy greed.

Why do we try for so much so hard with such
little time? Why do we turn to countries warmed
by a different sun? What exile from home
    escapes himself too?

The disease of worry boards the bronze-prowed ship,
and troops of horsemen cannot leave it behind,
swifter than stags and swifter than the Eastwind
    driving the stormclouds.

Joyful here and now, may the spirit despise
concern for what lies beyond and dilute the

[17]A primitive region north of Greece.

[18]Parthia was an imperial successor to Persian power in the Middle East; it was, perhaps,
the most feared and hated rival of Rome during Horace's lifetime.

[19]Horace's friend, an aristocrat, who owned estates in Sicily.

[20]An attendant who bore symbols of authority (*fasces*) in front of the consuls, the highest
Roman elected officials, and cleared the way for them.

bitter with a calm smile. Nothing is wholly
  filled with happiness.

Sudden death took Achilles[21] in his glory,
his long old age wasted Tithonus[22] away,
and to me perhaps this hour will offer
  what you are denied.

You are surrounded by a hundred mooing
herds of Sicilian cattle, you can hear
your racehorse whinny, you are dressed in wool
  double-dyed with Af-

rican purple; I was not cheated by Fate,
who gave me a little farm[23] and a spirit
sensitive to Grecian poetry, above
  the crowd and its spite.

III: 6

You, the guiltless, will pay for your fathers' sins,
Roman, until you repair the decaying
  temples and shrines of the gods and their
    images, filthy with blackening smoke.

When you act as servant of the gods, you rule:
from them all beginning, leave them the ending;
  neglected, the gods have brought many
    sorrows to suffering Italy.

Twice now Monaeses and Pacorus' army,[24]
when omens were evil, have smashed our attack

---

[21]The greatest of the warriors who fought at Troy; he died there. (See Homer's *Iliad*, selection 1.)

[22]The goddess Aurora had given Tithonus immortality, but not eternal youth; thus, although he remained alive like his divine love, he aged, growing ever more wrinkled and emaciated.

[23]The small estate given to Horace by Maecenas.

[24]The Parthian army that, in Horace's lifetime, inflicted two severe defeats on Roman troops in the region of Roman-ruled Syria.

to bits, and they grin as they fasten
    our trophies to their skimpy necklaces.

In the grip of civil conflicts the city
was nearly wiped out by Egypt and Dacia,
    the one with a frightening fleet, and
        the other with superior archers.[25]

Breeder of vices, our age has polluted
first marriage vows and the children and the home;
    from this spring, a river of ruin
        has flooded our country and our people.

The blossoming virgin enjoys her course in
Ionic dancing,[26] and even now practices
    all the tricks, and thoughts of sinful loves
        fill her to the tender tips of her toes.

Soon she is after, at her husband's parties,
younger lovers, and is not particular
    about the one she hastily gives
        the forbidden thrills when the lights go out;

then called for, her husband there and knowing it,
she responds, whether a salesman summons her
    or the master of a Spanish ship,
        a wealthy trader in adulteries.

Not from parents like these were the young men born
who stained the sea with Carthaginian blood
    and struck down Pyrrhus and the mighty
        Antiochus and dreadful Hannibal;[27]

[25]After the murder of Julius Caesar, the ensuing Civil War brought an end to the Roman Republic. The victorious Octavian, Caesar's adopted son, acquired the title of Augustus as the first Roman emperor. Cleopatra of Egypt had opposed him with her navy in 31 B.C. at the decisive battle of Actium. At the same time, archers from Dacia (modern Romania) attacked Octavian's troops on land.

[26]Wild, sensual dances from Asia Minor.

[27]Three powerful enemy generals who had invaded Roman territory in earlier centuries.

no, they were men, the descendants of farm-bred
soldiers, who were raised to turn over the clods
    with their Sabine hoes, and to chop wood
        and carry it in at their stern mother's

orders, as the Sungod shifted the shadows
of the mountains, and gave the weary oxen
    relief from the yoke, bringing an hour
        of rest as his chariot departed.

What does time's decaying leave undiminished?
Our parent's age, worse than their parents,' brought
forth
    us, who are still worse, who soon will breed
    descendants even more degenerate.

IV: 15

Of stricken fields and conquered towns I planned
High singing; but Apollo[28] on his lyre
    Twanged a warning, not to aspire
So high, nor risk my skiff too far from land.

Thine age, great Caesar[29] to our fields restores
Their fatness; now in Jove's avengèd shrine
    Once more the captured eagles shine
That blazed our shame on Parthia's temple doors.[30]

And Janus' Gates of War[31] stand shut. Thy rein
Hath curbed the stubborn passions that had brought
    Our honour and our pride to nought,
And to the ancient arts we turn again

Which nursed the strength of Italy, and spread
Far forth her empire's majesty and fame,

[28]The patron god of poetry and music (especially the lyre, a harp-like instrument).

[29]Augustus Caesar, the emperor—a patron of Horace.

[30]The Romans had suffered a defeat from the Parthians in 53 B.C., but Augustus has now
restored the lost army standards ("eagles") to the temple of Jove (Jupiter).

[31]The gates of the temple of Janus stood open in time of war and closed in time of peace.

Emblazoning the Latin name
From the sun's rising to his Western bed.

Under thy guardian hand, no storm of hate
Shall banish peace, no kindred blood outpoured,
    Nor wrath, fell anvil of the sword,
Mover of woeful strife in city and state,

No tribe that drinks of Danube or of Don,[32]
Nor Tartar fire nor Persian treachery,
    The Julian edict[33] shall defy;
No Thracian highland but thy sway shall own.

And we, on work-a-day and holy days,
Blessing good Bacchus[34] for his gifts of mirth,
    With wives and children round our hearth,
Paying the Gods their due of prayer and praise,

Will sing our storied names with rites of yore
And jocund harmony of voice and lyre,
    Telling of Troy and our great sire[35]
Whom bounteous Venus to Anchises bore.

---

[32]The geographical names in this stanza all refer to places on the outer margins of the empire.

[33]The treaty conditions imposed by Augustus who had been adopted into the Julian (Julius Caesar's) family line.

[34]God of wine and revelry.

[35]Aeneas, survivor of ancient Troy and—according to Roman legend—ancestor of the Roman people. Aeneas was the son of the goddess Venus and the Trojan hero Anchises.

19

Lucretius

On the Nature of Things

*W*HATEVER *the private opinions of educated Romans during the last century of the Republic, they publicly supported the official state religion. It was seen by the ruling minority as a prop to their privileged status. Rarely, then, does Roman literature express sentiments subversive of traditional beliefs about the gods.*

Titus Lucretius Carus (ca. 99–55 B.C.)—in his attack on the superstitious fears and unscientific notions embedded in the state religion—was, perhaps, the most remarkable exception to this Roman conformism. Of his life we can be sure only that, unlike the typical Roman of good birth, he renounced a public career, pursued philosophy instead, and found the meaning of things in the teachings of Epicurus, the third century B.C. Athenian philosopher. Hailing Epicurus as "father" and "glory of the Greek race," Lucretius gave himself with missionary fervor to proclaiming Epicurus' "liberating" gospel; he set it forth in his long poem On the Nature of Things (De Rerum Natura). *It is the most eloquent poem ever written—for what is, essentially, a scientific and philosophical text. The following passages present some of Lucretius' views regarding nature, the soul, happiness, and death.*

In all these passages a single-minded aim may be seen: to deliver the human spirit from imaginary fears by presenting a purely naturalistic, materialistic interpretation of the world. True morality, Lucretius held, consists in "contemplating all things with a tranquil mind." He believed that fear of the supernatural and "the dread of something after death" are the greatest of all terrors.

ON THE NATURE OF THINGS   Lucretius, *The Way Things Are [On the Nature of Things],* the *De Rerum Natura* of Titus Lucretius Carus, trans. Rolfe Humphries (Bloomington: Indiana University Press, 1968), pp. 21–22, 24–27, 29–31, 34–36, 81–82, 87, 89–93, 52–53, 116–117, 110–111, 113–114. Copyright © 1968 by Indiana University Press. Reprinted by permission of the publisher.

Once released from these fears by the materialistic philosophy of atomism, men might, as Epicurus said, "go dancing round the world in unclouded happiness." (Atomism is the the belief that the universe—even the soul or mind—is composed only of tiny indestructible bits of matter called "atoms," and of empty space, or "void," through which the atoms move.) Since the universe is ultimately material, Lucretius believed, pleasure and pain are the only real guides to conduct. We experience pleasure in the calm that comes from the absence of pain, fear, and desire.

Authentic Epicureanism, even when expressed as poetry, did not fit the general Roman temper. Lucretius' views attracted few public supporters in his own time, and in the Middle Ages he was either ignored or scorned as the devil's disciple. Rediscovered in the Renaissance, Lucretius stirred additional interest during the scientific revolution that began in Europe in the seventeenth century. His doctrine of atomism was taken up then as never before, and his poem has gained recognition as a unique expression of the many-sided Roman genius.

When human life, all too conspicuous,
Lay foully grovelling on earth, weighed down
By grim Religion looming from the skies,
Horribly threatening mortal men, a man,
A Greek,[1] first raised his mortal eyes
Bravely against this menace. No report
Of gods, no lightning-flash, no thunder-peal
Made this man cower, but drove him all the more
With passionate manliness of mind and will
To be the first to spring the tight-barred gates
Of Nature's hold asunder. So his force,
His vital force of mind, a conqueror
Beyond the flaming ramparts of the world
Explored the vast immensities of space
With wit and wisdom, and came back to us
Triumphant, bringing news of what can be
And what cannot, limits and boundaries,
The borderline, the bench mark, set forever.
Religion, so, is trampled underfoot,
And by his victory we reach the stars.

[1]The materialist philosopher Epicurus (341–270 B.C.).

I fear that, in these matters, you may think
You're entering upon a path of crime,
The ABC's of godlessness. Not so.
The opposite is true. Too many times
Religion mothers crime and wickedness.
Recall how once at Aulis, when the Greeks,
Those chosen peers, the very first of men,
Defiled, with a girl's blood, the altar-stone
Sacred to Artemis.[2] The princess stood
Wearing the sacred fillets or a veil,
And sensed but could not see the king her father,
Agamemnon, standing sorrowful
Beside the altar, and the priests near-by
Hiding the knife-blade, and the folk in tears
At what they saw. She knelt, she spoke no word,
She was afraid, poor thing. Much good it did her
At such a time to have been the very first
To give the king that other title, *Father*!
Raised by men's hands and trembling she was led
Toward the altar, not to join in song
After the ritual of sacrifice
To the bright god of marriage. No; she fell
A victim by the sacrificing stroke
Her father gave, to shed her virgin blood—
Not the way virgins shed it—but in death,
To bring the fleet a happy exodus!
A mighty counselor, Religion stood
With all that power for wickedness.

•   •   •

Our terrors and our darknesses of mind
Must be dispelled, not by the sunshine's rays,
Not by those shining arrows of the light,

[2]This story is recalled from the Greek legend of the Trojan War. The princess is Iphigeneia, a daughter of King Agamemnon, commander of the Greek forces at Troy (see Homer's *Iliad*, selection 1). Before his expedition sailed from the port of Aulis, Agamemnon had offended the goddess Artemis; he was required to atone for this by sacrificing his daughter. Only then were favorable winds provided for the departure of Agamemnon's fleet toward Troy.

But by insight into nature, and a scheme
Of systematic contemplation. So
Our starting-point shall be this principle:
Nothing at all is ever born from nothing
By the gods' will. Ah, but men's minds are frightened
Because they see, on earth and in the heaven,
Many events whose causes are to them
Impossible to fix; so, they suppose,
The gods' will is the reason. As for us,
Once we have seen that *Nothing comes from nothing,*
We shall perceive with greater clarity
What we are looking for, whence each thing comes,
How things are caused, and no "gods' will" about it.

Now, if things come from nothing, all things could
Produce all kinds of things; nothing would need
Seed[3] of its own. Men would burst out of the sea,
And fish and birds from earth, and, wild or tame,
All kinds of beasts, of dubious origin,
Inhabit deserts and the greener fields,
Nor would the same trees bear, in constancy,
The same fruit always, but, as like as not,
Oranges would appear on apple-boughs.
If things were not produced after their kind,
Each from its own determined particles,
How could we trace the substance to the source?
But now, since all created things have come
From their own definite kinds of seed, they move
From their beginnings toward the shores of light
Out of their primal motes. Impossible
That all things issue everywhence; each kind
Of substance has its own inherent power,
Its own capacity. Does not the rose
Blossom in spring, the wheat come ripe in summer,
The grape burst forth at autumn's urge? There must be
A proper meeting of their seeds in time
For us to see them at maturity
Grown by their season's favor, living earth

---

[3]*Seed, atom, mote, firstling,* and *particle* are used by Lucretius interchangeably. They refer to his concept of the smallest, indestructible units of matter.

Bringing them safely to the shores of light.
But if they came from nothing, they might spring
To birth at any unpropitious time,—
Who could predict?—since there would be no seeds
Whose character rules out untimely union.
Thirdly, if things could come from nothing, time
Would not be of the essence, for their growth,
Their ripening to full maturity.
Babies would be young men, in the blink of an eye,
And full-grown forests come leaping out from the ground.
Ridiculous! We know that all things grow
Little by little, as indeed they must
From their essential nature.

• • •

Our second axiom is this, that nature
Resolves each object to its basic atoms
But does not ever utterly destroy it.
If anything could perish absolutely,
It might be suddenly taken from our sight,
There would be no need of any force to smash it,
Disrupt and shatter all its fastenings,
But as it is, since everything coheres
Because of its eternal seed, its essence,
Until some force is strong enough to break it
By violent impact, or to penetrate
Its void interstices, and so dissolve it,
Nature permits no visible destruction
Of anything.

Besides, if time destroys
Completely what it banishes from sight
With the procession of the passing years,
Out of what source does Venus[4] bring again
The race of animals, each after its kind,
To the light of life? and how, being restored,

[4]Roman name for the goddess of love.

Is each thing fed, sustained and given increase
By our miraculous contriving earth?
And what supplies the seas, the native springs,
The far-off rivers? And what feeds the stars?
By rights, if things can perish, infinite time
And ages past should have consumed them all,
But if, throughout this history, there have been
Renewals, and the sum of things can stay,
Beyond all doubt, there must be things possessed
Of an immortal essence. Nothing can
Disintegrate entirely into nothing.

An indiscriminate common violence
Would finish everything, except for this—
Matter is indestructible; it holds
All things together, though the fastenings
Vary in tightness. Otherwise, a touch,
The merest touch, would be a cause of death,
A force sufficient to dissolve in air
Textures of mortal substance. But here's the fact—
The elements are held, are bound together
In different degrees, but the basic stuff
Is indestructible, so things remain
Intact, unharmed, until a force is found
Proportionate to their texture, to effect
Reversion to their primal elements,
But never to complete annihilation.

Finally, when the fathering air has poured
His rainfall into mother earth, the drops
Seem to have gone, but look!—bright harvests rise,
Boughs on the trees bring greenery and growth
And are weighed down by fruit, by which, in turn,
Our race is fed, and so are animals,
And we see happy cities, flowering
With children, and we hear the music rise
As new birds sing all through the leafy woods.
Fat cows lie down to rest their weary sides
In welcome pastures, and the milk drops white
Out of distended udders; and the calves

Romp over the tender grass, or wobble, drunk
On that pure vintage, more than strong enough
For any such experience as theirs.
To sum it up: no visible object dies;
Nature from one thing brings another forth,
And out of death new life is born.

                         •   •   •

But not all bodily matter is tightly-packed
By nature's law, for there's a void in things.
This knowledge will be useful to you often,
Will keep you from the path of doubt, from asking
Too many questions on the sum of things,
From losing confidence in what I tell you.
By *void* I mean vacant and empty space,
Something you cannot touch. Were this not so,
Things could not move. The property of matter,
Its most outstanding trait, is to stand firm,
Its office to oppose; and everything
Would always be immovable, since matter
Never gives way. But with our eyes we see
Many things moving, in their wondrous ways,
Their marvelous means, through sea and land and sky.
Were there no void, they would not only lack
This restlessness of motion altogether,
But more than that—they never could have been
Quickened to life from that tight-packed quiescence.

Besides, however solid things appear,
Let me show you proof that even these are porous:
In a cave of rocks the seep of moisture trickles
And the whole place weeps its fat blobs of tears.
Food is dispersed all through a creature's body;
Young trees grow tall and yield their fruit in season,
Drawing their sustenance from the lowest roots
Through trunks and branches; voices penetrate
Walls and closed doors; the seep of stiffening cold
Permeates bone. Phenomena like these

Would be impossible but for empty spaces
Where particles can pass. And finally,
Why do we see that some things outweigh others
Which are every bit as large? If a ball of wool
Has the same substance as a ball of lead,
(Assuming the dimensions are the same)
They both should weigh as much, since matter tends
To exercise a constant downward pressure.
But void lacks weight. So, when two objects bulk
The same, but one is obviously lighter,
It clearly states its greater share of void,
And, on the other hand, the heavier thing
Proclaims it has less void and greater substance.
Certainly, therefore, what we're looking for
By logical deduction, does exist,
Is mixed with solid, and we call it *void*.

•   •   •

Bodies are partly basic elements
Of things, and partly compounds of the same.
The basic elements no force can shatter
Since, being solid, they resist destruction.
Yet it seems difficult to believe that objects
Are ever found to be completely solid.
A thunderbolt goes through the walls of houses,
As noise and voices do, and iron whitens
In fire, and steam at boiling point splits rocks,
Gold's hardnesses are pliant under heat,
The ice of bronze melts in the flame, and silver
Succumbs to warmth or chill, as our senses tell us
With the cup in our hands, and water, hot or cold,
Poured into the wine. No, there is nothing solid
In things, or so it seems; reason, however,
And science are compelling forces—therefore
Stay with me; it will not take many verses
For me to explain that there are things with bodies
Solid and everlasting; these we call

Seeds of things, firstlings, atoms, and in them lies
The sum of all created things.

                    To start with,
Since it has been established that the nature
Of things is different, dual, one being substance,
The other void, it follows that each one
Must, in its essence, be itself completely.
Where space exists, or what we call the void,
Matter cannot be found; what substance holds
Void cannot occupy. So atoms are
Solid and therefore voidless. Furthermore,
If there is void in things, there has to be
Solid material surrounding this.
Nothing, by logic, can be proved to hold
A void within its mass, unless you grant
It must itself be solid. There can be
Nothing except an organized composure
Of matter, which can hold a void within it.
And matter, therefore, being of solid substance,
Can last forever, while all else is shattered.
Then, were there nothing which we label *void,*
All would be solid substance; and again,
Were there no substance to fill up the spaces,
All would be void and emptiness. These, then,
Must alternate, substance and void, since neither
Exists to the exclusion of the other.
So there is substance, which marks off the limits
Between the full and the empty, and this substance
Cannot be broken if blows are struck against it
From anywhere outside it, not exploded
By dissolution from within, nor weakened
In any other way, as I have shown you.
It must be obvious that, lacking void,
Nothing can possibly be crushed or broken
Or split in two by cutting, or allow
Invasion by water, cold, or fire, those forces
Of dissolution. The more an object holds
Void space within it, the more easily

It weakens under stress and strain; and therefore,
As I have pointed out, when stuff is solid,
Without that void, it must be everlasting.
Were this not true of matter, long ago
Everything would have crumbled into nothing
And things we see today have been restored
From nothing; but remember, I have proved
Nothing can be created out of nothing.
Also, that nothing can be brought to nothing.
So basic elements must be immortal,
Impossible to dissolve in some last moment
Else there would be no matter for renewal.
They must be, then, completely singly solid,
For otherwise they could not through the ages
Be kept intact for restoration's work

●　●　●

There is no end,
No limit to the cosmos, above, below,
Around, about, stretching on every side.
This I have proven, but the fact itself
Cries loud in proclamation, nature's deep
Is luminous with proof. The universe
Is infinitely wide; its vastness holds
Innumerable seeds, beyond all count,
Beyond all possibility of number,
Flying along their everlasting ways.
So it must be unthinkable that our sky
And our round world are precious and unique
While all those other motes of matter flit
In idleness, achieve, accomplish nothing,
Especially since this world of ours was made
By natural process, as the atoms came
Together, willy-nilly, quite by chance,
Quite casually and quite intentionless
Knocking against each other, massed, or spaced
So as to colander [pass] others through, and cause
Such combinations and conglomerates

As form the origin of mighty things,
Earth, sea and sky, and animals and men.
Face up to this, acknowledge it. I tell you
Over and over—out beyond our world
There are, elsewhere, other assemblages
Of matter, making other worlds. Oh, ours
Is not the only one in air's embrace.

With infinite matter available, infinite space,
And infinite lack of any interference,
Things certainly ought to happen. If we have
More seeds, right now, than any man can count,
More than all men of all time past could reckon,
And if we have, in nature, the same power
To cast them anywhere at all, as once
They were cast here together, let's admit—
We really have to—there are other worlds,
More than one race of men, and many kinds
Of animal generations.

                         •   •   •

Since I have taught how everything begins,
The nature of those first particles, their shape,
Their differences, their voluntary course,
Their everlasting motion, and the ways
Things are created from them, I must now
Make use of poetry to clarify
The nature of intelligence and spirit,
Of mind and soul. The fear of Acheron[5]
Must, first and foremost, be dismissed; this fear
Troubles the life of man from its lowest depths,
Stains everything with death's black darkness, leaves
No pleasure pure and clear; it drives a man
To violate honor, or to break the bonds
Of friendship, and, in general, overthrow
All of the decencies. Men have betrayed

[5]A river in the underworld (the Greek Hades).

Their country or their parents, desperate
To avoid the realms of Acheron.

. . .

          First,
The mind—the intellect, we sometimes call it—
The force that gives direction to a life
As well as understanding, is a part
Of a man's make-up, every bit as much
As are his hands and feet and seeing eyes.

. . .

          Now pay heed,
I have more to say. To start with, I maintain
That mind and spirit are held close together,
Compose one unity, but the lord and master
Holding dominion over all the body
Is purpose, understanding—in our terms
Mind or intelligence, and this resides
In the region of the heart. Hence we derive
Terror and fear and panic and delight.
Here therefore dwell intelligence and mind.
The rest of spirit is dispersed all through
The entire frame, and it obeys the mind,
Moves, gains momentum, at its nod and beck,
And mind alone is sensible or wise
Or glad all by itself, when body and soul
Are quite unmoved by anything; and as an eye
Or head can hurt us, though we feel no pain
In any other part, so now and then
The mind can suffer or rejoice, while spirit
Is nowhere stirred in any part by strangeness;
But when the mind is deeply moved by fear
We see the spirit share that panic sense
All through the body: sweat breaks out, and pallor comes;
The tongue grows thick, the voice is choked, the eyes
Grow dark, ears ring, the limbs collapse. Men faint,

We have often seen, from a terror in the mind;
From this example all can recognize
That spirit and mind are closely bound together,
And spirit, struck by the impulse of the mind,
Propels and thrusts the body.

       This same doctrine
Shows that the nature of both mind and spirit
Must be corporeal. We are bound to admit
That spirit and mind are properties of body
When they propel the limbs, arouse from sleep,
Change an expression, turn a man around,
Control him utterly, but none of this
Is possible without contact, nor is touch
Possible without body. Furthermore,
You see that mind can sympathize with body,
Share its emotions. If a weapon drives
Deep into bone and sinew, and yet fails
To shatter life entirely, still it brings
Weakness, collapse, and turbulence of mind
Within the fallen victim, a desire,
Half-hearted and confused, to rise again.
So mind, which suffers under wounds and blows,
Must have a bodily nature.

       I'll explain,
At this point, what that body's like, what forms it:
First, it [mind] is very delicate indeed,
Made of the most diminutive particles.
That this is so requires no argument
Beyond the fact that nothing seems to move
With such velocity as mind intends
Or mind anticipates; mind acts, we know,
Quicker than anything natural we see.
But anything so mobile must consist
Of particles very round and smooth indeed,
And very small indeed, to be so stirred,
So set in motion by the slightest urge.
Water is moved in just this way, and flows
With almost no impulsion, being formed

Of tiny little round motes, adaptable
Most easily for rolling. Honey, though,
Is more cohesive, less disposed to flow,
More sluggish, for its whole supply of matter
Is more condensed; its motes are not as smooth,
As round, as delicate. The slightest stir
Of air disturbs a cone of poppy seeds,
Sends the top sliding downward; no such breath
Is adequate to disturb a pile of pebbles
Or even a heap of wheat-ears. Bodies move
With speed proportionate to their size and weight,
If small, then swift. The heavy or the rough
Are the more stable, solid, hard to move.
Now, since the nature of the mind appears
Mobile, extremely so, it must consist
Of particles which are small and smooth and round.
This knowledge, my good scholar, you will find
To your advantage in more ways than one.
Another fact gives evidence how frail,
How delicate spirit is, or soul, or mind,
How almost infinitesimal its compass
Even supposing it were massed together:
When death's calm reassurance takes a man,
And mind and spirit have left him, you perceive
Nothing at all subtracted from the body,
Nothing of weight, of semblance, gone. Death shows
All that was his except the vital sense,
The warming breath. And so the spirit must
Consist throughout of very tiny seeds,
All sown minutely in sinew, flesh, and veins—
So tenuous that when it leaves the body
There seems no difference, no diminution
Of outward contour nor of inward weight.
The same thing happens when the scent of wine,
Or nard's[6] aroma, or any effluence,
Vanishes into air, and still its source
Appears no less substantial to our eyes,
Especially since nothing of its weight
Is lost—so many and such tiny seeds

---

[6]An aromatic plant.

Imparting scent and flavor in all things.
Let me repeat: infinitesimal motes
Must form both mind and spirit, since we see
No loss of weight when these depart the body.

•   •   •

How sweet it is, when whirlwinds roil great ocean,
To watch, from land, the danger of another,
Not that to see some other person suffer
Brings great enjoyment, but the sweetness lies
In watching evils you yourself are free from.
How sweet, again, to see the clash of battle
Across the plains, yourself immune to danger.
But nothing is more sweet than full possession
Of those calm heights, well built, well fortified
By wise men's teaching, to look down from here
At others wandering below, men lost,
Confused, in hectic search for the right road,
The strife of wits, the wars for precedence,
The everlasting struggle, night and day,
To win towards heights of wealth and power. O wretched,
O wretched minds of men! O hearts in darkness!
Under what shadows and among what dangers
Your lives are spent, such as they are. But look—
Your nature snarls, yaps, barks for nothing, really,
Except that pain be absent from the body
And mind enjoy delight, with fear dispelled,
Anxiety gone. We do not need so much
For bodily comfort, only loss of pain.
I grant you, luxuries are very pleasant,
But nature does not really care if houses
Lack golden statues in the halls, young men
Holding out fiery torches in their hands
To light the all-night revels. Let the house
Gleam silver and gold, the music waken echoes
In gilded panel and crossbeam—never mind.
Much poorer men are every bit as happy,
Are quite well-off, stretched out in groups together
On the soft grass beside a running brook,
Under a tall tree's shade, in lovely weather,

Where flowers star green meadows. Fever's heat
Departs no sooner if your bodies toss
On crimson sheets, or under figured covers,
Than if you have to lie on a poor blanket.
So, since our bodies find in wealth no profit,
And none in rank or power, it must be mind
Is no more profited. You may see your hosts
Make mimic wars, surging across the drill-ground,
Flanked by their cavalry and well-supported
By strong reserves, high in morale. You may
Behold your fleet churn wide across great seas—
And does all this frighten religious terror
In panic from your heart? does the great fear
Of death depart, and leave you comforted?
What vanity, what nonsense! If men's fears,
Anxieties, pursuing horrors, move,
Indifferent to any clash of arms,
Untroubled among lords and monarchs, bow
Before no gleam of gold, no crimson robe,
Why do you hesitate, why doubt that reason
Alone has absolute power? Our life is spent
In shadows, and it suffers in the dark.
As children tremble and fear everything
In their dark shadows, we, in the full light,
Fear things that really are not one bit more awful
Than what poor babies shudder at in darkness,
The horrors they imagine to be coming.
Our terrors and our darknesses of mind
Must be dispelled, then, not by sunshine's rays,
Not by those shining arrows of the light,
But by insight into nature, and a scheme
Of systematic contemplation.

•   •   •

Men seem to feel some burden on their souls,
Some heavy weariness; could they but know
Its origin, its cause, they'd never live
The way we see most of them do, each one
Ignorant of what he wants, except a change,
Some other place to lay his burden down.

One leaves his house to take a stroll outdoors
Because the household's such a deadly bore,
And then comes back, in six or seven minutes—
The street is every bit as bad. Now what?
He has his horses hitched up for him, drives,
Like a man going to a fire, full-speed,
Off to his country-place, and when he gets there
Is scarcely on the driveway, when he yawns,
Falls heavily asleep, oblivious
To everything, or promptly turns around,
Whips back to town again. So each man flees
Himself, or tries to, but of course that pest
Clings to him all the more ungraciously.
He hates himself because he does not know
The reason for his sickness; if he did,
He would leave all this foolishness behind,
Devote his study to the way things are,
The problem being his lot, not for an hour,
But for all time, the state in which all men
Must dwell forever and ever after death.

•   •   •

        Death
Is nothing to us, has no relevance
To our condition, seeing that the mind
Is mortal. Just as, long ago, we felt
Not the least touch of trouble when the wars
Were raging all around the shaken earth
And from all sides the Carthaginian hordes[7]
Poured forth to battle, and no man ever knew
Whose subject he would be in life or death,
Which doom, by land or sea, would strike him down,
So, when we cease to be, and body and soul,
Which joined to make us one, have gone their ways,
Their separate ways, nothing at all can shake
Our feelings, not if earth were mixed with sea
Or sea with sky. Perhaps the mind or spirit,

[7]The Carthaginians, holding an empire in North Africa, sought to conquer Rome in the third and second centuries B.C.

After its separation from our body,
Has some sensation; what is that to us?
Nothing at all, for what we knew of being,
Essence, identity, oneness, was derived
From body's union with spirit, so, if time,
After our death, should some day reunite
All of our present particles, bring them back
To where they now reside, give us once more
The light of life, this still would have no meaning
For us, with our self-recollection gone.
As we are now, we lack all memory
Of what we were before, suffer no wound
From those old days. Look back on all that space
Of time's immensity, consider well
What infinite combinations there have been
In matter's ways and groupings. How easy, then,
For human beings to believe we are
Compounded of the very selfsame motes,
Arranged exactly in the selfsame ways
As once we were, our long-ago, our now
Being identical. And yet we keep
No memory of that once-upon-a-time,
Nor can we call it back; somewhere between
A break occurred, and all our atoms went
Wandering here and there and far away
From our sensations. If there lies ahead
Tough luck for any man, he must be there,
Himself, to feel its evil, but since death
Removes this chance, and by injunction stops
All rioting of woes against our state,
We may be reassured that in our death
We have no cause for fear, we cannot be
Wretched in nonexistence. Death alone
Has immortality, and takes away
Our mortal life. It does not matter a bit
If we once lived before.

                    So, seeing a man
Feel sorry for himself, that after death
He'll be a rotting corpse, laid in a tomb,

Succumb to fire, or predatory beasts,
You'll know he's insincere, just making noise,
With rancor in his heart, though he believes,
Or tries to make us think so, that death ends all.
And yet, I'd guess, he contradicts himself,
He does not really see himself as gone,
As utter nothingness, but does his best—
Not really understanding what he's doing—
To have himself survive, for, in his life,
He will project a future, a dark day
When beast or bird will lacerate his corpse.
So he feels sorry for himself; he fails
To make the real distinction that exists
Between his castoff body, and the man
Who stands beside it grieving, and imputes
Some of his sentimental feelings to it.
Resenting mortal fate, he cannot see
That in true death he'll not survive himself
To stand there as a mourner, stunned by grief
That he is burned or mangled.

·   ·   ·

          Hark! The voice of Nature
Is scolding us: "What ails you, little man,
Why this excess of self-indulgent grief,
This sickliness? Why weep and groan at death?
If you have any sense of gratitude
For a good life, if you can't claim her gifts
Were dealt you in some kind of riddled jar
So full of cracks and holes they leaked away
Before you touched them, why not take your leave
As men go from a banquet, fed to the full
On life's good feast, come home, and lie at ease,
Free from anxiety? Alas, poor fool,
If, on the other hand, all of your joys
Are gone, and life is only wretchedness,
Why try to add more to it? Why not make
A decent end? There's nothing, it would seem,

My powers can contrive for your delight.
The same old story, always. If the years
Don't wear your body, don't corrode your limbs
With lassitude [weariness], if you keep living on
For centuries, if you never die at all,
What's in it for you but the same old story
Always, and always?"

          •   •   •

Such a rebuke from Nature would be right,
For the old order yields before the new,
All things require refashioning from others.
No man goes down to Hell's black pit; we need
Matter for generations yet to come,
Who, in their turn, will follow you, as men
Have died before you and will die hereafter.
So one thing never ceases to arise
Out of another; life's a gift to no man
Only a loan to him. Look back at time—
How meaningless, how unreal!—before our birth.
In this way Nature holds before our eyes
The mirror of our future after death.
Is this so grim, so gloomy? Is it not
A rest more free from care than any sleep?

20

Petronius

The Satyricon

*T*HE *vast wealth of the Roman Empire
made possible the emergence of a new class of rich entrepreneurs eager to enjoy
the material pleasures and social status they could readily purchase. A satirical
chronicler of this new class, believed to be the author of this earliest Latin
novel, was Gaius Petronius (d. A.D. 66). We have little knowledge of this
man beyond a brief and fascinating narrative in Tacitus'* Annals:

> He spent his days sleeping, his nights working and enjoying
> himself. Others achieve fame by energy, Petronius by laziness.
> Yet he was not, like others who waste their resources, regarded
> as dissipated or extravagant, but as a refined voluptuary. People
> liked the apparent freshness of his unconventional and unself-
> conscious sayings and doings. Nevertheless, as governor of
> Bithynia [a province in Asia Minor] and later as consul, he had
> displayed a capacity for business.
>
> Then, reverting to a vicious or ostensibly vicious way of
> life, he had been admitted into the small circle of Nero's inti-
> mates, as Arbiter of Taste: to the blasé emperor nothing was
> smart and elegant unless Petronius had given it his approval.
> So Tigellinus [Nero's treacherous henchman], loathing him as
> a rival and a more expert hedonist, denounced him on the
> grounds of his friendship with Flavius Scaevinus [a conspirator
> against Nero]. This appealed to the emperor's outstanding pas-
> sion—his cruelty. A slave was bribed to incriminate Petronius.
> No defence was heard. Indeed, most of his household were
> under arrest. . . .

THE SATYRICON   From *The Satyricon* by Petronius, translated by William Arrowsmith. Copyright © 1959 by William Arrowsmith. Reprinted by arrangement with New
American Library, New York, New York. [Pp. 39–84]

Petronius . . . had reached Cumae [near Naples]; and there he was arrested. Delay, with its hopes and fears, he refused to endure. He severed his own veins. Then, having them bound up again when the fancy took him, he talked with his friends—but not seriously, or so as to gain a name for fortitude. And he listened to them reciting, not disclosures about the immortality of the soul or philosophy, but light lyrics and frivolous poems. Some slaves received presents—others beatings. He appeared at dinner, and dozed, so that his death, even if compulsory, might look natural.

Even his will deviated from the routine death-bed flatteries of Nero, Tigellinus, and other leaders. Petronius wrote out a list of Nero's sensualities—giving names of each male and female bed-fellow and details of every lubricious novelty—and sent it under seal to Nero. Then Petronius broke his signet-ring, to prevent its subsequent employment to incriminate others.

If this man really was the author of The Satyricon, *then Tacitus' description shows an appropriately sophisticated personality—one with a great appetite for sensual pleasure, but also courageous, likable, and discriminating. Such a man would have the wit to puncture the pretensions of the* nouveaux *riches.*

Although Petronius also wrote lyric poetry, his literary works probably were not well known to his contemporaries. Tacitus, in fact, does not even mention them. Substantial portions of the still fragmentary manuscript of The Satyricon—*including that excerpted here—were not rediscovered until 1663. The title of this novel appears to be a pun that plays on the Latin words* satura, *a mixture or satire;* satyrus, *a satyr, who is a lecherous, goat-like companion of the wine god, Bacchus; and* satyrion, *a plant used as a Roman aphrodisiac. Thus, the title implies a collection of lustful, satirical stories.*

The following excerpt, "Dinner with Trimalchio," is the longest surviving story. It is set in an unnamed city of southern Italy and reveals considerable information about social conditions and relationships of the mid-first century A.D. *Two young men, Encolpius ("Crotch," in Greek)—the narrator, and Ascyltus ("Tireless")—his companion and sexual rival, compete for the affections of the beautiful youth Giton ("Neighbor"). After a series of comic—often lascivious—adventures, they find themselves as dinner guests at the house of Trimalchio, a former slave now enormously wealthy. His gross vulgarity only makes more comic the desire of Trimalchio to be thought of as a person of literary culture and sensual refinement. He mixes up mythological stories and wastes enormous quantities of food and precious serving vessels. The narrator, though leading a dissolute life himself, views the uneducated Trimalchio with an amused "college boy's" contempt. Trimalchio and his friends, nevertheless, know they have grabbed the money-power of the earth and turn fiercely on the young men when they sense their disdain.*

Beneath the caricature and the satire of manners the story carries a serious message. The last arrival at the dinner is Habinnas, an undertaker. Drunken Trimalchio proceeds to act out his own funeral, complete with shroud, expensive senatorial robe (to which he is not entitled), ointment, wine, and funeral music. The showy materialism of Trimalchio's life cannot respond in any other way to the overwhelming fact of approaching death.

. . . we wandered around at first without getting undressed. Or rather we went joking around, mixing with various groups of bathers at their games. Suddenly we caught sight of an old, bald man in a long red undershirt, playing ball with a bunch of curly-headed slave boys. It wasn't so much the boys who took our eyes—though they were worth looking at—as the old man himself. There he stood, rigged out in undershirt and sandals, nothing else, bouncing a big green ball the color of a leek. When he dropped one ball, moreover, he never bothered to stoop for it, but simply took another from a slave who stood beside him with a huge sack tossing out fresh balls to the players. This was striking enough, but the real refinement was two eunuchs standing on either side of the circle, one clutching a chamber pot of solid silver, the other ticking off the balls. He was not, however, scoring the players' points, but merely keeping count of any balls that happened to drop on the ground. While we were gawking at these elegant gymnastics, Menelaus[1] came rushing up. "That's *him!*" he whispered, "that's the fellow who's giving the meal. What you're seeing now is just the prelude to the show." These words were hardly out when Trimalchio[2] gave a loud snap with his fingers. The eunuch came waddling up with

---

[1]Petronius frequently satirizes the lofty terms of epic poetry and myth. In Homer's *Iliad*, for example, Menelaus is Helen's offended husband and brother of Agamemnon, commander of the Greek armies at Troy. (See selection 1.) In *The Satyricon*, however, Menelaus is an assistant to Agamemnon, a parasitical teacher of rhetoric. Similarly, many of Trimalchio's vulgar dinner guests have names of mythological—even divine— origin.

[2]The name appears to mean "triply fortunate."

the chamber pot, Trimalchio emptied his bladder and went merrily on with his game. When he was done, he shouted for water, daintily dipped the tips of his fingers and wiped his hands in the long hair of a slave.

But the details of his performance would take too long to tell. We quickly undressed, went into the hot baths, and after working up a sweat, passed on to the cold showers. There we found Trimalchio again, his skin glistening all over with perfumed oil. He was being rubbed down, not with ordinary linen, but with cloths of the purest and softest wool. During this rubdown, right before his eyes, the three masseurs were guzzling away at the finest of his rare Falernian wines. In a minute, moreover, they were squabbling and in the next second the wine had spilled all over the floor. "Tut, a mere trifle," said Trimalchio, "they were merely pouring me a toast."[3] He was then bundled into a blazing scarlet wrapper, hoisted onto a litter and trundled off. Before him went four runners in spangled harness and a little wheelbarrow in which the old man's favorite rode, a little boy with a wrinkled face and bleary, crudded eyes, even uglier than his master. A musician with a miniature flute trotted along at Trimalchio's head and during the entire trip played into his master's ear as though whispering him little secrets.

Drunk with admiration, we brought up the rear and Agamemnon joined us when we reached Trimalchio's door. Beside the door we saw a sign:

ANY SLAVE LEAVING THE PREMISES
WITHOUT AUTHORIZATION FROM THE MASTER
WILL RECEIVE ONE HUNDRED LASHES!

At the entrance sat the porter, dressed in that same leek-green that seemed to be the livery of the house. A cherry-colored sash was bound around his waist and he was busily shelling peas into a pan of solid silver. In the doorway hung a cage, all gold, and in it a magpie was croaking out his welcome to the guests. . . .

We approached the dining room next where we found the steward at the door making up his accounts. I was particularly struck by the

---

[3]It was Roman custom, when drinking to someone's health, to pour some of the wine under the table as an offering to the gods.

doorposts. For fixed to the jamb were fasces, bundles of sticks with axes protruding from them;[4] but on the lower side the bundles terminated in what looked like the brass ram of a ship, and on the brass this inscription had been engraved:

> TO GAIUS POMPEIUS TRIMALCHIO,
> OFFICIAL OF THE IMPERIAL CULT,
> FROM HIS STEWARD
> CINNAMUS.

Hanging from the ceiling on a long chain was a two-bracket lamp with the same inscription, and on each of the doorposts a wooden tablet had been put up. On one of these, if I remember rightly, this memo was written:

> "The Master will be dining in town
> on the 30th and 31st of December."

On the other tablet was a diagram of the orbits of the moon and the seven planets, with the lucky and unlucky days[5] all indicated by knobs of different colors.

We duly noted these refinements and were just about to step into the dining room when suddenly a slave—clearly posted for this very job—shouted, "RIGHT FEET FIRST!" Well, needless to say, we froze. Who wants to bring down bad luck on his host by walking into his dining room in the wrong way? However, we synchronized our legs and were just stepping out, right feet first, when a slave, utterly naked, landed on the floor in front of us and implored us to save him from a whipping. He was about to be flogged, he explained, for a trifling offense. He had let someone steal the steward's clothing, worthless stuff really, in the baths. Well, we pulled back our right feet, faced about and returned to the entry where we found the steward counting a stack of gold coins. We begged him to let the servant off. "Really, it's not the money I mind," he replied with enormous condescension, "so much as the idiot's carelessness. It was my dinner-suit he lost, a birthday

---

[4]Fasces were traditional symbols of Roman authority; the sticks signified the power to flog; the ax, the power of life and death.

[5]Trimalchio is an extremely superstitious man.

present from one of my dependents. Expensive too, but then I've already had it washed. Well, it's a trifle. Do what you want with him." We thanked him for his gracious kindness, but when we entered the dining room up ran the same slave whom we'd just begged off. He overwhelmed us with his thanks and then, to our consternation, began to plaster us with kisses. "You'll soon see whom you've helped," he said. "The master's wine will prove the servant's gratitude."

At last we took our places. Immediately slaves from Alexandria came in and poured ice water over our hands. These were followed by other slaves who knelt at our feet and with extraordinary skill pedicured our toenails. Not for an instant, moreover, during the whole of this odious job, did one of them stop singing. This made me wonder whether the whole menage was given to bursts of song, so I put it to the test by calling for a drink. It was served immediately by a boy who trilled away as shrilly as the rest of them. In fact, anything you asked for was invariably served with a snatch of song, so that you would have thought you were eating in a concert-hall rather than a private dining room.

Now that the guests were all in their places, the *hors d'oeuvres* [appetizers] were served, and very sumptuous they were. Trimalchio alone was still absent, and the place of honor—reserved for the host in the modern fashion—stood empty. But I was speaking of the *hors d'oeuvres*. On a large tray stood a donkey made of rare Corinthian bronze; on the donkey's back were two panniers, one holding green olives, the other, black. Flanking the donkey were two side dishes, both engraved with Trimalchio's name and the weight of the silver, while in dishes shaped to resemble little bridges there were dormice,[6] all dipped in honey and rolled in poppyseed. Nearby, on a silver grill, piping hot, lay small sausages, while beneath the grill black damsons[7] and red pomegranates had been sliced up and arranged so as to give the effect of flames playing over charcoal.

We were nibbling at these splendid appetizers when suddenly the trumpets blared a fanfare and Trimalchio was carried in, propped up on piles of miniature pillows in such a comic way that some of us couldn't resist impolitely smiling. His head, cropped close in a recognizable slave cut, protruded from a cloak of blazing scarlet; his neck,

---

[6]Small rodents, regarded as a delicacy in the ancient world.

[7]Small dark plums.

heavily swathed already in bundles of clothing, was wrapped in a large napkin bounded by . . . a purple stripe with little tassels dangling down here and there. On the little finger of his left hand he sported an immense gilt ring; the ring on the last joint of his fourth finger looked to be solid gold of the kind the lesser nobility wear, but was actually, I think, an imitation, pricked out with small steel stars. Nor does this exhaust the inventory of his trinkets. At least he rather ostentatiously bared his arm to show us a large gold bracelet and an ivory circlet with a shiny metal plate.

He was picking his teeth with a silver toothpick when he first addressed us. "My friends," he said, "I wasn't anxious to eat just yet, but I've ignored my own wishes so as not to keep you waiting. Still, perhaps you won't mind if I finish my game." At these words a slave jumped forward with a board of juniper wood and a pair of crystal dice. I noticed one other elegant novelty as well: in place of the usual black and white counters, Trimalchio had substituted gold and silver coins. His playing, I might add, was punctuated throughout with all sorts of vulgar exclamations. . . .

By this time Trimalchio had finished his game. He promptly sent for the same dishes we had had and with a great roaring voice offered a second cup of mead [an alcoholic drink] to anyone who wanted it. Then the orchestra suddenly blared and the trays were snatched away from the tables by a troupe of warbling waiters. But in the confusion a silver side dish fell to the floor and a slave quickly stooped to retrieve it. Trimalchio, however, had observed the accident and gave orders that the boy's ears should be boxed and the dish tossed back on the floor. Immediately the servant in charge of the dishware came pattering up with a broom and swept the silver dish out the door with the rest of the rubbish. Two curly-haired Ethiopian slaves followed him as he swept, both carrying little skin bottles like the circus attendants who sprinkle the [gladiatorial] arena with perfume, and poured wine over our hands. No one was offered water.

We clapped enthusiastically for this fine display of extravagance. "The god of war," said Trimalchio, "is a real democrat. That's why I gave orders that each of us should have a table to himself. Besides, these stinking slaves will bother us less than if we were all packed in together."

Glass jars carefully sealed and coated were now brought in. Each bore this label:

GENUINE FALERNIAN WINE
GUARANTEED ONE HUNDRED YEARS
OLD!
BOTTLED
IN THE CONSULSHIP
OF
OPIMIUS.[8]

While we were reading the labels, Trimalchio clapped his hands for attention. "Just think, friends, wine lasts longer than us poor suffering humans. So soak it up, it's the stuff of life. I give you, gentlemen, the genuine Opimian vintage. Yesterday I served much cheaper stuff and the guests were much more important." While we were commenting on it and savoring the luxury, a slave brought in a skeleton, cast of solid silver, and fastened in such a way that the joints could be twisted and bent in any direction. The servants threw it down on the table in front of us and pushed it into several suggestive postures by twisting its joints, while Trimalchio recited this verse of his own making:

> *Nothing but bones, that's what we are.*
> *Death hustles us humans away.*
> *Today we're here and tomorrow we're not,*
> *so live and drink while you may! . . .*

Suddenly the orchestra gave another flourish and four slaves came dancing in and whisked off the top of the tray. Underneath, in still another tray, lay fat capons and sowbellies and a hare tricked out with wings to look like a little Pegasus.[9] At the corners of the tray stood four little gravy boats, all shaped like the satyr Marsyas,[10] with phalluses for spouts and a spicy hot gravy dripping down over several large fish swimming about in the lagoon of the tray. The slaves burst out clapping, we clapped too and turned with gusto to these new

---

[8]Wine was customarily labelled with the name of the man who was consul in the year it was bottled; Opimius had been consul in 121 B.C. Assuming the date of Trimalchio's dinner to be sometime during Nero's reign, the wine—if genuinely Opimian—would have been over 175 years old and, therefore, much deteriorated.

[9]A mythological winged horse.

[10]Satyrs were lecherous, goat-like creatures. Marsyas was a flute-playing satyr who foolishly challenged the lyre-playing god Apollo to a musical competition.

delights. Trimalchio, enormously pleased with the success of his little *tour de force,* roared for a slave to come and carve. The carver appeared instantly and went to work, thrusting with his knife like a gladiator practicing to the accompaniment of a water-organ. But all the time Trimalchio kept mumbling in a low voice, "Carver, carver, carver carver . . . " I suspected that this chant was somehow connected with a trick, so I asked my neighbor, an old hand at these party surprises. "Look," he said, "you see that slave who's carving? Well, he's called Carver, so every time Trimalchio says 'Carver,' he's also saying 'Carve 'er!' and giving him orders to carve."

This atrocious pun finished me: I couldn't touch a thing. So I turned back to my neighbor to pick up what gossip I could and soon had him blabbing away, especially when I asked him about the woman who was bustling around the room. "Her?" he said, "why, that's Fortunata, Trimalchio's wife. And the name couldn't suit her better. She counts her cash by the cartload. And you know what she used to be? Well, begging your Honor's pardon, but you wouldn't have taken bread from her hand. Now, god knows how or why, she's sitting pretty: has Trimalchio eating out of her hand. If she told him at noon it was night, he'd crawl into bed. As for him, he's so loaded he doesn't know how much he has. But that bitch has her finger in everything—where you'd least expect it too. A regular tightwad, never drinks, and sharp as they come. But she's got a nasty tongue; get her gossiping on a couch and she'll chatter like a parrot. If she likes you, you're lucky; if she doesn't, god help you.

"As for old Trimalchio, that man's got more farms than a kite could flap over. And there's more silver plate stuffed in his porter's lodge than another man's got in his safe. As for slaves, whoosh! So help me, I'll bet not one in ten has ever seen his master. Your ordinary rich man is just peanuts compared to him; he could knock them all under a cabbage and you'd never know they were gone.

"And buy things? Not him. No sir, he raises everything right on his own estate. Wool, citron, pepper, you name it. By god, you'd find hen's milk if you looked around. Now take his wool. The home-grown strain wasn't good enough. So you know what he did? Imported rams from Tarentum, bred them into the herd. Attic honey he raises at home. Ordered the bees special from Athens. And the local bees are better for being crossbred too. And, you know, just the other day he sent off to India for some mushroom spawn. Every mule he owns had a wild ass for a daddy. And you see those pillows there? Every last one is stuffed with purple or scarlet wool. That boy's loaded!

"And don't sneer at his friends. They're all ex-slaves, but every one of them's rich. You see that guy down there on the next to last couch? He's worth a cool half-million. Came up from nowhere. Used to tote wood on his back. People say, but I don't know, he stole a cap off a hob-goblin's head and found a treasure. He's the god's fair-haired boy. That's luck for you, but I don't begrudge him. Not so long ago he was just a slave. Yes sir, he's doing all right. Just a few days ago he advertised his apartment for rent. The ad went like this:

APARTMENT FOR RENT AFTER THE FIRST OF JULY.
AM BUYING A VILLA. SEE G. POMPEIUS DIOGENES.

"And you see that fellow in the freedman's seat? He's already made a pile and lost it. What a life! But I don't envy him. After the first million the going got sticky. Right now I'll bet he's mortgaged every hair on his head. But it wasn't his fault. He's too honest, that's his trouble, and his crooked friends stripped him to feather their own nests. One thing's sure: once your little kettle stops cooking and the business starts to slide, you get the brushoff from your friends. And, you know, he had a fine, respectable business too. Undertaking. Ate like a king: boars roasted whole, pastry as tall as buildings, pheasants, chefs, pastrycooks—the whole works. Why, he's had more wine spilled under his table than most men have in their cellars. Life? Hell, it was a dream! Then when things started sliding, he got scared his creditors would think he was broke. So he advertised an auction:

GAIUS JULIUS PROCULUS
WILL HOLD
AN AUCTION
OF HIS
SPARE FURNITURE! . . .

At this point Trimalchio heaved himself up from his couch and waddled off to the toilet. Once rid of our table tyrant, the talk began to flow more freely. Damas called for larger glasses and led off himself. "What's one day? Bah, nothing at all. You turn round and it's dark. Nothing for it, I say, but jump right from bed to table. Brrrr. Nasty spell of cold weather we've been having. A bath hardly warmed me up. But a hot drink's the best overcoat of all; that's what I always say. Whoosh, I must have guzzled gallons. I'm tight and no mistake. Wine's gone right to my head . . . "

"As for me," Seleucus broke in, "I don't take a bath every day. Your bath's a fuller;[11] the water's got teeth like a comb. Saps your vital juices. But once I've had a slug of mead, then bugger the cold. Couldn't have had a bath today anyway. Had to go to poor old Chrysanthus' funeral. Yup, he's gone for good, folded his tent forever. And a grand little guy he was; they don't make 'em any better these days. I might almost be talking to him now. Just goes to show you. What are men anyway but balloons on legs, a lot of blown-up bladders? Flies, that's what we are. No, not even flies. Flies have something inside. But a man's a bubble, all air, nothing else. And, you know, Chrysanthus might still be with us if he hadn't tried that starvation diet. Five days and not a crumb of bread, not a drop of water, passed his lips. Tch, tch. And now he's gone, joined the great majority. Doctors killed him. Maybe not doctors, call it fate. What good's a doctor but for peace of mind? But the funeral was fine, they did it up proper: nice bier, fancy drapes, and a good bunch of mourners turned out too. Mostly slaves he'd set free, of course.[12] But his old lady was sure stingy with the tears. Not that he didn't lead her a hard life, mind. But women, they're a race of kites. Don't deserve love. You might as well drop it down a well. And old love's a real cancer . . . "

He was beginning to be tiresome and Phileros shouted him down. "Whoa there," he cut in, "let's talk about the living. He got what was coming to him. He lived well, he died well. What the hell more did he want? And got rich from nothing too. And no wonder, I say. That boy would have grubbed in the gutter for a coin and picked it out with his teeth too. God knows what he had salted away. Just got fatter and fatter, bloated with the stuff. Why, that man oozed money the way a honeycomb oozes honey. But I'll give you the lowdown on him, and no frills either. He talked tough, sure, but he was a born gabber. And a real scrapper too, regular pair of fists on legs. But you take his brother: now that's a real man for you, friendly and generous as they come, and what's more, he knows how to put on a spread. Anyway,

[11]A cleaner of woolen cloaks who employs very strong solvents.

[12]Slaves were frequently set free in a man's will.

as I was saying, what does our boy do but flop on his first big deal and end up eating crow? But come the vintage and he got right back on his feet and sold his wine at his own figure. What really gave him a boost was some legacy he got. And I don't mind telling you, he milked that legacy for all it was worth and then some. So what does the sap do next but pick a fight with his own brother and leave everything to a total stranger? I mean, it just shows you. Run from your kin and you run a damn long way, as the saying goes. Well, you know, he had some slaves and he listened to them as though they were a lot of oracles, so naturally they took him in the end. It's like I always say, a sucker gets screwed. And that goes double when a man's in business. But there's a saying, it isn't what you're given, but what you can get that counts. Well, he got the meat out of that one all his life. He was Lady Luck's fair-haired boy and no mistake. Lead turned to gold in his hand. Of course, it's easy when the stuff comes rolling in on its own. And you know how old he was when he died? Seventy and then some. But carried it beautifully, hard as nails and his hair as black as a crow. I knew him for ages, and he was horny, right to the end. By god, I'll bet he even pestered the dog. Boys were what he really liked, but he wasn't choosy: he'd jump anything with legs. I don't blame him a bit, you understand. He won't have any fun where he's gone now."

But Ganymedes struck in, "Stuff like that doesn't matter a bit to man or beast. But nobody mentions the real thing, the way the price of bread is pinching. God knows, I couldn't buy a mouthful of bread today. And this damn drought goes on and on. Nobody's had a bellyful for years now. It's those rotten officials, you take my word for it. They're in cahoots with the bakers: you scratch me and I'll scratch you. So the little people get it in the neck, but in the rich man's jaws it's jubilee all year. By god, if we only had the kind of men we used to have, the sort I found here when I arrived from Asia. Then life was something like living. Man, milk and honey day in and day out, and the way they'd wallop those blood-sucking officials, you'd have thought old Jupiter[13] was having himself a tantrum. I remember old Safinius now. He used to live down by the old arch when I was a boy. More peppercorn than man. Singed the ground wherever he went. But honest and square and a real friend! Why, you could have matched coins with him in the dark. And in the townhall he'd lay it right on the

[13]Greek Zeus, chief among the Olympian gods.

line, no frills at all, just square on the target. And when he made a speech in the main square, he'd let loose like a bugle blowing. But neat as a pin all the time, never ruffled, never spat: there was something Asiatic about him. And you know, he always spoke to you, even remembered your name, just as though he were one of us. And bread was dirt-cheap in his day. For a penny you got a loaf that two men couldn't finish. Nowadays bulls' eyes come bigger than bread. But that's what I mean, things are just getting worse and worse. Why, this place is running downhill like a heifer's ass. You tell me, by god, the good of this three-fig official of ours who thinks more of his graft than what's happening to us. Why, that boy's just living it up at home and making more in a day than most men ever inherit. If we had any balls, let me tell you, he'd be laughing out of the other side of his face. But not us. Oh no, we're big lions at home and scared foxes in public. Why, I've practically had to pawn my clothes and if bread prices don't drop soon, I'll have to put my houses on the market. Mark my words, we're in for bad times if some man or god doesn't have a heart and take pity on this place. I'll stake my luck on it, the gods have got a finger in what's been happening here. And you know why? Because no one believes in the gods, that's why. Who observes the fast days any more, who cares a rap for Jupiter? One and all, bold as brass, they sit there pretending to pray, but cocking their eyes on the chances and counting up their cash. Once upon a time, let me tell you, things were different. The women would dress up in their best and climb barefoot up to the temple on the hill. Their hair was unbound and their hearts were pure and they went to beg Jupiter for rain. And you know what happened? Then or never, the rain would come sloshing down by the bucket, and they'd all stand there like a pack of drowned rats, just grinning away. Well, that's why the gods have stuffed their ears, because we've gotten unreligious. The fields are lying barren and . . . "

"For god's sake," the ragseller Echion broke in, "cut out the damned gloom, will you? 'Sometimes it's good, sometimes it's bad,' as the old peasant said when he sold the spotted pig. Luck changes. If things are lousy today, there's always tomorrow. That's life, man. Sure, the times are bad, but they're no better anywhere else. We're all in the same boat, so what's the fuss? If you lived anywhere else, you'd be swearing the pigs here went waddling around already roasted. And don't forget, there's a big gladiator show coming up the day after tomorrow. Not the same old fighters either; they've got a fresh shipment in and there's not a slave in the batch. You know how old Titus[14] works. Nothing's too good for him when he lets himself go. Whatever it is, it'll be something special. I know the old boy well, and he'll go whole hog. Just wait. There'll be cold steel for the crowd, no quarter, and the amphitheater will end up looking like a slaughterhouse. He's got what it takes too. When the old man died—and a nasty way to die, I'm telling you—he left Titus a cool million. Even if he spent ten thousand, he'd never feel it, and people won't forget him in a hurry either. He's already raked together a troupe of whirling dervishes, and there's a girl who fights from a chariot. And don't forget that steward that Glyco caught in bed with his wife. You just wait, there'll be a regular free-for-all between the lovers and the jealous husbands. But that Glyco's a cheap bastard. Sent the steward down to be pulled to pieces by the wild beasts, you know.[15] So that just gave his little secret away, of course. And what's the crime, I'd like to know, when the poor slave is told to do it? It's that piss-pot-bitch of his that ought to be thrown to the bulls, by god! Still, those who can't beat the horse must whop the saddle. But what stumps me is why Glyco ever thought old Hermogenes' brat would turn out well anyway. The old man would have pared a hawk's claws in mid-air, and like father, like daughter, as I always say. But Glyco's thrown away his own flesh and blood; he'll carry the marks of this mess as long as he lives and only hell will burn it away. Yes sir, that boy has dug his own grave and no mistake.

"Well, they say Mammaea's going to put on a spread.[16] Mmmm, I can sniff it already. There'll be a nice little handout all around. And if he does, he'll knock old Norbanus out of the running for good. Beat him hands down. And what's Norbanus ever done anyway, I'd like to know. A lot of two-bit gladiators and half-dead at that: puff at them and they'd fall down dead. Why, I've seen better men tossed to the wild animals. A lot of little clay statues, barnyard strutters, that's what they were. One was an old jade, another was a clubfoot, and the replacement they sent in for him was half-dead and hamstrung to boot. There was one Thracian with some guts but he fought by the book. And after the fight they had to flog the whole lot of them the way the

[14]A wealthy Roman who sponsored gladiatorial spectacles.

[15]Masters could punish their household slaves by forcing them to fight wild beasts in the arena.

[16]A public feast given by Mammaea as part of his election campaign; his rival, Norbanus, has been presenting gladiatorial shows.

mob was screaming, 'Let 'em have it!' Just a pack of runaway slaves. Well, says Norbanus, at least I gave you a show. So you did, says I, and you got my cheers for it. But tot it up and you'll see you got as much as you gave. So there too, and tit for tat, says I.

"Well, Agamemnon, I can see you're thinking, 'What's that bore blabbing about now?' You're the professor here, but I don't catch you opening your mouth. No, you think you're a cut above us, don't you, so you just sit there and smirk at the way we poor men talk. Your learning's made you a snob. Still, let it go. I tell you what. Someday you come down to my villa and look it over. We'll find something to nibble on, a chicken, a few eggs maybe. This crazy weather's knocked everything topsy-turvy, but we'll come up with something you like. Don't worry your head about it, there'll be loads to eat.

"You remember that little shaver of mine? Well, he'll be your pupil one of these days. He's already doing division up to four, and if he comes through all right, he'll sit at your feet someday. Every spare minute he has, he buries himself in his books. He's smart all right, and there's good stuff in him. His real trouble is his passion for birds. I killed three of his pet goldfinches the other day and told him the cat had got them. He found some other hobby soon enough. And, you know, he's mad about painting. And he's already started wading into Greek and he's keen on his Latin. But the tutor's a little stuck on himself and won't keep him in line. The older boy now, he's a bit slow. But he's a hard worker and teaches the others more than he knows. Every holiday he spends at home, and whatever you give him, he's content. So I bought him some of those big red lawbooks. A smattering of law, you know, is a useful thing around the house. There's money in it too. He's had enough literature, I think. But if he doesn't stick it out in school, I'm going to have him taught a trade. Barbering or auctioneering, or at least a little law. The only thing that can take a man's trade away is death. But every day I keep pounding the same thing into his head: 'Son, get all the learning you can. Anything you learn is money in the bank. Look at Lawyer Phileros. If he hadn't learned his law, he'd be going hungry and chewing on air. Not so long ago he was peddling his wares on his back; now he's running neck and neck with old Norbanus. Take my word for it, son, there's a mint of money in books, and learning a trade never killed a man yet.'"

Conversation was running along these lines when Trimalchio returned, wiping the sweat from his brow. He splashed his hands in perfume and stood there for a minute in silence. "You'll excuse me, friends," he began, "but I've been constipated for days and the doctors are stumped. I got a little relief from a prescription of pomegranate rind and resin in a vinegar base. Still, I hope my tummy will get back its manners soon. Right now my bowels are bumbling around like a bull. But if any of you has any business that needs attending to, go right ahead; no reason to feel embarrassed. There's not a man been born yet with solid insides. And I don't know any anguish on earth like trying to hold it in. Jupiter himself couldn't stop it from coming.— What are you giggling about, Fortunata? You're the one who keeps me awake all night with your trips to the potty. Well, anyone at table who wants to go has my permission, and the doctors tell us not to hold it in. Everything's ready outside—water and pots and the rest of the stuff. Take my word for it, friends, the vapors go straight to your brain. Poison your whole system. I know of some who've died from being too polite and holding it in." We thanked him for his kindness and understanding, but we tried to hide our snickers in repeated swallows of wine.

As yet we were unaware that we had slogged only halfway through this "forest of refinements," as the poets put it. But when the tables had been wiped—to the inevitable music, of course—servants led in three hogs rigged out with muzzles and bells. According to the headwaiter, the first hog was two years old, the second three, but the third was all of six. I supposed that we would now get tumblers and rope dancers and that the pigs would be put through the kind of clever tricks they perform for the crowds in the street. But Trimalchio dispelled such ideas by asking, "Which one of these hogs would you like cooked for your dinner? Now your ordinary country cook can whip you up a chicken or make a . . . mincemeat or easy dishes of that sort. But my cooks frequently broil calves whole." With this he had the cook called in at once, and without waiting for us to choose our pig, ordered the oldest slaughtered. Then he roared at the cook, "What's the number of your corps, fellow?"

"The fortieth, sir," the cook replied.

"Were you born on the estate or bought?"

"Neither, sir. Pansa left me to you in his will."

"Well," barked Trimalchio, "see that you do a good job or I'll have you demoted to the messenger corps."

The cook, freshly reminded of his master's power, meekly led the hog off toward the kitchen, while Trimalchio gave us all an indulgent smile. "If you don't like the wine," he said, "we'll have it changed for you. I'll know by the amount you drink what you think of it. Luckily too I don't have to pay a thing for it. It comes with a lot of other good things from a new estate of mine near town. I haven't seen it yet, but I'm told it adjoins my lands at Terracina and Tarentum. Right now what I'd really like to do is buy up Sicily. Then I could go to Africa without ever stepping off my own property. . . .

By now Trimalchio was drinking heavily and was, in fact, close to being drunk. "Hey, everybody!' he shouted, "nobody's asked Fortunata to dance. Believe me, you never saw anyone do grinds the way she can." With this he raised his hands over his forehead and did an impersonation of the actor Syrus singing one of his numbers, while the whole troupe of slaves joined in on the chorus. He was just about to get up on the table when Fortunata went and whispered something in his ear, probably a warning that these drunken capers were undignified. Never was a man so changeable: sometimes he would bow down to Fortunata in anything she asked; at other times, as now, he went his own way.

But it was the secretary, not Fortunata, who effectively dampened his desire to dance, for quite without warning he began to read from the estate records as though he were reading some government bulletin.

"Born," he began, "on July 26th, on Trimalchio's estate at Cumae, thirty male and forty female slaves.

"Item, five hundred thousand bushels of wheat transferred from the threshing rooms into storage.

"On the same date, the slave Mithridates crucified alive for blaspheming the guardian spirit of our master Gaius.

"On the same date, the sum of three hundred thousand returned to the safe because it could not be invested.

"On the same date, in the gardens at Pompeii, fire broke out in the house of the bailiff Nasta . . . "

"What?" roared Trimalchio. "When did I buy any gardens at Pompeii?"

"Last year," the steward replied. "That's why they haven't yet appeared on the books."

"I don't care what you buy," stormed Trimalchio, "but if it's not reported to me within six months, I damn well won't have it appearing on the books at all!"

The reading was then resumed. First came the directives of the superintendents on various estates and then the wills of the gamekeepers, each one excluding Trimalchio by a special clause.[17] There followed a list of his overseers, the divorce of a freedwoman by a nightwatchman for being caught *in flagrante* with an attendant from the baths, and the banishment of a steward to Baiae.[18] It closed with the accusation against a cashier and the verdict in a dispute between several valets.

At long last the tumblers appeared. An extremely insipid clown held up a ladder and ordered a boy to climb up and do a dance on top to the accompaniment of several popular songs. He was then commanded to jump through burning hoops and to pick up a big jug with his teeth. No one much enjoyed this entertainment except Trimalchio who claimed that the stunts were extremely difficult. Nothing on earth, he added, gave him such pleasure as jugglers and buglers; everything else, such as animal shows and concerts, was utter trash. "I once bought," he bragged, "several comic actors, but I used them for doing farces and I told my flutist to play nothing but Latin songs, the funny ones."

Just at this point the ladder toppled and the boy on top fell down, landing squarely on Trimalchio. The slaves shrieked, the guests screamed. We were not, of course, in the least concerned about the boy, whose neck we would have been delighted to see broken; but we dreaded the thought of possibly having to go into mourning for a man who meant nothing to us at all. Meanwhile, Trimalchio lay there groaning and nursing his arm as though it were broken. Doctors came rushing in, Fortunata at their head, her hair flying, a goblet in her hand, and filling the room with wails of distress. As for the boy, he was already clutching us by the legs and begging us to intercede for him. My own reaction was one of suspicion. I was afraid, that is, that these pleas for pity were simply the prelude to one more hoax; for the incident of the slave who had forgotten to gut the pig was still fresh in my mind. So I started to examine the room rather uneasily, half expecting, I suppose, that the walls would split open and god knows what contraption would appear. And these suspicions were somewhat confirmed when they began flogging a servant for having bound up his master's wounded arm with white, rather than scarlet, bandages. Actually, as it turned out, I was not far wrong, for instead of having

---

[17]Trimalchio wished to be excluded from their wills in order to demonstrate that he had no need of the wealth of mere gamekeepers.

[18]A fashionable resort—a pleasant place, indeed, for exile.

the boy whipped, Trimalchio ordered him to be set free, so that nobody could say that the great Trimalchio had been hurt by a mere slave.

We gave this ample gesture our approval and remarked on the uncertainties of human existence. "Yes," said Trimalchio, "it would be a shame to let an occasion like this pass by without some enduring record of it." He then called for writing materials and after a brief but harrowing effort produced the following lines:

> We think we're awful smart, we think we're awful wise,
> but when we're least expecting, comes the big surprise.
> Lady Luck's in heaven and we're her little toys,
> so break out the wine and fill your glasses, boys! . . .

Ascyltus, however, was no longer able to swallow his snickers and he finally tossed back his head and roared and guffawed until he was almost in tears. At this one of Trimalchio's freedmen[19] friends, the man just above me at the table, took offense and flared out in wild rage. "You cheap muttonhead," he snarled, "what are you cackling about? Entertainment isn't good enough for the likes of you, I suppose? You're richer, huh? And eat better too? I'll bet! So help me, if you were down here by me, I'd stop your damn bleating!

"Some nerve he's got, laughing at us. Stinking runaway, that's what he is. A burglar. A bum. Bah, he's not worth a good boot in the ass. By god, if I tangle with him, he won't know where he's headed! So help me, I don't often fly off the handle like this. Still, if the flesh is soft, I say, the worms will breed.

"Still cackling, are you? Who the hell are you to snicker? Where'd your daddy buy you? Think you're made out of gold, eh? So that's it, you're a Roman knight?[20] That makes me a king's son. Then why was I a slave? Because I wanted to be. Because I'd rather be a Roman slave than a tax-paying savage.[21] And as I live and breathe, I hope no man thinks I'm funny. I walk like a free man. I don't owe any man a thing. I've never been hauled into court. That's right: no man ever had to tell me to pay up. I've bought a few little plots of land and a nice bit of silver plate. I feed twenty stomachs, not counting the dog. I bought

[19]Former slaves.

[20]A social-legal classification including all who had property above a specified amount.

[21]In the empire at this time, Roman citizens were not taxed; this created a major inducement for gaining citizenship (even by the degrading transitional step of Roman slavery).

my wife's freedom so no man could put his dirty paws on her. I paid a good two hundred for my own freedom. Right now, I'm on the board for the emperor's worship, and I hope when I die I won't have to blush for anything. But you're so damn busy sneering at us, you don't look at your own behind. You see the lice on us but not the ticks on yourself. Nobody but you thinks we're funny. Look at your old professor there: he appreciates us. Bah, you're still sucking tit; you're limp leather, limper, no damn better. Oh you're rich, are you? Then cram down two lunches; bolt two suppers, sonny. As for me, I'd rather have my credit than all your cash. Who ever had to dun me twice? Forty years, boy and man, I spent as a slave, but no one could tell now whether I was slave or free. I was just a curly-headed kid when I came to this place. The town hall wasn't even built then. But I did everything I could do to please my master. He was a good man, a real gentleman, whose fingernail was worth more than your whole carcass. And there were some in that house who would have liked to see me stumble. But thanks to my master I gave them the slip. Those are real trials, those are real triumphs. But when you're born free everything's as easy as saying, 'Hurry on down.' Well, what are you gaping at now, like a goat in vetch?"[22]

At these last words, Giton, who was sitting at our feet, went rudely off into a great gale of whooping laughter which he had been trying to stifle for some time. Ascyltus' tormentor promptly trained his fire on the boy. "So you're snorting too, are you, you frizzle-headed scallion? You think it's time for capers, do you, carnival days and cold December?[23] When did you pay your freedom tax, eh?[24] Well, what are you smirking at, you little gallowsbird? Look, birdbait, I'll give it to you proper and the same for that master who won't keep you in line. May I never eat bread again, if I let you off for anyone except our host here; if it weren't for him, I'd fix you right now. We were all feeling good, nice happy party, and then those half-baked masters of yours let you cut out of line. Like master, like slave, I always say.

"Damnation, I'm so hopping mad, I can't stop. I'm no sorehead either, but when I let go, I don't give a damn for my own mother. Just

[22]The irate speaker accuses Ascyltus of looking as bewildered as a goat in a rich pasture with unlimited grazing choice.

[23]During the riot of the winter Carnival, or Saturnalia, the normal social order was reversed; slaves and children were allowed to make fun of their masters.

[24]When a slave was freed, a five percent tax on his assessed value had to be paid to the treasury.

you wait, I'll catch you out in the street someday. You mouse, you little potato! And when I do, if I don't knock your master into the cabbage patch, my name's not Hermeros. You can holler for Jupiter on Olympus as loud as you like, and it won't help you one little bit. By god, I'll fix those frizzle-curls of yours, and I'll fix your two-bit master too! You'll feel my teeth, sonny boy. And you won't snicker then, or I don't know who I am. No, not if your beard were made out of gold! By god, I'll give you Athena's own anger, and that goes for the blockhead who set you free! I never learned geometry or criticism or hogwash of that kind, but I know how to read words carved in stone and divide up to a hundred, money, measure, or weights. Come on, I'll lay you a little bet. I'll stake a piece of my silver set. You may have learned some rhetoric in school, but let me prove your daddy wasted his money educating you. . . . And isn't he something, that professor who taught you your manners? Him a professor? A bum, that's what he is. In my time, a teacher was a teacher. Why, my old teacher used to say, 'Now, boys, is everything in order? Then go straight home. No dawdling, no gawking on the way. And don't be sassy to your elders.' But nowadays teachers are trash. Not worth a damn. As for me, I'm grateful to my old teacher for what he taught me . . ."

Ascyltus was on the point of replying, but Trimalchio, charmed by his friend's eloquence, broke in first: "Come on now. That's enough. No more hard feelings. I want everyone feeling good. As for you, Hermeros, don't be too hard on the boy. He's a little hotheaded, so show him you're made of better stuff. It's the man who gives in in arguments like this who wins every time. Besides, when you were just a little bantam strutting around the yard, you were all cockadoodledoo and no damn sense. So let bygones be bygones. Come on, everybody, smile!" . . .

By now Fortunata was almost desperate to dance and Scintilla was clapping her hands even more frequently than she opened her mouth. Suddenly Trimalchio had an idea. "You there, Philargyrus," he called out to a slave, "I know you're a fan of the Greens[25] in the races, but come and sit with us anyway. You too, Cario, and tell your wife to do the same." Well, you can imagine what happened. The dining room was by now so packed with slaves that in the rush for seats the guests were almost shoved bodily from the couches. For my part, I had to

[25]At the chariot races in the Roman Circus, horses and drivers were marked by their colors. Supporters passionately identified themselves with the color carried by their favorite drivers.

endure seeing the cook—the one who had made the goose out of pork and who reeked of pickles and hot sauce—installed just above me on the couch. Worst of all, not content with a place at the table, he had to do an imitation of the tragic actor Ephesus and then had the brass to bet his master that the Greens would win the next race in the circus.

But Trimalchio was charmed by the challenge. "My friends," he brayed, "slaves are human too. They drink the same mother's milk that we do, though an evil fate grinds them down. But I swear that it won't be long—if nothing happens to me—before they all taste the good water of freedom. For I plan to free them all in my will. To Philargyrus here I leave a farm and his woman. Cario inherits a block of flats and the tax on his freedom and his bed and bedding. To my dear Fortunata I leave everything I have, and I commend her to the kindness of my friends. But I'm telling you the contents of my will so my whole household will love me as much when I'm still alive as after I'm dead."

Once the slaves heard this, of course, they burst out with cheers and effusive thanks. But Trimalchio suddenly began to take the whole farce quite seriously and ordered his will brought out and read aloud from begining to end while the slaves sat there groaning and moaning. At the close of the reading, he turned to Habinnas. "Well, old friend, will you make me my tomb exactly as I order it? First, of course, I want a statue of myself. But carve my dog at my feet, and give me garlands of flowers, jars of perfume and every fight in Petraites' career.[26] Then, thanks to your good offices, I'll live on long after I'm gone. In front, I want my tomb one hundred feet long, but two hundred feet deep. Around it I want an orchard with every known variety of fruit tree. You'd better throw in a vineyard too. For it's wrong, I think, that a man should concern himself with the house where he lives his life but give no thought to the home he'll have forever. But above all I want you to carve this notice:

THIS MONUMENT DOES NOT PASS INTO
THE POSSESSION OF MY HEIRS.[27]

In any case I'll see to it in my will that my grave is protected from damage after my death. I'll appoint one of my ex-slaves to act as custodian to chase off the people who might come and crap on my

[26] A popular gladiator.
[27] Presumably, so his heirs would not be able to sell distrustful Trimalchio's tomb.

tomb. Also, I want you to carve me several ships with all sail crowded and a picture of myself sitting on the judge's bench in official dress with five gold rings on my fingers and handing out a sack of coins to the people. For it's a fact, and you're my witness, that I gave a free meal to the whole town and a cash handout to everyone. Also make me a dining room, a frieze maybe, but however you like, and show the whole town celebrating at my expense. On my right I want a statue of Fortunata with a dove in her hand. And oh yes, be sure to have her pet dog tied to her girdle. And don't forget my pet slave. Also I'd like huge jars of wine, well stoppered so the wine won't slosh out. Then sculpt me a broken vase with a little boy sobbing out his heart over it. And in the middle stick a sundial so that anyone who wants the time of day will have to read my name. And how will this do for the epitaph?

> HERE LIES GAIUS POMPEIUS TRIMALCHIO
> MAECENATIANUS,
> VOTED IN ABSENTIA AN OFFICIAL OF THE
> IMPERIAL CULT.
> HE COULD HAVE BEEN REGISTERED
> IN ANY CATEGORY OF THE CIVIL SERVICE AT ROME
> BUT CHOSE OTHERWISE.
> PIOUS AND COURAGEOUS,
> A LOYAL FRIEND,
> HE DIED A MILLIONAIRE,
> THOUGH HE STARTED LIFE WITH NOTHING.
> LET IT BE SAID TO HIS ETERNAL CREDIT
> THAT HE NEVER LISTENED TO PHILOSOPHERS.
> PEACE TO HIM.
> FAREWELL.

At the end he burst into tears. Then Fortunata started wailing, Habinnas began to cry, and every slave in the room burst out sobbing as though Trimalchio were dying then and there. The whole room throbbed and pulsed to the sound of mourning. I was almost in tears myself, when Trimalchio suddenly cried, "We all have to die, so let's live while we're waiting! Come on, everybody, smile, be happy. We'll all go down to the bath for a dip. The water's hot as an oven." . . .

At this moment an incident occurred on which our little party almost foundered. Among the incoming slaves there was a remarkably pretty boy. Trimalchio literally launched himself upon him and, to Fortunata's extreme annoyance, began to cover him with rather prolonged kisses. Finally, Fortunata asserted her rights and began to abuse him. "You turd!" she shrieked, "you hunk of filth." At last she used the supreme insult: "Dog!" At this Trimalchio exploded with rage, reached for a wine cup and slammed it into her face. Fortunata let out a piercing scream and covered her face with trembling hands as though she'd just lost an eye. Scintilla, stunned and shocked, tried to comfort her sobbing friend in her arms, while a slave solicitously applied a glass of cold water to her livid cheek. Fortunata herself hunched over the glass heaving and sobbing.

But Trimalchio was still shaking with fury. "Doesn't that slut remember what she used to be? By god, *I* took her off the sale platform and made her an honest woman. But she blows herself up like a bullfrog. She's forgotten how lucky she is. She won't remember the whore she used to be. People in shacks shouldn't dream of palaces, I say. By god, if I don't tame that strutting Cassandra,[28] my name isn't Trimalchio! And to think, sap that I was, that I could have married an heiress worth half a million. And that's no lie. Old Agatho, who sells perfume to the lady next door, slipped me the word: 'Don't let your line die out, old boy,' he said. But not me. Oh no, I was a good little boy, nothing fickle about me. And now I've gone and slammed the axe into my shins good and proper.—But someday, slut, you'll come scratching at my grave to get me back! And just so you understand what you've done, I'll remove your statue from my tomb. That's an order, Habinnas. No sir, I don't want any more domestic squabbles in my grave. And what's more, just to show her I can dish it out too, I won't have her kissing me on my deathbed."

After this last thunderbolt, Habinnas begged him to calm himself and forgive her. "None of us is perfect," he said, "we're men, not gods." Scintilla burst into tears, called him her dear dear Gaius and implored him by everything holy to forgive Fortunata. Finally, even Trimalchio began to blubber. "Habinnas," he whined, "as you hope to make a fortune, tell me the truth; if I've done anything wrong, spit right in my face. So I admit I kissed the boy, not because of his looks, but because he's a good boy, a thrifty boy, a boy of real character. He can divide up to ten, he reads at sight, he's saved his freedom price from his daily allowance and bought himself an armchair and two

[28]Trojan prophetess of doom.

ladles out of his own pocket. Now doesn't a boy like that deserve his master's affection? But Fortunata says no.—Is that your idea, you high-stepping bitch? Take my advice, vulture, and keep your own nose clean. Don't make me show my teeth, sweetheart, or you'll feel my anger. You know me. Once I make up my mind, I'm as stubborn as a spike in wood.

"But the hell with her. Friends, make yourselves comfortable. Once I used to be like you, but I rose to the top of my ability. Guts are what make the man; the rest is garbage. I buy well, I sell well. Others have different notions. But I'm like to bust with good luck.—You slut, are you still blubbering? By god, I'll give you something to blubber about.

"But like I was saying, friends, it's through my business sense that I shot up. Why, when I came here from Asia, I stood no taller than that candlestick there. In fact, I used to measure myself by it every day; what's more, I used to rub my mouth with lamp oil to make my beard sprout faster. Didn't do a bit of good, though. For fourteen years I was my master's pet. But what's the shame in doing what you're told to do? But all the same, if you know what I mean, I managed to do my mistress a favor or two. But mum's the word: I'm none of your ordinary blowhards.

"Well, then heaven gave me a push and I became master in the house. I was my master's brains. So he made me joint heir with the emperor[29] to everything he had, and I came out of it with a senator's fortune. But we never have enough, and I wanted to try my hand at business. To cut it short, I had five ships built. Then I stocked them with wine—worth its weight in gold at the time—and shipped them off to Rome. I might as well have told them to go sink themselves since that's what they did. Yup, all five of them wrecked. No kidding. In one day old Neptune swallowed down a cool million. Was I licked? Hell, no. That loss just whetted my appetite as though nothing had happened at all. So I built some more ships, bigger and better and a damn sight luckier. No one could say I didn't have guts. But big ships make a man feel big himself. I shipped a cargo of wine, bacon, beans, perfume and slaves. And then Fortunata came through nicely in the nick of time: sold her gold and the clothes off her back and put a hundred gold coins in the palm of my hand. That was the yeast of my wealth. Besides, when the gods want something done, it gets done in a jiffy. On that one voyage alone, I cleared about five hundred thou-

[29]It was customary (for fear of total imperial confiscation) to include a gift to the emperor in one's will.

sand. Right away I bought up all my old master's property. I built a house, I went into slave-trading and cattle-buying. Everything I touched just grew and grew like a honeycomb. Once I was worth more than all the people in my home town put together, I picked up my winnings and pulled out. I retired from trade and started lending money to ex-slaves. To tell the truth, I was tempted to quit for keeps, but on the advice of an astrologer who'd just come to town, I decided to keep my hand in. He was a Greek, fellow by the name of Serapa, and clever enough to set up as consultant to the gods. Well, he told me things I'd clean forgotten and laid it right on the line from A to Z. Why, that man could have peeked into my tummy and told me everything except what I'd eaten the day before. You'd have thought he'd lived with me all his life.

"Remember what he said, Habinnas? You were there, I think, when he told my fortune. 'You have bought yourself a mistress and a tyrant,' he said, 'out of your own profits. You are unlucky in your friends. No one is as grateful to you as he should be. You own vast estates. You nourish a viper in your bosom.' There's no reason why I shouldn't tell you, but according to him, I have thirty years, four months, and two days left to live. And soon, he said, I am going to receive an inheritance. Now if I could just add Apulia[30] to the lands I own, I could die content.

"Meanwhile, with Mercury's help, I built this house. As you know, it used to be a shack; now it's a shrine. It has four dining rooms, twenty bedrooms, two marble porticoes, an upstairs dining room, the master bedroom where I sleep, the nest of that viper there, a fine porter's lodge, and guestrooms enough for all my guests. In fact, when Scaurus[31] came down here from Rome, he wouldn't put up anywhere else, though his father has lots of friends down on the shore who would have been glad to have him. And there are lots of other things I'll show you in a bit. But take my word for it: money makes the man. No money and you're nobody. But big money, big man. That's how it was with yours truly: from mouse to millionaire.

"In the meantime, Stichus," he called to a slave, "go and fetch out the clothes I'm going to be buried in. And while you're at it, bring along some perfume and a sample of that wine I'm having poured on my bones."

[30]A Roman province in southeastern Italy.

[31]Trimalchio is name dropping; Scaurus' family was one of the greatest in Rome.

Stichus hurried off and promptly returned with a white grave-garment and a very splendid robe with a broad purple stripe. Trimalchio told us to inspect them and see if we approved of the material. Then he added with a smile, "See to it, Stichus, that no mice or moths get into them, or I'll have you burned alive. Yes sir, I'm going to be buried in such splendor that everybody in town will go out and pray for me." He then unstoppered a jar of fabulously expensive spikenard[32] and had us all anointed with it. "I hope," he chuckled, "I like this perfume as much after I'm dead as I do now." Finally he ordered the slaves to pour the wine into the bowl and said, "Imagine that you're all present at my funeral feast."

The whole business had by now become absolutely revolting. Trimalchio was obviously completely drunk, but suddenly he had a hankering for funeral music too and ordered a brass band sent into the dining room. Then he propped himself on piles of cushions and stretched out full length along the couch. "Pretend I'm dead," he said, "say something nice about me." The band blared a dead march, but one of the slaves belonging to Habinnas—who was, incidentally, one of the most respectable people present—blew so loudly that he woke up the entire neighborhood. Immediately the firemen assigned to that quarter of town, thinking that Trimalchio's house was on fire, smashed down the door and rushed in with buckets and axes to do their job. Utter confusion followed, of course, and we took advantage of the heaven-sent opportunity, gave Agamemnon the slip, and rushed out of there as though the place were really in flames.

[32]Fragrant oil.

21
Juvenal

Satires: The Third Satire

*T*HE *wealthy aristocracy of the Roman Empire, deprived of any real participation in its government and of any serious public responsibilities, often led a parasitic and useless existence. The dangers of such luxurious idleness had been pointed out by a number of writers, but it was a poet of the early second century* A.D. *who voiced an angry disgust unequalled except for the Christian writings of his day.*

This poet was Decimus Junius Juvenalis (ca. A.D. *60–ca. 135), born to a middle-class family near Rome. Little of his biography is known with certainty; but it is believed that, failing of advancement in a military career, Juvenal published a criticism of the Emperor Domitian's favorite actor—and so was exiled to Egypt. Returning to Rome in* A.D. *96 under a new emperor, his career and fortune gone, he led the life of an embittered man, sponging upon wealthy patrons. He managed to write poetry and, after about twenty years of this difficult existence, somehow acquired a farm near fashionable Tivoli (sixteen miles from Rome). More secure now, but still full of anger, he continued writing his famous* Satires *(*A.D. *110–130).*

The theme of the Third Satire, presented in full here, is the age-old fear and hatred of megalopolis, the giant city, with its public corruption and private vice. The keynote is struck in the setting of the poem. In search of quiet, Juvenal meets a friend, Umbricius, another poor hanger-on, in a once-sacred grove, only to find that it has been pretentiously "improved"; the area is also

SATIRES: THE THIRD SATIRE   Juvenal, *The Satires of Juvenal*, trans. Rolfe Humphries (Bloomington: Indiana University Press, 1958), 33–45. Copyright © 1958 by Indiana University Press. Reprinted by permission of the publisher.

crowded with grasping, deceitful foreigners who are swarming into the city. The poem then becomes a complaining, sharply worded monologue by Umbricius, blasting the dangers of Rome and the bored, selfish, sex-crazy rich in the city he is leaving forever. (The speaker complains that no one can survive in Rome who is honest, poor, and a native Roman; but he appears to give no consideration to becoming, himself, a productive worker. For Umbricius/Juvenal a career seems to mean being a rich man's client.)

The moral chaos of second-century Rome, described from a pessimistic "loser's" point of view by Umbricius, helps to explain the growing appeal of Christianity and other religiously inspired ethical codes. Juvenal offered his readers a literary escape into the idealized Roman past and the supposed simplicity of the countryside; Christianity offered to Romans a new way of life.

AGAINST THE CITY OF ROME[1]

Troubled because my old friend is going, I still must commend him
For his decision to settle down in the ghost town of Cumae,[2]
Giving the Sibyl one citizen more. That's the gateway to Baiae[3]
There, a pleasant shore, a delightful retreat. I'd prefer
Even a barren rock in that bay to the brawl of Subura.[4]
Where have we ever seen a place so dismal and lonely
We'd not be better off there, than afraid, as we are here, of fires,
Roofs caving in, and the thousand risks of this terrible city
Where the poets recite all through the dog days of August?

While they are loading his goods on one little four-wheeled wagon,
Here he waits, by the old archways which the aqueducts moisten.

[1]It should be noted that while this translation is a modern version, the satire still contains many references to conditions of the poet's time and place; but, in general, what excited Juvenal's anger is what still arouses disgust today.

[2]An ancient coastal town south of Rome, founded by the Greeks, the home of a legendary Sibyl, a prophetess.

[3]A fashionable resort near Cumae.

[4]A noisy main street of Rome, running east from the Forum through a "red light" district.

This is where Numa,[5] by night, came to visit his goddess.
That once holy grove, its sacred spring, and its temple,
Now are let out to the Jews,[6] if they have some straw and a basket.
Every tree, these days, has to pay rent to the people.
Kick the Muses[7] out; the forest is swarming with beggars.
So we go down to Egeria's vale, with its modern improvements.
How much more close the presence would be, were there lawns by
    the water,
Turf to the curve of the pool, not this unnatural marble!

Umbricius has much on his mind. "Since there's no place in the
    city,"
He says, "For an honest man, and no reward for his labors,
Since I have less today than yesterday, since by tomorrow
That will have dwindled still more, I have made my decision. I'm
    going
To the place where, I've heard, Daedalus put off his wings,[8]
While my white hair is still new, my old age in the prime of its
    straightness,
While my fate spinner still has yarn on her spool, while I'm able
Still to support myself on two good legs, without crutches.
Rome, good-bye! Let the rest stay in the town if they want to,
Fellows like A, B, and C, who make black white at their pleasure,
Finding it easy to grab contracts for rivers and harbors,
Putting up temples, or cleaning out sewers, or hauling off corpses,
Or, if it comes to that, auctioning slaves in the market.
Once they used to be hornblowers, working the carneys;
Every wide place in the road knew their puffed-out cheeks and their
    squealing.

---

[5]The legendary second king of Rome (eighth century B.C.), noted for piety and the inspiration given to him by the nymph Egeria.

[6]After the destruction of the temple at Jerusalem by Roman legions, A.D.70, the number of Jews in Rome increased. Many of them were poor "displaced persons," originally brought back as prisoners from the subjugated province. Apparently, for a small rent, they were allowed to settle in the woods close to Rome's walls.

[7]Patron goddesses of literature and the arts.

[8]Daedalus was the most famous craftsman of ancient mythology. In order to escape from confinement inside the labyrinth he had constructed on the island of Crete, Daedalus made himself wings of feathers and wax. He landed first at Cumae.

Now they give shows of their own. Thumbs up! Thumbs down![9]
  And the killers
Spare or slay, and then go back to concessions for private privies.
Nothing they won't take on. Why not?—since the kindness of For-
  tune
(Fortune is out for laughs) has exalted them out of the gutter.

"What should I do in Rome? I am no good at lying.
If a book's bad, I can't praise it, or go around ordering copies.
I don't know the stars; I can't hire out as assassin
When some young man wants his father knocked off for a price; I
  have never
Studied the guts of frogs,[10] and plenty of others know better
How to convey to a bride the gifts of the first man she cheats with.
I am no lookout for thieves, so I cannot expect a commission
On some governor's staff. I'm a useless corpse, or a cripple.
Who has a pull these days, except your yes men and stooges
With blackmail in their hearts, yet smart enough to keep silent?
No honest man feels in debt to those he admits to his secrets,
But your Verres[11] must love the man who can tattle on Verres
Any old time that he wants. Never let the gold of the Tagus,[12]
Rolling under its shade, become so important, so precious
You have to lie awake, take bribes that you'll have to surrender,
Tossing in gloom, a threat to your mighty patron forever.

"Now let me speak of the race that our rich men dote on most
  fondly.
These I avoid like the plague, let's have no coyness about it.
Citizens, I can't stand a Greekized Rome. Yet what portion
Of the dregs of our town comes from Achaia only?
Into the Tiber pours the silt, the mud of Orontes,[13]

[9]Signals given by spectators in the amphitheater, indicating mercy or death for defeated
gladiators.

[10]Fortune-tellers, supposedly, could predict the future by observing the heavenly constellations and the entrails of sacrificed animals.

[11]A Roman governor of Sicily infamous for his cruelty and greedy corruption; he was
successfully prosecuted by Cicero in 70 B.C.

[12]A river of Spain whose sands were supposed to be rich in gold.

[13]That is, the dregs of Syria. Orontes is a river there. Juvenal's ethnocentric bias is loud
and clear.

Bringing its babble and brawl, its dissonant harps and its timbrels,
Bringing also the tarts who display their wares at the Circus.
Here's the place, if your taste is for hat-wearing whores, brightly
  colored!
What have they come to now, the simple souls from the country
Romulus[14] used to know? They put on the *trechedipna*
(That might be called, in our tongue, their running-to-dinner outfit),
Pin on their *niketeria* (medals), and smell *ceromatic*
(Attar of wrestler). They come, trooping from Samos and Tralles,
Andros, wherever that is, Azusa and Cucamonga,
Bound for the Esquiline or the hill we have named for the vineyard,[15]
Termites, into great halls where they hope, some day, to be tyrants.
Desperate nerve, quick wit, as ready in speech as Isaeus,[16]
Also a lot more long-winded. Look over there! See that fellow?
What do you take him for? He can be anybody he chooses,
Doctor of science or letters, a vet or a chiropractor,
Orator, painter, masseur, palmologist, tightrope walker.
If he is hungry enough, your little Greek stops at nothing.
Tell him to fly to the moon and he runs right off for his space ship.
Who flew first? Some Moor, some Turk, some Croat, or some
  Slovene?
Not on your life, but a man from the very center of Athens.[17]

"Should I not run away from these purple-wearing freeloaders?[18]
Must I wait while they sign their names? Must their couches always
  be softer?
Stowaways, that's how they got here, in the plums and figs from
  Damascus.[19]
I was here long before they were: my boyhood drank in the sky

[14]Legendary founder and first king of Rome (see selection 14).

[15]That is, the Greeks are swarming from all parts of their world into Rome. The Esquiline was one of the Seven Hills of ancient Rome, where many houses of the rich were located.

[16]A teacher of public speaking who came to Rome from Syria, *ca.* A.D.97, and made a great sensation by his eloquence.

[17]The birthplace of Daedalus. (See footnote 8.)

[18]For the Romans, the expensive purple dye was a symbol of power and luxury. High officials wore clothing with a purple border.

[19]The chief city of Syria.

Over the Aventine[20] hill; I was nourished by Sabine olives[21]
Agh, what lackeys they are, what sycophants! See how they flatter
Some ignoramus's talk, or the looks of some horrible eyesore,
Saying some Ichabod Crane's long neck reminds them of muscles
Hercules strained when he lifted Antaeus aloft on his shoulders,[22]
Praising some cackling voice that really sounds like a rooster's
When he's pecking a hen. We can praise the same objects that they
    do,
Only, they are believed. Does an actor do any better
Mimicking Thais, Alcestis, Doris without any clothes on?
It seems that a woman speaks, not a mask; the illusion is perfect
Down to the absence of bulge and the little cleft under the belly.[23]
Yet they win no praise at home, for all of their talent.
Why?—Because Greece is a stage, and every Greek is an actor.
Laugh, and he splits his sides; weep, and his tears flow in torrents
Though he's not sad; if you ask for a little more fire in the winter
He will put on his big coat; if you say 'I'm hot,' he starts sweating.
We are not equals at all; he always has the advantage,
Able, by night or day, to assume, from another's expression,
This or that look, prepared to throw up his hands, to cheer loudly
If his friend gives a good loud belch or doesn't piss crooked,
Or if a gurgle comes from his golden cup when inverted
Straight up over his nose—a good deep swig, and no heeltaps![24]

"Furthermore, nothing is safe from his lust, neither matron nor
    virgin,
Not her affianced spouse, or the boy too young for the razor.
If he can't get at these, he would just as soon lay his friend's
    grandma.
(Anything, so he'll get in to knowing the family secrets!)

[20]One of the Seven Hills of Rome.

[21]That is, locally grown food. (The Sabines were a tribe living near Rome in its earliest days.)

[22]Antaeus was a legendary giant with whom the hero Hercules wrestled. (Whenever Antaeus was thrown, he arose stronger than before from contact with his divine earthmother, Gaea. Finally, Hercules held Antaeus up in the air and squeezed him to death.)

[23]Umbricius is referring to the skill of Greek male actors who played female roles in their dramas.

[24]That is, he drains his cup completely, without pausing.

Since I'm discussing the Greeks, let's turn to their schools and
    professors,
The crimes of the hood and gown. Old Dr. Egnatius, informant,
Brought about the death of Barea, his friend and his pupil,[25]
Born on that riverbank where the pinion of Pegasus landed.[26]
No room here, none at all, for any respectable Roman
Where a Protogenes rules, or a Diphilus, or a Hermarchus,[27]
Never sharing their friends—a racial characteristic!
Hands off! he puts a drop of his own, or his countryside's poison
Into his patron's ear, an ear which is only too willing
And I am kicked out of the house, and all my years of long service
Count for nothing. Nowhere does the loss of a client[28] mean less.

"Let's not flatter ourselves. What's the use of our service?
What does a poor man gain by hurrying out in the nighttime,
All dressed up before dawn, when the praetor nags at his troopers
Bidding them hurry along to convey his respects to the ladies,
Barren, of course, like Albina, before any others can get there?[29]
Sons of men freeborn give right of way to a rich man's
Slave; a crack, once or twice, at Calvina or Catiena[30]
Costs an officer's pay, but if you like the face of some floozy
You hardly have money enough to make her climb down from her
    high chair.
Put on the stand, at Rome, a man with a record unblemished,
No more a perjurer than Numa was, or Metellus,[31]
What will they question? His wealth, right away, and possibly, later,
(Only possibly, though) touch on his reputation.
'How many slaves does he feed? What's the extent of his acres?

[25]P. Egnatius Celer taught Stoic philosophy to Barea Soranus, a Roman aristocrat, and then brought a charge of treason against him. As the "informant," Egnatius was rewarded with a fourth of the victim's property.

[26]Egnatius came from Tarsus on the river Cydnus in Asia Minor (Turkey), where a feather ("pinion") of the mythological winged horse, Pegasus, was supposed to have landed.

[27]Common Greek names.

[28]A person paid for "service" to a rich patron.

[29]The Roman official (praetor) is sending his servants to pay a call on the rich childless Albina in hope of acquiring her fortune.

[30]Ladies of high rank.

[31]Legendary Romans of heroic virtue.

How big are his platters? How many? What of his goblets and wine
  bowls?'
His word is as good as his bond—if he has enough bonds in his
  strongbox.
But a poor man's oath, even if sworn on all altars
All the way from here to the farthest Dodecanese island,[32]
Has no standing in court. What has he to fear from the lightnings
Of the outraged gods?[33] He has nothing to lose; they'll ignore him.

"If you're poor, you're a joke, on each and every occasion.
What a laugh, if your cloak is dirty or torn, if your toga
Seems a little bit soiled, if your shoe has a crack in the leather,
Or if more than one patch attests to more than one mending!
Poverty's greatest curse, much worse than the fact of it, is that
It makes men objects of mirth, ridiculed, humbled, embarrassed.
'Out of the front-row seats!' they cry when you're out of money,
Yield your place to the sons of some pimp, the spawn of some
  cathouse,
Some slick autioneer's brat, or the louts some trainer has fathered
Or the well-groomed boys whose sire is a gladiator.
Such is the law of place, decreed by the nitwitted Otho:
All the best seats are reserved for the classes who have the most money.[34]
Who can marry a girl if he has less money than she does?
What poor man is an heir, or can hope to be? Which of them ever
Rates a political job, even the meanest and lowest?
Long before now, all poor Roman descendants of Romans
Ought to have marched out of town in one determined migration.
Men do not easily rise whose poverty hinders their merit.
Here it is harder than anywhere else: the lodgings are hovels,
Rents out of sight; your slaves take plenty to fill up their bellies
While you make do with a snack. You're ashamed of your earthen-
  ware dishes—
Ah, but that wouldn't be true if you lived content in the country,
Wearing a dark-blue cape, and the hood thrown back on your shoul-
  ders.

[32]Islands off the coast of Asia Minor.

[33]Lightning was thought to be the punishment from Jupiter against perjurers.

[34]In 67 B.C. the tribune L. Roscius Otho had introduced a law reserving the first fourteen
  rows of theater seats for those with the social rank of "knights." By Juvenal's time,
  however, only the qualification of money—not rank—was enforced.

"In a great part of this land of Italy, might as well face it,
No one puts on a toga unless he is dead.[35] On festival days
Where the theater rises, cut from green turf, and with great pomp
Old familiar plays are staged again, and a baby,
Safe in his mother's lap, is scared of the grotesque mask,[36]
There you see all dressed alike, the balcony and the front rows,
Even His Honor content with a tunic of simple white.
Here, beyond our means, we have to be smart, and too often
Get our effects with too much, an elaborate wardrobe, on credit!
This is a common vice; we must keep up with the neighbors,
Poor as we are. I tell you, everything here costs you something.
How much to give Cossus the time of day, or receive from Veiento
One quick glance, with his mouth buttoned up for fear he might
    greet you?[37]
One shaves his beard, another cuts off the locks of his boy friend,
Offerings fill the house, but these, you find, you will pay for.
Put this in your pipe and smoke it—we have to pay tribute
Giving the slaves a bribe for the prospect of bribing their masters.

"Who, in Praeneste's cool, or the wooded Volsinian uplands,
Who, on Tivoli's heights, or a small town like Gabii, say,
Fears the collapse of his house? But Rome is supported on pipestems,
Matchsticks; it's cheaper, so, for the landlord to shore up his ruins,
Patch up the old cracked walls, and notify all the tenants
They can sleep secure, though the beams are in ruins above them.
No, the place to live is out there, where no cry of *Fire!*
Sounds the alarm of the night, with a neighbor yelling for water,
Moving his chattels and goods, and the whole third story is smok-
    ing.
This you'll never know: for if the ground floor is scared first,
You are the last to burn, up there where the eaves of the attic
Keep off the rain, and the doves are brooding over their nest eggs.
Codrus owned one bed, too small for a midget to sleep on,
Six little jugs he had, and a tankard adorning his sideboard,

---

[35]That is, away from Rome the country people wear the full-dress toga only for their
own funerals.

[36]The actors in all Roman plays wore masks to indicate their type of character.

[37]That is, even the slaves of such rich men as Cossus and Veiento have to be bribed in
order that one may meet their master (in hope of becoming a client). And, later, one is
expected to tip the slaves for the refreshments available at their master's house.

Under whose marble (clay), a bust or a statue of Chiron,[38]
Busted, lay on its side; an old locker held Greek books
Whose divinest lines were gnawed by the mice, those vandals.
Codrus had nothing, no doubt, and yet he succeeded, poor fellow,
Losing that nothing, his all. And this is the very last straw—
No one will help him out with a meal or lodging or shelter.
Stripped to the bone, begging for crusts, he still receives nothing.

"Yet if Asturicus' mansion burns down, what a frenzy of sorrow!
Mothers dishevel themselves, the leaders dress up in black,
Courts are adjourned. We groan at the fall of the city, we hate
The fire, and the fire still burns, and while it is burning,
Somebody rushes up to replace the loss of the marble,
Some one chips in toward a building fund, another gives statues,
Naked and shining white, some masterpiece of Euphranor
Or Polyclitus'[39] chef d'oeuvre; and here's a fellow with bronzes
Sacred to Asian gods. Books, chests, a bust of Minerva,
A bushel of silver coins. *To him that hath shall be given!*
This Persian, childless, of course, the richest man in the smart set,
Now has better things, and more, than before the disaster.
How can we help but think he started the fire on purpose?

"Tear yourself from the games,[40] and get a place in the country!
One little Latian town, like Sora, say, or Frusino,
Offers a choice of homes, at a price you pay here, in one year,
Renting some hole in the wall. Nice houses, too, with a garden,
Springs bubbling up from the grass, no need for a windlass or
      bucket,
Plenty to water your flowers, if they need it, without any trouble.
Live there, fond of your hoe, an independent producer,
Willing and able to feed a hundred good vegetarians.
Isn't it something, to feel, wherever you are, how far off,
You are a monarch? At least, lord of a single lizard.

"Here in town the sick die from insomnia mostly.
Undigested food, on a stomach burning with ulcers,

---

[38]In Greek mythology, a wise and kind centaur (half-man, half-horse)—a learned teacher
  of such famous heroes as Achilles.

[39]Famous Greek sculptors.

[40]Chariot races.

Brings on listlessness, but who can sleep in a flophouse?
Who but the rich can afford sleep and a garden apartment?
That's the source of infection. The wheels crack by on the narrow
Streets of the wards, the drivers squabble and brawl when they're
    stopped.
More than enough to frustrate the drowsiest son of a sea cow.
When his business calls, the crowd makes way, as the rich man,
Carried high in his car, rides over them, reading or writing,
Even taking a snooze, perhaps, for the motion's composing.
Still, he gets where he wants before we do; for all of our hurry
Traffic gets in our way, in front, around and behind us.
Somebody gives me a shove with an elbow, or two-by-four scantling.
One clunks my head with a beam, another cracks down with a beer
    keg.
Mud is thick on my shins, I am trampled by somebody's big feet.
Now what?—a soldier grinds his hobnails into my toes.

"Don't you see the mob rushing along to the handout?
There are a hundred guests, each one with his kitchen servant.
Even Samson himself could hardly carry those burdens,
Pots and pans some poor little slave tries to keep on his head, while
    he hurries
Hoping to keep the fire alive by the wind of his running.
Tunics, new-darned, are ripped to shreds; there's the flash of a fir
    beam
Huge on some great dray, and another carries a pine tree,
Nodding above our heads and threatening death to the people.
What will be left of the mob, if that cart of Ligurian marble
Breaks its axle down and dumps its load on these swarms?
Who will identify limbs or bones? The poor man's cadaver,
Crushed, disappears like his breath. And meanwhile, at home, his
    household
Washes the dishes, and puffs up the fire, with all kinds of a clatter
Over the smeared flesh-scrapers, the flasks of oil, and the towels.[41]
So the boys rush around, while their late master is sitting,
Newly come to the bank of the Styx,[42] afraid of the filthy

---

[41]Three items for the master's bath.

[42]A river flowing around the border of the underworld (Hades). The dead souls were
    ferried across it—if they had the proper fare.

Ferryman there, since he has no fare, not even a copper
In his dead mouth to pay for the ride through that muddy whirlpool.

"Look at other things, the various dangers of nighttime.
How high it is to the cornice that breaks, and a chunk beats my
    brains out,
Or some slob heaves a jar, broken or cracked, from a window.
Bang! It comes down with a crash and proves its weight on the side-
    walk.
You are a thoughtless fool, unmindful of sudden disaster,
If you don't make your will before you go out to have dinner.
There are as many deaths in the night as there are open windows
Where you pass by; if you're wise, you will pray, in your wretched
    devotions,
People may be content with no more than emptying slop jars.

"There your hell-raising drunk, who has had the bad luck to kill no
    one,
Tosses in restless rage, like Achilles mourning Patroclus,[43]
Turns from his face to his back, can't sleep, for only a fracas
Gives him the proper sedation. But any of these young hoodlums,
All steamed up on wine, watches his step when the crimson
Cloak goes by, a lord, with a long, long line of attendants,
Torches and brazen lamps, warning him, *Keep your distance!*
Me, however, whose torch is the moon, or the feeblest candle
Fed by a sputtering wick, he absolutely despises.
Here is how it all starts, the fight, if you think it is fighting
When he throws all the punches, and all I do is absorb them.
He stops. He tells me to stop. I stop. I have to obey him.
What can you do when he's mad and bigger and stronger than you
    are?
'Where do you come from?' he cries, 'you wino, you bean-bloated
    bastard?
Off what shoemaker's dish have you fed on chopped leeks and boiled
    lamb-lip?
What? No answer? Speak up, or take a swift kick in the rear.

[43]Achilles' best friend. His death before the gates of Troy at the hands of the Trojan
champion Hector caused Achilles, who had been sulking in his tent, to return to
combat. (See Homer's *Iliad*, selection 1.)

Tell me where you hang out—in some praying house with the Jew-
    boys?'[44]
If you try to talk back, or sneak away without speaking,
All the same thing: you're assaulted, and then put under a bail bond
For commiting assault. This is a poor man's freedom.
Beaten, cut up by fists, he begs and implores his assailant,
Please, for a chance to go home with a few teeth left in his mouth.

"This is not all you must fear. Shut up your house or your store,
Bolts and padlocks and bars will never keep out all the burglars,
Or a holdup man will do you in with a switch blade.
If the guards are strong over Pontine marshes and pinewoods
Near Volturno,[45] the scum of the swamps and the filth of the forest
Swirl into Rome, the great sewer, their sanctuary, their haven.
Furnaces blast and anvils groan with the chains we are forging:
What other use have we for iron and steel? There is danger
We will have little left for hoes and mattocks and ploughshares.
Happy the men of old, those primitive generations
Under the tribunes and kings, when Rome had only one jailhouse!

"There is more I could say, I could give you more of my reasons,
But the sun slants down, my oxen seem to be calling,
My man with the whip is impatient, I must be on my way.
So long! Don't forget me. Whenever you come to Aquino[46]
Seeking relief from Rome, send for me. I'll come over
From my bay to your hills, hiking along in my thick boots
Toward your chilly fields. What's more, I promise to listen
If your satirical verse esteems me worthy the honor."

---

[44]Juvenal, here, may have mistakenly identified Jews with Christians who were actively
    seeking converts in Rome. To most Romans of the early second century, there appeared
    little difference between the two religions. Both rejected the Roman gods and both,
    therefore, were distrusted.

[45]Thinly inhabited regions near Rome, containing many hiding places for thieves.

[46]The birthplace of Juvenal, a town about fifty miles from Cumae.

22

Marcus Aurelius

Thoughts

*P*LATO, in his Republic *(selection 10), had hoped for the joining of wisdom with political authority in the same person, and the philosophers known as Stoics later taught the idea of a cosmopolis or "universal city" for all people and gods. Many Stoics believed that the Roman Empire, despite its imperfections, was the nearest example on earth of that ideal. The philosophy of Stoicism provided some of Rome's most able leaders with moral justification for their imperial duties and provided its thinkers with the important concept of "natural law."*

Most of the second century A.D. *is thought of as the time of "the good emperors," and the one among them who most nobly personified Plato's "philosopher-king" was a Stoic, Marcus Aurelius Antoninus (*A.D. *121–180). Born and reared in Rome, Marcus so impressed Emperor Antoninus that he legally adopted him and named him as his successor. After Marcus became emperor (*A.D. *161–180) he personally led the hard fighting on the northern frontier against the Germanic barbarians (see selection 16); he died there, far from the physical comforts of Rome. Marcus Aurelius proved to be the last of the "good emperors." This was doubtless because he set aside the established practice of selecting the most able successor to be found—and yielded, instead, to choosing his own son, the weak and irresponsible Commodus (emperor, 180–192).*

The following selection is taken from the private thoughts of a man communing with his own soul, recording at the end of each busy day as soldier and administrator his innermost ideas and feelings. Marcus wrote down his reflec-

THOUGHTS   Marcus Aurelius, *The Thoughts of the Emperor Marcus Aurelius Antoninus,* trans. George Long (Boston: Little, Brown, and Co., 1892), *passim.* Adapted by the editor.

tions in Greek, the language of the philosophers, without any narrative or logical order. Each passage may be read, by itself, as that moment's meditation on some portion of the meaning of the universe or of mankind. The fact of the survival of this very private manuscript is a mystery. For centuries it disappeared, and only during the Renaissance (fifteenth century) did it become valued as one of the treasures of humanity.

Written when the emperor was past fifty, Thoughts reveals a man not a genius, but modest, unselfish, high-minded, and with the highest sense of duty. The chosen passages (arranged here in a topical order) echo the principles of Roman Stoicism: a philosophy of universal brotherhood through reason and without revelation, and an ethic of duty based on self-discipline and without hope of reward or fear of punishment in another world. Marcus's work is one of the last and most admirable products of the classical pagan mind.

ON NATURE

All things are connected with one another, and the bond is holy; and there is hardly anything unconnected with any other thing. For things have been co-ordinated, and they combine to form the same universe. For there is one universe made up of all things, one god who pervades all things, one substance, one law, one reason common to all intelligent beings, and one truth. . . .

• • •

The intelligence of the universe is social. Accordingly it has made the inferior things for the sake of the superior, and it has fitted the superior to one another. You see how it has subordinated, co-ordinated, and assigned to everything its proper portion, and has brought together into concord with one another the things which are the best.

ON LIVING IN HARMONY WITH NATURE

Everything harmonizes with me, which is harmonious to you, O Universe. Nothing for me is too early nor too late, which is in due time for you. Everything is fruit to me which your seasons bring, O Nature:

from you are all things, in you are all things, to you all things return. The poet says, Dear city of Cecrops;[1] and will you not say, Dear city of Zeus?

•   •   •

Judge every word and deed which are according to nature to be fit for you; and be not diverted by the blame which follows from any people nor by their words, but if a thing is good to be done or said, do not consider it unworthy of you. For those persons have their own leading principle and follow their own movement; which things you must not regard, but go straight on, following your own nature and the common nature; and the way of both is one.

•   •   •

No man will hinder you from living according to the reason of your own nature: nothing will happen to you contrary to the reason of the universal nature.

ON REASON

Whatever this is that I am, it is a little flesh and breath, and the ruling part [reason].

•   •   •

If our intellectual part is common, the reason also, because of which we are rational beings, is common: if this is so, common also is the reason which commands us what to do, and what not to do; if this is so, there is a common law also; if this is so, we are fellow-citizens; if this is so, we are members of some political community; if this is so, the world is in a manner a state. For of what other common political community will any one say that the whole human race are members?

[1]The legendary first king of Athens. Here the distinction made by Marcus is, of course, between devotion to a mere city-state (Athens) and devotion to the order of nature (symbolized by the reference to Zeus, mythical lord of the universe).

And from that, from this common political community comes also our very intellectual faculty and reasoning faculty and our capacity for law; or from what place do they come?

* * *

A man should always have these two rules in readiness; the one to do only what the reason of the ruling faculty may suggest for the use of men; the other, to change his opinion, if there is any one at hand who sets him right and moves him from any opinion. But this change of opinion must proceed only from a certain persuasion, as of what is just or of common advantage, and the like, not because it appears pleasant or brings reputation.

Have you reason? I have.—Why then not use it? For if this does its own work, what else do you wish?

* * *

Remember that the ruling faculty is invincible; when self-collected it is satisfied with itself, if it does nothing which it does not choose to do, even if it resist from mere obstinacy. What then will it be when it forms a judgment about anything aided by deliberate reason? Therefore the mind which is free from passions is a fortress, for man has nothing more secure to which he can fly for refuge and for the future be invincible. He then who has not seen this is an ignorant man; but he who has seen it and does not fly to this refuge is unhappy.

ON DUTY AND RESPONSIBILITY

Every moment think steadily as a Roman and a man to do what you have in hand with perfect and simple dignity, and feeling of affection, and freedom, and justice, and to give yourself relief from all other thoughts. And you will give yourself relief if you do every act of your life as it if were the last, laying aside all carelessness and passionate opposition to the commands of reason, and all hypocrisy, and self-love, and discontent with the portion which has been given to you. You see how few the things are, which, if a man lays hold of, he is able to live a life which flows in quiet, and is like the existence of the gods;

and the gods on their part will require nothing more from him who observes these things.

• • •

Do not disturb yourself by thinking of the whole of your life. Let not your thoughts at once embrace all the various troubles which you may expect to come, but on every occasion ask yourself, What is there in this which is intolerable and past bearing? for you will be ashamed to confess. In the next place remember that neither the future nor the past pains you, but only the present. And this is reduced to a very little, if you only limit it, and scold your mind if it is unable to hold out against even this.

• • •

If you work at that which is before you, following right reason seriously, vigorously, calmly, without allowing anything else to distract you, but keeping your divine part pure, as if you should be bound to give it back immediately; if you hold to this, expecting nothing, fearing nothing, but satisfied with your present activity according to nature, and with heroic truth in every word and sound which you utter, you will live happy. And there is no man who is able to prevent this.

ON THE MORAL LIFE

If you find in human life anything better than justice, truth, temperance, fortitude, and, in a word, anything better than your own mind's self-satisfaction in the things which it enables you to do according to right reason; if, I say, you see anything better than this, turn to it with all your soul, and enjoy that which you have found to be the best. But if nothing appears to be better than the Deity [Reason]which is planted in you, which has subjected to itself all your appetites, and carefully examines all the impressions, and, as Socrates[2] said, has detached itself from the persuasions of sense, and has submitted itself to the gods, and cares for mankind; if you find everything else smaller and of less value than this, give place to nothing else, for if you once diverge and incline to it, you will no longer without distraction be able to give the prefer-

[2]Athenian philosopher of the fifth century B.C.(see selections 8 and 9).

ence to that good thing which is your proper possession; for it is not right that anything of any other kind, such as praise from the many, or power, or enjoyment of pleasure, should come into competition with that which is rationally and politically [or, practically] good. . . . I say, do simply and freely choose the better, and hold to it. . . .

Never value anything as profitable to you which shall compel you to break your promise, to lose your self-respect, to hate any man, to suspect, to curse, to act the hypocrite, to desire anything which needs walls and curtains. For he who has preferred to everything else his own intelligence and daemon[3] and the worship of its excellence, acts no tragic part, does not groan, will not need either solitude or much company; and, what is chief of all, he will live without either pursuing or flying from death, and whether for a longer or a shorter time he shall have the soul enclosed in the body, he cares not at all. For even if he must depart immediately, he will go as readily as if he were going to do anything else which can be done with decency and order; taking care of this alone all through life, that his thoughts turn not away from anything which belongs to an intelligent animal and a member of a civil community.

• • •

Occupy yourself with few things, says the philosopher, if you would be tranquil.—But consider if it would not be better to say, Do what is necessary, and whatever the reason of the animal, which is naturally social, requires. For this brings not only the tranquillity which comes from doing well, but also that which comes from doing few things. For the greatest part of what we say and do being unnecessary, if a man takes this away, he will have more leisure and less uneasiness. Accordingly, on every occasion a man should ask himself, Is this one of the unnecessary things? Now a man should take away not only unnecessary acts, but also unnecessary thoughts, for thus superfluous acts will not follow after.

Try how the life of the good man suits you, the life of him who is satisfied with his portion out of the whole, and satisfied with his own just acts and benevolent feelings.

Have you seen those things? Look also at these. Do not disturb yourself. Make yourself all simplicity. Does any one do wrong? It is to

[3]Inner spirit, or conscience.

himself that he does the wrong. Has anything happened to you? Well; out of the universe from the beginning everything which happens has been apportioned and spun out to you. In a word, your life is short. You must turn to profit the present by the aid of reason and justice.

ON HUMILITY AND PATIENCE

When you are offended with any man's shameless conduct, immediately ask yourself, Is it possible, then, that shameless men should not be in the world? It is not possible. Do not, then, require what is impossible. For this man also is one of those shameless men who must of necessity be in the world. Let the same considerations be remembered in the case of the dishonest man, the faithless man, and every man who does wrong in any way. For at the same time that you remind yourself that it is impossible that such sort of men should not exist, you will feel more kindly towards every one individually. It is useful to perceive, too, when the occasion arises, what power nature has given to man to oppose to every wrongful act. For she has given to man, as an antidote against the stupid man, mildness, and against another kind of man some other power. And in all cases it is possible for you to correct by teaching the man who is gone astray; for every man who errs misses his object and is gone astray. Besides, wherein have you been injured? For you will find that no one among those who have irritated you has done anything that could injure your mind, but that which is evil to you and harmful has its foundation only in the mind. And what harm is done or what is there strange, if the man who has not been instructed does the acts of an uninstructed man? Consider whether you should not rather blame yourself because you did not expect such a man to err in such a way. For you had means given you by your reason to suppose that it was likely that he would commit this error, and yet you have forgotten and are amazed that he has erred. But most of all when you blame a man as faithless or ungrateful, turn to yourself. For the fault is plainly your own, whether you did trust that a man who had such a disposition would keep his promise, or when conferring your kindness you did not confer it absolutely, nor yet in such a way as to have received from your very act all the profit. For what more do you want when you have done a man a service? Are you not content that you have done something conformable to your nature, and do you seek to be paid for it? just as if the eye demanded a payment for seeing, or the feet for walking. For as these members are formed for a particular purpose, and by working according to their several constitutions obtain what is their own; so also a man is formed by nature to acts of benevolence. When he has done anything benevolent or in any other way helpful to the common interest, he has acted comformably to his constitution, and he gets what is his own.

ON BALANCE AND SERENITY

Hippocrates,[4] after curing many diseases, himself fell sick and died. The Chaldeans[5] foretold the deaths of many, and then fate caught them too. Alexander and Pompey and Julius Caesar, after so often completely destroying whole cities, and in battle cutting to pieces many ten thousands of cavalry and infantry, themselves too at last departed from life. Heraclitus,[6] after so many speculations on the conflagration of the universe, was filled with water internally and died smeared all over with mud. And lice destroyed Democritus;[7] and other lice[8] killed Socrates. What means all this? You have embarked, you have made the voyage, you have come to shore; get out. If indeed to another life, there is no lack of gods, not even there; but if to a state without sensation, you will cease to be held by pains and pleasures, and to be a slave to the body, which is as much inferior as that which serves it is superior: for the one is intelligence and deity; the other is earth and corruption.

• • •

Labor not unwillingly, nor without regard to the common interest, nor without due consideration, nor with distraction; nor let fancy words set off your thoughts, and be not either a man of many words, or busy about too many things. And further, let the deity which is in you be the guardian of a living being, manly and of ripe age, and

[4]Famous Greek physician of the fifth century B.C.

[5]The ancient Chaldeans (of Mesopotamia) enjoyed a high reputation as astrologers and sorcerers—thus, the biblical phrase "Wise Men of the East."

[6]Greek "nature" philosopher of the sixth century B.C., who believed that all things are in a state of flux and originated in fire. He is alleged to have died of dropsy (marked by swelling from internal bodily fluids), while living on a dunghill.

[7]A Greek philosopher who conceived the "atomic" theory of matter, in the fifth century B.C. He chose, for the sake of his studies, to live in poverty. Thus, the legend arose that Democritus had been devoured by lice.

[8]A play on words; Marcus here refers to the mean-spirited men ("lice") who convicted Socrates on charges of inventing his own gods and corrupting the youth (see selection 8).

engaged in matter political. Be a Roman and a ruler, who has taken his post like a man waiting for the signal which summons him from life, and ready to go, having need neither of oath nor of any man's advice. Be cheerful also, and seek not external help nor the tranquillity which others give. A man, then, must stand erect, not be kept erect by others.

* * *

This is the chief thing: Be not agitated, for all things are according to the nature of the universal; and in a little time you will be nobody and nowhere, like Hadrian and Augustus.[9] In the next place, having fixed your eyes steadily on your business, look at it; and at the same time remembering that it is your duty to be a good man, and what man's nature demands, do that without turning aside; and speak as it seems to you most just, only let it be with a good disposition and with modesty and without hypocrisy.

* * *

Things themselves touch not the soul,[10] not in the least degree; nor have they admission to the soul, nor can they turn or move the soul. But the soul turns and moves itself alone, and whatever judgments it may think proper to make, such it makes for itself the things which present themselves to it.

* * *

Pain is either an evil to the body—then let the body say what it thinks of it—or to the soul; but it is in the power of the soul to maintain its own serenity and tranquillity, and not to think that pain is an evil. For every judgment and movement and desire and dislike is within, and no outside evil can force itself upon the soul.

ON RETIREMENT INTO ONE'S SELF

I have often wondered how it is that every man loves himself more

[9]Deceased Roman emperors.

[10]By "soul," Marcus means, essentially, the mind.

than all the rest of men, but yet sets less value on his own opinion of himself than on the opinions of others.

• • •

Men seek retreats for themselves, houses in the country, seashores, and mountains; and you too are accustomed to desire such things very much. But this is altogether a mark of the most ordinary sort of men, for it is in your power whenever you choose to retire into *yourself*. For nowhere either with more quiet or more freedom from trouble does a man retire than into his own soul, particularly when he has within him such thoughts that can bring him immediate tranquillity; and I affirm that tranquillity is nothing else than the good ordering of the mind. Constantly, then, give yourself this retreat and renew yourself; and let your principles be brief and fundamental, which, as soon as you apply them, will cleanse the soul completely, and send you back free from all discontent with the things to which you return. For with what are you discontented? With the badness of men? Recall to your mind this conclusion, that rational animals exist for one another, and that to endure is a part of justice, and that men do wrong involuntarily; and consider how many already, after mutual suspicion, hatred, and fighting, have been stretched dead, reduced to ashes; and be quiet at last. But perhaps you are dissatisfied with that which is assigned to you out of the universe.—Recall to your recollection this alternative: either there is divine providence or atoms [chance concurrence of things]; or remember the arguments by which it has been proved that the world is a kind of political community. But perhaps bodily things will still fasten upon you.—Consider then further that the mind mingles not with the breath, whether moving gently or violently, when it has once drawn itself apart and discovered its own power, and think also of all that you have heard and assented to about pain and pleasure.—But perhaps the desire of the thing called fame will torment you.—See how soon everything is forgotten, and look at the chaos of infinite time on each side of the present and the emptiness of applause, and the changeableness and lack of judgment in those who pretend to give praise, and the narrowness of the space within its limits. For the whole earth is a point, and how small a nook in it is this your dwelling, and how few there are in it, and what kind of people they are who will praise you.

This then remains: Remember to retire into this little territory of your own, and above all do not distract or strain yourself. But be free, and look at things as a man, as a human being, as a citizen, as a mortal. But among the things readiest to your hand to which you will turn, let there be these two. One is that *things* do not touch the soul, for they are external and remain outside the soul; but our agitations come only from our perception, which is within. The other is that all these things, which you see, change immediately and will no longer be; and constantly bear in mind how many of these changes you have already witnessed. The universe is change; life is your perception of it.

THE GODS

Since it is possible that you may depart from life this very moment, direct every act and thought accordingly. But to go away from among men, if there are gods, is not a thing to be afraid of, for the gods will not involve you in evil; and if indeed they do not exist, or if they have no concern about human affairs, what is it to me to live in a universe without gods or without providence? But in truth they do exist, and they do care for human things, and they have put all the means in man's power to enable him not to fall into real evils.

• • •

What do you wish,—to continue to exist? Well, do you wish to have sensation, movement, growth, and then cease to grow, to use your speech, to think? What is there of all these things which seems to you worth desiring? But if it is easy to set little value on all these things, turn to that which remains, which is to follow reason and the gods. But it is inconsistent with honoring reason and the gods if one is troubled because by death a man will be deprived of the other things.

• • •

As physicians have always their instruments and knives ready for cases which suddenly require their skill, so do you have principles ready for the understanding of things divine and human, and for doing everything, even the smallest, while remembering the bond which unites the divine and human to one another. For you will not do anything well affecting humans without at the same time referring to things divine; or the contrary.

23

Apuleius

The Golden Ass

*B*Y the second century A.D. many re-
*ligions, including Christianity, were rivals for converts within the relatively
tolerant Roman Empire. Among the most popular of those groups that—
despite vigorous conservative opposition—attracted many initiates from the old
Roman state religion was the cult of the Egyptian goddess Isis. She represented
the female generative force of nature. With her brother-husband, Osiris, she
was also ruler of the lower world of the dead. The clearest description we have
of this cult's rituals can be found in* The Metamorphoses, *or* The Golden
Ass, *of Lucius Apuleius (born ca. A.D. 125), Platonic philosopher, Latin
orator and novelist.*

*Apuleius, born in the city of Madaura in North Africa, was educated at
Carthage and in the philosophical schools of Athens. He travelled widely in
the east where, apparently, he was initiated into the "mystery" religion of Isis-
Osiris. Journeying to Rome he made a living as a teacher of oratory and as a
lawyer. After returning to Africa, Apuleius married a rich widow considerably
older than himself. She was the mother of his friend. Some of her kinsmen
prosecuted Apuleius on the charge that he had gained the love of the widow
through magical means and caused the death of her son, his friend. Apuleius'*
Apologia *still survives as a dazzlingly learned and successful courtroom
defense. He was acquitted of all charges. Subsequently settling in Carthage,
Apuleius also travelled extensively around the other cities of northern Africa,
lecturing mainly on philosophical topics. His point of view can be seen in the*

title of one of his existing speeches, "On the God of Socrates." Apuleius' fame suffced to have statues of him erected in Carthage and in his birthplace of Madaura.

The work for which Apuleius is best known is The Metamorphoses *[transformations], or* The Golden Ass, *the only Latin novel to survive complete. In it he tells the story of Lucius who sets out on a journey through Thessaly, a region of northern Greece known for its witches. In the town of Hypata he plunges into a wild sexual affair with his host's female servant, Fotis. She steals her mistress's magical ointment for Lucius in order to change her lover into the winged owl he wishes to become temporarily. As often happens to impulsive servants in the ancient stories, however, she makes a mistake and hands him the wrong ointment. Fotis then sees Lucius's handsome physical appearance transformed into that of an ugly beast of burden, a jackass (donkey).*

Although the antidote is simply to eat roses, the asinine Lucius is dragged off by a violent band of robbers before Fotis can bring the fragrant cure to him. The rapid series of wild adventures that befall the transformed young man delights the reader with a variety of tales from the licentious and the macabre to the spiritual. (The "Golden" of the title refers to the entertainment value of the tales.) After twelve miserable months in his ass's skin, from one rose-season to the next, Lucius escapes at full gallop from the Corinthian arena where he is scheduled to be part of a sexual exhibition with a condemned murderess who will then be torn apart by wild beasts. With tears running down his hairy face Lucius, incapable of human speech, offers a soundless prayer and falls asleep.

The following excerpt begins in an atmosphere of religious revelation as the Egyptian goddess Isis appears to him, identifies herself as the true source of all the forms of female divinity, and tells Lucius of his forthcoming return to human form. Lucius awakens, watches an elaborate procession of Isis-worshippers pass by, and eats the garland of roses held by her High Priest. His bestial form is transformed back into his human form. Dedicating himself to his savior goddess, Lucius (in the concluding section that follows this excerpt) eventually goes to Rome where he is initiated into the deepest mysteries of both Isis and Osiris. Like his creator, Apuleius, Lucius becomes a famous lawyer.

Although The Golden Ass *is a work of fiction, the conversion scenes clearly reflect the author's deeply felt personal experiences. The symbolism is clear: when man serves his lusts, he becomes a brute animal like the lowliest ass; when man turns toward the spirituality represented by Isis, he achieves his truly human form. Later, Christians were to discuss Apuleius' meaning with some care. The great Saint Augustine, in his* City of God *(selection*

28), suggested that Apuleius might have himself actually turned into an ass, a victim of his own "demonic art or power."

THE GODDESS ISIS INTERVENES

When I had finished my prayer and poured out the full bitterness of my oppressed heart, I returned to my sandy hollow, where once more sleep overcame me. I had scarcely closed my eyes before the apparition of a woman began to rise from the middle of the sea with so lovely a face that the gods themselves would have fallen down in adoration of it. First the head, then the whole shining body gradually emerged and stood before me poised on the surface of the waves. Yes, I will try to describe this transcendent vision, for though human speech is poor and limited, the Goddess herself will perhaps inspire me with poetic imagery sufficient to convey some slight inkling of what I saw.

Her long thick hair fell in tapering ringlets on her lovely neck, and was crowned with an intricate chaplet in which was woven every kind of flower. Just above her brow shone a round disc, like a mirror, or like the bright face of the moon, which told me who she was. Vipers rising from the left-hand and right-hand partings of her hair supported this disc, with ears of corn bristling beside them. Her many-coloured robe was of finest linen; part was glistening white, part crocus-yellow, part glowing red and along the entire hem a woven bordure of flowers and fruit clung swaying in the breeze. But what caught and held my eye more than anything else was the deep black lustre of her mantle. She wore it slung across her body from the right hip to the left shoulder, where it was caught in a knot resembling the boss of a shield; but part of it hung in innumerable folds, the tasselled fringe quivering. It was embroidered with glittering stars on the hem and everywhere else, and in the middle beamed a full and fiery moon.

In her right hand she held a bronze rattle, of the sort used to frighten away the God of the Sirocco;[1] its narrow rim was curved like a sword-belt and three little rods, which sang shrilly when she shook the handle, passed horizontally through it. A boat-shaped gold dish hung from her left hand, and along the upper surface of the handle writhed an asp with puffed throat and head raised ready to strike. On her divine feet were slippers of palm leaves, the emblem of victory.

[1]The sirocco is a hot, dry, dust-laden wind blowing north from Africa.

All the perfumes of Arabia floated into my nostrils as the Goddess deigned to address me: 'You see me here, Lucius, in answer to your prayer. I am Nature, the universal Mother, mistress of all the elements, primordial child of time, sovereign of all things spiritual, queen of the dead, queen also of the immortals, the single manifestation of all gods and goddesses that are. My nod governs the shining heights of Heaven, the wholesome sea-breezes, the lamentable silences of the world below. Though I am worshipped in many aspects, known by countless names, and propitiated with all manner of different rites, yet the whole round earth venerates me. The primeval Phrygians call me Pessinuntica, Mother of the gods; the Athenians, sprung from their own soil, call me Cecropian Artemis; for the islanders of Cyprus I am Paphian Aphrodite; for the archers of Crete I am Dictynna; for the trilingual Sicilians, Stygian Proserpine; and for the Eleusinians their ancient Mother of the Corn.

'Some know me as Juno, some as Bellona of the Battles; others as Hecate, others again as Rhamnubia, but both races of Aethiopians, whose lands the morning sun first shines upon, and the Egyptians who excel in ancient learning and worship me with ceremonies proper to my godhead, call me by my true name, namely, Queen Isis. I have come in pity of your plight, I have come to favour and aid you. Weep no more, lament no longer; the hour of deliverance, shone over by my watchful light, is at hand.

'Listen attentively to my orders.

'The eternal laws of religion devote to my worship the day born from this night. Tomorrow my priests offer me the first-fruits of the new sailing season by dedicating a ship to me: for at this season the storms of winter lose their force, the leaping waves subside and the sea becomes navigable once more. You must wait for this sacred ceremony, with a mind that is neither anxious for the future nor clouded with profane thoughts; and I shall order the High Priest to carry a garland of roses in my procession, tied to the rattle which he carries in his right hand. Do not hesitate, push the crowd aside, join the procession with confidence in my grace. Then come close up to the High Priest as if you wished to kiss his hand, gently pluck the roses with your mouth and you will immediately slough off the hide of what has always been for me the most hateful beast in the universe.[2]

[2]Isis particularly hates the ass because it was identified with the demonic god Seth, who had murdered Osiris, brother-husband of the good Isis. Thus, in having been turned into an ass, Lucius had been captured by the black magic of evil forces.

'Above all, have faith: do not think that my commands are hard to obey. For at this very moment, while I am speaking to you here, I am also giving complementary instructions to my sleeping High Priest; and tomorrow, at my commandment, the dense crowds of people will make way for you. I promise you that in the joy and laughter of the festival nobody will either view your ugly shape with abhorrence or dare to put a sinister interpretation on your sudden return to human shape. Only remember, and keep these words of mine locked tight in your heart, that from now onwards until the very last day of your life you are dedicated to my service. It is only right that you should devote your whole life to the Goddess who makes you a man again. Under my protection you will be happy and famous, and when at the destined end of your life you descend to the land of ghosts, there too in the subterrene hemisphere you shall have frequent occasion to adore me. From the Elysian fields[3] you will see me as queen of the profound Stygian realm, shining through the darkness of Acheron[4] with a light as kindly and tender as I show you now. Further, if you are found to deserve my divine protection by careful obedience to the ordinances of my religion and by perfect chastity, you will become aware that I, and I alone, have power to prolong your life beyond the limits appointed by destiny.'

With this, the vision of the invincible Goddess faded and dissolved.

THE ASS IS TRANSFORMED

I rose at once, wide awake, bathed in a sweat of joy and fear. Astonished beyond words at this clear manifestation of her godhead, I splashed myself with sea water and carefully memorized her orders, intent on obeying them to the letter. Soon a golden sun arose to rout the dark shadows of night, and at once the streets were filled with people walking along as if in a religious triumph. Not only I, but the whole world, seemed filled with delight. The animals, the houses, even the weather itself reflected the universal joy and serenity, for a calm sunny morning had succeeded yesterday's frost, and the songbirds, assured that spring had come, were chirping their welcome to the queen of the stars, the Mother of the seasons, the mistress of the universe. The trees, too, not only the orchard trees but those grown

[3]That place in the underworld (Hades) where dwell the spirits of those favored by the gods.

[4]The Styx and the Acheron are rivers in Hades.

for their shade, roused from their winter sleep by the warm breezes of the south and tasselled with green leaves, waved their branches with a pleasant rustling noise; and the crash and thunder of the surf was stilled, for the gales had blown themselves out, the dark clouds were gone and the calm sky shone with its own deep blue light.

Presently the vanguard of the grand procession came in view. It was composed of a number of people in fancy dress of their own choosing; a man wearing a soldier's sword-belt; another dressed as a huntsman, a thick cloak caught up to his waist with hunting knife and javelin; another who wore gilt sandals, a wig, a silk dress and expensive jewellery and pretended to be a woman. Then a man with heavy boots, shield, helmet and sword, looking as though he had walked straight out of the gladiators' school; a pretended magistrate with purple robe and rods of office; a philosopher with cloak, staff, clogs and billy-goat beard; a bird-catcher, carrying lime and a long reed; a fisherman with another long reed and a fish-hook. Oh, yes, and a tame she-bear, dressed like a woman, carried in a sedan chair; and an ape in a straw hat and a saffron-coloured Phrygian cloak with a gold cup grasped in its paws—a caricature of Jupiter's[5] beautiful cup-bearer Ganymede. Finally an ass with wings glued to its shoulders and a doddering old man seated on its rump; you would have laughed like anything at that pair, supposed to be Pegasus and Bellerophon.[6] These fancy-dress comedians kept running in and out of the crowd, and behind them came the procession proper.

At the head walked women crowned with flowers, who pulled more flowers out of the folds of their beautiful white dresses and scattered them along the road; their joy in the Saviouress appeared in every gesture. Next came women with polished mirrors tied to the backs of their heads, which gave all who followed them the illusion of coming to meet the Goddess, rather than marching before her. Next, a party of women with ivory combs in their hands who made a pantomime of combing the Goddess's royal hair, and another party with bottles of perfume who sprinkled the road with balsam and other precious perfumes; and behind these a mixed company of women and men who addressed the Goddess as 'Daughter of the Stars' and propitiated her by carrying every sort of light—lamps, torches, wax-candles and so forth.

[5]Jupiter (Greek Zeus) is chief among the gods.
[6]Bellerophon is a mythical Greek hero, rider of Pegasus, the winged horse.

Next came musicians with pipes and flutes, followed by a party of carefully chosen choir-boys singing a hymn in which an inspired poet had explained the origin of the procession. The temple pipers of the great god Serapis were there, too, playing their religious anthem on pipes with slanting mouth-pieces and tubes curving around their right ears; also a number of beadles and whifflers crying: 'Make way there, way for the Goddess!' Then followed a great crowd of the Goddess's initiates, men and women of all classes and every age, their pure white linen clothes shining brightly. The women wore their hair tied up in glossy coils under gauze head-dresses; the men's heads were completely shaven, representing the Goddess's bright earthly stars, and they carried rattles of brass, silver and even gold, which kept up a shrill and ceaseless tinkling.

The leading priests, also clothed in white linen drawn tight across their breasts and hanging down to their feet, carried the oracular emblems of the deity. The High Priest held a bright lamp, which was not at all like the lamps we use at night banquets; it was a golden boat-shaped affair with a tall tongue of flame mounting from a hole in the centre. The second priest held an *auxiliaria,* or sacrificial pot, in each of his hands—the name refers to the Goddess's providence in helping her devotees. The third priest carried a miniature palm-tree with gold leaves, also the serpent wand of Mercury.[7] The fourth carried the model of a left hand with the fingers stretched out, which is an emblem of justice because the left hand, with its natural slowness and lack of any craft or subtlety, seems more impartial than the right. He also held a golden vessel, rounded in the shape of a woman's breast, from the nipple of which a thin stream of milk fell to the ground. The fifth carried a winnowing fan woven with golden rods, not osiers. Then came a man, not one of the five, carrying a wine-jar.

Next in the procession followed those deities that deigned to walk on human feet. Here was the frightening messenger of the gods of Heaven, and of the gods of the dead: Anubis with a face black on one side, golden on the other, walking erect and holding his herald's wand in one hand, and in the other a green palm-branch. Behind, danced a man carrying on his shoulders, seated upright, the statue of a cow, representing the Goddess as the fruitful Mother of us all. Then along came a priest with a box containing the secret implements of her wonderful cult. Another fortunate priest had an ancient emblem of her

[7]Greek Hermes, winged messenger of the gods.

godhead hidden in the lap of his robe: this was not made in the shape of any beast, wild or tame, or any bird or human being, but the exquisite beauty of its workmanship no less than the originality of its design called for admiration and awe. It was a symbol of the sublime and ineffable mysteries of the Goddess, which are never to be divulged: a small vessel of burnished gold, upon which Egyptian hieroglyphics were thickly crowded, with a rounded bottom, a long spout, and a generously curving handle along which sprawled an asp, raising its head and displaying its scaly, wrinkled, puffed-out throat.

At last the moment had come when the blessing promised by the almighty Goddess was to fall upon me. The High Priest in whom lay my hope of salvation approached, and I saw that he carried the rattle and the garland in his right hand just as I had been promised—but, oh, it was more than a garland to me, it was a crown of victory over cruel Fortune, bestowed on me by the Goddess after I had endured so many hardships and run through so many dangers! Though overcome with sudden joy, I refrained from galloping forward at once and disturbing the calm progress of the pageant by a brutal charge, but gently and politely wriggled my way through the crowd which gave way before me, clearly by the Goddess's intervention, until at last I emerged at the other side. I saw at once that the priest had been warned what to expect in his vision of the previous night but was none the less astounded that the fulfilment came so pat. He stood still and held out the rose garland to the level of my mouth. I trembled and my heart pounded as I ate those roses with loving relish; and no sooner had I swallowed them than I found that the promise had been no deceit. My bestial features faded away, the rough hair fell from my body, my sagging paunch tightened, my hind hooves separated into feet and toes, my fore hooves now no longer served only for walking upon, but were restored, as hands, to my human uses. Then my neck shrank, my face and head rounded, my great hard teeth shrank to their proper size, my long ears shortened, and my tail which had been my worst shame vanished altogether.

A gasp of wonder went up and the priests, aware that the miracle corresponded with the High Priest's vision of the Great Goddess, lifted their hands to Heaven and with one voice applauded the blessing which she had vouchsafed me: this swift restoration to my proper shape.

When I saw what had happened to me I stood rooted to the ground with astonishment and could not speak for a long while, my mind unable to cope with so great and sudden a joy. I could find no words good enough to thank the Goddess for her extraordinary loving-kindness. But the High Priest, who had been informed by her of all my miseries, though himself taken aback by the weird sight, gave orders in dumb-show that I should be lent a linen garment to cover me; for as soon as I regained my human shape, I had naturally done what any naked man would do—pressed my knees closely together and put both my hands down to screen my private parts. Someone quickly took off his upper robe and covered me with it, after which the High Priest gazed benignly at me, still wondering at my perfectly human appearance.

'Lucius, my friend,' he said, 'you have endured and performed many labours and withstood the buffetings of all the winds of ill luck. Now at last you have put into the harbour of peace and stand before the altar of loving-kindness. Neither your noble blood and rank nor your education sufficed to keep you from falling a slave to pleasure; youthful follies ran away with you. Your luckless curiosity earned you a sinister punishment. But blind Fortune, after tossing you maliciously about from peril to peril has somehow, without thinking what she was doing, landed you here in religious felicity. Let her begone now and fume furiously wherever she pleases, let her find some other plaything for her cruel hands. She has no power to hurt those who devote their lives to the honour and service of our Goddess's majesty. The jade! What use was served by making you over to bandits, wild dogs and cruel masters, by setting your feet on dangerous stony paths, by holding you in daily terror of death? Rest assured that you are now safe under the protection of the true Fortune, all-seeing Providence, whose clear light shines for all the gods that are. Rejoice now, as becomes a wearer of white linen. Follow triumphantly in the train of the Goddess who has delivered you. Let the irreligious see you and, seeing, let them acknowledge the error of their ways. Let them cry: "Look, there goes Lucius, rescued from a dreadful fate by the intervention of the Goddess Isis; watch him glory in the defeat of his ill luck!" But to secure today's gains, you must enrol yourself in this holy Order as last night you pledged yourself to do, voluntarily undertaking the duties to which your oath binds you; for her service is perfect freedom.'

When the High Priest had ended his inspired speech, I joined the throng of devotees and went forward with the procession, an object of curiosity to all Corinth. People pointed or jerked their heads at me and said: 'Look, there goes Lucius, restored to human shape by the power of the Almighty Goddess! Lucky, lucky man to have earned her compassion on account of his former innocence and good behaviour, and now to be reborn as it were, and immediately accepted into her most sacred service!' Their congratulations were long and loud.

Meanwhile the pageant moved slowly on and we approached the sea shore, at last reaching the very place where on the previous night I had lain down as an ass. There the divine emblems were arranged in due order and there with solemn prayers the chaste-lipped priest consecrated and dedicated to the Goddess a beautifully built ship, with Egyptian hieroglyphics painted over the entire hull; but first he carefully purified it with a lighted torch, an egg and sulphur. The sail was shining white linen, inscribed in large letters with the prayer for the Goddess's protection of shipping during the new sailing season. The long fir mast with its shining head was now stepped, and we admired the gilded prow shaped like the neck of Isis's sacred goose, and the long, highly-polished keel cut from a solid trunk of citrus-wood. Then all present, both priesthood and laity, began zealously stowing aboard winnowing-fans heaped with aromatics and other votive offerings and poured an abundant stream of milk into the sea as a libation. When the ship was loaded with generous gifts and prayers for good fortune, they cut the anchor cables and she slipped across the bay with a serene breeze behind her that seemed to have sprung up for her sake alone. When she stood so far out to sea that we could no longer keep her in view, the priests took up the sacred emblems again and started happily back towards the temple, in the same orderly procession as before.

On our arrival the High Priest and the priests who carried the oracular emblems were admitted into the Goddess's sanctuary with other initiates and restored them to their proper places. Then one of them, known as the Doctor of Divinity, presided at the gate of the sanctuary over a meeting of the Shrine-bearers, as the highest order of the priests of Isis are called. He went up into a high pulpit with a book and read out a Latin blessing upon 'our liege lord, the Emperor, and upon the Senate, and upon the Order of Knights, and upon the Commons of Rome, and upon all sailors and all ships who owe obedience to the aforesaid powers.' Then he uttered the traditional Greek formula, 'Ploeaphesia,' meaning that vessels were now permitted to sail, to which the people responded with a great cheer and dispersed happily to their homes, taking all kinds of decorations with them: such as olive boughs, scent shrubs and garlands of flowers, but first kissing the feet of a silver statue of the Goddess that stood on the temple steps. I did not feel like moving a nail's breadth from the place, but stood with my eyes intently fixed on the statue and relived in memory all my past misfortunes.

Meanwhile, the news of my adventures and of the Goddess's wonderful goodness to me had flown out in all directions; eventually it reached my own city of Madaura,[8] where I had been mourned as dead. At once my slaves, servants and close relatives forgot their sorrow and came hurrying to Corinth in high spirits to welcome me back from the Underworld, as it were, and bring me all sorts of presents. I was as delighted to see them as they were to see me—I had despaired of ever doing so—and thanked them over and over again for what they had brought me: I was especially grateful to my servants for bringing me as much money and as many clothes as I needed.

I spoke to them all in turn, which was no more than my duty, telling them of troubles now past and of my happy prospects; then returned to what had become my greatest pleasure in life—contemplation of the Goddess. I managed to obtain the use of a room in the temple and took constant part in her services, from which I had hitherto been excluded. The brotherhood accepted me almost as one of themselves, a loyal devotee of the Great Goddess.

Not a single night did I pass, nor even doze off during the day, without some new vision of her. She always ordered me to be initiated into her sacred mysteries, to which I had long been destined. I was anxious to obey, but religious awe held me back, because after making careful enquiries I found that to take Orders was to bind oneself to a very difficult life, especially as regards chastity: and that an initiate has to be continuously on his guard against accidental defilement. Somehow or other, though the question was always with me, I delayed the decision which I knew I must sooner or later take.

One night I dreamed that the High Priest came to me with his lap full of presents. When I asked: 'What have you there?' he answered: 'Something from Thessaly. Your slave Candidus has just arrived.' When I awoke, I puzzled over the dream for a long time, wondering what it meant, especially as I had never owned a slave of that name. However, I was convinced that whatever the High Priest offered me must be something good. When dawn approached I waited for the

---

[8]Madaura is also the author's birthplace; the clear implication is that Apuleius, like his fictional Lucius, has become a worshipper of Isis.

opening of the temple, still in a state of anxious expectation. The white curtains of the sanctuary were then drawn and we adored the august face of the Goddess. A priest went the round of the altars, performing the morning rites with solemn supplications and, chalice in hand, poured libations of water drawn from a spring within the temple precincts. When the service was over a choir saluted the breaking day with the loud hymn that they always sing at the hour of prime.[9]

The doors opened and who should come in but the two slaves whom I had left behind at Hypata when Fotis by her unlucky mistake had put a halter around my neck. They had heard the tale of my adventures and brought me all my belongings. They had even managed to recover my white horse, after its repeated changes of hand, by identifying my brand on its haunch. Now I understood the meaning of my dream: not only had they brought me something from Thessaly, but I had recovered my horse, plainly referred to in the dream as 'your slave Candidus'; for Candidus means 'white.'

Thereafter I devoted my whole time to attendance on the Goddess, encouraged by these tokens to hope for even greater marks of her favour, and my desire for taking holy orders increased. I frequently spoke of it to the High Priest, begging him to initiate me into the mysteries of the holy night. He was a grave man, remarkable for the strict observance of his religious duties, and checked my restlessness, as parents calm down children who are making unreasonable demands, but so gently and kindly that I was not in the least discouraged. He explained that the day on which a postulant might be initiated was always indicated by signs from the Goddess herself, and that it was she who chose the officiating priest and announced how the incidental expenses of the ceremony were to be paid. In his view I ought to wait with attentive patience and avoid the two extremes of over-eagerness and obstinacy; begin neither unresponsive when called nor importunate while awaiting my call. 'No single member of the brotherhood,' he said, 'has ever been so wrong-minded and sacrilegious, in fact so bent on his own destruction, as to partake of the mystery without direct orders from the Goddess, and so fall into deadly sin. The gates of the Underworld and the guardianship of life are in her hands, and the rites of initiation approximate to a voluntary death from which there is only a precarious hope of resurrection. So she usually chooses old men who

[9]Dawn.

feel that their end is fast approaching yet are not too senile to be capable of keeping a secret; by her grace they are, in a sense, born again and restored to new and healthy life.'

He said, in fact, that I must be content to await definite orders, but agreed that I had been foreordained for the service of the Goddess by clear marks of her favour. Meanwhile I must abstain from forbidden food, as the priests did, so that when the time came for me to partake of their most holy mysteries I could enter the sanctuary with unswerving steps.

I accepted his advice and learned to be patient, taking part in the daily services of the temple as calmly and quietly as I knew how, intent on pleasing the Goddess. Nor did I have a troublesome and disappointing probation. Soon after this she gave me proof of her grace by a midnight vision in which I was plainly told that the day for which I longed, the day on which my greatest wish would be granted, had come at last. I learned that she had ordered the High Priest, . . . whose destiny was linked with mine by planetary sympathy, to officiate at my initiation.

These orders and certain others given me at the same time so exhilarated me that I rose before dawn to tell the High Priest about them, and reached his door just as he was coming out. I greeted him and was about to beg him more earnestly than ever to allow me to be initiated, as a privilege that was now mine by right, when he spoke first. 'Dear Lucius,' he said, 'how lucky, how blessed you are that the Great Goddess has graciously deigned to honour you in this way. There is no time to waste. The day for which you prayed so earnestly has dawned. The many-named Goddess orders me to initate you into her most holy mysteries.'

He took me by the hand and led me courteously to the doors of the vast temple, and when he had opened them in the usual solemn way and performed the morning sacrifice he went to the sanctuary and took out two or three books written in characters unknown to me: some of them animal hieroglyphics, some of them ordinary letters protected against profane prying by having their tops and tails wreathed in knots or rounded like wheels or tangled together in spirals like vine tendrils. From these books he read me out instructions for providing the necessary clothes and accessories for my initiation.

I at once went to my friends the priests and asked them to buy part of what I needed, sparing no expense: the rest I went to buy myself.

In due time the High Priest summoned me and took me to the nearest public baths, attended by a crowd of priests. There, when I had enjoyed my ordinary bath, he himself washed and sprinkled me with holy water, offering up prayers for divine mercy. After this he brought me back to the temple and placed me at the very feet of the Goddess.

It was now early afternoon. He gave me certain orders too holy to be spoken above a whisper, and then commanded me in everyone's hearing to abstain from all but the plainest food for the ten succeeding days, to eat no meat and drink no wine.

I obeyed his instructions in all reverence and at last the day came for taking my vows. As evening approached a crowd of priests came flocking to me from all directions, each one giving me congratulatory gifts, as the ancient custom is. Then the High Priest ordered all uninitiated persons to depart, invested me in a new linen garment and led me by the hand into the inner recesses of the sanctuary itself. I have no doubt, curious reader, that you are eager to know what happened when I entered. If I were allowed to tell you, and you were allowed to be told, you would soon hear everything; but, as it is, my tongue would suffer for its indiscretion and your ears for their inquisitiveness.

However, not wishing to leave you, if you are religiously inclined, in a state of tortured suspense, I will record as much as I may lawfully record for the uninitiated, but only on condition that you believe it. *I approached the very gates of death and set one foot on Proserpine's threshold,*[10] *yet was permitted to return, rapt through all the elements. At midnight I saw the sun shining as if it were noon; I entered the presence of the gods of the underworld and the gods of the upper-world, stood near and worshipped them.*

Well, now you have heard what happened, but I fear you are still none the wiser.

The solemn rites ended at dawn and I emerged from the sanctuary wearing twelve different stoles, certainly a most sacred costume but one that there can be no harm in my mentioning. Many uninitiated people saw me wearing it when the High Priest ordered me to mount into the wooden pulpit which stood in the centre of the temple, immediately in front of the Goddess's image. I was wearing an outer garment of fine linen embroidered with flowers, and a precious scarf hung down from my shoulders to my ankles with sacred animals worked in colour on every part of it; for instance Indian serpents and

[10]Proserpine (Greek Persephone) is queen of the underworld.

Hyperborean griffins, which are winged lions generated in the more distant parts of the world. The priests call this scarf an Olympian stole. I held a lighted torch in my right hand and wore a white palm-tree chaplet with its leaves sticking out all round like rays of light.

The curtains were pulled aside and I was suddenly exposed to the gaze of the crowd, as when a statue is unveiled, dressed like the sun. That day was the happiest of my initiation, and I celebrated it as my birthday with a cheerful banquet at which all my friends were present. Further rites and ceremonies were performed on the third day, including a sacred breakfast, and these ended the proceedings. However, I remained for some days longer in the temple, enjoying the ineffable pleasure of contemplating the Goddess's statue, because I was bound to her by a debt of gratitude so large that I could never hope to pay it.

24

The Epic of Gilgamesh

*T*HE *oldest known literature is poetry, and the oldest poetry is epic in form—describing mighty struggles of legendary heroes and gods. An excellent example is Homer's* Iliad *(selection 1), the earliest surviving poetry of the ancient Greeks. More ancient still is the Middle Eastern* Epic of Gilgamesh: *the story of a mythological king and demigod (half-human, half-divine). His name is Gilgamesh, and there was also a real king of the same name who ruled the important city-state of Uruk (biblical Erech), about 2700* B.C. *Uruk was located in ancient Sumer (in southern Mesopotamia), site of the world's first civilization. Long after this historical Gilgamesh, but more than a thousand years before Homer sang in Greek of the Trojan War—and long before the Hebrew Old Testament had been written— Gilgamesh had become the hero of a cycle of poems, first passed on by word of mouth.*

The content of this sophisticated and beautiful poetic tradition was unknown in the modern world until late in the nineteenth century when English scholars translated from the text inscribed on twelve clay tablets—just discovered in the ruins of the library of an Assyrian king (Ashurbanipal, reigned 669–630? B.C.). Since that time many other tablets telling parts of Gilgamesh's story have also been found. Some are far more ancient than Ashurbanipal's collection. The earliest poems about Gilgamesh were recorded in the Sumerian language. The legends, however, spread widely through time and place. Ver-

sions have been discovered in several ancient languages, although the hero's name, Gilgamesh, remained Sumerian. It means "father, hero" or "the old one, the hero."

The text of the tablets found in Assyria begins with praise of Gilgamesh, king of Uruk, son of the goddess Ninsun and a local temple-priest. Gilgamesh is a builder of great walls and a courageous warrior, but he becomes too proud and brutish. The gods hear the lament of his subjects and create Enkidu, a wild man who lives with untamed beasts. A temple-prostitute, sent by Gilgamesh, initiates Enkidu into city ways. He journeys to Uruk, confronts Gilgamesh, and they grapple. Gilgamesh throws Enkidu to the ground. Enkidu admits Gilgamesh's superior strength, and they embrace.

Now close friends, the two heroes, defying all cautionary advice, set out together against Humbaba, the fierce, divinely appointed giant who guards a remote cedar forest. Gilgamesh's motive is the gaining of immortal fame; he wishes to transcend his own human destiny. The two kill Humbaba and return to Uruk, where Gilgamesh rejects an offer of marriage from Ishtar, goddess of love and fertility. In revenge Ishtar sends down the destructive Bull of Heaven which the two friends slay. Enkidu dreams that the gods will kill him for having slain the Bull and then, lying mortally ill, dreams of the dark "house of dust" which awaits him.

After bitter weeping and a state funeral for Enkidu, Gilgamesh searches for the secret of everlasting life. Completing a difficult journey he finds Utnapishtim, a survivor of the Great Flood, the one man to whom the gods have granted immortality. Utnapishtim tells Gilgamesh the story of the flood, tests him, and shows him where to find a plant that will renew his youth. After Gilgamesh obtains the plant, however, it is snatched away by a serpent. Gilgamesh returns to Uruk, his "strong-walled city, . . . weary, worn out with labour, and . . . engraves on a stone the whole story." Although the Assyrian tablets do not advance the narrative much beyond this point, in other ancient sources Gilgamesh now dies.

A feature of The Epic of Gilgamesh especially interesting to Western readers is its parallel to passages in the Old Testament. The most remarkable and obvious similarity is in the stories of the Great Flood. (The tale is told fully in a number of the surviving tablets.) In the Old Testament's Book of Genesis (selection 25) the flood is described as a just punishment by the One God for the sins of the corrupt, while righteous Noah and his family are saved. In the story of Gilgamesh, on the other hand, the moral message is less clear. The many quarreling "gods agreed to exterminate mankind" because their sleep was being disturbed by the growing clamor of human voices. The obedient hero, Utnapishtim, is saved by a warning-dream sent by one of the gods—and *is then granted immortality. Many of the details of this earlier flood story, according to some modern scholars, clearly influenced the version in Genesis. Above all,* The Epic of Gilgamesh *is deeply pessimistic. No concept emerges of an enduring covenant between the divine and the human—a concept basic to the Bible. Also, there is no hint of human salvation; all must enter death's "house of dust."*

The following excerpt is taken from a modern translation that, for clarity's sake, combines a number of differing ancient versions of the poem into a straightforward prose narrative.

Then Gilgamesh said to Utnapishtim the Faraway, 'I look at you now, Utnapishtim, and your appearance is no different from mine; there is nothing strange in your features. I thought I should find you like a hero prepared for battle, but you lie here taking your ease on your back. Tell me truly, how was it that you came to enter the company of the gods and to possess everlasting life?' Utnapishtim said to Gilgamesh, 'I will reveal to you a mystery, I will tell you a secret of the gods.'

THE STORY OF THE FLOOD[1]

'You know the city Shurrupak, it stands on the banks of Euphrates?[2] That city grew old and the gods that were in it were old. There was Anu, lord of the firmament, their father, and warrior Enlil their counsellor, Ninurta the helper, and Ennugi watcher over canals; and with them also was Ea. In those days the world teemed, the people multiplied, the world bellowed like a wild bull, and the great god was aroused by the clamour. Enlil heard the clamour and he said to the gods in council, "The uproar of mankind is intolerable and sleep is no longer possible by reason of the babel." So the gods agreed to exterminate mankind. Enlil did this, but Ea because of his oath warned me in a dream. He whispered their words to my house of reeds, "Reed-

---

[1]Told to Gilgamesh by Utnapishtim, whom the god Ea saved, with his family and helpers, from the world flood. Utnapishtim is thus the preserver of all humankind (and of the animals) that survived the disaster; he and his wife were themselves granted eternal life by the god Enlil. Gilgamesh has sought out Utnapishtim in the hope of learning from him the secret of immortality.

[2]The chief river of the Mesopotamian valley.

house, reed-house! Wall, O wall, hearken reed-house, wall reflect; O man of Shurrupak, son of Ubara-Tutu; tear down your house and build a boat, abandon possessions and look for life, despise worldly goods and save your soul alive. Tear down your house, I say, and build a boat. These are the measurements of the barque as you shall build her: let her beam equal her length, let her deck be roofed like the vault that covers the abyss; then take up into the boat the seed of all living creatures."

'When I had understood I said to my lord, "Behold, what you have commanded I will honour and perform, but how shall I answer the people, the city, the elders?" Then Ea opened his mouth and said to me, his servant, "Tell them this: I have learnt that Enlil is wrathful against me, I dare no longer walk in his land nor live in his city; I will go down to the Gulf to dwell with Ea my lord. But on you he will rain down abundance, rare fish and shy wild-fowl, a rich harvest-tide. In the evening the rider of the storm will bring you wheat in torrents."

'In the first light of dawn all my household gathered round me, the children brought pitch and the men whatever was necessary. On the fifth day I laid the keel and the ribs, then I made fast the planking. The ground-space was one acre, each side of the deck measured one hundred and twenty cubits,[3] making a square. I built six decks below, seven in all, I divided them into nine sections with bulkheads between. I drove in wedges where needed, I saw to the punt-poles, and laid in supplies. The carriers brought oil in baskets, I poured pitch into the furnace and asphalt and oil; more oil was consumed in caulking, and more again the master of the boat took into his stores. I slaughtered bullocks for the people and every day I killed sheep. I gave the ship-wrights wine to drink as though it were river water, raw wine and red wine and oil and white wine. There was feasting then as there is at the time of the New Year's festival; I myself anointed my head. On the seventh day the boat was complete.

'Then was the launching full of difficulty; there was shifting of ballast above and below till two thirds was submerged. I loaded into her all that I had of gold and of living things, my family, my kin, the beast of the field both wild and tame, and all the craftsmen. I sent them on board, for the time that Shamash[4] had ordained was already fulfilled

---

[3] A cubit is an ancient unit of measure, equal to the length of a man's forearm from the elbow to the tip of his middle finger (usually about eighteen inches).

[4] God of the sun, a wise judge and righteous lawgiver; husband-brother of Ishtar, goddess of love and fertility.

when he said, "In the evening, when the rider of the storm sends down the destroying rain, enter the boat and batten her down." The time was fulfilled, the evening came, the rider of the storm sent down the rain. I looked out at the weather and it was terrible, so I too boarded the boat and battened her down. All was now complete, the battening and the caulking; so I handed the tiller to Puzur-Amurri the steersman, with the navigation and the care of the whole boat.

'With the first light of dawn a black cloud came from the horizon; it thundered within where Adad, lord of the storm was riding. In front over hill and plain Shullat and Hanish, heralds of the storm, led on. Then the gods of the abyss rose up; Nergal pulled out the dams of the nether waters, Ninurta the war-lord threw down the dykes, and the seven judges of hell, the Annunaki, raised their torches, lighting the land with their livid flame. A stupor of despair went up to heaven when the god of the storm turned daylight to darkness, when he smashed the land like a cup. One whole day the tempest raged, gathering fury as it went, it poured over the people like the tides of battle; a man could not see his brother nor the people be seen from heaven. Even the gods were terrified at the flood, they fled to the highest heaven, the firmament of Anu; they crouched against the walls, cowering like curs. Then Ishtar the sweet-voiced Queen of Heaven cried out like a woman in travail: "Alas the days of old are turned to dust because I commanded evil; why did I command this evil in the council of all the gods? . . . Now like the spawn of fish [the people] float in the ocean." The great gods of heaven and of hell wept, they covered their mouths.

'For six days and six nights the winds blew, torrent and tempest and flood overwhelmed the world, tempest and flood raged together like warring hosts. When the seventh day dawned the storm from the south subsided, the sea grew calm, the flood was stilled; I looked at the face of the world and there was silence, all mankind was turned to clay. The surface of the sea stretched as flat as a roof-top; I opened a hatch and the light fell on my face. Then I bowed low, I sat down and I wept, the tears streamed down my face, for on every side was the waste of water. I looked for land in vain, but fourteen leagues distant there appeared a mountain, and there the boat grounded; on the mountain of Nisir the boat held fast, she held fast and did not budge. One day she held, and a second day on the mountain of Nisir she held fast and did not budge. A third day, and a fourth day she held fast on the mountain and did not budge; a fifth day and a sixth day she held fast on the mountain. When the seventh day dawned I loosed a dove and let her go. She flew away, but finding no resting-place she returned. Then I loosed a swallow, and she flew away but finding no resting-place she returned. I loosed a raven, she saw that the waters had retreated, she ate, she flew around, she cawed, and she did not come back. Then I threw everything open to the four winds, I made a sacrifice[5] and poured out a libation[6] on the mountain top. Seven and again seven cauldrons I set up on their stands, I heaped up wood and cane and cedar and myrtle. When the gods smelled the sweet savour, they gathered like flies over the sacrifice. Then, at last, Ishtar also came, she lifted her necklace with the jewels of heaven that once Anu had made to please her. 'O you gods here present, by the lapis lazuli round my neck I shall remember these days as I remember the jewels of my throat; these last days I shall not forget. Let all the gods gather round the sacrifice, except Enlil. He shall not approach this offering, for without reflection he brought the flood; he consigned my people to destruction."

'When Enlil had come, when he saw the boat, he was wrath and swelled with anger at the gods, the host of heaven, "Has any of these mortals escaped? Not one was to have survived the destruction." Then the god of the wells and canals Ninurta opened his mouth and said to the warrior Enlil, "Who is there of the gods that can devise without Ea? It is Ea alone who knows all things." Then Ea opened his mouth and spoke to warrior Enlil, "Wisest of gods, hero Enlil,[7] how could you so senselessly bring down the flood?

> *Lay upon the sinner his sin,*
> *Lay upon the transgressor his transgression[8]*
> *Punish him a little when he breaks loose,*
> *Do not drive him too hard or he perishes;*
> *Would that a lion had ravaged mankind*
> *Rather than the flood,*
> *Would that a wolf had ravaged mankind*
> *Rather than the flood,*
> *Would that famine had wasted the world*

[5]An animal is killed and then burnt.

[6]A wine-offering to the gods, poured on the ground.

[7]Ea's use of "wisest" is here intended ironically.

[8]Although the Old Testament's flood story, with its concluding covenant of righteousness, is not present in this epic, there is, nevertheless, a moral message in Ea's criticism of Enlil: punish only the one who commits the transgression.

> *Rather than the flood,*
> *Would that pestilence had wasted mankind*
> *Rather than the flood.*

It was not I that revealed the secret of the gods; the wise man learned it in a dream. Now take your counsel what shall be done with him."

'Then Enlil went up into the boat, he took me by the hand and my wife and made us enter the boat and kneel down on either side, he standing between us. He touched our foreheads to bless us saying, "In time past Utnapishtim was a mortal man; henceforth he and his wife shall live in the distance at the mouth of the rivers." Thus it was that the gods took me and placed me here to live in the distance, at the mouth of the rivers.'

25

The Bible: Old Testament

*T*HE *Old Testament, as the collection of Jewish sacred books is called by Christians, is accepted by both faiths as the divinely inspired account of God's dealings with his "chosen witnesses," the Jews. In a wider sense it is viewed by its believers as the revelation of God's will to all humanity. Originally written in Hebrew, the Old Testament (like the Sumerian* Epic of Gilgamesh, *selection 24) is many centuries older than Christianity. It is presented at this point in the* Classics *because it was accepted by the Christians as the essential prologue of their own gospel (the New Testament). Through Christianity, Jewish religious ideas became widely known throughout the Roman Empire. The Old Testament is still the com-plete* Scriptures *for Jews. The following passages tell the Jewish version of some crucial events in the developing relationship between the human and the divine; they also show the growing human comprehension of God's presence and plan.*

The early books of the Old Testament, known to Jews as the Torah (Law), begin with the creation of the universe and then immediately focus on a garden. This garden is part of the world as God had planned it—full of good things where man and woman enjoy the intimacy of their creator. This right relation-

ship is broken by their proud and rebellious self-will, their "original" sin, followed by the first murder. Evil, then, lies deep in human nature; therefore, judgment falls upon mankind in the great Flood, which only Noah and his family survive. Thus, the themes that will run through the Jewish-Christian epic are set forth: a recurring pattern of sin, divine judgment and punishment, and—because of the merits of one only, or of a few—divine mercy.

The Hebrew people, through their founding patriarch Abraham, are then selected as the instrument of the divine purpose. God establishes a special covenant (binding agreement) with them. They pledge obedience to God and then, through Moses, are given God's Law at Mount Sinai. With the establishment of that Law, the Jewish religion develops far beyond its tribal origins. Once again, however, many humans prove unequal to the divine challenge. Exposed to the competing ways and faiths of neighboring peoples, some Jews follow strange gods and adopt a life of self-indulgence. God's anger at this breaking of the covenant is expressed through his spokesmen, the prophets (moralizing believers in the One God), who warn in his name. Gradually, the prophets give shape and direction to the religious experience of the Jews. The books named for the prophets make up more than a third of the books of the Old Testament. The earliest prophet was Amos, who, in the eighth century B.C., denounced luxury and social injustice among the Jews and predicted the coming judgment. Amos clearly reveals a god who is universal—not for the Jews alone. This God demands moral purity, rather than merely the rituals and burnt offerings of organized religion.

Historically, God's judgment took various forms. First, for example, the northern kingdom, called Israel, was wiped out by the Assyrians in 721 B.C. Later, the southern kingdom, called Judah, which included the city of Jerusalem, fell to the Babylonians in 586 B.C. Many of these Hebrews were brought into captivity in Babylon (the period of "Exile"). Reflecting upon these disasters and guided by the insights of the "Second Isaiah," a prophet who wrote chapters 40–66 of Isaiah about 540 B.C., the Jews acquired a clearer understanding of God's nature and of their role in history. The prophetic tradition continued even after many of the exiles were able to return to Judah. The inspired messages of the prophets mark the peak of Jewish religious literature.

Still another literary tradition in the Old Testament is called wisdom literature. Job is one book in that tradition. It deals with a question that has always troubled thoughtful religious people: why does the divine plan appear to allow the suffering of the righteous and innocent? No satisfactory intellectual answer to that question is stated in Job. God's response to Job, however, offers a *resounding statement of infinite power and purpose, as well as God's personal communion with the suffering, questioning, and righteous individual.*

GENESIS[1]

The Beginnings of History
1:1–4:16

In the beginning God created the heavens and the earth. The earth was without form and void, and darkness was upon the face of the deep; and the Spirit of God was moving over the face of the waters.

And God said, "Let there be light"; and there was light. And God saw that the light was good; and God separated the light from the darkness. God called the light Day, and the darkness he called Night. And there was evening and there was morning, one day.

And God said, "Let there be a firmament in the midst of the waters, and let it separate the waters from the waters." And God made the firmament and separated the waters which were under the firmament from the waters which were above the firmament. And it was so.[2] And God called the firmament Heaven. And there was evening and there was morning, a second day.

And God said, "Let the waters under the heavens be gathered together into one place, and let the dry land appear." And it was so. God called the dry land Earth, and the waters that were gathered together he called Seas. And God saw that it was good. And God said, "Let the earth put forth vegetation, plants yielding seed, and fruit trees bearing fruit in which is their seed, each according to its kind, upon the earth."

---

[1] A Greek word meaning "origin" or "birth." Genesis is the first book of the Bible and begins with two versions of the Creation story. It then tells about the expulsion of the first humans from Eden, the first murder, the flood, and the Hebrew founders down to the settling of some of their people in Egypt. Genesis thus introduces the ancestry of the Israelites (Hebrews)—first, like all humanity, from Adam, and then, more particularly, from "Father" Abraham. The book also describes the special relationship and *covenant* (agreement) that God established with Noah, and later with Abraham and his descendants.

[2] This description of God's creative action on the second day rests upon the belief that the world was created out of a watery chaos. The "firmament" was imagined as a sort of solid dome, which separated the "waters above" from the "waters under."

And it was so. The earth brought forth vegetation, plants yielding seed according to their own kinds, and trees bearing fruit in which is their seed, each according to its kind. And God saw that it was good. And there was evening and there was morning, a third day.

And God said, "Let there be lights in the firmament of the heavens to separate the day from the night; and let them be for signs and for seasons and for days and years, and let them be lights in the firmament of the heavens to give light upon the earth." And it was so. And God made the two great lights, the greater light to rule the day, and the lesser light to rule the night; he made the stars also. And God set them in the firmament of the heavens to give light upon the earth, to rule over the day and over the night, and to separate the light from the darkness. And God saw that it was good. And there was evening and there was morning, a fourth day.

And God said, "Let the waters bring forth swarms of living creatures, and let birds fly above the earth across the firmament of the heavens." So God created the great sea monsters and every living creature that moves, with which the waters swarm, according to their kinds, and every winged bird according to its kind. And God saw that it was good. And God blessed them, saying, "Be fruitful and multiply and fill the waters in the seas, and let birds multiply on the earth." And there was evening and there was morning, a fifth day.

And God said, "Let the earth bring forth living creatures according to their kinds: cattle[3] and creeping things and beasts of the earth according to their kinds." And it was so. And God made the beasts of the earth according to their kinds and the cattle according to their kinds, and everything that creeps upon the ground according to its kind. And God saw that it was good.

Then God said, "Let us make man in our image, after our likeness; and let them have dominion over the fish of the sea, and over the birds of the air, and over the cattle, and over all the earth, and over every creeping thing that creeps upon the earth."

So God created man in his own image, in the image of God he created him; male and female he created them. And God blessed them, and God said to them, "Be fruitful and multiply, and fill the earth and subdue it; and have dominion over the fish of the sea and over the birds of the air and over every living thing that moves upon the earth." And God said, "Behold, I have given you every plant yielding seed which

[3]All domestic animals.

is upon the face of all the earth, and every tree with seed in its fruit; you shall have them for food. And to every beast of the earth, and to every bird of the air, and to everything that creeps on the earth, everything that has the breath of life, I have given every green plant for food." And it was so. And God saw everything that he had made, and behold, it was very good. And there was evening and there was morning, a sixth day.

Thus the heavens and the earth were finished, and all the host of them. And on the seventh day God finished his work which he had done, and he rested on the seventh day from all his work which he had done. So God blessed the seventh day and hallowed it, because on it God rested from all his work which he had done in creation.

These are the generations of the heavens and the earth when they were created.[4]

In the day that the Lord God made the earth and the heavens, when no plant of the field was yet in the earth and no herb of the field had yet sprung up—for the Lord God had not caused it to rain upon the earth, and there was no man to till the ground; but a mist went up from the earth and watered the whole face of the ground—then the Lord God formed man of dust from the ground, and breathed into his nostrils the breath of life; and man became a living being. And the Lord God planted a garden in Eden, in the east; and there he put the man whom he had formed. And out of the ground the Lord God made to grow every tree that is pleasant to the sight and good for food, the tree of life also in the midst of the garden, and the tree of the knowledge of good and evil.

A river flowed out of Eden to water the garden, and there it divided and became four rivers. The name of the first is Pishon; it is the one which flows around the whole land of Hav'ilah, where there is gold; and the gold of that land is good; bdellium and onyx stone are there. The name of the second river is Gihon; it is the one which flows around the whole land of Cush. And the name of the third river is Tigris, which flows east of Assyria. And the fourth river is the Euphra'tes.

The Lord God took the man and put him in the garden of Eden to till it and keep it. And the Lord God commanded the man, saying, "You may freely eat of every tree of the garden; but of the tree of the knowledge of good and evil you shall not eat, for in the day that you eat of it you shall die."

[4]This sentence begins a second version of the creation; it differs in some significant ways from the first.

Then the Lord God said, "It is not good that the man should be alone; I will make him a helper fit for him. So out of the ground the Lord God formed every beast of the field and every bird of the air, and brought them to the man to see what he would call them; and whatever the man called every living creature, that was its name. The man gave names to all cattle, and to the birds of the air, and to every beast of the field; but for the man there was not found a helper fit for him. So the Lord God caused a deep sleep to fall upon the man, and while he slept took one of his ribs and closed up its place with flesh; and the rib which the Lord God had taken from the man he made into a woman and brought her to the man. Then the man said,

> "This at last is bone of my bones
>   and flesh of my flesh;
> she shall be called Woman,
>   because she was taken out of Man."[5]

Therefore a man leaves his father and his mother and cleaves to his wife, and they become one flesh. And the man and his wife were both naked, and were not ashamed.

Now the serpent was more subtle than any other wild creature that the Lord God had made. He said to the woman, "Did God say, 'You shall not eat of any tree of the garden'?" And the woman said to the serpent, "We may eat of the fruit of the trees of the garden; but God said, 'You shall not eat of the fruit of the tree which is in the midst of the garden, neither shall you touch it, lest you die.'" But the serpent said to the woman, "You will not die. For God knows that when you eat of it your eyes will be opened, and you will be like God, knowing good and evil." So when the woman saw that the tree was good for food, and that it was a delight to the eyes, and that the tree was to be desired to make one wise, she took of its fruit and ate; and she also gave some to her husband, and he ate. Then the eyes of both were opened, and they knew that they were naked; and they sewed fig leaves together and made themselves aprons.

And they heard the sound of the Lord God walking in the garden in the cool of the day, and the man and his wife hid themselves from the presence of the Lord God among the trees of the garden. But the Lord God called to the man, and said to him, "Where are you?" And he said, "I heard the sound of thee in the garden, and I was afraid, because I

---

[5]In Hebrew, a word for "man" is *ish*; for "woman," *ishshah*.

was naked; and I hid myself." He said, "Who told you that you were naked? Have you eaten of the tree of which I commanded you not to eat?" The man said, "The woman whom thou gavest to be with me, she gave me the fruit of the tree, and I ate." Then the Lord God said to the woman, "What is this that you have done?" The woman said, "The serpent beguiled me, and I ate." The Lord God said to the serpent,

> "Because you have done this,
>> cursed are you above all cattle,
>> and above all wild animals;
> upon your belly you shall go,
>> and dust you shall eat
>> all the days of your life.
> I will put enmity between you and the woman,
>> and between your seed [descendants] and her
>> seed;
> he shall bruise your head,
>> and you shall bruise his heel."

To the woman he said,

> "I will greatly multiply your pain in childbearing;
>> in pain you shall bring forth children,
> yet your desire shall be for your husband,
>> and he shall rule over you."

And to Adam[6] he said,

> "Because you have listened to the voice of your wife,
>> and have eaten of the tree
> of which I commanded you,
>> 'You shall not eat of it,'
> cursed is the ground because of you;
>> in toil you shall eat of it all the days of your life;
> thorns and thistles it shall bring forth to you;
>> and you shall eat the plants of the field.
> In the sweat of your face
>> you shall eat bread

[6]Another Hebrew word for "man" or "mankind" is *adam*.

> till you return to the ground,
>> for out of it you were taken;
> you are dust,
>> and to dust you shall return."

The man called his wife's name Eve, because she was the mother of all living.[7] And the Lord God made for Adam and for his wife garments of skins, and clothed them.

Then the Lord God said, "Behold, the man has become like one of us, knowing good and evil; and now, lest he put forth his hand and take also of the tree of life, and eat, and live for ever"—therefore the Lord God sent him forth from the garden of Eden, to till the ground from which he was taken. He drove out the man; and at the east of the garden of Eden he placed the cherubim,[8] and a flaming sword which turned every way, to guard the way to the tree of life.

Now Adam knew[9] Eve his wife, and she conceived and bore Cain, saying, "I have gotten a man with the help of the Lord." And again, she bore his brother Abel. Now Abel was a keeper of sheep, and Cain a tiller of the ground. In the course of time Cain brought to the Lord an offering of the fruit of the ground, and Abel brought of the firstlings of his flock and of their fat portions. And the Lord had regard for Abel and his offering, but for Cain and his offering he had no regard.[10] So Cain was very angry, and his countenance fell. The Lord said to Cain "Why are you angry, and why has your countenance fallen? If you do well, will you not be accepted? And if you do not do well, sin is couching at the door; its desire is for you, but you must master it."

Cain said to Abel his brother, "Let us go out to the field." And when they were in the field, Cain rose up against his brother Abel, and killed him. Then the Lord said to Cain, "Where is Abel your brother?" He said, "I do not know; am I my brother's keeper?" And the Lord said, "What have you done? The voice of your brother's blood is crying to me from the ground. And now you are cursed from the ground, which has opened its mouth to receive your brother's blood from your hand. When you till the ground, it shall no longer yield to you its strength; you shall be a fugitive and a wanderer on the earth." Cain said to the

[7]Eve's name, in Hebrew, resembles the word for "living."

[8]Winged, semi-divine creatures who served as guardians of sacred areas.

[9]That is, had sexual intercourse.

[10]The Cain and Abel story may personify a social conflict between settled farmers and seminomadic shepherds. No reason is given for the Lord's acceptance only of Abel's offering.

Lord, "My punishment is greater than I can bear. Behold, thou hast driven me this day away from the ground; and from thy face I shall be hidden; and I shall be a fugitive and a wanderer on the earth, and whoever finds me will slay me." Then the Lord said to him, "Not so! If anyone slays Cain, vengeance shall be taken on him sevenfold." And the Lord put a mark[11] on Cain, lest any who came upon him should kill him. Then Cain went away from the presence of the Lord, and dwelt in the land of Nod, east of Eden.

The Flood
6:1–22

When men began to multiply on the face of the ground, and daughters were born to them, the sons of God saw that the daughters of men were fair; and they took to wife such of them as they chose. Then the Lord said, "My spirit shall not abide in man for ever, for he is flesh, but his days shall be a hundred and twenty years." The Nephilim [giants]were on the earth in those days, and also afterward, when the sons of God came in to the daughters of men, and they bore children to them.[12] These were the mighty men that were of old, the men of renown.

The Lord saw that the wickedness of man was great in the earth, and that every imagination of the thoughts of his heart was only evil continually. And the Lord was sorry that he had made man on the earth, and it grieved him to his heart. So the Lord said, "I will blot out man whom I have created from the face of the ground, man and beast and creeping things and birds of the air, for I am sorry that I have made them." But Noah found favor in the eyes of the Lord.

These are the generations of Noah. Noah was a righteous man, blameless in his generation; Noah walked with God. And Noah had three sons, Shem, Ham, and Japheth.

Now the earth was corrupt in God's sight, and the earth was filled with violence. And God saw the earth, and behold, it was corrupt; for all flesh had corrupted their way upon the earth. And God said to Noah, "I have determined to make an end of all flesh; for the earth is filled with violence through them; behold, I will destroy them with

[11]A protective mark, perhaps a tattoo.

[12]This story of the mating of "the sons of God" with "the daughters of men" reveals the survival of an earlier, non-Hebrew mythology. Unlike those earlier myths, however, this biblical account of a divine parent does not grant semi-divine status to the off-spring. The story attempts, rather, to explain the origin of a legendary race of giants.

the earth. Make yourself an ark of gopher wood; make rooms in the ark, and cover it inside and out with pitch. This is how you are to make it: the length of the ark three hundred cubits,[13] its breadth fifty cubits, and its height thirty cubits. Make a roof for the ark, and finish it to a cubit above; and set the door of the ark in its side; make it with lower, second, and third decks. For behold, I will bring a flood of waters upon the earth, to destroy all flesh in which is the breath of life from under heaven; everything that is on the earth shall die. But I will establish my covenant with you; and you shall come into the ark, you, your sons, your wife, and your sons' wives with you. And of every living thing of all flesh, you shall bring two of every sort into the ark, to keep them alive with you; they shall be male and female. Of the birds according to their kinds, and of the animals according to their kinds, of every creeping thing of the ground according to its kind, two of every sort shall come in to you, to keep them alive. Also take with you every sort of food that is eaten, and store it up; and it shall serve as food for you and for them." Noah did this; he did all that God commanded him.[14]

EXODUS[15]

The Covenant
19:1–20:21

On the third new moon after the people of Israel had gone forth out of the land of Egypt, on that day they came into the wilderness of Sinai. And when they set out from Reph'idim and came into the wilderness

[13]A cubit is an ancient unit of measurement based on the length of a man's forearm, usually about eighteen inches.

[14]God then sends the great flood as a punishment for human wickedness. (Many details of the biblical flood story resemble the account in the earlier *Epic of Gilgamesh*, selection 24, with the essential difference that the biblical flood represents a single, divine moral judgment—not the whims of many gods.) God's mercy will be shown by his saving of a "righteous remnant" (Noah and his family), by whom humanity can begin anew. Through Noah, God will make a covenant with all humanity that "never again shall there be a flood to destroy the earth."

[15]A Greek word meaning "a going out." The book of Exodus tells of the departure, under hostile circumstances (*ca.* 1300 B.C.), of an oppressed community of Hebrews from Egypt. It begins the story of their forty years journey through the desert back to the land of their ancestors—Abraham, his son Isaac, and Isaac's son Jacob (also called Israel). Their religious and political leader is Moses. The book's climactic event is God's reassertion of his covenant with the Hebrew people through his giving of the Law to Moses at Mount Sinai. With the establishment of this law, the *Jewish religion* assumes a clear identity.

of Sinai, they encamped in the wilderness; and there Israel encamped before the mountain. And Moses went up to God, and the Lord called to him out of the mountain, saying, "Thus you shall say to the house of Jacob, and tell the people of Israel: You have seen what I did to the Egyptians, and how I bore you on eagles' wings and brought you to myself. Now therefore, if you will obey my voice and keep my covenant, you shall be my own possession among all peoples; for all the earth is mine, and you shall be to me a kingdom of priests and a holy nation.[16] These are the words which you shall speak to the children of Israel."

So Moses came and called the elders of the people, and set before them all these words which the Lord had commanded him. And all the people answered together and said, "All that the Lord has spoken we will do." And Moses reported the words of the people to the Lord. And the Lord said to Moses, "Lo, I am coming to you in a thick cloud, that the people may hear when I speak with you, and may also believe you for ever."

Then Moses told the words of the people to the Lord. And the Lord said to Moses, "Go to the people and consecrate them today and tomorrow, and let them wash their garments, and be ready by the third day; for on the third day the Lord will come down upon Mount Sinai in the sight of all the people. And you shall set bounds for the people round about saying, 'Take heed that you do not go up into the mountain or touch the border of it; whoever touches the mountain shall be put to death; no hand shall touch him, but he shall be stoned or shot; whether beast or man, he shall not live.' When the trumpet sounds a long blast, they shall come up to the mountain." So Moses went down from the mountain to the people, and consecrated the people; and they washed their garments. And he said to the people, "Be ready by the third day; do not go near a woman."

On the morning of the third day there were thunders and lightnings, and a thick cloud upon the mountain, and a very loud trumpet blast, so that all the people who were in the camp trembled. Then Moses brought the people out of the camp to meet God; and they took their stand at the foot of the mountain. And Mount Sinai was wrapped in smoke, because the Lord descended upon it in fire; and the smoke of it went up like the smoke of a kiln, and the whole mountain quaked

---

[16]The first part of this sentence identifies the Hebrews as God's chosen people or "own possession"—on the condition that they follow God's law. The second part emphasizes that their God is also the God of the whole universe and that they are "a holy nation" in the sense of being the consecrated carrier of God's word.

greatly. And as the sound of the trumpet grew louder and louder, Moses spoke, and God answered him in thunder. And the Lord came down upon Mount Sinai, to the top of the mountain; and the Lord called Moses to the top of the mountain, and Moses went up. And the Lord said to Moses, "Go down and warn the people, lest they break through to the Lord to gaze and many of them perish. And also let the priests who come near to the Lord consecrate themselves, lest the Lord break out upon them." And Moses said to the Lord, "The people cannot come up to Mount Sinai; for thou thyself didst charge us, saying, 'Set bounds about the mountain, and consecrate it.' " And the Lord said to him, "Go down, and come up bringing Aaron [Moses' brother] with you; but do not let the priests and the people break through to come up to the Lord, lest he break out against them." So Moses went down to the people and told them.

And God spoke all these words, saying,[17]

> "I am the Lord your God, who brought you out of the land of Egypt, out of the house of bondage.
> "You shall have no other gods before me.
> "You shall not make for yourself a graven image,[18] or any likeness of anything that is in heaven above, or that is in the earth beneath, or that is in the water under the earth; you shall not bow down to them or serve them; for I the Lord your God am a jealous God, visiting the iniquity of the fathers upon the children to the third and fourth generation of those who hate me, but showing steadfast love to thousands of those who love me and keep my commandments.
> "You shall not take the name of the Lord your God in vain; for the Lord will not hold him guiltless who takes his name in vain.
> "Remember the sabbath day, to keep it holy. Six days you shall labor, and do all your work; but the seventh day is a sabbath to the Lord your God; in it you shall not do any work, you, or your son, or your daughter, your manservant, or your maidservant, or your cattle, or the sojourner who is within your gates; for in six days the Lord made heaven and earth, the sea, and all that is in them, and rested the seventh day; therefore the Lord blessed the sabbath day and hallowed it.

[17]The following "Ten Commandments" state the essence of Jewish duties to God and to the rest of humanity. The Commandments are given as the basic requirements if the Hebrews are to enter into covenant with God and become his "holy nation."

[18]The second commandment, prohibiting worship of any "graven image" (carved statue), was unique in the ancient world.

"Honor your father and your mother, that your days may be long in the land which the Lord your God gives you.

"You shall not kill.[19]

"You shall not commit adultery.

"You shall not steal.

"You shall not bear false witness against your neighbor.

"You shall not covet your neighbor's house; you shall not covet your neighbor's wife, or his manservant, or his maidservant, or his ox, or his ass, or anything that is your neighbor's."

Now when all the people perceived the thunderings and the lightnings and the sound of the trumpet and the mountain smoking, the people were afraid and trembled; and they stood afar off, and said to Moses, "You speak to us, and we will hear; but let not God speak to us, lest we die." And Moses said to the people, "Do not fear; for God has come to prove you, and that the fear of him may be before your eyes, that you may not sin."

And the people stood afar off, while Moses drew near to the thick darkness where God was.

The Torah, or Law[20]
20:22–23:33

And the Lord said to Moses, "Thus you shall say to the people of Israel: 'You have seen for yourselves that I have talked with you from heaven. You shall not make gods of silver to be with me, nor shall you make yourselves gods of gold. An altar of earth you shall make for me and sacrifice on it your burnt offerings and your peace offerings, your sheep and your oxen; in every place where I cause my name to be remembered I will come to you and bless you. And if you make me an altar of stone, you shall not build it of hewn stones; for if you wield your tool upon it you profane it. And you shall not go up by steps to my altar, that your nakedness be not exposed on it.'

[19]The sixth commandment is sometimes translated, "You shall not commit murder." (Capital punishment for crimes, and war, are *not* absolutely forbidden in the Old Testament.)

[20]In addition to the basic principles established in the Ten Commandments, the Old Testament lists 603 other commandments. They regulate many details in the daily lives of the faithful. Some of these regulations can be seen in the following passage. Many are taken from neighboring societies, but reflect distinctive ethical and ritual practices of the Hebrews.

"Now these are the ordinances which you shall set before them. When you buy a Hebrew slave, he shall serve six years, and in the seventh he shall go out free, for nothing. If he comes in single, he shall go out single; if he comes in married, then his wife shall go out with him. If his master gives him a wife and she bears him sons or daughters, the wife and her children shall be her master's and he shall go out alone. But if the slave plainly says, 'I love my master, my wife, and my children; I will not go out free,' then his master shall bring him to God, and he shall bring him to the door or the doorpost; and his master shall bore his ear through with an awl; and he shall serve him for life.

"When a man sells his daughter as a slave, she shall not go out as the male slaves do. If she does not please her master, who has designated her for himself, then he shall let her be redeemed; he shall have no right to sell her to a foreign people, since he has dealt faithlessly with her. If he designates her for his son, he shall deal with her as with a daughter. If he takes another wife to himself, he shall not diminish her food, her clothing, or her marital rights. And if he does not do these three things for her, she shall go out for nothing, without payment of money.

"Whoever strikes a man so that he dies shall be put to death. But if he did not lie in wait for him, but God let him fall into his hand, then I will appoint for you a place to which he may flee. But if a man willfully attacks another to kill him treacherously, you shall take him from my altar, that he may die.

"Whoever strikes his father or his mother shall be put to death.

"Whoever steals a man, whether he sells him or is found in possession of him, shall be put to death.

"Whoever curses his father or his mother shall be put to death.

"When men quarrel and one strikes the other with a stone or with his fist and the man does not die but keeps his bed, then if the man rises again and walks abroad with his staff, he that struck him shall be clear; only he shall pay for the loss of his time, and shall have him thoroughly healed.

"When a man strikes his slave, male or female, with a rod and the slave dies under his hand, he shall be punished. But if the slave survives a day or two, he is not to be punished; for the slave is his money.

"When men strive together, and hurt a woman with child, so that there is a miscarriage, and yet no harm follows, the one who hurt her shall be fined, according as the woman's husband shall lay upon him; and he shall pay as the judges determine. If any harm follows, then you shall give life for life, eye for eye, tooth for tooth, hand for hand, foot for foot, burn for burn, wound for wound, stripe for stripe.

"When a man strikes the eye of his slave, male or female, and destroys it, he shall let the slave go free for the eye's sake. If he knocks out the tooth of his slave, male or female, he shall let the slave go free for the tooth's sake.

"When an ox gores a man or woman to death, the ox shall be stoned, and its flesh shall not be eaten; but the owner of the ox shall be clear. But if the ox has been acustomed to gore in the past, and its owner has been warned but has not kept it in, and it kills a man or a woman, the ox shall be stoned, and its owner also shall be put to death. If a ransom is laid on him, then he shall give for the redemption of his life whatever is laid upon him. If it gores a man's son or daughter, he shall be dealt with according to the same rule. If the ox gores a slave, male or female, the owner shall give to their master thirty shekels of silver, and the ox shall be stoned.

"When a man leaves a pit open, or when a man digs a pit and does not cover it, and an ox or an ass falls into it, the owner of the pit shall make it good; he shall give money to its owner, and the dead beast shall be his.

"When one man's ox hurts another's, so that it dies, then they shall sell the live ox and divide the price of it; and the dead beast also they shall divide. Or if it is known that the ox has been accustomed to gore in the past, and its owner has not kept it in, he shall pay ox for ox, and the dead beast shall be his.

"If a man steals an ox or a sheep, and kills it or sells it, he shall pay five oxen for an ox, and four sheep for a sheep. He shall make restitution; if he has nothing, then he shall be sold for his theft. If the stolen beast is found alive in his possession, whether it is an ox or an ass or a sheep, he shall pay double.

"If a thief is found breaking in, and is struck so that he dies, there shall be no bloodguilt for him; but if the sun has risen upon him, there shall be bloodguilt for him.

"When a man causes a field or vineyard to be grazed over, or lets his beast loose and it feeds in another man's field, he shall make restitution from the best in his own field and in his own vineyard.

"When fire breaks out and catches in thorns so that the stacked grain or the standing grain or the field is consumed, he that kindled the fire shall make full restitution.

"If a man delivers to his neighbor money or goods to keep, and it is stolen out of the man's house, then, if the thief is found, he shall pay double. If the thief is not found, the owner of the house shall come near to God, to show whether or not he has put his hand to his neighbor's goods.

"For every breach of trust, whether it is for ox, for ass, for sheep, for clothing, or for any kind of lost thing, of which one says, 'This is it,' the case of both parties shall come before God; he whom God shall condemn shall pay double to his neighbor.

"If a man delivers to his neighbor an ass or an ox or a sheep or any beast to keep, and it dies or is hurt or is driven away, without any one seeing it, an oath by the Lord shall be between them both to see whether he has not put his hand to his neighbor's property; and the owner shall accept the oath, and he shall not make restitution. But if it is stolen from him, he shall make restitution to its owner. If it is torn by beasts, let him bring it as evidence; he shall not make restitution for what has been torn.

"If a man borrows anything of his neighbor, and it is hurt or dies, the owner not being with it, he shall make full restitution. If the owner was with it, he shall not make restitution; if it was hired, it came for its hire.

"If a man seduces a virgin who is not bethrothed, and lies with her, he shall give the marriage present for her, and make her his wife. If her father utterly refuses to give her to him, he shall pay money equivalent to the marriage present for virgins.

"You shall not permit a sorceress to live.

"Whoever lies with a beast shall be put to death.

"Whoever sacrifices to any god, save to the Lord only, shall be utterly destroyed.

"You shall not wrong a stranger or oppress him, for you were strangers in the land of Egypt. You shall not afflict any widow or orphan. If you do afflict them, and they cry out to me, I will surely hear their cry; and my wrath will burn, and I will kill you with the sword, and your wives shall become widows and your children fatherless.

"If you lend money to any of my people with you who is poor, you shall not be to him as a creditor, and you shall not exact interest from him. If ever you take your neighbor's garment in pledge, you shall restore it to him before the sun goes down; for that is his only covering, it is his mantle for his body; in what else shall he sleep? And if he cries to me, I will hear, for I am compassionate.

"You shall not revile God, nor curse a ruler of your people.

"You shall not delay to offer from the fulness of your harvest and from the outflow of your presses.

"The first-born of your sons you shall give to me. You shall do likewise with your oxen and with your sheep: seven days it shall be with its dam; on the eighth day you shall give it to me.[21]

"You shall be men consecrated to me; therefore you shall not eat any flesh that is torn by beasts in the field; you shall cast it to the dogs.

"You shall not utter a false report. You shall not join hands with a wicked man, to be a malicious witness. You shall not follow a multitude to do evil; nor shall you bear witness in a suit, turning aside after a multitude, so as to pervert justice; nor shall you be partial to a poor man in his suit.

"If you meet your enemy's ox or his ass going astray, you shall bring it back to him. If you see the ass of one who hates you lying under its burden, you shall refrain from leaving him with it, you shall help him to lift it up.

"You shall not pervert the justice due to your poor in his suit. Keep far from a false charge, and do not slay the innocent and righteous, for I will not acquit the wicked. And you shall take no bribe, for a bribe blinds the officials, and subverts the cause of those who are in the right.

"You shall not oppress a stranger; you know the heart of a stranger, for you were strangers in the land of Egypt.

"For six years you shall sow your land and gather in its yield; but the seventh year you shall let it rest and lie fallow, that the poor of your people may eat; and what they leave the wild beasts may eat. You shall do likewise with your vineyard, and with your olive orchard.

"Six days you shall do your work, but on the seventh day you shall rest; that your ox and your ass may have rest, and the son of your bondmaid, and the alien, may be refreshed. Take heed to all that I have

---

[21]In many ancient cultures the first-born male offspring had a special value. Some religious groups, neighbors of the Hebrews, actually sacrificed their children, but that was never a part of the Jewish religion. This passage states that the first-born male oxen and sheep would be part of a sacrificial meal. The sons would be consecrated to God's service. Shortly afterwards, in the biblical narrative (in the book of Numbers), the Jewish tribe of Levites assumed the priestly duties in place of all the other Hebrew first-born males.

said to you; and make no mention of the names of other gods, nor let such be heard out of your mouth.

"Three times in the year you shall keep a feast to me. You shall keep the feast of unleavened bread; as I commanded you, you shall eat unleavened bread for seven days at the appointed time in the month of Abib, for in it you came out of Egypt. None shall appear before me empty-handed. You shall keep the feast of harvest, of the first fruits of your labor, of what you sow in the field. You shall keep the feast of ingathering at the end of the year, when you gather in from the field the fruit of your labor. Three times in the year shall all your males appear before the Lord God.

"You shall not offer the blood of my sacrifice with leavened bread, or let the fat of my feast remain until the morning.

"The first of the first fruits of your ground you shall bring into the house of the Lord your God.

"You shall not boil a kid in its mother's milk.

"Behold, I send an angel before you, to guard you on the way and to bring you to the place which I have prepared. Give heed to him and hearken to his voice, do not rebel against him, for he will not pardon your transgression; for my name is in him.

"But if you hearken attentively to his voice and do all that I say, then I will be an enemy to your enemies and an adversary to your adversaries.

"When my angel goes before you, and brings you in to the Amorites, and the Hittites, and the Per'izzites, and the Canaanites, the Hivites, and the Jeb'usites, and I blot them out, you shall not bow down to their gods, nor serve them, nor do according to their works, but you shall utterly overthrow them and break their pillars in pieces. You shall serve the Lord your God, and I will bless your bread and your water; and I will take sickness away from the midst of you. None shall cast her young or be barren in your land; I will fulfil the number of your days. I will send my terror before you, and will throw into confusion all the people against whom you shall come, and I will make all your enemies turn their backs to you. And I will send hornets before you, which shall drive out Hivite, Canaanite, and Hittite from before you. I will not drive them out from before you in one year, lest the land became desolate and the wild beasts multiply against you. Little by little I will drive them out from before you, until you are increased and possess the land. And I will set your bounds from the Red Sea to the sea of the Philistines, and from the wilderness to the Euphra'tes; for I will deliver the inhabitants of the land into your hand, and you shall drive them out before you. You shall make no covenant with them or with their gods. They shall not dwell in your land lest they make you sin against me; for if you serve their gods, it will surely be a snare to you."

AMOS[22]

The Prophecy
1:1–2; 2:4–3:8; 5:14–27; 7:10–8:10; 9:1–4, 8–15

The words of Amos, who was among the shepherds of Teko'a, which he saw concerning Israel in the days of Uzzi'ah king of Judah and in the days of Jerobo'am the son of Jo'ash, king of Israel, two years before the earthquake. And he said:

"The LORD roars from Zion,
    and utters his voice from Jerusalem;
the pastures of the shepherds mourn,
    and the top of [Mount] Carmel withers."

• • •

Thus says the LORD:
"For three transgressions of Judah,
    and for four, I will not revoke the punishment;
because they have rejected the law of the LORD,
    and have not kept his statutes,

---

[22]The earliest of the "writing" prophets after the Exodus from Egypt. The Hebrew nation had divided into the northern kingdom of Israel and the southern kingdom of Judah, which included Jerusalem. Amos was an eighth-century B.C. shepherd from Tekoa, in Judah, who first preached at a festival in the town of Bethel, in Israel. He blasted the luxurious living and corrupt morals of the rich, their exploitation of the poor, and religious observance based only on outward ritual. The local priest, Amaziah, then reported him to Jeroboam, king of Israel. Amos prophesied the destruction of that kingdom (which would fall to the Assyrians in 721 B.C.), but also stated that a remnant of the Jews would "rebuild the ruined cities and inhabit them." God judges all nations, Amos preached, but his special covenant with the Jews makes special moral demands upon them.

but their lies have led them astray,
    after which their fathers walked.
So I will send a fire upon Judah,
    and it shall devour the strongholds of Jerusalem."

Thus says the LORD:
"For three transgressions of Israel,
    and for four, I will not revoke the punishment;
because they sell the righteous for silver,
    and the needy for a pair of shoes—
they that trample the head of the poor into the dust of the earth,
    and turn aside the way of the afflicted;
a man and his father go in to the same maiden,
    so that my holy name is profaned;
they lay themselves down beside every altar
    upon garments taken in pledge;
and in the house of their God they drink
    the wine of those who have been fined.

"Yet I destroyed the Amorite[23] before them,
    whose height was like the height of the cedars,
    and who was as strong as the oaks;
I destroyed his fruit above,
    and his roots beneath.
Also I brought you up out of the land of Egypt,
    and led you forty years in the wilderness,
    to possess the land of the Amorite.
And I raised up some of your sons for prophets,
    and some of your young men for Nazirites.[24]
    Is it not indeed so, O people of Israel?"
                    says the LORD.

"But you made the Nazirites drink wine,
    and commanded the prophets,
    saying, 'You shall not prophesy.'

[23]Earlier inhabitants of the same land.

[24]A group of men who took ascetic religious vows. Among their prohibitions, they did not drink intoxicating beverages and did not cut their hair.

"Behold, I will press you down in your place,
   as a cart full of sheaves presses down.
Flight shall perish from the swift,
   and the strong shall not retain his strength,
   nor shall the mighty save his life;
he who handles the bow shall not stand,
   and he who is swift of foot shall not save himself,
   nor shall he who rides the horse save his life;
and he who is stout of heart among the mighty
   shall flee away naked in that day,"
                          says the LORD.

Hear this word that the LORD has spoken against you, O people of Israel, against the whole family which I brought up out of the land of Egypt:

"You only have I known
   of all the families of the earth
therefore I will punish you
   for all your iniquities.

"Do two walk together,
   unless they have made an appointment?
Does a lion roar in the forest,
   when he has no prey?
Does a young lion cry out from his den,
   if he has taken nothing?
Does a bird fall in a snare on the earth,
   when there is no trap for it?
Does a snare spring up from the ground,
   when it has taken nothing?
Is a trumpet blown in a city,
   and the people are not afraid?
Does evil befall a city,
   unless the LORD has done it?
Surely the Lord GOD does nothing,
   without revealing his secret
   to his servants the prophets.
The lion has roared;
   who will not fear?

The Lord GOD has spoken;
  who can but prophesy?"

. . .

Seek good, and not evil,
  that you may live;
and so the LORD, the God of hosts, will be with you,
  as you have said.
Hate evil, and love good,
  and establish justice in the gate;
it may be that the LORD, the God of hosts,
  will be gracious to the remnant of Joseph. [25]

Therefore thus says the LORD, the God of hosts, the Lord:
"In all the squares there shall be wailing;
  and in all the streets they shall say, 'Alas! alas!'
They shall call the farmers to mourning
  and to wailing those who are skilled in lamentation,
and in all vineyards there shall be wailing,
  for I will pass through the midst of you,"
                                   says the LORD.

Woe to you who desire the day of the LORD!
  Why would you have the day of the LORD?
It is darkness, and not light;
  as if a man fled from a lion,
  and a bear met him;
or went into the house and leaned with his hand against the wall,
  and a serpent bit him.
Is not the day of the LORD darkness, and not light,
  and gloom with no brightness in it?

"I hate, I despise your feasts,
  and I take no delight in your solemn assemblies.
Even though you offer me your burnt offerings and cereal offerings,
  I will not accept them,

[25]Jacob's son, who had begun the Hebrew sojourn in Egypt.

and the peace offerings of your fatted beasts
    I will not look upon.
Take away from me the noise of your songs;
    to the melody of your harps I will not listen.
But let justice roll down like waters,
    and righteousness like an ever-flowing stream.

"Did you bring to me sacrifices and offerings the forty years in the wilderness, O house of Israel? You shall take up Sakkuth your king, and Kaiwan[26] your star-god, your images, which you made for yourselves; therefore I will take you into exile beyond Damascus," says the LORD, whose name is the God of hosts.

• • •

Then Amazi'ah the priest of Beth'el sent to Jerobo'am king of Israel, saying, "Amos has conspired against you in the midst of the house of Israel; the land is not able to bear all his words. For thus Amos has said,

> 'Jerobo'am shall die by the sword,
>   and Israel must go into exile
>   away from his land.'"

And Amazi'ah said to Amos, "O seer, go, flee away to the land of Judah, and eat bread there, and prophesy there; but never again prophesy at Beth'el, for it is the king's sanctuary, and it is a temple of the kingdom."

Then Amos answered Amazi'ah, "I am no prophet, nor a prophet's son; but I am a herdsman, and a dresser of sycamore trees, and the LORD took me from following the flock, and the LORD said to me, 'Go, prophesy to my people Israel.'

"Now therefore hear the word of
    the LORD.
You say, 'Do not prophesy against
    Israel,
and do not preach against the
    house of Isaac.'

[26]Sakkuth and Kaiwan were Assyrian gods, worshipped in the form of carved images.

Therefore thus says the LORD:
'Your wife shall be a harlot in the
    city,
and your sons and your daughters
    shall fall by the sword,
and your land shall be parceled
    out by line;
you yourself shall die in an unclean
    land,
and Israel shall surely go into
    exile away from its land.' "

Thus the Lord GOD showed me: behold, a basket of summer fruit.
And he said, "Amos, what do you see?" And I said, "A basket of
summer fruit." Then the LORD said to me,

"The end has come upon my people Israel;
I will never again pass by them.
The songs of the temple shall become wailings in that day,"
says the Lord GOD;

"the dead bodies shall be many;
    in every place they shall be cast out in silence."

Hear this, you who trample upon the needy,
    and bring the poor of the land to an end,
saying, "When will the new moon be over,
    that we may sell grain?
And the sabbath,
    that we may offer wheat for sale,
that we may make the ephah small and the shekel great,
    and deal deceitfully with false balances,
that we may buy the poor for silver
    and the needy for a pair of sandals,
    and sell the refuse of the wheat?"

The Lord has sworn by the pride of Jacob:
    "Surely I will never forget any of their deeds.
Shall not the land tremble on this account,
    and every one mourn who dwells in it,
and all of it rise like the Nile,
    and be tossed about and sink again, like the Nile of Egypt?"

"And on that day," says the Lord GOD,
   "I will make the sun go down at noon,
   and darken the earth in broad daylight.
I will turn your feasts into mourning,
   and all your songs into lamentation;
I will bring sackcloth upon all loins
   and baldness on every head;
I will make it like the mourning for an only son,
   and the end of it like a bitter day."

● ● ●

   I saw the LORD standing beside the altar, and he said:
"Smite the capitals until the thresholds shake,
   and shatter them on the heads of all the people;
and what are left of them I will slay with the sword;
   not one of them shall flee away,
   not one of them shall escape.

"Though they dig into She'ol,[27]
   from there shall my hand take them;
though they climb up to heaven,
   from there I will bring them down.
Though they hide themselves on the top of Car'mel,
   from there I will search out and take them;
and though they hide from my sight at the bottom of the sea,
   there I will command the serpent, and it shall bite them.
And though they go into captivity before their enemies,
   there I will command the sword, and it shall slay them;
  and I will set my eyes upon them for evil and not for good.". . .

"Behold, the eyes of the Lord GOD are upon the sinful kingdom,
   and I will destroy it from the surface of the ground;
except that I will not utterly destroy the house of Jacob,"
               says the LORD.

"For lo, I will command,
   and shake the house of Israel among all the nations

---

[27]The underground place of the dead, similar to the Greek idea of Hades.

as one shakes with a sieve,
　　but no pebble shall fall upon the earth.
All the sinners of my people shall die by the sword,
　　who say, 'Evil shall not overtake or meet us.'

"In that day I will raise up
　　the booth of [King]David that is fallen
and repair its breaches,
　　and raise up its ruins,
　　and rebuild it as in the days of old;
that they may possess the remnant of E'dom
　　and all the nations who are called by my name,"
　　says the LORD who does this.

"Behold, the days are coming," says the LORD,
　　"when the plowman shall overtake the reaper
　　and the treader of grapes him who sows the seed;
the mountains shall drip sweet wine,
　　and all the hills shall flow with it.
I will restore the fortunes of my people Israel,
　　and they shall rebuild the ruined cities and inhabit them;
they shall plant vineyards and drink their wine,
　　and they shall make gardens and eat their fruit.
I will plant them upon their land,
　　and they shall never again be plucked up
　　out of the land which I have given them,"
　　　　　　　　says the LORD your God.

ISAIAH[28]

The Prophecy
45:8–25; 52:13–53:12

"Shower, O heavens, from above,
　　and let the skies rain down righteousness;

[28]The following passages from the latter part of the book of Isaiah were written by a famous prophet toward the end of the "Babylonian Exile." (After the fall of the southern kingdom of Judah, many Jews had been taken into captivity in Babylon, 586 B.C.) With the approach of a mighty Persian army, which will defeat the forces of Babylon (539 B.C.), the prophet joyfully anticipates the return to his homeland (Judah). The liberating Persians are viewed as a part of the universal God's historical plan.

let the earth open, that salvation may sprout forth,
    and let it cause righteousness to spring up also;
    I the Lord have created it.

"Woe to him who strives with his Maker,
    an earthen vessel with the potter!"
Does the clay say to him who fashions it, 'What are you making?'
    or 'Your work has no handles'?
Woe to him who says to a father, 'What are you begetting?'
    or to a woman, 'With what are you in travail?' "
Thus says the LORD,
    the Holy One of Israel, and his Maker:
"Will you question me about my children,
    or command me concerning the work of my hands?
I made the earth,
    and created man upon it;
it was my hands that stretched out the heavens,
    and I commanded all their host.
I have aroused him in righteousness,
    and I will make straight all his ways;
he shall build my city
    and set my exiles free,
not for price or reward,"
    says the LORD of hosts.

Thus says the LORD:
"The wealth of Egypt and the merchandise of Ethiopia,
    and the Sabe'ans, men of stature,
shall come over to you and be yours,
    they shall follow you;
    they shall come over in chains and bow down to you.
They will make supplication to you, saying:
    'God is with you only, and there is no other,
    no god besides him.' "
Truly, thou art a God who hidest thyself,
    O God of Israel; the Savior.
All of them are put to shame and confounded,
    the makers of idols go in confusion together.
But Israel is saved by the LORD
    with everlasting salvation;

you shall not be put to shame or confounded
    to all eternity.

For thus says the LORD,
who created the heavens
    (he is God!),
who formed the earth and made it
    (he established it;
he did not create it a chaos,
    he formed it to be inhabited!):
"I am the LORD, and there is no other.
I did not speak in secret,
    in a land of darkness;
I did not say to the offspring of Jacob,
    'Seek me in chaos.'
I the LORD speak the truth,
    I declare what is right.

"Assemble yourselves and come,
    draw near together,
    you survivors of the nations!
They have no knowledge
    who carry about their wooden idols,
and keep on praying to a god
    that cannot save.
Declare and present your case;
    let them take counsel together!
Who told this long ago?
    Who declared it of old?
Was it not I, the LORD?
    And there is no other god besides me,
a righteous God and a Savior;
    there is none besides me.

"Turn to me and be saved,
    all the ends of the earth!
    For I am God, and there is no other.
By myself I have sworn,
    from my mouth has gone forth in righteousness
    a word that shall not return:

'To me every knee shall bow,
        every tongue shall swear.'

"Only in the LORD, it shall be said of me,
        are righteousness and strength;
to him shall come and be ashamed,
        all who were incensed against him.
In the LORD all the offspring of Israel
        shall triumph and glory."

• • •

Behold, my servant shall prosper,
        he shall be exalted and lifted up,
        and shall be very high.[29]
As many were astonished at him—
        his appearance was so marred, beyond human semblance,
        and his form beyond that of the sons of men—
so shall he startle many nations;
        kings shall shut their mouths because of him;
for that which has not been told them they shall see,
        and that which they have not heard they shall understand.

Who has believed what we have heard?
        And to whom has the arm of the LORD been revealed?
For he grew up before him like a young plant,
        and like a root out of dry ground;
he had no form or comeliness that we should look at him,
        and no beauty that we should desire him.
He was despised and rejected by men;
        a man of sorrows, and acquainted with grief;
and as one from whom men hide their faces
        he was despised, and we esteemed him not.

Surely he has borne our griefs
        and carried our sorrows;

---

[29]This passage, often called the Song of the Suffering Servant, describes the Jewish people, collectively, as God's "servant"—a humiliated individual who endures his bruises without complaint. But now the Jews, who have suffered for all mankind, will be restored to their rightful place as God's chosen nation. (Christians would later interpret this passage as a prophecy of the coming and sacrifice of Jesus Christ.)

yet we esteemed him stricken,
  smitten by God, and afflicted.
But he was wounded for our transgressions,
  he was bruised for our iniquities;
upon him was the chastisement that made us whole,
  and with his stripes we are healed.
All we like sheep have gone astray;
  we have turned every one to his own way;
and the Lord has laid on him
  the iniquity of us all.

He was oppressed, and he was afflicted,
  yet he opened not his mouth;
like a lamb that is led to the slaughter,
  and like a sheep that before its shearers is dumb,
  so he opened not his mouth.
By oppression and judgment he was taken away;
  and as for his generation, who considered
that he was cut off out of the land of the living,
  stricken for the transgression of my people?
And they made his grave with the wicked
  and with a rich man in his death,
although he had done no violence,
  and there was no deceit in his mouth.

Yet it was the will of the LORD to bruise him;
  he has put him to grief;
when he makes himself an offering for sin,
  he shall see his offspring, he shall prolong his days;
the will of the LORD shall prosper in his hand;
  he shall see the fruit of the travail of his soul and be satisfied;
by his knowledge shall the righteous one, my servant,
  make many to be accounted righteous;
  and he shall bear their iniquities.
Therefore I will divide him a portion with the great,
  and he shall divide the spoil with the strong;
because he poured out his soul to death,
  and was numbered with the transgressors;
yet he bore the sin of many,
  and made intercession for the transgressors.

JOB[30]

Prologue
1:1—2:13

There was a man in the land of Uz, whose name was Job; and that man was blameless and upright, one who feared God, and turned away from evil. There were born to him seven sons and three daughters. He had seven thousand sheep, three thousand camels, five hundred yoke of oxen, and five hundred she-asses, and very many servants; so that this man was the greatest of all the people of the east. His sons used to go and hold a feast in the house of each on his day; and they would send and invite their three sisters to eat and drink with them. And when the days of the feast had run their course, Job would send and sanctify them, and he would rise early in the morning and offer burnt offerings according to the number of them all; for Job said, "It may be that my sons have sinned, and cursed God in their hearts." Thus Job did continually.

Now there was a day when the sons of God[31] came to present themselves before the LORD, and Satan[32] also came among them. The LORD said to Satan, "Whence have you come?" Satan answered the LORD, "From going to and fro on the earth, and from walking up and down on it." And the LORD said to Satan, "Have you considered my servant Job, that there is none like him on the earth, a blameless and upright man, who fears God and turns away from evil?" Then Satan answered the LORD, "Does Job fear God for nought? Hast thou not put a hedge about him and his house and all that he has, on every side? Thou hast blessed the work of his hands, and his possessions have

---

[30]The date and author of this work are unknown. Portions of it were passed on as an ancient folktale, but the story of Job may not have achieved its present form in Hebrew until about 400 B.C. The book's central religious concern is the defense of God's justice in a world where good people sometimes suffer terribly. There is literary irony in that readers of the story know what the tormented central character does *not* know: God is using Job as a demonstration of human faith to Satan, presented here as God's agent.

[31]Divine beings, like angels, members of the heavenly court. The author here uses a description resembling the court of an ancient monarch; nevertheless, God is single and undivided.

[32]In Hebrew, "the adversary." In the book of Job, Satan is man's adversary—not God's. He is presented as coming *among* "the sons of God," but not as being one of them. Satan here serves as God's investigator and the tester of humans. In later centuries, in both Judaism and Christianity, Satan would become the demonic personification of evil.

increased in the land. But put forth thy hand now, and touch all that he has, and he will curse thee to thy face." And the LORD said to Satan, "Behold, all that he has is in your power; only upon himself do not put forth your hand." So Satan went forth from the presence of the LORD.

Now there was a day when his sons and daughters were eating and drinking wine in their eldest brother's house; and there came a messenger to Job, and said, "The oxen were plowing and the asses feeding beside them; and the Sabe'ans fell upon them and took them, and slew the servants with the edge of the sword; and I alone have escaped to tell you." While he was yet speaking, there came another, and said, "The fire of God fell from heaven and burned up the sheep and the servants, and consumed them; and I alone have escaped to tell you." While he was yet speaking, there came another, and said, "The Chalde'ans formed three companies, and made a raid upon the camels and took them, and slew the servants with the edge of the sword; and I alone have escaped to tell you." While he was yet speaking, there came another, and said, "Your sons and daughters were eating and drinking wine in their eldest brother's house; and behold, a great wind came across the wilderness, and struck the four corners of the house, and it fell upon the young people, and they are dead; and I alone have escaped to tell you."

Then Job arose, and rent his robe, and shaved his head, and fell upon the ground, and worshiped. And he said, "Naked I came from my mother's womb, and naked shall I return; the LORD gave, and the LORD has taken away; blessed be the name of the LORD."

In all this Job did not sin or charge God with wrong.

Again there was a day when the sons of God came to present themselves before the LORD, and Satan also came among them to present himself before the LORD. And the LORD said to Satan, "Whence have you come?" Satan answered the LORD, "From going to and fro on the earth, and from walking up and down on it." And the LORD said to Satan, "Have you considered my servant Job, that there is none like him on the earth, a blameless and upright man, who fears God and turns away from evil? He still holds fast his integrity, although you moved me against him, to destroy him without cause." Then Satan answered the LORD, "Skin for skin! All that a man has he will give for his life. But put forth thy hand now, and touch his bone and flesh, and he will curse thee to thy face." And the LORD said to Satan, "Behold, he is in your power; only spare his life."

So Satan went forth from the presence of the LORD, and afflicted Job with loathsome sores from the sole of his foot to the crown of his head. And he took a potsherd with which to scrape himself, and sat among the ashes.

Then his wife said to him, "Do you still hold fast your integrity? Curse God, and die." But he said to her, "You speak as one of the foolish women would speak. Shall we receive good at the hand of God, and shall we not receive evil?" In all this Job did not sin with his lips.

Now when Job's three friends heard of all this evil that had come upon him, they came each from his own place, Eli'phaz the Te'manite, Bil'dad the Shu'hite, and Zo'phar the Na'amathite. They made an appointment together to come to condole with him and comfort him. And when they saw him from afar, they did not recognize him; and they raised their voices and wept; and they rent their robes and sprinkled dust upon their heads toward heaven. And they sat with him on the ground seven days and seven nights, and no one spoke a word to him, for they saw that his suffering was very great.

Job's Complaint to God
3:1–7, 11–13, 20–26

After this Job opened his mouth and cursed the day of his birth.
And Job said:
"Let the day perish wherein I was born,
    and the night which said,
    'A man-child is conceived.'
Let that day be darkness!
    May God above not seek it,
    nor light shine upon it.
Let gloom and deep darkness claim it.
    Let clouds dwell upon it;
    let the blackness of the day terrify it.
That night—let thick darkness seize it!
    let it not rejoice among the days of the year,
    let it not come into the number of the months.
Yea, let that night be barren;
    let no joyful cry be heard in it. . . .

"Why did I not die at birth,
    come forth from the womb and expire?

Why did the knees receive me?
    Or why the breasts, that I should suck?
For then I should have lain down and been quiet
    I should have slept; then I should have been at rest. . . .

"Why is light given to him that is in misery,
    and life to the bitter in soul,
who long for death, but it comes not,
    and dig for it more than for hid treasures;
who rejoice exceedingly,
    and are glad, when they find the grave?
Why is light given to a man whose way is hid,
    whom God has hedged in?
For my sighing comes as my bread,
    and my groanings are poured out like water.
For the thing that I fear comes upon me,
    and what I dread befalls me.
I am not at ease, nor am I quiet;
    I have no rest; but trouble comes."

*The Speeches of Job's Friends and his Answers
Excerpted from 4:1–13:24*

Then Eli'phaz the Te'manite answered:
"If one ventures a word with you, will you be offended?
    Yet who can keep from speaking?
Behold, you have instructed many,
    and you have strengthened the weak hands.
Your words have upheld him who was stumbling,
    and you have made firm the feeble knees.
But now it has come to you, and you are impatient;
    it touches you, and you are dismayed.
Is not your fear of God your confidence,
    and the integrity of your ways your hope?

"Think now, who that was innocent ever perished?
    Or where were the upright cut off?
As I have seen, those who plow iniquity
    and sow trouble reap the same.

By the breath of God they perish,
    and by the blast of his anger they are consumed.
The roar of the lion, the voice of the fierce lion,
    the teeth of the young lions, are broken.
The strong lion perishes for lack of prey,
    and the whelps of the lioness are scattered.

"Now a word was brought to me stealthily,
    my ear received the whisper of it.
Amid thoughts from visions of the night,
    when deep sleep falls on men,
dread came upon me, and trembling,
    which made all my bones shake.
A spirit glided past my face;
    the hair of my flesh stood up.
It stood still,
    but I could not discern its appearance.
A form was before my eyes;
    there was silence, then I heard a voice:
'Can mortal man be righteous before God?
    Can a man be pure before his Maker?
Even in his servants he puts no trust,
    and his angels he charges with error;
how much more those who dwell in houses of clay,
    whose foundation is in the dust,
    who are crushed before the moth.
Between morning and evening they are destroyed;
    they perish for ever without any regarding it. . . .

"Call now; is there any one who will answer you?
    To which of the holy ones will you turn?
Surely vexation kills the fool,
    and jealousy slays the simple. . . .
For affliction does not come from the dust,
    nor does trouble sprout from the ground;
but man is born to trouble
    as the sparks fly upward.

"As for me, I would seek God,
    and to God would I commit my cause;

who does great things and unsearchable,
    marvelous things without number:
he gives rain upon the earth
    and sends waters upon the fields;
he sets on high those who are lowly,
    and those who mourn are lifted to safety.
He frustrates the devices of the crafty,
    so that their hands achieve no success.
He takes the wise in their own craftiness;
    and the schemes of the wily are brought to a quick end. . . .

"Behold, happy is the man whom God reproves;
    therefore despise not the chastening of the Almighty.
For he wounds, but he binds up;
    he smites, but his hands heal.
He will deliver you from six troubles;
    in seven there shall no evil touch you.
In famine he will redeem you from death,
    and in war from the power of the sword.
You shall be hid from the scourge of the tongue,
    and shall not fear destruction when it comes.
At destruction and famine you shall laugh,
    and shall not fear the beasts of the earth.
For you shall be in league with the stones of the field,
    and the beasts of the field shall be at peace with you.
You shall know that your tent is safe,
    and you shall inspect your fold and miss nothing.
You shall know also that your descendants shall be many,
    and your offspring as the grass of the earth.
You shall come to your grave in ripe old age,
    as a shock of grain comes up to the threshing floor in its season.
Lo, this we have searched out; it is true.
    Hear, and know it for your good."

    Then Job answered:
"O that my vexation were weighed,
    and all my calamity laid in the balances!
For then it would be heavier than the sand of the sea;
    therefore my words have been rash.

For the arrows of the Almighty are in me;
    my spirit drinks their poison;
    the terrors of God are arrayed against me. . . .

"O that I might have my request,
    and that God would grant my desire;
that it would please God to crush me,
    that he would let loose his hand and cut me off!
This would be my consolation;
    I would even exult in pain unsparing;
    for I have not denied the words of the Holy One.
What is my strength, that I should wait?
    And what is my end, that I should be patient?
Is my strength the strength of stones,
    or is my flesh bronze?
In truth I have no help in me,
    and any resource is driven from me.

"He who withholds kindness from a friend
    forsakes the fear of the Almighty.
My brethren are treacherous as a torrent-bed,
    as freshets that pass away,
which are dark with ice,
    and where the snow hides itself.
In time of heat they disappear;
    when it is hot, they vanish from their place.
The caravans turn aside from their course;
    they go up into the waste, and perish.
The caravans of Te'ma look,
    the travelers of Sheba hope.
They are disappointed because they were confident;
    they come thither and are confounded.
Such you have now become to me;
    you see my calamity, and are afraid.
Have I said, 'Make me a gift'?
    Or, 'From your wealth offer a bribe for me'?
Or, 'Deliver me from the adversary's hand'?
    Or, 'Ransom me from the hand of oppressors'?

"Teach me, and I will be silent;
    make me understand how I have erred.
How forceful are honest words!
    But what does reproof from you reprove?
Do you think that you can reprove words,
    when the speech of a despairing man is wind?
You would even cast lots over the fatherless,
    and bargain over your friend.

"But now, be pleased to look at me;
    for I will not lie to your face.
Turn, I pray, let no wrong be done.
    Turn now, my vindication is at stake.
Is there any wrong on my tongue?
    Cannot my taste discern calamity?

"Has not man a hard service upon earth,
    and are not his days like the days of a hireling?
Like a slave who longs for the shadow,
    and like a hireling who looks for his wages,
so I am alloted months of emptiness,
    and nights of misery are apportioned to me.
When I lie down I say, 'When shall I arise?'
    But the night is long,
    and I am full of tossing till the dawn.
My flesh is clothed with worms and dirt;
    my skin hardens, then breaks out afresh.
My days are swifter than a weaver's shuttle,
    and come to their end without hope. . . .

"Therefore I will not restrain my mouth;
    I will speak in the anguish of my spirit;
    I will complain in the bitterness of my soul. . . .
I loathe my life; I would not live for ever.
    Let me alone, for my days are a breath.
What is man, that thou dost make so much of him,
    and that thou dost set thy mind upon him,
dost visit him every morning,
    and test him every moment?
How long wilt thou not look away from me,

nor let me alone till I swallow my spittle?
If I sin, what do I do to thee, thou watcher of men?
　　Why hast thou made me thy mark?
　　Why have I become a burden to thee?
Why dost thou not pardon my transgression
　　and take away my iniquity?
For now I shall lie in the earth;
　　thou wilt seek me, but I shall not be."

　　Then Bil'dad the Shu'hite answered:
"How long will you say these things,
　　and the words of your mouth be a great wind?
Does God pervert justice?
　　Or does the Almighty pervert the right?
If your children have sinned against him,
　　he has delivered them into the power of their transgression.
If you will seek God
　　and make supplication to the Almighty,
if you are pure and upright,
　　surely then he will rouse himself for you
　　and reward you with a rightful habitation.
And though your beginning was small,
　　your latter days will be very great.

"For inquire, I pray you, of bygone ages,
　　and consider what the fathers have found;
for we are but of yesterday, and know nothing,
　　for our days on earth are a shadow.
Will they not teach you, and tell you,
　　and utter words out of their understanding? . . .

"Behold, God will not reject a blameless man,
　　nor take the hand of evildoers.
He will yet fill your mouth with laughter,
　　and your lips with shouting.
Those who hate you will be clothed with shame,
　　and the tent of the wicked will be no more."

　　Then Job answered:
"Truly I know that it is so:

But how can a man be just before God?
If one wished to contend with him,
    one could not answer him once in a thousand times. . . .

"I will say to God, Do not condemn me;
    let me know why thou dost contend against me.
Does it seem good to thee to oppress,
    to despise the work of thy hands
    and favor the designs of the wicked?
Hast thou eyes of flesh?
    Dost thou see as man sees?
Are thy days as the days of man,
    or thy years as man's years,
that thou dost seek out my iniquity
    and search for my sin,
although thou knowest that I am not guilty,
    and there is none to deliver out of thy hand?
Thy hands fashioned and made me;
    and now thou dost turn about and destroy me.
Remember that thou hast made me of clay;
    and wilt thou turn me to dust again?

•   •   •

Then Zo'phar the Na'amathite answered;
"Should a multitude of words go unanswered,
    and a man full of talk be vindicated?
Should your babble silence men,
    and when you mock, shall no one shame you?
For you say, 'My doctrine is pure,
    and I am clean in God's eyes.'
But oh, that God would speak,
    and open his lips to you,
and that he would tell you the secrets of wisdom!
    For he is manifold in understanding.
Know then that God exacts of you less than your guilt deserves."

•   •   •

Then Job answered:
"No doubt you are the people,
    and wisdom will die with you.

But I have understanding as well as you;
   I am not inferior to you.
   Who does not know such things as these?
I am a laughingstock to my friends;
   I, who called upon God and he answered me,
   a just and blameless man, am a laughingstock.
In the thought of one who is at ease there is contempt for misfortune;
   it is ready for those whose feet slip. . . .

"Lo, my eye has seen all this,
   my ear has heard and understood it.
"What you know, I also know;
   I am not inferior to you.
But I would speak to the Almighty,
   and I desire to argue my case with God.
As for you, you whitewash with lies;
   worthless physicians are you all.
Oh that you would keep silent,
   and it would be your wisdom!
Hear now my reasoning,
   and listen to the pleadings of my lips.
Will you speak falsely for God,
   and speak deceitfully for him?
Will you show partiality toward him,
   will you plead the case for God?
Will it be well with you when he searches you out?
   Or can you deceive him, as one deceives a man?
He will surely rebuke you
   if in secret you show partiality.
Will not his majesty terrify you,
   and the dread of him fall upon you?
Your maxims are proverbs of ashes,
   your defenses are defenses of clay.

"Let me have silence, and I will speak,
   and let come on me what may. . . .
Behold, he will slay me; I have no hope;
   yet I will defend my ways to his face.
This will be my salvation,
   that a godless man shall not come before him.
Listen carefully to my words,
   and let my declaration be in your ears.

Behold, I have prepared my case;
   I know that I shall be vindicated.
Who is there that will contend with me?
   For then I would be silent and die.
Only grant two things to me,
   then I will not hide myself from thy face:[33]
withdraw thy hand far from me,
   and let not dread of thee terrify me.
Then call, and I will answer;
   or let me speak, and do thou reply to me.
How many are my iniquities and my sins?
   Make me know my transgression and my sin.
Why dost thou hide thy face,
   and count me as thy enemy?

• • •

[Editor's note: Each of Job's friends has assumed that Job is being punished for
his sins. Their explanations of his torments are in keeping with conventional
Jewish beliefs of the time: since Job is suffering, he *must* have sinned. Their
limited minds can imagine no other cause. After all, they state, if Job had really
been "blameless and upright," he would have remained prosperous. All Job
has to do is admit his guilt and ask God for pardon; or else, according to his
wife, "Curse God, and die." Job, however, has retained his intellectual honesty
and the conviction of his own righteousness. ("I will defend my ways to his
face.") He still believes in a just God and—after listing his own righteous acts
and recent misery—awaits God's explanation.]

God's Answer and Job's Submission
Excerpted from 38:1–42:6

Then the LORD answered Job out of the whirlwind:
"Who is this that darkens counsel by words without knowledge?
Gird up your loins like a man,
   I will question you, and you shall declare to me.

"Where were you when I laid the foundation of the earth?
   Tell me, if you have understanding.

---

[33]Job is now speaking directly to God.

Who determined its measurements—surely you know!
    Or who stretched the line upon it?
On what were its bases sunk,
    or who laid its cornerstone,
when the morning stars sang together,
    and all the sons of God shouted for joy?

"Or who shut in the sea with doors,
    when it burst forth from the womb;
when I made clouds its garment,
    and thick darkness its swaddling band,
and prescribed bounds for it,
    and set bars and doors,
and said, 'Thus far shall you come, and no farther,
    and here shall your proud waves be stayed'?

"Have you commanded the morning since your days began,
    and caused the dawn to know its place,
that it might take hold of the skirts of the earth,
    and the wicked be shaken out of it?
It is changed like clay under the seal,
    and it is dyed like a garment.
From the wicked their light is withheld,
    and their uplifted arm is broken.

"Have you entered into the springs of the sea,
    or walked in the recesses of the deep?
Have the gates of death been revealed to you,
    or have you seen the gates of deep darkness?
Have you comprehended the expanse of the earth?
    Declare, if you know all this. . . .

"Who has cleft a channel for the torrents of rain,
    and a way for the thunderbolt,
to bring rain on a land where no man is,
    on the desert in which there is no man;
to satisfy the waste and desolate land,
    and to make the ground put forth grass?

"Has the rain a father,
    or who has begotten the drops of dew?

From whose womb did the ice come forth,
    and who has given birth to the hoarfrost of heaven?
The waters become hard like stone,
    and the face of the deep is frozen.

"Can you bind the chains of the Plei′ades,
    or loose the cords of Ori′on?
Can you lead forth the Maz′zaroth in their season,
    or can you guide the Bear with its children?[34]
Do you know the ordinances of the heavens?
    Can you establish their rule on the earth? . . .

"Can you hunt the prey for the lion,
    or satisfy the appetite of the young lions,
when they crouch in their dens,
    or lie in wait in their covert?
Who provides for the raven its prey,
    when its young ones cry to God,
    and wander about for lack of food?

"Do you know when the mountain goats bring forth?
    Do you observe the calving of the hinds?
Can you number the months that they fulfill,
    and do you know the time when they bring forth,
when they crouch, bring forth their offspring,
    and are delivered of their young?
Their young ones become strong, they grow up in the open;
    they go forth, and do not return to them.

"Who has let the wild ass go free?
    Who has loosed the bonds of the swift ass,
to whom I have given the steppe for his home,
    and the salt land for his dwelling place?
He scorns the tumult of the city;
    he hears not the shouts of the driver.
He ranges the mountains as his pasture,
    and he searches after every green thing.

[34]Pleiades, Orion, Mazzaroth, and Bear are references to heavenly constellations visible
in the night skies.

"Is the wild ox willing to serve you?
    Will he spend the night at your crib ?
Can you bind him in the furrow with ropes,
    or will he harrow the valleys after you?
Will you depend on him because his strength is great,
    and will you leave to him your labor?
Do you have faith in him that he will return,
    and bring your grain to your threshing floor? . . .

"Do you give the horse his might?
    Do you clothe his neck with strength?
Do you make him leap like the locust?
    His majestic snorting is terrible.
He paws in the valley, and exults in his strength;
    he goes out to meet the weapons,
He laughs at fear, and is not dismayed
    he does not turn back from the sword.
Upon him rattle the quiver,
    the flashing spear and the javelin.
With fierceness and rage he swallows the ground;
    he cannot stand still at the sound of the trumpet.
When the trumpet sounds, he says 'Aha!'
    He smells the battle from afar,
    the thunder of the captains, and the shouting.

"Is it by your wisdom that the hawk soars,
    and spreads his wings toward the south?
Is it at your command that the eagle mounts up
    and makes his nest on high?
On the rock he dwells and makes his home
    in the fastness of the rocky crag.
Thence he spies out the prey;
    his eyes behold it afar off.
His young ones suck up blood;
    and where the slain are, there is he."

And the LORD said to Job:
    "Shall a faultfinder contend with the Almighty?
    He who argues with God, let him answer it."

Then Job answered the LORD:
"Behold, I am of small account; what shall I answer thee?
   I lay my hand on my mouth.
I have spoken once, and I will not answer;
   twice, but I will proceed no further."

Then the LORD answered Job out
   of the whirlwind:
"Gird up your loins like a man;
   I will question you, and you declare to me.
Will you even put me in the wrong?
   Will you condemn me that you may be justified?
Have you an arm like God,
   and can you thunder with a voice like his?
Deck yourself with majesty and dignity;
   clothe yourself with glory and splendor.
Pour forth the overflowings of your anger,
   and look on every one that is proud, and abase him.
Look on every one that is proud, and bring him low;
   and tread down the wicked where they stand.
Hide them all in the dust together;
   bind their faces in the world below.
Then will I also acknowledge to you,
   that your own right hand can give you victory. . . .

"Can you draw out Levi'athan[35] with a fishook,
   or press down his tongue with a cord?
Can you put a rope in his nose,
   or pierce his jaw with a hook?
Will he make many supplications to you?
   Will he speak to you soft words?
Will he make a covenant with you
   to take him for your servant for ever?
Will you play with him as with a bird,
   or will you put him on a leash for your maidens?
Will traders bargain over him?
   Will they divide him up among the merchants?
Can you fill his skin with harpoons,
   or his head with fishing spears?

[35]A legendary sea monster; also a symbol of chaos.

Lay hands on him;
   think of the battle; you will not do it again!
Behold, the hope of a man is disappointed;
   he is laid low even at the sight of him.
No one is so fierce that he dares to stir him up,
   Who then is he that can stand before me?
Who has given to me, that I should repay him?
   Whatever is under the whole heaven is mine. . . ."

Then Job answered the LORD:
   I know that thou canst do all things,
   and that no purpose of thine can be thwarted. . . .
Therefore I have uttered what I did not understand,
   things too wonderful for me,
   which I did not know. . . .
I had heard of thee by the hearing of the ear,
   but now my eye sees thee;
therefore I despise myself,
   and repent in dust and ashes."

Epilogue
42:7–17

After the LORD had spoken these words to Job, the LORD said to Eli′phaz the Te′manite: "My wrath is kindled against you and against your two friends; for you have not spoken of me what is right, as my servant Job has. Now therefore take seven bulls and seven rams, and go to my servant Job, and offer up for yourselves a burnt offering; and my servant Job shall pray for you, for I will accept his prayer not to deal with you according to your folly; for you have not spoken of me what is right, as my servant Job has." So Eli′phaz the Te′manite and Bil′dad the Shu′hite and Zo′phar the Na′amathite went and did what the LORD had told them; and the LORD accepted Job's prayer.

And the LORD restored the fortunes of Job, when he had prayed for his friends; and the LORD gave Job twice as much as he had before. Then came to him all his brothers and sisters and all who had known him before, and ate bread with him in his house; and they showed him sympathy and comforted him for all the evil that the LORD had brought upon him; and each of them gave him a piece of money and a ring of gold. And the LORD blessed the latter days of Job more than his beginning; and he had fourteen thousand sheep, six thousand camels, a thousand yoke of oxen, and a thousand she-asses. He had also seven sons and three daughters. And he called the name of the first Jemi'mah; and the name of the second Kezi'ah; and the name of the third Ker'en-hap'puch. And in all the land there were no women so fair as Job's daughters; and their father gave them inheritance among their brothers. And after this Job lived a hundred and forty years, and saw his sons, and his sons' sons, four generations. And Job died, an old man, and full of days.

26

The Bible: New Testament

*T*HE *New Testament is a Christian addition (first written in Greek) to the Hebrew Old Testament. Christians believe that the appearance and teachings of Jesus represented a new covenant or testament (the words are the same in Greek), superseding the old one between God and the Jews (see selection 25). The twenty-seven books that make up the New Testament were written independently during the late first century and early second century of the Christian era. They were among many Christian writings circulating at the time and were not regarded as sacred, as were the scriptures of the Jews, until more than a century after Jesus. And it was not until A.D. 367 that their texts, as we know them now, were officially established by the Church. The New Testament is thus the result of a winnowing-out process from a large body of early Christian writings. Although, as with the older Hebrew scriptures, the New Testament was not originally a product of Western thought, after centuries of historical development the Jewish-Christian tradition and Western culture have become inseparably interwoven.*

The following passages deal with some of the most fundamental matters of Christian faith. They were highly colored, in those early centuries, by traditional thought-forms and language. Their place of origin is ancient Palestine, occupied at the time by Roman imperial forces. They focus on the life, teachings, and divine significance of a unique personality, Jesus of Nazareth.

The expression of the Christian story underwent changes from the outset. The gospel (the "good news" about Jesus' life) was first preached in a strictly Jewish atmosphere in the Roman-conquered provinces of Judea and Galilee, where ideas of a "Messiah," a "Kingdom of God," and a "Son of Man" were well known. As the Christian movement shifted from its Jewish roots and became increasingly identified with non-Jews (Gentiles), its message was restated in a way more suited to the Greek-speaking peoples around the eastern Mediterranean. Such terms as "Savior," "Son of God," and "Body of Christ" then appeared. In general, the earlier gospels emphasize Jesus' role as a human ethical teacher and prophet favored by God. These books are those named for Mark, written ca. 70–80, and Matthew and Luke, both written ca. 90. The gospel named for John, written ca. 100, on the other hand, stresses the divine nature of Jesus.

All the gospels should be read in the light of the disturbed condition of Judea during the years between Jesus' crucifixion and the unsuccessful Jewish revolt against Rome, 66–73. The Roman destruction of Jerusalem in 70 apparently destroyed the earliest Christian records (in the local languages of Hebrew and Aramaic). Thus, the gospels, as we know them now, were set down after the revolt failed, and they reflect the need to prove to the Roman officials that the Christians were separate from the rebellious Jews.

The "Sermon on the Mount," from The Gospel According to Matthew, shows the ethical side of the Christian tradition. Jesus' teachings go beyond the Law of Moses (see selection from Exodus, pp. 554–61). They summon individuals to put inwardness of religious life before the outward forms. The three chapters of Matthew's twenty-eight included here are among the most popular in the Bible, despite the demands they make upon those who have chosen to serve God rather than self.

The crucifixion of Jesus had first seemed to his friends and enemies as the end of an ill-fated religious mission. His disciples, however, soon became convinced of his return from death and awaited him. Seven weeks after the reported resurrection (Easter Sunday), on the day of Pentecost in the Christian calendar, the disciples were "filled with the Holy Spirit." Thus, the Christian Church was born, and the disciples went forward with the world-wide work of converting others. The story of these missionary beginnings is told in the fifth book of the New Testament, the Acts of the Apostles.

The most influential of the apostles (earliest Christian missionaries) was Paul, a vigorous convert to the new faith. He proved to be a fearless preacher and organizer, founding and guiding new congregations in Asia Minor and Greece and giving instructions through numerous visits and letters. Paul's letters, ca. 51–63, may be the earliest writings of the New Testament. Two of his most significant letters are excerpted here. The First Letter of Paul to the Corinthians, written in a style typical of his letters, answers questions from the Christian congregation at Corinth. It gives advice on such matters as Christian sexual morality, the proper conduct of religious services, and the differing roles of men and women. The letter also explains the Lord's Supper (the earliest sacrament), the supreme value of Christian love, and the nature of the resurrection of bodies after death. The Letter of Paul to the Romans deals with such essential matters of doctrine as "justification by faith" and the relation of the old Jewish covenant to the new Christian covenant. Later, when established as part of Holy Scripture, the letters of Paul would exercise immense and continuing influence on the thinking and practices of all Christians.

THE GOSPEL ACCORDING TO MATTHEW[1]

The Sermon on the Mount[2]
4:23–7:29

And he went about all Galilee, teaching in their synagogues and preaching the gospel of the kingdom and healing every disease and every infirmity among the people. So his fame spread throughout all Syria, and they brought him all the sick, those afflicted with various diseases and pains, demoniacs, epileptics, and paralytics, and he healed

---

[1]Of unknown authorship, this gospel may have acquired its title because the writer possibly used, as one of his sources, a collection of Jesus' sayings prepared by the disciple Matthew. Like the other gospels it was written in Greek for a mainly non-Jewish audience after the Roman destruction of Jerusalem in A.D.70. It attempts to distinguish the new religion of Christianity from its Jewish roots. Nevertheless, this gospel assumes the reader's knowledge of the Old Testament and of Jewish history and religious ideas. Many of Jesus' sayings are, in fact, quotations or adaptations of the older Hebrew scriptures.

[2]This passage is often described as the essence of Christian ethical teaching. The sermon's delivery on a mountain suggests Jesus' relationship to the Law of Moses, delivered on Mount Sinai.

them. And great crowds followed him from Galilee and the Decapolis[3] and Jerusalem and Judea and from beyond the Jordan.

Seeing the crowds, he went up on the mountain, and when he sat down[4] his disciples came to him. And he opened his mouth and taught them, saying:

"Blessed are the poor in spirit, for theirs is the kingdom of heaven.

"Blessed are those who mourn, for they shall be comforted.

"Blessed are the meek, for they shall inherit the earth.

"Blessed are those who hunger and thirst for righteousness, for they shall be satisfied.

"Blessed are the merciful, for they shall obtain mercy.

"Blessed are the pure in heart, for they shall see God.

"Blessed are the peacemakers, for they shall be called sons of God.

"Blessed are those who are persecuted for righteousness' sake, for theirs is the kingdom of heaven.

"Blessed are you when men revile you and persecute you and utter all kinds of evil against you falsely on my account. Rejoice and be glad, for your reward is great in heaven, for so men persecuted the prophets[5] who were before you.

"You are the salt of the earth; but if salt has lost its taste, how shall its saltness be restored? It is no longer good for anything except to be thrown out and trodden under foot by men.

"You are the light of the world. A city set on a hill cannot be hid. Nor do men light a lamp and put it under a bushel, but on a stand, and it gives light to all in the house. Let your light so shine before men, that they may see your good works and give glory to your Father who is in heaven.

"Think not that I have come to abolish the law and the prophets; I have come not to abolish them but to fulfil them.[6] For truly, I say to you, till heaven and earth pass away, not an iota, not a dot, will pass from the law until all is accomplished. Whoever then relaxes one of the least of these commandments and teaches men so, shall be called least in the kingdom of heaven; but he who does them and teaches them shall be called great in the kingdom of heaven. For I tell you, unless

[3] A region—also occupied by Rome—just east of the Jordan River.

[4] The usual posture of Jewish rabbis (religious leaders) while teaching.

[5] The Jewish prophets of the Old Testament. (See, for example, Amos and Isaiah, pp. 561–72).

[6] The relation of Jesus' message to the Jewish Law (given at Mount Sinai) obviously was of great concern to his followers, who were mostly of Jewish heritage. Here he clearly states the enduring force of that law.

your righteousness exceeds that of the scribes and Pharisees,[7] you will never enter the kingdom of heaven.

"You have heard that it was said to the men of old,[8] 'You shall not kill; and whoever kills shall be liable to judgment.' But I say to you that every one who is angry with his brother shall be liable to judgment; whoever insults his brother shall be liable to the council, and whoever says, 'You fool!' shall be liable to the hell of fire. So if you are offering your gift at the altar, and there remember that your brother has something against you, leave your gift there before the altar and go; first be reconciled to your brother, and then come and offer your gift. Make friends quickly with your accuser, while you are going with him to court, lest your accuser hand you over to the judge, and the judge to the guard, and you be put in prison; truly, I say to you, you will never get out till you have paid the last penny.

"You have heard that it was said, 'You shall not commit adultery.' But I say to you that every one who looks at a woman lustfully has already committed adultery with her in his heart. If your right eye causes you to sin, pluck it out and throw it away; it is better that you lose one of your members than that your whole body be thrown into hell. And if your right hand causes you to sin, cut it off and throw it away; it is better that you lose one of your members than that your whole body go into hell.

"It was also said, 'Whoever divorces his wife, let him give her a certificate of divorce.' But I say to you that every one who divorces his wife, except on the ground of unchastity, makes her an adulteress; and whoever marries a divorced woman commits adultery.

"Again you have heard that it was said to the men of old, 'You shall not swear falsely, but shall perform to the Lord what you have sworn.' But I say to you, Do not swear at all, either by heaven, for it is the throne of God, or by the earth, for it is his footstool, or by Jerusalem, for it is the city of the great King. And do not swear by your head, for you cannot make one hair white or black. Let what you say be simply 'Yes' or 'No'; anything more than this comes from evil.

"You have heard that it was said, 'An eye for an eye and a tooth for a tooth.' But I say to you, Do not resist one who is evil. But if any one strikes you on the right cheek, turn to him the other also; and if any

[7]The Pharisees, one of the main Jewish sects in Jesus' time, had become the principal interpreters of Judaism after the fall of Jerusalem. Their "scribes" (specialists in religious law) conducted prayers in the synagogues and explained the Hebrew bible.

[8]That is, the men who received the Law at Mount Sinai.

one would sue you and take your coat, let him have your cloak as well; and if any one forces you to go one mile, go with him two miles. Give to him who begs from you, and do not refuse him who would borrow from you.

"You have heard that it was said, 'You shall love your neighbor and hate your enemy.' But I say to you, Love your enemies and pray for those who persecute you, so that you may be sons[9] of your Father who is in heaven; for he makes his sun rise on the evil and on the good, and sends rain on the just and on the unjust. For if you love those who love you, what reward have you? Do not even the tax collectors do the same? And if you salute only your brethren, what more are you doing than others? Do not even the Gentiles[10] do the same? You, therefore, must be perfect, as your heavenly Father is perfect.

"Beware of practicing your piety before men in order to be seen by them; for then you will have no reward from your Father who is in heaven.

"Thus, when you give alms, sound no trumpet before you, as the hypocrites do in the synagogues and in the streets, that they may be praised by men. Truly, I say to you, they have received their reward. But when you give alms, do not let your left hand know what your right hand is doing, so that your alms may be in secret; and your Father who sees in secret will reward you.

"And when you pray, you must not be like the hypocrites; for they love to stand and pray in the synagogues and at the street corners, that they may be seen by men. Truly, I say to you, they have received their reward. But when you pray, go into your room and shut the door and pray to your Father who is in secret; and your Father who sees in secret will reward you.

"And in praying do not heap up empty phrases as the Gentiles do; for they think that they will be heard for their many words. Do not be like them, for your Father knows what you need before you ask him. Pray then like this:

> Our Father who art in heaven,
> Hallowed be thy name.
> Thy kingdom come,
> Thy will be done,

---

[9]That is, worthy followers of God's Law.

[10]Non-Jews, who did *not* receive the Law at Mount Sinai.

On earth as it is in heaven.
Give us this day our daily bread;
And forgive us our debts,
As we also have forgiven our debtors;
And lead us not into temptation,
But deliver us from evil.

For if you forgive men their trespasses, your heavenly Father also will forgive you; but if you do not forgive men their trespasses, neither will your Father forgive your trespasses.

"And when you fast, do not look dismal, like the hypocrites, for they disfigure their faces that their fasting may be seen by men. Truly, I say to you, they have received their reward. But when you fast, anoint your head and wash your face, that your fasting may not be seen by men but by your Father who is in secret; and your Father who sees in secret will reward you.

"Do not lay up for yourselves treasures on earth, where moth and rust consume and where thieves break in and steal, but lay up for yourselves treasure in heaven, where neither moth nor rust consumes and where thieves do not break in and steal. For where your treasure is, there will your heart be also.

"The eye is the lamp of the body. So, if your eye is sound, your whole body will be full of light; but if your eye is not sound, your whole body will be full of darkness. If then the light in you is darkness, how great is the darkness!

"No one can serve two masters; for either he will hate the one and love the other, or he will be devoted to the one and despise the other. You cannot serve God and mammon.[11]

"Therefore I tell you, do not be anxious about your life, what you shall eat or what you shall drink, nor about your body, what you shall put on. Is not life more than food, and the body more than clothing? Look at the birds of the air: they neither sow nor reap nor gather into barns, and yet your heavenly Father feeds them. Are you not of more value than they? And which of you by being anxious can add one cubit[12] to his span of life? And why are you anxious about clothing? Consider the lilies of the field, how they grow; they neither toil nor spin; yet I tell you, even Solomon in all his glory was not arrayed like one of these. But if God so clothes the grass of the field, which today

[11]A Semitic word for money or material possessions.

[12]A measuring unit of about eighteen inches.

is alive and tomorrow is thrown into the oven, will he not much more clothe you, O men of little faith? Therefore do not be anxious, saying, 'What shall we eat?' or 'What shall we drink?' or 'What shall we wear?' For the Gentiles seek all these things; and your heavenly Father knows that you need them all. But seek first his kingdom and his righteousness, and all these things shall be yours as well.

"Therefore do not be anxious about tomorrow, for tomorrow will be anxious for itself. Let the day's own trouble be sufficient for the day.

"Judge not, that you be not judged. For with the judgment you pronounce you will be judged, and the measure you give will be the measure you get. Why do you see the speck that is in your brother's eye, but do not notice the log that is in your own eye? Or how can you say to your brother, 'Let me take the speck out of your eye,' when there is the log in your own eye? You hypocrite, first take the log out of your own eye, and then you will see clearly to take the speck out of your brother's eye.

"Do not give dogs what is holy; and do not throw your pearls before swine, lest they trample them under foot and turn to attack you.

"Ask, and it will be given you; seek, and you will find; knock, and it will be opened to you. For every one who asks receives, and he who seeks finds, and to him who knocks it will be opened. Or what man of you, if his son asks him for bread, will give him a stone? Or if he asks for a fish, will give him a serpent? If you then, who are evil, know how to give good gifts to your children, how much more will your Father who is in heaven give good things to those who ask him! So whatever you wish that men would do to you, do so to them; for this is the law and the prophets.

"Enter by the narrow gate; for the gate is wide and the way is easy, that leads to destruction, and those who enter by it are many. For the gate is narrow and the way is hard, that leads to life, and those who find it are few.

"Beware of false prophets, who come to you in sheep's clothing but inwardly are ravenous wolves. You will know them by their fruits. Are grapes gathered from thorns, or figs from thistles? So, every sound tree bears good fruit, but the bad tree bears evil fruit. A sound tree cannot bear evil fruit, nor can a bad tree bear good fruit. Every tree that does not bear good fruit is cut down and thrown into the fire. Thus you will know them by their fruits.

"Not every one who says to me, 'Lord, Lord,' shall enter the kingdom of heaven, but he who does the will of my Father who is in heaven. On that day many will say to me, 'Lord, Lord, did we not prophesy in your name, and cast out demons in your name, and do many mighty works in your name?' And then will I declare to them, 'I never knew you; depart from me, you evildoers.'

"Every one then who hears these words of mine and does them will be like a wise man who built his house upon the rock; and the rain fell, and the floods came, and the winds blew and beat upon that house, but it did not fall, because it had been founded on the rock. And every one who hears these words of mine and does not do them will be like a foolish man who built his house upon the sand; and the rain fell, and the floods came, and the winds blew and beat against that house, and it fell; and great was the fall of it."

And when Jesus finished these sayings, the crowds were astonished at his teaching, for he taught them as one who had authority, and not as their scribes.[13]

THE ACTS OF THE APOSTLES[14]

The Beginnings of the Church
1:1–2:47

In the first book,[15] O Theophilus,[16] I have dealt with all that Jesus began to do and teach, until the day when he was taken up, after he had given commandment through the Holy Spirit to the apostles whom he had chosen. To them he presented himself alive after his passion [death on the cross] by many proofs, appearing to them during forty days, and speaking of the kingdom of God. And while staying with them he charged them not to depart from Jerusalem, but to wait for the promise

---

[13]That is, as one who speaks on his own responsibility, as did the prophets—*not* as one who conforms to earlier authorities, as did the scribes.

[14]Written by the same person who had already written The Gospel According to Luke. This book traces the story of the Christian movement from the resurrection of Jesus to the time when the apostle Paul, as a prisoner, first travelled to Rome. We see in The Acts of the Apostles the broadening of the early Church from a small Jewish group centered in Jerusalem to a universal movement spreading throughout the Roman world. The time-span described is about A.D.30–60.

[15]The Gospel According to Luke.

[16]Literally, in Greek, "lover of God," who might be any devout reader—or, possibly, an individual patron of the early Church.

of the Father, which, he said, "you heard from me, for John baptized with water, but before many days you shall be baptized with the Holy Spirit."

So when they had come together, they asked him, "Lord will you at this time restore the kingdom to Israel?"[17] He said to them, "It is not for you to know times or seasons which the Father has fixed by his own authority. But you shall receive power when the Holy Spirit has come upon you; and you shall be my witnesses in Jerusalem and in all Judea and Samaria and to the end of the earth." And when he had said this, as they were looking on, he was lifted up, and a cloud took him out of their sight. And while they were gazing into heaven as he went, behold, two men stood by them in white robes, and said, "Men of Galilee, why do you stand looking into heaven? This Jesus, who was taken up from you into heaven, will come in the same way as you saw him go into heaven."

Then they returned to Jerusalem from the mount called Olivet, which is near Jerusalem, a sabbath day's journey away;[18] and when they had entered, they went up to the upper room, where they were staying, Peter and John and James and Andrew, Philip and Thomas, Bartholomew and Matthew, James the son of Alphaeus and Simon the Zealot and Judas the son of James. All these with one accord devoted themselves to prayer, together with the women and Mary the mother of Jesus, and with his brothers.[19]

In those days Peter stood up among the brethren (the company of persons was in all about a hundred and twenty), and said, "Brethren, the scripture had to be fulfilled, which the Holy Spirit spoke beforehand by the mouth of David, concerning Judas who was guide to those who arrested Jesus. For he was numbered among us, and was allotted his share in this ministry. (Now this man bought a field with the reward of his wickedness; and falling headlong he burst open in the middle and all his bowels gushed out. And it became known to all the inhabitants of Jerusalem, so that the field was called in their language

---

[17]His followers are asking Jesus, since he had been promised the throne of his claimed ancestor, King David (tenth century B.C.), if he would restore the ancient kingdom of the Jews, now under Roman rule.

[18]The travel permitted Jews on the Sabbath, about a half-mile.

[19]Protestants believe that Mary had four sons—James, Joseph, Simon, and Judas—younger than Jesus. Catholic tradition regards them as relatives—but not blood brothers—of Jesus.

Akeldama, that is, Field of Blood.)[20] For it is written in the book of Psalms [in the Old Testament],

> 'Let his habitation become desolate,
> and let there be no one to live in it';

and

> 'His office let another take.'

So one of the men who have accompanied us during all the time that the Lord Jesus went in and out among us, beginning from the baptism of John until the day when he was taken up from us—one of these men must become with us a witness to his resurrection." And they put forward two, Joseph called Barsabbas, who was surnamed Justus, and Matthias. And they prayed and said, "Lord, who knowest the hearts of all men, show which one of these two thou hast chosen to take the place in this ministry and apostleship from which Judas turned aside, to go to his own place." And they cast lots for them, and the lot fell on Matthias; and he was enrolled with the eleven apostles.

When the day of Pentecost[21] had come, they were all together in one place. And suddenly a sound came from heaven like the rush of a mighty wind, and it filled all the house where they were sitting. And there appeared to them tongues as of fire, distributed and resting on each one of them. And they were all filled with the Holy Spirit and began to speak in other tongues,[22] as the Spirit gave them utterance.

Now there were dwelling in Jerusalem Jews, devout men from every nation under heaven. And at this sound the multitude came together, and they were bewildered, because each one heard them speaking in his own language. And they were amazed and wondered, saying, "Are not all these who are speaking Galileans? And how is it that we hear, each of us in his own native language? Parthians and Medes and Elamites and residents of Mesopotamia, Judea and Cappadocia, Pontus and Asia, Phrygia and Pamphylia, Egypt and the parts of Libya belonging to Cyrene, and visitors from Rome, both Jews and

[20]The disciple Judas, who had betrayed Jesus to the Roman officials, had killed himself in this field. Now the sacred number of twelve disciples, corresponding to the ancient number of tribes among the Hebrews, must be restored.

[21]Fifty days after Passover, the Jewish festival of Pentecost (Shavuot) celebrated the harvesting of the first fruits; at this time in Jewish history, Pentecost also celebrated the giving of the Law at Mount Sinai.

[22]That is, other languages. This ability is explained as a miracle from the Holy Spirit.

proselytes, Cretans and Arabians, we hear them telling us in our own tongues the mighty works of God." And all were amazed and perplexed, saying to one another, "What does this mean?" But others mocking said, "They are filled with new wine."

But Peter, standing with the eleven, lifted up his voice and addressed them, "Men of Judea and all who dwell in Jerusalem, let this be known to you, and give ear to my words. For these men are not drunk, as you suppose, since it is only the third hour of the day;[23] but this is what was spoken by the prophet Joel:[24]

> 'And in the last days it shall be, God declares,
> that I will pour out my Spirit upon all flesh,
> and your sons and your daughters shall prophesy,
> and your young men shall see visions,
> and your old men shall dream dreams;
> yea, and on my menservants and my maidservants in those days
> I will pour out my Spirit; and they shall prophesy.
> And I will show wonders in the heaven above
> and signs on the earth beneath,
> blood, and fire, and vapor of smoke;
> the sun shall be turned into darkness
> and the moon into blood,
> before the day of the Lord comes, the great and manifest day.
> And it shall be that whoever calls on the name of the Lord shall
> be saved.'

"Men of Israel, hear these words: Jesus of Nazareth, a man attested to you by God with mighty works and wonders and signs which God did through him in your midst, as you yourselves know—this Jesus, delivered up according to the definite plan and foreknowledge of God, you crucified and killed by the hands of lawless men. But God raised him up, having loosed the pangs of death, because it was not possible for him to be held by it. For David[25] says concerning him,

> 'I saw the Lord always before me,
> for he is at my right hand that I may not be shaken;
> therefore my heart was glad, and my tongue rejoiced;
> moreover my flesh will dwell in hope.

[23]About 9 a.m.

[24]Peter quotes the following passage from the Old Testament prophet Joel (2:28–32).

[25]Peter paraphrases from Psalm 16 in the Old Testament, credited to King David.

> For thou wilt not abandon my soul to Hades,
> nor let thy Holy One see corruption.
> Thou hast made known to me the ways of life;
> thou wilt make me full of gladness with thy presence.'

"Brethren, I may say to you confidently of the patriarch David that he both died and was buried, and his tomb is with us to this day. Being therefore a prophet, and knowing that God had sworn with an oath to him that he would set one of his descendants upon his throne, he foresaw and spoke of the resurrection of the Christ, that he was not abandoned to Hades, nor did his flesh see corruption. This Jesus God raised up, and of that we all are witnesses. Being therefore exalted at the right hand of God, and having received from the Father the promise of the Holy Spirit, he has poured out this which you see and hear. For David did not ascend into the heavens; but he himself says,

> 'The Lord said to my Lord, Sit at my right hand,
> till I make [of] thy enemies a stool for thy feet.'[26]

Let all the house of Israel therefore know assuredly that God has made him both Lord and Christ, this Jesus whom you crucified."[27]

Now when they heard this they were cut to the heart, and said to Peter and the rest of the apostles, "Brethren, what shall we do?" And Peter said to them, "Repent, and be baptized every one of you in the name of Jesus Christ for the forgiveness of your sins; and you shall receive the gift of the Holy Spirit. For the promise is to you and to your children and to all that are far off, every one whom the Lord our God calls to him." And he testified with many other words and exhorted them, saying, "Save yourselves from this crooked generation." So those who received his word were baptized, and there were added that day about three thousand souls. And they devoted themselves to the apostles' teaching and fellowship, to the breaking of bread[28] and the prayers.

And fear came upon every soul; and many wonders and signs were done through the apostles. And all who believed were together and had all things in common; and they sold their possessions and goods

---

[26]From Psalm 110.

[27]That is, the human Jesus was not only Christ the Messiah ("anointed" savior who will rule Israel on earth), but also the heavenly Lord.

[28]Apparently, a common meal which included the Lord's Supper (see Paul's First Letter to the Corinthians, pp. 607–609).

and distributed them to all, as any had need. And day by day, attending the temple together and breaking bread in their homes, they partook of food with glad and generous hearts, praising God and having favor with all the people. And the Lord added to their number day by day those who were being saved.

• • •

The Conversion of Saul[29]
8:1–4; 9:1–20

And on that day a great persecution arose against the church in Jerusalem; and they were all scattered throughout the region of Judea and Samaria, except the apostles. Devout men buried Stephen,[30] and made great lamentation over him. But Saul laid waste the church, and entering house after house, he dragged off men and women and committed them to prison.

Now those who were scattered went about preaching the word. . . .

But Saul, still breathing threats and murder against the disciples of the Lord, went to the high priest and asked him for letters to the synagogues at Damascus, so that if he found any belonging to the Way, men or women, he might bring them bound to Jerusalem. Now as he journeyed he approached Damascus, and suddenly a light from heaven flashed about him. And he fell to the ground and heard a voice saying to him, "Saul, Saul, why do you persecute me?" And he said, "Who are you, Lord?" And he said, "I am Jesus, whom you are persecuting; but rise and enter the city, and you will be told what you are to do." The men who were travelling with him stood speechless, hearing the voice but seeing no one. Saul arose from the ground; and when his eyes were opened, he could see nothing; so they led him by the hand and brought him into Damascus. And for three days he was without sight, and neither ate nor drank.

Now there was a disciple at Damascus named Ananias. The Lord

[29]Saul was a Greek-speaking Jew from Tarsus in Asia Minor. Originally employed as a persecutor of the Christians in Jerusalem and Damascus, *ca.* A.D.36, he was converted on the road to Damascus by the blinding vision described here. After the conversion he was usually known by his Greek name, Paul. Most of The Acts of the Apostles concerns Paul's travels to organize local congregations of Christians.

[30]The first Christian martyr, Stephen, had been stoned to death while Saul looked on.

said to him in a vision, "Ananias." And he said, "Here I am, Lord." And the Lord said to him, "Rise and go to the street called Straight, and inquire in the house of Judas for a man of Tarsus named Saul; for behold, he is praying, and he has seen a man named Ananias come in and lay his hands on him so that he might regain his sight." But Ananias answered, "Lord, I have heard from many about this man, how much evil he has done to thy saints at Jerusalem; and here he has authority from the chief priests to bind all who call upon thy name." But the Lord said to him, "Go, for he is a chosen instrument of mine to carry my name before the Gentiles and kings and the sons of Israel; for I will show him how much he must suffer for the sake of my name." So Ananias departed and entered the house. And laying his hands on him he said, "Brother Saul, the Lord Jesus who appeared to you on the road by which you came, has sent me that you may regain your sight and be filled with the Holy Spirit." And immediately something like scales fell from his eyes and he regained his sight. Then he rose and was baptized, and took food and was strengthened.

For several days he was with the disciples at Damascus. And in the synagogues immediately he proclaimed Jesus, saying, "He is the Son of God."

THE FIRST LETTER OF PAUL TO THE CORINTHIANS[31]

Salutation [Greeting]
1:1–3

Paul, called by the will of God to be an apostle of Christ Jesus. . . .

To the Church of God which is at Corinth, to those sanctified in Christ Jesus, called to be saints together with all those who in every place call on the name of our Lord Jesus Christ, both their Lord and ours:

Grace to you and peace from God our Father and the Lord Jesus Christ.

---

[31]After his conversion Paul travelled untiringly throughout the eastern part of the Roman-controlled Mediterranean world, spreading the Christian message (mainly to non-Jews). This letter, written about A.D.55, shows Paul in his typical stern role as the sender of doctrinal and moral advice to the backsliding Christian congregation at Corinth in Greece. Many of its new believers were illiterate slaves or freedmen, the lowest elements of a city noted for its vices, hostile factions, and a great variety of gods. (Corinth was the city where Lucius was transformed and became a worshipper of the pagan goddess Isis; see *The Golden Ass,* selection 23.)

On Sexual Morality and Marriage
5:1–2; 7:1–11

It is actually reported that there is immorality among you, and of a kind that is not found even among pagans; for a man is living with his father's wife. And you are arrogant! Ought you not rather to mourn? Let him who has done this be removed from among you.

• • •

Now concerning the matters about which you wrote. It is well for a man not to touch a woman. But because of the temptation to immorality, each man should have his own wife and each woman her own husband. The husband should give to his wife her conjugal rights, and likewise the wife to her husband. For the wife does not rule over her own body, but the husband does; likewise the husband does not rule over his own body, but the wife does. Do not refuse one another except perhaps by agreement for a season, that you may devote yourselves to prayer; but then come together again, lest Satan tempt you through lack of self-control. I say this by way of concession, not of command. I wish that all were as I myself am.[32] But each has his own special gift from God, one of one kind and one of another.

To the unmarried and the widows I say that it is well for them to remain single as I do. But if they cannot exercise self-control, they should marry. For it is better to marry than to be aflame with passion.

To the married I give charge, not I but the Lord, that the wife should not separate from her husband (but if she does, let her remain single or else be reconciled to her husband)—and that the husband should not divorce his wife.

On Roles of Men and Women
11:2–12; 14:34–35

I commend you because you remember me in everything and maintain the traditions even as I have delivered them to you. But I want you to understand that the head of every man is Christ, the head of a woman is her husband, and the head of Christ is God. Any man who prays or prophesies with his head covered dishonors his head, but any woman

---

[32]That is, unmarried.

who prays or prophesies with her head unveiled dishonors her head—
it is the same as if her head were shaven. For if a woman will not veil
herself, then she should cut off her hair; but if it is disgraceful for a
woman to be shorn or shaven, let her wear a veil. For a man ought not
to cover his head, since he is the image and glory of God; but woman
is the glory of man. (For man was not made from woman, but woman
from man. Neither was man created for woman, but woman for man.)
That is why a woman ought to have a veil on her head, because of the
angels.[33] (Nevertheless, in the Lord woman is not independent of man
nor man of woman; for as woman was made from man, so man is now
born of woman. And all things are from God.)

•　•　•

As in all the churches of the saints, the women should keep silence
in the churches. For they are not permitted to speak, but should be
subordinate, as even the law says. If there is anything they desire to
know, let them ask their husbands at home. For it is shameful for a
woman to speak in church.

The Lord's Supper
10:1–5, 14–22; 11:17–27

I want you to know, brethren, that our fathers were all under the cloud,
and all passed through the sea,[34] and all were baptized into Moses in the
cloud and in the sea, and all ate the same supernatural food and all
drank the same supernatural drink. For they drank from the supernatural Rock which followed them, and the Rock was
Christ.[35] Nevertheless with most of them God was not pleased; for they
were overthrown in the wilderness.[36]. . . Therefore, my beloved, shun
the worship of idols. I speak as to sensible men; judge for yourselves
what I say. The cup of blessing which we bless, is it not a participation

---

[33]The angels were thought to carry out God's law.

[34]In Exodus the Jews were led by Moses away from Egypt; God guided them by day
with a "pillar of cloud" and divided the water of the Red Sea so they could cross over
to the Sinai desert.

[35]According to a Hebrew legend, the Rock had followed the Jews in the desert; Paul
asserts that the source of this life-giving water was the pre-existent Christ.

[36]That is, baptism and taking of the Lord's Supper are, by themselves, not enough to
guarantee salvation, any more than similar acts provided salvation for most of the Jews
of Exodus.

in the blood of Christ? The bread which we break, is it not a participation in the body of Christ? Because there is one bread, we who are many are one body, for we all partake of the one bread. Consider the people of Israel; are not those who eat the sacrifices partners in the altar? What do I imply then? That food offered to idols is anything, or that an idol is anything? No, I imply that what pagans sacrifice they offer to demons and not to God.[37] I do not want you to be partners with demons. You cannot drink the cup of the Lord and the cup of demons. You cannot partake of the table of the Lord and the table of demons. Shall we provoke the Lord to jealousy? Are we stronger than he?

• • •

But in the following instructions I do not commend you, because when you come together it is not for the better but for the worse. For, in the first place, when you assemble as a church, I hear that there are divisions among you; and I partly believe it, for there must be factions[38] among you in order that those who are genuine among you may be recognized. When you meet together, it is not the Lord's supper that you eat. For in eating, each one goes ahead with his own meal, and one is hungry and another is drunk. What! Do you not have houses to eat and drink in? Or do you despise the church of God and humiliate those who have nothing? What shall I say to you? Shall I commend you in this? No, I will not.

For I received from the Lord what I also delivered to you, that the Lord Jesus on the night when he was betrayed took bread, and when he had given thanks, he broke it, and said, "This is my body which is for you. Do this in remembrance of me." In the same way also the cup, after supper, saying, "This cup is the new covenant in my blood.[39] Do this, as often as you drink it, in remembrance of me." For as often as you eat this bread and drink the cup, you proclaim the Lord's death until he comes.

Whoever, therefore, eats the bread or drinks the cup of the Lord in

---

[37]That is, carved idols are nothing, but demons (pagan gods) use them as camouflage. Thus, eating food consecrated to demons is defiance of God.

[38]Rival cliques, perhaps corresponding to the differing social classes at the common meal that took place in connection with the Lord's Supper.

[39]The old covenant with God at Mount Sinai had also been sealed with blood—from the sacrificed animals of the burnt offerings (Exodus 24:8).

an unworthy manner will be guilty of profaning the body and blood of the Lord.

On Love
13:1–13

If I speak in the tongues of men and of angels, but have not love, I am a noisy gong or a clanging cymbal. And if I have prophetic powers, and understand all mysteries and all knowledge, and if I have all faith, so as to remove mountains, but have not love, I am nothing. If I give away all I have, and if I deliver my body to be burned, but have not love, I gain nothing.

Love is patient and kind; love is not jealous or boastful; it is not arrogant or rude. Love does not insist on its own way; it is not irritable or resentful; it does not rejoice at wrong, but rejoices in the right. Love bears all things, believes all things, hopes all things, endures all things.

Love never ends; as for prophecies, they will pass away; as for tongues, they will cease; as for knowledge, it will pass away. For our knowledge is imperfect and our prophecy is imperfect; but when the perfect comes, the imperfect will pass away. When I was a child, I spoke like a child, I thought like a child, I reasoned like a child; when I became a man, I gave up childish ways. For now we see in a mirror dimly, but then face to face. Now I know in part; then I shall understand fully, even as I have been fully understood. So faith, hope, love abide, these three; but the greatest of these is love.

Life After Death
15:1–58

Now I would remind you, brethren, in what terms I preached to you the gospel, which you received, in which you stand, by which you are saved, if you hold it fast—unless you believed in vain.

For I delivered to you as of first importance what I also received, that Christ died for our sins in accordance with the scriptures, [40] that he was buried, that he was raised on the third day in accordance with the scriptures, and that he appeared to Cephas, then to the twelve. Then

[40]Probably, Paul means the Old Testament in general when he refers to "the scriptures." However, later tradition specifically cited The Song of the Suffering Servant from Isaiah (pp. 571–72) as an Old Testament prophecy of Jesus' death—and Psalm 16:10 for prophecy of his resurrection ("For thou dost not give me up to Sheol [the underworld of the dead], or let thy godly one see the Pit").

he appeared to more than five hundred brethren at one time, most of whom are still alive, though some have fallen asleep. Then he appeared to James, then to all the apostles. Last of all, as to one untimely born, he appeared also to me. For I am the least of the apostles, unfit to be called an apostle, because I persecuted the church of God. But by the grace of God I am what I am, and his grace toward me was not in vain. On the contrary, I worked harder than any of them, though it was not I, but the grace of God which is with me. Whether then it was I or they, so we preach and so you believed.

Now if Christ is preached as raised from the dead, how can some of you say that there is no resurrection of the dead? But if there is no resurrection of the dead, then Christ has not been raised; if Christ has not been raised, then our preaching is in vain and your faith is in vain. We are even found to be misrepresenting God, because we testified of God that he raised Christ, whom he did not raise if it is true that the dead are not raised. For if the dead are not raised, then Christ has not been raised. If Christ has not been raised, your faith is futile and you are still in your sins. Then those also who have fallen asleep in Christ have perished.[41] If for this life only we have hoped in Christ, we are of all men most to be pitied.

But in fact Christ has been raised from the dead, the first fruits of those who have fallen asleep. For as by a man came death, by a man has come also the resurrection of the dead. For as in Adam all die, so also in Christ shall all be made alive. But each in his own order: Christ the first fruits, then at his coming[42] those who belong to Christ. Then comes the end, when he delivers the kingdom to God the Father after destroying every rule and every authority and power. For he must reign until he has put all his enemies under his feet. The last enemy to be destroyed is death. "For God has put all things in subjection under his feet." But when it says, "All things are put in subjection under him," it is plain that he is excepted who put all things under him. When all things are subjected to him, then the Son himself will also be subjected to him who put all things under him, that God may be everything to every one.

---

[41]That is, those who have died as Christians are utterly lost unless Christ was raised from the dead.

[42]The *second* coming of Christ, which will end the present age of humankind and establish his kingdom after a great struggle.

Otherwise, what do people mean by being baptized on behalf of the dead?[43] If the dead are not raised at all, why are people baptized on their behalf? Why am I in peril every hour? I protest, brethren, by my pride in you which I have in Christ Jesus our Lord, I die every day![44] What do I gain if, humanly speaking, I fought with beasts at Ephesus? If the dead are not raised, "Let us eat and drink, for tomorrow we die." Do not be deceived: "Bad company ruins good morals." Come to your right mind, and sin no more. For some have no knowledge of God. I say this to your shame.

But some one will ask, "How are the dead raised? With what kind of body do they come?" You foolish man! What you sow does not come to life unless it dies. And what you sow is not the body which is to be, but a bare kernel, perhaps of wheat or of some other grain. But God gives it a body as he has chosen, and to each kind of seed its own body. For not all flesh is alike, but there is one kind for men, another for animals, another for birds, and another for fish. There are celestial bodies and there are terrestrial bodies; but the glory of the celestial is one, and the glory of the terrestrial is another. There is one glory of the sun, and another glory of the moon, and another glory of the stars; for star differs from star in glory.

So is it with the resurrection of the dead. What is sown is perishable, what is raised is imperishable. It is sown in dishonour, it is raised in glory. It is sown in weakness, it is raised in power. It is sown a physical body, it is raised a spiritual body. If there is a physical body, there is also a spiritual body. Thus it is written, "The first man Adam became a living being";[45] the last Adam became a life-giving spirit. But it is not the spiritual which is first but the physical, and then the spiritual. The first man was from the earth, a man of dust; the second man is from heaven. As was the man of dust, so are those who are of the dust; and as is the man of heaven, so are those who are of heaven. Just as we have born the image of the man of dust, we shall also bear the image of the man of heaven. I tell you this, brethren: flesh and blood cannot inherit the kingdom of God, nor does the perishable inherit the imperishable.

[43]Apparently, some of the early Christians accepted baptism in the names of their loved ones who had died without being baptized, in order to insure their loved ones' resurrection.

[44]That is, I risk death every day.

[45]See the second version of creation in Genesis, p. 547.

Lo! I tell you a mystery. We shall not all sleep, but we shall all be changed, in a moment, in the twinkling of an eye, at the last trumpet.[46] For the trumpet will sound, and the dead will be raised imperishable, and we shall be changed. For this perishable nature must put on the imperishable, and this mortal nature must put on immortality. When the perishable puts on the imperishable, and the mortal puts on immortality, then shall come to pass the saying that is written:

> "Death is swallowed up in victory."
> "O death, where is thy victory?
> O death, where is thy sting?"

The sting of death is sin, and the power of sin is the law.[47] But thanks be to God, who gives us the victory through our Lord Jesus Christ.

Therefore, my beloved brethren, be steadfast, immovable, always abounding in the work of the Lord, knowing that in the Lord your labor is not in vain.

THE LETTER OF PAUL TO THE ROMANS[48]

Salutation
1:1–7

Paul, a servant of Jesus Christ, called to be an apostle, set apart for the gospel of God which he promised beforehand through his prophets in the holy scriptures, the gospel concerning his Son, who was descended from David according to the flesh and designated Son of God in power according to the Spirit of holiness by his resurrection from the dead, Jesus Christ our Lord, through whom we have received grace[49] and

---

[46]That is, many Christians, alive now, will survive until Christ returns, but all—whether living or dead—will receive spiritual bodies.

[47]That is, although the Law reflects God's intentions, in practice it is often powerless against sin and even encourages it by focusing a person's thoughts on sin.

[48]This letter, probably written from Corinth early in 57, tells of Paul's intention to visit Rome on his way to begin a new mission in Spain. In Rome there was a Christian community Paul had not founded or even seen. Paul's religious thinking is here clearly set forth. He argues for the doctrine of "justification": that forgiveness from the penalty of sin comes only through *faith in Christ*. Paul also deals with the role in the *new* covenant of his Jewish kindred, for justification applies equally to Jew and Gentile.

[49]The freely given, undeserved favor and love of God.

apostleship to bring about the obedience of faith for the sake of his name among all the nations, including yourselves who are called to belong to Jesus Christ;

To all God's beloved in Rome, who are called to be saints:

Grace to you and peace from God our Father and the Lord Jesus Christ.

Salvation Through Faith Alone
1:16–25

For I am not ashamed of the gospel: it is the power of God for salvation to every one who has faith, to the Jew first and also to the Greek.[50] For in it the righteousness of God is revealed through faith for faith; as it is written, "He who through faith is righteous shall live."

For the wrath of God is revealed from heaven against all ungodliness and wickedness of men who by their wickedness suppress the truth. For what can be known about God is plain to them, because God has shown it to them. Ever since the creation of the world his invisible nature, namely, his eternal power and deity, has been clearly perceived in the things that have been made. So they are without excuse; for although they knew God they did not honor him as God or give thanks to him, but they became futile in their thinking and their senseless minds were darkened. Claiming to be wise, they became fools, and exchanged the glory of the immortal God for images resembling mortal man or birds or animals or reptiles.

Therefore God gave them up in the lusts of their hearts to impurity, to the dishonoring of their bodies among themselves, because they exchanged the truth about God for a lie and worshiped and served the creature rather than the Creator, who is blessed for ever! Amen.

God Is For Every Person, Without Partiality
2:1–3:9

Therefore you have no excuse, O man, whoever you are, when you judge another; for in passing judgment upon him you condemn yourself, because you, the judge, are doing the very same things. We know that the judgment of God rightly falls upon those who do such things.

[50]Non-Jews in general; the eastern end of the Mediterranean was culturally Hellenistic (Greek). Thus, the entire New Testament was written in the Greek language.

Do you suppose, O man, that when you judge those who do such things and yet do them yourself, you will escape the judgment of God? Or do you presume upon the riches of his kindness and forbearance and patience? Do you not know that God's kindness is meant to lead you to repentance? But by your hard and impenitent heart you are storing up wrath for yourself on the day of wrath when God's righteous judgment will be revealed. For he will render to every man according to his works: to those who by patience in well-doing seek for glory and honor and immortality, he will give eternal life; but for those who are factious and do not obey the truth, but obey wickedness, there will be wrath and fury. There will be tribulation and distress for every human being who does evil, the Jew first and also the Greek,[51] but glory and honor and peace for every one who does good, the Jew first and also the Greek. For God shows no partiality.

All who have sinned without the law will also perish without the law, and all who have sinned under the law will be judged by the law. For it is not the hearers of the law who are righteous before God, but the doers of the law who will be justified. When Gentiles who have not the law do by nature what the law requires, they are a law to themselves, even though they do not have the law. They show that what the law requires is written on their hearts, while their conscience also bears witness and their conflicting thoughts accuse or perhaps excuse them on that day when, according to my gospel, God judges the secrets of men by Christ Jesus.

But if you call yourself a Jew and rely upon the law and boast of your relation to God and know his will and approve what is excellent, because you are instructed in the law, and if you are sure that you are a guide to the blind, a light to those who are in darkness, a corrector of the foolish, a teacher of children, having in the law the embodiment of knowledge and truth—you then who teach others, will you not teach yourself? While you preach against stealing, do you steal? You who say that one must not commit adultery, do you commit adultery? You who abhor idols, do you rob temples? You who boast in the law, do you dishonor God by breaking the law? For, as it is written, "The name of God is blasphemed among the Gentiles because of you."

Circumcision indeed is of value if you obey the law; but if you break

---

[51]The Jew *first* because the special relationship granted to the people who had received the earlier covenant increased their responsibility. Both Jews and Gentiles, however, are *judged* equally by their actions, the Jews under the Law of Moses as found in the Old Testament, the Gentiles by the same standard as "written on their hearts."

the law, your circumcision becomes uncircumcision.[52] So, if a man who is uncircumcised keeps the precepts of the law, will not his uncircumcision be regarded as circumcision? Then those who are physically uncircumcised but keep the law will condemn you who have the written code and circumcision but break the law. For he is not a real Jew who is one outwardly, nor is true circumcision something external and physical. He is a Jew who is one inwardly, and real circumcision is a matter of the heart, spiritual and not literal. His praise is not from men but from God.

Then what advantage has the Jew? Or what is the value of circumcision? Much in every way. To begin with, the Jews are entrusted with the oracles of God. What if some were unfaithful? Does their faithlessness nullify the faithfulness of God? By no means! Let God be true though every man be false, as it is written,[53]

> "That thou mayest be justified in thy words,
> and prevail when thou art judged."

But if our wickedness serves to show the justice of God, what shall we say? That God is unjust to inflict wrath on us? (I speak in a human way.) By no means! For then how could God judge the world? But if through my falsehood God's truthfulness abounds to his glory, why am I still being condemned as a sinner? And why not do evil that good may come?—as some people slanderously charge us with saying. Their condemnation is just.

What then? Are we Jews any better off? No, not at all; for I have already charged that all men, both Jews and Greeks, are under the power of sin. . . .

*Justification[54] through Faith by God's Grace—Not Through Works
3:21–31*

But now the righteousness of God has been manifested apart from law, although the law and the prophets bear witness to it, the righteousness of God through faith in Jesus Christ for all who believe. For

[52]That is, the Jewish violator of the Law stands before God precisely where the pagan violator stands. (Circumcision is the physical symbol of God's covenant with the Hebrews, Genesis 17.)

[53]In Psalm 51.

[54]Pardon, forgiveness by God of humans' sinful guilt—necessary for individual salvation.

there is no distinction; since all have sinned and fall short of the glory of God, they are justified by his grace as a gift, through the redemption[55] which is in Christ Jesus, whom God put forward as an expiation by his blood,[56] to be received by faith. This was to show God's righteousness, because in his divine forbearance he had passed over former sins; it was to prove at the present time that he himself is righteous and that he justifies him who has faith in Jesus.

Then what becomes of our boasting? It is excluded. On what principle? On the principle of works? No, but on the principle of faith.[57] For we hold that a man is justified by faith apart from works of law. Or is God the God of Jews only? Is he not the God of Gentiles also? Yes, of Gentiles also, since God is one; and he will justify the circumcised on the ground of their faith and the uncircumcised through their faith. Do we then overthrow the law by this faith? By no means! On the contrary, we uphold the law.

---

[55]Payment (for sin), liberation, deliverance.

[56]Christ's death is a sacrificial atonement (expiation) for human sin; it is God's way of cleansing away the sins of the faithful.

[57]That is, if salvation could be achieved by human "works" (deeds), there might be a reason for boasting; but since salvation is through *faith,* there is no reason for pride.

27

Saint Jerome

Letter CXXV

*I*N *the early fourth century (A.D. 313)
Christianity achieved legal status among the other religions of the Roman
Empire. Near the end of that same century (381) Christianity became the
official religion of the state, and worship of the old Greco-Roman gods was
forbidden. That conflict with classical culture was not only religious; there
were also intellectual and social consequences. For example, many devout
Christian men and women of the upper classes, disgusted by the continuing
immorality of many Romans, gave up the life of the cities—along with its
traditional civic and social responsibilities. They thus rejected the urban
achievement of the ancient world—for a withdrawn religious life. This desire
to pursue the "ascetic ideal," often in isolated places, was fast becoming a major
force in the Church.*

*One of the most famous and influential of these ascetics was Saint Jerome
(Eusebius Hieronymus), ca. 345–420, born of Christian parents in the Roman province of Dalmatia (in modern Yugoslavia). Although a scholar, educated in Rome, Jerome withdrew to the Syrian desert near Antioch, living
austerely for five years among other Christian hermits. There he studied Christian theology, Greek and Hebrew, the languages of the Bible. Returning to
Antioch in 379 he was ordained a priest but never performed priestly duties.*

*Travelling to Rome for a Church council in 382, he became the secretary of
Pope Damasus, who commissioned him to make a new Latin translation of the
Bible. Jerome also became the spiritual adviser to a pious group of aristocratic
women. Hostile reactions to his verbal attacks upon the growing involvement
of churchmen in worldly affairs, as well as the death of his protector, Pope
Damasus, caused Jerome in 385 to leave Rome forever. He finally settled for*

LETTER CXXV   *Select Letters of St. Jerome*, trans. F.A. Wright (Loeb Classical Library—
London: Heinemann and Cambridge: Harvard University Press, 1933), 407–419,
423–429, 435–439. Reprinted by permission of Harvard University Press.

the rest of his life in Bethlehem, where he founded a monastery for men, a convent for women (under one of his Roman female followers), and a hostel for Christian pilgrims. Devoted as ever to study and writing, he produced there (among many other works) the famous Latin translation of the Bible known as the Vulgate. It was to become the official ("authorized") version of the Catholic Church and was one of the last important literary achievements of the ancient world.

Over 150 of Jerome's letters survive. The one excerpted here was written in 411 and is a rather moderate expression of his asceticism. It states the established arguments for monasticism (life in a secluded religious community). Rusticus, the person to whom Jerome addressed the letter, took his advice and entered a monastery, but afterward became a bishop. The many biblical quotations and references in the letter—too many to footnote fully—show, of course, the deep well of Jerome's primary inspiration. At the same time, his references to classical literature show his divided spirit. Once, in fact, in a feverish nightmare, the ill Jerome heard God pronouncing judgment upon him—saying that he followed not Christ but Cicero (the Roman pagan writer)! The letter is notable, too, for revealing the decay of the classical ideal of citizenship—that of Pericles and Plato, Cato and Cicero. It also shows the spiritual preoccupation of many able individuals who, in pre-Christian times, would have served as leaders of the state.

If you wish to be, and not merely seem, a monk, have regard not for your property—you began your vows by renouncing it—but for your soul. Let a squalid garb be the evidence of a clean heart: let a coarse tunic prove that you despise the world; provided only that you do not pride yourself on such things nor let your dress and language be at variance. Avoid hot baths: your aim is to quench the heat of the body by the help of chilling fasts. But let your fasts be moderate, since if they are carried to excess they weaken the stomach, and by making more food necessary to make up for it lead to indigestion, which is the parent of lust. A frugal, temperate diet is good both for body and soul.

See your mother often, but do not be forced to see other women when you visit her. Their faces may dwell in your heart and so
            'A secret wound may fester in your breast.'[1]

---

[1] From Virgil's *Aeneid* (IV, 67), the Roman national epic (19 b.c.). In the poem, Queen Dido of Carthage begins to brood deeply about the handsome hero Aeneas. She falls in love with him and kills herself when he leaves her.

You must remember too that the maids who wait upon her are an especial snare; the lower they are in rank, the easier it is to ruin them. John the Baptist had a saintly mother and his father was a priest; but neither his mother's love nor his father's wealth could prevail upon him to live in his parents' house at the risk of his chastity. He took up his abode in the desert, and desiring only to see Christ refused to look at anything else. His rough garb, his skin girdle,[2] his diet of locusts and wild honey were all alike meant to ensure virtue and self-restraint. The sons of the prophets, who are the monks of the Old Testament, built huts for themselves by the stream of Jordan, and leaving the crowded cities lived on porridge and wild herbs.

As long as you stay in your native city, regard your cell as Paradise, gather in it the varied fruits of the Scriptures, make them your delight, and rejoice in their embrace. If your eye or your foot or your hand offend you, cast it off. Spare nothing, provided that you spare your soul. 'Whosoever looketh on a woman to lust after her hath committed adultery with her already in his heart.' 'Who can boast "I have made my heart clean"?' The stars are not pure in God's sight: how much less are men, whose life is one long temptation! Woe to us, who commit fornication whenever we have lustful thoughts! . . . The chosen vessel, from whose mouth we hear Christ's own words, keeps his body under and brings it into subjection; but still he perceives that the natural heat of the body fights against his fixed purpose, and he is compelled to do what he will not. Like a man suffering violence he cries aloud and says: 'O wretched man that I am, who shall deliver me from the body of this death?' And do *you* think then that you can pass through life without a fall and without a wound, if you do not keep your heart with all diligence and say with the Saviour: 'My mother and my brethren are these which hear the word of God and do it'? Such cruelty as this is really love. Nay, what greater love can there be than to guard a holy son for a holy mother? She desires your eternal life: she is content not to see you for the moment, provided that she may see you for ever with Christ. She is like Hannah, who brought forth Samuel,[3] not for her own comfort, but for the service of the tabernacle.[4]

The sons of Jonadab drank no wine nor strong drink and lived in tents which they pitched whenever night came on. Of them the psalm

[2] A covering made of animal hides.

[3] A prophet, judge, and political leader of the Jews in the Old Testament.

[4] The sanctuary which contained the two tablets of the Law on which were inscribed the Ten Commandments from Mount Sinai. (See Exodus selection, pp. 554–55.)

says that they were the first to undergo captivity, for when the Chaldean host was devastating Judaea they were compelled to enter cities. Let others think as they will—every one follows his own bent—but to me a town is a prison, and the wilderness a paradise. What do we monks want with crowded cities, we whose very name bespeaks loneliness?[5] Moses was trained for forty years in the desert to fit him for the task of leading the Jewish people, and from being a shepherd of sheep he became a shepherd of men. The apostles left their fishing on Lake Gennesaret to fish for human souls. Then they had a father, nets, and a little boat: but they followed the Lord straightway and abandoned everything, carrying their cross every day, without so much as a stick in their hands.

I say this, so that if you are tickled by a desire to become a clergyman, you may learn now what you will then be able to teach others,[6] offering a reasonable sacrifice to Christ. You must not think yourself an old soldier while you are still a recruit, a master while you are still a pupil. It would not become my lowly rank to pass judgment on others, or to say anything unfavourable about those who serve in churches.[7] Let them keep their proper place and station, and if you ever join them, my treatise written for Nepotian [Letter LII] will show you how you ought to live in that position. For the moment I am discussing a monk's early training and character, a monk, moreover, who after a liberal education in his early manhood placed upon his neck the yoke of Christ.

The first point with which I must deal is whether you ought to live alone or in a monastery with others. I would prefer you to have the society of holy men and not to be your own teacher. If you set out on a strange road without a guide you may easily at the start take a wrong turning and make a mistake, going too far or not far enough, running till you weary yourself or delaying your journey for a sleep. In solitude pride quickly creeps in, and when a man has fasted for a little while and has seen no one, he thinks himself a person of some account. He forgets who he is, whence he comes, and where he is going, and lets his body run riot within, his tongue abroad. Contrary to the apostle

---

[5]The Latin word for "monk" is *monachus*, derived from the Greek word *monachos* meaning "solitary, alone."

[6]Actually, by Jerome's time monks were usually not totally solitary, but were organized in *communities*—devoted to prayer, meditation, and useful work.

[7]Those ordained as priests, presbyters, or deacons who served in the churches of the cities. If a monk wished to enter the *ministry* of the Church, he first had to be ordained (a religious ritual conveying special spiritual powers).

[Paul's] wishes, he judges another man's servants; he stretches out his hand for anything that his gullet craves; he does what he pleases and sleeps as long as he pleases; he fears no one, he thinks all men his inferiors, spends more time in cities than in his cell, and though among the brethren he makes a pretence of modesty, in the crowded squares he ruffles it with the best. What then, you will say? Do I disapprove of the solitary life? Not at all: I have often commended it. But I wish to see the soldiers who march out from a monastery-school men who have not been frightened by their early training, who have given proof of a holy life for many months, who have made themselves last that they might be first, who have not been overcome by hunger or satiety, who take pleasure in poverty, whose garb, conversation, looks and gait all teach virtue, and who have no skill—as some foolish fellows have—in inventing monstrous stories of their struggles with demons, tales invented to excite admiration of the ignorant mob and to extract money from their pockets.

Just lately, to my sorrow, I saw the fortune of a Croesus[8] brought to light at one man's death, and beheld a city's alms collected ostensibly for the poor's benefit left by will to his sons and their descendants. . . . Nor need we wonder at his avarice: his partner and teacher was a man who turned the hunger of the needy into a source of wealth for himself, and to his own wretchedness kept back the legacies that were left to the wretched. But at last their cries reached heaven and were too much for God's patient ears, so that he sent an angel to say to this villainous Nabal the Carmelite:[9] 'Thou fool, this night thy soul shall be required of thee: then whose shall those things be which thou has provided?'

For the reasons then which I have given above, I wish you not to live with your mother. And there are some further considerations. If she offers you a dainty dish, you would grieve her by refusing it, while if you take it you would be throwing oil on the fire. Moreover, in a house that is full of girls you would see things in the day-time that you would think about in the night. Always have a book in your hand and before your eyes; learn the psalms word by word, pray without ceasing, keep your senses on the alert and closed against vain imaginings. Let your mind and body both strain towards the Lord, overcome wrath by patience; love the knowledge of the Scriptures and you will not love the sins of the flesh.

[8]A king of Lydia in the sixth century B.C., widely known for his vast wealth. (See the selection from Herodotus, pp. 148–59.)

[9]In the Old Testament, a wealthy, rude, and ungrateful owner of sheep and goats. (In Hebrew *nabal* means "fool.")

Do not let your mind offer a lodging to disturbing thoughts, for if they once find a home in your breast they will become your masters and lead you on into fatal sin. Engage in some occupation, so that the devil may always find you busy. If the apostles[10] who had the power to make the Gospel their livelihood still worked with their hands that they might not be a burden on any man, and gave relief to others whose carnal possessions they had a right to enjoy in return for their spiritual benefits, why should you not provide for your own future wants? Make creels[11] of reeds or weave baskets of pliant osiers. Hoe the ground and mark it out into equal plots, and when you have sown cabbage seed or set out plants in rows, bring water down in channels and stand by like the onlooker in the lovely lines:

> 'Lo, from the channelled slope he brings the stream,
> Which falls hoarse murmuring o'er the polished stones
> And with its bubbling flood allays the heat
> Of sun-scorched fields.'[12]

Graft barren trees with buds or slips, so that you may, after a little time, pluck sweet fruit as a reward for your labours. Make hives for bees, for to them the Proverbs of Solomon send you, and by watching the tiny creatures learn the ordinance of a monastery and the discipline of a kingdom. Twist lines too for catching fish, and copy out manuscripts, so that your hand may earn you food and your soul be satisfied with reading. 'Every one that is idle is a prey to vain desires.' Monasteries in Egypt make it a rule not to take any one who will not work, thinking not so much of the necessities of life as of the safety of men's souls, lest they should be led astray by dangerous imaginings, and be like Jerusalem in her whoredoms, who opened her feet to every chance comer.

•   •   •

No art is learned without a master. Even dumb animals and herds of wild beasts follow leaders of their own. Bees have rulers, and cranes

[10]Earliest Christian missionaries.

[11]Wicker containers.

[12]From Virgil's *Georgics*, a long Latin poem, 30 B.C., on the beauty and dignity of agricultural labor.

fly behind one of their number in the shape of the letter Y. There is one emperor, and one judge for each province. When Rome was founded it could not have two brothers reigning together, and so it was inaugurated by an act of fratricide.[13] Esau and Jacob warred against one another in Rebecca's womb.[14] Each church has but one bishop, one arch-presbyter, one archdeacon; every ecclesiastical order is subjected to its own rulers. There is one pilot in a ship, one master in a house; and however large an army may be, the soldiers await one man's signal.

I will not weary my reader with further repetition, for the purpose of all these examples is simply this. I want to show you that you had better not be left to your own discretion, but should rather live in a monastery under the control of one father and with many companions. From one of them you may learn humility, from another patience; this one will teach you silence, that one meekness. You will not do what you yourself wish; you will eat what you are ordered; you will take what you are given; you will wear the dress allotted to you; you will perform a set amount of work; you will be subordinate to some one you do not like; you will come to bed worn out with weariness and fall asleep as you walk about. Before you have had your fill of rest, you will be forced to get out of bed and take your turn in psalm-singing, a task where real emotion is a greater requisite than a sweet voice.

The apostle [Paul] says: 'I will pray with the spirit and I will pray with the understanding also,' and, again: 'Make melody in your hearts.' He had read the precept: 'Sing ye praises with understanding.' You will serve the brethren; you will wash the feet of guests; if you suffer wrong you will say nothing; the superior of the monastery you will fear as a master and love as a father. Whatever precepts he gives, you will believe to be wholesome for you. You will not pass judgment upon your elder's decisions, for it is your duty to be obedient and carry out orders, according to the words of Moses: 'Keep silence and hearken, O Israel.' You will be so busy with all these tasks that you will have no time for vain imaginings, and while you pass from one occupation to the next you will only have in mind the work that you are being forced to do.

---

[13]Brother-killing. According to Roman legend, Romulus killed his twin brother, Remus, and thereby became sole ruler of the new city of Rome. (See selection 14, Livy's *History*, p. 390.)

[14]Isaac and Rebecca were the parents of the twins Esau and Jacob, who fought (it was said) even in the womb. Eventually, Esau sold his inheritance to Jacob (Genesis 25).

I myself have seen some men who after they had renounced the world—in garb, at least, and in verbal professions, but not in reality—changed nothing of their former mode of life. Their household has increased rather than diminished; they have the same number of servants to wait upon them and keep the same elaborate table; though they drink from glass and eat from plates of earthenware, it is gold they swallow, and amidst crowds of servants swarming round them they claim the name of hermit. Others, who are poor and of slender means and think themselves full of wisdom, pass through the streets like the pageants in a procession, to practise a cynical eloquence. Others shrug their shoulders and croak indistinctly to themselves, and with glassy eyes fixed upon the earth they balance swelling words upon their tongues, so that if you add a crier, you might think it was his excellency the governor who was coming along. Some, too, by reason of damp cells and immoderate fasts, added to the weariness of solitude and excessive study, have a singing in their ears day and night, and turning melancholy mad need Hippocrates'[15] medications more than any advice of mine.

Very many cannot forgo their previous trades and occupations, and though they change its name carry on the same pedlar's traffic as before, seeking for themselves not food and raiment, as the apostle directs, but greater profits than men of the world expect. In the past the mad greed of sellers was checked by the aediles, or as the Greeks call them, market-inspectors, and men could not cheat with impunity: to-day under the cloak of religion such men hoard up unjust gains, and the good name of Christianity does more wrong than it suffers. I am ashamed to say it, but I must—at least we ought to blush at our disgrace—we hold out our hands in public for alms while we have gold hidden under our rags, and to every one's surprise after living as poor men we die rich with purses well filled.

In your case, since you will be in a monastery, such conduct will not be allowed; habits will gradually grow on you, and finally you will do of your own accord what was at first a matter of compulsion; you will take pleasure in your labours, and forgetting what is behind you will reach out to that which is before; you will not think at all of the evil that others do, but only of the good which it is your duty to perform.

---

[15]Hippocrates was a famous physician of ancient Greece (fifth century B.C.).

Do not be influenced by the number of those that sin, or disturbed by the host of the perishing [damned], so as to have the unspoken thought: 'What? Shall all then perish who live in cities? Behold, they enjoy their property, they serve in the churches, they frequent the baths, they do not disdain unguents [skin lotions], and yet they flourish and are universally respected.' To such reasonings I have replied before, and will now do so briefly again, merely remarking that in this present short treatise I am not discussing the behaviour of the clergy, but laying down rules for a monk. The clergy are holy men, and in every case their life is worthy of praise. Go then and so live in your monastery that you may deserve to be a clergyman, that you may keep your youth free from all stain of defilement, and that you may come forth to Christ's altar as a virgin steps from her bower; that you may be well spoken of abroad, and that women may know your reputation but not your looks. When you come to ripe years, that is, if life be granted you, and have been appointed as a clergyman either by the people or by the bishop of the city, then act as becomes a cleric, and among your colleagues choose the better men as your models. In every rank and condition of life the very bad is mingled with the very good.

• • •

Truth does not love corners nor does she seek out whisperers. To Timothy[16] it is said: 'Against an elder receive not an accusation suddenly; but him that sinneth rebuke before all, that others also may fear.' When a man is of ripe years you should not readily believe evil of him; his past life is a defence and so is the honourable title of elder. Still, as we are but men and sometimes in spite of our mature age fall into the sins of youth, if I do wrong and you wish to correct me, rebuke me openly and do not indulge in secret backbiting. 'Let the righteous smite me, it shall be a kindness, and let him reprove me; but let not the oil of the sinner enrich my head.' 'Whom the Lord loveth, he chasteneth, and scourgeth every son whom he receiveth.' By the mouth of Isaiah, God makes proclamation: 'O my people, they who call you happy cause you to err and destroy the way of your paths.' What benefit is it to me if you tell other people of my misdeeds, if without my knowledge you hurt another by the story of my sins or rather by your

---

[16]A younger associate of Saint Paul. The quotation is from The First Letter of Paul to Timothy (5:19–20) on Church discipline.

slanders, if while really eager to tell your tale to all you speak to each individual as though he were your only confidant? Such conduct seeks not my improvement but the satisfaction of your own vice. The Lord gave commandment that those who sin against us should be arraigned privately or else in the presence of a witness, and that if they refuse to listen they should be brought before the Church, and those who persist in wickedness should be regarded as heathens and publicans.[17]

I have spoken thus definitely because I wish to free a young friend of mine from an itching tongue and itching ears, so that I may present him born again in Christ without a spot or roughness as a chaste virgin, holy both in body and in mind. I would not have him boast in name alone, or be shut out by the Bridegroom [Christ] because his lamp has gone out for want of the oil of good works. You have in your town a saintly and most learned prelate, Proculus,[18] and he by the living sound of his voice can do more for you than any pages I can write. By daily homilies he will keep you in the straight path and not suffer you to turn right or left and leave the king's highway, whereby Israel undertakes to pass on its hasty journey to the promised land. May the voice of the Church's supplication be heard: 'Lord, ordain peace for us, for thou hast wrought all our works for us.' May our renunciation of the world be a matter of free will and not of necessity! May we seek poverty as a glorious thing, not have it forced upon us as a punishment!

However, in our present miseries, with swords raging fiercely all around us, he is rich enough who is not in actual want of bread, he is more powerful than he needs be who is not reduced to slavery. Exuperius, the saintly bishop of Toulouse, like the widow of Zarephath[19] feeds others and goes hungry himself. His face is pale with fasting, but it is the craving of others that torments him, and he has spent all his substance on those that are Christ's flesh. Yet none is richer than he; for in his wicker basket he carries the body of the Lord and in his glass cup His blood.[20] He has driven greed from the temple; without scourge of ropes or chiding words he has overthrown the tables of mammon

---

[17]Tax collectors. In the Gospels the "publicans" were often Jews who served the Roman conquerors in Judea and, therefore, were detested by their countrymen. They were frequently classified with "sinners."

[18]Bishop of Marseilles.

[19]An Old Testament figure.

[20]That is, the bread and wine of the Lord's Supper (sacrament of the Eucharist).

of those that sell doves, that is, the gifts of the Holy Spirit; he has scattered the money of the moneychangers, so that the house of God might be called a house of prayer and not a den of robbers.

Follow closely in his steps and in those of others like him in virtue, men whom their holy office only makes more humble and more poor. Or else, if you desire perfection, go out like Abraham from your native city and your kin, and travel whither you know not. If you have substance, sell it and give it to the poor. If you have none, you are free from a great burden. Naked yourself[21] follow a naked Christ. The task is hard and great and difficult, but great also are the rewards.

[21]That is, without property.

28

Saint Augustine

The City of God

As the heirs of Greco-Roman civili-
zation, imbued with its forms of thought and expression, fourth- and fifth-
century Christians still thought of themselves as part of that thousand-year
tradition. Instead of turning their backs on classical civilization, Christian
thinkers generally struggled to give it a new moral and spiritual direction, thus
achieving a kind of synthesis of Christianity and classicism. The most important of these thinkers, the dominant Western "Father of the Church," was
Aurelius Augustinus (A.D. 354–430).

Born in northern Africa near ancient Carthage, Augustine received the best
education his middle-class father, a pagan, could afford. His mother was a
devout Christian who influenced him greatly. After attending an advanced
school at Carthage, Augustine became a teacher of rhetoric (literature and
speech) at Carthage, then at Rome, and then Milan. There, impressed by
Milan's learned and eloquent Bishop Ambrose, he was converted (A.D. 386)
to Christianity. In his autobiography called the Confessions, Augustine
describes the errors of his youth, his intense spiritual and psychological struggles, and his philosophical path to conversion. A few years after his return to
Africa from Milan, he was made bishop of Hippo Regius, a small coastal town
near his birthplace. Even from there, his personality and constant flow of
writings spread his fame so that he became the outstanding figure in the entire
Western Church—his enduring influence second only to Saint Paul's.

Augustine's most important and longest work, The City of God (written

THE CITY OF GOD   Saint Augustine, *The City of God*, trans. Demetrius B. Zema
and Gerald G. Walsh (Washington, D.C.: The Catholic University of America Press,
1962–64). Copyright 1950–54. Reprinted by permission of the Catholic University of
American Press.

between 413 and 426), was meant to "combat the blasphemies and errors" of those who, bewildered by the collapse of their former security, laid the blame for the capture of Rome by the Visigoths (410) upon the Romans' rejection of their old gods. (In 381 Christianity had become the official religion of the Empire.) Deeply versed in the philosophies of the pagan world and admiring much of it, especially Platonism, Augustine answered Christianity's attackers with his idea of the "two cities." This, "the most famous of all philosophic meditations on history," as it has been called, is excerpted in the following passages.

History, Augustine states, is the unfolding result of God's will—moving from Creation to the Last Judgment. Individuals "choose" one of the two communities that embrace all of humanity: the "heavenly city" or the "earthly city." But they make their choice in accordance with God's will (predestination) and God's grace (mercy). (For the reader's convenience, book and chapter numbers for these excerpts are shown in the subtitles. Augustine's favorite sources of biblical quotation—too many to footnote fully here—are the Psalms, the Gospels, and Paul's Letters.) In The City of God *we see clearly the intellectual process whereby Judaism and the Christianity that grew from it became integrated into a new world-view equal in its comprehensiveness to the classical philosophies that it largely replaced.*

THE VICES OF THE ROMANS WHICH THE OVERTHROW OF THEIR COUNTRY DID NOT SERVE TO REFORM (I,33)

Are your minds bereft of reason? You are not merely mistaken; this is madness. Here are people in the East bewailing Rome's humiliation, and great states in remote regions of the earth holding public mourning and lamentation—and you Romans are searching for theaters, pouring into them, filling them, behaving more irresponsibly than ever before. It is this spiritual disease, degeneration, decline into immorality and indecency that Scipio[1] feared when he opposed the erection of theaters. He saw how easily ease and plenty would soften and ruin you. He did not wish you to be free from fear.

---

[1]Publius Cornelius Scipio Nasica, a conservative Roman aristocrat, consul (138 B.C.) and general of the republican era.

He did not think that the republic could be happy while walls were standing, yet morals were collapsing. But, you were more attached to the seductions of foul spirits than to the wisdom of men with foresight. That is why you take no blame for the evil you do, but blame Christianity for the evil you suffer. Depraved by prosperity and unchastened by adversity, you desire, in your security, not the peace of the State but liberty for license. Scipio wanted you to have a salutary fear of the enemy, lest you should rot in debauchery. Though crushed by the enemy, you put no check on immorality, you learned no lessons from calamity; in the depths of sorrows you still wallow in sin.

AN INTRODUCTION TO THE PART OF THIS WORK IN WHICH THE RESPECTIVE ORIGINS AND THE ENDS OF THE TWO CITIES, THE HEAVENLY AND THE EARTHLY, ARE TO BE DISCUSSED (XI,1)

The expression, 'City of God,' which I have been using is justified by that Scripture whose divine authority puts it above the literature of all other people and brings under its sway every type of human genius—and that, not by some casual intellectual reaction, but by a disposition of Divine Providence. For, in this Scripture, we read: 'Glorious things are said of thee, O city of God'; and, in another psalm: 'Great is the Lord, and exceedingly to be praised in the city of our God, in His holy mountain, increasing the joy of the whole earth'; and, a little later in the same psalm: 'As we have heard, so have we seen, in the city of the Lord of hosts, in the city of our God: God hath founded it for ever'; and in another text: 'The stream of the river maketh the city of God joyful: the most High hath sanctified his own tabernacle. God is in the midst thereof, it shall not be moved.'[2]

Through these and similar passages too numerous to quote, we learn of the existence of a City of God whose Founder has inspired us with a love and longing to become its citizens. The inhabitants of the earthly city who prefer their own gods to the Founder of the holy City do not realize that He is the God of gods—though not, of course, of those false, wicked and proud gods who, because they have been deprived of that unchangeable light which was meant for all, are reduced to a pitiful power and, therefore, are eager for some sort of influence

[2]Augustine, as he often does, is quoting from the Old Testament's book of Psalms. In this case, Psalms 87, 48, and 46.

and demand divine honors from their deluded subjects. He is the God of those reverent and holy gods who prefer to obey and worship one God rather than to have many others obeying and worshiping them.[3]

In the ten preceding Books, I have done my best, with the help of our Lord and King, to refute the enemies of this City. Now, however, realizing what is expected of me and recalling what I promised, I shall begin to discuss, as well as I can, the origin, history, and destiny of the respective cities, earthly and heavenly, which, as I have said, are at present inextricably intermingled, one with the other. First, I shall explain how these two cities originated when the angels took opposing sides.

THE ESSENTIAL DIFFERENCE BETWEEN THE TWO CITIES, BETWEEN WORLDLY SOCIETY AND THE COMMUNION OF SAINTS (XIV,28)

What we see, then, is that two societies have issued from two kinds of love. Worldly society has flowered from a selfish love which dared to despise even God, whereas the communion of saints is rooted in a love of God that is ready to trample on self. In a word, this latter relies on the Lord, whereas the other boasts that it can get along by itself. The city of man seeks the praise of men, whereas the height of glory for the other is to hear God in the witness of conscience. The one lifts up its head in its own boasting; the other says to God: 'Thou art my glory, thou liftest up my head.'

In the city of the world both the rulers themselves and the people they dominate are dominated by the lust for domination; whereas in the City of God all citizens serve one another in charity, whether they serve by the responsibilities of office or by the duties of obedience. The one city loves its leaders as symbols of its own strength; the other says to its God: 'I love thee, O Lord, my strength.' Hence, even the wise men in the city of man live according to man, and their only goal has been the goods of their bodies or of the mind or of both; though some of them have reached a knowledge of God, 'they did not glorify

[3]By "those false, wicked and proud gods" Augustine means the fallen angels who, in Christian teachings, had rebelled against God. The earthly city had originated with those rebellious angels, now demons, who caused people to believe in the old pagan gods, considered by Augustine to be mere fictions. "Those reverent and holy gods" are, of course, the good angels who had remained faithful to God.

him as God or give thanks but became vain in their reasonings, and their senseless minds have been darkened. For while professing to be wise' (that is to say, while glorying in their own wisdom, under the domination of pride), 'they have become fools, and they have changed the glory of the incorruptible God for an image made like to corruptible man and to birds and four-footed beasts and creeping things' (meaning that they either led their people, or imitated them, in adoring idols shaped like these things), 'and they worshipped and served the creature rather than the Creator who is blessed forever.' In the City of God, on the contrary, there is no merely human wisdom, but there is a piety which worships the true God as He should be worshiped and has as its goal that reward of all holiness whether in the society of saints on earth or in that of angels of heaven, which is 'that God may be all in all.'

ON THE TWO LINES OF DESCENT, DISTINGUISHED BY THEIR RESPECTIVE DESTINIES, WHICH CAN BE TRACED, FROM THE BEGINNING ON, IN THE HISTORY OF MANKIND (XV,1)

Regarding the Garden of Eden, the happiness that was possible there, the life of our first parents, their sin and their punishment, a great deal has been thought, said, and written.[4] In the foregoing Books I myself have said something on these subjects, setting forth what can be found in the text of Scripture and adding only such reflections as seemed in harmony with its authority. The discussion could be pursued in greater detail, but it would raise so many and such varied problems that I would need for their solution more books than our present purpose calls for; nor is there so much time at my disposal that I feel obliged to waste it in satisfying the curiosity of those persons with nothing to do who are more captious in putting their questions than capable of grasping the answers.

Actually, I think I have said enough on the really great and difficult problems concerning the origin of the world, the soul, and the human race. In regard to mankind I have made a division. On the one side are those who live according to man; on the other, those who live according to God. And I have said that, in a deeper sense, we may speak of two cities or two human societies, the destiny of the one being an

[1]See Genesis, pp. 547–50, in the selection from the Old Testament.

eternal kingdom under God while the doom of the other is eternal punishment along with the Devil.

Of the final consummation of the two cities I shall have to speak later. Of their original cause among the angels whose number no man knows and then in the first two human beings, I have already spoken. For the moment, therefore, I must deal with the course of the history of the two cities from the time when children were born to the first couple until the day when men shall beget no more. By the course of their history, as distinguished from their original cause and final consummation, I mean the whole time of world history in which men are born and take the place of those who die and depart.

Now, the first man born of the two parents of the human race was Cain. He belonged to the city of man. The next born was Abel, and he was of the City of God. Notice here a parallel between the individual man and the whole race. We all experience as individuals what the Apostle [Paul] says: 'It is not the spiritual that comes first, but the physical, and then the spiritual.' The fact is that every individual springs from a condemned stock and, because of Adam, must be first cankered and carnal, only later to become sound and spiritual by the process of rebirth in Christ. So, too, with the human race as a whole, as soon as human birth and death began the historical course of the two cities, the first to be born was a citizen of this world and only later came the one who was an alien in the city of men but at home in the City of God, a man predestined by grace[5] and elected by grace. By grace an alien on earth, by grace he was a citizen of heaven. In and of himself, he springs from the common clay, all of which was under condemnation from the beginning, but which God held in His hands like a potter, to borrow the metaphor which the Apostle so wisely and deliberately uses. For, God could make 'from the same mass one vessel for honorable, another for ignoble use.' The first vessel to be made was 'for ignoble use.' Only later was there made a vessel for honorable use. And as with the race, so, as I have said, with the individual. First comes the clay that is only fit to be thrown away, with which we must begin, but in which we need not remain. Afterwards comes what is fit for use, that into which we can be gradually molded and in which, when molded, we may remain. This does not mean that every one who is wicked is to become good, but that no one becomes good who was not once wicked. What is true is that the sooner a man makes a change

[5]In Christian theology, the freely given and undeserved favor and love of God.

in himself for the better the sooner he has a right to be called what he has become. The second name hides the first.

Now, it is recorded of Cain that he built a city, while Abel, as though he were merely a pilgrim on earth, built none. For, the true City of the saints is in heaven, though here on earth it produces citizens in whom it wanders as on a pilgrimage through time looking for the Kingdom of eternity. When that day comes it will gather together all those who, rising in their bodies, shall have that Kingdom given to them in which, along with their Prince, the King of Eternity, they shall reign for ever and ever.

ON PRUNING THE LOVE OF HUMAN PRAISE BECAUSE THE GLORY OF THE SAINTS IS ALL IN GOD (V,14)

. . . . After the Apostles[6] came the martyrs[7] . . . a vast multitude of them with true piety and, therefore, with true virtue endured what other men made them suffer. It was different with pagan heroes. They were citizens of the earthly city, of a kingdom not in heaven but on earth, and the only purpose of all their duties was the city's temporal security. They knew nothing of everlasting life, but only of a succession of living and dying mortals. What other glory could they love but the fame by which, when they were dead, they might seem to live on the lips of those who praised them?

GOD'S TEMPORAL REWARD FOR THE NATURAL MORALITY OF THE ROMANS (V,15)

For these pagan heroes there was not to be the divine grace of everlasting life along with His holy angels in His heavenly City, for the only road to this Society of the Blessed is true piety, that is, that religious service or *latreía* (to use the Greek word) which is offered to the One true God. On the other hand, if God did not grant them at least the temporal glory of a splendid Empire, there would have been no reward for the praiseworthy efforts or virtues by which they strove to attain that glory. When our Lord said: 'Amen I say to you they have received their reward,' He had in mind those who do what seems to be good in order to be glorified by men.

After all, the pagans subordinated their private property to the com-

---

[6]The earliest Christian missionaries.

[7]Those who went to their deaths because of their service to Christ.

mon welfare, that is, to the republic and the public treasury. They resisted the temptation to avarice. They gave their counsel freely in the councils of the state. They indulged in neither public crime nor private passion. They thought they were on the right road when they strove, by all these means, for honors, rule, and glory. Honor has come to them from almost all peoples. The rule of their laws has been imposed on many peoples. And in our day, in literature and in history, glory has been given them by almost everyone. They have no right to complain of the justice of the true and supreme God. 'They have received their reward.'

THE REWARD OF THE SAINTS WHO ARE CITIZENS OF THE ETERNAL CITY, AND FOR WHOM THE EXAMPLES OF ROMAN VIRTUES WERE NOT WITHOUT VALUE (V,16)

The reward of the saints[8] is altogether different. They were men who, while on earth, suffered reproaches for the City of God which is so much hated by lovers of this world. That City is eternal. There, no one is born because no one dies. There, there reigns that true and perfect happiness which is not a goddess, but a gift of god—toward whose beauty we can but sigh in our pilgrimage on earth, though we hold the pledge of it by faith. In that City, the sun does not 'rise upon the good and bad' for the Sun of Justice cherishes the good alone. There, where the Truth is a treasure shared by all, there is no need to pinch the poor to fill the coffers of the state.

It was, then, not only to reward the Roman heroes with human glory that the Roman Empire spread. It had a purpose for the citizens of the Eternal City during their pilgrimage on earth. Meditating long and seriously on those great examples, they could understand what love of their Heavenly Fatherland should be inspired by everlasting life, since a fatherland on earth has been so much loved by citizens inspired by human glory.

ON WAR AND PEACE IN THE ASSOCIATIONS OF EARTHLY MINDED MEN (XV,4)

As for the city of this world, it is neither to last forever nor even to be a city, once the final doom of pain is upon it. Nevertheless, while

---

[8]All those whose first loyalty is to God.

history lasts, it has a finality of its own; it reaches such happiness by sharing a common good as is possible when there are no goods but the things of time to afford it happiness. This is not the kind of good that can give those who are content with it any freedom from fear. In fact, the city of man, for the most part, is a city of contention with opinions divided by foreign wars and domestic quarrels and by the demands for victories which either end in death or are merely momentary respites from further war. The reason is that whatever part of the city of the world raises the standard of war, it seeks to be lord of the world, when, in fact, it is enthralled in its own wickedness. Even when it conquers, its victory can be mortally poisoned by pride, and if, instead of taking pride in the success already achieved, it takes account of the nature and normal vicissitudes of life and is afraid of future failure, then the victory is merely momentary. The fact is that the power to reach domination by war is not the same as the power to remain in perpetual control.

Nevertheless, it is wrong to deny that the aims of human civilization are good, for this is the highest end that mankind of itself can achieve. For, however lowly the goods of earth, the aim, such as it is, is peace. The purpose even of war is peace. For, where victory is not followed by resistance there is a peace that was impossible so long as rivals were competing, hungrily and unhappily, for something material too little to suffice for both. This kind of peace is a product of the work of war, and its price is a so-called glorious victory; when victory goes to the side that had a juster cause it is surely a matter for human rejoicing, and the peace is one to be welcomed.

The things of earth are not merely good; they are undoubtedly gifts from God. But, of course, if those who get such goods in the city of men are reckless about the better goods of the City of God, in which there is to be the ultimate victory of an eternal, supreme, and untroubled peace, if men so love the goods of earth as to believe that these are the only goods or if they love them more than the goods they know to be better, then the consequence is inevitable: misery and more misery.

THE CHRISTIAN VIEW OF THE SUPREME GOOD AND THE ULTIMATE EVIL, AS DISTINGUISHED FROM THE PHILOSOPHERS' VIEW THAT THE SUPREME GOOD IS IN MEN THEMSELVES (XIX,4)

If I am asked what stand the City of God would take on the issues raised and, first, what this City thinks of the supreme good and ultimate evil, the answer would be: She holds that eternal life is the supreme good and eternal death the supreme evil, and that we should live rightly in order to obtain the one and avoid the other. Hence the Scriptural expression, 'the just man lives by faith'[9]—by faith, for the fact is that we do not now behold our good and, therefore, must seek it by faith; nor can we of ourselves even live rightly, unless He who gives us faith helps us to believe and pray, for it takes faith to believe that we need His help.

Those who think that the supreme good and evil are to be found in this life are mistaken. It makes no difference whether it is in the body or in the soul or in both—or, specifically, in pleasure or virtue or in both—that they seek the supreme good. They seek in vain whether they look to serenity, to virtue, or to both; whether to pleasure plus serenity, or to virtue, or to all three; or to the satisfaction of our innate exigencies, or to virtue, or to both. It is in vain that men look for beatitude on earth or in human nature. Divine Truth, as expressed in the Prophet's words, makes them look foolish: 'The Lord knows the thoughts of men' or, as the text is quoted by St. Paul: 'The Lord knows the thoughts of the wise that they are vain.'

ON THE AREAS OF AGREEMENT AND DISAGREEMENT BETWEEN THE TWO CITIES (XIX,17)

While the homes of unbelieving men are intent upon acquiring temporal peace out of the possessions and comforts of this temporal life, the families which live according to faith look ahead to the good things of heaven promised as imperishable, and use material and temporal goods in the spirit of pilgrims, not as snares or obstructions to block their way to God, but simply as helps to ease and never to increase the burdens of this corruptible body which weighs down the soul. Both types of homes and their masters have this in common, that they must use things essential to this mortal life. But the respective purposes to which they put them are characteristic and very different.

So, too, the earthly city which does not live by faith seeks only an earthly peace, and limits the goal of its peace, of its harmony of authority and obedience among its citizens, to the voluntary and collective attainment of objectives necessary to mortal existence. The heavenly City, meanwhile—or, rather, that part that is on pilgrimage in mortal life and lives by faith—must use this earthly peace until such

[9]See the selection from the Letter of Paul to the Romans, p. 613

time as our mortality which needs such peace has passed away. As a consequence, so long as her life in the earthly city is that of a captive and an alien (although she has the promise of ultimate delivery and the gift of the Spirit as a pledge), she has no hesitation about keeping in step with the civil law which governs matters pertaining to our existence here below. For, as mortal life is the same for all, there ought to be common cause between the two cities in what concerns our purely human living.

Now comes the difficulty. The city of this world, to begin with, has had certain 'wise men' of its own mold, whom true religion must reject, because either out of their own daydreaming or out of demonic deception these wise men came to believe that a multiplicity of divinities was allied with human life, with different duties, in some strange arrangement, and different assignments: this one over the body, that one over the mind; in the body itself, one over the head, another over the neck, still others, one for each bodily part; in the mind, one over the intelligence, another over learning, another over temper, another over desire; in the realities, related to life, that lie about us, one over flocks and one over wheat, one over wine, one over oil, and another over forests, one over currency, another over navigation, and still another over warfare and victory, one over marriage, a different one over fecundity and childbirth, so on and so on.[10]

The heavenly City, on the contrary, knows and, by religious faith, believes that it must adore one God alone and serve Him with that complete dedication which the Greeks call *latreía* and which belongs to Him alone. As a result, she has been unable to share with the earthly city a common religious legislation, and has had no choice but to dissent on this score and so to become a nuisance to those who think otherwise. Hence, she has had to feel the weight of their anger, hatred, and violence, save in those instances when, by sheer numbers and God's help, which never fails, she has been able to scare off her opponents.

So long, then, as the heavenly City is wayfaring on earth, she invites citizens from all nations and all tongues, and unites them into a single pilgrim band. She takes no issue with that diversity of customs, laws, and traditions whereby human peace is sought and maintained. Instead of nullifying or tearing down, she preserves and appropriates whatever

---

[10]Augustine is referring to the many gods of the pre-Christian Greeks and Romans. Different gods had power over different aspects of humanity and the environment.

in the diversities of divers races is aimed at one and the same objective of human peace, provided only that they do not stand in the way of faith and worship of the one supreme and true God.

Thus, the heavenly City, so long as it is wayfaring on earth, not only makes use of earthly peace but fosters and actively pursues along with other human beings a common platform in regard to all that concerns our purely human life and does not interfere with faith and worship. Of course, though, the City of God subordinates this earthly peace to that of heaven. For this is not merely true peace, but, strictly speaking, for any rational creature, the only real peace, since it is, as I said, 'the perfectly ordered and harmonious communion of those who find their joy in God and in one another in God.'

When this peace is reached, man will be no longer haunted by death, but plainly and perpetually endowed with life, nor will his body, which now wastes away and weighs down the soul, be any longer animal, but spiritual, in need of nothing, and completely under the control of our will.

This peace the pilgrim City already possesses by faith and it lives holily and according to this faith so long as, to attain its heavenly completion, it refers every good act done for God or for his fellow man. I say 'fellow man' because, of course, any community life must emphasize social relationships.

THE SOCRATIC SCHOOL OF PHILOSOPHY (VIII,3)

To Socrates goes the credit of being the first one to channel the whole of philosophy into an ethical system for the reformation and regulation of morals.[11] His predecessors without exception had applied themselves particularly to physics or natural science. I do not think that it can be definitely decided just why Socrates chose to follow this course. It has been suggested that he did so because he had become wearied of obscure and uncertain investigations, and preferred to turn his mind to a clean-cut objective, to that secret of human happiness which seems to have been the sole purpose of all philosophical research. Others have claimed, more kindly, that he did not think it right for minds darkened with earthly desires to reach out beyond their limits to the realm of the divine.

[11]See selection 8, the *Apology*, in which Socrates (469–399 B.C.) defends his life's philosophical work at his trial.

Socrates realized that his predecessors had been seeking the origin of all things, but he believed that these first and highest causes could be found only in the will of the single and supreme Divinity and, therefore, could be comprehended only by a mind purified from passion. Hence his conclusion, that he must apply himself to the acquisition of virtue, so that his mind, freed from the weight of earthly desires, might, by its own natural vigor, lift itself up to eternal realities and, with purified intelligence, contemplate the very nature of that immaterial and immutable light in which the causes[12] of all created natures abidingly dwell. Nevertheless, with his marvelous combination of wit and words, pungency and politeness, and with his trick of confessing ignorance and concealing knowledge he used to tease and poke fun at the folly of ignoramuses who talked as though they knew the answers to those moral problems in which he seemed wholly absorbed.

The result was that he incurred their enmity. He was falsely accused and condemned to death. However, the very city of Athens that had publicly condemned him began publicly to mourn his loss, and the wrath of the people was so turned against his two accusers that one[13] of them was killed by an angry mob and the other[14] escaped a similar death only by voluntary and perpetual exile.

Socrates was thus so highly distinguished both in life and in death that he left behind him numerous disciples. They rivaled one another in zealous discussions of those ethical problems where there is question of the supreme good and, hence, of human happiness.

In his discussions, Socrates had a way of proposing and defending his theories and then demolishing them. No one could make out exactly what he believed. Consequently, each of his followers picked what he preferred and sought the supreme good in his heart's desire.

Now the truth is that the supreme good is that which, when attained, makes all men happy. Yet, so varied in regard to this good were the views of the Socratics that is seems hardly credible that all of them were followers of one and the same master.

[12]Plato, (429–347 B.C.), Socrates' most brilliant disciple, wrote of the eternal Forms or Ideas as "causes." See his "Allegory of the Cave," pp. 345–48 in selection 10, the *Republic*.

[13]Meletus, prosecutor in the trial of Socrates.

[14]Anytus, the politician who remained in the background but pressed Meletus to carry on the prosecution. (Augustine's information on both of these accusers of Socrates is of doubtful accuracy.)

ON THE MOST DISTINGUISHED DISCIPLE OF SOCRATES, PLATO, THE ONE WHO DIVIDED PHILOSOPHY INTO THREE PARTS (VIII,4)

Of the pupils of Socrates, Plato was so remarkable for his brilliance that he has deservedly outshone all the rest. He was born in Athens of a good family and by his marvelous ability easily surpassed all his fellow disciples. Realizing, however, that neither his own genius nor Socratic training was adequate to evolve a perfect system of philosophy, he traveled far and wide to wherever there was any hope of gaining some valuable addition to knowledge. Thus, in Egypt he mastered the lore which was there esteemed. From there he went to lower Italy, famous for the Pythagorean School, and there successfully imbibed from eminent teachers all that was then in vogue in Italian philosophy.

However, Plato's special affection was for his old master—so much so that in practically all the Dialogues he makes Socrates, with all his charm, the mouthpiece not only of his own moral arguments but of all that Plato learned from others or managed to discover himself.

Now, the pursuit of wisdom follows two avenues—action and contemplation. Thus, one division of philosophy may be called active; the other part, contemplative. The former deals with the conduct of life; that is to say, with the cultivation of morals. Contemplative philosophy considers natural causality and truth as such. Socrates excelled in practical wisdom; Pythagoras favored contemplation, and to this he applied his whole intelligence.

It is to Plato's praise that he combined both in a more perfect philosophy, and then divided the whole into three parts: first, moral philosophy which pertains to action; second, natural philosophy whose purpose is contemplation; third, rational philosophy which discriminates between truth and error. Although this last is necessary for both action and contemplation, it is contemplation especially which claims to reach a vision of truth. Hence, this threefold division in no way invalidates the distinction whereby action and contemplation are considered the constituent elements of the whole of philosophy. Just what Plato's position was in each of these three divisions—that is to say, just what he knew or believed to be the end of all action, the cause of all nature, the light of all reason—I think it would be rash to affirm and would take too long to discuss at length.

Plato was so fond of following the well-known habit of his master of dissimulating his knowledge or opinions that in Plato's own works (where Socrates appears as a speaker) it is difficult to determine just what views he held even on important questions. However, of the views which are set forth in his writings, whether his own or those of others which seemed to have pleased him, a few must be recalled and included here. In some places, Plato is on the side of the true religion which our faith accepts and defends. At other times he seems opposed; for example, on the respective merits of monotheism and polytheism in relation to genuine beatitude after death.

Perhaps this may be said of the best disciples of Plato—of those who followed most closely and understood most clearly the teachings of a master rightly esteemed above all other pagan philosophers—that they have perceived, at least, these truths about God: that in Him is to be found the cause of all being, the reason of all thinking, the rule of all living. The first of these truths belongs to natural, the second to rational, the third to moral philosophy.

Now, if man was created so that by his highest faculty he might attain to the highest of all realities, that is, to the one, true and supreme God, apart from whom no nature exists, no teaching is true, no conduct is good, then let us seek Him in whom all we find is real, know Him in whom all we contemplate is true, love Him in whom all things for us are good.